Chinese Contract Law—Theory and Practice

Chinese Contract Law—
Theory and Practice

SECOND EDITION

By

Mo Zhang

BRILL
NIJHOFF

LEIDEN | BOSTON

Library of Congress Cataloging-in-Publication Data

Names: Zhang, Mo (Law teacher), author.
Title: Chinese contract law—theory and practice / Mo Zhang.
Description: Boston : BRILL, 2020. | Includes bibliographical references
   and index. | Summary: "The modern Chinese law and legal system, though
   bearing strong resemblance to the civil law heritage, are in fact in an
   evolving stage without a definite model of tradition. After the fall of
   the last emperor in 1911, China experienced nearly forty years of
   warlord chaos, the anti-Japanese war, and then civil law"– Provided by
   publisher.
Identifiers: LCCN 2019043768 | ISBN 9789004414761 (hardback) |
   ISBN 9789004414785 (ebook)
Subjects: LCSH: Contracts–China.
Classification: LCC KNQ858 .Z43 2020 | DDC 346.5102/2–dc23
LC record available at https://lccn.loc.gov/2019043768

Typeface for the Latin, Greek, and Cyrillic scripts: "Brill." See and download: brill.com/brill-typeface.

ISBN 978-90-04-41476-1 (hardback)
ISBN 978-90-04-41478-5 (e-book)

Copyright 2020 by Koninklijke Brill NV, Leiden, The Netherlands.
Koninklijke Brill NV incorporates the imprints Brill, Brill Hes & De Graaf, Brill Nijhoff, Brill Rodopi, Brill Sense, Hotei Publishing, mentis Verlag, Verlag Ferdinand Schöningh and Wilhelm Fink Verlag.
All rights reserved. No part of this publication may be reproduced, translated, stored in a retrieval system, or transmitted in any form or by any means, electronic, mechanical, photocopying, recording or otherwise, without prior written permission from the publisher.
Authorization to photocopy items for internal or personal use is granted by Koninklijke Brill NV provided that the appropriate fees are paid directly to The Copyright Clearance Center, 222 Rosewood Drive, Suite 910, Danvers, MA 01923, USA. Fees are subject to change.

This book is printed on acid-free paper and produced in a sustainable manner.

Printed by Printforce, the Netherlands

Contents

Preface to the Second Edition XI
Acknowledgments XIV

Introduction 1
1 Mao's "Plain Paper" Theory and Legal Nihilism in China 2
2 Post-Mao Reconstruction of the Legal System 6
3 Contract Law Legislation 8
    3.1 *Enactment of the General Principles of Civil Law* 9
    3.2 *Adoption of the Unified Contract Law* 11
    3.3 *The 2017 General Provisions of Civil Law* 14
    3.4 *The 2019 Foreign Investment Law* 16
4 Judicial Interpretation and Guiding Cases 17
5 The Ideology of "Governing the Country by Law" 28
6 Unsolved Issue: Judicial Independence 29

1 Contract Law in the Chinese Tradition 33
1 Concept of Contract 34
    1.1 *Chinese Tradition* 34
    1.2 *Civil Law Influence* 36
    1.3 *Theories of Contract Law* 39
        1.3.1 Economic Means Theory 39
        1.3.2 Civil Act Theory 40
        1.3.3 Agreement Theory 41
        1.3.4 Exchange Theory 42
    1.4 *Definition of Contract* 42
2 Contract Classification 49
    2.1 *Named and Unnamed Contracts* 49
    2.2 *Formal and Informal Contracts* 50
    2.3 *Consensual and Real Contracts* 51
    2.4 *Onerous and Gratuitous Contracts* 52
    2.5 *Unilateral and Bilateral Contracts* 54
3 Application of the Contract Law 55
4 Contract and the Socialist Market Economy 59
5 Contracts and the State Plan 64

2 Freedom of Contract in China 68
1 Conception of Freedom 71
2 Right of Parties to a Contract 73

3 Limitations on Party Autonomy 77
3.1 Legal Compliance 79
3.2 State Plan Mandate 81
3.3 Administrative Supervision 81
3.4 Government Approval and Other Special Requirements 84

3 Enforceability of Contracts 87
1 Obligatio and Contract Obligations 90
2 Governing Principles of Contracts 93
2.1 Equality and Voluntariness 93
2.2 Fairness and Good Faith 96
2.3 Legality and Public Interests 102
2.4 Observance of Contract 106
3 Pre-Contractual Liabilities 107

4 Formation of Contracts 115
1 Offer 115
1.1 Offer and Invitation for Offer 117
1.2 Legal Effect of Offers 123
1.3 Termination of an Offer 124
1.3.1 Withdrawal of Offer 124
1.3.2 Revocation of Offer 125
1.3.3 Void Offers 126
2 Acceptance 128
2.1 Requirements for Acceptance 128
2.2 Withdrawal of Acceptance 132
2.3 Late Acceptance 132
2.4 Late Arrival of Acceptance 133
2.5 Acceptance and Conclusion of Contract 134
3 Conclusion and Effectiveness of Contracts 136
4 Formality of Contracts 138
5 Incorporation of the State Plan and Government Approval 147

5 Terms of Contracts 150
1 Terms Generally Included in a Contract 151
2 Interpretation of a Contract 155
2.1 Contract Interpretation Approaches 155
2.2 Contract Interpretation Theories 158
2.3 Contract Interpretation under the Contract Law 159
3 Supplementary Agreement for Uncertain or Missing Terms 162

CONTENTS VII

    4 Proof of the Terms of a Contract   167
    5 Standard Terms   168
    6 Disclaimers   177

6 **Contract Defenses—Validity Issues**   178
    1 Issues at Stake   181
    2 Capacity of the Parties—Effect-to-be-Determined Contract   185
        2.1 *Contract by a Person with Limited Capacity for Civil Conduct*   188
        2.2 *Contract by an Agent without Due Authorization*   190
        2.3 *Right to Request Ratification and to Rescind a Contract*   195
        2.4 *Contract by a Person with No-Right-to-Dispose*   197
    3 Void Contracts   201
        3.1 *Fraud or Duress*   203
            3.1.1 Fraud   206
                3.1.1.1 Intent to Deceive   206
                3.1.1.2 Conduct of Deceit   207
                3.1.1.3 Reliance   208
                3.1.1.4 Mistaken Manifestation of the Consent of the Deceived   209
            3.1.2 Duress   210
        3.2 *Malicious Collusion to Damage the Interests of the State, a Collective, or a Third Party*   213
        3.3 *Use of a Contract for Illegal Purpose*   215
        3.4 *Harm to the Social Public Interest*   217
        3.5 *Violation of Compulsory Provisions of Law or Regulations*   218
    4 Voidable Contracts   221
        4.1 *Exploitation of the Other Party's Precarious Position*   223
        4.2 *Material Misunderstanding*   224
        4.3 *Obvious Unfairness*   227
    5 Consequences of Void and Voidable Contracts   230
        5.1 *Avoidance from the Very Beginning*   231
        5.2 *Partial Avoidance and the Remaining Part of the Contract*   231
        5.3 *Independence of a Dispute Settlement Clause*   232
        5.4 *Restitution and Compensation*   233
    6 Conditions Affecting the Validity of Contacts   235

7 **Performance of Contracts**   240
    1 Performance Principles   240
        1.1 *Complete and Adequate Performance*   241

        1.2   *Good Faith Performance*   242
   2   Determination of the Obligations to Be Performed   246
   3   Right of Defense to Non-Performance   249
        3.1   *Fulfillment Plea*   251
        3.2   *Unrest Defense*   254
   4   Protective Measures for Performance   257
        4.1   *Right of Subrogation*   258
                4.1.1   Conditions for Subrogation   259
                4.1.2   Action to Seek Subrogation   261
                4.1.3   Defenses of the Obligor's Debtor   262
                4.1.4   Legal Effect of Subrogation   262
        4.2   *Right of Cancellation*   263
   5   Guarantee of Performance   269
        5.1   *Suretyship*   270
        5.2   *Security Interest*   271
        5.3   *Money Deposit*   272
        5.4   *Lien*   273
   6   Changes of Circumstances during Performance   273
        6.1   *Changes Related to the Parties*   274
        6.2   *Rebus Sic Stantibus*   274

8   Modification of Contract and Assignment   278
   1   Modification   279
   2   Assignment   282
        2.1   *Assignment of Contractual Rights*   286
                2.1.1   Formality of Assignment   290
                2.1.2   Non-Assignable Rights   292
                2.1.3   Effect of Assignment   294
                2.1.4   Right of Defense in Assignment   296
        2.2   *Delegation of Contractual Obligations*   297
                2.2.1   Delegation as a Transfer of Debts in Whole or in Part   297
                2.2.2   Subordinate Duties   302
                2.2.3   Non-Delegable Duties   303
                2.2.4   Transfer of Obligor's Defenses against Obligee   304
   3   Comprehensive Assignment   304

9   Rescission and Termination of Contracts   307
   1   Rescission   308
        1.1   *Rescission by Agreement*   309

    1.2   *Rescission by the Provisions of Law*   312
        1.2.1   Force Majeure   313
        1.2.2   Breach of Contract   315
            1.2.2.1   Anticipatory Repudiation   316
            1.2.2.2   Unreasonable Delay in Performance   318
            1.2.2.3   Frustration of the Contract Purpose   319
        1.2.3   Other Reasons Provided by the Law   320
    1.3   *Rescission Notice*   323
    1.4   *Legal Consequences of Rescission*   325
2   Termination   327
    2.1   *Performance*   329
    2.2   *Offset*   331
    2.3   *Deposit*   333
    2.4   *Exemption*   340
    2.5   *Merger*   342

10   Breach of Contracts and Remedies   345

1   Liability for Breach: a Chinese Concept   345
2   Liability Imputation   347
3   Breach   351
    3.1   *Anticipatory Repudiation*   351
    3.2   *Actual Breach*   353
4   Remedies   356
    4.1   *Continuing Performance*   357
        4.1.1   Monetary Obligation   359
        4.1.2   Non-Monetary Obligation   360
            4.1.2.1   Impossibility Rule   361
            4.1.2.2   Impracticability Rule   363
            4.1.2.3   Rule of Timing   364
    4.2   *Remedial Measures*   366
    4.3   *Damages*   367
        4.3.1   Compensatory Damages   371
        4.3.2   Liquidated Damages   372
        4.3.3   Punitive Damages   375
        4.3.4   Earnest Money   376
5   Mitigation Duty   378
6   Exemption of Liability   378

11   Third Party Interests   381

1   Third Party Receiving Performance   383

- 2 Third Party Performing the Contract 387
- 3 Breach Caused by a Third Party 389
- 4 *Bona Fide* Third Party 392

12 International Contracts 395
- 1 Foreign Elements 395
- 2 Choice of Law in International Contracts 397
  - 2.1 *Choice of Law by the Parties* 398
  - 2.2 *Application of Law Absent the Parties' Choice* 408
  - 2.3 *Application of International Law* 412
- 3 Choice of Forum in International Contracts 419
- 4 Dispute Settlement Mechanism 424
  - 4.1 *Reconciliation* 425
  - 4.2 *Mediation* 425
  - 4.3 *Arbitration* 429
  - 4.4 *Litigation* 432
- 5 Statute of Limitations 434

13 Labor Contracts 439
- 1 Labor Contract Legislation and Legal Framework 440
- 2 Concept of Labor Contract 442
  - 2.1 *Definition* 443
  - 2.2 *Categories* 444
- 3 Formation 445
  - 3.1 *Requirements* 445
  - 3.2 *Probationary Period* 448
  - 3.3 *Collective Contract* 449
  - 3.4 *Labor Dispatch* 451
- 4 Validity and Enforceability 452
- 5 Performance and Modificatiom 454
  - 5.1 *Performance* 454
  - 5.2 *Modification* 457
- 6 Rescission and Termination 458
  - 6.1 *Rescission* 458
  - 6.2 *Termination* 462
- 7 Legal Liabilities 466
- 8 Dispute Settlement 469
- 9 Government Supervision and Review 472

Index 475

Preface to the Second Edition

There have been important developments in the area of contracts both in terms of legislation as well as practices in China since the publication of the first edition of this book in 2006. In the preface of the first edition, a historical feature of Chinese law and the Chinese legal system was described as follows:

> The modern Chinese law and legal system, though bearing strong resemblance to the civil law heritage, are in fact in an evolving stage without a definite model of tradition. After the fall of the last emperor in 1911, China experienced nearly forty years of warlord chaos, the anti-Japanese war, and then civil law. During that period, the development of the law and legal system was overshadowed by the country's constant struggles for peace and stability both internally and externally. Although the Nationalist government adopted a series of laws known as the Code of Six Laws (*Liu Fa Quan Shu*), those laws had very limited application and ultimately were abolished by the Communist government in 1949. After 1949 until 1979, China deeply indulged in pursuance of Chairman Mao's philosophy of class struggle, and was eventually dragged into the edge of bankruptcy economically. Since 1979, China has changed dramatically with the opening-up policy and vast reforms, moving toward prosperity. In the meantime, the country has been making efforts to rebuild its legal system under the doctrine of "Chinese reality with reference to foreign laws and legal systems." As a result, numerous laws and regulations are being adopted and many of them, as they can be easily discerned, are the mixture of legal rules and methodologies of different countries or legal systems.

In 2010, China proclaimed that the country had established a "socialist legal system with Chinese characteristics." Both the term "socialist" and the concept of "Chinese characteristics" are subject to various interpretations, but the legal system is currently structured under a platform of one core (Constitution), seven branches (Constitution and related laws; civil and commercial laws; administrative laws; economic laws; social laws; criminal laws; and litigation and non-litigation procedure laws), and three layers (laws, administrative regulations, and local rules and decrees). Moreover, China has a long-desired legislative agenda to adopt a comprehensive Civil Code. Contract law is not only an important component of the civil law branch, but also an indispensable part of the comprehensive Civil Code.

The new developments in the area of contract legislation and judicial practices during the past thirteen years are multi-faceted. First, there are several new pieces of legislation that are related to contracts, including, among others, (a) the 2007 Labor Contract Law and the 2008 State Council Rules of Implementation of the Labor Contract Law; (b) the 2007 Property Law; (c) the 2011 Choice of Law Statute; (d) the 2012 Revised Civil Procedural Law; and most importantly, (e) the 2017 General Provisions of Civil Law and the 2019 Foreign Investment Law.

Second, the Supreme People's Court (SPC) of China has issued a number of judicial Interpretations pertaining to the application of the Contract Law. Among the interpretations are (a) the 2009 Interpretation on Several Questions Concerning the Application of the Contract Law (II); (b) the 2012 Interpretation on the Application of Law in Adjudicating Disputes over Sale of Goods Contract; (c) the 2014 Interpretation on the Application of Law in Adjudicating Disputes Over the Contracts of Financial Leasing; (d) the 2015 Interpretation on the Application of Civil Procedure Law; (e) the 2015 Interpretation on Several Issues Concerning Adjudication of the Private Lending Cases; and (f) the 2018 Interpretation on the Application of Law in Adjudicating the Cases Involving Disputes Over Operation Contract of Construction Project.

Third, the country has put in place an initiative to establish a "Guiding Case" system in the judiciary. Guiding cases are the cases selected nationwide and published by the SPC to guide Chinese courts in their adjudication of the same or similar cases. The very purpose of having guiding cases, as stated by the SPC, is to help unify the application of law, enhance the quality of adjudication, and maintain judicial justice. A practical implication of buiding the case law system is that China is moving toward adoption of case law. As of February 2019, a total of 112 guiding cases have been published, and a quite number of them involve contracts.

The second edition of the book incoporates all those developments. Like the previous edition, this edition remains to focus on the general provisions of the Contract Law. It begins with a review of the history of contract legislation in the country, and then turns into a detailed analysis of the law of contracts with Chinese characteristics. From Chapter 3, each chapter of the book has a special concentration on a certain subject of the law of contract, such as formation, terms, defenses, performance, assignment, rescission and termination, breach and remedies, as well as third parties. Chapter 12 of the book addresses issues in international contracts since those issues are provided in particularity in the Contract Law due to the foreign nature of such contracts.

A new chapter in the second edition is Chapter 13, Labor Contracts. In China, labor contracts are treated differently from civil and commercial contracts, and are governed by a separate set of laws—notwithstanding that certain general principles of the Contract Law remain applicable to labor contracts. In addition, the formation of labor contracts must meet certain statutory requirements, and the enforcement of labor contracts is closely scrutinized by the government through the process of supervision and review.

The second edition also contains certain structural changes in several chapters in order to help examine and discuss all legal issues as thoroughly as possible while continuing to focus on the theories and practices in the application of the Contract Law. Some new cases, including guiding cases, are added to illustrate legal rules governing the contracting process and to address practical matters involved in contract disputes.

Mo Zhang
Temple University Beasley School of Law
Philadelphia, USA
July 2019

Acknowledgments

The publication of this book would not be possible without assistance and inspiration from scholars, practitioners, students, and friends both at home and abroad. Special thanks are due to Temple University Beasley School of Law and Dean Gregory Mandel for their great support. I am truly grateful to my colleagues at Temple and Tsinghua University School of Law for their comments and suggestions.

Once again, I am deeply indebted to Professor Robert J. Reinstein of Temple, Professor Jiang Ping of China University of Political Science & Law, Professor Jacques deLisle of University of Pennsylvania Law School, and late Professor Whitmore Gray of the University of Michigan Law School for their invaluable advice and mentorship. My thanks also go to Professor Wang Liming of Renmin University for his guidance.

A particular debt of gratitude is owed to Tracey Kline, JD '19, who provided editing assistance. All errors are mine.

Introduction

"The Contract Law of the People's Republic of China" ("Contract Law") was adopted on March 15, 1999 at the plenary meeting of the National People's Congress of China ("NPC")—the Chinese National Legislative body. The promulgation of the Contract Law was of significance in all aspects.[1] It not only unified all previous contract law legislation, but also marked the beginning of the comprehensive contract regulation in modern China since 1949, when the People's Republic of China was founded. Taking effect on October 1, 1999, the Contract Law is the primary piece of contract legislation in China that forms a statutory framework governing contracts in the country. In addition to the legislation, the judicial interpretations of the Supreme People's Court of China ("SPC") constitute an important part of the contract legal scheme, particularly in the implementation of the Contract Law.

In Chinese history, a contract was commonly termed as agreement or "Qi Yue" in Chinese. As it is explained in China, "Qi" denotes an "agreement" while "Yue" infers the effect of binding.[2] The written form of "Qi Yue" made to deal with civil affairs in the country can be found in as early as the Western Zhou (1100 to 770 BC).[3] During the Western Zhou period, "Qi Yue" was used to record the consent of two parties to their exchange of goods or purchase of lands, and it was also employed to document the other civil activities between the parties such as loans and leases. On certain occasions where the exchange was deemed important, the process and the terms of the exchange were engraved in the bronze tripod as the evidence of the exchange. The engraved agreement was then called the "Certificate of Agreement" ("Qi Juan").[4]

Ever since Western Zhou, "Qi Yue" had become the major form representing the consent of the parties in their civil activities and serving as the evidence of the agreement entered into by the parties concerned. Under Tang Code, for example, a "Qi Yue" was required for the sale of homestead or livestock, and

---

1 See Gu Angran, *A Talk on Contract Law of the People's Republic of China*, 1–5 (Law Publ'g House 1999).
2 See Wang Liming, CONTRACT LAW OF CHINA 2 (Hein Wells 2016).
3 For general information, see Zhang Jinfan, *Evolution of the Chinese Legal Civilization*, 55–56 (China Univ. of Political Sci. & Law Press 1999).
4 See id.

any such sale that occurred without a "Qi Yue" would be punished.[5] During the Republic period of 1911 to 1949, "Qi Yue" was a major form of civil obligations in the Civil Code, one of the Six Codes that made up the main body of the law of the Republic.[6]

Ironically, however, the contract did not play any active role after the founding of the People's Republic of China in 1949 until the 1980's. During that period, the contract regulation, if any, was made basically in lieu of government policies. There were many factors attributive to this phenomenon. The most notable one was the planned economy dominating the country. Another significant factor was the ideology that the private interest should unconditionally be subordinated to the public interest—a rigid rule that profoundly governed the nation for decades.

1   Mao's "Plain Paper" Theory and Legal Nihilism in China

When the Communist Party of China ("CPC") took power in October 1949, all then existing laws and regulations (old laws) promulgated by the Nationalist government were regarded as anti-revolution evils that ought to be eliminated. The process of "cleaning-up" the old laws in fact began in January 1949, when the CPC issued the "Statement of the Present Situation," which contained eight conditions for the peace talk with Kuomingtong ("Nationalist Party") or the KTM.[7] One of the conditions was to abolish the Constitution and laws adopted under the KMT regime. One month later, in February 1949, the Central Committee of the CPC promulgated the "Directives on the Annulment of the Code of Six Laws[8] and the Establishment of Judicial Principles in the Liberated Areas." The Directives repealed all laws and regulations then effective under the KMT government.[9]

---

5   See generally Geoffrey MacCormack, *The Law of Contract in China under the T'ang and Song Dynasties*, available at http://local.droit.ulg.ac.be/sa/rida/file/1985/03.%20MacCormack.pdf.
6   See 1929 CIVIL CODE, available at http://ishare.iask.sina.com.cn/f/25306726.html.
7   See Mao Tsetung, Statement of the Present Situation (Jan. 4, 1949) (English translation), available at https://www.marxists.org/reference/archive/mao/selected-works/volume-4/mswv4_50.htm.
8   The Six Laws were Constitutional Law, Civil Law, Criminal Law, Civil Procedure Law, Criminal Procedure Law, and Administrative Law. Note that the early version of the Six Laws had Commercial law instead of Administrative Law.
9   See Xin Chunying, CHINESE LEGAL SYSTEM AND CURRENT LEGAL REFORM 325–27 (Law Publ'g House 1999).

Mao Tse-tung, Chairman of the CPC, highly appraised the abolition of the KMT legal system and poetically described the new system to be established to replace the old one as a piece of "Plain Paper" (a blank sheet of white paper). According to Mao, "there would be no burden bearing with a piece of plain paper, on which the newest and most beautiful words could be written and the newest and most beautiful pictures could be drawn."[10] Under this "Plain Paper" philosophy, Mao started his ambitious socialist construction in China, and built Chinese economy under the model of the former Soviet Union— known as the planned economy.

In the early years of the 1950's, attempting to help China recover from the debris of the civil war (1946–1949), the central government of China made efforts to regulate the economy through certain legal means, many of which were actually based on the practices that were developed in the "liberated areas" the CPC had controlled before 1949. In September 1950, for example, in order to help stabilize the state economy, the State Administration Council (later replaced by the State Council in 1954), through its Commission of Finance and Economy, issued "Provisional Methods on Contractual Agreement Made between Government Agencies, State Enterprises, and Cooperatives" (the "1950 Methods").[11]

Under the 1950 Methods, it was required that a contractual agreement be made for major business activities between government agencies, state enterprises, and cooperatives. The major business activities as listed in the Methods included loans, agency receipts and payments, sales of goods, custom-made goods, barters, sales by commission, consigned processing, commission-lent money or in kind, entrusted transportation, renovation and construction, concessionary business operations, as well as joint ventures.[12]

On September 20, 1954, the first Constitution of China was adopted.[13] According to the 1954 Constitution, the National People's Congress ("NPC") was

---

10   *Selected Papers of Mao Tze-tung*, INTRODUCTION OF A COOPERATIVE UNIT 1 (People's Publ'g House 1985).

11   See State Admin. Council, *Provisional Methods on Making Contractual Agreement Among Government Agencies, State Enterprises, and Cooperatives* (Sep. 27, 1950), a full text is available at http://blog.sina.com.cn/s/blog_88c9839f010138jg.html.

12   See id.; see also Wang Liming, *Understanding Contract Law—General Principles*, 11–12 (China Univ. of Political Science & Law Publ'g House 1996).

13   From 1954 to 1982, there were four constitutions that were adopted in China—in 1954, 1975, 1978, and 1982, respectively. The current Constitution is the 1982 Constitution, which has been amended five times since it was adopted on December 4, 1982. The five amendments to the 1982 Constitution were made in 1988, 1993, 1999, 2004 and 2018 respectively.

the top legislative body of the nation.[14] Empowered by the 1954 Constitution, the NPC began to work on drafting major laws, one of which was the "Civil Code." In October 1955, the "General Principles of Civil Law of China" was first drafted. The draft contained such provisions as "basic principles," "subject of rights (person)," "object (subject matter) of rights," "legal acts," and "statute of limitations."[15] In December 1956, the first draft "Civil Code" was complete. It had four parts with a total of 525 articles. The four parts were "General Principles," "Ownership," "*Obligatio* (zhai)," and "Inheritance." In the *Obligatio*, contract was the major component. Unfortunately, however, the process of drafting was interrupted in 1958 as result of the Anti-Rightist Campaign against intellectuals that was launched in 1957.[16] Consequently and inevitably, the drafting work of the "Civil Code" was aborted.[17]

After the Anti-Rightist Campaign, China entered into a period of legal vacuum. In August 1958, Chairman Mao, in a special session of CCP's political bureau meeting in Bei Daihe, made notorious remarks: "the law was something we should have, but we did have our own stuff."[18] According to Mao, it would be impossible to rule the majority on the basis of law, but the customs to which people already got used. In Mao's opinion, customs were important because they were the daily practices commonly accepted, while the provisions in a law were often too numerous to be remembered. Mao took himself as an example and said, "Though I participated in the drafting of Constitution, I even could not remember it."[19]

In addition, Chairman Mao attached great importance to the policy of the CPC. It was Mao's belief that every decision made by CCP was the law,

---

14 The power to legislate was later delegated to local people's congresses (e.g., the provincial congress) with regard to local matters or affairs. Under Article 58 of the 1982 Constitution, the National People's Congress and its Standing Committee exercise the legislative power of the state.

15 See He Qinghua et al., *General View of Civil Code Drafts of New China*, Vo. I, 3–11 (Law Press 2003).

16 The anti-rightist campaign was the national "class struggle" launched by Chairman Mao against intellectuals in 1957 in response to the criticism the intellectuals made to the CPC and the central government at Mao's invitation. The criticism began in 1956 when Mao initiated a policy of "Letting Hundreds of Flowers Blossom and Letting Hundreds of Thoughts Contend" in order to promote "people's democracy." *See* Yin Xiaohu, *New China's Road of Constitutionalism* (1949–1999), 87–90 (Shanghai Univ. of Commc'n Press 2000).

17 *See* Wang Jiafu, *Civil Law Obligatio*, 21 (Law Publ'g House 1991).

18 *See* Yin Xiaohu, *supra* note 16, at 90.

19 *See* Xiang Chunyi, *The Leadership of Party and the Building of Legal System*, JURIS. 4 (2009).

INTRODUCTION 5

and even the party's meeting minutes would also become the law.[20] As an echo to Mao's remarks, the CCP Working Group of Politics and Law sent a report to Mao and the CCP Central Committee on December 20, 1958. The group's report emphasized that under the reality or actual situations in China, there had been no need at all to adopt civil law, criminal law, or procedural laws.[21]

The nationwide "crop failure" in the early 1960's,[22] which resulted in the most severe famine in modern Chinese history and which caused millions of people to die of starvation, shocked the CPC and the central government of China. In an attempt to put the nation back on the right track from class struggle zealotry to economic construction, Mao offered to step aside and play a secondary role in the government as a gesture of self-blame for the disaster. As a result, Liu Shaoqi came to the front to lead the country's recovery from the economic drawback. Under Liu, the national legislative work resumed. In July 1964, the second draft "Civil Code" was complete. In the second draft, there were fifteen chapters, including a chapter on sales.[23] Unfortunately, however, the effort to adopt the "Civil Code" in the country once again failed due to the "Cultural Revolution" that Mao launched in 1966 in order to knock out Liu and his followers, whom Mao labeled as the "representatives of capitalism."

---

20   *See id.* A well-known story about Mao's marital life with his wife Jiang Qin may help illustrate further how Mao treated himself *vis-a-vis* the law and judiciary. At one time when Mao talked to his guards about his depression over his relationship with Jiang, Mao said, "If you want to divorce your wife, you could go to a court, but if I want to do the same, where should I go?".
21   *See* Yin Xiaohu, *supra* note 16, at 94–95.
22   During the three years of 1960 to 1962, the country nearly collapsed because of the starvation. The official explanation was that the starvation was caused by the natural disaster plus the former Soviet Union's sudden withdrawal of its aids to China. However, it was believed that the tragedy was to a great extent the sequelae of the government's mismanagement during the "great leap forward" campaign nationwide from 1958 to 1960. *See* Stanley Lubman, BIRD IN CAGE, LEGAL REFORM IN CHINA AFTER MAO 80 (Stanford Univ. Press 1999).
23   Under the 1964 draft, "sales" was defined as the relation that occurs between units, units and individuals, or individuals for purposes of meeting the needs of production and living, to sell commodities and other things according to the principles of voluntariness and equal value within the limits allowed by laws. See He Qinghua, *supra* note 15, Vol. III, 124–26.

2 Post-Mao Reconstruction of the Legal System

It was not until 1979, when China finally came out of the shadow of the chaos of the Cultural Revolution, that the nation began to rebuild its legal system along with the vast economic reform. Beginning in 1979, legislative activities started to move forward as the country returned to its normal legislative processes.[24] In 1982, four different versions of the "Civil Code" were drafted in an attempt to catch up with the changes attendant to the rapid economic reform that began in 1979. In each of these drafts, contract was considered an important and indispensable part of the Civil Code.

However, the effort to enact the "Civil Code" was suspended in 1982. Suspension was attributed to uncertainty facing the NPC and its Standing Committee as to what would should to be included in the Code and how the Code would need to be structured given the economic reform which the nation had underwent. In order to more pragmatically deal with the substantial changes that resulted from the economic reform, the legislature turned its focus away from adopting a general and comprehensive "Civil Code" and instead, moved the legislative efforts toward promulgating separate pieces of legislation for specific areas, such as contract and torts.

The underlying rationale was simple and intuitive: a separate piece of legislation for a specific legal area would be more efficiently and effectively adapted to the changing economy than would a single comprehensive "Civil Code." In addition, separate legislation would help provide an experimental basis for more sophisticated legislation at a later time. As a result of this new focus on adopting area-specific pieces of legislation, contract law became an independent piece on the legislative agenda.

The economic reform that was aimed at opening China to the outside world (the developed economy in particular) significantly changed China in many ways. First of all, China moved from a centrally-planned economy to a market-oriented economy,[25] which greatly helped the nation move into the mainstream of the world economy, and become one of the fastest growing countries

---

24 In July of 1979, the Second Session of the Fifth National People's Congress passed seven major laws, including Criminal Law, Criminal Procedural Law, as well as the Law of Chinese-Foreign Equity Joint Ventures. By the end of 1982, twenty-six new laws were adopted, the most important of which was the 1982 Constitution.

25 In 1992, the 14th National Conference of the CCP set as the goal of China's economic reform the establishment of a socialist market economy in China. One year later in 1993, the 1982 Constitution was amended to provide that the state was to pursue developing a socialist market economy. The amendment also provided that the state shall enhance economic legislation and improve macro-control of the economy.

globally in terms of economic development.²⁶ The economic reform eventually paved the way for China to become a member of the World Trade Organization ("WTO") in 2001, after fifteen years of tough negotiations with the West.

Secondly, China entered into a massive legislation period in which many laws were adopted to regulate the politically and economically changing society. During the thirty years from 1949 to 1979, there were about 134 laws that were adopted at the national level. In 1979, only about twenty-three were still effective. From 1979 to 1999, when the Contract Law was adopted, thousands of laws and regulations were promulgated, and most of them were in the economic areas. For instance, in the first three years of economic reform from 1979 to 1982, the NPC and the State Council adopted more than 300 laws and regulations, and some 250 of them dealt with economic matters.²⁷

Thirdly, China began to more eagerly and readily absorb foreign "ideas and concepts" or "factors." Most notably, foreign direct investment (FDI) became the major component of the nation's economy. By the end of 2004, over 50,000 FIEs were approved in China with a cumulated total FDI of $562.1 billion. More than 400 Fortune 500 companies have investments in China.²⁸ In 2010, FDI in China surpassed $100 billion, reaching $105.74 billion.²⁹ In 2017, China's FDI inflows increased to over $136 billion, making China the world's second largest FDI recipient after United States.³⁰ In the legal area, it has become a common scenario that foreign laws and legal systems are often referred in the law-making process of the country. As a result, the legislation proceedings are no long kept secret to the foreigners. On the contrary, foreign lawyers and businessmen are given the opportunity, though on a selective basis, to express their concerns and make comments about the draft laws. The purpose was to "get connected with the world"—a mission that demonstrated China's stated commitment to joining the mainstay of the world economy.

---

26 According to Chinese President Hu Jingtao, China's GDP grew at an average rate of 9.4 percent annually for the past twenty-six years from 1978 to 2004. See Hu Jintao, Keynote Speech at 2005 Fortune Global Forum (Beijing May 16, 2018). A full text of the speech is available at http://politics.people.com.cn/GB/1024/3392948.html. For more detailed statistics, see http://www.stats.gov.cn.
27 See Xin Chuying, *supra* note 19, at 348–49.
28 See Hu Jingtao, *supra* note 26. For the details of the statistics, see the Ministry of Commerce of China (formerly MOFTEC), Statistics of Foreign Investment in China, available at http://www.mofcom.gov.cn.
29 See China Daily (Jan. 18, 2011), China's 2010 FDI hits $106b, up 17%, available at http://www.chinadaily.com.cn/bizchina/2011-01/18/content_11873206.htm.
30 See the UNCTAD, the 2018 World Investment Report, available at https://unctad.org/en/PublicationsLibrary/wir2018_en.pdf.

3 Contract Law Legislation

The promulgation of contract law legislation began in China in 1980 with the drafting of the Economic Contract Law ("ECL"). Drafting work on the ECL commenced in October 1980 and, on September 29, 1981, a draft of the law was sent to NPC for its review. The ECL was adopted on December 13, 1981 and went into effect on July 1, 1982. In essence, the ECL regulated contracts that were entered into for business purposes between legal persons, other economic organizations, individual businesses, and rural business households.[31]

It is important to note that, under the ECL, the contract was phrased as "economic contract" because at that time the contract was still viewed as the legal means to realize economic goals as stipulated by the state plans.[32] Also important to note was that the ECL excluded natural persons from making economic contracts, and thus no individual was eligible to be a contractual party. The ECL was amended in 1993 to reflect China's ongoing economic reform. The most striking change in the amended ECL was the deletion of the provision that defined the purpose of economic contracting as to guarantee the implementation of the state plans. However, the exclusion of natural persons from making a contract remained intact.

The second important piece of contract legislation was the Foreign Economic Contract Law ("FECL"), which was promulgated by the NPC on March 21, 1985. The FECL was designed to apply to the contracts in which a foreign party or foreign element was involved. Under Article 2 of the FECL, foreign economic contracts referred to the contracts entered into between enterprises or other economic organizations of the People's Republic of China and foreign enterprises, other foreign economic organizations, or individuals.[33] Once again, no Chinese citizen was allowed to enter into a foreign economic contract. In addition, the FECL did not apply to contracts of international transportation.

On June 23, 1987, the Technology Contract Law ("TCL") was adopted with a stated purpose of providing impetus to scientific and technical development in China. The application of TCL, however, was limited to contracts between legal persons, legal persons and citizens, or citizens, which were entered into

---

31 See Economic Contract Law of the People's Republic of China. An English translation is available at http://www.qis.net/chinalaw/prclaw19.htm.
32 See Wang Shengming, INTRODUCTION TO THE CONTRACT LAW OF CHINA AND IMPORTANT DRAFTS OF THE CONTRACT LAW 3 (Law Publ'g House 2000).
33 See Foreign Economic Contract Law of the People's Republic of China. An English translation is available at http://www.qis.net/chinalaw/prclaw20.htm.

for the purpose of establishing civil rights and obligations in technical development, technology transfer, and technical consulting and services. Promulgation of the TCL signified the first time that Chinese contract law legislation permitted Chinese individuals to enter into contracts. Due to the law's intended domestic nature, however, the TCL did not apply to contracts in which there was a foreign party, regardless of whether the foreign party was an enterprise, other organization, or an individual.[34] Moreover, the TCL's application was limited to technology contracts.[35]

The adoption of the TCL marked the beginning of China's "triarchy" period of contract law legislation, in which three contract laws simultaneously operated to govern contracting in different legal areas. The concurrent operation of these three laws caused a great deal of confusion regarding each law's applicability, particularly when a contract involved overlapping domestic, foreign, and technology matters. It also created legal inconsistency, as each of the three contract laws differs from one another in terminology, content, structure, and wording of contractual principles. Inevitably, there had been a strong voice all over the country calling for a unified contract law ever since the ECL was amended in 1993.[36]

3.1 Enactment of the General Principles of Civil Law

Prior to its adoption of the TCL, the NPC passed the "General Principles of Civil Law of the People's Republic of China" on April 12, 1986 ("1986 Civil Code"). The reasons for the adoption of the 1986 Civil Code were multi-faceted. The most compelling reason for adopting the 1986 Civil Code was the need for a piece of national legislation that would regulate the civil affairs that were taking place during the economic reform and establish a common legal norm for the nation's booming civil activities.[37] Another reason was that promulgation of both the ECL and the FECL had provided legislators useful experiences for how to identify the legal issues involved in civil matters as well as how to regulate civil matters in a relatively comfortable way.

As noted, a comprehensive Civil Code originally was intended. In fact, between 1980 and 1982, four drafts of the Civil Code were made, all entitled "Civil Law of People's Republic of China." The 1980 draft, dated August 15, 1980, had

---

34   See *Technology Contact Law of the People's Republic of China*. An English translation of the law is available at http://www.qis.net/chinalaw/prclaw21.htm.
35   The Technology Contract Law was not supposed to supersede any part of the Economic Contract Law.
36   *See* Wang Shengming, *supra* note 32, at 4–5.
37   *See* Wang Jiafu, *supra* note 17, at 24–25.

six parts and 501 articles,[38] and the 1982 draft, dated May 1, 1982, consisted of eight parts and 465 articles.[39] Throughout this time period, however, many argued that it was still too early to adopt a comprehensive Civil Code because of the many uncertain factors arising from the ongoing economic reform. As a compromise, the legislature adopted a simplified Civil Code, which covered only the general provisions of the Civil Code, named the "General Principles."

The 1986 Civil Code, which became effective on January 1, 1987, was an important piece of civil law legislation in modern China. The enactment of the 1986 Civil Code hallmarked a new era in Chinese civil law legislation—an era in which China began to develop its statutory civil law since 1949. According to Professor James Gordley at Boat Hall in Berkeley, "with the enactment of the Chinese Civil Code, systems of private law modeled on those of the West will govern nearly the entire world."[40] Although termed "General Principles," the 1986 Civil Code from its adoption became the fundamental law governing and regulating personal and property relationships between citizens, citizens and legal persons, or legal persons in China.[41]

The 1986 Civil Code contains ten articles on contracts, most of which deal with major contractual rights and obligations. Following the civil law tradition, the 1986 Civil Code characterizes contract as a major component of *obligatio* (Zhai). Unlike the term "obligations" in the common law, the civil law concept of *obligatio*, which originated in Roman law, refers to a civil relationship that contains both rights and obligations (*obligatio civilis*). *Obligatio* can be created either by agreement, namely by means of a contract (*obligatio ex contractu*), or by the operation of law, which may implicate the law of torts (*obligatio ex delicto*), unjust enrichment (*obligatio quasi ex contractu*), voluntary service (*negotiorum gestio*), as well as pre-contractual obligation (*culpa in contrahendo*).

Under the 1986 Civil Code, the *obligatio* is a special relationship of rights and obligations established between the parties concerned, under either the

---

38 See He Qinghua, *supra* note 15, at 371–435.
39 See *id.* at 560–622.
40 See James Gordley, *The Philosophical Origins of Modern Contract Doctrine* 1 (Clarendon Press, Oxford 1991).
41 On April 2, 1988, the Supreme People's Court issued "Opinions (Provisional) on Several Matters Concerning Application of the General Principles of the Civil Law of China." The Opinions consist of eight parts and 200 articles, and together were deemed the primary legal document guiding the courts all over the nation for civil law matters. The Opinions were revised on December 5, 1990, and the revised Opinions contain 230 articles in total. Full context for the 1990 Opinions in Chinese is available at http://www.law-lib.com/law/law_view.asp?id=15743.

agreed terms (contract) or legal provisions (torts).[42] The party entitled to the rights shall be the "obligee" (creditor), while the party assuming the obligations shall be the "obligor" (debtor).[43] Since rights and obligations mutually exist between parties to the *obligatio*, the terms "obligee" and "obligor" may be used interchangeably to refer to either party in the relationship depending on how the issue is framed. In a sales contract, for example, the buyer is an obligee in terms of the right to receive the goods ordered, and is also an obligor in terms of making payment. With regard to the legal relationship between obligee and obligor, the 1986 Civil Code provides that the obligee shall have the right to demand that the obligor fulfill his obligations as specified by the contract or stipulated by law.[44]

3.2   Adoption of the Unified Contract Law

China's fast-going economic reform posed great challenges for the application of the nation's three concurrently operating contract laws. In 1993, the Standing Committee of the NPC began drafting the Contract Law in order to unify the nation's contract law regime. The first draft of the Contract Law was submitted to the Legislative Affairs Commission of the Standing Committee of the NPC in January 1995. Thereafter, another four drafts were made, in October 1995, June 1996, May 1997, and August 1998, respectively. The August 1998 draft of the Contract Law was also published nationwide for comments and suggestions from the public on September 7, 1998. The Standing Committee of the NPC had four readings of the draft before the draft was submitted to the NPC's General Assembly Meeting for a vote in March 1999.[45] Under Chinese Legislative Law, a process of three readings in the congress is required for a draft law to be adopted.[46]

---

42   A criticism is that Article 84 of the 1986 Civil Code is incomplete because, it is believed, certain legal acts (e.g., a reward advertisement) may also create *obligatio*. Some then suggest that the *obligatio* should be defined as the relationship of rights and obligations under which a specified performance is requested between the specific parties and which arises from legal acts or provisions of law. See Wang Liming, *The Proposed Draft of the Civil Code of China and Legislative Reasons—Contracts*, 12 (Law Press 2004).
43   See General Principles of Civil Law of the People's Republic of China [hereinafter "GPCL"], art. 84. An English translation of the full text of the GPCL is available at http://www.qis.net/chinalaw/prclaw27.htm.
44   *See id.*
45   See Mo Zhang, *Freedom of Contract with Chinese Characteristics: A Closer Look at China's New Contract Law*, 14 TEMPLE INT'L & COMP. L.J. 2, 237 (2000).
46   *See* The Legislative Law of China, art. 29 (2000) (amended Mar. 15, 2015), available at http://www.law-lib.com/law/law_view.asp?id=490890.

As the Contract Law was in its drafting phase, the Standing Committee of the NPC, for the first time, invited comment from Western scholars and lawyers. In addition, from October 1997 to December 1998, the Legislative Affairs Commission of the Standing Committee sent two delegations to the United States, Canada, the United Kingdom, and Germany respectively to meet with scholars, judges, officials, and practicing lawyers in universities, institutes, government agencies, courts, companies, and law firms. The stated reason for these visits was to "learn from foreign laws and reference foreign legislation" [47] Moreover the Office of Legislative Affairs Commission directly invited a group of American lawyers through Amcham—Beijing (American Chamber of Commerce in Beijing) to discuss the draft Contract Law. and provide advisory opinions on certain matters in the draft, such as the draft's provisions on "offer and acceptance."

As noted, the NPC passed the Contract Law on March 15, 1999. The Contract Law consists of twenty-three chapters and 428 articles and is divided into three parts: "General Provisions," "Specific Provisions," and "Supplementary Provisions."[48] In the Specific Provisions, fifteen types of the contracts are listed and addressed separately. In Chinese jargon, these fifteen contracts are the "named contracts"; all other contracts not listed in the Specific Provisions are the "unnamed contracts."[49] Literally speaking, the named contracts are considered to be used more frequently than the unnamed contracts. With regard to the law applicable to the unnamed contracts, the Contract Law follows the doctrine of "application by analogy." Under Article 124 of the Contract Law, for any contract that is not addressed explicitly in the Specific Provisions or in other laws, the General Provisions of the Contract Law, as well as the most similar provisions in either the Specific Provisions or other laws, apply.

Historically, as discussed, modern Chinese law follows the civil law (continental law) tradition. As a result, many of the legal principles embodied in Chinese legislation are rooted in Roman law. The use of the term *"obligatio"* in Chinese civil law legislation, for example, typically implicates the civil law brand. However, this seems to have changed quite dramatically in recent years

---

47 *See* Wang Shengming, *supra* note 32, at 102–03.
48 The General Provisions cover purposes, applications, and principles of the Contract Law; formation, effect, performance, or termination of the contract; and remedies for breach of contract. The Specific Provisions deal with fifteen different contracts such as sales, technology, and transportation. The supplementary Provisions state residual matters such as effective day of the Contract Law as well as repeal of three existing contract laws.
49 The fifteen named contracts are: Sales; Supply and Use of Electricity, Water, Gas and Heating; Donation; Loans; Lease; Financial Leasing; Work; Construction; Transportation; Technology; Storage; Warehousing; Commission, Brokerage; and Intermediation.

as China has increasingly shown interest in borrowing from, and referencing, rules and legal concepts of the common law system.[50] The Contract Law in many aspects reflects this trend.

The Contract Law is distinguishable in several respects from China's previous contract law legislation. First, the Contract Law embodies a hybrid of civil law and common law principles, though its civil law roots still dominate. For example, the concept of "anticipatory repudiation," which is borrowed from common law (American contract law in particular), is adopted in the Contract Law.[51] Article 94(b) of the Contract Law provides that a contracting party may rescind the contract if, before the performance period expires, the other party to the contract explicitly expresses, or otherwise indicates through its acts, that it will not perform its major contractual obligations. Article 108 further provides that, where one party to a contract so demonstrates that it will not perform the contract, the other party to the contract may hold that party responsible for the breach of the contract before the performance period expires. Detailed discussion of these articles will be seen in other chapters of this book.

Another example is the Contract Law's provision on offer and acceptance, the first of its kind in Chinese contract legislation.[52] Under Article 13 of the Contract Law, formation of a contract requires offer and acceptance. Under Article 14, the offer is a manifestation of intent to contract, and its contents must be definite and certain, indicating that the offeror will be bound upon acceptance. Article 15 classifies as an invitation for offer the price quotation form, auction notice, public notice for bids, prospectus, as well as commercial advertisement. Acceptance is defined in Article 21 as the manifestation of the offeree's assent to an offer.

Second, the Contract Law attempts to be more market economy-oriented than previous contract legislation. China previously had a centrally planned economy where the government played a decisive role in the nation's economy. Since opening itself up to the outside world, China has made great efforts to transform from a planned economy to a market economy. In line with this

---

50 During the drafting the Contract Law in 1998 and 1999, the Legislation Affairs Commission of the Standing Committee of the National People's Congress of China unprecedentedly invited a group of American attorneys in Beijing to discuss the draft contract law. It clearly signaled that taking foreign law as references has become a major part in China's legislative process.

51 *See also* Liming Wang, *China's Proposed Uniform Contract Code*, 31 ST. MARY'S L.J. 7, 7–17 (1999).

52 Note that consideration is not required for contract formation in China. Therefore, mutual assent through offer and acceptance need not be supported by consideration in order for a contract to be valid.

endeavor, the Contract Law reflects a seeming abandonment of the notion that contracts are merely a vehicle for effectuating the state economic plan and the contracting parties must therefore implement the state economic plan through their contracts.

Nevertheless, the taint of the planned economy remains discernable in the Contract Law. Article 38 is an example. That article provides that, when the state issues a mandatory task or a state purchasing order, the legal persons or other organizations impacted shall enter into contracts between each other in accordance with their rights and obligations as stipulated by relevant laws and administrative regulations. Article 38 is subject to three limitations: (1) it only applies to legal persons or other organizations, not natural persons; (2) the legal persons or other organizations must be those that are affected by the state task or purchasing order; and (3) the state task must be mandatory and the purchasing order must be made by the state. Despite these limitations, however, the state plan as provided in Article 38 could still affect the contract making power of the parties.

Third, the Contract Law has incorporated within its provisions certain rules of relevant international treaties or conventions in the legislature's effort to fulfill China's treaty obligations and keep in line with internationally accepted practices. For instance, Articles 17 (Withdrawal of Offer), 18 (Revocation of Offer), and 31 (Acceptance with Additional or Modified Terms) of the Contract Law are in substance China's domestic version of Articles 15(b), 16(a), and 19(a)(b) of the 1980 UN Convention on Contracts for the International Sale of Goods (CISG). China has been a member of the CISG since December 1986.

In addition, under Article 11 of the Contract Law, written contracts must take a form that visibly displays the contract's contents, such as the form of a written contractual agreement, a letter, or electronic data text (including telegram, telex, fax, EDI, and E-mails). This provision is basically borrowed from the 1996 E-Commerce Model Law of United Nations Commission on International Trade Law (UNCITRAL). Moreover, Chapter 9 (Contract for Sales) of the Contract Law is primarily based on the provisions of the CISG as well as the UNIDROIT Principles of International Commercial Contracts.

3.3 The 2017 General Provisions of Civil Law

In March 2017, the NPC made a major stride toward adoption of a comprehensive civil code by enacting the General Provisions of Civil Law ("2017 GPCL"). As the general part of the future comprehensive civil code, the 2017 GPCL is primarily based on the 1986 Civil Code, though it contains more detailed provisions which reflect both improvement and development made in regulating civil affairs throughout the past decades. Effective October 1, 2017, the 2017

GPCL contains a total of 206 articles, fifty-five articles more than the 1986 Civil Code. Interestingly, the 2017 GPCL was not promulgated to replace the 1986 Civil Code; the two "codes" operate simultaneously. According to the Standing Committee of the NPC, if there is a conflict between the 1986 Civil Code and the 2017 GPCL, the latter controls under the "last in time" rule.

The 2017 GPCL consists of eleven chapters, encompassing general principles for civil activities, rules of person, agency, civil rights and acts, civil obligations, and statute of limitations. In contrast to the 1986 Civil Code, the 2017 GPCL divides the person into three categories: natural person, legal person, and non-legal person organization. With regard to the civil capacity of a natural person, the 2017 GPCL reduces the minimum age of the person with limited civil capacity from ten to eight years old. The 2017 GPCL also adds a provision for the protection of a fetus. Under Article 16 of the 2017 GPCL, with respect to such rights and interests of a fetus as inheritance and acceptance of donation, the fetus is viewed as possessing the capacity for entitlement to civil rights unless the fetus is dead at birth.

A notable feature of the 2017 GPCL with regard to civil rights is the law's protection of the right of personality. Article 109 of the 2017 GPCL provides that the personal liberty and human dignity of a natural person are protected by law. Under Article 110, the right of personality of a natural person includes the right to life, body, health, name, image, reputation, honor, privacy, marital autonomy, and etc. In recognition of the right of personality of a non-natural person, Article 110 further provides that a legal person or non-legal-person organization shall enjoy the rights of name, reputation, honor, and others as such. In addition to the right of personality, civil rights under the 2017 GPCL include property rights as well as the right of intellectual property.

Among the property rights protected by the 2017 GPCL are the right of thing, creditor right, right of succession, right of equity, and other investment right. A major legal cause of the creditor right is the contract. As a "civil act," the contract is subject to the provisions of the 2017 GPCL. As defined in Article 133 of the 2017 GPCL, a "civil act" is conduct in which civil actors/entities establish, modify, or terminate civil legal relationships through the manifestation of their intent. Thus, pursuant to Article 136, a civil act may not be modified or rescinded without the consent of the parties involved. The 2017 GPCL also contains a special section that governs the manifestation of intent for civil acts. For a civil act, such as a contract, to be valid and effective, three requirements must be met under Article 143 of the 2017 GPCL: (a) the actor must have the capacity for civil conduct; (b) intention must be manifested genuinely; and (c) there is no violation of mandatory provisions of the law or regulations, public order, or good social morals.

One last point regards the provision of *obligatio* under the 2017 GPCL. As noted, *obligatio* under the 1986 Civil Code is a special relationship of rights and obligations established between the parties concerned, under either agreed-upon terms or legal provisions. Under Article 118 of the 2017 GPCL, *obligatio* is the right of an obligee to request a specific obligor to perform or not to perform a certain act,[53] and such a right is derived from contract, tort, *negotiorum gestio*,[54] unjust enrichment,[55] or other provisions of law.[56] It is also emphasized in Article 118 that civil parties enjoy the right of *obligatio* in accordance with the law.[57]

3.4 The 2019 Foreign Investment Law

Another recent major legislation in China is the Foreign Investment Law (FIL), which was promulgated by the NPC on March 15, 2019. Effective on January 1. 2020, the FIL reshapes China's foreign investment legal regime and adopts a "pre-entry national treatment plus negative list" mechanism to replace the existing scheme regulating foreign investment enterprises known as FIEs. In the past decades, the FIEs were established in the country in three different forms, including equity joint ventures (EJV), contractual (or cooperative) joint ventures (CJV) and wholly foreign owned enterprises (WFOE), subject respectively to three different FIE laws.

The FIL unifies the FIEs legislations and streamlines the legal framework of foreign investment. The pre-entry national treatment is a market access system that grants to foreign investors a national treatment before their presence or establishment in the country. Under this system, foreign investors and their investments at the stage of investment admission are given the treatment no less than that given to the domestic investors and their investments. The negative list refers to the special measures that are used to control admission of foreign investment in specific areas. Under the FIL, pre-entry national treatment is granted only to the foreign investments in the areas outside the negative list. In other words, the pre-entry national treatment does not apply to the foreign investments in the industries or sectors contained in the negative list.

---

53 See 2017 GPCL, art. 118.
54 Under Article 121 of the GPCL, a *negotiorum gestio* means service provided under neither statutory nor contractual obligations to the other person in order to prevent the damage to the interests of the other person.
55 In Article 122 of the GPCL, unjust enrichment occurs when a person unjustly benefits without any legal basis.
56 See 2017 GPCL, art. 118.
57 See id.

The enactment of the FIL will affect the approval requirements for the FIE contracts. Under the Contract Law and the FIE laws, all EJV and CJV contracts require government approval after their conclusion in order to take effect. Under the FIL, however, if the Sino-Foreign joint ventures are not covered by the negative list, no government approval will be needed for the effectiveness of their contracts as a result of the operation of pre-entry national treatment. In addition, as it will be discussed later in the book, the FIL makes the application of international treaty optional, which is at adds with the existing statutory provisions.

4 Judicial Interpretation and Guiding Cases

China has a unitary state system. The Chinese judiciary consists of four levels of courts. At the national level is the SPC, the top judicial body of the country, followed by the high people's court at the provincial level. The next level is the intermediate people's court, followed by the basic people's court, which is commonly referred to as the trial court, at the county level.[58] In late 2014, China began to create circuit (tribunal) courts and, as of 2016, a total of six circuit courts, covering twenty-six provinces and municipalities in the mainland, had been established.[59] Note, however, that the circuit courts are merely the dispatched branches of the SPC and thus do not add any additional level to the current court system of China.

The Chinese judiciary plays a unique role in the development of Chinese contract law, as well as Chinese law generally. Chinese courts are distinctive in several aspects from the courts in many other countries. First, Chinese courts do not have the power to make or even to interpret law. Under the Chinese constitution, the Chinese judiciary has only the power to implement and apply the law. Second, an important function of the Chinese judiciary in the implementation of law is judicial interpretation. In China, legal interpretation contemplates both legislative interpretation and judicial interpretation. The

---

58 As of 2017, there are thirty-two high people's courts (excluding Hong Kong and Macao), 409 intermediate people's courts, and 3,117 basic people's courts in China.

59 The First Circuit, located in Shenzhen, covers Guangdong, Guangxi, Hainan, and Hunan; the Second Circuit in Shenyang is responsible for Liaoning, Jilin and Hei Long Jiang; the Third Circuit in Nanjing deals with Jiangsu, Shanghai, Zhejiang, Fujian and Jiangxi; the Fourth Circuit in Zhengzhou handles Henan, Sanxi, Hubei, and Anhui; the Fifth Circuit in Chongqing takes cases from Chongqing, Sichuan, Guizhou, Yunnan, and Tibet; and the Sixth Circuit has jurisdiction over Shanxi, Gansu, Qinghai, Ningxia, and Xinjiang.

legislative interpretation is the power rested with the State legislature and the judiciary only has the power to offer judicial interpretation. The former is purposed to tell what the law is, while the latter is aimed at ensuring that the law is applied as intended by the legislature. Third, under the Chinese legal system, only the SPC has the power to make judicial interpretation.[60] Therefore, judicial interpretation in China is actually SPC interpretation.

According to the SPC, judicial interpretation can take four different forms: "interpretation," "provision," "reply," and "decision."[61] Another form that is considered to have the same effect of judicial interpretation is "notice" issued by the SPC.[62] Although it remains debatable whether judicial interpretation is a source of law in China, judicial interpretation binds all people's courts.[63] The people's courts have often relied on judicial interpretation, especially in situations where the law is unclear.[64] Since the Contract Law was adopted in 1999, the SPC has issued four interpretations for the law's implementation. The latest one was issued in 2014, concerning financial lease contracts.[65]

In addition to judicial interpretation, the SPC has in recent years developed a "guiding case" system. According to the SPC's *Provisions Concerning the Work*

---

60   *See* Standing Committee of the NPC, *Resolution on Strengthening the Work of Interpretation of Law* (1981), available at http://www.npc.gov.cn/wxzl/gongbao/2000_12/06/content_5004401.htm.

61   According to the SPC, "interpretation" is intended to handle the issue of how to specifically apply a certain piece of law or how to apply the law to a specific type of case or matter in judicial practices. The "provisions" refer to judicial interpretation made in lieu of regulations or opinions adopted on the basis of need for judicial work pursuant to the legislative spirit. The "reply" is an interpretation in response to the request from the higher people's courts or the military courts for direction on the specific application of laws in the trial. The "decision" is the form employed by the Supreme People's Court to amend or repeal a judicial interpretation. *See* Supreme People's Court, PROVISIONS ON THE WORK OF JUDICIAL INTERPRETATION, art. 5, at http://www.eastlaw.net/chineselaws/judicial/JudicialInterpretation2007.htm. The Provisions were issued on March 23, 2007 and became effective on April 1, 2007. *See id.*

62   *See* Zhang Weiping, CIVIL PROCEDURE LAW 16 (Law Press, 3d ed. 2013).

63   *See* Mo Zhang, *Pushing the Envelope: Application of Guiding Cases in Chinese Courts and Development of Case Law in China*, 26 WASH. INT'L L.J. 269, 284 (2017), (hereinafter referred to as Guiding Cases).

64   *See id.*

65   The four interpretations include: (a) the SPC's "Interpretation on Several Issues Concerning Implementation of the Contract Law of China (I)," issued on December 19, 1999; (b) the SPC's "Interpretation on Several Issues Concerning Implementation of the Contract Law of China (II)," issued on April 24, 2009; (c) the SPC's "Interpretation on the Issues of Application of Law in Adjudicating Disputes over Sales Contracts," issued on May 10, 2012; and (d) the SPC's "Interpretation on the Issues of Application of Law in Adjudicating Disputes of Financial Lease Contracts," issued on February 24, 2014.

of Guiding Cases (Guiding Case Provisions) issued in November 2010, development of the guiding case system in the people's courts was intended to help unify the application of law, enhance the quality of adjudication, and maintain judicial justice.[66] China is known as a civil law country where the courts generally do not follow precedent.[67] The establishment of the guiding case system in the people's courts, however, turned a great deal of focus to the role of cases in judicial proceedings.

The guiding cases are the cases selected nationwide and published periodically by the SPC. The primary purpose of publishing the selected cases is to help guide the lower courts in their adjudication of the same or similar cases. As a matter of fact, case publication by the SPC began as early as in 1985,[68] and at that time, publication of cases was considered to be part of China's judicial reform to promote judicial efficiency and transparency. The issuance of the 2010 Guiding Case Provisions systemizes the application of guiding cases in the Chinese judiciary. In 2015, the SPC adopted the Detailed Rules for the Implementation of the Guiding Case Provisions to further provide judges with instructions on how to use guiding cases in the court adjudications.[69]

Since the first four guiding cases were made public by the SPC in December 2011, a total of 112 cases, as noted, have been published as of February 25, 2019.[70] Although there have been debates on whether the guiding cases have any binding force, the holdings of and reasoning employed in the guiding cases

---

66   *See* the SPC, Provisions Concerning the Work of Guiding Cases (Nov. 26, 2010) [hereinafter "Guiding Case Provisions"].

67   *See generally* John H. Merryman & Rogelio P. Perdomo, THE CIVIL LAW TRADITION 1–38 (3d ed., 2007).

68   The *Gazette of the Supreme People's Court* is an official publication of the Supreme People's Court and is published monthly. Prior to the publication of the *Gazette*, the Supreme People's Court already started compiling cases. However, such compilation was issued in the form of internal documents within the courts. In 1983, for example, the Supreme People's Court compiled seventy-five selected criminal cases and sent them to the lower courts for reference. From 1983 to 1989, the total number of cases complied reached 293. *See* Hu Yunteng & Yu Tongzhi, *Study on Several Important and Complicated Issues Concerning the System of Case Guidance*, 6 JURIS. RES. 3 (2008).

69   *See* the SPC, the Detailed Rules for the Implementation of the Guiding Case Provisions, adopted on June 2, 2015, available at http://openlaw.cn/news/14db70aa-f878a9952d12351480f964dd.

70   The last six guiding cases are all related disputes with the countries participating in China's "Belt and Road" initiative. The cases involve the disputes over international sale of goods contract, international shipping contract, letter of guarantee fraud, shipwreck rescue contract, issuance of a letter of credit, and the application for the establishment of a maritime liability limitation fund. See SPC, Guiding Case Status Report, February 25, 2019, available at https://www.chinacourt.org/article/detail/2019/02/id/3736851.shtml.

are believed to have great influence on the trials and judgments of the future cases bearing similarities or even the cases in general.[71]

The Chinese Constitution mandates that the SPC be supervised by the NPC.[72] Each year, the SPC is required to deliver an annual work report to the General Assembly of the NPC. The same is true at all local levels. What has become troublesome is the difference between legislative interpretation and judicial interpretation. Confusion arises in several aspects. First of all, it is unclear where the line is between interpretation of law and application of law because, in judicial practices, the issue of application of law often involves what a provision of law actually means and how such provision should be applied.[73] Secondly, a question commonly encountered is whether judicial interpretation has the same effect as legislative interpretation. Put differently, the question is whether judicial interpretation can be deemed as law.[74] Thirdly, from a practical viewpoint, judges in making their judgments often struggle with the issue of whether their judgment can rely solely on judicial interpretation.[75] In other words, it is questionable whether a court may explain (interpret) the meaning of the law that is to be applied in the way intended by the judicial interpretation without referring to the law.

The lack of clarity as to the distinctions between legislative interpretation *vis-a-vis* judicial interpretation often results in a "clash" between the legislature and the judiciary. On the one hand, the ambiguity makes it possible for the judiciary to step over into the realm of interpreting the law. On the other hand, the legislatures seem very sensitive about being offended by the judiciary, and in many cases appear to be antagonistic to the possible intrusion by the judiciary into the legislative areas during the judicial proceedings that involve the application of law. The "Corn Seeds" case might best illustrate the kind of conflict between the two governmental bodies and the dilemma facing the people's courts. For purposes of discussion, the full text of the court decision is translated as follows:

---

71 Fore detailed discussion about guiding cases, see Mo Zhang, Guiding Cases, *supra* note 62.
72 See the Constitution of People's Republic of China, 1982(as amended 2018), art. 3 & 128, a full text of English translation is available at http://en.pkulaw.cn/display.aspx?cgid=311950&lib=law (hereinafter referred to as 1982 Chinese Constitution).
73 See Cao Shibing, *The Legal Status of the Judgment and Judicial Interpretation of the Supreme People's Court*, 3 CHINESE SCI. L. [first page on which article begins], 175–81 (2006), available at http://www.iolaw.org.cn/showNews.asp?id=16296.
74 *See generally* Ji Cheng, JUDICIAL INTERPRETATION OF THE SUPREME PEOPLE'S COURT: A PRELIMINARY STUDY (China Univ. of Political Sci. & Law 2007).
75 *See id.*

Luo Yang Intermediate People's Court of Henan Province
Civil Judgment Document

(2003) Luo Min Chu Zhi No. 6

Plaintiff: Ru Yang County Seeds Co.
Official Representative: Cui Hao Xian, Manager of Plaintiff
Legal Counsel: Chen Zhan Jun, Attorney from Luo Yang Ju Xing He Law Firm

Defendant: Yi Cun County Seeds Co.
Official Representative: Zhang Xia Lei, Manage of Defendant
Legal Counsel: Wang Xiang Ru, Attorney from Luo Yang Da Xin Law Firm
Agent *ad litem*: Song Yan Jun, Head of Commodity Pricing Division of Commodity Pricing Bureau of Yi Cun County

This case is filed by plaintiff Ru Yang County Seeds Co. (hereinafter referred to as Ru Yang Co.) to sue defendant Yi Cuan County Seeds Co. (hereinafter referred to as Yi Cuan Co.) for the disputes involving a contract on entrusted reproduction of corn seeds. After taking the case, this Court has formed a collegial panel according to the law and the panel has held open court hearings, attended by Chen Zhan Jun, Legal Counsel for plaintiff, and Zhang Xia Lei, Official Representative of defendant, Wang Xiang Ru, Legal Counsel and Song Yan Jun, Agent *ad litem* for defendant. The court hearings now have come to an end.

Plaintiff Yu Yang Co. claimed that on May 22, 2001, plaintiff entered into the "Contract on Entrusted Reproduction of Corn Seeds" with defendant. Under the contract, plaintiff agreed to provide defendant with 4,857 *jin* of parent corn seeds (1 Chinese *jin* is equivalent to 0.5kg or 1.1lb, note added) and defendant agreed to use them to reproduce 200,000 *jin* of hybrid corn seeds specified as Nong Da 108 with a quality matching the national standard of second grade or above. The term for the reproduction expired on October 31, 2002. The contract also contained explicit provisions with regard to other rights and obligations of the parties.

Plaintiff asserted that during the course of actual performance of the contract, defendant failed to fulfill its obligations and did not deliver to plaintiff any hybrid corn seeds reproduced. As a result, on the basis of market profit margin between RMB 3.4 to 3.9 Yuan per *jin*, plaintiff has suffered a loss of expectation interest for about RMB 680,000 to 780,000 Yuan, and plus other economic damages, the total actual loss was around RMB 1,000,000 Yuan. After several unsuccessful negotiations, plaintiff brought this lawsuit, and asked the court to order: (1) defendant pay plaintiff RMB 1,000,000 for contract damages and other economic loss, and (2) defendant bear all litigation costs. During the court hearings, plaintiff modified its claims to request instead to recover from defendant (1) RMB 12,185 for the cost of parent seeds, and (2) RMB 703,784.60 for contract damages.

Defendant argued that its failure to perform the contract was caused by the significant drop in production resulting from the severe drought, and plaintiff should also bear certain liability for breach of contract because during the production and processing of the seeds plaintiff did not conduct any on-site inspection nor did plaintiff participate in any seeds purchasing. Defendant further argued that the "Regulations for Administration of Crop Seeds of He Nan Province" explicitly provided that purchasing and selling of seeds must strictly follow the provincial policy of unified pricing, and that the "Notice of Methods for Administration of Major Crop Seeds" jointly issued by the Commodity Pricing Bureau of Henan Province and the Bureau of Agriculture of Henan Province clearly provided a formula for calculating the selling price of seeds. Defendant contended that under the formula, the overall profit rate for the hybrid seeds shall be within 23% margin, and the net profit should be between 8% and 10%, and therefore even if Yi

Cuan Co. had fully performed the contract, plaintiff's retainable interest should be within RMB 16,800 and 25,000 Yuan.

During the hearings, the Court found that:

Plaintiff and defendant entered into the "Contract on Entrusted Reproduction of Corn Seeds" on May 22, 2001. Under the contract, plaintiff would at its own cost purchase 4,875 *jin* of Nong Da 108 hybrid corn seeds, and entrust defendant to reproduce 650 *mu* (about 97 acres, note added) with a total output of 200,000 *jin* hybrid cord seeds meeting the quality standard of the State Second Grade or above. The period for performance of the contract would end on October 30, 2002. It was also provided in the contract that after receiving the produced hybrid corn seeds, plaintiff would pay defendant a seeds reproduction fee at RMB 0.2 Yuan per *jin* (including the expenses of reproduction management, purchasing, shelling, short-distance transportation to plaintiff's processing factory, and other expenses). The price for plaintiff to accept the seeds (the contract price, note added) would be the base-purchasing price plus reproduction fee and the base-purchasing price would be calculated at 2.2 to 2.5 times as much as local corn seeds market price at the time of purchasing. Plaintiff's expenses for purchasing the parent seeds would be offset from the contract price when it received the reproduced seeds.

According to the contract, defendant would be responsible for the reproduction management, technical instruction, purchasing and shelling, and transporting of the seeds to plaintiff's processing factory. During the course of reproduction, plaintiff would visit the site 3 to 4 times. When purchasing the reproduced seeds, plaintiff would send one person to participate in examining the quality of the seeds. The total weight of the reproduced seeds receipted by plaintiff would be the net weight after deducting the water content of the seeds at the ratio of 3–5% of gross weight. It was also provided in the contract that plaintiff would unconditionally accept all seeds reproduced by defendant while defendant would unconditionally provide plaintiff with total output of the reproduced seeds regardless of the corn seeds market situation.

On the day when the contract was signed, plaintiff provided defendant with 3,899 *jin* of Nong Da 108 maternal corn seeds and 975 *jin* of paternal corn seeds at a cost of RMB 12,185 Yuan. Defendant then under the contract planted these seeds into 650 *Mu* of the seed reproduction field. As of today after the harvest of the seeds, however, defendant did not make any delivery of the reproduced corn seeds of Nong Da 108 to plaintiff as required by the contract.

The Court further found that:

1. The accounting records of defendant from May 1, 2002 to June 30, 2002 revealed that during the same period of time, the price defendant used to purchase Nong Da 108 corn seeds from farmers at the reproduction field was RMB 2.904 Yuan/kg. The "Monitor Report of Yi Cuan County of Luo Yang Municipality on the Standard of Price and Fees for Major Agricultural Products" also showed that the medium corn market price at Yi Cuan County in October 2001 was RMB 1.00 Yuan/kg. In the meantime, defendant's accounting ledgers during April 1, 2002 and June 30, 2002 indicated that the wholesale price for the coated corn seeds of Nong Da 108 was RMB 10.60 Yuan/kg, and the wholesale price of the bare corn seeds was 10.00/kg. For the same period, the wholesale price for coated and bare corn seeds at each of the retail stations of Ru Yang County was the same as that of Yi Cuan County.

2. The accounting books of Yi Cuan County (from May 1, 2002 to June 30, 2002) evidenced that the cost of the corn seeds sun-drying was RMB 8 Yuan/ton, the cost of turnover for shelling was RMB 8 Yuan/ton, the labeling fee was RMB5.253 Yuan/ton, the packaging fee RMB 30 Yuan/ton, and the unloading fee RMB 3.5/ton. On this basis, the processing cost for the corn seeds was RMB 0.062154 Yuan/kg. Plaintiff agreed to compute this cost into the price of the reproduced corn seeds.

3. Defendant Ru Yang Co. was exempted from paying Business Income Tax and Value Added Tax for the year 2002 under the State Policy.

4. The "Regulations for Administration of Crop Seeds of Henan Province" (Provisional) took effect on Aril 27, 1884, and its successor "Regulations for Administration of Crop Seeds of Henan Province" (Regulations), which was amended on October 22, 1993, was effective on November 8, 1989. Article 36 of the Regulations provides: "the purchase and sale of seeds shall strictly comply with the provincial policy of unified price, and no price can be raised without authorization. With regard to the seeds for which there is no provincially unified price, the price shall be determined jointly by the city (district) or county administrative department of agriculture and department of pricing."

On August 20, 1998, the Henan Provincial Bureau of Commodity Pricing and the Provincial Bureau of Agriculture together issued the "Yu Jia Nong Zhi (1998) No. 188 Document," namely the "Notice of Methods for Administration of Major Crop Seeds" (Notice). The first paragraph of the Notice required that the method for price administration of major crop seeds be the government-guided price, and the price management be conducted under the principle of "unified leadership and level-by-level management." Under the Notice, the calculating formula for the sale price of seeds is set as "sale price = (cost of purchase + seed-selecting process fee) x (1 + rate of composite deviation) + tax." On July 8, 2000, "the Seeds Law of the People's Republic of China," which repealed the "Regulation of Seeds Administration of the People's Republic of China" promulgated by the State Council on March 13, 1989, was adopted, and it went into effect on December 1, 2000.

The Seeds Law is silent about the price of purchase and sale of seeds, and in addition, the price category made by the State Commission of Planning and other relevant departments of the State Council does not make the price of corn seeds the state fixed price or the state guided price. Moreover, there is no provincial price category in Henan Province. Therefore, the price of goods and services that are not listed in the price category at both the state and provincial levels shall be determined by the market.

5. The book "Fine Seeds of Crops in China" tells that Nong Da 108 corn seeds will produce about 600 kg corns per *mu* if planted in the spring, or around 500 kg/*mu* if planted in the summer. The "Yearbook of Luo Yang Statistics" indicates that in 2001 the production output of corns per *mu* was about 208 kg.

It is therefore held that:

The contract entered into by and between plaintiff and defendant is a valid contract because it is a manifestation of the true intent of the parties, and its contents do not violate any prohibitive provisions of law or regulation. Once the contract is established, the parties shall fulfill their respective contractual obligations conscientiously. In the case at bench, after plaintiff provided defendant with the parent corn seeds under the requirements of the contract, defendant failed to deliver to plaintiff the corn seeds in the agreed quantity and quality in accordance with the contract. Such failure constitutes a breach of contract, for which defendant shall be held liable. According to the "Yearbook of Luo Yang Statistics," the production output of corns per *mu* was about 208 kg in 2001, which was lower than the average output during past years. In addition, the drought situation in the three-month period of May, June, and July 2001 can be proved by the meteorological records provided by the Meteorology Bureau of Yu Cuan County. Therefore, the agreed output of corn seeds per *mu* by the parties should be reduced accordingly by 10%, and defendant's argument in this regard is sustained.

With regard to the agreed 3–4 times onsite inspection by plaintiff, it shall be regarded as plaintiff's right, of which plaintiff shall be free to choose not to exercise. Thus, plaintiff's choice to give up the inspection right does not constitute a breach of contract, and thus defendant's assertion against plaintiff in this regard must be denied. After the Seeds Law took effect, the corn price is to be determined on the basis of the market situation. *Since the "Regulations for Administration of Crop Seeds of Henan Province" is a local law subordinate to national law in terms of legal effect, any of its provisions that are in conflict with the Seeds Law shall necessarily be void. Furthermore, the "Notice" of Henan Provincial Bureau of Commodity Pricing and Provincial Bureau of Agriculture was issued under the "Regulations," and any provision contained in the "Notice" that is inconsistent with the Seeds Law must also be void* (emphasis added). Consequently, defendant's argument about using the formula provided in the "Notice" to calculate the actual loss of plaintiff's expected interest has no legal ground and should not be supported by the Court.

The Court concludes that, because defendant never delivered to plaintiff any reproduced corn seeds under the contract, defendant shall pay plaintiff for the cost of RMB 12,285 Yuan for the purchased parent corns seeds, and defendant shall also be liable for the loss of plaintiff's expected interest on the ground of breach of contract. Therefore, in accordance with Article 4 of General Principles of Civil Law of People's Republic of China, and Articles 109, 112, 113, and 118 of Contract Law of the People's Republic of China, it is so ordered:

1. Defendant, within 10 days after this judgment becomes effective, pay plaintiff for the cost of parent corn seeds in the amount of RMB 12,185 Yuan;
2. Defendant, within 10 days after this judgment becomes effective, pay plaintiff for its economic loss in the amount of RMB 59,7001 Yuan;
3. Plaintiff's other claims be dismissed.

The cost for hearing the case is RMB 12,170 Yuan, the property attachment cost RMB 3,520 Yuan, and other costs RMB 2,434 Yuan. Of the three above items with a total cost of RMB 18,124 Yuan, defendant shall bear RMB 16,500 Yuan, and plaintiff RMB 1,624 Yuan.

If any party disagrees with this judgment, it may appeal to the High People's Court of Henan Province within 15 days after being served with this judgment by handing over to this Court the petition for appeal with copies of the appeal to the other party according to the number of participants.

Head Judge: Li Hui Juan
Judge: Zai Tao
Acting Judge: Zhu Meng
(Sealed)
May 27, 2003
Clerk: Zhang Yan Jun

This judgment, though not perfect, is among the judgments that are clearly written and employ some analytical reasoning. The most relevant part of this judgment is the challenge that the judge made to the local regulations that conflict with the State Seeds Law (national law). In reaching the conclusion, the trial judge examined the local regulations in light of the national law and made rational efforts to preserve the authority of the national law. Such efforts in every respect are within the four corners of the Legislation Law of China. Article 79 of the Legislation Law explicitly provides that the legal authority of state law is higher than that of local law and regulations.[76] Thus, any existing

---

76   Adopted on March 15, 2000, the "Legislation Law of China" regulates the enactment, amendment, and repeal of laws, administrative regulations, local laws and regulations, regulations of autonomy region, and specific regulation.

local law or regulation that contradicts the newly enacted national law shall be void. In addition, under the Judge Law of China, judges are required to faithfully implement the Constitution and laws and it is the obligation of the judges to strictly observe the Constitution and laws.[77]

Unfortunately, however, when the judgment in the "Corn Seeds" case was handed down, it was immediately interpreted as being offensive to the local government. The judge's opinion concerning the application of the Seeds Law over local regulations was blamed as an intrusion into local government power and, even more seriously, a violation of Chinese people's congress system. On October 13, 2003, both the Office and Legal System Division of the Standing Committee of the People's Congress of Henan Province issued a flamingly worded notice condemning the judgment and urging the High People's Court of Henan to vigorously look into and handle this "serious matter."[78]

On October 21, 2003, the High People's Court circulated a Notice of Criticism among its court system characterizing the judgment as law-breaking conduct of the court which threatened the authority of local law and regulations as well as the unified legal system. Ironically, when warning that if the same conduct ever happened again, the judge and her direct superior both would be seriously held liable, the High People's Court of Henan unequivocally stated that preventing the incident from happening again was essential to maintaining "judicial justice and efficiency."[79]

Under the tremendous pressure from the local government, the Luo Yang Intermediate People's Court issued a self-criticism Notice internally on October 28, 2003 in which it directly blamed Judge Li Hui Juan and her supervisor, deputy chief judge of the First Civil Division of the Court, for their failure to duly perform their duties as judges. In its Notice, the Court stated that, during the trial, the people's court may only apply the law and has no authority to question the validity of local law and regulations. Considering this incident to be a serious political matter, the Court further stressed that no judgment shall ever contain anything that would render local laws and regulations void.[80] Consequently, Judge Li Hui

---

77 See the Law of Judges of China, adopted on February 28, 1995 and amended on June 30, 2001, art. 3 & 7 (hereinafter referred to as Judge Law).
78 See Official Document of the Office of the Standing Committee of the People's Congress of Henan Province, Yu Fa Chang Ban, No. 78 (2003); Official Document of Legal System Division of the Standing Committee of the People's Congress of Henan Province, Yu Ren Chang Fa, No. 18 (2003).
79 See Official Notice of the High People's Court of Henan Province, Yu Gao Fa, No. 187 (2003).
80 See Official Notice of Luo Yang Intermediate People's Court, Luo Zhong Fa, No. 147 (2003).

Juan's employment with the court was suspended for months and, although her employment was later reinstated, she was precluded from being the head judge that directly hears cases (at least for quite a period of time). Clearly this incident may jeopardize her promotion in the court or even her career as a judge.

It is without doubt that the Luo Yang case exemplifies how judges may be treated in China when they attempt to be independent. The case also illustrates the limits placed on Chinese judges and courts as to their ability to engage in legal interpretation. Of course, there arose great sympathy for Judge Li in the Chinese legal community and many people openly offered strong support for Judge Li and her decision not to apply the local law and regulations that contradicted the national law. Indeed, the issue of whether the people's court may question the validity of local law and regulations is clearly debatable under the Chinese Constitution, particularly when there is an obvious conflict between the national law and the local law.

As a matter of fact, in early 1993, the Supreme People's Court made an attempt in this regard. On March 11, 1993, in its "Answer to the High People's Court of Fu Jian Province Concerning Application of Law When There Is a Conflict Between National Administrative Law and Local Law," the Supreme People's Court made it clear that, when hearing administrative cases, if local law and regulations are inconsistent with national law or administrative regulations, the latter shall be applied. According to the Supreme People's Court, this Answer was made after consulting with the Standing Committee of the National People's Congress.[81]

Applying the Supreme People's Court's "Answer" to the Luo Yang case, there was nothing wrong with Judge Li's refusal to apply the local law. But the spark that caused the fire seemed to be Judge Li's opinion on the validity of the local law—intolerable because it was deemed to have broken an unalterable rule: "You may not apply the local law but you should not say so." This necessarily raises many legitimate questions that deserve serious discussions. The questions include: (1) Which law should the judges follow in their decision making—national law or local law? (2) What does the "unified legal system" really mean? (3) What is judicial power under the Constitution? (4) Should a judge be held liable for his or her judgments? (5) What is the real relationship between national law and local law? (6) Does the legislative body have the power to interfere with judicial matters?[82] The outcome of the Luo Yang case

---

81   See the SPC, Answer to the High People's Court of Fujian Province on the Question Which Law Shall Be Applied When in Administrative Cases the Provisions of Local Law and Regulations Were Inconsistent with the Law and Regulations, Fa Han, No. 16 (1993).

82   In November of 2003, a roundtable discussion on the Luo Yang case was held at the Tsinghua University School of Law in Beijing. Attended by a number of constitutional

may also best explain why many judges in Chinese courts are reluctant to offer detailed reasons for their decisions—because there are so many minefields lying ahead.

Interestingly, the trial court decision in the Lou Yang case was appealed by both plaintiff and defendant to the High People's Court of Henan Province. In a decision entered on May 9, 2004, the High People's Court affirmed the trial court's opinion concerning the legal effect of the National Seeds Law over the local regulations in question. The High People's Court held that, since the contract in the case was concluded on May 22, 2001, the contract's validity had to be viewed in the light of the Contract Law and related judicial interpretations.

On that ground, the court stated that the validity of the contract had to be assessed under Article 52(5) of the Contract Law as well as Article 4 of the Supreme People's Court "Explanations to the Questions Concerning Application of the Contract Law of the People's Republic of China." Under Article 52(5), a contract is null and void if it violates mandatory provisions of law or regulations. As required by Article 4, after the Contract Law took effect, the people's court, when determining the voidance of a contract, was to apply the law passed the National People's Congress as well as regulations adopted by the State Council, but not local rules or regulations.

The High People's Court upheld the trial court decision on the basis that the facts on which the trial court's judgment was entered were clearly ascertained, the trial court's application of law was correct, and there was no improper handling of the substance of the case. Notwithstanding, the High People's Court

---

law scholars, lawyers, and judges, the discussion dealt with several interesting questions arising from the Luo Yang case. Some of the questions seemed both controversial and sensitive:
- **Constitutional Question**: (a) The relationship between the legislature and the judiciary—who deals with what? (b) Review of law and constitutionality—should the people's court have judicial review power? (c) What should be the division between national legislative power and local legislative power, as well as between central governmental authority and local governmental authority? (d) Judicial effect of constitutionally legal questions—what judicial effect should the Legislation Law have? (e) Understanding of the unified legal system—who has the obligation to maintain the unified legal system?
- **Judicial Question**: (a) Are the judges the state judges or local judges and what should the judges protect? (b) Should there be legal reasoning in court judgments and, if so, how should such legal reasoning be written? (c) Is judicial independence the independence of courts or the independence of judges, and should the "trial committee" be abolished? (d) Relationship between a higher people's court and the lower people's courts—should the High People's Court be responsible for the conduct of the lower people's courts?

noted in its opinion that the trial court made two inappropriate statements: (1) that, after the adoption of the Seeds Law, the price of the corn seeds is to be determined by the market; and (2) that the "Regulations for Administration of Crop Seeds of Henan Province" is a local law subordinate to national law in terms of legal effect, such that any of its provisions that conflict with the Seeds Law is necessarily void. The High Court held that such statements had to be corrected.[83]

5 The Ideology of "Governing the Country by Law"

Contract law legislation in China is considered part of the country's endeavor to establish a rule-based regime for civil matters. Since the early 1990s, China has endeavored to re-construct its national legal infrastructure and to uphold the idea that the country is governed by law. This initiative, which was later stated as the building of a socialist legal system with Chinese characteristics, was not only a result of lessons learned from the ten-year Cultural Revolution chaos, but was also an symbol intended to indicate China's commitment to the rule of law. The Chinese characteristics inherent in China's new legal system suggest that the country will develop its legal system in a uniquely Chinese way, rather than following Western legal and political systems.

From the West's viewpoint, what is generally lacking in China from a legal perspective is the "rule of law"—a commonly used but poorly defined phrase in the West.[84] From China's point of view, however, developing the rule of law preliminarily requires making laws, and China remains in this preliminary stage.[85] In China, the concept of the rule of law is normally referred to as "governing the country by law." Modern Chinese leaders commonly use this rhetoric to differentiate themselves from leaders of the nation's past, such as Mao, during whose eras the country was actually ruled by men. Under Chinese law, the core of a rule-based legal system consists of four basic elements: (1) there must be laws to follow, (2) laws must be observed, (3) enforcement of laws must be strict, and (4) violation of laws must be dealt with.[86]

---

[83] See Civil Judgment of the High People's Court of He Nan Province, Yu Fa Min 2 Zhong Zhi, No. 153 (2003).

[84] See Barry M. Hager, *The Rule of Law: Defining It and Defending It in the Asian Context*, in THE RULE OF LAW: PERSPECTIVES FROM THE PACIFIC RIM 1, 1–10 (2000).

[85] See Xin Chunying, *supra* note 9, at 338–53.

[86] See also Albert H.Y. Chen, *Toward A Legal Enlightenment: Discussion in Contemporary China on the Rule of Law*, in THE RULE OF LAW: PERSPECTIVES FROM THE PACIFIC RIM, *supra* note 83, at 13–14.

INTRODUCTION   29

   In order to implement the ideology of "governing the country by law," China took several steps. In 1997, the CPC set as a goal for the country the establishment of a socialist legal system with Chinese characteristics by 2010.[87] In 1999, the NPC amended the Constitution of China (1982) by inserting a provision in Article 5 that states that the People's Republic of China is committed to governing the country in accordance with the law and building China into a socialist country ruled by law.[88] In 2011, China announced that a socialist system of laws with Chinese characteristics had been formed in the country. Per the State Council's White Paper, the system consists of one core, three levels, and seven major branches of laws, with the Constitution being supreme, the laws being the main body, and administrative and local regulations being the major components.[89]

   Among the seven braches of laws is the civil and commercial law. Contract Law is a major law in the civil and commercial law arenas. To the extent that the country is to be ruled by law, the law of contract is expected to play a vital role in regulating China's civil affairs. More generally, China's decades-long legal reform has helped put into place more than 240 laws, over 706 administrative regulations, and some 8,600 local regulations. In other words, there has been significant progress in China in terms of legislation enactment, and the number of laws and regulations keeps growing. What is critical, however, is not China has many laws and regulations, but that the laws and regulations that are promulgated are strictly observed and effectively enforced. Enforcement remains the greatest challenge facing the nation.

6   Unsolved Issue: Judicial Independence

A fundamental issue that remains unsolved in China concerns judicial independence. Despite the differences in the understandings of the concept of the rule of law which persist in China, there is a general consensus in the country

---

87   See Jiang Zemin, REPORT AT THE 15TH NATIONAL CONGRESS OF THE CPC (Sep. 12, 1997), available at http://www.fas.org/news/china/1997/970912-prc.htm.
88   See the 1982 Chinese Constitution, *supra* note 72, art.5.
89   See Information Office of the State Council, White Paper on the Socialist Legal System with Chinese Characteristics (Nov. 11, 2011). According the White Paper, there are one core, three levels, and seven branches in the system—the core is the Constitution; the seven branches include the Constitution and related laws, civil and commercial laws, administration laws, economic laws, social laws, criminal laws, and litigation and non-litigation procedural laws; and the three levels represent the hierarchy of laws, namely laws, regulations, and local rules/decrees.

that an impartial and independent judiciary is an indispensable part of the rule of law. Chinese courts, however, are viewed both at home and abroad as lacking independence, something which has vitally threatened the judiciary's capacity to effectuate justice. In response to mounting public outcry and criticism, the SPC since 1999 has made building "justice and efficiency" the main priority of the courts.[90] Notwithstanding the SPC's efforts, however, the people's courts still encounter insurmountable hurdles when attempting to exercise their judicial power independently.

Indeed, judicial independence is a recognized principle in the Chinese Constitution and Chinese laws. The first Chinese Constitution, which was adopted in 1954,[91] provided that the people's courts shall adjudicate cases independently and abide only by laws.[92] Article 126 of the 1982 Constitution, as amended in 2004, provides that the people's courts shall exercise judicial power independently according to stipulations of laws, free of any interference by administrative agencies, social organizations, or individuals.[93] This constitutional provision is also embodied in the 1979 Organic Law of the People's Courts, as amended in 1983,[94] as well as the 1995 Law of Judges, as amended in 2001.[95]

Therefore, by the text of the Chinese Constitution and laws, the people's courts are afforded independent judicial power. The question remains, however, whether the Chinese judiciary will actually become independent. The quick answer, unfortunately, may be "no" or "not yet." First of all, under CPC's leadership, separation of powers is viewed as contrary to Chinese characteristics, and therefore is not allowed. A major political function of the SPC is to safeguard and ensure the implementation of the policies of the CPC.

---

90   See Supreme Court President Xiao Yang, Working Report of the Supreme People's Court to the First Session of the 10th National People's Congress (Mar. 11, 2003). The full text of the report is available at http://www.court.gov.cn/work/200303280001.htm.
91   China adopted four Constitutions in 1954, 1975, 1978, and 1982, respectively. See *supra* note 13".
92   See the Constitution of the People's Republic of China 1954.
93   See the 1982 Chinese Constitution, *supra* note 72, art. 126.
94   Article 4 of the Organic Law of the People's Courts is exactly a copy of Article 126 of the 1982 Constitution.
95   The Law of Judges of China was adopted on February 28, 1995 and amended on June 30, 2001. In Article 1 of the law (as amended), it is stated that the purpose of this law is to safeguard the independent exercise of judicial power and judicial justice by the people's courts. Article 8 provides that a people's court judge shall have the right to adjudicate cases independently without interference by administrative agencies, social organizations, and individuals.

Secondly, under the people's congress system, the judiciary is subordinate to the legislature, which is controlled by the CPC, and courts must report to the people's congress and even to the politburo of the CPC. According to the Constitution of 1982, the NPC is the highest body of the state,[96] and is required to be under the leadership of the CPC.[97] The SPC, as noted, is responsible to the NPC.[98] Under this institutional structure, the local courts at both provincial and county levels must also report to the local people's congresses at each corresponding level.[99]

Thirdly, the current organizational structure of the judiciary obviously has an institutional defect, which makes judicial independence extremely difficult, if not impossible. As noted, China maintains a unitary judicial system with four levels, from the SPC down to the basic trial courts. However, the SPC has no control over any of the lower courts except for judicial work related supervision. All judges of the lower people's courts are selected and appointed by local people's congresses, which are heavily influenced by local Communist Party chiefs and government heads.

More importantly, courts' operation expenses, which include judge salaries, come from local government budgets. In addition, judges in China do not have a statutory term, and can be replaced or removed anytime at will by people's congresses. It is therefore quite common for judges of local people's courts to follow the "instructions" or "opinions" of local governments in particular cases. Moreover, it has been a long tradition throughout Chinese history that government power and judicial power are always intertwined.[100]

This book is not intended to explore answers to questions regarding judicial independence in China, and it should not be expected that such answers can be easily found. As the foregoing has emphasized, China is a country wherein the courts are under the CPC's absolute leadership and there is no system of checks and balances. Although, as noted, Chinese Constitution recognizes the people's courts' independence in adjudicating cases, the recognition is premised on the notion that the CPC's leadership should not be weakened or compromised. Of course, there may be different views about what judicial independence in China would exactly mean. But given the reality in China, it is not difficult to understand why the Luo Yang case transpired in such a unique

---

96 *See* the 1982 Chinese Constitution, *supra* note 72, art. 57.
97 *See* Xu *Congde*, Constitution, 117–18 (People's University Press, 1999).
98 *See* the 1982 Chinese Constitution, *supra* note 72, art. 128.
99 *See id.*
100 For thousand years in Chinese history, judicial power rested with the executive branch. Thus, a mayor was not only the administrative head but also the chief judge.

way. Under the Chinese Constitution, the people's courts are to exercise judicial power independently, in accordance with the provisions of law and not subject to interference by any administrative organ, public organization, or individual.[101] In reality, however, the road toward judicial independence in China is still considerably long.

---

101   See the 1982 Chinese Constitution, *supra* note 72, art. 126.

CHAPTER 1

Contract Law in the Chinese Tradition

Once again, the most well known term equivalent to "contract" in China is "Qi Yue" (commonly translated as "agreement"). In Chinese language, "Qi Yue" consists of two words: "Qi" and "Yue." The "Qi" means "carved character," indicating a formal record of consent. "Yue," as noted, denotes an agreement to be bound.[1] According to Chinese legal history scholars, the term "contract" (He Tong) actually appeared in ancient China 2,000 years ago, but was soon replaced by the term "Qi Yue." At that time, contract was regarded as a form of Qi Yue, and therefore, contract itself was not a Qi Yue; rather, it was used as a mark or symbol evidencing the existence of the Qi Yue between the parties.[2] In that sense, therefore, "contract" was once translated in Chinese as "Qi Ju"—certificate or written document of Qi Yue.

In modern China, the term "contract" was not used independently to refer to an agreement reached by the parties until the late 1970's, when the Western literature on contract was introduced into the nation. For many years before that, the term "contract," when used, was always associated with "Qi Yue" and thus was phrased as "He Tong Qi Yue" (contractual agreement). Scholars in China had debated the difference between He Tong (contract) and Qi Yue (agreement),[3] but most now believe that differentiating the terms bears no practical significance.[4]

As noted, in Chinese contract law, an important concept that prescribes the contractual relationship between the parties is "*obligatio*." Again, the *obligatio* represents a legal relationship under which one party (obligor) is obligated to the other (obligee). An "*obligatio*" that is created by an agreement of the parties is known as a contract. Under this *obligatio,* the obligee (creditor) has the right to request the obligor (debtor) to perform its obligation under the contract and the obligor (debtor) is liable for what he promised to the obligee (creditor).[5]

---

1 See Wang Liming, *Contract Law of China*, 2 (William S. Hein & Co. 2016).
2 See He Weifang, *Analytical Differentiation between "Contract" and "Agreement,"* Jurisprudence Research 2 (1992).
3 Some scholars argued that "contract" refers to the meeting of minds in the same direction of the parties involved while "agreement" means the declaration of wills between the parties, which includes a meeting of the minds but not necessarily in the same direction. See Zhou Linbing, *Comparative Contract Law*, 80–81 (Lanzhou Univ. Press 1989).
4 See Wang Liming, *Contract Law, Fundamentals and Case Analysis*, 7 (People's Univ. Publ'g House 2001).
5 See *id.* at 13–14.

1   Concept of Contract

Although the concept of Qi Yue was used in China for many centuries, it was never clearly defined.[6] In many cases, as a normal practice, a Qi Yue, once signed, would be torn into two half pieces and each party would keep a half piece as evidence of the agreement that existed between them. A Qi Yue, once made, would implicate a legal relationship under which an obligation was created.[7] In addition, when the term *"obligatio"* was initially used in the country, it was often to mean contractual obligation, referring mostly to the monetary obligation under which a debtor was responsible for paying a creditor.[8]

1.1   *Chinese Tradition*

The law of contract in ancient China took the form of rules of Qi Yue, which governed Qi Yue, its making-process, and enforcement. In the more than 2,000 years of Chinese history, the rules of Qi Yue, though different from dynasty to dynasty, had three characteristics in common. First, most of the rules in their formality were the compilation of customs or common usages. Second, the rules were patriarchal in nature and focused on obligations without specifying rights. The underlying proposition was that the law was mainly intended to impose duties and obligations rather than to recognize rights and protect entitlements. Third, the punishment for breaching an agreement or violating an obligation was harsh, and was mostly punitive under the penal law.[9]

The most notable feature of Chinese legal tradition was its concomitance with Confucian philosophy. In China, beginning in the Han Dynasty (206 BC), Confucianism was upheld as the orthodox of ideology, something which lasted for almost whole period of Chinese imperial history. A center piece of Confucianism was the idea of *"Li"*—norms of conduct. An essential factor of *"Li"* was filial piety requiring obedience and loyalty. The idea was that, in each of the dynasties, the whole country was like a family where the emperor, who was

---

6   In 1955 and 1956, the drafters of the proposed Civil Code once tried to define *"Qi Yue"* as "an agreement made between two or more people in order to create, modify, or terminate the *obligatio* relation of right and liability." Many drafters argued against adopting this definition, however. *See* He Qinghua et al., *An Overview of Civil Code Drafts of New China*, Vol. I, 175 (Law Press 2003).
7   *See* Zhang Jifan, *Evolution of the Chinese Legal Civilization*, 287 (China Univ. of Poli. Science & Law Press 1999).
8   *See* Wang Jiafu, *Civil Law Obligatio*, 16 (Law Publishing House 1991).
9   *See id.*, at 17.

deemed the son of heaven, was the head of the family, and everyone else was a family member subject to his absolute control.[10]

Speaking broadly, one of the major defining features of the traditional Chinese legal system was that laws or rules were structured pursuant to a comprehensive and monolithic model which combined civil and criminal rules.[11] Because of the traditional legal system's focus on punishment, the civil law was largely overshadowed by the criminal law and, as noted, law to a great extent was synonymous with penalty. Although there is an ongoing debate among Chinese scholars about whether civil and criminal law were distinct in the traditional Chinese legal system,[12] the commonly accepted notion is that criminal law served as the backbone of the entire legal system.[13] For that reason, in Chinese legal history, the word "law" was normally interpreted to mean "penalty" or "punishment" (Xing).[14]

Another distinctive characteristic of Chinese legal history was that the law was to a great extent interwoven with the philosophy of Confucianism as well as the feudal ethic rules.[15] For example, in the arena of contract law, the enforcement of contractual obligations relied more on moral standards than on legal requirements. In other words, a contractual obligation was enforceable because the parties to the agreement were morally bound by what they had promised to each other. To keep the promise was a basic requirement of Confucian virtue. According to an old Chinese saying, "a promise shall be worth a thousand ounces of gold"—meaning that a person's actions were as good as his words or his promises. Therefore, a violation of an agreement would be deemed a violation of virtue and the moral standard and would accordingly warrant punishment.[16]

---

10 See Wang Chengguang, *An Emerging Legal System, in* INTRODUCTION TO CHINESE LAW, 4–8 (Sweet & Maxwell Asia 1997).
11 See *id.* at 5.
12 In general, the traditional Chinese legal system in the 2,000 years of Chinese history was characterized as a "combination of all kinds of laws into one scheme and no separation between civil and criminal laws." This characterization has been criticized as misleading by those who argue that the traditional Chinese legal system is more properly described as a "coexistence of all laws and differentiation of civil law from criminal law." See Zhang Jinfan, *supra* note 7, at 7–8.
13 See Wang Chengguang, *supra* note 10, at 6.
14 See Xin Chuying, *Chinese Legal System and Current Legal Reform*, 313 (Law Publishing House 1999).
15 See Wang Chengguang, *supra* note 10, at 7.
16 See Wang Jiafu, *supra* note 8, at 17.

1.2   *Civil Law Influence*

The modern Chinese legal system, however, has a civil law origin against the backdrop of its own tradition. Historically, China once quite actively reached the outside world through trade, diplomatic interaction, and cultural exchange, especially in the Han (206 BC–220) and Tang (618–907) dynasties. Beginning with the Ming Dynasty (1368), however, China gradually became a closed and self-sufficient country. The "Great China" glory that shined in many dynasties was suddenly diminished when the imperial power and dignity were shattered by the cannons of the Western powers emerging from the Industrial Revolution. In the two Opium wars (1840–42 and 1856–60), China was defeated. As a result, the invasion of foreign troops immediately brought to an end China's isolation.

After the Opium wars, Western influence began to take hold in China. Under the "unequal treaties," Western countries were able to establish "extraterritoriality" on Chinese soil that allowed the foreign forces to administer "Western justice" in their respective "foreign ports" or "spheres of influence" within China.[17] In those occupied territories, Western nations formed their own courts and applied their own laws. Consequently, Western legal concepts and practices started to become an external force greatly impacting the Chinese legal tradition.

Notwithstanding, many in the Forbidden City, awakened by the loss in the Opium wars, began to search for possible cures for revitalizing the ailing country. A group of reformers calling for political and legal reform to reshape the legal system of the nation emerged. Realizing the impact of the Western Industrial Revolution, the reformers launched a campaign of learning from the West which aimed to fortify the country's political and legal infrastructure. Advocated for by the reformers, Emperor Guangxu in 1902 issued an "Imperial Edict" to revise and amend existing laws (the Great Qin Codes) through the means of referencing foreign laws. For purposes of the reform, the Emperor appointed jurists Shen Jiaben and Wu Tingfang as the commissioners of legal revision.[18]

---

17   *See* Jerome A. Cohen, *Forward, in* THE RULE OF LAW, PERSPECTIVES FROM THE PACIFIC RIM, xi (Mansfield Center for Pacific Affairs 2000).

18   *See* Wang Jiafu, *supra* note 8, at 17–18. Also in 1904, Emperor Guangxu issued an edict to Prince Tsa Tchen, which stated: "[T]he development of commercial relations, the encouragement to industry have always been the primary duty of the Government, and must be carefully attended to. We hereby order that Tsai Tchen, Yuan Chih Kai and Wu Ting Fang be commissioned to compile a commercial code which will constitute the rule to be observed in commercial transactions." *See* Joseph An-Pao Wang, *China Studies, Studies in Chinese Government and Law, Civil Code of the Republic of China*, x–xi (Kelly and Walsh, Ltd. 1930) (reprinted by Univ. Pubs. of Am., Inc. 1976).

In the meantime, the imperial government selected a number of students to study abroad, mostly in Europe.

Several years later, in 1907, the Office of Legal Revision was established and became responsible for revising existing laws and drafting new laws. The Office of Legal Revision was comprised of students who had recently returned to China after studying in Europe, Japan, and the United Stated. Strikingly, the Office of Legal Revision even hired a Japanese jurist as an advisor to assist with the drafting of new laws for the nation. The drafting was mainly focused on civil law or the law regulating civil affairs. The first draft of the Civil Code was complete in December 1910 and finalized in 1911. However, that draft did not become the law due to the fall of the Qing Dynasty in 1911.

The first draft of the Civil Code contained five parts—general principles, rights of *obligatio*, property rights, domestic relations, and inheritance. Distinctively, the draft was primarily based on the German and Japanese law models and its first three parts were actually drafted by the Japanese jurist in the Office of Legal Revision.[19] Although the first draft never became the law, many of its provisions were taken by the Nationalist Government after that government was formed until 1925, when the second draft of the Civil Code was made. The second draft essentially followed the blueprint of the first draft. Part II of the second draft was named "*Obligatio*" and contained four chapters and 521 articles in total. Unfortunately, the second draft of the Civil Code met the same fate as the first draft and was never promulgated due to political chaos in the nation.[20]

China's first codified law of *Obligatio* was adopted in 1930 as part of the Civil Code of the Republic of China (1930 Civil Code). The drafters of the 1930 Civil Code followed the 1925 draft and took into consideration the comments from members of the drafting committee and advisers. In addition to its German and Japanese origins, the 1930 Civil Code had a number of influences from the codes of other major European countries, such as France and Italy. Reflecting a combination of influences from then-existing civil statutes as well as the reality of the country, the 1930 Civil Code had five parts, which were entitled "General Principles," "*Obligatio*," "Right of Things" (Property), "Family," and "Successions."[21] Under the 1930 Civil Code, the sources that would cause *obligatio* to occur included Qi Yue (agreement), conferring of authority of agency,

---

19 See id., Joseph An-Pao Wang, at xi
20 See id. at 19.
21 In Joseph An-Pao Wang's book, *obligatio* was translated as "obligations" and "property rights" as "rights over things." See id.

management of affairs without mandate (*negotiorum gestio*), unjust enrichment (*Culpa in Contrahendo*), and torts (*delict*).[22]

Interestingly, the five parts of the 1930 Civil Code took effect at different times. Part I was adopted on May 23, 1929 and took effect on October 10, 1929. Parts II and III were promulgated in November 1929 and came into force on May 30, 1930. Parts IV and V were enacted by the end of 1930.[23] Consistent with the Chinese tradition, the 1930 Civil Code still used the term Qi Yue (agreement), rather than Hetong (contract). According to Article 153 of the 1930 Civil Code, "a Qi Yue (agreement) [was] made when the parties ... reciprocally declared either expressly or tacitly their concordant intentions."[24] However, the 1930 Civil Code did not define the term Qi Yue, nor did it state the nature of the Qi Yue reached by the parties (i.e., the purpose that a Qi Yue would serve and the legal basis on which the Qi Yue would be enforced).

As noted, the 1930 Civil Code, along with other laws adopted by the Nationalist Government, was abandoned in 1949 by the Communist Government of China. That abandonment, however, did not change the civil law nature of the Chinese legal system that had been inherited from the decades-long influences of civil law literature. In addition, during the 1950s, China was driven to establish its legal system on the model of the former Soviet Union. Although the law in the era of the Soviet Union was labeled as socialist, it historically had a strong French influence,[25] which further embedded into the Chinese legal system the civil law brand.

There are several distinctive features of the Chinese legal system that reflect the system's civil law root. First, statutes are the primary source of law in China, and Chinese courts must therefore follow the black letter rules set forth by statutes in all legal proceedings. This differs significantly from the legal system of the United States—while, for example, contract law in China is governed by a statute adopted by the national legislative body, contract law in the United States is basically common law, embodied in court decisions. Second, as noted, Chinese courts do not have lawmaking power and the SPC only has the power to interpret specific questions concerning the application of a law.[26] Third, Chinese courts are not bound by precedent, as court decisions by

---

22 See *id*. at 45–57. Note that the term "unjust enrichment" was translated as "undue enrichment," and the term "torts" was translated as "wrongful acts."
23 See *id*. at xiv–xv.
24 See 1930 Civil Code (English Translation); *id*. at 45.
25 For general information, see John Henry Merryman, *The Civil Law Tradition* (Stanford Univ. Press, 2nd ed., 1985).
26 See 1979 Organic Law of People's Courts of China, art. 33.

higher Chinese courts have no binding effect on lower courts. In other words, a higher court's decisions may not be cited as legal authority for a lower court's decisions.[27]

In the past decades, a trend has emerged in China to incorporate common law elements into both legislation and judicial practice. The establishment of a guiding case system within Chinese courts represents this trend to focus on the role of cases in the judicial proceedings. As noted, with the publication of guiding cases that courts are required to refer to in all same or similar cases, the SPC has virtually created a precedent-like model for courts to follow. Although it might be too early to say that China now has a case law system, the application of this guiding case system constitutes a move toward the adoption of case law in the country.[28]

1.3 *Theories of Contract Law*

Over the development of contract law in China, Chinese scholars as well as legislators have debated over contract theories. The debates have mainly revolved around the nature and function of contract law. Although in general there has been a consensus in the country that contract law regulates the legal relationships pertaining to civil and commercial matters and that contract is in essence a mutual dealing between the parties, differences have existed as to what the theory underlying the contract is and how contract rules should be addressed. During the development of contract law legislation, four different contract theories dominated many of the discussions and debates in this regard.

1.3.1 Economic Means Theory

Originating from the former Soviet Union, the economic means theory posits business transactions as a series of economic activities among business entities in the different stages of production. Under this approach, a contract is viewed as an economic means employed by the State to manage and facilitate economic activities. Maintenance of economic order and state control

---

27 Note, however, that, with regard to procedural matters concerning court proceedings, the SPC's opinions must be followed by all lower courts. In addition, although the Supreme People's Court's "interpretations" are not the "laws" in China, they have played a significant role in providing courts with "urgently needed gap-fillers." *See* Wang Chenguang, *supra* note 10, at 21.

28 For a general discussion of guiding cases, see Mo Zhang, *Pushing the Envelope: Application of Guiding Cases in Chinese Courts and Development of Case Law in China*, 26 WASH. INT'L L.J., 269 (2017).

(management) constitutes the basis for the law of contract. Thus, a contract is enforceable so long as it does not adversely affect the economic order of the state.

The notion of the economic means theory lies with its contract definition. Under the economic means theory, "contract" is defined as a device to undertake economic activities between enterprises in the process of production. Based on that definition, contract is termed "economic contract." Further, the term "economic contract" is interpreted to mean a number of things. First, the parties to an economic contract are limited to legal persons, meaning no individual or private person may be a party to such contract. Second, the economic contract basically serves as a tool to implement the economic plan of the State, and its contents and formality are all subject to and affected by the State plan. Third, the purpose of the economic contract is to meet the needs of production and reproduction as well as business management.[29]

Until the late 1980's, the economic means theory was dominant in China and significantly influenced the nation's first two contract laws—the 1981 Economic Contract Law and the 1985 Foreign Economic Contract Law. As Professor William Jones of Washington University observed, for decades in China, a contract was viewed as (a) a device for making the economic plan concrete, (b) the essential basis of the state economic plan, (c) a means for making the state economic plan accurate, and (4) an essential complement to the state economic plan.[30] A notable commonality between the 1981 Economic Contract Law and the 1985 Foreign Economic Contract Law, which characteristically represented the economic means theory, was that individuals were excluded from being a party to the contract.[31]

1.3.2 Civil Act Theory

The civil act theory bears the influence of Roman law. This theory takes the view that there are three fundamental elements embedded in a contract. First, a contract is created by the mutual act of parties; second, a contract represents the consensus of the parties; and third, a contract is the cause for the occurrence of civil obligation. Therefore, under the civil act theory, contract is a civil

---

29 See Su Huixiang, *Theory of Economic Contract Law*, 3–5 (Liao Ning People's Press 1990).
30 See William C. Jones, *Basic Principles of Civil Law in China*, 201–202 (M.E. Sharpe Inc. 1989).
31 In the 1985 Foreign Economic Contract Law, an individual, but only a foreign individual, may be a party to a contract.

act that creates rights and obligations between the parties, and contract law is the law that regulates and enforces that civil act. The theory then stresses that the civil act as such shall and should be honored because it is based on the consensus of the parties.[32]

The focus of the civil act theory is on activity. When the parties reach an agreement, they become obligated to undertake certain activity as agreed. It is such activity that creates a civil relationship between the parties such that they are responsible to each other within the scope of their agreement. In order to reach their respective goals, each part to the agreement must fulfill his or her respective obligations pursuant to the agreed terms and conditions. The failure of one party to act as agreed frustrates the goal expected by the other party, and the law imposes liability in order to compensate that other party.

1.3.3   Agreement Theory

The agreement theory focuses on the manifestation of consent of the parties. Focusing on whether a meeting of the minds of the parties actually occurs, the proponents of agreement theory argue that contract law is meant to enforce agreements that reflect the intentions and expected benefits of the parties. The agreement theory makes mutual assent the core element of a contract and emphasizes that the intent of the parties to reach an agreement must be ascertained in order to form a contract. In other words, the existence of a contract is dependent on whether the parties intend to be bound.

Under the agreement theory, for an agreement to constitute an enforceable contract, the intent of the parties needs to be manifested in a certain concrete way. The argument is that a contract embodies a promise or expression of intent, but the promise alone is not sufficient to make a contract. According to the agreement theory, a contract is an agreement consisting of both promises and actions—because, in order to make a contract, parties have to take certain actions, such as formalizing promises and compromising differences. Therefore, from the viewpoint of the agreement theory, a promise is no more than a preliminary element to the making of an agreement, while a contract not only involves an agreement but also deals with how the agreement is to be made, modified, as well as terminated.[33]

---

32   See Li Guoguang, *Explanation and Application of the Contract Law*, 10–12 (Xinghua Publ'g House 1999).
33   See Jiang Ping, *A Detailed Explanation of the Contract Law of China*, 2–4 (China Univ. of Political Science & Law Press 1999).

1.3.4 Exchange Theory

The exchange theory premises the making of a contract on the exchange of goods or products, and its whole idea is that a contract helps realize economic operation and growth in any given society. The starting point of the exchange theory is that market circulation depends on the exchange of products, and a contract facilitates such an exchange. Thus, under the exchange theory, contract law is intended to establish a legal norm making the exchange of goods or products occur in a smoothly and acceptable order.[34]

The Contract Law does not follow any of the above theories exclusively, but rather takes a combination of maxims of both the civil act theory and the agreement theory. The Contract Law makes it clear that a contract is an agreement—specifically, an agreement aimed at forming a civil relationship wherein both parties to the relationship bear contractual rights and obligations. Moreover, many Chinese scholars define the Contract Law as the law regulating business transactions among civil actors with equal status. They argue that the Contract Law applies only to agreements entered into between parties that are on equal footing.[35]

As stated in Article 1 of the Contract Law, the law of contract is intended to serve a three-fold purpose: (a) to protect lawful rights and the interests of the parties, (b) to maintain the social economic order, and (c) to promote the construction of socialist modernization.[36] With respect to what constitutes the basis for the enforceability of a contract, however, the Contract Law seemingly contains no readily answer—instead emphasizing that a contract, once established according to law, shall be legally binding on the parties.[37]

1.4 *Definition of Contract*

There was no clear definition of "contract" in China until 1986, when the 1986 Civil Code was adopted. Nonetheless, prior to 1986, there was a commonly-held notion that "contract in essence is an agreement." For example, the 1981 Economic Contract Law described the economic contract as "an agreement between legal persons to ascertain their mutual rights and obligations for purposes of achieving a certain economic goal."[38] This description had at least two flaws. First, it limited the purpose of a contract to the achievement of a "certain economic goal," a discernible *sequela* of the decades-long planned economy.

---

34   *See* Wang Jiafu, *supra* note 8, at 12–16.
35   *See* Wang Liming, *Study on Contract Law*, Vol. 1, 56–57 (People's Univ. Press 2003).
36   *See* Contract Law, art. 1.
37   *See id.*, art. 8.
38   *See* Economic Contract Law of China (1981), art. 4.

Second, it excluded natural persons from the pool of those capable of making a contract, which rendered the Contact Law a piece of "broken" legislation.

The 1986 Civil Code provided for the first time a formal definition of contract. Under Article 85 of the 1986 Civil Code, a contract is defined as an agreement establishing, modifying, and terminating the civil relations between the parties. Following that concept, Article 2 of the 1999 Contract Law further defines contract as an agreement establishing, modifying, and terminating the relations of civil rights and obligations between natural persons, legal persons, or other organizations of equal status. This definition of contract as set forth in Article 2 of the 1999 Contract Law has become the standard official definition of contract in China.

Article 2 of the 1999 Contract Law is distinguishable from Article 85 of the 1986 Civil Code in two key aspects. First, by recognizing natural persons as possible parties to a contract, the Contract Law departed from previous contract law legislation, where Chinese citizens were precluded from making contracts and were not covered by any law of contract. Second, the Contract Law makes it imperative that all parties to a contract be equal civil subjects regardless of their respective status. A common view in China is that, for purposes of Article 2 of the 1999 Contract Law, a contract by definition shall in generally include the following legal characteristics:

i. Contract is a "civil legal act" performed by natural persons, legal persons, and other organizations of equal status;
ii. Contract is an agreement manifesting the will of the parties to be bound by what they mutually consented to; and
iii. Contract creates, modifies, or terminates a legal relationship between the parties concerning their civil rights and obligations.[39]

In light of the Contract Law, the "civil legal act" is to stress that a contract signifies the parties' expression of their will for civil and economic benefits, and it must serve a lawful purpose. Scholars in China try to differentiate a "legal act" from a "de facto act." In their view, a "legal act" is premised on the expectation of actors (parties) and will produce anticipated results while a "*de facto* act" does not lead to any mutually expected outcomes. Therefore, a contract, as a legal act, requires the mutual assent of parties, which fundamentally requires a meeting of the minds. By contrast, a "*de facto* act," such as a tort or an act resulting in unjust enrichment, does not demand such mutuality.[40]

---

39 See Wang Liming, *A Novel Discussion on Contract Law—General Principles*, 6–7 (China Univ. of Political Sci. & Law Publ'g House) (1996).
40 See Wang Liming, *Study on Contract Law, supra* note 35 at 7–14; *see also* Wang Jiafu, *supra* note 8, at 15–18.

Where parties consent to being mutually bound by an agreement, that agreement must serve a lawful purpose to qualify as a contract. Stated differently, only if the expression of the will of the parties is made for a lawful purpose and does not violate any law, may a contract so concluded become binding and enforceable. For this reason, a contract is also described as a "lawful civil act." If an agreement is made for the purpose of achieving an illegal goal, that agreement, despite being based on "mutual consent" or "expression of wills," does not having the binding effect of a contract. Pursuant to this notion, a contract is not simply an agreement, but rather is an agreement that is both legally enforceable and for a lawful purpose.

Another important element of a contract, as defined in the Contract Law, is the equal status of the parties. The Contract Law divides contractual parties into three categories: natural persons, legal persons, and other organizations. The term "natural persons" refers to Chinese citizens, foreigners, as well as stateless persons. Note that in the 2017 GPCL, the definition of natural persons was extended to include "individual industrials and commercial households," as well as "rural contracted operation households." Pursuant to Article 54 of the 2017 GPCL, an "individual industrial and commercial household" is a natural person conducting an industrial or commercial operation in accordance with the law.[41] Under Article 55 of the 2017 GPCL, a "rural contracted operation household" is defined as a member of a rural collective economic organization who has legally obtained an usufruct on rural land for a contracted household farm operation.[42]

The term "other organizations" is not defined in the law. However, according to judicial interpretations of the SPC, the term encompasses those organizations that are formed under the law with certain assets and an organizational structure but that have no independent civil ability and capacity.[43] The 2017 GPCL classifies "other organizations" as non-legal-person organizations. Under Article 102 of the 2017 GPCL, a non-legal-person organization is an organization that does not have the status of a legal person but is nonetheless able to

---

41 *See* the 2017 GPCL, art. 54.
42 *See id.*, art. 55. In China, under the household responsibility system adopted in the early 1980s for rural areas, the property right of rural land is divided into two parts: the ownership right that is collectively owned by a rural community (i.e., a village), and the right of use (i.e., usufruct) that is held by an individual household who contracts a piece of land from the village for harming.
43 *See* the SPC, *Opinions on the Matters Concerning Application of the Law of Civil Procedures of the People's Republic of China.* Under the Opinions, "other organizations" would include partnerships, social organizations not organized as legal persons, branches of a legal person, and village enterprises.

conduct civil activities in its own name in accordance with the law.[44] Article 102 further provides that non-legal-person organizations include sole proprietorships, partnerships, as well as professional service entities without legal person status.

Under the 1986 Civil Code, a "legal person" is an association that has the capacity for civil rights and civil activities and that independently enjoys civil rights while assuming civil obligations in accordance with the law.[45] A similar definition is also provided in the 2017 GPCL. The 2017 GPCL, however, divides legal persons into three categories: for-profit legal person, non-profit legal person, and special legal person.[46] The difference between a legal and a non-legal person lies with the person's civil liability-bearing capacity. A legal person has the capacity to independently enjoy civil rights and assume civil liabilities while a non-legal person does not. Under Article 104 of the 2017 GPCL, if the property of a non-legal-person organization is insufficient to pay the organization's debts, the organization's investor or promoter shall bear unlimited liability for those debts.[47] Thus, a creditor can reach the owner or shareholder of a non-legal-person entity for the debts owed by such entity, unless otherwise provided by the law.[48]

The following case may help illustrate the difference between a legal person and a non-legal-person organization in the determination of civil liabilities.

> Zhejiang Provincial Logistic Bureau Truck Fleet
> v.
> Wenzhou Lucheng Transportation Co-op and Wuma Labor Services Co.
> September 12, 1988 [1988] Zhefa Jingshang Zhi No. 38

On November 15, 1986, Plaintiff, Zhejiang Provincial Logistic Burear Truck Fleet (LBTF), and Defendant, Wenzhou Lucheng Transportation Co-op (WLT), signed a bus rental contract. Under the contract, LBTF rented out two forty-five-seat buses to WLT for one and half years and WLT agreed to pay LBTF a rental fee in the amount of RMB 5,000 per month plus RMB 1,050 road preservation fees.[49] WLT picked up the buses from LBTF in December 1986 and paid RMB 5,000 for that month on December 31, 1986.

Incorporated in 1984, Wuma Labor Services Co. (WLS) endorsed WLT's application for a business license and registration. In return, WLT paid WLS administrative fees. Shortly after WLT put the rented buses in operation, two of the buses were heavily damaged in a traffic accident.

---

44 *See* the 2017 GPCL, art. 102.
45 *See* the 1986 Civil Code, art. 36.
46 *See* the 2017 GPCL, art. 96.
47 *See id.*, art. 104.
48 *See id.*
49 In late 1980s, the exchange rate between US dollar and Chinese RMB was about 1:4.70. Under that rate, RMB 5000 was about $ 1,064. The exchange rate now is 1:8.25.

The accident affected WLT's operation, and WLT subsequently defaulted on rental payments to LBTF. LBTF thereafter brought suit against WLT, seeking compensation for the unpaid rents as well as for the damage to the buses.

During the trial, it was found that WLT was in a very bad financial situation and had no money to pay for anything. LBTF consequently amended its complaint and added WLS as a related third party on the ground that WLS received administrative fees from WLT. In its decision, the trial court granted LBTF's request to add WLS as a third party to the litigation and ultimately held WLS jointly and severally liable for WLT's debts. WLS appealed.

On appeal, two legal issues were submitted to the Zhejiang High People's Court for clarification. The first issue was whether WLS should be named as a third party or co-defendant in the proceeding. The second issue was whether WLS should be jointly and severally liable for WLT's debts. The High People's Court split on these two issues. One opinion was that WLT was actually a branch of WLS and had no legal person status, and therefore, WLS should be held liable. According to this opinion, the lower court's decision warranted affirmance with the modification that WLS should have been named as a co-defendant, not a third party. An opposite opinion, though recognizing that WLT's status was very special, tends to hold that WLT should have been deemed a legal person and therefore WLS should have been separated from WLT. This opinion recommended remanding the case on the grounds that there was no legal basis for holding WLS liable.

Because the High People's Court could not reach a consensus on how the case should be decided, the case was reported to the Supreme People's Court for opinion.[50] In its reply, the Supreme People's Court requested more evidence relating to the legal status of WLT. According to the Supreme People's Court, if WLT was proven to be an independent enterprise, not a branch of the WLS, it would be inappropriate to hold WLS jointly and severally liable. If, however, it was proven that WLT was indeed a branch of WLS, WLS was to be named as a co-defendant and held jointly and severally liable in the event that WLT proved unable to pay its debts.

In the WLT case, the Supreme People's Court made legal person status a decisive factor in determining an entity's liability and litigation standing. The Supreme People's Court's opinion in its reply further implicated that an "other organization," though not a legal person," may conduct civil activities, such as contracting, in its own name with others, but that whoever forms or creates such an organization will be held jointly and severally liable if the organization is unable to pay for its debts arising from the civil activities.[51] As noted, the 2017 GPCL changed the term "other organization" to the "non-legal-person organization."

The term "legal person" used to include an "enterprise legal person" as well as a "non-enterprise legal person." "Enterprise legal person" included state-owned enterprises, collectively- and privately-owned enterprises, publicly

---

50   In Chinese court proceedings, it is common for a lower court to ask a higher court to opine on certain legal issues that are regarded as substantially important and especially difficult.

51   *See*, Kong Xiangjun, *Analysis and Jurisprudential Research on Difficult Cases in Contract Law*, 16–17 (People's Court Press 2000).

listed enterprises, and foreign investment enterprises (known as FIES). "Non-enterprise legal persons" included government agencies, institutional units, and other social entities organized as legal persons. As discussed, the 2017 GPCL re-defined the term "legal person" to mean a "for profit," "non-profit," or "special" legal person. This change was said to represent a shift of focus from the social status of a legal person to the business function.

Under Article 76 of the 2017 GPCL, a for-profit legal person is a legal person formed for the purpose of making profits and distributing profits to shareholders or other investors. For-profit legal persons include limited liability companies, join stock limited companies, and other enterprise legal persons.[52] A non-legal person is defined in Article 87 of the 2017 GPCL as a legal person formed for the public welfare or another non-profit purpose, with no distribution of any profits to its investors, promoters, or members. Included in non-profit legal persons are public institutions, social groups, foundations, and social service organizations.[53] As specified in Article 96 of the 2017 GPCL, a special legal person refers to government agency legal persons, rural collective economic organization legal persons, urban and rural cooperative economic organization legal persons, or grass-root self-governing mass organization legal persons.[54]

Since a contract is deemed to be a civil legal act, all participants in such an act shall be equal regardless of their respective status. Article 4 of the 2017 GPCL reiterates the principle that all civil actors are equal in legal status in their civil activities. The underlying purpose of this principle is to promote the idea that a contract is the result of free bargaining, without coercion or fear on the basis of social or other status, between the parties. Equal status is vitally important particularly in contract dispute cases where a governmental entity and a private party are parties to the contract at issue. In such cases, the equal status principle ensures that the governmental entity and the private party are treated in the same manner and to the same extent.

Not surprisingly, the concept of contract embodied in the Contract Law has clear civil law tradition roots. The basic notion is that a contract is (a) a mutual act of the parties, (b) a manifestation of the will of the parties, and (c) a cause of *obligatio*. Partly because of this tradition, the Contract Law explicitly provides that contract is "an agreement." It is interesting to note that most Chinese

---

52   *See* the 2017 GPCL, art. 76.
53   *See id.*, art. 87.
54   *See id.*, art. 96.

contract scholars describe the United States as having a typical common law contract system where a contract is defined as "a promise or a set of promises."[55] Those scholars accordingly believe that the defining distinction between the contract theory of civil law and common law systems is that a contract is promised-based in a common law system whereas it is agreement-based in a civil law system.[56]

In the United States, the study of contract is often regarded as the study of the legal enforcement of a promise.[57] In China, by contrast, the study of contract is regarded as the study of how agreements are made and enforced. From the viewpoint of Chinese contract law scholars, a "promise" is not a mutual act and it, at least on its face, does not necessarily require mutual assent. Perhaps a closer look at the gist of contract law in each system will help illuminate the difference. In the United States, contract law focuses on "why a promise or a set of promises should be enforced," while in China, contract law emphasizes "what constitutes an agreement and how an agreement should be enforced." Additionally, a contract in China is generally regarded as an act to create, modify, or terminate civil relations through an agreement between the parties.[58]

It is also noteworthy that, in Chinese contract law, there is no concept tantamount to that of "quasi-contract" in U.S. contract law. Again, under the concept of *"obligatio,"* in addition to contract and torts, both unjust enrichment and *negotiorum gestio* (voluntary service) can be an independent cause of action to support a civil claim. As noted, under Article 118 of the 2017 GPCL, the right to request fulfillment of an obligation can be created by contract, torts, unjust enrichment or *negotiorum gestio*.[59] For example, in China, the obligation to return money paid in error to a person to whom it is not owed is an obligation arising under the doctrine of unjust enrichment, while in the United States, it is characterized as a quasi-contact obligation.

55　The Restatement defines a "contract" as "a promise of a set of promises for the reach of which the law gives a remedy, or performance of which the law in some way recognizes as a duty." *Restatement (Second) of Contracts* § 1.
56　*See* Wang Jiafu, *supra* note 8, at 254–258.
57　*See* Robert E. Scott & Jody S. Kraus, *Contract Law and Theory*, 1 (3d ed., 2002).
58　*See* Li Guoguang, *supra* note 32, at 11.
59　See the 2017 GPCL, art. 118. Also to illustrate, under Article 93 of the 1986 Civil Code, if a person provides management or services in order to protect another person's interests when he or she is not legally or contractually obligated to do so, he or she shall be entitled to claim from the beneficiary the expenses necessary for such management or services.

2 Contract Classification

Contracts in China are classified into different types. This classification scheme, however, is not set forth in the Contract Law but rather was formulated by scholars. In Chinese contract literature, the contract classification is believed to serve a multi-faceted purpose: (a) it helps advance the rationale of contract legislation by requiring the adoption of rules closely tailored to the characteristics of different types of contracts; (b) it helps facilitate proper application of the Contract Law, especially in judicial proceedings wherein a judge needs to differentiate contracts of different natures; and (c) it helps courts ascertain the respective rights and obligations of the parties to a contract because the type of contract affects the scope, as well as the order of performance, of contractual obligations.[60]

Note, however, that contract-type classifications often overlap depending upon the perspective from which contracts are viewed. In addition, the way contracts are classified in China may differ from the way they would be classified in other counties. In the United States, for example, contracts can be divided into bilateral contracts and unilateral contracts. In China, however, the terms "bilateral" and "unilateral" may mean different things. A contract in American contract law is generally considered to be a "promise." Thus, if a contract in the U.S. involves two promises, the contract is bilateral; if the contract involves only one promise, the contract is unilateral.[61]

By contrast, there is no uniform contract classification in China. Chinese contract law scholars disagree on how contracts should be classified. Notwithstanding, the major types of contracts commonly recognized include: named and unnamed contracts, formal and informal contracts, consensual and real contracts, onerous and gratuitous contracts, and bilateral and unilateral contracts.

2.1 Named and Unnamed Contracts

"Named contracts" are those listed in the Contract Law or regulations and that have particular names as prescribed by law. "Unnamed contracts" are those contracts that are not specified in the Contract Law. The Contract Law currently recognizes fifteen named contracts.[62] Given their statutory prescription,

---

60 See Cui Jianyuan, *General Theories of Contract Law*, Vol. I, 53–54 (Renmin Univ. Press, 2nd ed., 2012).
61 See Jeff Ferriell, *Understanding Contracts*, 7 (2nd ed., 2009).
62 The fifteen named contracts include Sales, Utility Supplies, Gift and Donation, Loans, Leases, Financial Leases, Work-For-Hire, Construction Projects, Transportation, Technology, Storage, Warehousing, Entrust, Brokerage, and Intermediation.

such named contracts are also called "typical contracts." The contracts are "typical" because their name, nature, and substance are all provided by the law. By contrast, unnamed contracts are considered atypical since they are not listed in, or provided names by, the law.

Because contracts involve various civil relations and transactions, it is hard, if not impossible, for the law to provide for all kinds of contracts. To maximize the effectiveness of their regulation, contracts that are frequently used and are governed by a well-developed body of law must be named in statutes. According to Chinese scholars, naming such contracts in statutes serves at least two functions. First, the most provisions of named contracts are non-mandatory and can help supplement the agreement reached by the parties because courts often rely on those provisions in interpreting contracts. Second, through named contracts, certain mandatory rules may be provided so as to ensure that the parties' exercise of contract-making power does not harm the public interest or social morals.[63]

Unnamed contracts, on the other hand, are all the other contracts that parties may make for any particular purpose. In many cases, these contracts involve certain transactions that either are newly-developed or are governed by readily-applicable laws or regulations. Unnamed contracts have two notable features. First, an unnamed contract may turn into a named contract when it gets sufficiently matured to be named by the law. Second, unnamed contracts are subject to the general provisions of the Contract Law. Article 124 of the Contract Law requires that any contract that is not explicitly prescribed in the Specific Provisions of the Contract Law or in other law must apply the General Provisions of the Contract Law. The Article further provides that courts, when dealing with unnamed contracts, may apply *mutatis mutandis* (the necessary changes having been made), namely, the most similar provisions in the Specific Provisions of the Contract Law or in other laws.[64] In other words, the court may analogously apply the most provisions in the existing laws.

2.2 *Formal and Informal Contracts*

Whether a contract is formal or informal is a matter of formality. A contract is formal if the law requires it to comply with certain formalities. A contract is informal if the parties have the freedom to choose its formality at-will. In addition to dictating how a contract should be made, this formality requirement directly affects contract validity. In the common law system, for example,

---

63 *See* Han Shiyuan, *The Law of Contract*, 48 (3d ed., 2011).
64 *See* Contract Law, art. 124.

the statute of frauds' demand of a "writing" for certain contracts is basically a statutory requirement of contract formality. Thus a contract is invalid and thus unenforceable if it violates such a formality requirement.

Under the Contract Law, all contracts may be made in the formality chosen by the parties unless otherwise provided by the law. Put differently, the statute makes all contracts "informal" as a basic rule and makes "formal" contracts the exception. Pursuant to Article 10 of the Contract Law, a contract may be established in writing, orally, or in other forms. If, however, a written form is required by the law or is agreed to by the parties, the contract must be in writing.[65] In addition to this framework, certain contracts are required by law to be subjected to approval or registration prior to taking effect.[66]

In general, the formality requirement is mandatory. The mandatory nature of the formality requirement may be overcome by actual performance, however. Pursuant to Article 36 of the Contract Law, if a contract that is required either by law or by agreement of the parties to be made in writing is not in fact made in writing, but one party nevertheless performs the party's principal obligation under that contract and the other party accepts that performance, the contract is effective.[67] In this regard, actions (i.e, performance) speak louder than words (i.e., required writings).

2.3 Consensual and Real Contracts

In civil law, a contract can be either "consensual" or "real," depending on whether the mere consent of the parties is sufficient to form the contract. A "consensual contract" does not require anything external or symbolic beyond the parties' consent and it is formed at the moment the parties reach an agreement pursuant to the terms and conditions they negotiated for. A contract of sale is a common example of a consensual contract. A "real contract," by contrast, requires a repositioning of things affixing to the obligation, in addition to the consent of the parties, in order to be formed. In Roman law, typical types of real contracts included *mutuum* (loan for consumption), *commodatum* (loan for use), *depositum* (deposit), and *pignus* (pledge). In those contracts, the delivery of the thing (*res*) was required before the contract would be deemed completed.[68]

---

65 See id., art. 10.
66 See id., art. 44.
67 See id., art. 36.
68 See generally Reinhard Zimmermann, *The Law of Obligations: Roman Foundations of the Civilian Tradition* (1990).

Chinese Contract Law follows this civil law tradition and contains provisions reflecting the distinctive nature of different types of contracts. For example, Article 130 of the Contract Law defines "sales contract" as a contract by which the seller transfers ownership of the subject matter of the contract to the buyer in exchange for the buyer paying a certain price.[69] Article 138 further provides that the seller must deliver the subject matter of the contract according to the agreed-upon time limit, and that, if the parties have agreed upon a time period for delivery, the seller may make such delivery at any time within said period.[70]

In contrast, Article 365 of the Contract Law defines a "bailment contract" as a contract under which the bailee (warehouser) keeps in store a chattel (article) handed over by the owner (depositor), before ultimately returning said chattel.[71] Under Article 367, a bailment contract is formed at the time the chattel is handed over, except as otherwise agreed upon by the parties.[72] Thus, a sales contract is concluded on the basis of the parties' consent while a bailment contract requires for its formation both the consent of the parties as well as the delivery of the subject matter of the contract.

The significance of the distinction between consensual and real contracts lies with how courts both evaluate contract formation as well as ascertain the respective obligations of the parties to a contract. If a contract is consensual, the determinative factor is the parties' consent. If, however, a contract is real, delivery of the subject matter of the contract is a prerequisite for the formation of the contract. With regard to contractual obligations, failure to deliver (perform) the item (obligation) under the agreed-upon terms and conditions in a consensual contract constitutes a breach of contract. In a real contract, by contrast, such delivery is a "pre-contractual" obligation, and failure to perform it may therefore amount to only a contracting fault, not a breach.

2.4 Onerous and Gratuitous Contracts

An "onerous contract," alternatively referred to in China as a "contract for value" or "non-gratuitous contract," is a contract wherein parties agree to mutually exchange benefits. Through an onerous contract, one party is obligated to perform in the manner agreed upon and, in return, that party is entitled to receive counter-performance in the manner agreed upon from the other party. What is exchanged in an onerous contract can be monetary obligations or

---

69   See Contract Law, art. 130.
70   See id., art. 138.
71   See id., art. 365.
72   See id., art. 367.

services. For example, in a service contract, a contractor is required to provide a certain service for a client and the client, in turn, is required to pay for that service in the agreed-upon amount and method.

A "gratuitous contract" is a contract, the subject matter of which is the benefit of the person with whom the contract is made. The party who makes performance in a gratuitous contract is not entitled to seek any profit or advantage in exchange for the performance. A gratuitous contract is one that is made solely for the benefit of the other party. A typical gratuitous contract is a contract to make a gift or donation. In Article 185 of the Contract Law, a "contract for donation" is defined as a contract in which a donor gives his property gratis to a donee and the donee expresses an acceptance of the property.[73] Though parties to a gratuitous contract may agree on certain conditions, those conditions may only affect how the contract is to be performed and they cannot impose any reciprocal "giving" obligation on the party receiving the benefit.

According to Chinese contract law scholars, the differentiation between onerous and gratuitous contracts serves three major functions. First, it implicates the level or degree of the liabilities of the obligor. The obligor in an onerous contract assumes a higher level of duty of care during the contract's performance than does the obligor in a gratuitous contract. The duties of an obligor to an entrust contract are illustrative. "Entrust contract" is defined in Article 396 of the Contract Law as a contract by which the entrusting and entrusted parties agree that the entrusting party will handle the matters of the entrusted party.

Under the Contract Law, an entrust contract can be either onerous or gratuitous.[74] According to Article 406 of the Contract Law, if the entrust contract is onerous, the entrusting party may seek damages for any loss caused by the fault of the entrusted party. If, however, the entrust contract is gratuitous, the entrusting party may only seek damages for any loss caused by the deliberate intention or gross negligence of the entrusted party.[75]

Second, whether a contract is onerous or gratuitous affects the contract-making capacities of certain parties that the law is intended to protect. In China, if a contract is entered into by a person who has a limited civil capacity of conduct, the contract will take effect only after being ratified by the agent *ad litem*. Such ratification is not required, however, if the contract is one of a pure profit-obtaining nature.[76] Thus, under the Contract Law, any person whose

---

73   See id., art. 185.
74   See id., art. 396.
75   See id., art. 406.
76   See id., art. 47.

civil capacity of conduct is limited may not make an onerous contract without a consent of the agent *ad litem*. This restriction, however, does not apply to a contract that is gratuitous.

Third, the distinction between onerous and gratuitous contracts helps determine the legal consequences of certain transactions. One emblematic situation involves a debtor's transfer of assets. If this transfer is made gratuitously and it affects the debtor's ability to fulfill its debt obligations, a creditor of the debtor has a right under the Contract Law to ask a court to cancel the transfer. If, conversely, this transfer is made onerously but at an obviously low price, a court will only cancel the transfer in the event that the transfer adversely affects the creditor and the transferee is aware of it. Another typical situation concerns the status of a *bona fide* purchaser of property that is sold by a person other than the property's owner. If the transfer of property in such a situation is made gratuitously, the purchaser of the property is not considered to be *bone fide* and the property must therefore be returned.

2.5 *Unilateral and Bilateral Contracts*

The concepts of unilateral and bilateral contracts are understood differently in China than they are in common law countries such as the United States. In U.S. contract law, a bilateral contract is a contract that involves two promises and is formed at the moment the promises are exchanged. A unilateral contract, contrastingly, involves only one promise and is formed only once the performance of that promise is completed.[77] In short, a bilateral contract is a promise for promise contract, while a unilateral contract is a promise for performance contract. In a unilateral contract, a promisor's offer may only be accepted by means of the promisee's performance.

In China, by contrast, the difference between a bilateral contract and a unilateral contract lies in whether there are mutual obligations between the parties. If the contractual parties owe each other a mutual obligation to perform (e.g., delivery v. payment, service v. payment, or act v. commission), such an agreement constitutes a bilateral contract. If, on the other hand, only one party to the contract has a duty to perform for the benefit of the other party, such an agreement constitutes a unilateral contract. A contract to make a gift or a donation is a common example of a unilateral contract. Because of the mutuality of obligations it creates, bilateral contracts are often referred to by Chinese scholars as "reciprocal contracts."[78]

---

77 See Jeff Ferriell, *supra* note 61, at 7–8.
78 See Han Shiyuan, *The Law of Contract*, *supra* note 63, at 53.

The designation of a contract in China as "unilateral" has nothing to do with what bargains were struck between the parties under the contract. Rather, the designation signifies that only one party to the contract has an obligation to perform.[79] Because both create non-mutual obligations, unilateral contracts and gratuitous contracts substantially overlap in many aspects. Nevertheless, unilateral contracts are distinct in several respects. First, given the singular nature of the obligation it imposes, a unilateral contract is not subject to legal defense mechanisms such as fulfillment pleas or unrest defenses. Second, the rules of contract dissolution are generally not applicable to unilateral contracts because the performances mandated by such contracts are not mutual. Third, where a unilateral contract is breached as a result of something that is beyond the control of the parties, the issue of risk allocation between the parties does not arise.

3 Application of the Contract Law

Since a contract in China is characterized as a kind of *obligatio,* it does not cover civil relations concerning personal status. Therefore, the Contract Law does not apply to any agreement that involves marriage, adoption, or guardianship. Such exclusion is entirely based on the rationale that, for purposes of the Contract Law, a contract is an agreement dealing with relations of non-personal or non-family status. Under the 2017 GPCL, the status of a person is governed by the law of personality, which covers the right of a natural person to life, body, health, name, portrait, reputation, honor, privacy, and marital autonomy, as well as the right of a legal or non-legal person to name, reputation, and honor.[80]

On the other hand, according to Chinese contract law scholars, the main purpose of contract law is to deal with property-related civil relations and to regulate civil matters concerning business transactions. Thus, although an agreement may be made in relation to personal status such as marriage, adoption, or guardianship, such an agreement is not governed by the Contract Law because it does not involve business transactions. More importantly, a historically-rooted legal principle in China is that marriage is not a contract.[81] Notwithstanding, an agreement concerning distribution of family property, though involving personal status, is governed by the Contract Law.

---

79 *See* Wang Liming, *Contract Law of China, supra* note 1, at 3.
80 *See* the 2017 GPCL, art.110.
81 In China, marriage, including divorce, is exclusively governed by the Marriage Law.

In addition, the Contract Law is not applicable to agreements of an administrative nature. An agreement that is of an administrative nature is the opposite of one that is of a civil nature. In other words, an administrative agreement is the means by which the government supervises the fulfillment of agreements for the public interest. An example in this regard is an environmental protection agreement, through which a party (e.g., a real estate developer) promises a government authority that it will comply with environmental protection requirements.[82] Like an environmental protection agreement, negotiated arrangements such as family planning agreements or agreements concerning governmental appropriation, taxation, or fee schedules are not within the ambit of the Contract Law because they are clearly of an administrative nature.

The internal managerial relationships of legal persons and other business organizations are also outside the scope of the Contract Law. Take, for example, a production agreement between a company or its production plant and the company's employees. Under the Contract Law, such an agreement is not a contract. Rather, it is categorized as a work arrangement because it is made as a result of the company's production responsibility system and basically serves as a managerial device for internal production of the company.[83] Thus, a failure to perform as agreed in this regard gives no ground for a breach of contract claim.

A related issue is the labor (employment) contract. When the Contract Law was in its drafting stage, some people argued that the statute should cover labor contracts. Labor departments, however, disagreed and insisted there was no need to include labor contracts in the Contract Law because such contracts were already regulated by the Labor Law. On the other hand, some people argued that labor contract law was part of economic law—in that it regulated relationships between employers and employees—while the law of contract was a branch of civil law—in that it dealt with civil matters.[84] As a result, the

---

82 See Gu Angran, *Talks on the Contract Law of China*, 8 (Legal Publ'g Hous 1999).

83 See Gu Angran, *Explanations to the Contract Law of People's Republic of China* (Draft). The Explanation was made to delegates of the Second Session of the National Conference of the Ninth National People's Congress on March 9, 1999. It was on this Session that the Contract Law was passed.

84 The Labor Law of China was promulgated by the Standing Committee of the National People's Congress of China on July 5, 1994 and took effect on January 1, 1995. Chapter 3 of the Labor law directly deals with labor contracts and collective contracts. Under Article 16, a labor contract is an agreement that establishes the labor relationship between a laborer and an employing unit and that defines the respective rights and obligations of those parties. It is also required that a labor contract shall be concluded where a labor relationship is established.

Labor Contract Law was promulgated separately in 2007.[85] One year later, in 2008, the State Council adopted the Rules of Implementation of the Labor Contract Law.[86]

A major difference between contract and labor contract is the dispute settlement mechanism. In a contract dispute, either party to the contract may file a claim directly with a court absent an arbitration clause or agreement. In a labor contract dispute, by contrast, the dispute must first be submitted for arbitration unless otherwise provided by the law and a party may only bring the case to a court if it disagrees with the arbitral decision. A detailed discussion of the Labor Contract Law and its Implementation Rules will be made in Chapter 13 of this book.

A contract for transfer of the right to the use of land presents a thorny issue in the law of contract. Unlike many other countries, China is a country wherein no private person may own any piece of land. An individual in China may own a house or building, but the ownership does not reach the land where the house or building stands. Thus, real estate or real property rights in China refer only to land use rights and rights to structures permanently affixed to land, such as buildings. Under the 1982 Chinese Constitution (as amended in 2004), land in the cities is owned by the State and land in the rural and suburban areas (except those portions that belong to the State as prescribed by law) is owned by collectives.[87]

The 1982 Constitution prohibits any organization or individual from appropriating, buying, selling, or otherwise engaging in the transfer of, land by unlawful means. Organizations or individuals, however, may acquire the right to use land and such right may be transferred according to law.[88] The land use right is also provided in the 1986 Land Management Law of China (as amended in 1998).[89] In 2007, China adopted for the first time ever since 1949 its Property Law. Under the Property Law, the land use right is an usufruct right, which is defined in Article 117 of the Property Law as a right to possess, use, and receive proceeds from the immovable and movable owned by others.[90] The land use

---

85   The Labor Contract Law of China was adopted by the Standing Committee and the NPC on June 29, 2007 and took effect on January 1, 2008.
86   The State Council's Rules of Implementation of the Labor Contract Law of China was promulgated on September 18, 2008.
87   *See* the 1982 Chinese Constitution, art.10.
88   See *id.*
89   The "Law of Land Management of People's Republic of China" (Land Management Law) was adopted on June 25, 1986 and was amended on August 29, 1998. The amended Land Management Law took effect on January 1, 1999.
90   The Property Law of China was adopted by the NPC on March 16, 2007.

right includes the right to the contracted management of land, the right to use constructed land, as well as the right to use house sites and easements. Each of these rights has a term limit.[91] For urban residential housing, for example, the term of land use right is seventy years.[92]

During the drafting of the Contract Law, the right to the use of land was heavily debated. The major issue was whether a contract concerning transfer or sale of the right to the use of land should be governed by the Contract Law. Proponents argued that a contract for the transfer or sale of the right to the use of land should be governed by the Contract Law because the parties to such a contract are engaged in civil activities and possess equal status in the transaction. Opponents, however, contended that a contract involving the transfer or sale of the right to the use of land should be outside the scope of the Contract Law's application given that the land use right is granted by the government.

According to these opponents, the parties to a contract concerning the transfer or sale of the right to the use of the land do not necessarily have the equal civil status because the right to the use of land is created through government action. A contract involving the right to the use of land, these opponents maintain, is unique because (1) the government, as the owner of the land, retains the ultimate control over the land; (2) the right to the use of land is subject to a term limit though the term may be extended; and (3) the government has the right to interfere with the use of the land if it believes that the land is not being used as intended.[93] Because of the highly controversial nature of this issue, the Contract Law is silent about the contract for the transfer of the land use right.

On March 24, 2003, the SPC issued an "Explanation to the Application of Law to the Cases Involving Disputes over the Contract of Sale of Marketable Residential Housing" (2013 Explanation).[94] Under the 2013 Explanation, a contract for the sale of marketable residential housing is governed by the Contract Law. According to the SPC, a contract for the sale of marketable residential housing is defined as a contract by which a real estate developer sells housing

---

91   See Property Law of China, art. 117 (2007).
92   Under Article 149 of the Property Law, when the term of the right to use the land for dwelling houses expires, it shall be renewed automatically.
93   See Sun Lihai, *Selection of Legislative Materials of the Contract Law of China*, 205–06 (Legal Press 1999).
94   The Explanation took effect on June 1, 2003. See SPC, *Explanation to the Application of Law to the Cases Involving Disputes over the Contract of Sale of Marketable Residential Housing*. A Chinese version of the Explanation is available at http://www.law-lib.com.cn/law/law_view.asp?id=74535.

that is going to be built or that has already been built to the public and thereafter transfers the title of the housing to the buyer.[95]

However, under the *Law of Urban Real Estate Management of China*, which was adopted on June 5, 1994, when real estate is transferred or mortgaged, the title of the housing and the right to the use of the land to which the housing is affixed must be simultaneously transferred or mortgaged.[96] Thus, pursuant to its 2013 Explanation, the SPC has seemingly extended the application of the Contract Law to encompass the transfer of the land use right when such transfer is associated with the transfer of a building affixed to the land. In *Hu Baiqin v. Linyi Yixing Real Estate Development Inc.* (2015), the plaintiff entered into a contract to purchase a condominium built by the defendant. After the contract was signed, the defendant sold the unit to a third party. The plaintiff subsequently sued the defendant for breach of contract. In its decision granting the plaintiff' claim for damages, the Linyi county people's court relied on both the Contract Law as well as the SPC's 2013 Explanation. This case was published in the SPC's website as a typical (i.e., sample) case.[97]

4   Contract and the Socialist Market Economy

As noted, from the founding of the People's Republic of China in 1949 until 1978, when the nation's economic reforms began, China had a highly centralized planned economy. This economy, which was modeled upon the economy of the former Soviet Union, developed throughout China's first "five-year plan period" (1953–1958). Among the key elements of the planned economy were the State plan mandates and the dominance of public (i.e., state and collective) ownership. The planned economy prohibited private ownership of property.[98] Because the state pursuant to law was the sole actor in the planned economy, the State Plan under the economy controlled business transactions in virtually

---

95   *See id.*, art. 1.
96   *See Law of Urban Real Estate Management of China*, art. 31 (eff. Jan. 1, 1995), http://www.law-lib.com.cn/law/law_view.asp?id=253.
97   *See* the SPC, *Collection of Typical Cases involving Contract Disputes* (Dec. 4, 2015), http://www.court.gov.cn/fabu-xiangqing-16210.html.
98   In the mid-1950s, China launched a national campaign to "transform private ownership into socialist ownership." Aimed at extinguishing all "capitalist elements," this nationwide "socialist transformation" helped establish the absolute control of public ownership over the economy. By the end of the first five-year plan (1958), the state-owned enterprises amounted to about eighty percent of the national economy. *See* Wu Jinglian, *A Road to the Market Economy*, 129 (Beijing Univ. of Indus. Press 1992).

all aspects. Though state-owned enterprises were occasionally asked to deal with each other through agreements, such agreements were considered to be mere tools to implement the State Plan, and the parties to such agreements barely had any choice in the matters. Effectively, the State Plan rendered contracting meaningless.[99]

In 1978, China—learning from the bitter experience of the Cultural Revolution, during which the country was ravaged by political chaos and economic disorder—began to consider taking its economy in a different direction. A bold proposed step was to adopt a policy of "economic reform and opening-up to the outside." The economic reform contemplated by this policy was geared toward establishing a new economic system and building a modern enterprise scheme. Three interrelated concepts, all of which the country's lawmakers had been grappling with, were at the center of such economic reform: the "socialist system," "private ownership," and the "market economy." Questions that puzzled everyone at the outset of this economic reform included:

a. Was private ownership necessarily contradictory to China's socialist system? In other words, could the socialist system embrace private ownership, in addition to public ownership?
b. Did the market economy have to be established in the private ownership economy, or could it be adopted in a public ownership-based socialist system?
c. Could public and private ownership co-exist in a market economy with the public ownership as the core?

There was no immediately apparent answer to these questions when the economic reform began. Nevertheless, driven by the urgent need to make the country prosperous, the Chinese government followed Mr. Deng Xiaoping's philosophy of "walking across a river by touching the stones underneath" and cautiously moved forward. Along with the economic reform, China gradually redefined its economic system from a "socialist planned economy" to a "socialist planned commodity economy" in 1984, then to "socialist commodity economy" in 1987, and finally to a "socialist market economy" in 1992. One year later, in 1993, China amended the 1982 Constitution by formally adopting a "socialist market economy." The significance of this adoption of a socialist market economy was not simply linguistic; rather, it signified a change in the county's economic system as well as ideology.

Recognition of private ownership in China can be best explained by looking at the changes in the Chinese Constitution. Since 1954, China has adopted four

---

99 *See* Zhang Guangxing, *General Introduction to the Law of Obligations*, 14 (Law Press 1997).

constitutions. The current one is the 1982 Constitution.[100] Prior to 1982, private ownership had long been deemed an evil harmful to the socialist system that had to be rooted out. Even the 1982 Constitution, at the time it was adopted, did not explicitly recognize private ownership. The 1982 Constitution did, however, provide in Article 11 that the State would protect the lawful interest of " urban and rural workers' individual businesses." This provision signaled that outside of public ownership, there was something of an "ownership nature" that would also need to be protected.

On April 12, 1988, Article 11 was amended to clearly provide that the State permits the private sector of the economy to exist and develop within the limits prescribed by law, and that the private sector of the economy is a complement to the socialist public economy.[101] Eleven years later, on March 15, 1999, Article 11 was amended again. In its current version, the Article provides that non-public sectors of the economy—such as individual or private sectors— operating within the limits prescribed by law, constitute an important component of the socialist market economy.[102]

The 2004 Amendment to the 1982 Constitution made a substantial move toward protection of private ownership in China. First, it provides, like Article 11, that the State protects the lawful rights and interests of non-public sectors of the economy such as individual and private sectors.[103] Second, it requires compensation to be made whenever the private property of a citizen, including the right to the use of land, is expropriated or requisitioned by the government for the public interest. Third, it emphasizes that the citizen's lawful private property is inviolable, which provides legal assurance against infringement.[104] In 2007, China adopted, for the first time in its modern history, the Property Law. Under Article 3 of the Property Law, the State maintains a socialist market economy and guarantees the equal legal status as well as the right to development of all the mainstays of the market.[105] Article 4 of the Property

---

100 The four Constitutions were adopted in 1954, 1975, 1978, and 1982, respectively. The 1982 Constitution was amended in 1988, 1993, 1999 and 2004. The latest amendment to the 1982 Constitution was made in March 2018.
101 *See* the 1988 Amendment to the Chinese Constitution.
102 *See* the 1999 Amendment to the Chinese Constitution.
103 *See* the 1982 Constitution, art. 11 (as amended in 2018).
104 *See id.*, art. 13 (as amended in 2018).
105 The Property Law of China was adopted on March 16 2007 and took effect on October 1, 2007. An English version of the statute is available at http://www.npc.gov.cn/englishnpc/Law/2009-02/20/content_1471118.htm. In Article 2 of the Property Law, the property right is defined as the exclusive right—which consists of the right of ownership, the usufruct, and the security interest on property—enjoyed by the owner to directly dominate a given thing according to law.

Law further provides that the property right of the State, collectives, individual persons, and other owners is protected by law, and no units or individuals shall encroach on it.[106]

The socialist market economy system was formally adopted in the 1993 Amendment. Article 15 of the 1982 Constitution (as amended) provides that the State adheres to a socialist market economy and prohibits any organization or individual from disturbing the socio-economic order.[107] As an important indication of the socialist market economy's implementation, the 1993 Amendment changed the term "State-run enterprises" in the original 1982 Constitution to "State-owned enterprises." Although the term "socialist market economy" was never well-defined in the Constitution, it did implicate the ideology of the Chinese government, which is that on the one hand, the country had to stay with socialism where public ownership (or state ownership) remained dominant, and on the other hand, in order to aid further economic development, the country had to be driven mainly by market forces other than governmental plans of an administrative nature.

There was a belief in China that the market economy might also serve socialist needs because the market economy, though originating as a free enterprise system, actually took different forms.[108] Since the concept of a "socialist market economy" was introduced in China in 1980s, the nation's lawmakers have continually grappled to reach an "equilibrium" between socialism and a market economy.[109] Concurrently, the Chinese government, in order to advance the economic reforms, positioned the country as being in the "preliminary stage of socialism" wherein the market remained the primary force of the economy.[110]

---

106 See id., art. 4.
107 See id., art. 15.
108 Chinese scholars divide the market economy of the world into different models. The major ones are the US Model (i.e., free market economy), the French Model (i.e., administrative market economy), and the German Model (i.e., social market economy). See Liu Shiming, *Market Economy Models in the Modern World*, 648–649 (Guangdong Tourism Press 1998).
109 In November 1979, when Den Xiaoping introduced his idea that "socialism may also practice market economy," the term "market economy"—which had previously been taboo in China—became first associated with the term "socialism." In October 1982, Deng Xiaoping again pointed out that there existed no fundamental contradiction between socialism and a market economy. Thereafter, during his famous tour to the south in 1992, Mr. Deng further emphasized that a market economy was not the line that differentiates socialism and capitalism. See Ding Bangkai, *The Law of Socialist Market Economy*, 6 (South East Univ. Press 2002).
110 When the 1982 Constitution was amended in 1993, a new paragraph was added to its Preamble. This paragraph provided that the country was now in the preliminary stage of

Interestingly, China, after joining the WTO in 2001, has been making all efforts to promote its "market economy" status and to have that status recognized by other nations. In April 2004, New Zealand became the first county to recognize China's market economy status. According to Chinese sources, by the end of 2017, eighty-one countries—including Russia, Australia, Brazil, and a number of European countries—announced their recognition of China's market economy status.[111] But as of early 2019, several major countries and political bodies—including the United States, Japan, Canada, and the European Union—have yet to recognize China's market economy status.

It is important to keep in mind that China's pursuance of a market economy, or of the socialist market economy, was not for the purpose of transforming the nation's economy into one of private ownership, nor was it intended to eliminate the State plan. As many Chinese scholars have pointed out, the socialist market economy has three important elements: (1) though private and other forms of ownership exist under the socialist market economy, the pillar of that economy is public ownership; (2) the distribution system in the socialist market economy contains multi–distribution forms but its focus is on the principle of "from each according to his ability to each according to his work"; and (3) the ultimate goal of the socialist market economy is to achieve common wealth.[112]

Nevertheless, the adoption of the socialist market economy necessarily demanded a change in the way that businesses in China operated and were managed. A significant change was the shift in business decision-making functions from planning authorities to individual entities or private persons. Consequent to that change, contract-based transactions became the major components of the Chinese economy, though the State plan still played an economic role. Contracts replaced the State plan and became the basic legal devices for business activities.

In the early phase of the nation's economic reform, contracts were specially referred to as " economic contracts" because the sole purpose of contracts was considered to be to implement the State plan and also because the relationship between the parties to contracts was regarded as purely economic in nature. Since contracts have become the major means of dealing with civil and commercial affairs, however, "equality" and "mutual benefit" between the parties have become widely-recognized as fundamental elements of contract-making.

---

socialism and that the fundamental task of the nation was to combine all of its sources to facilitate the nation's socialism-oriented modernization.
111   See http://www.mnw.cn/news/world/1184105.html.
112   See Ding Bangkai, *supra* note 109, at 7.

In this regard, the "equal status" of the parties to a contract has been hailed as a critical component of making a contract. This requires, in turn, that the will of the parties to a contract be respected.[113]

Based on the foregoing, it is fair to say that—though the exact meaning of the socialist market economy is subject to further debates—contracts have undoubtedly functioned as primary players in the Chinese economy. Moreover, contract law, pursuant to the Chinese legislature's belief, is the basic legal framework of the market economy.[114] As noted, however, the socialist market economy is not intended to disregard State plans. To the contrary, State plans remain, to certain extent, influential in the process of making contracts in the socialist market economy.

5   Contracts and the State Plan

In the early stages of modern Chinese contract law legislation, there remained a strong preference for prioritizing implementation of the State plan. Underlying this preference was the conceived distinction between the brand of market economy that China sought to adopt and the free market economy that existed in many western countries. At this time, it was believed that contracts would become a useful tool to help implement the State plan. The simple reason for this belief was that all business activities were supposed to be under the control of the State plan.

Thus, in the 1981 Economic Contract Law, contracts were deemed to be subject to the supremacy of the State plan. Article 4 of the Economic Contract Law explicitly provided that the making of economic contracts had to comport with the requirements of the State plan. Moreover, according to Article 7 of the 1981 Economic Contract Law, an economic contract would be null and void if it violated the state plan. Under the 1981 Economic Contract Law, no contract could function as an obstacle to the implementation of the State plan. Indeed, a stated purpose of the 1981 Economic Contract Law was to ensure that the State plan would be fully implemented.[115]

---

113   "Equal status" is a basic principle in both the 2017 GPCL and the Contract Law. Article 3 of the GPCL provides that parties to a civil activity shall have equal status. Under Article 3 of the Contract Law, the parties to a contract shall have equal legal status and no party may impose its will on the other party.

114   See Hu Kangsheng, *Explanation to the Contract Law (Draft) of the People's Republic of China*, published in *Selection of Legislative Materials of Contract Law of the People's Republic of China*; see also Sun Lihai, *supra* note 93, at 3–7.

115   See 1981 Economic Contract Law of China, art. 1.

The State plan in China is normally divided into two categories: the mandatory State plan and the directory State plan (or State guidance plan). The mandatory State plan refers to the plan that must be carried out and is the device through utilization of which the State directly manages the nation's economy. The mandatory State plan is implemented through "administrative orders" of the State planning authority. By contrast, the directory State plan serves as guidance for how enterprises should conduct their businesses. Under it, enterprises retain certain a flexibility to make their business plans according to their business needs.

Generally, the State plan in the course of its implementation is operated in the form of quota. In accordance with 1981 Economic Contract Law, for business transactions concerning products and items that are within the scope of the mandatory State plan, any economic contracts attendant to those transactions must be made under the quota provided by the State. If the parties to such an economic contract cannot not reach an agreement, the matter should be handled by their superior authorities. If, contrastingly, business transactions involve products or items that fall into the category of the directory State plan, any economic contracts entered into through such transactions may be formed according to the business situation of the entities concerned in light of the State quota.[116]

When the Civil Code was adopted in 1986, an effort was made to separate contracts from the State plan by affording parties to contracts greater autonomy and power to make business decisions on their own. The 1986 Civil Code prohibits any civil activity undermining the State economic plan, but it does not require that contracts be made under the State plan. The 1981 Economic Contract Law was amended in 1993 and eliminated the preference for the State plan. In Article 1 of the amended Economic Contract Law, a stated purpose of the Contract Law was changed from "ensuring the implementation of State plan" to "ensuring a sound development of the socialist market economy."[117]

The Contract Law is said to have departed from the planned economy tradition and to be more market-oriented than previous contract legislation. First, the Contract Law further strengthens the principle of "equal status" by emphasizing that no party may impose its will on the other. The purpose underlining the "equal status" principle is to ensure that a contract is the result of the free will of the parties to the contract. Second, the Contract Law does not use the term "State plan," but instead employs the term "State mandatory task or State

---

116 The 1981 Economic Contract Law of China was amended on September 2, 1993. An English translation is available at http://en.pkulaw.cn/Display.aspx?lib=law&Cgid=44361.
117 See id., art. 11.

purchase order" to refer to the State mandate in the making of contracts. Third, the Contract Law defines "contracting party" as including natural persons, legal persons, or other organizations, and thereby signifies the end of China's exclusion of individuals (i.e., natural persons) from the pool of those capable of entering into contacts. [118]

Under Article 38 of the Contract Law, when the State issues a mandatory task or a state purchasing order based on necessity, the legal persons or organizations affected by that task or order must conclude contracts between themselves in accordance with their rights and obligations as stipulated by relevant laws and administrative regulations. Article 38 is the only provision in the Contract Law that addresses the State plan; a contract concluded under Article 38 is also called a "State mandatory task contract" or a "State purchasing order contract."[119] From this, it can be inferred that the impact of the State plan on contracts still exists in China.

Despite the Article 38 provision, the State plan appears to be playing an increasingly less active role in China's developing market economy.[120] The State has been shifting its planning authority from micro-control to macro-control of the nation's economy, and has been relying more on economic and legal means to manage the economy. In the contract law legislation, the State has

---

118   In the 1981 Economic Contract Law, "contract" was defined as an agreement determining the mutual relationship of rights and obligations between legal persons in order to realize certain economic goals. In 1993, when the Economic Contract Law was amended, it was provided that the statute applied to contracts entered into between legal persons who were equal civil parties; other economic organizations; self-employed workers or traders; and rural households operating on contracts for the purpose of realizing certain economic goals and clarifying each other's rights and obligations. It was clear that, under the Economic Contract Law, natural persons were not eligible to be parties to a contract. *See id.* Although the Technology Contract Law that was adopted in 1987 applied to contracts establishing civil rights and obligations in technical development, technology transfer, technical consultancy and technical service that were entered into between legal persons, between legal persons and citizens, and between citizens, the statute excluded from its purview contracts in which one party was a foreign enterprise, another foreign organization, or a foreign individual. An English translation of the Technology Contract Law is available at http://www.qip.net/chinalaw/prclaw21.htm.
119   *See* Contract Law, art. 38.
120   The numbers of state-owned or state-controlled enterprises have been declining over the years. In 1998, there were 238,000 state-owned or -controlled enterprises. By the end of 2003, that number decreased to about 150,000. As of October 2004, there were only 31,500 state-owned industrial enterprises, which amounted (approximately) to merely fifteen percent of the county's total industrial enterprises. *See State-Owned Assets Supervision and Administration Commission of the State Council,* http://www.sasac.gov.cn/gzjg/qygg/200412010040.htm.

largely focused on State-owned or State-controlled enterprises.[121] Under Article 38, the "State mandatory task contract" or "State purchasing order contract" only applies to "relevant legal persons or other organizations."[122] Most of such "relevant legal persons" are State-owned or -controlled enterprises.

---

121 A state-controlled enterprise is referred to as a publicly held company when the State owns a majority of the enterprise's shares. Under the Company Law of China—which was adopted on December 29, 1993, took effect on July 1, 1994, and was amended first on December 25, 1999 and again on August 28, 2004—companies in China can take two alternative forms: limited liability or limited by shares. A company that is limited by shares is referred to as a "stock company." A State-owned enterprise may be structured as a limited liability company (i.e., wholly State owned) or a company limited by shares. In the latter case, the State is a shareholder in the company.
122 *See* Contract Law, art. 38.

CHAPTER 2

Freedom of Contract in China

It is a widely-held belief in western countries that it is in the public interest to accord individuals broad powers to determine their affairs through agreements reached among themselves.[1] This proposition rests upon the notion of freedom of contract. Derived from Roman law and developed in the nineteenth century,[2] the concept of freedom of contract has become the cornerstone of modern contract law, constituting the most important principle in contract law since the French Civil Code was adopted in 1804.[3] To be more explicit, in an open market economy, it is essential that businessmen and entities have the right to freely decide to whom they will offer their goods or services and by whom they wish to be supplied, as well as to freely agree on the terms of individual transactions.[4]

The concept of freedom of contract, as illustrated by western contract theories, contains "two closed related" elements: mutual agreement of the parties and free choice without external intervention.[5] A commonly accepted notion is that freedom of contract is not only a key aspect of a free society, but also a great engine of commerce in the world.[6] Although legislatures since the twentieth centrury have increased restrictions on parties' power to make contracts as they wish, freedom of contract (or freedom to bargain) remains a basic principle of many societies that is premised on the free market.[7]

---

1 Farnsworth, Contracts, 321–22 (Aspen Law & Bus., 3d ed., 1999).
2 Under the Roman law concept of *contractus consensus*, contracts were formed by mere consent of the parties. Thus, only consensus between the parties was required by law to produce any one of these contracts. See P.J. du Plessis, Roman Legal Tradition, 73–94 (2006); *see also* G.H.L. Fridman, *Freedom of Contract*, 2 OTTAWA L. REV. 1 (1965).
3 The idea of freedom of contract was derived from Adam Smith's theory of a free economy where individuals were regarded as the best judges of their own affairs. Inspired by free market incentives, classic contract law theory posited contract as the convergence of the wills of the contracting parties, which was later interpreted as "meeting of the minds." *See generally* Peter Linzer, A Contracts Anthology (Anderson Publishing Co., 2nd ed., 1995).
4 See Article 1.1 of UNIDROIT Principles, at https://www.unidroit.org/instruments/commercial-contracts/unidroit-principles-2010/414-chapter-1-general-provisions/863-article-1-1-freedom-of-contract.
5 *See generally* P.S. Atiyah, The Rise and Fall of Freedom of Contract (1979).
6 *See* Jeff Ferriell, Understanding Contracts, 1 (2nd ed., 2009).
7 *See* Joseph M. Perillo, Contracts, 5 (7th ed., 2014).

Unfortunately, however, the concept of freedom of contract was not accepted in China until recently. Although a great deal of Chinese contract theory is derived intellectually from the civil law (or continental law), especially French and German laws, the idea of freedom of contract is an exception. Even in the early 1980s, when China decided to revitalize its economy by introducing western legal and economic concepts into the nation, freedom of contract was not embraced because of concerns about both the influence of "capitalist ideology" as well as the unwanted impacts on State plans. This concern was clearly reflected in the 1981 Economic Contract Law, which did not provide for freedom of contract.[8]

There are a number of factors that contributed to China's rejection of the concept of freedom of contract. First, under the centrally planned economy, it was impossible for individuals or business entities to have free access to the market. Every business sector was strictly tied to the State's economic plan, and development of the economy was not driven by market forces but rather by the central government through pre-determined plans.[9] Second, because the State plan was the major player in China's economy, there was barely any room for freedom of contract in that economy. Therefore, it was inconceivable that anyone in China would think of having the right to freely enter into a contract with others. Moreover, as noted, under the 1981 Economic Contract Law, no individual could become a party to a contract. Third, the concept of freedom of contract had long been criticized in China as a capitalist concept—an "enemy" to the socialist system.

The Contract Law reversed this course. It expressly grants contracting parties the right to enter into contracts on a voluntary basis, and prohibits any unlawful interference with that right. The most noteworthy provision in the Contract Law is Article 4, which is widely acclaimed by the Chinese legislators as the statutary rule of "party autonomy" in contracting.[10] Under Article

---

8   When the Economic Contract Law was amended twelve years later in 1993, a progress made toward recognition of the concept of freedom of contract was the requirement that, in concluding an economic contract, the parties must implement the principles of equality and mutual benefit, and must achieve agreement thought negotiation. No party could impose its will on the other party and no unit or individual could unlawfully interfere. *See* Economic Contract Law, art. 5 (1993). An English translation of the Economic Contract Law is available at http://www.qip.net/chinalaw/prclaw19.htm.

9   This type of economy (also described as a "bird-cage economy") was modeled after the economy of the former Soviet Union and was advocated by late Chinese vice premier Chen Yun. Mr. Chen was in charge of the nation's economy for decades, except for the period of the Cultural Revolution.

10 Sun Lihai et al., A Practical Explanation to the Contract Law, 22–24 (Industry & Commerce Press, 1999) [hereinafter "Explanation"].

4, parties have the right to voluntarily enter into contracts in accordance with the law, and no unit or individual may unlawfully interfere. It is commonly recognized in China that Article 4 of the Contract Law represents a dramatic change in favor of freedom of contract in the country's contract legislation.[11]

When the drafting of the Contract Law started in 1993, there was a strong voice from many Chinese legal scholars and some legislators advocating that freedom of contract should be incorporated as a general principle into the Contract Law. As a matter of fact, in the first draft of the Contract Law in January 1995, freedom of contract was a general principle of the Contract Law. The January 1995 draft of the statute stated that "the parties shall have the freedom of contract within the boundary of law and no unit, organization, or individual shall unlawfully interfere with that freedom."[12] However, that provision was completely rephrased in the 1997 draft, which was released on May 14, 1997. The updated provision read: "the parties shall have the right equally and voluntarily to make contracts according to law. None of the parties shall impose its own will on the other and no unit or individual shall unlawfully interfere with the parties' right."[13] One year later, this provision was changed again in the 1998 draft of the Contract Law, which was finalized on August 20, 1998 and adopted in 1999, and which constitutes the current provision of Article 4 of the Contract Law.[14]

Interestingly, in almost all of the published materials that offer explanations of the Contract Law, the principle of "making contracts voluntarily" is interpreted to mean that the parties have the freedom to make contracts in accordance with the law.[15] Many believe in China that, although Article 4 does not explicitly use the term "freedom of contact" (i.e., the term commonly accepted

---

11   Han Shiyuan, The Law of Contract, 37–39 (2011).
12   See *The Introduction to the Contract of Law of China and its Major Drafts*, 8–18 (Civil Law Office, Legal Affairs Comm. of Standing Comm. of National People's Congress, ed., Law Publ'g House, 2000).
13   *Id.* at 113.
14   *Id.* at 173.
15   See, e.g., Jiang Ping et al., *A Detailed Explanation of the Contract Law of China*, (China Univ. of Political Sci. & Law Press 1999); Yang Lixin et al., *Implementation and Application of the Contract Law of China*, (Jilin People's Publ'g House, 1999); Liu Wenhua et al., *Detailed Explanation and Typical Cases of the New Contract Law*, (Word Books Press, Co. 1999); Sun Lihai et al., Explanation, *supra* note 10; Research and Economic Law Offices of the General Office of the Standing Committee of NPC, *Explanation and Practical Guidance of the Contract Law of China*, (China Democracy & Legality Press,1999); Research Office of the General Office of the Standing Committee of NPC, *A Practical Guidance of the Contract Law of China* (Huawen Publ'g House 1999); Zhao Xudong et al., *Interpretation of Terms and Phrases Related to the Contract Law*, (People's Court Publ'g House 1999).

by western countries and international organizations),[16] Chinese contract legislation clearly recognizes the concept of freedom of contract as a general principle.

1   Conception of Freedom

Freedom, individual freedom in particular, was previously considered to be a bourgeois philosophy in China. A prevalent notion dominating the nation for quite a long time was that freedom would serve the sole purpose of promoting individualism. Although the 1954 Constitution provided both that Chinese citizens enjoyed the freedom of speech, press, religion as well as demonstration, and that the personal liberty of citizens was not to be infringed, such freedom was never well-respected or protected, and therefore barely existed. Historical reasons aside,[17] this phenomenon was an inevitable consequence of the overly-stated supremacy of State interests.

Under the 1982 Chinese Constitution (as amended), the State protects three different interests—namely State, collective, and private interests. The State and collective interests are also jointly called "public interests." In the decades following the communist party's ascenscion to power in China, an infallible principle was that State interests controlled all other interests. Under this principle, a "golden rule" for maintaining the supremacy of State interests developed. This "golden rule" requires the subordination of all private interests to both State and collective interests, and the subordination of all private and collective interests to State interests. Thus, whenever there is a conflict between private interests and State or collective interests, the former must yield to the latter, without exception.

In western countries, individual freedom or liberty is the right "enshrined in nature that cannot be legitimately modified by any human power."[18] In China, by contrast, such freedom or liberty is viewed as a special privilege granted by

---

16   See UNIDROIT, *supra* note 4. Freedom of Contract is provided in UNIDROIT Principles as a basic principle in the context of international trade. Realizing the paramount importance of the principle of freedom of contract, Article 1.1 of UNIDROIT Principles (Freedom of Contract) stipulates that the parties are free to enter into a contract and to determine its contents.
17   Under Confucianism, three cardinal guides must be observed in order to maintain the stability of the country. The three cardinal guides were "ruler over subject, father over son, and husband over wife."
18   *See* 15 Am. Jur. 2d, Civil Rights, §2 (2000).

the ruling authority. Accordingly, the extent to which people enjoy freedom in China is very much dependent on the leniency of the government. In this context, the concern about whether people have freedom or have really enjoyed freedom has hardly been paramount in China. For example, throughout the ten-year Cultural Revolution, millions of people were deprived of personal freedom or liberty and all private interests were totally ignored. Since 1979, China has made efforts to bolster and respect private interests. Still, there is a long way to go.

A fundamental difference between China and the western world in their understandings of the concept of freedom is that, in China, freedom is conceptualized as a given right while, in the western world, it is considered to be an inherent right. The focal point of this distinction is how the government deals with people's freedom. When freedom is inherent, people naturally have it unless the law imposes restrictions on the exercise of freedom. If freedom, by contrast, is given, people do not have freedom until it is granted by the government. In addition, where freedom is inherent, it may not be taken away without due process of law or other compelling grounds. Where freedom is granted, however, this protection does not exist.

Broadly speaking, China has historically been an obligation-based rather than a right-based country. In Chinese history, obligations were weighted significantly more than rights and barely any right was deemed natural. Under Confucian creed, which was upheld as the ruling orthodox of the country in many dynasties, the social order may only remain in the good course when the ruler is ruler, the ruled is ruled, the father is father, and the son is son, and each fulfills the role assigned and acts accordingly with others. It was this creed that posed an insurmountable boundary to defining the propriety of a person's behavior in reference to the person's status. Clearly, the very focus of the creed was on the obligations of loyalty and filial piety. Reflected in law, the main theme was to impose obligations through pubishment rather than to recognize rights.

The development of a market economy in China prompted a drive for change. Since China's economic reform, there had been a growing demand in the nation for protecting individuals' rights. In the drafting of the Contract Law, the issue of how to address the concept of freedom of contract became highly debated. Many scholars strongly advocated for the view that freedom of contract should be embodied in the Contract Law. However, these scholars encountered resistance from others who argued against employing the term of freedom of contract in the Contract Law. Underlying this resisitance was a fear that freedom of contract may mean something beyond what the Contract Law intended in terms of the parties' rights to make a contract.

In its official explanation for the 1998 draft Contract Law, the Legal Affairs Committee (LCA) of the Standing Committee of NPC stated that the concept of freedom of contract referred primarily to party autonomy, meaning that the parties have the right to freely enter into a contract and to determine the contents of the contract. The LCA further pointed out, however, that freedom of contract was not absolute and, in many countries, such freedom was limited to the legally allowable extent. Hence, the LCA concluded that it might not be proper in China to simply adopt the concept of freedom of contract.[19] In the Committee's opinion, the freedom of contract principle in the Contract Law would need to be addressed to embrace Chinese characteristics. As a result, the term "freedom of contract" was replaced with "making a contract voluntarily" in the Contract Law.

Despite this term change, a number of Chinese scholars believed that the concept of freedom of contract would empower parties to determine their own affairs through negotiated agreements, and would require that the parties' freely expressed will be honored and protected. It therefore seems undisputable that the concept of freedom of contract has been very well received among Chinese scholars, notwithstanding the differences in how China has understood the essence of this long-established contract principle in comparison with western nations. Given the impact of China's ex-system of a planned economy, freedom of contract in China emphasizes two major points: respect for parties' wills and no government interference.[20]

2 Right of Parties to a Contract

The main tenet of the concept of freedom of contract is that parties to a contract have the right to determine and arrange their business affairs among themselves without interference.[21] Although there has been an increasing trend in modern society in imposing restrictions on freedom of contract, the right of contractual parties to decide freely to whom they will offer their goods

---

19 Sun Lihai et al., *Selection of Legislative Materials in the Contract Law of the People's Republic of China*, 8–12 (Legal Publ'g House 1999).

20 *See id.*, *see also* Wang Liming, *Study on the Contract Law (Vol. 1)*, 154–155 (People's Univ. Press 2002).

21 In western countries, freedom of contract was regarded as embodying some of the cardinal principles of law. These principles were: (a) citizens enjoy a broad discretion to make contracts, (b) the law routinely respects citizens' choices of terms in contracts, and (c) the voluntariness of citizens' choices is protected against coercion and fraud. *See* Patrick S. Atiyah, *The Rise and Fall of Freedom of Contract*, (Oxford Univ. Press, 1979).

or services and by whom they wish to be supplied, and the possibility for the parties to freely agree on the terms of individual transactions, remain fundamental elements of an open, market-oriented, and competitive international economic order.[22] Even though the tension between individual freedoms and social or governmental control grows, the idea of private autonomy remains influential.[23]

Because of China's extensive government control, party autonomy in the nation's contract-making process entails more obstacles in comparison with many other countries. Facing this reality, those Chinese scholars that support freedom of contract argue that Article 4 of the Contract Law should by implication include at least two basic notions. The first notion is that the consensual agreement of the parties should have an effect that is superior to that of permissive (i.e., non-mandatory) provisions of law (*jus dispositivum*). Under this notion, whenever there is an agreement reached by the parties, the agreement should control if no compulsory provision applies. Another situation where the parties' agreement dominates is the case in which the law permits something to be "otherwise agreed by the parties."[24]

The second notion is that the choice made voluntarily by the parties concerning every aspect of a contract shall be respected. The basic view in this regard embraces two points. First, "made voluntarily" under Article 4 shall mean that the choice must be made freely by the parties—not arranged by or chosen for the parties by any authority or through administrative means. Second, free choice so made shall implicate that the parties to a contract—natural persons, legal persons, and other organizations alike—have the right on the basis of their free will to determine whether to enter into a contract, how a contract is to be made, and what is to be contained in the contract.[25]

According to Chinese legislators and scholars, the effect of the "making a contract voluntarily" provision in Article 4 is significant in Chinese contract legislation because the provision essentially grants the parties the freedom to contract. As noted, some legislators and scholars even deem "voluntarily" to be equivalent to the "freedom of contract." Many in China have also made efforts to address Article 4 in a more specific way. Nowadays, as illustrated by a majority of Chinese scholars, the freedom that the parties to a contract may have under Article 4 of the Contract Law includes the following aspects:

---

22 *See* UNIDROIT, art. 1.1, *supra* note 4.
23 *See* Friedrich Kessler, *Contract as a Principle of Order*, in A Contracts Anthology (Anderson Publ'g Co., 2nd ed., 1995).
24 *See* Wang Liming, *supra* note 20, at 155.
25 *See* Sun Lihai, Explanation, *supra* note 10, at 22.

- The freedom to decide whether or not to enter into a contract. As a general principle, nobody can interfere with, or unduly influence, the parties' contracting power. It has become a common belief in China that the provision of "no unit or individual may unlawfully interfere" under Article 4 is key to the assurance of freedom of contract. Since a contract represents the expression of the free will of the parties, the relationship of the parties to the contract should be established on a voluntary basis without influence by any external forces. It is also believed that, although the parties' right to make a contract may still be limited, the limit as such should be kept at minimum.
- The freedom to determine with whom to contract. Under the concept of freedom of contract, any party to a contract has the right to freely decide who will be the other party to the contract. This right is practically significant because, in China's past, parties were frequently given no choice but to enter into deals with each other through "marriages" pre-arranged by relevant authorities. Such pre-arranged-marriages were also seen in a number of company merger and acquisition cases. In this situation, the parties are actually under government pressure to make a contract between themselves.
- The freedom to determine the contents of the contract. "Contents" in this context refer to a contract's terms and conditions, as well as all other items that are deemed necessary by the parties. Article 12 of the Contract Law provides that the contents of a contract shall be agreed upon by the parties. Article 12 also provides a list of terms that comprise the general contents of a contract, but does not specify which items are essential.[26] Thus, under the Contract Law, the inclusion of Article 12 terms is not a required prerequisite for a contract to be valid; rather, such terms serve merely as guidance for the parties. In this way, parties have the right to create contents that may vary from contract to contract.

In addition, Article 12 of the Contract Law allows parties to use model text for each kind of contract. Moreover, pursuant to Article 61, parties may enter into a supplementary agreement if there is no agreement in the contract regarding such terms as quality, price or remuneration, place of performance, etc. These terms may also be determined from the context of relevant clauses of the contract or in accordance with transaction practices. Article 62 of the Contract Law further provides in detail the methods by

---

26 There are eight terms, including (a) title or name and domicile of the parties; (b) contract subject; (c) quantity; (d) quality; (e) price or remuneration; (f) time, place and method of performance; (g) liability for breach of contract; and (h) methods to solve disputes.

which the unclear terms are to be determined if they cannot be ascertained under Article 61.
- The freedom to choose the contract form. The Contract Law is flexible pertaining to the form a contract may take. Under Article 10 of the Contract Law, a contract may be made in writing, orally, or in other forms. Pursuant to Article 10, a writing is required only if the laws or regulations so provide or if the parties agree to such a mandate. Thus, absent statutory requirements, the parties may enter into a contract orally, unless the parties specify otherwise.

  In addition, the performance doctrine as set forth in Article 36 of the Contract law trumps the writing requirement. According to Article 36, a contract, which must be concluded in writing only if required, is enforceable if one party has performed its principal obligations under the contract and the other party has received the performance required by the contract. This performance doctrine also applies, under Article 37, to contracts that have been made in writing but that are not signed or stamped before the performance begins.
- The freedom to modify or rescind a contract. Article 77 of the Contract Law provides that the parties may modify a contract by consent through negotiation. The parties may also rescind a contract the same way in accordance with Article 93 of the Contract Law. The right of rescission under Article 93 may be provided by the parties in the contract or by a separate agreement. The conditions under which a contract may be rescinded are also subject to the agreement of the parties.
- The freedom to decide what remedy or relief should be sought when the contract is breached. In accordance with Article 107 of the Contract Law, if one party to a contract fails to perform its obligations under the contract or if one party's performance fails to satisfy the terms of the contract, that party will bear such responsibilities for breaching the contract as to continue to perform its obligations, to take remedial measures, or to compensate for any loss. Article 107, as interpreted, allows the non-breaching party to choose what relief it is entitled to. The non-breaching party may at its own choice ask for liquidated damages, seek compensation, or demand specific performance if such performance is permitted under the law.
- The freedom to choose the methods of dispute settlement. Under Article 128 of the Contract law, parties have different alternatives for settling contractual disputes. In addition to litigation, the parties may obtain a dispute resolution through conciliation, mediation, or arbitration. In general, the parties are encouraged, but are not required, to seek conciliation or mediation as a first resort to the settlement of disputes. Litigation is available only if there is no arbitration agreement or if the arbitration agreement is

invalid. Once the parties agree to arbitration, they will be bound by the arbitral award and no litigation concerning the same dispute is allowed.[27]

Nevertheless, criticism that the Contact Law only has a limited recognition of freedom of contract perists, on the basis that the term "making a contract voluntarily" in the Contract Law is different from the term "freedom of contract."[28] The argument is premised on the notion that "freedom of contract" focuses on maximum economic efficiency, and promotes the parties' ability to exercise their full creative potential and to establish appropriate business relationships that possess all the specific nuances required in such relationships.[29] The term "making a contract voluntarily," however, emphasizes primarily the parties' wills, which are the prerequisite for manifestation of the intent to make a contract.[30]

There is also a concern that, though parties under the Contract Law may enter into contracts voluntarily, the government retains the ability to intervene in the contract-making process. Because of this possibility of government intervention, the parties may still be subject to certain unpredictable forces that could restrain their contract-making power. Therefore, many people believe that, to effectively prevent government interference, the concept of freedom of contract must be constantly emphasized and further respected along with the "voluntary" provision of Article 12 of the Contract Law.[31]

3   Limitations on Party Autonomy

Even if Article 4 of the Contract Law implicates a recognition of freedom of contract in China, the parties' right to freely enter into a contract remains restricted. Article 4 has two aspects. On the one hand, it is intended to ensure that contracts will be made on a voluntary basis, free from any external coersion. On the other hand, however, Article 4 imposes two conditions on the

---

27 Under the Arbitration Law of China (1994), if the parties have concluded an arbitration agreement and one party initiates an action in a People's Court, the People's Court shall not take the case unless the arbitration agreement is void (Article 4). In addition, if, after the arbitration award is made, one party institutes a judicial proceeding in a People's Court concerning the same dispute, the People's Court shall not hear the case (Article 9).
28 See Jiang Ping, supra note 15, at 5; Yang Lixing, supra note 15, at 14.
29 When invited to offer comments on the draft Contract Law, the legal committee of the American Chamber of Commerce (Beijing) stressed the importance of "freedom of contract" being drafted into the general principles of the Contract Law.
30 See Jiang Ping, supra note 15, at 7–8.
31 See Wang Liming, supra note 20, at 16.

parties' exercise of their contract-making power: (1) a contract must be entered into according to law; and (2) only ulawful interference with the parties' right to freely make a contract is prohibited.

Freedom of contract is not unrestricted in today's world and a party's right to make a contract is subject to the limitations prescribed by law or for the sake of public policy. From the legislative perspective, it is believed in contract literature that "while the parties' power to contract as they please for lawful purposes remains a basic principle of contract law today, it is hemmed in by increasing legislative restrictions."[32] The most notable areas in which the growing trend to set limits on freedom of contract is clearly descernible include employment, consumer protection, environment, as well as natural resources.[33]

As far as public policy is concerned, the imposition of restrictions on freedom of contract serves a twofold purpose. First, it ensures that the parties to a contract deal with each other in a manner not in conflict with the public interest so that unfairness and and unjustice will not occur. This requires, among others, that the bargaining process not be abused by misleading or coercive conduct by any party. Second, it is an appropriate mechanism for discouraging undesirable conduct, either by the parties or others, and for averting unsavory agreements.[34]

Therefore, in modern contract law, the autonomy parties enjoy with respect to making contracts pursuant to the principle of freedom of contract is not unlimited. In China, the limits on the right of parties to make a contract bear the "Chinese distinction." "Bird in cage," a popular metaphor often used in the country to describe the relationship between business entities and government, may best state the kind of freedom of contract accorded parties in China.[35] This metaphor implies that contractual parties have the freedom to contract but that the exercise of such freedom must be within boundaries prescribed by the government. This comports with the Chinese notion that freedom is a granted, rather than an inherent, right.

---

32 *See* John D. Calamari & Joseph M. Perillo, The Law of Contracts, 5 (4th ed., 1998).
33 In the United States, in addition to legislative restrictions, freedom of contract is also subject to judicial restrictions "imposed by the courts in the exercise of their function of developing the common law." *See* Joseph M. Perillo, Contract, 5 (Hornbook, 7th ed., 2014).
34 *See* Farnsworth, *supra* note 1, at 223–25, 321–23.
35 This is the term that was used to describe the economic model promoted by the late Chinese leader Chen Yun, who was famous as a primary designer of China's state economic plans. Under Chen's economic model, State plans functioned as a cage that defined the dimension of the business activities of all enterprises (the birds).

The "Chinese distinction" is often referred to as the "Chinese reality." In general, the "Chinese reality" in business settings has at least four unique characteristics: (a) public ownership dominance, (b) supremacy of State interest, (c) limited choices available to private parties, and (d) excessive government role. With respect to contracts, the limitations on a individual's freedom to contract, as implicated in Article 4 of the Contract Law, is further characterized by the following aspects.

3.1 *Legal Compliance*

Legal compliance involves the issue of legality. There is a statutory requirement in China that a contract must comply with laws and regulations both substantively and procedurally. Substantive compliance requires that the contents of a contract conform to the provisions of laws and regulations; any violation of such laws or regulations renders the contract invalid or unenforceable. Procedural compliance concerns restrictions imposed on the formality of a contract, which means that conclusion of a contract must follow certain procedures stipulated by laws and regulations. In addition, to be legal under the Contract Law, a contract must conform with social ethics and the State plan. It is typical in China that, for certain contracts, the State plan must be observed.

The most important provision in the Contract Law that restricts the parties' freedom in making a contract is Article 7. As a governing principle of legal compliance, Article 7 provides that, in concluding and performing a contract, the parties must abide by the laws and administrative regulations, and must observe social ethics.[36] The 2017 GPCL contains a similar provision that applies to all civil matters, including contracts. Under Article 8 of the 2017 GPCL, parties engaging civil activites must not act in violation of the law or contrary to public order or good morals.[37]

Thus, pursuant to Article 7, parties' freedom to contract is subject to statutory limitations in two aspects: compliance with the law and observance of social ethics. Note that the law and administration regulations referred to in Article 7 denote legal provisions in both contract areas as well as areas that have the effect of limiting the parties' contract-making power.[38] In addition, under Article

---

36 For purposes of the Contract Law, "laws" refer to statutes or legal codes adopted by the National People's Congress and its Standing Committee, and "administrative regulations" are regulations issued by the State Council or approved to issue by the State Council. *See* Sun Lihai, Explanation, *supra* note 10, at 27–28.
37 *See* 2017 General Provisions of Civil Law of China, art. 8.
38 For example, the Consumer Interest Protection Law imposes certain restrictions upon manufacturers or business operators in their dealings with consumers.

7, neither party to contract may disrupt the social-economic order or damage the public interest. But both the social economic order and public interest as provided in Article 7 are considerably vaque.

The requirement of legal compliance was first provided in the 1986 Civil Code. Under the Civil Code, however, parties to a contract are both required to comply with the law and also bound by State policy absent applicable law.[39] The Contract Law does not contain such a policy compliance requirement because of the concerns about the uncertainty and unpredictability of the policy, particularly from foreign investors.[40] The deletion of the policy compliance requirement in the Contract Law is indeed a positive move away from the 1986 Civil Code. Notwithstanding, the potential influence of government policies on business activities should not be underestimated. It thus remains questionable whether parties in China may effectively protect themselves from policy interference.

The observance of social ethics requirement originated from the 1986 Civil Code.[41] However, neither the Contract Law nor the Civil Code define "social ethics." The term "social ethics" basically means commonly accepted moral norms. The term is not used in the 2017 GPCL. Instead, the 2017 GPCL, as noted, requires that the public order and good morals be observed in conducting civil activites. In addition, under Article 10 of the 2017 GPCL, civil disputes must be resolved in accordance with the law, and absent any applicable provison of law requiring otherwise, customs may apply, though not if they are contary to the public order and good morals. Many in China believe that the terms "good morals" and "social ethics" are substantively synonymous.[42]

---

39   Under Article 6 of the Civil Code, civil activities must conform to the law and, where there are no relevant provisions in the law, State policies shall be observed.
40   A significant issue concerning policy is transparency. Since the policies in many cases are addressed in the "internal documents" or "red letterhead documents" of the government and may be changed at any time without notice, with regard to the parties to a contract, the possible impacts of the policies on their business transactions or operations are totally unpredictable and unmanageable.
41   Article 7 of the 1986 Civil Code requires that civil activities defer to social ethics.
42   See Yang Yongchun, *Upholding Public Order and Social Morals under Civil Law Principle*, PEOPLE'S DAILY (Mar. 24, 2017), http://opinion.people.com.cn/n1/2017/0324/c1003-29165441.html. The concept of "public order and social morals" was first ued in the Interpreation of the Standing Committee of the NPC on Article 19 (1) of the 1986 Civil Code and Article 22 of the Marriage Law, which was issued on November 1, 2014.

3.2 *State Plan Mandate*

Once again, a significant change in China that resulted from the nation's vast economic reform was the shift from the planned economy to the market economy. As a consequence of this shift, the role of State plans was dramatically reduced. However, the adoption of the market economy in the country did not eliminate all State plans. To the contrary, State plans still play a part in certain arenas. As noted, under the Contract Law, the parties' contract-making power may still be affected by State mandatory tasks or State purchasing orders. The key article in the Contract Law that retains State plans is Article 38.

Despite the reforms moving toward the market economy, the State ownership remains predominant, especially in China's "pillar" industries. As of 2017, the revenue of State-owned or State-controlled enterprises amounted to over sixty percent of the nation's GDP. Among the Chinese Fortune 500 enterprises, more than 295 are State-owned or -controlled enterprises.[43] In addition, the State retains direct control over pillar industries (i.e., industries producing products essential to the nation's economy). In the past, contracts were subject to the absolute control of the government and were required to serve the purpose of implementing State plans. Now, governmental control over contracts under State plans is exercised through State mandatory tasks or State purchasing orders.

Pursuant to Article 38 of the Contract Law, companies or enterprises that receive by allocation State mandatory tasks or State purchase orders are required to make contracts to implement those tasks or orders. In general, user / supplier contracts are made between companies or enterprises that are affected by State mandatory tasks or purchasing orders. It is clear under the Contract Law that a contract may not be enforceable if it is in violation of a State mandatory task or purchasing order. But, what seems problematical is the extent to which the parties may seek judicial remedies when a breach of a contract concerning a State mandatory task or purchasing order occurs.[44]

3.3 *Administrative Supervision*

A unique characteristic of the Contract Law concerns administrative supervision. Resting mainly with the administrations of industry and commerce

---

43 The 2017 Chinese Fortune 500 available at http://www.xuesai.cn/jianzaoshi2/hangye/1519568.html.
44 In the past, all disputes involving State mandatory plan-related contracts were adjudicated primarily by administrative departments rather than by courts.

(AIC) as well as other relevant government agencies (RGA),[45] "administrative supervision" essentially refers to administrative interference with parties' contractual rights. Before the Contract Law was adopted, the AIC and the RGA had broad administrative powers to supervise contracts—powers that were often abused.[46] The Contract Law places certain limits on the exercise of such administrative powers, though it still empowers the AIC and the RGA to act as government watchdogs over contracts.

In accordance with Article 127 of the Contract Law, contract supervision by the AIC and the RGA is intended to deal with illegal conducts that are committed under color of contract to endanger and harm State and public interests. The two key terms in Article 127 are "illegal conduct" and "the State and public interests." Obviously, the primary purpose of Article 127 is to help protect the State's interests in maintaining the economic order and social stability of the nation. Thus, parties whose conduct is found to have caused harm to the State's interests face administrative penalties in the form of fines and/or revocation of their business licenses.[47]

The Contract Law contains no provisions with regard to how administrative supervision must be conducted, however. In addition, both "illegal conduct" and "the State and public interest" are quite vague terms. Moreover, there is a lack of a clear distinction between supervision and interference. Therefore, many people are concerned about the possible overreach of administrative supervision pertaining to government action under Article 127 of the Contract Law. As a matter of fact, in addition to the imposition of sanctions for illegal conduct involving contracts, administrative supervision in practice includes issuance of model contracts, certifications of contract, inspections of contract performance, as well as administrative mediations of contractual disputes.[48]

Model contracts are normally drafted and issued jointly by the AIC and the RGA for the purpose of helping parties draft their contracts. With regard to international contracts, the Ministry of Commerce (known as MOFCOM) has also provided a set of model contracts for parties' guidance.[49] According to

---

45 Generally, the RGA contains planning departments, construction administrations, supervising authorities of enterprises, departments in charge of exclusive trades, and real estate administrations. See *A Practical Guidance of the Contract Law of China,* 126–27.
46 Under the 1981 Economic Contract Law, the AIC and RGA at county or higher levels had authority to supervise economic contracts.
47 Article 127 of the Contract Law further provides that, if crime is committed, criminal responsibility shall be imposed.
48 See Sun Lihai, Explanation, *supra* note 10, at 201–213.
49 The MOFTEC was renamed as "MOFCOM" (Ministry of Commerce) in March 2003 as a result of a restructuring of the central government.

Article 12 of the Contract Law, parties may conclude a contract with reference to the model text of each kind of contract. Although the use of model contract forms provided by government gencies is not mandatory under the Contract Law, parties often feel somewhat compelled to employ such forms due to pressure from relevant government authorities.

Contract certification is the means by which the AIC or the RGA review the truthfulness and legality of contracts upon the application of parties. Contract certfication was first provided in the 1985 AIC Provisions of Certification of Economic Contracts ("1985 Provisions") to prevent contract fraud or sham contracts, and to strengthen the evidentiary effect of a contract's existence. Under the 1985 Provisions, contract certification was to be made by the county office of the AIC at the place at which the contract either formed or performed. The 1985 Provisions were amended in 1998 by the AIC Methods of Contract Certification ("1998 Methods"). Pursuant to the 1998 Methods, contract certification may be made either upon the application of the parties or as required by law. Although the 1998 Methods were repealed in 2004, this contract certification framework remained intact with respect to certain contracts (e.g., construction contracts). In addition, in certain areas, contracts are required to be filed with the relevant government agency for record.

Contract certification empowers the AIC or the RGA to review the substance (i.e., contents) of contracts. There are certain controversial issues relating to this, howerver. One issue is the status of certification. Under the Contract Law, certification is not a prerequisite for contract validity, and is not even an element of the contract-making process. But the effectiveness of a contract may become uncertain if the contract is found to contain defects during the process of certification, because of which the validity of the contract might be challenged. Another issue involves whether the contract takes effect upon the parties' signature (i.e., requiring no government approval) or only comes into force after it is cerified. A compounding issue concerns parties' remedies in cases where the AIC or the RGA make a mistake in the certification.

A derivative function of administration supervision is administrative mediation of contractual disputes. Such mediation may be conducted by the AIC or by the superior authority of the parties involved. Most cases in which an administrative mediation is called involve disputes between State-owned enterprises, particularly when State purchasing orders are at issue. Additionally, as indicated, administrative supervision may culminate with sanctions against a party or parties for wrongdoing. Such sanctions generally include a warning, fine, confiscation of illegal gains, expropriation of part or all of goods and/or deposit, as well as revocation of business license.

3.4 *Government Approval and Other Special Requirements*

Perhaps the most direct government involvement in contracting in China is the requirement of contract approval. For certain kinds of contracts in China, government approval must be sought before the contracts can become effective. Approval is the mechanism through which contracts are under the screening of government authorities, and it normally consists of two steps—namely, review (i.e., examination) and approval. During the review step, the reviewing authority looks into the contents and formality of the contract to determine if they are in compliance with applicable laws and regulations. The approval step depend on the result of this review. Therefore, review is actually the basis for approval. In other words, no approval will be granted if a contract fails to pass the review.

At present, there are a number of contracts for which governmental approval is mandatory. The most striking examples are contracts involving foreign investments, such as joint venture contracts. In accordance with Article 3 of the Law of the People's Republic of China on Chinese-Foreign Equity Joint Ventures (as revised in 1990), the joint venture agreement, contract, and articles of association shall be subject to review and approval by the competent State department in charge of foreign economic relations and trade. Similarly, under the Law of the People's Republic of China on Chinese-Foreign Contractual Joint Venture Law (1988), an agreement and contract reached by parties to the joint venture will not take effect until they are reviewed and approved by competent authorities. However, as noted, the adoption of the 2019 Foreign Investment Law lifts the approval requirement for the Sino-Foreign joint ventures that are not within the negative list concerning the restrictions on certain industrial sectors or areas for foreign investment.

In addition, according to Regulations on Administration of Contract for Introduction of Technology (1985), contracts entered into by and between a recipient and a supplier for introduction of technology must be submitted for review and approval to the Ministry of Commerce (MOFCOM) or any other agency authorized by the MOFCOM. The requirements of government review and approval also apply to contracts concerning exploitation of offshore petroleum resources in cooperation with foreign enterprises, transfers of patent rights by Chinese enterprises or individuals, first-time imports of pharmaceutics, as well as transfers of the right of land use.

The Contract Law concolidates all previously existing approval requirements, and restates the basic rule that, if administrative review and approval are required, a contract will not have effect unless and until such approval is obtained. Under Article 44 of the Contract Law, a contract subject to approval pursuant to laws or regulations shall become effective upon approval.

Moreover, in its opinions implementing the Contract Law, the Supreme People's Court makes clear that any contract for which State approval is required shall be invalid without obtaining the approval.[50]

In addition, when a contract is subject to government review and approval, the requirements of review and approval are extended with respect to the modification and assignment of the contract. Articles 77 and 87 of the Contract Law provide that, if governmental approval is required for a contract, modification or assignment of the contract will equally require an approval from the approving authority or other designated authority. Under these provisions, government approval is a prerequisite for the valid and enforceable modification or assignment of the contract.

For certain types of contract, approval is also needed when the contract is to be terminated. For example, under Article 14 of the Chinese-Foreign Equity Joint Venture Law (as amended in 2001), in the case of a heavy loss, if a party in a joint venture fails to perform its obligations under the contract and the articles of association, or *force majeure* etc., the parties may terminate the contract by agreement, but the agreement for termination of the contract must be submitted to the approving authorities for approval. Thus, failure to obtain such approval jeopardizes the desired termination.

Other special requirements for a contract to be valid and enforceable include registration, filing, as well as filing and recording. "Registration" refers to the process of registering a contract or agreement with authorized government agencies before the contract or agreement takes effect. For example, under Article 10 of the Patent Law of China, a transfer of a patent application right or a patent right must be made through a written contract, and the contract takes effect only after the contract is registered with, and announced to the public by, the competent patent bureau. Registration also applies to contracts concerning Chinese-foreign joint exploration of China's mineral resources.[51] For any of these contracts, the Chinese contractual party must register with the relevant registration authority after the contract is signed.

Filing is required when the parties enter into a license agreement for trademark use under the trademark law and regulations. A filing with approving authority is also required when parties terminate a foreign economic contract that has been approved by the government. Additionally, contracts concerning

---

50 See SPC, *Answers to Several Questions Concerning Application of Foreign Economic Contract Law* (Oct. 19, 1987); Supreme People's Court, *Opinions on Questions Regarding Implementation of Economic Contract Law* (Sept. 17, 1984).
51 See Provisional Methods of Registration and Administration of Mineral Resources Exploration.

private dwelling house rentals must be filed with local real estate administration authorities, and contracts for hiring of temporary works must be filed with local labor departments.

Filing and recording apply to contracts that involve real estate. Under Article 9 of the Property Law of China, which was adopted in 2007, the creation, alteration, transfer, or extinction of a property right becomes valid upon filing and recording with the recording authority. Without such filing and recording, any change with regard to the property right shall be invalid, unless otherwise provided for by the law. According to Article 15 of the Property Law, a contract made between the parties concerning the creation, alteration, transfer, or extinction of the right of real property takes effect at the time when the contract is made, unless otherwise provided by the law or agreed upon by the parties. But if the said property right is not filed and recorded, the contract, though valid, will have no effect pertaining to the change of the property right.[52]

---

52   *See* Property Law of China, promulgated by the NPC on March 16, 2007, and effective on October 1, 2007, available at http://www.npc.gov.cn/englishnpc/Law/2009-02/20/content_1471118.htm.

CHAPTER 3

Enforceability of Contracts

As discussed, a contract in China refers to an agreement made by the parties for undertaking certain civil activities. From the Chinese viewpoint, an agreement represents the mutual consensus of the parties involved, which is more than merely a promise or set of promises.[1] Thus, the Contract Law is intended to enforce an agreement that is the product of mutual promises made by the parties. It is commonly understood in China that the very focus of the Contract Law is on voluntary undertakings by both parties to a contract, not simply one promise made by either party.

In contract literature, attempts have been made to draw a line between a promise and a contract. In one respect, a contract is considered to represent a social institution of agreement-making, while a promise is seen as a social institution of a more informal kind. In another respect, a contract, once made, is backed by the coercive power of the State. A promise, however, is supported by moral arguments and its enforceability is based on "an artificial virtue" or morality.[2] In China, courts typically require contracts to be the product of mutual commitments from the two sides in contrast to promises, which are basically one-sided.[3]

Though a contract is an agreement, not every agreement is an enforceable contract. Under the Contract Law's definition, a contract must contain at least two elements: 1) it must be a voluntary undertaking by parties of equal status, and 2) it must be for the purpose of creating, modifying, or terminating relations of civil rights and obligations. Note that like the contract legislation in all other civil countries, the Contract Law does not require a consideration for the formation of a contract.

Therefore, to be enforced as a contract, an agreement must meet the statutory requirements. To be more specific, to be enforceable, an agreement must

---

1 In the United States, the Restatement (Second) of Contracts defines a contract as "a promise or a set of promises for the breach of which the law gives a remedy, or the performance of which the law in some way recognizes as a duty." § 1. Also under the Restatement, a promise is termed as "a manifestation of intention to act or refrain from acting in a specified way, so made as to justify a promisee in understanding that a commitment has been made." § 2(a).
2 *See* T. M. Scanlon, *Promises and Contracts*, *in* Peter Benson, The Theory of Contract Law 86–117 (Cambridge Univ. Press 2001).
3 *See* Wang Liming, Studies on Contract Law, VOL. I. 5–6 (Renmin Univ. Press 2002).

not involve any improper activities such as criminal offences and must not be used to further any illegal purposes. In addition, for purposes of the Contract Law, an agreement, to be enforced as a contract, must not involve relationships of personal status such as marriage, adoption, or guardianship.[4]

A contract, once made, is generally enforceable unless its enforceability is precluded under the law. Regarding the enforceability of contracts, Article 8 of the Contract Law specifically provides that, when a contract is established in accordance with the law, it is legally binding on the parties. Article 8 further provides that the parties must perform their respective obligations in accordance with the terms of the contract and neither party may unilaterally modify or rescind the contract without the other party's consent.

The text of Article 8 of the Contract Law is adopted *verbatim* in Article 119 of the 2017 GPCL, which reiterates the binding force of a contract that is legally formed. Article 8 of the Contract Law and Article 119 of the 2017 GPCL both emphasize that a contract concluded in accordance with the law is fully enforceable. A contract being fully enforceable means that the law protects the rights arising out of the contract and also safeguards the performance of the contract so that the parties' expectations will be met.

The Contract Law deals with the issue whether a contract is enforceable in different aspects. First, the statute contains provisions that specifically address the enforceability of contracts. Pursuant to the Contract Law, a contract is enforceable if it is made by the mutual assent of the parties. As noted, the mutuality between the parties is considered to be the essence of a contract. The Contract Law requires that a contract be made on the basis of equality and voluntariness. Article 13 of the Contract Law explicitly provides that parties must conclude a contract in the form of an offer and acceptance. Article 25 further provides that a contract is concluded when the acceptance becomes effective. Again, it is important to bear in mind that, in China, a contract need not be supported by consideration to be enforceable.

Second, the Contract Law adopts the doctrine of performance to deal situations where there is imperfection in contract formation. Under this doctrine, a contract that is otherwise unenforceable becomes enforceable if one party has performed its principal obligations under the contract and the other party has accepted that performance. The application of this performance doctrine mainly cures any formality defects in contracts. The Contract Law requires certain formalities to be observed in order for a contract to be valid.

---

4 Under Article 2 of the Contract Law, agreements involving marriage, adoption, and guardianship shall apply the provisions of other laws.

Under Article 10, a contract may be formed by a writing, orally, or through other means.

However, if laws and administrative regulations require a certain contract to be concluded in writing, or if the parties to a certain contract agree that it will be written, that contract must be in written form to be valid. Moreover, Article 32 provides that a written contract is concluded when both parties sign or affix a seal on the contract. Notwithstanding these provisions, Articles 36 and 37 prescribe that, if a contract is not in written form when it is required to be by law, regulations, or the parties, or if a written contract is not signed or affixed with a seal, but one party has performed its principal obligations under the contract and the other party has accepted that performance, the contract will be deemed enforceable.

Third, the Contract Law makes reasonable reliance a factor for courts to consider when they are determining whether a contract exists. Although there is no such concept as "promissory estoppel" in the Chinese legal tradition, the concept of reasonable reliance has been incorporated into the Contract Law. Thus, a contract may be found to exist if one party reasonably relies on the other party's promise or conduct and changes its position accordingly.

Under Article 19 (2) of the Contract Law, an offer may not be revoked if the offeree has reasonsably relied on the offer being irrevocable and prepared for the fulfillment of the contract.[5] In this situation, a contract is deemed concluded if an offeree accepts the offer and all other requirements for the contract to be valid are met, regardless of the fact that the offeror intended or even acted to revoke the offer. Note, however, that, under Article 19 (2), the reasonable reliance test requires two key elements: (a) reasonable belief and (b) performance preparation.

Another aspect of the Contract Law dealing with contract enforceability involves the issue of contract validity. The validity of a contract in essence concerns the legal effect of a contract concluded by the parties. Since, under the Contract Law, a contract is considered enforceable only if it is made in accordance with the law, the primary focus of validity is on what agreements the law will enforce or recognize as creating, modifying, or terminating civil rights and obligations between the parties involved.

---

5 Interestingly, Article 19 (2) at first glance looks similar to Section 87 (2) of Restatement (Second) of Contracts. But the latter has a clear focus on the offeror while the former is concerned about the offeree. Section 87 (2) provides: "An offer which the offeror should reasonably expect to induce action or forbearance of a substantial character on the part of the offeree before acceptance and which does induce such action or forbearance is binding as an option contract to the extent necessary to avoid injustice."

Thus, a contract, in order to be binding, must be legally valid. In this regard, unlike previous contract legislation, the Contract Law differentiates between contracts that are concluded and contracts that are valid under the law. In China, the conclusion of a contract does not necessarily mean that the contract is valid because the validity may be affected by other factors such as the conditions under which the contract is to take effect. Moreover, the validity of a contract may be affected by the contract's formation, which will be further discussed in the relevant chapter of this book.

In addition, it is important to note that the enforceability of a contract must be viewed within the four conors of the basic principles provided in the Contract Law governing contracts. In China, contract principles serve as the foundation for contract law legislation and also as guidance for the application of the Contract Law. In practice, those principles are generally used as the benchmark for determining the rules of bargaining in contract-making as well as the standard by which terms of a contract are interpreted.[6]

A very common feature of Chinese legislation, as with the civil law tradition, is that each law contains certain stated principles, and such principles are treated as the fundamental norms or imperative guidance imbedded the law. It is believed in China that, under the umbrella of the principles, every provision in the law is integrated with all other provisions in the law, which preserves the unity of the law. In this connection, contract principles in China, despite being quite abstract and vague, are compulsory and must be followed by the parties.

1   *Obligatio* and Contract Obligations

Before looking at the contract principles, it is necessary to review the concept of *obligatio*. As discussed, a contract in China is regarded as one of the causes for *obligatio* to arise. In fact, the law of *obligatio* and the law of property are the counterparts of civil legislation in civil law countries. A distinctive feature of *obligatio* is that it gives one party the right to make a claim against the other party. Unlike the terms of an obligation that mainly refer to duties or commitments, an *obligatio* contains both rights and obligations, under which one party (obligee) is entitled to ask, for its own benefit or a third party's interest, the other party to do or not to do something, and the other party (obligor) is obligated to perform accordingly to satisfy the obligee's request.

---

6   *See* Wang Liming, *supra* note 3 at pp137–39.

ENFORCEABILITY OF CONTRACTS 91

Arising from the *obligatio*, the obligee's right is three-pronged, consisting of (1) the right to demand performance, including payment; (2) the right to receive performance, including payment; and (3) the right to request protection when the obligor defaults in fulfillment of its obligations. An obligor has the duty to perform under the terms and conditions agreed upon by the parties. The obligor's failure to perform creates a legal gound for remedies. In addition, the rights and obligations under *obligatio* exist on a mutual basis and this mutuality determines the obligee-obligor relationship.

The obligee-obligor relationship between contracting parties is established when the contract is made. The parties to a contract are, respectively,the obligee and the obligor because their positions change over the course of the contract's performance. For example, Party A entered into a contract with Party B where Party A agreed to provide computer software services to Party B, and Party B agreed in turn to pay Party A. From a services perspective, Party B is an obligee and Party A is an obligor. However, after the services are done, Party A becomes an obligee because it is entitled to receive payment and Party B becomes an obligor because it is obligation to make the agreed-upon payment.

Again in China, *obligatio* as a legal term is provided in the 1986 Civil Code. Under Article 84 of the 1986 Civil Code, the *obligatio* represents a special relationship of rights and obligations established between the parties concerned, either by the agreed terms of a contract or according to the provisions of law.[7] It is further provided in Article 84 that the party entitled to the rights shall be the obligee and the party assuming the obligations shall be the obligor. Since contract triggers *obligatio*, the contratual parties are mutually obligated to each other.

The law of *obligatio* is aimed at providing legal assurance that rights will be protected and obligations will be performed. Perhaps for that reason, the law of *obligatio* is also called the law of obligations. According to Article 84 of the 1986 Civil Code, the obligee shall have the right to demand that the obligor fulfill his or her obligations as specified by the contract or under the provisions of law.[8] Fulfillment of *obligatio* requires no less than complete performance of all the obligations arising from the contract or from other legal grounds. Thus, to perform the obligor's obligation is to realize the rights of the obligee. In China, it is commonly recognized that enforcement of a valid contract meets the requirements of *obligatio*.[9] Article 106 of the 1986 Civil Code explicitly provides

---

7   *See* 1986 Civil Code, art. 84.
8   *See id.*
9   *See* Tong Rou et al., Chinese Civil Law 299–303 (Law Publ'g House 1998); Zhang Guangxing, General Introduction to the Law of Obligations 15–17 (Law Publ'g House 1997); Wang Jiafu, Obligatio in Civil Law 128–30 (Law Publ'g House 1998).

that citizens and legal persons who breach a contract or fail to fulfill other obligations shall bear civil liability.

Scholars in China attach great importance to the performance of obligations. They argue that, in order to satisfy *obligatio*, performance of obligations must follow three basic rules. The first rule is actual performance. The basic notion of the actual performance rule is that the parties to a contract must fulfill their obligations on the agreed subject matter (commonly called "object" in China), and should not arbitrarily substitute the subject mater with liquidated damages or an equivalent thereof unless the actual performance is excused. In addition, under the actual performance rule, one party who fails to perform his obligations shall be obligated to continue performing, and the other party has the right to demand the continuing performance.[10]

The second rule is proper performance. The thrust of the proper performance rule is that, in addition to the agreed subject matter, the parties under their mutual obligations are required to perform in accordance with the agreed-upon terms and conditions. To the extent that obligations are satisfied, the proper performance rule serves as a safeguard for the performance so that the performance will be made as agreed with regard to essential aspects of the contract such as quantity, quality, time, place, as well as formality. Since it is often the case that a contract may not actually be performed properly, proper performance is the standard for determining whether and to what extent a breach of an obligation occurs.[11]

The third rule is known as the cooperative performance rule. This rule is intended to encourage parties in an obligee-obligor relationship to perform their mutual obligations in a cooperative way. Also, under the cooperative performance rule, the parties owe to each other the mitigation duty. Article 114 of the 1986 Civil Code is regarded to have underscored the cooperative performance rule as applied to contracts. According to Article 114, if one party is suffering losses caused by the other party's breach of contract, that party must take prompt measures to prevent the losses from increasing. If the party does not promptly take any measures, and this failure causes the losses to increase, the party will not have the right to claim compensation for the increased losses.

---

10   See id., Tong Rou, at 310.
11   See id. at 311.

2 Governing Principles of Contracts

As provided in the Contract Law, the principles that govern contracts include "equality of parties," "voluntariness," "fairness," "good faith," "legality," and "observance of contract obligations." In many cases, the enforceability of a contract depends on whether these principles have been observed. Thus, a contract will be held invalid if it is found to violate any of these principles. Additionally, when hearing contract cases, the people's courts often make decisions on the basis of these contract principles. In this context, the contract principles are indeed the authoritative legal sources through utilization of which the Chinese courts adjudicate contractual disputes.

In judicial practice, the foregoing contract principles are considered to serve several functions. First, unlike most provisions in contract law that are non-mandatory, the contract pinciples are mandatory in nature and therefore must be followed. Second, the contract principles are gap-fillers that help supplement, and aid courts in interpreting, Contract Law provisions that appear to be vague or unclear. Third, the contract principles function as the legal benchmark for construction of contract terms or missing contents.[12] Given their importance, the contract principles are discussed in details as follows.

2.1 *Equality and Voluntariness*

Equality and voluntariness are considered to be the fundamental standards governing civil activities in China. Under Article 4 of the 2017 GPCL, all parties to civil legal relations are equal in legal status. It is further provided in Article 5 that the parties to civil legal relations shall conduct civil activities under the principle of voluntariness and create, modify, or terminate civil legal relations according to their own wills.[13] The 2017 GPCL makes equality and voluntariness the civil principles that govern all civil activities in general.

Equality deals with the status of parties in civil legal relations. Under the civil law tradition, the law of *obligatio* is classified as private law, where parties are in a horizontal relationship, as opposed to public law, where the relation of parties involved is vertical and in most cases is between a state and its citizens. The civil law tradition is deeply embedded in Chinese civil law legislation. Article 2 of the 1986 Civil Code unequivocally provides that the civil law of the People's Republic of China regulates both property and personal relationships between citizens, between legal persons, and between citizens and legal

---

12   See Han Shiyuan, The Law of Contract, 35 (Law Press, 3d ed., 2011).
13   See General Provisions of the Civil Law of the People's Republic of China (2017), art. 4 & 5 [hereinafter " 2017 GPCL"].

persons. Moreover, Article 3 of the 1986 Civil Code mandates that parties to a civil activity shall have equal status.

The Contract Law follows the equality principle by emphasizing that a contract is an agreement made between parties having equal status. Article 3 of the Contract Law provides that the parties to a contract are equal in legal status and therefore must deal with each other on an equal footing. Simultaneously, Article 3 of the Contract Law prohibits any party from imposing its will on the party. Thus, under Article 3 of the Contract Law, equality in legal status is the prerequisite for parties to enter into a contract. This provision also reflects the notion that parties in civil activities have a horizontal relationship.

In China, the equal legal status rule embraces three principal requirements. The first requirement is that parties to a civil activity shall have equal capacity for civil rights. Equal capacity means that each party in a civil activity, regardless of the party's age, religion, position or physical or economic condition, shall have the same capacity for civil rights, which rights shall not be deprived of or restricted by anybody. Under Article 10 of the 1986 Civil Code, all citizens are equal with respect to their capacity for civil rights.[14] Article 10 also applies to non-Chinese citizens through Article 8, which provides that the stipulations of the Code as applied to citizens apply to foreigners and stateless persons within the territory of the People's Republic of China except as otherwise provided by law.[15]

The second requirement concerns equal treatment of parties in civil activities. The key point of this requirement is that parties with different backgrounds or positions, when dealing with each other in civil areas, shall have equal legal status and shall be treated equally. Speaking literally, if the State, a State agency, or a State-owned enterprise is engaged in a civil activity, it shall be deemed the same as a civil party, and shall have no privilege over any other person. Interestingly, according to many Chinese contract law scholars, the equal treatment requirement is derived from the belief that all men are equal before the law.[16] An important implication of the equal treatment is to promote fair dealing and prevent administrative or governmental abuse of power.[17]

---

14 See 1986 Civil Code, art. 10.
15 See id., art. 8.
16 See Han Shiyuan *supra* note 12, at p 23.
17 It is quite common in China that the State, a State agency, or State-owned enterprise uses its position economically or politically to influence business activities, and in many cases such influence is exercised through administrative means to downplay the role or status of the other party involved.

The third requirement embodied in the equal legal status focuses on equality in negotiating or bargaining. Such equality implicates that parties in civil activities equally have the right to determine their affairs through fair negotiation, and that such negotiation must be conducted in the way that ensures that no party will overtake the will of the other. This requirement not only applies to the creation of civil relationships between relevant parties, but also governs the modification and termination of such relationships. The whole idea of the requirement is to ensure that parties in civil activities such as contract-making will deal with each other fairly and freely.

A significant feature of equality is that it focuses on mutual assent and mutual benefit. Under the Contract Law, mutual assent is the key to a contract. The requirement of mutual assent guarantees that the contracting parties have every opportunity to express their will freely. Mutual benefit requires that parties to a contract enjoy their respective contractual rights that correspond to their contractual obligations. In other words, no party may be entitled to contractual rights disproportionately to the party's contractual obligations and no party shall take advantage of the other party.

Essentially, the principle of equality as applied to contracts means that contractual parties have equal legal status regardless of their backgrounds or positions in every aspects of contracting, including contract formation, contract performance, the assumption of contractual obligations, and liabilities for breach of the contract. In this context, it is fair to conclude that, with an emphasis on the equal status of the parties to a contract, Article 3 of the Contract Law is intended to enforce the rule of "non-imposition of one party's will on the other."

At issue in maintaining equality, however, is the governmental interest that any contract might affect. For example, in a contract between a private company and a State-owned enterprise, the private company will hardly be treated the same as the State-owned enterprise. This is particularly true when a local governmental interest is involved or where the government has a clear preference for protecting the State-owned enterprises in which it has interest. Take, for example, remedies. A private company might not have the same access to remedies as a State-owned enterprise because the government generally tends to protect State-owned enterprises through whatever means the government sees fit.

Voluntariness is mainly about the free will of the parties in making a contract and it primarily involves the self-determination power or autonomy of the parties. As explained, because of the concerns about being tainted by western ideology, the Contract Law shies away from the term "freedom of contract," instead setting forth voluntariness as a principle in an attempt to safeguard the legitimate rights of the parties to a contract. Under Article 5 of the 2017 GPCL and Article 4 of the Contract Law, the principle of voluntariness contains two parts: the first part is about the rights of the parties to voluntarily enter into a contract within the limits of law, and the second part prohibits any unit or individual from unlawfully interfering with the contract.

2.2   Fairness and Good Faith

Article 5 of the Contract Law requires parties to a contract to abide by the principle of fairness in determining their respective rights and obligations. Article 4 of the 1986 Civil Code mandates that, in civil activities, the principle of fairness must be observed. Article 6 of the 2017 GPCL also makes it imperative that the parties to civil legal relations conduct civil activities under the principle of fairness in order to reasonably determine each other's rights and obligations. However, no legislation has ever defined "fairness." There are two possible reasons: (1) because it is difficult to define fairness, and (2) because it is better to let courts to deal with the meaning of fairness on a case-by-case basis.

Nevertheless, in general, fairness as applied to contracts is mainly concerned about the contents of a contract, and it is geared toward achieving a balance of rights and obligations between the parties. As explained by Chinese scholars, the concept of fairness has its root in the idea that the relationship between contractual parties shall be maintained to the extent that the parties' respective rights and obligations are reasonably and justly allocated and shared. Specifically, the benefits a party has acquired shall proportionally match the obligations the party has born or is supposed to bear.[18] In this regard, it seems that the principle of fairness resembles the principle of equity that is popular in Western countries—although the concept of equity is rarely used in a civil law country like China.

In judicial practices, the Chinese courts employ several tests to determine whether fairness has been achieved. The first test is "obvious unfairness." This test is developed from Article 59 of the 1986 Civil Code. In accordance with Article 59, a party shall have the right to request a People's Court or an arbitration institution to alter or rescind a civil act that is obviously unfair.[19] In general, unfairness is obvious if it is found that a party has taken advantage of the other party in order to cause the parties' respective rights and obligations to be clearly unbalanced in favor of the former.[20] Under Article 151 of the 2017 GPCL, if a

---

18   *See* Jiang Ping et al., A Detailed Explanation of the Contract Law of Law 6–7 (China Univ. of Pol. Science & Law Press 1999).
19   *See* 1986 Civil Code, art. 59.
20   *See* Economic Trial Chamber of the Supreme People's Court, Explanation and Application of Contract Law, 28–29 (Xinghua Publ'g Press 1999).

civil act is evidently unfair because it is formed as a result of one party taking advantage of the other party being in a difficult situation or lacking the capacity to make judgments, the aggrieved party has the right to request a People's Court or arbitration institution to revoke the act.[21]

The second test is "reasonable allocation of risks." Resting on the market theory,[22] the reasonable allocation of risks test revolves around the notion that each business transaction consists of both predicable and unpredictable risks. Fairness requires that the parties to a contract share risks fairly and justly, though not necessarily equally. Therefore, it is unfair if one party, against its will, assumes more risks than the other party in the parties' contractual dealings. To determine whether there is a violation of the fairness principle, a court looks at whether the possible risks stemming from a contract are reasonably allocated between the parties to the contract.[23]

The third test is called "fair distribution of rights and obligations." Under this test, a party to a contract is required to bear obligations that are proportionate to the rights the party has or claims to have. A typical example concerns the validity of the disclaimer clause in a contract. In dealing with the effect of such a disclaimer, a court assesses whether the distribution of rights and obligations between the parties is unfairly affected by the disclaimer. Another example is the standard contract. A court will normally analyze a standard contract against the drafter of the contract, particularly where the standard contract is simply a "take it or leave it" deal.[24]

Because the fairness principle is fundamental to contract-based business transactions, some scholars in China view it as the equivalent of the principle of justice. Such scholars believe that a striking feature of every contract is the concept of "exchange for equal value," which requires the preservation of justice in the contract-making process.[25] In its application, the principle of justice requires that the parties to a contract treat, and deal with, each other fairly in both concluding and perfoming a contract.[26]

"Good faith" is mainly about business ethics. As a principle governing civil acts in China, good faith was first provided for in the 1986 Civil Code, where

---

21 See 2017 GPCL, art. 151.
22 The market is the place where risks and opportunities, which are shared by the players, co-exist.
23 See Li Guoguang, Explanation and Application of the Contract Law 28–33 (Xinhua Press 1999).
24 See Wang Liming, Study in Contact Law, *supra* note 3, at 181–186.
25 See Gui Jianyuan, General Commentaries on Contract Law (I), 44–45 (Renmin Univ. Press, 2011).
26 See id.

it was termed as "honesty and credibility." The Contract Law follows the 1986 Civil Code and makes good faith a contract principle. Under Article 6 of the Contract Law, the parties to a contract must observe the principles of honesty and credibility in exercising their rights and fulfilling their obligations. The 2017 GPCL rephrases the good faith principle and provides that the parties to civil affairs, when conducting civil activities, must follow the principle of good faith, adhere to honesty, and fulfill their promises.[27]

Good faith is not readily defined in Chinese statutes. In the United States, good faith is defined in UCC §1–201 (19) as "honesty in fact in the conduct or transaction concerned."[28] Chinese scholars criticize this definition on the basis that it lacks consideration of the parties' interests. They believe that a major function of good faith is to maintain a balance of interests between parties as well as between parties and society.[29] Another American doctrine widely discussed in China is Professor Robert Summers' notion of exclusion. According to Professor Summers, good faith is best left undefined and is best understood as excluding activities that constitute bad faith.[30] Most Chinese scholars find this notion unpersuasive, reasoning that, in many cases, "non-bad faith" does not necessarily mean "good faith."

In Chinese legal history, good faith under the Confucian tradition was considered to be a moral norm governing society. The popular dogma representing good faith was "faithful to promise"—a rule that focused on faithfulness, trustworthiness, and honesty. Confucius had a strong belief that "people could not live without credibility" (*Min Wu Xin Bu Li*). This belief became a long lasting "gentleman rule" in Chinese history. Unfortunately, this tradition was devastated during the Cultural Revolution. China has been making efforts to restore it since the economic reforms started.

Although scholars in China differ in their views concerning how good faith should be defined, the term good faith is generally interpreted to mean that people in civil activities must be honest to each other without abusing their rights, and must perform their obligations faithfully with sincerity. In addition, in order to comply with the good faith principle, the interests between the parties as well as between the parties and society must be balanced. To illustrate

---

27 *See* the 2017 GPCL, art. 7.
28 *See* UCC, §1–201(19).
29 *See* Xu Guodong, *Concept and Historical Evolution of Good Faith Principle*, 4 LEGAL RESEARCH (1989).
30 *See* Robert S. Summers, *The General Duty of Good Faith—Its Recognition and Conceptualization*, 67 CORNELL L. REV. 810 (1982).

what good faith is in reality, Chinese scholars understand this principle in the context of the Contract Law as containing the following aspects:
(a) During contract negotiations, the parties are obligated to deal with each other truthfully and to make collaberative efforts to enter into the contract;
(b) After the contract is formed, the parties shall take all necessary steps to prepare for the performance of the contract;
(c) When performing the contract, the parties shall each faithfully fulfill their contractual obligations, and provide the assistance and notice necessary to the contract's performance;
(d) If a contract needs to be modified or terminated due to a change in circumstances, the party seeking modification or termination shall provide the other party with proper notice in order to minimize the possible damages that might incur.
(e) After the contract is performed, the parties must not disclose any business secrets they obtained from one another during the contract period; and
(f) When a dispute arises out of a contract provision, the parties shall fairly and reasonably interpret the provision so that the mutual benefits of the parties is protected.[31]

In addition to Article 6, the Contract Law has two more articles that are directly related to the good faith principle. One is Article 42, under which a party shall be liable for damages if, during the contract-making process, it performs any act that violates the principle of good faith and causes losses to the other party. Under the SPC's Interpretations on Several Questions Concerning Application of the Contract Law (II) issued on April 20, 2009 (2009 Contract Law Interpretations), if a contract requires registration or governmental approval in order to become effective and the responsible party fails to obtain such registration or approval, the party's failure to act constitutes a violation of the good faith principle.[32]

The other one is Article 60, which requires that the parties observe the principle of good faith and fulfill the obligations of notification, assistance, and confidentiality in accordance with the nature and purposes of the contract as well as trade practices. The following case helps illustrate how the good faith principle is interpreted and applied in the People's Courts.

---

31 *See* Jiang Ping, *supra* note 18, at 7.
32 See the SPC, Intrpreations of Several Questions Concerning Application of the Contract Law of the People's Republic of China (II), art. 8, issued on April 20, 2009 (2009 Contract Law Interpretations).

Wen Zaolun v. Guang Xi Movies Studio and Guang Dong Full Stars Movie & TV Entertainment Inc.

Beijing High People's Court[33]

On September 20, 1999, Defendant Guangxi Movies Studio (Guangxi Movies) and Defendant Guang Dong Full Stars Movie & TV Entertainment Inc. (Full Stars) entered into a contract to jointly make a thirty-episode TV series drama entitled "No Other Alternatives." Under the contract, Full Stars would invest all funds for making the drama and would be responsible for recruiting the production team. In addition, during the drama-making process, Full Stars would be solely responsible for handling any disputes with a third party concerning copyrights and other economic interests, without causing any liability to Guang Xi Movies. The responsibility of Guang Xi Movies mainly included the obtaining of government approval of the scripts of the drama and related work. On this basis, the "'No other Alternatives' Production Group" (Production Group) was formed under Guang Xi Movies Studio / Full Stars Movie & TV Entertainment Inc.

On November 8, 1999, the Production Group and Plaintiff signed an agreement under which Plaintiff agreed to play the male leading role in the drama. The term of the agreement was from October 25, 1999 to February 29, 2000, and the Plaintiff would be paid RMB 50,000 per episode, or RMB 1,500,000 in total. The payment would be made in three installments: RMB 500,000 up front at the time of agreement, RMB 500,000 to be made sixty days after the agreement was signed, and the final payment of RMB 500,000 to be made fourteen days before the production ended.

Plaintiff was actually paid RMB 500,000 on September 14, 1999 for the role he would play in the drama. However, after the first ten episodes were completed, on December 7, Plaintiff felt sick and asked for a day leave. On the next day, Plaintiff visited the doctor and was diagnosed with proteinuria, which was a sign of kidney disease. As a result, Plaintiff was advised to rest for two weeks. On the same day, Plaintiff asked his assistant to give the doctor's diagnosis to Li Baoguo, the director of the production group. Li Baoguo then told Chen Zecheng, the drama director, that Plaintiff was sick and could not attend the drama filming. Under this circumstance, Chen Zecheng had to adjust the filming schedule.

Plaintiff then was absent from the drama filming for about two weeks. On December 21, 1999, the Production Group retained a lawyer to send a "lawyer's letter" to Plaintiff, stating that due to Plaintiff's uncooperative conduct, the Production Group had suffered heavy economic loss, and therefore, the Production Group had to terminate the agreement with Plaintiff, and in the meantime reserved the right to hold Plaintiff liable for damages. Consequently, the Production Group did not make any further payment to Plaintiff.

In response, Plaintiff brought the lawsuit against both Guang Xi Movies and Full Stars. Plaintiff claimed that under the agreement, he was entitled to the payment of RMB 1,500,000, but was only paid RMB 500,000. To support his claim, Plaintiff argued that he played the first ten episodes and that he developed his illness, for which he had to see the doctor, because of the overloaded filming work. Defendant insisted that his sick leave from the drama filming was pursuant to the doctor's advice and was approved by director Chen Zecheng. Plaintiff then alleged that the Production Group's abrupt termination of the agreement without negotiating with him constituted a breach of contract, and that, therefore, both Guang Xi Movies and Full Stars should be held liable for his economic damages of RMB 1,000,000, which would be his expected interest.

---

33 The case was reported in the First Civil Division of Beijing High People's Court, *A In-depth Analysis of Beijing Civil Cases* 203–10 (Law Press 2003).

Guang Xi Movies moved to dismiss Plaintiff's action on the ground of its contract with Full Stars. Guang Xi Movies argued that, since Full Stars was solely responsible for dealing with any disputes between the Production Group and a third party, the disputes between the Production Group and Plaintiff had nothing to do with Guang Xi Movies.

Full Stars argued that it paid Plaintiff RMB 500,000 under the contract, but Plaintiff did not perform his duties during his fifteen days' absence on a personal health excuse without approval by the Production Group. Full Stars also argued that Plaintiff's notice of absence to the Production Group and his actual leave from the drama filming unequivocally demonstrated his inability to timely fulfill his obligations under the contract, and therefore the Production Group had the right to terminate the contract with him.

In addition, both Guang Xi Movies and Full Stars filed a joint counterclaim against Plaintiff. They asserted that, under the contract, Plaintiff would be with the Production Group daily for four months but his work would be no more than twelve hours a day, and therefore, he would not take any leave during the four-month period. They argued that plaintiff's absence from December 7 to December 21, 1999 constituted a breach of the contract, and the breach caused great damages in the amount of RMB 1,471,030.22 to the Production Group, which included overhead expenses of RMB 283,175.22, Plaintiff's substitute cost of RMB 2,405, additional actor's cost of RMB 510,000, script revision cost of RMB 189,750, director's time extension compensation fee of RMB 207,000, and actors' time extension compensation fee of RMB 224,700.

Beijing Second Intermediate People's Court (trial court) found that Plaintiff's failure to perform the contract during the period of December 8 to December 21, 1999 was caused by his illness, and he had informed the Production Group of his illness with a doctor's diagnosis and asked for leave, to which the Production Group expressed no objection. It was also found that, after receiving Plaintiff's request for sick leave, the Production Group made adjustments to the drama filming schedule accordingly, and the schedule adjustment served as an indication of the Production Group's acknowledgement of Plaintiff's sick leave. The trial court then held that, because of the Production Group's "no objection" and "acknowledgement," Plaintiff's sick leave should not be regarded as a breach of the contract. On this ground, the trial court dismissed Guang Xi Movies and Full Stars' claim for damages against Plaintiff.

The trial court, however, was of the opinion that, although Plaintiff's sick leave did not constitute a breach of the contract, given the fact that he was playing a leading role in the drama, the issue whether he could continue playing his role was critical to the performance of the contract so as to realize the objective of the contract. The trial court therefore held that as a leading role, Plaintiff's absence for fourteen days as well as the possibility of his continuing to take sick leave because of his "kidney disease" had made it uncertain whether he could play his role any more, and under this circumstance, it would be permissible for the Production Group to terminate the contract with Plaintiff in order to protect the Production Group's economic interest. For the reason that the Production Group's termination of the contract was not a breach of the contract either, the trial court rejected Plaintiff's claims as well.

All parties involved in the case appealed to Beijing High People's Court (appellate court). The appellate court affirms the trial court's judgment on the ground that, under the good faith standard, the trial court did not err in finding that Plaintiff's sick leave did not amount to a breach of the contract and, under the same standard, it is also reasonable to uphold the Production Group's termination of the contract for purposes of self-protection. The judgment below is therefore affirmed.

Aparently, the key issue in the above case was whether Plaintiff's sick leave or the Production Group's termination of the contract constituted a breach of the contract. According to the judge in the trial court, the case appeared to be distinctive in the following aspects: (1) the circumstance upon which the contract was based changed after the contract was made; (2) the change of the circumstance was unpredictable by the parties at the time the parties entered into the contract; (3) neither of the parties could be blamed for the change of the circumstance; and (4) it would be unfair for the contract to remain effective under the changed circumstance.

If the case was tried before the Contract Law was adopted, the courts might base their judgment on *"Rebus Sic Stantibus,"* a contract doctrine that allows a party to be excused from performance when the change of circumstances, which is beyond the contracting parties' expectation and control, has frustrated the original basis of the contract such that continuing performance would obviously render the contract unfair.[34] The Contract Law, however, does not recognize this doctrine because (1) there is no commonly accepted definition for *"rebus sic stantibus"*; and (2) it is very difficult, if not impossible, to draw a line between *"rebus sic stantibus"* and normal commercial risk. As a result, the courts will have to look into other doctrines.

Thus, when analyzing the case, the appellate court heavily relies on the "good faith" principle of Article 6 of the Contract Law. To determine whether there was a breach of the contract, the appellate court must determine if the judgment rendered below considered, among others, (a) whether Plaintiff made the "sick leave" in good faith, and (b) whether the Production Group honestly believed that the occurrence of the unexpected event would jeopardize its interest unless the contract was terminated. It is important for the court to make sure that it would be fair to require the parties to continue performing the contract.

2.3 *Legality and Public Interests*

The enforceability of a contract also depends on whether the contract complies with law and is consistent with social and public interests. Article 7 of the Contract Law mandates that the parties, in making and fulfilling the contract, must abide by law and administrative regulations and respect social ethics, and may neither disrupt the social-economic order nor impair social and public interests.[35] It is important to keep in mind that Article 7 of the Contract Law

---

34   This doctrine was upheld by the SPC. In its letter of judicial instruction issued on March 6, 1992, the Supreme People's Court held that for purposes of the instant case, due to the chance in circumstances that could not be foreseen and prevented by the parties during the performance of the contract, it would be obviously unfair if Defendant was asked to continue performing its obligations according to the original contract.

35   See the Contract Law, art. 7.

is significantly different from Articles 6 and 7 of the 1986 Civil Code. Under Article 6 of the 1986 Civil Code, civil activities must comply with the law; if there are no relevant provisions in the law, State policies must be observed.[36] Article 7 of the 1986 Civil Code also prohibits civil activities from undermining State economic plans.[37] The 2017 GPCL contains a general requirement that the parties engaged in civil affairs shall not conduct civil activities in violation of law or contrary to public order and good morals.[38]

Legal compliance involves the legality of a contract. It is essential that the contents, goals, as well as formality of a contract meet legal requirements. Under Article 54 of the 1986 Civil Code, for a civil act to have legal effect, it must be "the lawful act of a citizen or legal person to establish, change or terminate civil rights and obligations."[39] Article 58 of the 1986 Civil Code further provides that a civil act shall be null and void if it violates the law or the public interest.[40] For the purposes of the Contract Law, the law includes both law and administrative regulations. According to the Law of Legislation of China, law refers to the statute promulgated by the National People's Congress and its Standing Committee, while administrative regulation is the rule or regulation adopted by the State Council or Ministries with the approval of the State Council.[41]

Two questions relevant to the legality of a contract need to be further addressed. The first question concerns the scope or extent of legality, which involves what is deemed "lawful" or "legal." In general, legality means non-violation of laws and regulations that are compulsory or mandatory. Mandatory laws or regulations are those that the parties must apply and that cannot be derogated from by agreement. For example, under Article 40 of the Guaranty Law of China, in a mortgage contract, the mortgagor and mortgagee shall not provide in their agreement that the ownership of mortgaged property will be transferred to the creditor in case the mortagee's claim is not satisfied after maturity of the debt.[42] This provision excludes the parties' power to transfer by agreement the ownership of mortgaged property under this circumstance.[43]

In addition, the issue of legality is determined under the national laws or regulations. On December 19, 1999, in order to help implement the Contract

---

36 See the 1986 Civil Code, art 6.
37 See *id.*, art 7.
38 See the 2017 GPCL, art. 8.
39 See the 1986 Civil Code, art. 54.
40 See *id.*, art 58.
41 The Law of Legislation of the People's Republic of Law was adopted on March 15, 2000 and effective on July 1, 2000.
42 See the Guaranty Law of China, art. 40.
43 See the Guaranty Law of China, adopted on June 30, 1995, art. 40.

Law, the SPC issued Interpretations on Several Questions Concerning Application of the Contract Law of China (1999 Contract Law Interpretations). According to the SPC, after the Contract Law took effect, when determining whether a contract is null or vague, the People's Courts were to apply the laws stipulated by the National People's Congress or the administrative regulations adopted by the State Council, and the determination was not to be made under local laws or local administrative rules.[44]

The second question concerns State policy. Under the 1986 Civil Code, the legality of a civil act required compliance with State policy. As briefly discussed in Chapter 2 of this Book, policy compilance is highly controversial. On the one hand, policy is a manageable means for serving government interests and is a useful device for the government to consult where the law is unclear in a particular area. On the other hand, the policy compliance requirement often makes the consequences of civil activities unpredictable and therefore uncertain.

Policy compliance raises two issues. One issue is policy transparency. Since most policies in China take the form of internal documents or speeches of leaders, they are quite often not available to the general public. The other issue is the effect of policies, especially when a conflict occurs between a policy and the law. In the past, governmental policy superseded the law in many cases. Now, as a result of reforms, the role of governmental policy is not as important as it formerly was in controlling civil affairs. Notwithstanding, the potential impact of governmental policy should not be underestimated, since policy is considered to be not only a meaningful tool to help interpret the law but also authoritative guidance to be used in resolving civil disputes.

Nevertheless, the Contract Law does not make policy compliance a determinant of whether a contract is valid. In this respect, the Contract Law is generally regarded as being more rule-based than the 1986 Civil Code. The 2017 GPCL repeals the policy compliance requirement in the 1986 Civil Code. In its place, the 2017 GPCL mandates application of customs absent applicable provisions of law. As noted, under Article 10 of the 2017 GPCL, civil disputes must be resolved in accordance with the law; a custom may be applied if there is no applicable provision of law, provided that such application is not contrary to public order and good morals.

Customs, though not defined in the 2017 GPCL, are considered in China to be common usages or long-established practices that are repeatedly used by

---

44 See the SPC, *An Explanation to Several Questions Concerning Application of the Contract Law of China* (1999), available at http://www.law-lib.com/law/law-view.asp?id=70172.

many people with regard to a particular matter or thing. In Chinese legislation, there actually existed application of customs prior to the adoption of the 2017 GPCL. Article 60 of the Contract Law, for example, allows for use of transaction practices to determine the duties associated with the performance of a contract.[45]

In its 2009 Contract Law Interpretations, the SPC defines "transaction practices" to include (a) the common usage normally used at the place of transaction or in a particular area or industry, which is known or ought to be known to the other party at the time of contract; or (b) the conventional practice regularly employed by the parties.[46] This provision is of significance because it formally makes customs the authoritative legal source for People's Courts to consult in handling civil disputes. It is also expected that the SPC will provide further guidance on the application of customs in its interpretations yet to come.

Social and public interest are now generally referred to in China as public order and good morals. From the viewpoint of the People's Courts, application of social and public interests provision is a general rule that is quite elastic, and is within the courts' discretionary power, though exercise of such power is on the statutory basis.[47] The question, therefore, is how and when the social and public interest may be applied. One opinion is that, because the social and public interest is a generally normative provision, it normally may not be directly used as the legal basis for a court to render its decision.[48] Another opinion argues that the purpose of the social and public interest provision is to allow courts to directly apply this rule to nullify a contract if the contract is found to have damaged national or social interests or social morals, and no relevant law is readily applicable.[49]

In China's civil legislation, the social and public interests rule is scattered in different provisions of the laws. Some scholars have looked at these provisions and classified the social and public interests into different categories. In one publication, it is concluded that the civil conducts violating social and public

---

45 See the Contract Law, art. 60 (the parties shall abide by the principle of good faith and fulfill the duties of notice, assistance and confidentiality on the basis of the nature and purpose of contract, or the transaction practices).
46 See SPC, 2009 Contract Interpretations, art. 7.
47 As observed, in the Civil Law, judicial discretion is either within the civil codes, or within the particular rules of those codes. *See* Roberto G. MacLean, *Judicial Discretion in the Civil Law*, 43 LOUISIANA L. REV., 45, 49 (1982).
48 *See* Economic Trial Chamber of the SPC, Explanation *supra* note 20, at 43–44.
49 *See* Su Haopeng, Formation and Validity of Contract 69–70 (China Legal Publ'g House 1999).

interests include those that (a) damage national interest, (b) hamper family relations, (c) violate sexual morals, (d) violate or infringe human rights or human dignity, (e) restrict economic or business activities, (f) violate fair competition, (g) commit illegal gambling, (g) infringe consumer interests, (h) violate labor protection, and (i) seek usurious profits.[50]

2.4 Observance of Contract

Article 8 of the Contract Law establishes a principle of contract observance. Pursuant to Article 8, a valid contract is binding and must be observed. Thus, a legally formed contract has a binding effect between the parties. Binding in this context means that the parties must fulfill their obligations as set forth in the contract, and no party may alter or rescind the contract without the consent of the other party.[51] Article 8 further provides that a contract, once legally made, is under the protection of the law.[52] The very purpose of Article 8 is to ensure that contractual obligations will be performed as agreed. The observance principle is based on the long-established civil principle in China that an agreement shall be honored when it is reached. This principle also reflects the contract maxim of *pacta sunt servanda,* meaning that agreements must be kept.

In China, the binding effect of a contract is believed to come from two importance sources. The first source is the will of parties. Since a contract is an agreement made by the parties, the parties, when making the agreement, should be willing and prepared to be bound by it. The prerequisite for the binding force, of course, is that the agreement is made freely and voluntarily. Therefore, in order for a contract to be performed as agreed, it is important that the parties mutually trust each other and abide by the agreement reached between them.

The second source is the will of the State. Governmental will is intended to facilitate business transactions within the norms of law and regulations. A common view among Chinese scholars is that the law embraces moral imperatives, and for the sake of market order and social stability, it is in the strongest interest of the State that agreements are kept as promised by the parties—a moral standard that is enforced as a legal rule.[53]

---

50   See Liang Huixing, *Market Economy and the Principles of Public Order and Good Morals*, in Treatise on Civil and Commercial Law, Vol. 1, 57 (Law Publ'g House 1999).
51   See Contract Law, art. 8.
52   See id.
53   See Economic Trial Chamber of the Supreme People's Court, *supra* note 20, at 45.

In the context of the Contract Law, the binding effect of a contract contains the following aspects. First, the parties are required to properly and completely perform their obligations under the contract. In pursuit of the performance rule, a party not only has the obligation to perform its own contractual obligation, but also has the right to demand the other party to perform under the contract. Second, after a contract is made, a party may not modify or rescind the contract without the other party's consent. If there exists a necessity for a change of the contract, the change must be made through the parties' negotiations. Third, a party will be held liable if it fails to perform its contractual obligations unless the non-performance is excused under the provisions of law. In the case of a contract breach, the breaching party may be compelled to continue performing or to pay for damages. Finally, fourth, when a dispute arises between the parties, the contract shall serve as the basis on which the dispute is to be resolved.[54]

Note that in Chinese contract law, a very popular term that is used to describe the effect of a contract is "legally established" (or "*Yi Fa Cheng Li*" in Chinese). "Legally established" means that a contract is formed according to the law. For a contract to be legally established, it must be a product of a combination of both the will of the parties and the will of the State. In other words, the contract must be made voluntarily by the parties and in compliance with the law in all aspects, including, for example, the contents, formality, and purpose of the contract. In addition, it is an important feature under the Contract Law that a contract made by parties is subject to judicial or administrative review in light of legal compliance (e.g., the capacity of the party). In sum, pursuant to the Contract Law, only a legally established contract has a binding effect and thus is enforceable.

3 Pre-Contractual Liabilities

Traditionally, parties owed no contractual duties to each other unless a contractual relationship between them was formed. This doctrinal wisdom came from the classic proposition that, unless contractual responsibility arose, parties had no legal rights against each other at all.[55] However, during contract negotiations, parties normally had to disclose their business information to each other for purposes of making a contract. The problem then was how to

---

54   See Jiang Ping, *supra* note 18, at 18.
55   See Hugh Collins, The Law of Contact 168 (Butterworths, 2nd ed., 1993).

protect the respective interests of the parties during the negotiation process, particularly when a party's interest was (or was likely to be) damaged by the other party's improper conduct before the contract was formed.

A dilemma created by the above problem was the tension between freedom of contract and the imposition of pre-contractual liabilities. In common law countries, courts are reluctant to impose any responsibility on the parties to a contract without their consent. A major concern is that acceptance of the pre-contractual liability doctrine would diminish the basic value of the freedom to contract.[56] Accordingly, in many cases, the concept of negligence liability in torts is borrowed and applied to deals involving responsibilities that arise prior to the formation of the contract.

In China, pre-contractual liability is recognized as a special form of liability and is imposed on the party who during contract negotiations violates the good faith principle, causing the other party to suffer damages. In general, the imposition of pre-contractual liability is intended to deal with the situation where the liability that occurs may not be properly characterized as either contractual liability or tort liability. The sole purpose of the imposition of pre-contractual liability is to provide the parties with legal protection needed during the course of their making a contract.

Many in China consider Article 61 of the 1986 Civil Code as the initial provision of pre-contractual liability in the current Chinese law. Under Article 61, after a civil act has been determined to be null and void or has been rescinded, a party who acquired property as a result of the act must return it to the party who suffered a loss. The erring party must compensate for the loss that it has caused to the other party. If both parties are at fault, they must each bear their proper share of the responsibilities.[57] But Article 61 does not seem to provide for pre-contractual liability because it does not directly deal with the liabilities that arise prior to the conclusion of a contract. It is arguable whether a contract that is later declared null and void or rescinded is necessarily one that has not be concluded.

The Contract Law contains a specific provision that makes pre-contractual liability an important part of the contractual liability scheme. Article 42 of the Contract Law provides that a party is liable for damages if it does one of the following in concluding a contract, which results in losses to the other party: (a) disguises and pretends to conclude a contract and negotiates in bad faith; (b) conceals deliberately the important facts relating to the conclusion of

---

56 *See id.* at 169–70.
57 *See* 1986 Civil Code, art. 61.

the contract or provides deliberately false information; or (c) engages in other acts violating the principle of good faith.[58] Under Article 42, pre-contractual liability can be construed to mean liability for damages caused by one party to the other during the contract-making process, or simply put, the liability of the party at fault prior to the formation of a contract.

However, Article 42 seems too broad in terms of scope and contents. What remains an open question is the nature of liability parties may be subject to in the pre-contract stage. Ambiguity exists with respect to Article 42's actual application, particularly with regard to application of the "catch-all provision" of Article 42 (c). Therefore, in order to avoid any confusion that may arise from Article 42, further interpretations and judicial determinations were needed. For that purpose—as well as because of concerns that the application of Article 42 might be mishandled—the Research Office of the Standing Committee of the National People's Congress has offered a list of the pre-contractual liabilities that are covered under Article 42. According to the Research Office, under existing laws and judicial practices in China, pre-contractual liabilities are based on "fault" and refer to the following:

(a) Liability arising from arbitrary withdrawal of an offer, especially when the other party has relied on the offer;
(b) Damages caused by a failure to fulfill notice obligations during a contract's negotiation;
(c) Liability arising from infringement upon the personal or property right of the other party as a result of a failure to fulfill protection obligations during a contract's negotiation;
(d) Liability arising out of the failure to make contract;
(e) Liability occurring when a contract is void due to the negligence of the parties;
(f) Liability arising from the rescission of a contract; or
(g) Liability arising from the non-authorized representation of an agent.[59]

Similarly, some contract scholars in China have also tried to define the scope of pre-contract liability. In a leading contract law book, for example, pre-contract liabilities are stated to include the following obligations:
(a) Obligation not to withdraw an offer without due course;
(b) Obligation not to conceal material information such as the contracting party's financial situation as well as itsability to perform the contract;

---

58 The Contract Law, art. 42.
59 The Research Office of the General Office of the Standing Committee of the National People's Congress of China, Explanation and Application Guidance to the Contract Law of China, 50–52 (China Democracy & Legality Publ'g House 1999).

(c) Obligation to operate and provide necessary assistance;
(d) Obligation to be faithful;
(e) Obligation to keep secret all confidential information; and
(f) Obligation not to abuse the freedom to a contract. [60]

In addition, the imposition of pre-contractual liability under Article 42 requires four elements. First, in order for Article 42 to apply, there must be a breach of duties imposed by law prior to the conclusion of the contract. A notable feature of pre-contractual liability is that such liability does not arise from any agreement between the parties, but rather is created by the operation of law. Second, the breach must cause damages or losses to the other party. A difficult issue here is how to determine losses. A majority of Chinese scholars take the position that loss suffered by a party during the pre-contract stage is the party's reliance interest, which mainly refers to the costs incurred by the party in reliance on the contract to be concluded.[61] Third, there must exist fault, including intentional misconduct or negligence, for which a party can be blamed. A fundamental standard in determining whether a party is at fault is whether the good faith principle has been violated. Finally, fourth, there must be causation between the losses that are claimed and the fault of the liable party. It must also be proven that the losses the claiming party has suffered are necessarily caused by the fault of the other party.

In 2012, the SPC promulgated Interpretations on the Issues Involving Application of Law in Adjudicating Disputes over Sales Contracts. In Article 2 of the Interpretations, the SPC specifically addressed what liabilities arise before a contract of sales is made. According to the SPC, when parties sign a pre-contract document —such as a letter to prescribe, letter to purchase, letter of booking, letter of intent, or memorandum, under which they agree to conclude a contract of sales at a specified time in the future—if one party fails to fulfill the obligation to enter into the contract and the other party makes a request demanding the non-performing party to bear the liability for the breach of the pre-contractual duty or for a disolution of the pre-contractual relationship and claims damages therefrom, the People's Court must grant that request.[62]

The following case tells how a people's court determined the pre-contractual liability specifically. In this case, the trial court dismissed the plaintiff's claim

---

60 *See* Wang Liming, Study on the Contract Law, *supra* note 3, at 312–13.
61 *See* Wang Liming, Introduction to the Contract Law and Case Analysis 84–85 (People's Univ. Publ'g House 2001).
62 *See* SPC, Interpretation on the Issues Concerning Application of Law in Adjudicating Disputes over the Contracts of Sales, issued on March 31, 2012.

for pre-contractual liability against defendant on the ground that plaintiff failed to fulfill its burden of proof that defendant was at fault.

**Sichuan Yafeng Construction Engineering Company, Ltd., v.
Sichuan Green Pharmaceutical Technology Development, Inc.**

Pengzhou City People's Court, Sichuan Province Pengzhou Mingchu No. 511[63]

Plaintiff: Yafeng Construction Engineering Company, Ltd, Pengzhou City, Sichuan Province (hereinafter referred to as "Yafeng Company"), located in Bai Xian Jie Village, Longfeng Township of Pengzhou City;
Defendant: Sichuan Green Pharmaceutical Technology Development, Inc. (hereinafter referred to as "Green Pharmaceutical Company") whose principal business office is 10th Floor, International Plaza, 206 Chuncheng Jie, Chengdu City.

The facts of the case were as follows:
On April 6, 2001, plaintiff Yafeng Company attended the public bidding offered by defendant Green Pharmaceutical Company for the project of defendant's scientific research and quality testing building. After the bids contest, plaintiff was selected by the Bidding Evaluation Committee as the winner of the bid, and the result was also notarized by the Notary Public Office of Pengzhou City. A "Bid Winning Notice", numbered as 2001–019, was then issued to plaintiff by the Construction Bidding Management Office of Pengzhou City.

Although plaintiff received the Notice from the Bidding Evaluation Committee, defendant refused to sign a written contract with plaintiff, alleging that plaintiff lacked legitimate bidding capacity and therefore was incapable to perform the contract. Plaintiff then brought the lawsuit against defendant for pre-contractual liability. Plaintiff claimed that defendant's refusal to sign the contract with plaintiff violated the principle of good faith during the contract making process for which defendant shall be held liable. Plaintiff asked the court to order defendant to pay the damage in the amount of RMB 8,000 plus all litigation costs.

Defendant moved to dismiss by arguing that at the time of bidding, plaintiff had no legal capacity of making the bid. Defendant further argued that the winner of the bid should be determined by defendant, and the winning notice should also be sent to the winner by defendant. According to defendant, it never agreed that plaintiff was the bid-winner, and therefore it had every right not to sign the contract with plaintiff. Defendant also asserted that since it did no do anything wrong in the process of the bidding, and there was no fault or negligence on the defendant side, plaintiff's claim on the ground of pre-contractual liability should be denied.

The court finds that there is no evidence to prove that the Bidding Evaluation Committee was authorized by the defendant to determine the winner of the bid. The court also finds that the Bid Winning Notice issued by the Construction Bidding Management Office of Pengzhou City was not endorsed by the defendant who made the invitation for bid.

Based on the facts found, the court is of opinion that plaintiff attended the bidding activities but did not win the bid. Invitation for bid and submission of a bid are the means of making a contract. The public announcement of invitation for bid or notice of public auction is nothing more than an invitation for offer. In the bidding process, the submission of the bid is an offer, and

---

63 See National Judicial College and People's University School of Law, *An Overview of Trial Cases of China* (Civil and Commercial Cases of 2004), 7-11 (People's Court Press and People's Univ. Publ'g House 2005).

the confirmation of the bid winner is an acceptance. Since the acceptance will take effect upon receipt, there will be no effective contract between the parties involved until the winner receives the bid-winning confirmation. Therefore, the key issue of whether a contract has been formed is whether the bidder has won the bid. Also the public bidding shall be conducted under the provisions of the Law of Public Bidding and Submission of Bids of China (Public Bidding Law).

In the instant case, plaintiff did not win the bid and therefore no contract was ever formed between plaintiff and defendant. Then the whole issue is whether defendant did anything wrong during the bidding process for which defendant would be held liable pre-contractually. Plaintiff alleged that defendant violated the good faith principle and therefore should bear pre-contractual liability imposed by the law. The court holds that under Article 42 of the Contract Law, the pre-contractual liability provision will apply only if defendant during the course of contract-making committed bad faith negotiation, fraud or other conducts violating the good faith principle.

It is clear, then, that the pre-contractual liability under the Contract Law is based on the principle of fault liability. Applying this principle to this case, three factors must be ascertained in order to hold defendant liable. The first factor is whether defendant has breached its pre-contractual obligations. According to the provisions of Articles 7, 40 and 45 of the Public Bidding Law, the administrative supervision department shall supervise the public bidding activities, and investigate and punish illegal conducts in the public bidding process under the law. Also under those provisions, the inviter of bids may decide the bid-winner according to the written evaluation report or recommendation of the bid evaluation committee or authorize the committee to make the decision. After the bid-winner is determined, a notice of winning bid shall be issued by the inviter. Thus in this case, it is the defendant's right not to authorize the bid evaluation committee to directly determine the bid winner, to select plaintiff as the winner among all candidates, or to verify, and issue the notice of, the winning-bid to plaintiff. On the other hand, plaintiff did not provide any evidence to prove that defendant had violated its pre-contractual obligations.

The second factor is whether defendant itself had committed any fault. Plaintiff failed to prove that there existed fault on defendant side such as intentionally concealing important information pertaining to the conclusion of contract or providing false information. Absent such subjective fault, defendant shall bear no fault liability as imposed by the law.

The third factor concerns whether plaintiff had any reliance interest and lost such interest due to the defendant's fault. Plaintiff claimed that it had suffered RMB 8,000. But the evidence in the form of receipts only proved that the actual cost incurred to plaintiff for its participating in the public bidding was RMB 2,700. Of the cost, only RMB 300 for the notary public fees may constitute a reliance interest, and all other fees were the normal cost directly associated with the bidding activities. By normal cost, it means that plaintiff did not and had no reason to believe that it would win the bid by spending such money. In addition, the cost was clearly stated in the public bidding documents as the one to be born by plaintiff.

Based on the above facts and analysis, it is concluded that plaintiff does not meet the three-factor requirement for imposing pre-contractual liability on defendant, and therefore its claim must be denied for lack of legal grounds and sufficient evidence.

The case is then dismissed.

It is noteworthy that in *Sichuan Yafeng* the court established a three- factor test for the imposition of pre-contractual liability under Article 42 of the Contract Law. Under this test, in order to hold defendant liable on the ground of pre- contractual liability, plaintiff must prove with sufficient evidence the following factors: (1) defendant's obligations in the pre-contractual period and failure to fulfill such obligations, (2) defendant's fault causing the failure, and (3) the loss of plaintiff's reliance interest.

In addition to Article 42 of the Contract Law, another provision imposing pre-contractual liablities is Article 43, which applies to business secrets. In accordance with Article 43, neither party may disclose or inappropriately exploit business secrets obtained in the making of a contract regardless of whether the contract is formed or not.[64] If a party discloses or inappropriately exploits business secrets and consequently causes losses to the other party, the party is liable for those losses.

The Contract Law does not define "business secrets." Therefore, application of Article 43 with respect to business secret determinations requires cross-application of other laws. A frequently cited provision in this regard is Article 10 of the Unfair Competition Law,[65] under which business secrets are defined as any technological information or business operation information that satisfies the following four criteria: (a) the information is unknown to the public, (b) the owner of the business secrets has taken measures to keep them secret, (c) the information could bring economic benefits to the owner, and (d) the information has practical utility.[66]

An important issue concerning the imposition of pre-contractual liability is the burden of proof. In judicial proceedings in Chinese courts, to seek pre-contractual liability, the claiming party is required to prove damages as well as the fault of the other party. Under Article 64 of Civil Procedure Law of China (as amended in 2012), it is the duty of a party to a civil action to provide evidence in support of his claims or allegations. According to the SPC, a party to

---

64 *See* Contract Law, art. 43.
65 The Unfair Competition Law of China was adopted on September 2, 1993 was took effect on December 1, 1993.
66 In order to implement the Unfair Competition Law, on November 23, 1995, The State Administration of Industry and Commerce issued "[t]he Several Rules about Prohibition of Conducts Infringing Business Secrets." Under the Rules, "not known to the public" means that the information may not be obtained directly from public channels; "to bring about economic benefit and having practical utility" imply that the information in question has the definite applicability and could provide actual or potential economic benefits or competitive advantages; "secret-keeping measures" include the signing of security agreement, the establishing of security system as well as other reasonable security measures; "technology or business operation information consists of information containing design, program, recipe, production workmanship, production method, management know-how, customer list, sources of goods, production and marketing strategy, base amount of bid as well as the contents of bidding document.

a civil action is responsible for providing evidence to prove the facts on which his claim stands; if there is no evidence, or the evidence is not sufficient to prove the facts, the party who has the burden of proof will bear the adverse consequences[67] (i.e., the factual determination will be made against him).

---

67   On April 1, 2002, the Supreme People's Court adopted the Several Rules of Evidence Concerning Civil Litigation. For general information about the Evidence Rules, see Mo Zhang, *Burden of Proof: Developments in Modern Chinese Evidence Rules,* 10 TULSA J. COMP. & INT'L (2003). On January 30, 2015, the SPC issued the Interpretations on the Application of the Civil Procedural Law of China. Under Article 90 of the 2015 Interpretations, a party bears the burden to prove with evidence the facts on which its own claims or his rebutals to the other party's claims are relied, unless the law stipulates otherwise. Article 90 further provides that if before the judgment is made the party fails to produce evidence or the evidence produced is insufficient to prove the facts as alleged, the proving party shall face the consequences detrimental to him.

CHAPTER 4

Formation of Contracts

Formation of a contract requires mutual assent between the parties. Mutual assent is materialized and manifested by an offer and an acceptance. Under Article 13 of the Contract Law, in order to form a contract, one party must make an offer and the other party must accept that offer. As discussed in Chapter 2, in China, a contract need not be supported by consideration in order to be enforceable. Thus, what really matters is mutual assent of the parties. To achieve mutual assent, it is essential that the parties have agreed to the same terms through negotiations on a voluntary basis. The mutual assent upon which an agreement is made between the parties must take the form of offer and acceptance.

Interestingly, although the Contract Law is not the first contract legislation in modern China, its promulgation signified the first time that the law in China made offer and acceptance the two key elements for formation of a contract. In general, a contract is formed when an offer is accepted. As noted, however, certain types of contracts in China require governmental approval, and such contracts are therefore not effective until they are approved by the government. Article 44 of the Contract Law specifically deals with the formation and effect of contracts. Pursuant to Article 44, a contract legally made takes effect upon its formation; but if government approval or registration is required, the contract will become effective only after such approval or registration is obtained.[1]

1   Offer

Formation of a contract begins with an offer. In Article 14 of the Contract Law, an offer is defined as "a manifestation of intent showing the desire to enter into a contract with others." Under this definition, there are two elements that an offer must contain: manifestation of intent and desire to make a contract with others. In addition, to constitute an offer, the intent manifested must meet two requirements that are set forth in Article 14: (a) the contents must be concrete

---

1   Contract Law, art. 44.

and definite and (b) the offeror must be bound by his manifestation of intent upon acceptance by the offeree.[2]

For purposes of making an offer, the offeror's intent may be expressed either orally or in writing. In other words, the intent must be communicated in a certain way with the offeree. It is unclear under the Contract Law whether the intent can also be inferred from the offeror's conduct. According to scholarly interpretation, in the absence of express intent, intent can be presumed through the offeror's conduct in light of the usage of transactions.[3] Thus, if it can be reasonably believed from the offeror's conduct that the offeror has the intent to make a contract, a contractual obligation may arise upon effective acceptance by the other party.

In the West, there exist both subjective and objective tests for determining intent. The subjective test focuses on the actual intent of the parties, while the objective test relies on the outward manifestation of a party's intent. The difference between the two tests is that, under the subjective test, what really matters is what was intended, rather than what a party reasonably believed was said and done.[4] There are no such tests in China, though it seems that the Contract Law has made actual intent an essential element of an offer because the statute stresses the "desire to enter into a contract with others."

One question that arises with respect to offers concerns the identification of an offeree. Chinese scholars have been debating on whom an offer should be made to. At the center of the debate is the question of whether an offer must be made to a specific (or identified) person. One opinion is that, since an offer indicates the offeror's intent to make a contract, the offer should be made to the specific person with whom the offeror wishes to deal; otherwise there is no offer. The opposite opinion takes the view that the offeree does not have to be specific because, in a market economy, fair competition is the goal sought to be achieved, and therefore an offer should not necessarily be limited to specific persons.[5]

The Contract Law does not require that an offer be made to specific person(s). The majority opinion in China, nevertheless, is in favor of the "specific person" doctrine—though the person specified need not necessarily be just one person. An underlying reason is that, unless the offeree is specific, it would be hard to predict who is the intended person to whom the offer is made. In

---

2 *See id.*, art. 14.
3 *See* Wang Liming, Study on the Contract Law, Vol. I, 206–07 (People's Univ. Press 2002).
4 *See* Robert Scott & Jody Kraus, Contract Law and Theory 238–39 (3d ed., 2002).
5 *See* Wang Liming *supra* note 3, at 208.

addition, if an offer is allowed to be made to a non-specific person, it may result in a situation where the offeror faces multiple contracts if acceptances are made by several non-specific persons that are unknown to the offeror.[6]

It is also argued that the provision of the Contract Law concerning offers must be construed with reference to the 1980 United Nations Convention on Contracts for the International Sale of Goods (CISG). Under Article 14 (1) of the CISG, a proposal for concluding a contract that is addressed to one or more specific persons constitutes an offer if it is sufficiently definite and indicates the intention of the offeror to be bound in case of acceptance. Article 14 (2) explicitly provides that a proposal other than one addressed to one or more specific persons is to be considered merely as an invitation to make offers, unless the contrary is clearly indicated by the person making the proposal.[7]

Another question regards the contents of an offer. The Contract Law requires that the contents of an offer be concrete and definite but the statute does not specify what constitute "concrete and definite" contents. In general, an offer is considered to be concrete in China if it embraces the very basic items that are sufficient to form a contract. Moreover, the determination of whether an offer is definite depends on how a reasonable person with general knowledge related to the specific industry or products would think. According to some Chinese scholars, for purposes of the Contract Law, the "concrete and definite" requirement means that the contents of an offer must be clear enough such that the offeree can understand not only the offeror's true intent, but also the major terms that would be contained in the future contract.[8]

1.1 *Offer and Invitation for Offer*

Under the Contract Law, an offer is "a manifestation of intent." However, not every manifestation of intent constitutes an offer. To become an offer, manifestation must be made to the effect that it is understood by the other party that the intent so manifested is to ask for a deal. If a party's manifestation of intent does not clearly indicate that the party is intending to make a contract—or if it is simply to pass on business information or to advertise products or services—the manifestation will not be considered to be an offer.

A manifestation of intent that is not sufficient to constitute an offer is often labeled as an invitation for offer. The Contract Law has a special provision that

---

6 *See id.* at 208–09.
7 *See* United Nations Convention on Contracts for the International Sale of Goods (1980), O.R. 178–190; Docy. Hist. 766–78.
8 *See* Jiang Ping, Detailed Explanation to Contract Law of China 14–15 (China Univ. of Political Science & Law Publ'g House 1999).

explicitly involves invitations for offer. In Article 15 of the Contract Law, an invitation for offer is defined as a manifestation of intent indicating a desire to receive offers from others. According to Article 15, an invitation for an offer includes mailed or delivered price catalogs, public notices of auction, invitations for bid, prospectuses, and commercial advertisements.[9] But, it should be noted that Article 15 has made an exception to commercial advertisements. Under Article 15, though commercial advertisements are generally not offers, they will be deemed to be offers if their contents conform to the statute's provisions regarding offers and are found to be concrete and definite.

A debatable issue concerning advertisements is the effect of an advertisement for a reward. In the context of the Contract Law, Article 15 covers only commercial advertisements. Pursuant to the Advertisement Law of the People's Republic of China (1994), commercial advertisements refer to advertisements for which a commodity producer or service provider pays, and by which the commodity producer or service provider directly or indirectly, through certain media or forms, introduces its commodities to be sold or services to be provided.[10] Commcercial advertisements do not include advertisements for rewards. Therefore, it has become questionable what effect reward advertisements have in light of the Contract Law.

Chinese contract scholars are divided with respect to this question. One group argues that a reward advertisement is an offer because it is made to the public and requests performance. Under this argument, performance of what the reward has asked for constitutes acceptance, and a contractual relationship is established when the performance sought by the reward is complete. What seems unclear, however, is whether it is essential that the offeree, while performing according to the reward advertisement, must have knowledge of the offer in order to receive the reward.[11]

Another group of Chinese contract scholars take a different position. They argue that the contract theory of mutual consent does not apply to advertisements for rewards. Scholars upholding this view believe that a reward advertisement is not an offer but rather a unilateral conduct whereby the advertiser requests a specific performance from the general public.[12] Under the unilateral conduct doctrine, once an advertisement for a reward is made, the advertiser

---

9   *See* Contract Law, art. 15.
10 *See* Article 2 of Advertisement Law of the People's Republic of China. The Advertisement Law was adopted on October 27, 1994 and took effect on February 1, 1995.
11 *See* Kong Xiangjun, *Difficult Cases in Contract Law, Analysis and Legal Research*, 93–94 (People's Court Publ'g House, 2000).
12 In the U.S., a reward advertisement is generally considered as a unilateral contract.

is bound by the advertisement, regardless of the performer's actual knowledge of the advertisement. In addition, since an advertisement for a reward is not an offer, no acceptance is required. Therefore, an advertisement for a reward may not be withdrawn after it is made and whoever completes the required performance will be entitled to the reward.[13]

The following case is illustrative of how reward advertisements are dealt with in the People's Courts.

Li Min v. Zhu Jinhua and Li Shaohua

(Tian Jin Intermediate People's Court, 1984, cited by the Supreme People's Court as typical case reported in the Gazette of the Supreme People's Court, 11—1995)

On March 30, 1983, defendants Zhu Jinhua and Li Shaohua went to Tian Jin Peace Theater for a movie. After the movie, Zhu Jinhua left behind in the seat a portfolio that contained the document for the delivery of a car and other items totaling RMB 800,000. Zhu Jinhua was asked by defendant Li Shaohua to arrange for the delivery of the car on behalf of Luo Yang Electric Company in He Nan Province. Plaintiff found the portfolio in the theater. After the theater was empty and no one came back to claim the portfolio, plaintiff took it and put it in the custody of Wang Jiaping, who was a policeman (named as a third party in the case). When Zhu Jinhua realized that the portfolio was lost, he tried to retrieve it but was unsuccessful.

On April 4 and 5, Defendant Zhu Jinhua put a notice in the "lost and found" section of "Today's Evening Paper"—a very popular newspaper in the City of Tian Jin. The same notice was also made in "Tian Jin Daily" on April 7. In the notices, Zhu Jinhua indicated, respectively, that whoever found and returned the portfolio would receive "a reward" and "significant award." But nothing happened after the notices were made. On April 12, defendant Li Shaohua, who came to Tianjin from He Nan, put another notice in his name in the "Today's Evening Paper" for the same purpose, in which the term "significant reward" was changed to "the reward of RMB 15,000 to those who return the lost portfolio within a week after the notice."

In the evening on April 12, plaintiff Li Min saw Li Shaohua's notice in the newspaper. Li Min then told Wang Jiaping about the reward and asked him to contact Li Shaohua. On April 13, Wang Jiaping called Li Shaohua and the two of them agreed to exchange the lost portfolio for the reward of RMB 15,000. When they met at the agreed place, however, defendants changed their mind and refused to give plaintiff RMB 15,000. After an unsuccessful mediation by a local police department, plaintiff brought the lawsuit against defendant for the RMB 15,000 in the People's Court of He Ping District.

In his claim, plaintiff asserted that defendant's failure to make the payment of RMB 15,000 to plaintiff breached his obligation arising from the notice. Defendant Zhu Jinhua argued that, because nobody responded to his notices in the newspapers on April 4, 5 and 7, defendants believed that the only way to make the finder of the lost portfolio show up was to specify the reward amount. For that reason, Zhu Jinhua argued, the promise to give RMB 15,000 was not their true intent and therefore it was reasonable for them to refuse to pay. Defendant Li Shaohua also contended that, as a police officer, Wang Jiaping should not have kept the lost portfolio in his custody, but rather should have tried to find the owner or turn the lost item over to relevant

---

13   See Kong Xiangjun, *supra* note 11, at 93–94.

authorities. Defendant Li Shaohua moved to dismiss on the ground that, since Wang Jiaping did not fulfill his duty, plaintiff's request for the reward should be denied.

The trial court found that the document for the delivery of a car and other items in the lost portfolio belonged to Luo Yang Electric Company and was the property of the company. Based on its findings, the court held that plaintiff's failure to find the owner or to turn the lost property to a relevant authority was contrary to the public morale. According to the trial court, plaintiffs should have been able to find out who was the owner of the lost property because the document and items in the portfolio clearly indicated the name of Luo Yang Electric Company. The trial court further held that, as a policeman, Wang Jiahua should have made all efforts to find the owner, and failure to do so constituted a violation of his duty. The trial court then denied plaintiff's claim for the reason that the monetary reward in the notice was not the manifestation of the true intent of the defendants, and therefore should have no legal effect.

On appeal, the Intermediate People's Court of Tianjin reversed the trial court's judgment. The Intermediate Court was of opinion that the trial court's view of "not the manifestation of defendants' true intent" was not supported by sufficient evidence and lacked legal authority. In its reversal, the Intermediate Court held that, in accordance with the basic principle of the General Principles of Civil Law of China, defendants' notice indicating the reward as well as the money amount should be considered legally valid.[14]

It seemed that the Intermediate People's Court of Tian Jin in the *Li Min* case based its decision on contract theory. The rationale underlying its holding was that an advertisement for a reward, once made, creates a right-obligation relationship between the party who makes the advertisement and the party who performs the duty requested by the advertisement, and as long as this relationship does not violate law in its formality and contents, it should be held valid. Therefore, if a reward advertiser fails to perform what he has offered in the reward advertisement, the offeree has the right to demand the offeror to perform. An implication of the Court's holding was that it is not imperative for the offeree to have knowledge about the offer before the offeree's performance.

In its 2009 Contract Law Interpretations, the SPC formally recognizes the legal effect of a reward made to the public. According to the SPC, when the offeror of a reward publicly announces an offer to pay to a person who has performed certain acts, and then that person requests the payment, the People's Court shall grant the request, unless fraud, coercion, or other illegality is involved.[15] Apparently, the SPC regards a reward advertisement as an offer to form a reward contract. In China, a reward contract is categorized as a unilateral contract where acceptance is to perform what is asked in the offer.

Another point worthy of note is the distinction between an offer and an invitation for offer. As is often the case, the two terms are intertwined so closely

---

14 *See* Gazette of the Supreme People's Court (1995). The case was settled between the parties under the auspice of the Intermediate Court. Under the settlement, Plaintiff received a onetime payment of RMB 8,000.
15 *See* SPC 2009 Contract Interpretations, art. 3.

that it is difficult to differentiate them. For example, Article 16 of the Contract Law on one hand regards a commercial advertisement as an invitation for offer, and on the other hand intends to treat some commercial advertisements as offers by exception. This is a typical reflection of the open-ended nature of the issue as to what constitutes an offer and what constitutes an invitation for offer.

In an attempt to draw a line between an offer and an invitation for offer, Chinese contract law scholars have tried to provide a guideline for this matter from a doctrinal viewpoint. Although scholars differ as to what should be included in the guideline, a general consensus is that the following tests help determine whether there is an offer or an invitation for offer.[16]

The first test is the test of intent. Under this test, the question of whether there is an offer or an invitation for offer is to be determined by looking at the intent manifested by the party. If a party indicates, orally or in writing, that he will be bound by the terms and conditions in the proposal for a deal, the proposal constitutes an offer. If, however, the proposal only states the party's intent to invite the other party to make an offer, the proposal is not an offer. Such intent may also be determined by assessing the party's conduct or specific statements. For instance, if the phrase "for reference only" is used, no offer is made. Similarly, when there is a statement saying that the proposal so made shall not be interpreted as an "offer," there is no offer.

The second test is the contents test. The determinant under this test is whether the contents of a proposal contain the major terms of a contract. If the proposal specifies the major terms, it implies that the party making the proposal intends to enter into a contract with others. In that case, the proposal is an offer because it is made to invite an acceptance. The reason is that an offer is aimed at making a contract with others while an invitation for offer only represents an early stage of preparation for negotiation.

Major terms of an offer generally include name, quantity, as well as subject matter. Under the SPC's 2009 Contract Interpretations, when parties dispute whether a contract has been formed, the people's court should in general hold in favor of the contract being formed if the names of the parties, the subject matter, and the quantity can be ascertained, unless otherwise provided by the law or agreed by the parties.[17] Thus, even if a proposal contains the major terms, when the party making the proposal explicitly states in the proposal

---

16 See generally Wang Liming, supra note 3, at 213–22; Xiangjun, supra note 11, at 63–64; Yang Lixin, Implementation and Application of the Contract Law 39–40 (Jilin People's Publ'g House 1999).
17 See SPC 2009 Contract Interpretations, art. 1.

that he will not be bound by the terms of the proposal or that the terms need to be further negotiated, the proposal will still not be regarded as an offer.

The third test concerns the usage of transactions in the industry or prior dealings between the parties. This test essentially focuses on the history of the party's business dealings and common practices in those transactions. As an example illustrative of this test, assume that party A and party B have been engaged in purchasing a certain product for a long time, and the specification and price of the product have never changed during the parties' previous dealings. Under this circumstance, if party A proposes to buy the same product from party B without specifying the product (i.e., the subject matter) but only the quantity amount, party A's proposal will be deemed as an offer, though normally it would not be.

The fourth test is the provision of law. If there is a clear indication in the law as to what should be considered as an invitation for offer, the law must be followed. For instance, in Article 15 of the Contract Law, price catalogs mailed or delivered, public notices of auction, invitations for bid, and prospectuses are explicitly listed as invitations for offer. Also, as a practical matter, a commercial advertisement is generally deemed to be an invitation for offer. But since the Contract Law appears to be vague as what would constitute an exception to the general rule that a commercial advertisement constitutes an invitation for offer, scholars have attempted to clarify the situations under which the nature of a commercial advertisement can be readily identified. One proposal suggests that the supplier's manifestation of intent through public advertisements, price catalogs, or displays that are for purposes of supplying products or services at the special price should be presumed to be an offer.[18]

On June 1, 2003, the SPC issued "Explanations to Several Questions Concerning the Application of Law in Adjudicating the Disputes Arising from the Contracts for Sales of Commercial Housing."[19] In the Explanations, the SPC classified as offers certain advertisements for the sale of housing. According to the SPC, the advertisement or advertising materials for the sale of housing are generally invitations for an offer. However, advertisements or advertising materials shall be deemed to be offers if they contain specific and certain illustrations and promises made by the seller with regard to housing and related

---

18   *See* Liang Huixing, Proposed Draft of the Civil Code of China (Law Publ'g House 2003), art. 845.
19   The term "commercial housing" (Shang Pin Fang) means housing available for sale on the market. Most commercial housing is residence housing. Housing in China was previously allocated by government or work units to users, but now governmental and units-allocated housing are being replaced by commercial housing.

FORMATION OF CONTRACTS 123

facilities within the scope of a commercial housing development plan, and if these illustrations and promises materially affect the conclusion of a purchase contract of the housing or the purchase price.[20]

Also, under the SPC's Explanations, once an advertisement or advertising material is deemed as an offer, the terms or items specified in the advertisement or advertising material shall become the contents of the contract so entered even if the terms or items are not included in the contract. In this regard, if a party fails to fulfill its obligations arising from these terms or items, the party will be held liable for breach of the contract.[21] The underlying rationale is that an advertisement may constitute an offer, and an offer, if duly accepted, is binding.

1.2 *Legal Effect of Offers*

An issue concerning offers is the time for an offer to take effect. Under the Contract Law, an offer, once made, is not effective until it is received. Article 16 of the Contract Law provides that an offer becomes effective when it reaches the offeree.[22] A common term that is used in this regard is "arrival time." In Chinese judicial practice, to determine the time of "arrival," a court will look at whether the offer has arrived in a place that is controlled by the offeree, though the offer need not necessarily be in the hand of the offeree.[23]

If, however, an offer is made through means of data-telex, and the recipient has designated a specific system to receive the data-telex, the time of arrival of the offer will be the time when the data-telex enters into the system. But when no specific system is designated, the time when the data-telex first enters into any of the recipient's systems shall be deemed the time of arrival.[24] It is commonly understood that, though Article 16 does not specify what "system" means, the word "system" under Article 16 refers to a computer system.

Under the Contract Law, when an offer takes effect, it may not be withdrawn, and the offeror is bound by the offer unless he indicated in advance that he would not be bound by the offer. However, if the offeror does not intend to be bound by an offer, that offer is deemed to be an invitation for offer,

---

20   *See* Supreme People's Court, Explanations to Several Questions Concerning the Application of Law in Adjudicating the Disputes Arising from the Contracts for Sales of Commercial Housing, http://www.law-lib.com/law_view.asp?id=74535.
21   *See id.*
22   *See* Contract Law, art. 16.
23   *See* Economic Law Chamber of the Supreme People's Court, Contract Law Explanation and Application 116–17 (Xinghua Publ'g Press 1999).
24   *See* Contract Law, art. 16.

rather than an offer. Article 14 of the Contract Law requires that an offer must indicate the offeror's willingness to be bound by the offer upon acceptance by the offeree. In practice, an offeror's willingness to "be bound" is not always directly or unequivocally stated. Accordingly, willingness in this regard may often be inferred from the words or terms used in the offer or the sincerity of the offeror's intent to enter into the contract.

A related question is what effect of an offer has with respect to the offeree. This question necessitates consideration of who has the power to accept an offer and when that acceptance must be made. In general, acceptance must come from the person to whom the offer is made. In other words, the power to accept an offer may not be transferred unless such transfer is authorized or agreed to by the offeror. Timewise, if the offeree intends to accept the offer, the acceptance must be made within the valid period of the offer, which is either specified in the offer or, if no specific time is indicated in the offer, within a reasonable period of time.

A final point worth mentioning regards whether an offeree has an obligation to notify the offeror if the offeree does not want to accept the offer. Normally, an offeree is not obligated to send "non-acceptance" notice to the offeror. However, problems may arise when an offeree's silence could be considered to be implied acceptance. Quite often, this situation occurs where the parties dealt with each other in the past and, in such dealings, the offeree always promptly notified the offeror if the offeree did not accept the offer. In such a situation, the offeree must notify the offeror if it wants to turn down an offer; if the offeree does not, its silence may be deemed its acceptance of the offer.

1.3 Termination of an Offer

An offer is terminated when it is effectively withdrawn, revoked, or becomes void. Termination of an offer results in the loss of the offeree's power to accept the offer. Therefore, an offer cannot be accepted if it has been terminated. The Contract Law has special provisions that deal with how an offer is to be terminated.

1.3.1 Withdrawal of Offer

The Contract Law allows an offer to be withdrawn. Under Article 17, an offer may be withdrawn if the withdrawal notice reaches the offeree before, or at the same time as, the offer's arrival.[25] Hence, withdrawal of an offer may only take place before the offer becomes effective. Because the Contract Law does not

---

25 See Contract Law, art. 17.

impose any restriction on the withdrawal of offers, it is generally understood that any offer can be withdrawn before the offeree receives it.

For an offer to be withdrawn, it is important that a notice of withdrawal be timely made. The key is that an offeree receives the withdrawal notice before or at the same time the offer reaches the offeree. What is unclear, however, is whether the notice must be made in writing or can be made orally (e.g., by telephone). The Contract Law contains no provision in this regard, but a commonly accepted notion is that withdrawal should be made in a manner comparable to the way the offer was made. Specifically, if an offer is made in writing, a withdrawal notice of that offer should also be in writing. Conversely, if an offer is made orally, a withdrawal notice of that offer may be oral.

1.3.2   Revocation of Offer

An offer may not be withdrawn after it takes effect, but it may be revoked. Revocation of an offer, if made effectively, terminates the offer. Pursuant to Article 18 of the Contract Law, an offer may be revoked if the revocation reaches the offeree before the offeree dispatches an acceptance of the offer to the offeror.[26] Therefore, revocation may only occur after the offer becomes effective and before acceptance of the offer is sent out. Once again, it is questionable whether the revocation must be made in writing or whether it can be made orally, though the trend has been in favor of writing.

Not every offer may be revoked, however. Article 19 of the Contract Law explicitly provides that, under either of the following two circumstances, an offer may not be revoked: (a) the offeror has specified a time limit for acceptance, or has explicitly indicated through other means that the offer is irrevocable; or (b) the offeree has made preparations for fulfilling the contract in reasonable reliance on the offer as being irrevocable.[27] Article 19 (a) and (b) are exceptions to the general rules regarding offer revocation.

Article 19 (a) applies when an offer specifies a fixed time for acceptance. Under Article 19 (a), an offeror may not revoke an offer before expiration of such specified time for acceptance. The reason for this restriction is that, by providing a time limit for acceptance, the offeror has promised the offeree that the offer will remain effective during the specified time period. In reliance on that promise, the offeree may decide to accept the offer at any time within the time limit. It follows that Article 19 (a) has a focus on the offeror's intent because the

---

26   See id., art. 18.
27   See id., art 19.

whole issue is whether the offeror intends to keep an offer open for a specified period of time or to make the offer irrevocable.

Article 19 (b) makes the reasonable belief of the offeree determinative as to the question of whether an offer is irrevocable. There are three conditions under which the Article 19 (b) exception could be triggered. The first condition is that the offer contains no time limit for acceptance or any other language indicating that the offer is irrevocable. Otherwise, Article 19 (a) would apply. The second condition relates to the reasons for which the offeree believes that the offer is irrevocable. Nothing in the Contract Law touches on what reasons justify an offeree's belief that an offer is irrevocable. However, a general understanding is that an offer cannot be revoked pursuant to Article 19 (b) if the words or phrases used in the offer or the parties' previous dealings are so obvious or persuasive that they cause the offeree to believe that the offer is not revocable within a reasonable period of time. The third condition concerns the offeree's reliance. In order for the Article 19 (b) exception to be triggered, the offeree must be prepared to perform the contract in reliance on his belief that the offer is irrevocable.

Note that Article 19 is regarded by some scholars in China as a legal means for imposing pre-contractual liability upon at-fault parties. The argument is that, since the question of whether an offer is irrevocable arises in the negotiation stage of contracting, the fact that an offer is irrevocable does not necessarily mean that the offeror must fulfill his contractual obligations under the terms and conditions specified in the offer. Rather, it means only that the offeror may be held liable for damages that the offeree otherwise would not have suffered but for the offeror's revocation of the offer. Accordingly, the offeror's liability is based on the offeror's fault (i.e., the offeror's breach of her promise not to revoke the offer, which she made in the preliminary stages of the contract's formation).[28]

1.3.3 Void Offers

Under the Contract Law, an offer is terminated when the offer becomes null and void. According to Chinese scholars, an offer being void means that the offer has lost its legal effect and is not binding to anyone. Moreover, when an offer is null and void, the offeree's power to accept the offer ceases to be effective. Therefore, when an offer is void, its acceptance, even if timely made, does not result in a contract.[29] Simply put, the voidness of an offer deprives the offeree of the power or ability to accept the offer.

---

28   See Wang Liming, *supra* note 3, at 230–31.
29   See id. at 231.

As stipulated in Article 20 of the Contract Law, there are four situations under which the effect of an offer will be adversely affected. An offer becomes null and void if (a) a notice to reject the offer has reached the offeror; (b) the offeror has effectively revoked the offer in accordance with the law; (c) the offeree fails to accept the offer before the time for acceptance lapses; or (d) the offeree has substantially altered the contents of the offer.[30] If any of these situations occur, no acceptance of the offer will be effective.

Pursuant to Article 20 (a), an offer is terminated if it is rejected by the offeree. Such rejection takes place when the offeree does not accept the terms and conditions set forth in the offer. Since Article 20 (a) requires notice in the case of rejection, it is generally believed that rejection of an offer must be made expressly—though some argue that an offeree's inaction in response to an offer during the offer's time limit for acceptance may also constitute a rejection. Additionally, because Article 20 (a) prescribes that rejection may take effect only after the rejection notice has reached the offeror, some scholars argue that Article 20 (a) allows a rejection notice to be withdrawn before or at the same time the offeror receives the rejection notice.

Article 20 (b) essentially refers to the situation where an offer is revoked pursuant to Article 18 of the Contract Law. As discussed, Article 18 allows an offer to be revoked if the revocation is made before the offeree's acceptance notice is sent. Except for situations where the restrictions stipulated in Article 19 apply, an offer becomes null and void when it is effectively revoked. Therefore, an acceptance that is made after the offer is effectively revoked will not constitute acceptance, but rather a new offer. When "after revocation" acceptance constitutes a new offer, the offeree takes the place of the offeror, and acceptance of the new offer falls into the hands of the "former" offeror.

In accordance with Article 20 (c), a lapse of time in accepting an offer may also cause an offer to become null and void and therefore terminated. Article 20 (c) applies where the offer has specified a time limit for acceptance. For purposes of Article 20 (c), the offeree's failure to accept the offer within the allowed time period will be deemed as a rejection of the offer. Note, however, that since China applies the "arrival rule" rather than the "mailbox rule" to acceptances, it is essential that the acceptance reaches the offeror before the expiration day of the offer. The "arrival rule," in comparison with the "mailbox rule," as applied to acceptances will be further discussed later in this chapter.

Article 20 (d) is mainly about "material alteration." Under Article 20, an offer will be null and void if the offeree has materially changed the contents of

---

30   *See* Contract Law, art. 20.

the offer, and such change results in the termination of the offer. The term "material alteration" is defined in Article 30 of the Contract Law as a change in the contract's subject matter, quantity, quality, price or remuneration, time or place or method for performance, liability for breach of contract, or dispute settlement, etc. Hence, a change involving any of the above items contained in an offer would be considered "material," and as a result, the offeree's power of acceptance would be terminated.

2   Acceptance

The concept of acceptance is provided in Article 21 of the Contract Law, which defines acceptance as "a manifestation of the offeree's assent to an offer."[31] As noted, the Contract Law is the first contract legislation in modern China that contains provisions on offer and acceptance—though those two terms were actually used in practice for many years before the Contract Law was adopted. Indeed, though the concepts of both offer and acceptance did not originate in China, the concepts, as provided in the Contract Law, necessarily reflect some Chinese characteristics. First of all, offer and acceptance are premised on the notion that a contract is a mutual agreement. Secondly, acceptance, if valid, results in the conclusion of a contract, no consideration being needed. Thirdly, certain contracts' effectiveness is contingent upon administrative approval after acceptance.

2.1   *Requirements for Acceptance*

Pursuant to Article 21, acceptance basically signifies that the offeree agrees to the terms and conditions contained in the offer and wants to enter into a contract with the offeror accordingly. Article 25 further provides that a contract is concluded at the time acceptance takes effect.[32] Under the Contract Law, however, for an acceptance to be effective, the following three requirements must be met.

The first requirement is "contents in consistence" with the offer, which is called the consistence rule. As provided in Article 30 of the Contract Law, the consistence rule requires that the contents of the acceptance must match the contents of the offer. Thus, an alteration to the contents of an offer might affect the effect of the acceptance. However, in application of the consistence rule,

---

31   *See id.*, art. 21.
32   *See id.*, art. 25.

the Contract Law divides alterations into two categories: material alterations and non-material alterations. According to Article 30, as noted, any alteration to "the contract subject matter, quantity, quality, price or remuneration, time or place or method for performance, liability for breach of contract, or dispute settlement" is a material alteration.[33] All other alterations are non-material.

Under the consistence rule, if the offeree materially alters the contents of the offer, the acceptance shall constitute a new offer. With regard to the consequences of non-material alterations, Article 31 of the Contract Law explicitly provides that, unless the offeror timely rejects the alteration or the offer clearly indicates that the acceptance may not alter the contents of the offer at all, the acceptance shall be deemed valid despite the alteration, and the contents of the contract shall be whatever is contained in the acceptance.[34] Therefore, unlike material alterations, non-material alterations to the offer do not necessarily affect the effectiveness of an acceptance. Put differently, what the consistence rule actually requires is substantial consistence.

The second requirement is the "Arrival Rule." In contrast with the common law system, in which the acceptance of an offer is governed by the "Mailbox Rule," China follows the civil law tradition, pursuant to which acceptance takes effect on arrival. In accordance with Article 26 of the Contract Law, an acceptance becomes effective when notice of the acceptance reaches the offeree. The Contract Law mandates that the acceptance must arrive at the offeror in order for the acceptance to operate. In addition, under Article 22, the acceptance can be made either by a notice or through conduct.

In general, an acceptance should be made by means of notice. In case of notice, the acceptance will have no effect until the acceptance notice reaches the offeror. Acceptance can also be made through conduct under certain circumstances. As provided in Article 26, if there exists a transaction practice or if the offer allows the acceptance to be made through an act or conduct, the performance of such act (e.g., delivery of the goods) will then constitute an acceptance.[35]

Timely arrival of an acceptance notice is an important factor in the application of the "Arrival Rule." Article 23 of the Contract Law makes it a prerequisite for an acceptance to take effect that an acceptance must reach the offeror within the time limit specified in the offer. Furthermore, in accordance with Article 23, if no time limit for acceptance is specified in the offer, the arrival of the acceptance shall be determined in the following ways:

---

33 *See id.*, art. 30.
34 *See id.*, art. 31.
35 *See id.*, art. 26.

(a) If the offer is made orally, the acceptance shall be made promptly unless otherwise agreed upon by the parties; or
(b) It the offer is made in any other form, the acceptance shall arrive within a reasonable period of time.[36]

Often, courts determine what constitutes a reasonable period of time under Article 23 (b) by looking to industrial usages or transaction customs, previous dealings, or the nature of a particular business. In addition, courts consider the parties' methods of communication. Thus, the channel that the parties have used to dispatch the acceptance may become a relevant determinant as to what time period might be deemed reasonable. Further, it has been suggested that, to determine a reasonable time period, courts should take into consideration the length of time that the offeree would normally need to make a sound decision.[37] Moreover, under Article 26, if a contract is concluded in the form of data-telex, the arrival time for the acceptance will be the time when the data-telex enters the system.[38]

Equally important is when the time limit for an acceptance starts to run. Article 24 of the Contract Law provides three ways by which the time period for acceptance is to be calculated. First of all, if an offer is made in the form of a letter or telegram, the time limit for acceptance commences from the date shown on the letter or from the date the telegram is handed in for dispatch. The "date shown on the letter" refers to the time the letter of the offer is dated while the "date for dispatch" means the time the telegram is given to a post office or another office engaged in the telegram business of sending telegrams, which is normally indicated in the official receipt of such office. Secondly, if the letter is not dated, the beginning time of the time limit for an acceptance will be the date as shown on the envelope that contains the offer. And thirdly, if the offer is made by means of instantaneous communications such as by telephone or facsimile, the time limit for an acceptance starts at the moment the offer reaches the offeree, meaning the moment at which the offeree answers the phone or receives the fax.

The third requirement for acceptance is that the acceptance must be made by the offeree to the offeror. This requirement is derived from the definition of the acceptance contained in Article 21 of the Contract Law. Since an acceptance under Article 21 is a manifestation of the offeree's assent to the offer, it must be made by the offeree. Of course, the acceptance may not have to be made by the offeree personally. It may be made by an authorized agent of the

---

36 See id., art. 23.
37 See Wang Liming, *supra* note 3, at 233; *see also* Jiang Ping, *supra* note 8, at 20.
38 See Contract Law, art. 26.

offeree. On the other hand, the acceptance may not necessarily be made by just one offeree. It could be made by several offerees if the offer is made to more than one specified person. If, however, an acceptance is made by a third party—a non-intended offeree—it will be regarded as an offer.

Some contract scholars in China also suggest that the acceptance should comply with the format required by the offer. They argue that, though Article 22 of the Contract Law generally allows acceptances to take the form of notice unless otherwise permitted by business usages or the offer language to be made by conduct, the way a notice is sent to the offeror is subject to the requirements of the offer. For example, if an offer states that the acceptance must be made through telegram, a mailed acceptance of that offer will be deemed unacceptable. Therefore, a failure to follow the format specified in the offer for an acceptance may render the acceptance ineffective.[39]

From a general reading of the Contract Law, it is questionable whether an acceptance can be implied. The Contract Law, while defining acceptance as "a manifestation of the offeree's assent to the offer," is unclear as to whether such manifestation can be inferred from conduct (i.e., active or passive acts of the offeree). More precisely, there is no readily available answer to the question of whether an offeree's acceptance of an offer can be manifested by silence. Interestingly, in its "Opinions (Provisional) on the Questions Concerning Implementation of the General Principles of Civil Law of People's Republic of China," the SPC divided silence in the context of civil conduct into act-attached silence and non-act silence.

According Article 66 of the SPC Opinions, when one party makes certain claims of civil rights to the other party, and the other party does not express acceptance through either language or words but nevertheless takes certain acts in acknowledgement of the claims, acceptance can be implied. However, the silence attendant to that party's inaction may be deemed to constitute implied acceptance only if such is provided by the law or agreed upon by the parties.[40] Therefore, according to the SPC, non-act silence generally signifies neither consent nor acceptance.

Acceptance by silence was expressly excluded from the early drafts of the Contract Law. For example, under Article 21 (b) of the Draft Contract Law that was published in August 1998 for commenting by the general public, acceptance had to be made expressly; silence or inaction could not constitute

---

39 See Wang Liming, *supra* note 3, at 236–38.
40 See the SPC, Opinions (Provisional) on the Questions Concerning Implementation of the General Principles of Civil Law of the People's Republic of China (1988).

acceptance. This provision was deleted from the final draft of the Contract Law due to concerns that it might not be practical to eliminate the possibility of silence functioning as acceptance.[41] As a result, Article 22 of the Contract Law provides that acceptance may be made in the form of notice or by way of act. In judicial practice, the people's courts generally recognize acceptance by silence if it can be proved that such form of acceptance was specifically agreed to by the parties or is allowed by business usages.[42]

2.2   Withdrawal of Acceptance

Once again, the "mailbox" rule does not apply in China under the Contract Law. Since an acceptance does not become effective until it reaches the offeror, it follows that an acceptance may be withdrawn before such arrival. Pursuant to Article 27 of the Contract Law, withdrawal of acceptances is permitted and should be made through the means of notice. However, Article 27 prescribes that a withdrawal notice must reach the offeror before or at the same time as the acceptance notice reaches the offeror in order for a withdrawal of an acceptance to be valid.[43]

Therefore, the withdrawal of an acceptance, in accordance with Article 27, is effective under either of the following two circumstances: (a) the withdrawal notice reaches the offeror before the acceptance arrives, or (b) both the withdrawal notice and the acceptance notice reach the offoror at the same time. In both cases, time is the critical factor, and one that is a matter of burden of proof. Specifically, when circumstance (b) arises, the party claiming an effective withdrawal must prove that the withdrawal notice arrived at the offeror simultaneously with the acceptance's arrival.

2.3   Late Acceptance

As noted, under Article 20 (c) of the Contract Law, an offer may become void if it is not accepted within the time limit specified in the offer. There are two situations wherein no acceptance is made before the time for acceptance expires. One situation is that the offeree does not agree to the terms and conditions in the offer and has no desire to enter into a contract with the offeror. In this situation, there will never be an acceptance. The other situation is that, for whatever reasons, acceptance is not made until after the expiration of the time

---

41   There are several situations in which an acceptance might be made by silence: (1) agreed upon by the parties in advance; (2) previous dealings or transaction customs; (3) provided by laws.
42   See Economic Law Chamber of the SPC, Explanation, *supra* note 23, at 131–35.
43   See Contract Law, art. 27.

required for acceptance. The acceptance that is made after the fixed time for acceptance is commonly labeled as "late acceptance."

In contract theory, when an acceptance is made late there are two different approaches to the lateness of the acceptance. Pursuant to the traditional approach, the late acceptance constitutes a new offer that requires an acceptance from the offeror. The modern approach takes a different view and allows the offeror to decide the fate of the acceptance. Under the modern approach, it is up to the offeror to decide whether a late acceptance may be treated as a valid acceptance. The Contract Law follows the "up-to-offeror" approach, but requires that notice be timely made to the offeree. Under Article 28, if the offeree accepts the offer outside the time limit for acceptance, the acceptance shall be a new offer unless the offeror promptly notifies the offeree that the acceptance is effective.[44]

The effect of Article 28 is that late acceptance has no effect for purposes of contract-making unless the offeror accepts the late acceptance and timely informs the offeree of the effectiveness of the acceptance. In this respect, the late acceptance is still regarded as acceptance if so treated by the offeror. On the other hand, if the offeror chooses not to act (i.e., to send a notice to the offeree), the late acceptance becomes a new offer, which the offeror may decide whether to accept within a reasonable period of time.

Article 28 of the Contract Law grants the offeror the option to treat late acceptance as either timely made and thus effective, or as a new offer.[45] Given Article 28's notice requirement, it seems obvious that an offeror's silence with respect to a late acceptance does not lead to the formation of a contract—even though it might be unclear to the offeree that the acceptance was late. Note that Article 28 focuses on when acceptance is made, not the time at which acceptance is received. Thus, acceptance is late if it is made after the lapse of the fixed time.

2.4   *Late Arrival of Acceptance*

Again, under the "Arrival Rule" provided in the Contract Law, an acceptance does not take effect until it arrives at the offeror. An acceptance that is late may occur in two different situations: an acceptance that is made late and an acceptance that arrives late. The late arrival of an acceptance refers to the situation wherein the acceptance was made within the time limit, but it reached the offeror after the acceptance deadline. Unlike late acceptance, the late arrival of

---

44   *See* Contract Law, art. 28.
45   *See* Economic Law Chamber of the SPC, Explanation, *supra* note 23, at 242.

an acceptance creates a "half good and half bad" dilemma. In many cases, the late arrival of an acceptance is caused by a problem during the transmission. Thus, it would appear to be unfair to handle late arrival the same way as late acceptance.

The Contract Law recognizes the difference between late acceptance and late arrival of acceptance. It prescribes that an acceptance arriving late is presumably effective unless the offeror clearly indicates otherwise. Under Article 29, if the offeree dispatches the acceptance within the time limit and under normal circumstances the acceptance would reach the offeror within that time limit—but due to other reasons the acceptance arrives beyond the time limit—the acceptance shall be effective unless the offeror promptly informs the offeree that the acceptance is not acceptable because it exceeds the time allowed. [46] Thus, an acceptance that was timely sent but arrived late will generally be deemed effective absent the offeror's prompt rejection.

Questions remain as to what constitutes "normal circumstances" and "other reasons" for the delay in the arrival of acceptance under Article 29. As a practical matter, a general notion embraced in the people's courts is that "normal circumstances" are those that are commonly accepted pursuant to the customs or usages of business dealings or of particular industries. Thus, in actual cases, the determination of what constitutes "normal circumstances" largely depends on evidence proving customs or usages that support a timely arrival of acceptance. With regard to "other reasons," the term is construed differently from case to case, but is generally interpreted as referring to things that are not the offeree's fault and that usually would not happen.[47]

2.5   *Acceptance and Conclusion of Contract*

Conclusion of a contract is viewed in China as a prerequisite to (a) the establishment, modification, or termination of a contractual relationship between the parties involved, (b) the ascertainment of a contract's effectiveness, and (c) the determination of contractual liability.[48] Under Article 25 of the Contract Law, a contract is concluded when acceptance becomes effective. Article 25 states that the conclusion of a contract is dependent upon the effectiveness of the acceptance.

For purposes of the Contract Law, the conclusion of a contract means that the parties have reached a mutual assent that they will be bound by the terms

---

46   *See* Contract Law, art. 29.
47   *See* Economic Law Chamber of the SPC, Explanation, *supra* note 23, at 149.
48   *See* Second Civil Division of the SPC, Adjudication Guide of Contract Cases 5 (Law Press 2014).

and conditions agreed to in the contract. In addition, the conclusion of the contract signifies the institution of the parties' respective contractual rights and obligations. There are two factors that are important to the effectiveness of acceptance.

This first factor is timing. Timing is important because it determines when the contract is made or at what point the contract is formed. The Contract Law has several provisions that govern the timing of a contract. The general rule is set forth at Article 26 of the Contract Law, which prescribes that formation of a contract is subject to the "arrival" rule. Article 32 further provides that written contracts are concluded at the time both parties sign or affix a seal on the contract.[49] Although Article 32 does not specify whether the signature or the seal controls if the two are made at different times, the people's courts normally follow the doctrine of "first in time." Moreover, under Article 33, if a contract is concluded in the form of a letter or data-telex, etc., a sending party may request that the receiving party sign a letter of confirmation.[50] Under this circumstance, the contract is concluded when the confirmation letter is signed.

The second factor is the location of the contract's conclusion (i.e., the place of contract). The Contract Law more specifically incorporates this factor because the place where a contract is made is often an essential element in determinations of jurisdiction as well as the law governing contractual disputes. The general rule, set forth at Article 34 of the Contract Law, is that acceptance takes effect where the contract was concluded. Since an acceptance normally only becomes effective upon arrival, the place where the acceptance is received is considered to be the place of the contract.

There are two exceptions, set forth in sub-provisions of Article 34, to the general rule concerning the place of a contract. First, the place of a data-telex contract is the main business place of the recipient—if there is no main business place, however, the recipient's habitual residence is the place of such a contract. Second, if the parties have agreed to a certain place of the contract, that choice controls.[51]

In accordance with Article 35, if a contract is written, the contract is concluded at the place where both parties sign or affix a seal to it.[52] In many cases,

---

49 *See* Contract Law, art. 32.
50 *See id.*, art. 33.
51 *See id.*, art. 34.
52 Note that the Contract does not define the terms "main business place" or "habitual residence." In the Civil Code (1986), the term "domicile," rather than "main business place," is used for business entities. Under Article 39 of the 1986 Civil Code, the domicile of a business entity (generally termed a legal person) is the place where the entity's main administrative office is located. It is unclear whether the entity's main administrative office

however, the parties sign or affix a seal to a contract at different locations. To deal with this issue, the SPC in its 2009 Contract Law Interpretations adopted a special rule of conflict. Under Article 4 of the Interpretations, when a contract is concluded in writing and specifies the place of the contract, if the place of conclusion that was contractually agreed upon is different than the place where the contract was signed and/or sealed, the former is the place of the contract. If a written contract does not specify the place of its formation, and the parties sign or seal the contract in different places, the place of the contract is the place where the contract was last signed or sealed.[53]

Article 34 is regarded as a "general" provision among the Contract Law provisions governing the location of contracts. "General" in this context means that the provision applies by default; if Article 34 conflicts with any other provision in the Contract Law or in another statute, however, that other provision controls. The notion underlying this framework is that special provisions supersede general provisions unless the law provides otherwise.

3   Conclusion and Effectiveness of Contracts

A common view in contract theory is that effective acceptance of an offer results in a contract.[54] It follows under this view that a contract takes effect upon its conclusion. A different view prevails in China, however. In China, the conclusion of a contract and the effectiveness of a contract are treated as distinct matters, and the fact that a contract is concluded does not necessarily mean that it is effective. From the viewpoint of Chinese contract scholars, a contract being effective means that the contract meets all legal requirements and becomes legally binding, while a contract being concluded merely indicates that the parties have reached an agreement.[55]

---

can constitute the main business place. As far as a citizen (natural person) is concerned, Article 15 of the 1986 Civil Code provides that the domicile of a citizen shall be the place where his residence is registered, and if his habitual residence differs from his domicile, his habitual residence shall be regarded as his domicile. According to the Supreme Court's interpretation, the habitual residence of a citizen is the place where he has lived consecutively for more than one year after being away from his domicile. *See* the SPC's Opinions (Provisional) on Several Matters Concerning Implementation and Application of the General Principles of Civil Law of China, art. 9 (1988).

53   *See* the SPC, 2009 Contract Interpretations, art. 4.
54   *See* Jeff Ferriell, Understanding Contracts 189 (2nd ed., 2009).
55   *See* Liming, *supra* note 3, at 500–09.

Although contracts generally take effect upon their conclusions, in many cases contracts' effectiveness depends on other factors (e.g., approval). The Contract Law contains separate provisions for the conclusion of a contract and the effectiveness of a contract, respectively. Chapter 3 of the Contract Law governs contract conclusion while Chapter 4 deals with contract effectiveness.

The main provision regarding contract conclusion in the Contract Law is Article 44. Under Article 44, a contract takes effect upon its conclusion. If a contract, pursuant to law or administrative regulations, must be approved or registered in order to be effective, the contract will not be effective until all approval or registration requirements are met, even if the contract is legally concluded. As noted in Chapter 3, certain contracts in China require approval or registration in order to take effect. In addition, even if a contract is not subject to approval or registration requirements, the contract will not be effective if it is fails to satisfy the criteria for effectiveness.

The effectiveness of a contract is a matter of compliance. Pursuant to Article 55 of the 1986 Civil Code, a civil legal act must meet the following standards in order to be effective: (a) the person doing the act must have the relevant capacity for civil conduct, (b) his or her manifestation of intention must be genuine, and (c) the act must not violate the law or the public interest.[56] A contract is classified in China as a civil legal act, and must therefore comply with these standards in order to become effective and binding.

Given the difference between contract conclusion and contract effectiveness, in China a contract, in terms of validity, can be characterized as valid, voidable, or effect-to-be-determined.[57] As will be discussed in more detail in Chapter 6 of the book, an effect-to-be-determined contract is typically a contract that, though already concluded, is subject to a further determination of its effectiveness. Under the Contract Law, the effectiveness of a contract is furthermore affected by the conditions in the contract upon which the parties have agreed.

It should be noted that Chinese law and administrative regulations impose approval and registration requirements in two different ways. In some cases, approval or registration is required in order for a concluded contract to become effective. In other cases, registration is required but is not a prerequisite for the contract being effective. According to the SPC's 2009 Contract Law

---

56   *See* 1986 Civil Code, art. 55.
57   An effect-to-be-determined contract is a contract that has been concluded but that may not be effective—mainly because the party or parties to the contract lack capacity. The situations in which a contract is deemed valid, void, voidable, or effect-to-be-determined will be discussed in detail in Chapter 7.

Interpretations, in the former cases, the people's court will hold a contract to be ineffective if the party obligated under the contract to obtain approval or registration before the end of court arguments during the trial in the first instance fails to do so. In the latter cases, a failure to obtain registration does not affect the effectiveness of the contract, but the ownership of the subject matter of the contract or other property rights involved may not be transferred absent the required registration.[58]

An example is a change in the right of real property. Under Article 9 of the Property Law, the creation, change, transfer or elimination of a real property right must be registered in order to become effective.[59] Article 15 of the Property Law provides that contract entered into by the parties concerning creation, modification, transfer or elimination of the right of a real property shall become effective upon the conclusion of the contract unless otherwise provided by the law.[60] But it is further provided in Article 15 that the contract will remain effective whether or not a registration is made.[61] Thus, although a change in the real property right requires both a contract and a registration, the effectiveness of the contract has nothing to do with the registration.

4   Formality of Contracts

Contract formality is about how a contract should be formed. The Contract Law takes a more flexible approach to the formality requirement than China's prior contract laws.[62] The underlying notion is that a contract is an agreement between the parties, and it is therefore up to the parties to—within the boundaries of statutory requirements—choose the format they see fit for the contract. The Contract Law reflects the belief that flexibility in contract formality requirements has such benefits as (a) better serving the parties' needs in different transactions, (b) convenience, and (c) facilitating quick adaptation to new technological developments.

---

58   *See* the SPC, 2009 Contract Law Interpretations, art. 9.
59   See the Property Law of China, adopted in 2007, art. 9.
60   See *id.*, art. 15.
61   See *id.*
62   All previous contract legislation in China emphasized the need for contracts to be in writing, and made a writing a general requirement for every contract, with the exception of those made and executed instantly. For example, under Article 3 of the Economic Contract Law, an economic contract, if not made and executed instantly, must be in writing. The rigid writing requirement is said to comport with the idea that a contract is a tool to implement the State economic plan.

There are two points that are worth noting in regard to formality. First, there is no equivalent in Chinese contract legislation to the statute of frauds, pertaining to the writing requirement, in a country like the United States. In China, if a writing is required for a particular type of contract, that requirement will be set forth in a specific provision of the law. Second, although contract formality requirements under the Contract Law are less restrictive than they used to be, it is still generally preferred, and in some cases is required, that contracts be in writing. This practice is consistent with China's reservation made to Article 11 of the United Nations Convention on Contracts for the International Sale of Goods (CISG). Under Article 11 of the CISG, a writing is not required for contracts for sale of goods.[63]

Article 10 of the Contract Law governs the formality of contracts. Under Article 10, a contract may be made in writing, orally, or in other forms. Article 10 further provides that a contract must be in writing if laws or administrative regulations mandate that it be so.[64] There are certain contracts for which the law and administrative regulations contain specific writing requirements. An example is a real estate contract. Under Article 40 of the Law of the Urban Real Estate Management, the transfer of real estate requires a written contract that is signed by the parties.[65] Another example is a contract for the transfer of technology, for which writings are also required. In addition to the foregoing, a contract must be in writing if the parties agree that it will take a written form.

A question often raised concerning contract formality is the legal effect of formality. To be more precise, the question is whether noncompliance with formality requirements renders a contract void. Scholars in China are divided in their views surrounding this question. The first view is called the "effect approach." This approach regards formality as a mandatory requirement for a contract to be valid—unless the law contains optional language such as "may" or "can" in respect to the writing requirement. Therefore, under the "effect approach," a failure to follow the writing requirement necessarily makes a contract void.[66]

The second view is referred to as the "conclusion doctrine." Pursuant to this approach, formality affects the conclusion of a contract. The conclusion

---

63 Article 11 of the CISG provides that a contract of sale need not be concluded in or evidenced by a writing and is not subject to any other requirements as to form. Such a contract may be proved by any means, such as by witnesses.
64 *See* Contract Law, art. 10.
65 *See* Law of Urban Real Estate Management of China, art. 40 (adopted July 5, 1994, amended Aug. 30, 2007).
66 *See generally* Wang Liming, *supra* note 3, at 464–69.

doctrine considers formality to be a prerequisite for a contract. Under this doctrine, formation of a contract requires an agreement of the parties, and also that the agreement be manifested in certain forms if required to be done so by law. If a writing is required, the agreement must be shown on the paper. Otherwise, no contract exists, because the law does not recognize contracts that do not conform with applicable writing requirements.[67]

The third view is called the "evidentiary theory." Under this theory, the formality of a contract has nothing or little to do with either the conclusion or the effect of the contract, but rather serves mainly as evidence to prove the existence of the contract. The writing requirement affects the contract only to the extent that the existence of the contract or the existence of certain contents of the contract is disputed. The major difference between the evidentiary theory and the conclusion doctrine is that a violation of the writing requirement does not necessarily defeat the conclusion of a contract under the former theory, but it does under the latter theory.[68]

The Contract Law seems to have followed the "evidentiary theory." First, the Contract Law has departed from previous contract legislations by not making contract formalities mandatory. Second, the Contract Law allows parties to make decisions as to whether a contract for which a writing is not required by law shall be made in writing. Third, even if a writing is required for a contract either by law or by the parties, the transaction covered by the contract might be affected but the conclusion of the contract under certain circumstances would remain intact. Fourth, the Contract Law does not make a writing an element for the determination of a contract's effectiveness, whether or not a writing is required for a particular contract.

An important exception to the writing requirement is partial performance. Under Article 36 of the Contract Law, a contract, which is required to be in writing by laws or administrative regulations or by the parties' agreement, is formed—despite not being in writing—if one party has performed its principal obligation and the other party has accepted that performance.[69] Keep in mind that, to trigger this exception to the writing requirement, the performance must involve the principal obligation of the contract.

A similar provision is Article 37, which deals with written contracts without signatures or seals. Under Article 32 of the Contract Law, as noted, a written contract requires the signatures or seals of the parties in order to be formed. However, pursuant to Article 37, a written contract is formed before the signatures

---

67 See id.
68 See id.
69 See Contract Law, art. 36.

or seals are affixed if one party has performed the principal obligation of the contract and the other party has received that performance.[70] The following case is emblematic of when contracts are held enforceable under Article 37.

Zheng Dejun v. Beijing Dongxu Property Management Co. Ltd. and Beijing Zongji Real Estate Development Co. Inc.

Beijing Tongzhou District People's Court[71]

Defendant Dongxu Property Management (Dongxu) was entrusted by Defendant Zhongji Real Estate Development (Zhongji) to manage real property, named Huaxing Residence Quarter, that was developed by Zhongji. Dongxu's management was under the supervision of New Hua Lian Co. (New Hualian), a subsidiary of Zhongji.

Zhongji had three old boilers located in the Huaxing Residence Quarter. In 2001, Zhongji wanted to sell the three boilers and asked New Hualian to find a buyer. Mr. Li Zijing, the Vice President of New Hualian, who was in charge of supervising Dongxu's work, tasked Dongxu with identifying a buyer.

In an attempt to sell the boilers, Mr. Zhang Chenghua, a manager at Dongxu, contacted Mr. Li Zhenzhou, who used to work with Dongxu, and asked Li Zhenzhou to help find a buyer. Li Zhenzhou then contacted Zong Shaozeng and Gao Lianyong, who identified the Plaintiff as a potential buyer. On the Plaintiff's request, Zong and Gao, through Li Zhenzhou, went to Dongxu to meet with Zhang Chenghua. After initial negotiations, they agreed that the price of the boilers would be RMB 80,000 each. Zhang Chenghua then drafted an agreement for the boilers' transfer. Thereafter, Zhang Chenghua told Zong and Gao to wait for his further notice because he would have to report the sale to Li Zijing for approval.

On June 24, Zong, Gao and Li Zhenzhou went to New Hualian again to talk to Li Zijing. Upon Li Zijing's suggestion, a clause concerning the buyer's responsibility for disassembling the boilers was added to the Boilers Transfer Agreement and the purchase price remained unchanged. The Agreement was then fashioned into two printed copies. However, the signing party for the Plaintiff was Zong Shaozeng, instead of the Plaintiff. After the agreement was affixed with Dongxu's official seal, Zong and Gao took it to the Plaintiff. Upon receiving the agreement, the Plaintiff crossed out the name of Zong Shaozeng and wrote down his own name instead.

By the end of June, Li Zhenzhou informed Zong that Li Zhijing thought the purchase price was too low and wanted to renegotiate with Zong and Gao. Zong responded that the parties had signed the agreement and should go ahead with the agreement. During the meeting with Li Jingzhou, however, Li Jingzhou asserted that the agreement was invalid because the boilers belonged to Zhongji, not Dongxu, and also because the buyer's name was changed. Zong and Gao explained that the Plaintiff was the actual buyer. After further negotiations, the parties orally agreed that the Plaintiff would purchase the three boilers at a total price of RMB 260,000—RMB 20,000 more than originally agreed.

---

70   As noted, under Article 32 of the Contract Law, a written contract is concluded when both parties sign or affix a seal on it. Article 37 provides that a contract, which is made in writing, shall be concluded if one party has performed its principal obligation and the other party has received that performance before the contract is signed or the seal is affixed.

71   This case was reported in First Civil Division of Beijing High People's Court, A Precise Analysis of Beijing Civil Cases, 192–96 (Law Press 2003).

On July 1, Zong and Gao were invited to Li Zhijing's office to sign the revised agreement. Li Zhijing showed them the written agreement, which indicated that Zhongji was the seller and the Plaintiff the buyer, and that the purchase price was RMB 260,000. Li Zhijing told Zong and Gao that the agreement needed the signature of the company officers, but assured Zong and Gao that the contents of the agreement would not be changed. Li Zhijing then asked Zong and Gao to make a payment and said that the signed agreement would be made available to the buyer when the payment was made. On July 3, the Plaintiff had RMB 260,000 delivered to Li Zhenzhou, for which an acknowledgement bearing Zhongji's official seal was issued to the Plaintiff, and RMB 260,000 was deposited into New Hualian's bank account. On the same day, the Plaintiff dispatched his workers to start disassembling the boilers, and in the meantime, Dongxu had the documents of all three boilers handed over to the Plaintiff.

On July 5, Dongxu told the Plaintiff that Zhongji refused to sell the boilers to him. As a result, Dongxu prevented the Plaintiff from taking away the disassembled boilers. The Plaintiff then brought a lawsuit against the Defendants, asking the court to order the Defendants to continue performing and to pay the Plaintiff for economic damages in the amount of RMB 6,000. In addition, the Plaintiff asked the Defendant to refund him RMB 20,000 on the basis of the original agreement that had a purchase price of RMB 240,000.

Defendant Dongxu argued that the boilers in question were owned by Zhongji, and that, though Zhongji asked Dongxu to find it a buyer, it had not entrusted Dongxu with responsibility to sign the agreement with the Plaintiff on Zhongji's behalf. Defendant Dongxu further argued that the final agreement for purchase of the boilers was entered between Zhongji and the Plaintiff, and therefore, the previous agreement between Dongxu and the Plaintiff was void. In addition, Defendant Dongxu asserted that the Plaintiff had no cause of action against Dongxu since the Plaintiff remitted the purchase money directly to Zhangji.

Defendant Zhongji argued that it never endowed Dongxu with authority to sell the boilers. To the contrary, Zhongji maintained that it only asked Dongxu to help find a buyer, and there was no contractual relationship between Zhongji and the Plaintiff because Zhongji did not sign any agreement with the Plaintiff. Defendant Zhongji also stated that it did not receive the Plaintiff's payment and that the payment was kept in the account of New Hualian, who had no knowledge about the purchase. Defendant Zhongji then asserted that the acknowledgement of the receipt of the Plaintiff's payment issued by New Hualian was not Zhongji's official receipt.

The district court found that Li Zijing of New Hualian represented Zhongji in negotiating the purchase agreement with Zong and Cao, drafted and modified certain terms of the agreement, and, in particular, explicitly told the Plaintiff during the last negotiation to obtain the signed agreement upon payment of the purchase price. The district court then held that, though Li Zijing may have exceeded his "agency power" as authorized by Zhongji, he clearly had "apparent authority" to deal with the Plaintiff. With regard to the agreement, the district court found that Zhongji did not officially sign a written agreement with the Plaintiff, but did indeed, through New Hualian, receive the Plaintiff's payment for the boilers. The district court held that making a payment constitutes major performance in a sale contract, and therefore concluded that, because of the payment that Zhongji acknowledged, a valid agreement between the parties should be deemed to have existed.

Pursuant to Article 37 of the Contract Law, the district court denied Zhongji's argument that there existed no contractual relationship between Zhongji and the Plaintiff, and entered a judgment for the Plaintiff.

In *Zheng Dejun*, the rationale that the court employed in rendering its judgment was that as the buyer, the Plaintiff performed his principal obligation by making the payment in full, and as the seller Zhongji accepted the payment.

Despite the lack of a written agreement between the Plaintiff and Zhongji, Zhongji's receipt of the payment explicitly indicated Zhongji's knowledge of the sale and manifested Zhongji intention to sell the boilers to the Plaintiff.

As far as writings are concerned, the word writing is defined in Article 11 of the Contract Law as a form that can visibly show the described contents of the contract, such as a written contractual agreement, letters, and data-telex (including telegram, telex, fax, EDI—electronic data interchange, and e-mails).[72] Again, written contracts are generally required to bear the signatures of the parties or to have affixed seals. In China, the "seal" (commonly called the "chop") is an official ID of entities registered to do business or other activities. It is also considered to be the official signature of an entity or corporation in its business dealings.

Although Article 32 allows parties to sign or affix official seals on contracts, the seals are normally heavier than the signatures. Moreover, there has been a debate over whether Article 32 is optional. In other words, the debate questions whether parties may alter the Article 32 requirement. In one case—where a contract was signed by one party without the party's official seal and was affixed with the official seal of the other party without the other party's signature—the SPC affirmed the lower court decisions upholding the effectiveness of the contract. According to the SPC, since Article 32 includes the language "to sign or to affix a seal," either a signature or a seal satisfied the formality requirement.[73] The SPC made clear that, for purposes of Article 32 of the Contract Law, "to sign or to affix a seal" does not mean "to sign and to affix."[74]

In another case, parties provided in their contract that the contract would take effect upon the "signatures、seals of the parties," and one party signed the contract but did not affix its official seals on it. When the parties disputed the contract's effectiveness, the lower court held that the contract was effective because either signature or seal were sufficient to make the contract effective under Article 32 of the Contract Law. The SPC, however, disagreed. In its reversal, the SPC held that, since the "signatures" and "seals" were separated by a "pause" mark, the two words were in a conjunctive relation, and thus both were required in order for the contract to become effective. The SPC's opinion in this case suggests that Article 32 is mandatory but is a minimum requirement to which parties may add by agreement.

---

72   *See* Contract Law, art. 11.
73   *See Dayou Ke La Si Furniture Mall v. Beijing Mu Dan Yuan Apartments Co. Ltd.*, SPC, Min Shen Zi No. 27 (2013), http://www.court.gov.cn/wenshu/xiangqing-605.html.
74   *See id.*

A contract under Article 10 of the Contract Law can be made in forms other than orally or in writing. However, Article 10 does not specify what constitute the other acceptable forms of contracts. Some scholars suggest that other forms of contracts include notary public, verification, approval, as well as registration.[75] In the following case, the Beijing No.1 Intermediate People's Court applied Articles 10 and 11 of the Contract Law in its determination of the formality of an Internet service agreement.

Lai Yun Peng v. Beijing Stone Lifang Information Company, Inc.

Beijing No. 1 Intermediate People's Court[76]

Plaintiff Lai Yun Peng, twenty-seven years old, a resident of Heping District, Tian Jin. Defendant Beijing Stone, an information service corporation located in Haidian District, Beijing. The Plaintiff sued the defendant for specific performance of service for a 50 MB online free mailbox.

On April 22, 2001, the Plaintiff registered as a member of the Defendant-owned "Sina.com" through the Internet, and chose to use the "free mail" service provided by "Sina.com." When providing this service, "Sina.com" promised to offer a "free mailbox" with 50 MB capacity to a registered customer. On the date when the Plaintiff made the registration, he received from "Sina.com" an auto-reply message confirming his successful registration and eligibility to use the 50 MB free mailbox. During the use of the mailbox, "Sina.com" never charged any fees for the e-mails. The daily information services provided by "Sina.com" also included a large amount of commercial information, and when browsing information or sending personal emails, an end-user often interacted with auto pop-up commercials. The end-user could decide whether to read the commercials.

On August 2 and September 13, 2001, "Sina.com" sent a notice to all free mailbox users on the web, indicating that from September 16, 2001, the capacity of the free mailboxes would be adjusted and only 5 MB free mailbox service would be provided free of charge. The adjusted service was effective on September 16, and as a result the 50 MB free mailbox service was reduced to 5 MB.

The Plaintiff brought this lawsuit against the defendant, claiming that the defendant promised to provide 50 MB of free mailbox service, and the change of service to abruptly reduce the capacity of the mailbox from 50 MB to 5 MB without an agreement from all users constituted a breach of contract. The Plaintiff argued that although the service appeared to be free, it was actually not free because when the user sent emails from the mailbox, the commercial advertisement placed by defendant was always attached to the mails. The Plaintiff asked the trial court to order defendant to continue providing 50 MB free mailbox service as it promised.

To rebut, the Defendant asserted that "Sina.com" provided service to its users according to the service agreement. The full contents of the agreement were made available to each mailbox user when each user registered his or her membership. The user could become a member and start using the free mailbox only after the user clicked "I agree" in the space at the end of the agreement. In the agreement, it was clearly provided that "Sina.com" reserved the right to make necessary adjustments to the articles of the agreement, and that the Defendant was allowed to

---

75 *See* Jiang Ping, *supra* note 8, at 10–11.
76 This case was published as a distinctive case by the Supreme People's Court on March 31, 2003. It is also available at http://www.court.gov.cn/popular/20030033100082.htm.

change and even suspend the service. On that ground, the Defendant asked the trial court to dismiss the Plaintiff's claim, arguing that the adjustment made to the capacity of the free mailbox was not a breach of contract.

The trial court found that there were fifteen articles in the "Service Agreement of Sina.com Beijing Gateway," which contained such contents as the right to provide the service, the status of the web operator, the services to be provided, change of and amendment to the service agreement, as well as users' conduct rules. The provision of "confirmation and acceptance" read: "Sina.com has the right to amend the terms for services if necessary, and whenever a change is to be made, a notice shall be made on the important page of Sina.com's website. If a user disagrees with the changed terms, it may cancel the services. If, however, the user continues to use the mailbox after the change, the user shall be regarded to have accepted the changed terms. In addition, Sina.com reserves the right to amend or suspend the services at any time without bearing any responsibility for any user or third party."

The trial court held that the "Service Agreement of Sina.com Beijing Gateway" was a promise to offer information services to customers and the agreement set forth the rights and obligations of Sina.com in providing such services. Therefore, the agreement was actually an information services contract in the form of data-telex. Under Article 10(a) of the Contract Law, a contract may be concluded in writing, orally, or in other forms. Article 11 provides that the written form is the form that visibly shows the described contents, such as a written agreement, letter, or data-telex (including telegram, telex, fax, EDI, and e-mails). The trial court concluded that a contract between the Plaintiff and the Defendant for the use of the free mailbox was concluded when the Plaintiff clicked "I agree" at the bottom of the contents of the online agreement.

In reaching its conclusion, the trial court was of the opinion that, under the registration procedure provided by the Defendant for subscribing to the free mailbox membership, an applicant could complete the registration only after the applicant agreed to the terms of the services. When registering, the Plaintiff followed this procedure and chose "I agree." It was therefore reasonable to infer that the Plaintiff was aware of the contents of the agreement. The Plaintiff voluntarily clicked " I agree," which indicated that the Plaintiff was willing to be bound by the provisions of the agreement. Since the mailbox was a service provided to the Plaintiff free of charge, the Defendant, when offering the service, had the right to explain how such service was to be provided and to make certain reservations in order to maintain its business interests. In addition, the Defendant could make reasonable changes to the services by giving notice or according to the agreed terms if the changes did not violate mandatory rules of the law.

The trial court further held that, under the agreed terms of the agreement for the free mailbox between the Plaintiff and the Defendant, Sina.com could attach commercials to the Plaintiff's personal web-page, but this could not create a right-and-obligation relationship corresponding to the service for the use of the free mailbox. When offering the free mailbox to the Plaintiff, the Defendant did not deceive the Plaintiff. The Defendant did not conceal anything from the Plaintiff, nor did the Defendant impose on the Plaintiff any obligation or liability. Therefore, the agreement between the Plaintiff and the Defendant concerning the free mailbox services was valid. Under the provisions of the agreement, the Defendant made changes to the contents of the services without violating any regulations or law and with proper notice. Such changes did not constitute a breach of contract.

On November 15, 2001, the trial court entered judgment in favor of the Defendant, and dismissed the Plaintiff's claim. The Plaintiff appealed on the ground that the trial court erred in its determination of the facts because the service agreement was an invalid standard contract. The appellate court agreed that the service agreement in question was provided by the Defendant online, and was a standard contract because it was pre-made by one party and could be used repeatedly. The court further found that, for the information service on the Internet, the service provider and user communicated through the website. The use of a standard online contract, under which a right-and-obligation relationship is created between users and the provider, the court held, is not a violation of the law. Such a standard contract is valid as long as the agreed terms are not prohibited by the law. In the instant case, the court concluded, to invalidate the Service Agreement, the Plaintiff had to prove that the agreement (a) caused damage to the State, collective, or another party's interest, (b) harmed the social and public interest, or (c) exempted the Defendant from the liabilities, aggregated the liabilities of the Plaintiff, or deprived the Plaintiff of his major rights. Since the Plaintiff failed to provide any evidence in this regard, the agreement was legally binding on the parties.

The appellate court held that, since the free mailbox was a free service unilaterally provided by the Defendant, the Defendant had the right to make reasonable changes to the service according to the provisions of the agreement. When the free mailbox was adjusted from 50 MB to 5 MB, the Defendant fulfilled its obligations of explanation and notice set forth in the agreement by making an announcement about the change on its web page. Therefore, the Defendant's conduct was valid and there was no breach of contract. On this ground, Plaintiff's claim must be denied. The judgment from the trial court is affirmed.

What should be mentioned here in particular is the confirmation letter. There is no doubt that a confirmation letter is a type of writing. Under Article 33 of the Contract Law, however, a confirmation letter generally applies to cases where a contract is made through letters or EDI, and the parties request to sign the letter of confirmation before the contract is concluded. Interestingly, the language of Article 33 has generated debates among Chinese contract scholars over the legal effect of confirmation letters. The debates mainly center on whether a letter of confirmation constitutes a special condition for a contract to be concluded that is attached to the acceptance or is just part of the acceptance.[77] Nevertheless, scholars agree that a confirmation letter takes place in the stage of acceptance and may only be requested before the contract is concluded.[78]

A development concerning contract forms that occurred after the enactment of the Contract Law was the adoption of the Law of Electronic Signature. Promulgated on August 28, 2004 and taking effect on April 1, 2005, the Electronic Signature Law was promulgated to regulate signatory activities on the Internet and to establish the legal effect of electronic signatures as to contracts as well as other civil documents (excluding documents involving personal relations—such as marriage, adoption, and succession; transfer of real estate; and public utility services). Under the Electronic Signature Law, an electronic telex that could tangibly represent the contents it contains and could be obtained any time for review and use shall be deemed as a writing that meets all legal requirements.[79] In addition, an electronic telex shall be regarded as an

---

77 See Wang Liming, *supra* note 3, at 243–46.
78 See Economic Law Chamber of the SPC, Explanation, *supra* note 23, at 158–59.
79 See Law of Electronic Signature of the People's Republic of China, art. 4.

original if it could effectively represent the contents it contains, could be obtained any time for review and use, and could reliably ensure that its contents remain intact and unaltered from the time it is formed.[80]

In addition, the SPC has taken a more liberal approach to written contracts for the sale of goods. In its 2012 Contract Law Interpretations, the SPC instructed the people's courts to determine whether a sales contract was formed on the basis of the parties' transaction methods and business dealings—as well as other relevant evidence in cases where there was no written contract between the parties but one party claimed the existence of the contractual relationship on the basis of a document such as a delivery slip, receiving note, payment statement, or receipt.[81]

According the SPC, if in a case involving the sale of goods, a written document such as a letter of reconciliation confirmation or a letter of credit confirmation does not bear the creditor's name, but one party makes a claim by presenting the document as evidence that a contractual relationship exists, the people's court shall uphold the claim unless there is sufficient evidence proving to the contrary.[82]

Another issue concerning contract form is whether a contract may be formed by implication. In other words, the issue is whether the "other forms" contemplated by Contract Law include implication. One argument is that a contract can be formed by implication since Article 26 of the Contract Law allows an acceptance to take effect according to transaction practices. According to the SPC, a sale via a vending machine, automated ticketing system, or magcard should be considered to be a contract formed by implication. Another example is the automatic renewal of a lease contract, under which a lease is renewed automatically if none of the parties take an action to the contrary prior to the expiration of the current term.[83]

5 Incorporation of the State Plan and Government Approval

As addressed in previous chapters, the Contract Law differs sharply from previous contract law legislations in that the Contract Law has abandoned the idea that a contract is a tool to implement the State plan. Despite the difference

---

80 See id., art. 5.
81 See SPC, 2012 Contract Law Interpretations, art. 1.
82 See id.
83 See Second Civil Division of the SPC, Adjudication Guide, *supra* note 48, at 7.

however, the Contract Law does not depart completely from the State plan. Although the Contract Law attempts to provide parties with the freedom to make contracts by stressing the parties' right to enter into a contract voluntarily without unlawful interference, such freedom may still not be exercised in contravention of the State plan. If there is any conflict between a party's right to contract and the State plan, the State plan will prevail.

Because of the supremacy of the State plan, the Contract Law mandates that parties affected by the State plan must enter into contracts in compliance with the plan. As noted, the Contract Law refers to the State plan in terms of "mandatory tasks" and "State purchasing orders." "Mandatory task" refers to a task assigned by the State through administrative means, and such a task must be taken and accomplished by the entities involved. "State purchasing order," similar to the concept of government procurement, is an order placed by one business entity designated by the State to make a purchase from another business entity. With State purchasing orders, the contract is made between business entities, though the State plays a role in terms of placing the orders.

Again, under Article 38 of the Contract Law, when the State on the basis of necessity issues a mandatory task or State purchasing order, relevant legal persons and other organizations shall conclude contracts among themselves pursuant to the rights and obligations prescribed by laws and administrative regulations. With respect to State mandatory tasks and State purchasing orders, the State plan plays a dominant role and the parties to the contracts enjoy very limited freedom. For contract formation under Article 38, the State plan must be observed and implemented.

In addition to the State plan affecting the formation of contracts, another distinctive characteristic of the Chinese Contract Law relates to governmental approval. Pursuant to Article 44 of the Contract Law, if a contract is subject to government approval or registration in order to be effective, such a contract will not take effect unless approval or registration is obtained. Moreover, under the SPC's 2009 Contract Law Interpretations, if a party who is obligated to file an application for approval with a relevant government agency fails to fulfill that obligation, the party will be held to be in violation of the good faith principle and liability will accordingly be imposed.[84]

What seems problematical, however, is that the Contract Law itself does not specify what contracts are subject to government approval. Instead, the Contract Law provides a so-called "reference clause," which makes Article 44

---

84   *See* SPC, 2009 Contract Law Interpretations, art. 8.

subordinate to other legislations or regulations. Thus, whether government approval is needed for a contract depends on the provisions of other laws and administrative regulations. Under the "reference clause," the legislature or administrative agencies may from time to time determine what contracts require government surveillance through the approval mechanism.

CHAPTER 5

Terms of Contracts

In most Chinese contract law books, the terms of a contract are discussed in the context of the contract's contents. Chinese contract scholars have debated the relationship between a contract's terms and its contents, however. Under the majority view, "terms" of a contract and "contents" of a contract are not synonymous. Proponents of this view argue that the contents of a contract should be viewed from the perspective of civil legal relations and intrinsic structure. The contents of a contract may be the contract terms only with respect to the contract's intrinsic structure, because the contents are displayed by the terms. With respect to civil legal relations, however, the contents of contract refer to the contractual relationship created between the parties, which represents the parties' respective rights and obligations.[1]

The minority opinion, however, tends not to distinguish between the terms and the contents of a contract. Adherents to the minority view believe that the terms and the contents of a contract are the same thing and have the same meaning. One contract law book in China defines the contents of a contract as simply the contract's terms or the specific provisions setting forth the rights and obligations of the parties to the contract.[2] According to the minority opinion, the words "terms" and "contents" of a contract can be used interchangeably.

The Contract Law apparently makes no attempt to make a distinction between the contents of a contract and the terms of a contract. Instead, the Contract Law takes a quite liberal and pragmatic approach. In general, the Contract Law allows parties to decide the contents of their contracts. Additionally, the Contract Law provides a list of terms that are considered to be normally included in contracts. Moreover, the Contract Law suggests additional terms for particular contracts. Finally, the Contract Law contains special provisions applicable to cases wherein a contract has taken effect but some of its terms are either missing or are unclear.

---

1   *See* Wang Liming, Studies on Contract Law, Vol. I, 347–52 (People's Univ. Press 2002).
2   *See* Jiang Ping et al., A Detailed Explanation of the Contract Law of Law 12 (China Univ. of Political Science & Law Press 1999).

1 Terms Generally Included in a Contract

As noted, under the Contract Law, formation of a contract requires parties' mutual assent. In substance, mutual assent means that the parties have reached an agreement as to what the terms of the contract are. A question this creates is what terms a contract normally must have in order to be formed. Under Article 12 of the Contract Law, the contents of a contract are subject to the parties' agreement and generally include the following terms: (a) name and domicile of the parties; (b) contract object (also translated as subject matter of the contract); (c) quantity; (d) quality; (e) price or remuneration; (f) time limit, place, and method of contract; (g) liability for breach of contract; and (h) methods for dispute settlement.[3]

Chinese contract law scholars commonly view Article 12 as implicating the principle of freedom of contract that is set forth in Article 4 of the Contract Law. First, under Article 12 of the Contract Law, the contents of a contract are determined solely by the parties. The main theme of Article 12 is that parties to a contract may decide as they wish what should be included in the contract. Second, the terms listed in Article 12 are not mandatory. The parties may or may not use all of the Article 12 terms, and the parties may also add to those terms if necessary for a specific contract. Third, the parties may agree afterwards to change the terms. If they do, the post-agreement becomes part of the contract and supersedes any conflicting provisions previously contained in the contract.

An important feature of Article 12 is that there is no requirement that certain terms be included in the contract in order for the contract to be valid. Given their non-mandatory nature, the terms listed in Article 12 are intended to provide guidance to the parties for deciding what should be included in the contract. Thus, the fact that a contract does not have a certain term does not necessarily render the contract invalid or adversely affect the contract's conclusion.[4] In addition, terms may vary between different contracts and parties are free to make their own decisions on a case-by-case basis.

As noted, pursuant to the SPC 2009 Contract Law Interpretations, the people's courts will normally hold a contract to have been formed—unless the law or the parties' agreement requires otherwise—if the names of the parties to the contract, the subject matter of the contract, and the quantity can be ascertained.[5] The inference of the SPC's Interpretations is that among the terms

---

3   *See* Contract Law, art. 12.
4   In the United States, for a contract for the sale of goods to be valid, there must be a quantity term. The Contact Law in China contains no such requirement.
5   *See* SPC, 2009 Contract Law Interpretations, art. 1.

listed in Article 12 of the Contract Law, the most essential term in a contract is the quantity because, without the quantity term, the formation of the contract would be adversely affected.

Like Article 12, which suggests contract terms in a broad sense, the Specific Provisions of the Contract Law, governing specific contracts, also lists additional terms for particular contracts. For instance, within the Sales section of the Specific Provisions, Article 131 explicitly provides that a sales contract may contain terms other than those stipulated in Article 12, such as package manner, inspection standards and method, format of settlement and clearance, language used in contract, and contract authenticity.[6] Article 324, which governs technology contracts, contains a much more detailed provision concerning the terms of a contract, listing eleven contract terms.[7] Those terms, like the terms provided in Article 12, are not compulsory. Nevertheless, in practice the terms listed in the Contract Law are normally included in certain contracts.

There are a number of issues requiring further discussion with regard to the general terms of contracts. The first issue deals with the name and domicile of the parties. Under the Contract Law, a party to a contract can be either a natural person (i.e., an individual human being) or a legal person (i.e., a corporation or organization). The domicile of a person is defined in Article 15 of the 1986 Civil Code as well as Article 25 of the 2017 GPCL as the place where the person's residence is registered. If the person's habitual residence is not the same as his domicile (i.e., his registered residence), his habitual residence is regarded as his domicile.[8] Habitual residence is defined by the SPC as the place where a citizen has consecutively lived for more than one year after leaving his or her domicile.[9]

---

6 *See* Contract Law, art. 131.
7 Article 324 provides that the contents of a technology contract shall be agreed upon by the parties, and shall in general contain the following terms: (a) name of the project; (b) contents, scope, and requirements of the targeted project; (c) plan, schedule, time period, place, areas covered, and manners of performance; (d) maintenance of confidentiality of technical information and materials; (e) sharing of liability for risks; (f) ownership of technological achievements and method of sharing proceeds; (g) standards and method of inspection and acceptance; (h) price, remuneration or royalties, and method of payment; (i) damages for breach of contract or method for calculating the amount for compensation for losses; (j) methods for dispute settlement; and (k) interpretation of technical terms and expressions.
8 *See* the 1986 Civil Code, art. 15; 2017 GPCL, art. 25.
9 *See* the SPC, Opinions (Provisional) on Several Matters Concerning Application and Implementation of the General Principles of the Civil Law of China (1988).

A legal person's domicile is defined in Article 39 of the 1986 Civil Code as the place where the legal person's main administrative office is located.[10] Article 63 of the 2017 GPCL sets forth a similar definition. Under Article 63, a legal person's domicile is the principal place of its business administration. Article 63 requires that a legal person must register the principal place of its business administration as its domicile if the law requires the legal person to be registered.

The second issue with respect to general contract terms concerns contracts' subject matter (or *Biao Di* in Chinese). The term "subject matter" in this context is often used interchangeably in China with the term "contract object," referring to what the contract is intended to cover or the target of the right and obligation of the contract. For example, if a contract is to sell a box of wine, the wine is the subject matter of that contract. Each contract has its own subject matter. The subject matter of a contract can be either a thing (e.g., a particular product) or conduct (e.g., a specific service).

A question often raised is what the difference is between the subject matter of a contract and the purpose of a contract. Many people in China believe that the purpose of a contract is distinct from the subject matter of the contract in that the purpose is the ultimate goal or objective to be reached by the parties through their conclusion and performance of the contract while the subject matter is the matter about which the contract is concluded.[11] To illustrate, in a sales contract, the particular item (i.e., goods) is the subject matter of the contract; the purpose of the contract is to deliver the item as agreed to the buyer so that the seller will get paid.

The third issue regarding general contract terms involves the term of price. As noted, though China is moving toward a market economy, the State plan still pays an important role in the country's economy. The price that is set for products or services in China takes three forms: market pricing, government-mandated-pricing, and government-guided-pricing. Market pricing is the mechanism by which prices are determined according to the market situation, with no involvement of government (State or local) action. With government-mandated-pricing, by contrast, prices are pre-determined by the government, and may not be changed without government action. The pre-determined price normally applies to products that are essential to the nation's economy and social stability (e.g., gasoline). Finally, government-guided-pricing, an intermediary between marketing pricing and government-mandated pricing, is a

---

10   *See* the 1986 Civil Code, art. 39.
11   *See* Wang Liming, *supra* note 1, at 35–54; *see also* Cui Jianyuan, LAW OF CONTRACTS (I), 217 (2011) (explaining that the subject matter of a contract is the target of contractual rights and obligations, without which the contract would achieve no purpose).

pricing form by which prices are determined according to governmental guidance. With such pricing, the government normally provides a medium price as well as a range within which the actual price may fluctuate as a necessary response to market changes.

With its accession to the WTO, China made a commitment pursuant to which it allowed prices for traded goods and services in every sector to be determined by market forces, with certain exceptions. In addition, China promised to eliminate multi-tier pricing practices for such goods and services.[12] The exceptions referred to the products and services that were still subject to price controls with notification to the WTO. As listed in Annex 4 to the accession of China, there were a number of products and services for which government-mandated-pricing was required, and several other products and services were subject to government-guided-pricing.[13] Both government-mandated-pricing and government-guided-pricing can be conducted at the central or the local level. At the local level, pricing can be made by provincial or county government. In the past decades, China has reduced the number of items to which central pricing applies. As of September 2015, the categories of central pricing were decreased from thirteen to seven, and the items from some one hundred to two hundred. [14]

The fourth issue with respect to general contract terms is the quality term. In China, quality means not only the specifications of the subject matter of the contract as agreed upon by the parties, but also the standards set forth by the State that apply to certain products or services. Since the quality standard promulgated by the State is the minimum requirement for quality, the parties may agree on a higher quality standard than that required by the State. However, the quality as agreed upon by the parties in the contract may not be lower than

---

12   *See* Protocol on the Accession of the People's Republic of China, art. 9. WT/L/432 (Nov. 23, 2001).
13   According to the Annex 4, products subject to state pricing include tobacco, edible salt, natural gas, pharmaceuticals, and public utilities (e.g., gas, water, and electricity). Products subject to government guidance pricing are grain, vegetable oil, processed oil, fertilizer (Urea), silkworm cocoons, and cotton (not carded or combed). Services subject to government pricing include postal and telecommunication services charges, entrance fee for tour sites, and education services charges. Services subject to government guidance pricing are transportation services charges, professional services charges, charges for commission agents' services, charges for settlement, clearing and transmission services of banks, selling price and renting fee of residential apartments, and health related services. *See id.*, Annex 4.
14   The decision for the reduction was made by the State Council on September, 23, 2009. A report is available at http://w.huanqiu.com/r/MV8wXzc1NjA3ODRfMjM1XzE0NDM-wNjEyMzA=.

the State standard because a failure to meet the State standard would render the contract invalid.

Since the Contract Law leaves to the parties the ultimate right to choose a contract's terms and sets forth no mandatory terms for contracts, it is important that the parties have the terms, particularly the key terms, well defined or addressed in the contract. This will ensure that the contract best represents the true intentions of the parties, and will also aid courts in properly interpreting the contract if a dispute over a contract term arises. More importantly, it should be borne in mind that a contract in China will not necessarily be invalid or void simply because it lacks some key terms. As a matter of interpretation, a contract with any missing or unclear terms may be fixed under the provisions of the Contract Law.

2 Interpretation of a Contract

Interpretation of a contract becomes necessary when the parties dispute a certain word, expression, term, or clause of the contract, with each party advancing different interpretations of the word, expression, term, or clause. In general, courts employ contract interpretation in order to ascertain the true meaning of the word, expression, term, or clause that is in dispute. In this context, contract interpretation is a mechanism to help resolve the difference between the parties. The interpretation may also be extended to certain conduct or an event that may affect the contract.

2.1 *Contract Interpretation Approaches*

In China, there is no universal definition of the concept of contract interpretation. A simple definition is that contract interpretation is "the analysis and explanation of the meaning of a contract and related materials."[15] A more complicated definition is that contract interpretation is "the work to ascertain the real meaning of the terms of a contract and to look into the effective intention of the parties through all interpretation rules and means in order to resolve disputes."[16]

---

15 *See* Wang Liming & Cui Jianyuan, A New Commentary on Contract Law—General Provisions 471–74 (China Univ. of Political Science & Law Press, reversed edition, 2000).
16 *See* Li Guoguang, Explanation and Application of the Contract Law 518 (Xinghua Press 1999).

A difficult question concerning contract interpretation is how such interpretation should be made. The difficulty lies with the differences in approaches or standards that are employed to deal with issues related to contract interpretation. There are a number of issues that generate debates among Chinese contract scholars. The issues include (a) who can make the interpretation, (b) what should be interpreted, (c) what purpose the interpretation should serve, and (d) under what rule the interpretation should be made.

With regard to the issue of who can interpret a contract, two approaches have developed. One is called the "restrictive" approach, which limits contract interpretation to that made by certain authorities. Under the "restrictive" approach, only the court or arbitration body before which the contract dispute is brought may conduct contract interpretation.[17] Proponents of the "restrictive" approach take the position that contract interpretation becomes an issue only when the dispute over the contract term arises between the parties. The "restrictive" approach holds that, because the parties differ in their understanding of the disputed term, it is necessary to have a "referee" to interpret, and such referee should be either a court or an arbitration body.[18]

The other approach is termed the "broad" approach. As opposed to the "restrictive" approach, the "broad" approach believes that contract interpretation can be made by the parties and others, including, depending on the circumstances under which the interpretation is needed, a judge, arbitrator, agent *ad litem*, witness, notary public, or appraiser.[19] In addition, according to the "broad" approach, certain organizations, such as a consumer protection society, may also be qualified to interpret certain contract terms.[20] Despite its broadness, however, the "broad" approach agrees that contract interpretations by those other than a court or arbitration body, unless accepted by the parties, have no legally binding effect.

What should be interpreted is a quation about the contents and subject of contractual interpretation. In general, there is a consensus among Chinese scholars that contract interpretation is geared toward construing contractual terms that are in dispute, and therefore should focus on the literal meaning of the terms. However, scholars also believe that several other matters essential to contract interpretation should be considered in order to make the interpretation more meaningful or more closely aligned with the objective meaning of

---

17   See Liang Huixing, Rules of Contract Interpretation 539 (Law Publ'g House, 1997).
18   See Jiang Ping et al., *supra* note 2, at 102.
19   See Mang Liming, *supra* note 1, at 412–413.
20   See id.

the contract terms being interpreted. The argument is that in many cases the literal meaning of a contract term, standing alone, is not sufficient because the actual meaning of the term may also be affected by the intention of the parties and the circumstances surrounding the contract's formation. This is the case, for example, with contract terms setting forth the contract's purpose. When the parties enter into a contract, they have an intended goal for the contract. Therefore, contract interpretation should be made in accordance with that intended goal.

Another matter is the contract itself. Any term in a contract is a part of the contract. To interpret a contract term, it is therefore important, and often necessary, to consider the contract as a whole and to look into the relation of the term to the contract as well as the relationship between the term and other terms. In this regard, contract interpretation should be made in light of the whole contract in addition to the context in which the contract was made. The interpretation of a contract term may result in an interpretation of the contract that diverts from the plain meaning of the language used in the contract, but it helps ascertain the actual meaning of the language chosen by the parties.

A further matter that is important to contract interpretation has to do with such extrinsic circumstances as commercial usages or customs. In real business settings, commercial usages or customs possess commonly accepted meanings and are widely observed in business transactions or dealings. Thus, such usages or customs have great supplementary value to a contract's interpretation, particularly when the contract contains a term that is very vague.[21] In this sense, commercial usages or customs are often deemed to be "blank fillers" that help define the contractual terms in question.

The issue concerning the purpose that contract interpretation should serve involves the ultimate goal or objective of interpretation. Although on its face contract interpretation is intended to reveal the meaning of contract terms, the question is whether contract interpretation is aimed at ascertaining the real meaning of a contract term or, alternatively, digging out the meaning of the contract term that the parties actually intended. There is also a debate as to whether contract interpretation is limited to construing the meaning of terms or whether it has to do with the validity of a contract.

Some scholars in China argue that contract interpretation is intended to determine the real meaning of contract terms according to the intention of

---

21   *See generally* Jiang Ping et al., *supra* note 2, at 102–03; Wang Liming, *supra* note 1, at 420–28; Li Guoguang, *supra* note 16, at 518–26; Wang Liming & Chu Jianyuan, *supra* note 15, at 478–85; Cui Yunning, GENERAL VIEW ON CONTRACT LAW 34–38 (China Univ. of People's Public Sec. Press 2003).

the parties. To that end, interpretation is purposed to (a) make the uncertain contents of a contract reasonably certain, (b) provide supplements to the incomplete contents of the contract, and (c) solve conflicts among the terms.[22] Since the parties may attach different meanings to the same term, contract interpretation is the process of resolving the parties' difference.

Other scholars contend that the direct purpose of interpretation is to properly determine the rights and obligations of the parties so that the dispute between them can reasonably be solved. Therefore, such scholars argue, the purpose of contract interpretation is not only to ascertain the contents of the contract but also to make a determination on whether the contract has been concluded and whether the contract concluded is valid.[23] For example, according to some scholars, contract interpretation is premised on the conclusion of the contract, and thus the preliminary question concerning contract interpretation is whether the contract has been concluded—if the question of whether the contract has been concluded is not clear or is uncertain, an interpretation shall be made on the issue of conclusion first.[24]

The rule of contract interpretation is in fact a matter of the standard under which an interpretation is to be made. As noted, contract interpretation involves both the subjective intent of the parties and the objective meaning of the words chosen by the parties. In addition, the factors relevant to interpretation include the meaning of the contract term and the circumstances under which the contract is made. Thus, the rules that are applied to a contract's interpretation determine the way a disputed term within the contract is interpreted.

2.2   *Contract Interpretation Theories*

There are three theories widely discussed and debated in China pertaining to contract interpretation, each of which involves the intention of the parties as to the meaning of the words or terms used in the contract. At the two ends of the spectrum are the "objective expression" theory and the "subjective intention" theory. In the middle, there is the "comprehensive" theory that combines the two extremes.

---

22 *See id.*, Cui Yunning, at 32–33.
23 *See* Wang Liming, *supra* note 1, at 407–09.
24 A typical example used by Professor Wang to illustrate his point is as follows: A sent B a fax for a certain product, and B then immediately delivered the product to A. A refused to accept the product and a dispute arose between A and B. To resolve the dispute, a court must first look to the contents of the fax in order to determine whether the fax constituted an offer or was simply an invitation for offer. *See id.* at 407.

The "objective expression" theory focuses on the apparent intention of the parties. Under this theory, contract interpretation is to be made pursuant to an objective standard. Thus, when interpreting a contract term, one should look at what the parties' intention appears to be with respect to the term in question. The underlying idea is that conclusion of a contract is an overt act of the parties. Therefore, in order to determine the meaning of a term as intended by the parties in the contract, an inquiry must be made into how the parties reasonably act in expressing their intentions rather than what the parties may actually have in mind.[25]

In contrast to the "objective expression" theory, the "subjective intention" theory views the actual intention of the parties as being decisive to the interpretation of a contract. Under the "subjective intention" theory, to determine the meaning of a contract term, what really matters is not what the intention of the parties would reasonably look like, but rather, what the parties actually intended. Accordingly, if the meaning of the term that the parties intended is found to be different from the literal meaning of the language used or from the common understanding of a reasonable person, the parties' intention controls.[26]

The "comprehensive" theory is actually a mixture of the above two. This theory is considered eclectic because it does not follow either the "objective expression" theory or the "subjective intention" theory, but instead narrows the difference between the two opposite theories and mixes them into a single methodology. Under the comprehensive theory, contract interpretation should first and foremost focus on ascertaining the true intention of the parties because of the paramount significance of the parties' intentions with respect to the contract. If, however, the parties' true intentions cannot be determined or there is a lack of a common or joint intention of the parties, the interpretation should be made with recourse to the general understanding of reasonable persons in the same or similar situation.[27]

2.3 *Contract Interpretation under the Contract Law*

The Contract Law provisions that govern contract interpretation embody a combination of the different theories. On the one hand, the Contract Law attempts to appeal to the majority, and on the other hand, it is intended to avoid some controversial issues. Under Article 125 of the Contract Law, with regard to disputes between the parties to a contract as to the meaning of any term or

---

25 *See* Cui Yunning, *supra* note 21, at 33.
26 *See* Wang Liming & Cui Jianyuan, *supra* note 15, at 474–78.
27 *See* Wang Liming, *supra* note 1, at 419–20.

clause of the contract, the true meaning of such term or clause shall be determined according to the words and expressions of the contract, the contents of relevant clauses of the contract, the purpose of the contract, transaction usages, as well as the principle of good faith.[28]

The Contract Law provides no definition of contract interpretation. From Article 125, however, it can be inferred that contract interpretation is the process of ascertaining the "true meaning" of the contractual term or clause in question. In order to determine such "true meaning," contract interpretation shall be made in accordance with the words and expressions used, relevant clauses, the contract's purpose, usages, as well as good faith. On its face, the Contract Law does endorse either the "objective expression" or the "subjective intention" theory. However, many Chinese scholars believe that the Contract Law in fact favors the comprehensive theory based on its emphasis on both objective expressions and subjective intentions.[29]

In addition, the Contract Law contains no reference as to who may engage in contract interpretation. A prevailing understanding is that the Contract Law does not preclude the parties from interpreting their contract.[30] Put differently, it is commonly understood that the Contract Law does not exclusively rest the authority to make contract interpretation in the hands of courts or arbitration bodies. Consequently, a wide variety of relevant parties (including the parties to the contract) may interpret a contract. The difference lies in the legal effects of such interpretation. To be legally binding, contract interpretation must be made by the court or the arbitration body.

Under Article 125, contract interpretation should be made in three steps, which consider the plain meanings of words, context, and other circumstances. First, interpretation should begin with evaluating the words and expressions used in the contract. Thus, the "plain meaning" of the words and expressions seems to be the threshold of contract interpretation because no further efforts are needed if the meaning of a word or expression can be determined on the contract's face. Second, if the meaning of the word or expression cannot be ascertained, the meaning must be determined by looking at other relevant clauses in the contract. Third, if ambiguity still exists, the interpretation should

---

28   *See* Contract Law, art. 125.
29   For example, according to Li Guoguang, contract interpretation under the Contract Law should start with looking to the literal meaning of the words and expressions used in the contract, and then should ultimately determine the true meaning of the contract terms by examining the parties' intentions as expressed with a reference to the parties' actual thinking. *See* Li Guoguang, *supra* note 16, at 521.
30   *See* Wang Liming, *supra* note 1, at 412–13.

be made in consideration of other factors such as the purpose of the contract, transaction usages, and good faith.

It is interesting to note that Article 125 makes the principle of good faith an interpretation standard. Although it seems too abstract to consider how the good faith principle helps ascertain the meaning of a contract term or clause, most contract scholars in China argue that the good faith principle—though it is left undefined in the Contract Law—plays a significant role in contract interpretation and must be observed.[31] It is generally understood in China that good faith is the supreme rule of contracting and, as applied to contract interpretation, requires interpretation to be made according to commonly accepted business ethics in order to ensure fair dealing. In this respect, the application of good faith in contract interpretation is actually the application of fairness and business ethics.

For example, on March 14, 2004, in observance of "International Consumers Right Day,"[32] the Beijing Association of Consumers Protection, on the basis of complaints it received from customers in the year 2003, published a list of ten major bad faith and unethical business conducts that are in clear violation of the good faith principle. This list in one respect represents the public's general understanding of good faith in accordance with concepts of fairness and business ethics.

The ten major types of conduct that violate good faith are: (1) use of advertisements or other means to provide false information about products or services to mislead consumers; (2) illegal production and sale of substandard products; (3) use of the advantage of monopoly or exclusive business position to force consumers to buy products or services; (4) use of unfair standard contracts or terms to increase consumers' obligations and reduce business operators' liability; (5) use of deceiving means by malicious collaboration among business operators to allure consumers to buy; (6) intentional omission of product and service information that should be expressly stated; (7) use of inferior materials or cutting down of work for products or services; (8) intentional breach of an agreement with, or promise to, consumers; (9) intentional concealment of the specification, certificate, or other related information of products or services in order to evade legal obligations; and (10) revelation of consumers' personal information without authorization for purposes of making profits.[33]

---

31 See Jiang Ping et al., *supra* note 2, at 102–03.
32 In 1983, the Organization of International Consumers Union designated March 15 as International Consumers Right Day.
33 See Jin Hua Shi Bao, BEIJING TIMES, A12 (Mar. 15, 2004).

However, when contract interpretation is made in conformity with business and public ethics pursuant to the notion of good faith, the contents ascertained as such may not necessarily be the same as the parties actually intended them to be. To make contract interpretation more meaningful, it is subsequently argued that good faith should be considered only as a last resort. That is to say: if the true intention of the parties can be ascertained by other means of interpretation, such other means should be employed first. In this regard, the good faith principle actually functions as the "filler," filling in any holes in a contract's interpretation that may appear. To speak generally, good faith may be used as a "catch-all" means to deal with the interpretation of a contract.[34]

It should be emphasized that, under the Contract Law, the purpose of a contract is not only an important factor to be considered when interpreting a contract, but also a primary basis for interpreting any contract that is made in different language versions. The second paragraph of Article 125 provides that, where two or more versions of a contract are made, each in a different language, and it is agreed that both versions are equally authentic, it shall be presumed that the different versions' terms and expressions have the same meaning. Moreover, if the different versions' terms and expressions are inconsistent, they shall be interpreted so as to best reflect the contract's purpose.

3   Supplementary Agreement for Uncertain or Missing Terms

In addition to Article 125, which deals with contract interpretation, Articles 61 and 62 of the Contract Law contain provisions governing determinations of contract terms. However, Articles 61 and 62 apply only when some specific terms of a contract are missing or uncertain after the contract has taken effect. Articles 61 and 62 provide the mechanism for fixing a missing or uncertain term by means of a supplement made by the parties to the contract. For that reason, many in China label Articles 61 and 62 as "Contract Supplement Provisions." A different view, though, is that Articles 61 and 62 are the same as Article 125 in their function. Under this view, it is believed that Articles 61 and 62 are specific provisions for contract interpretation while Article 125 is a general one.[35]

---

[34]   In the United States, a distinction is made between contact interpretation and contract construction. The interpretation is to ascertain the meaning of the parties while construction relates the legal effect of words used. According to Professor John Calamari, the construction placed upon an agreement will not necessarily coincide the meaning of the parties. *See* Calamari & Perillo, THE LAW OF CONTRACTS 614–15 (5th ed., 1998).

[35]   *See* Wang Liming, *supra* note 1, at 428–31; *see also* Cui Yunning, *supra* note 21, at 159–63.

Under Article 61, if, after a contract has taken effect, the parties to the contract disagree as to any of its terms regarding quality, price, remuneration, or place of performance, or if the contract with respect to these terms is otherwise unclear, the parties may reach a supplementary agreement by means of negotiation in order the clarify the contract. If the parties fail to reach such a supplementary agreement, the terms of the contract shall be determined in the context of relevant clauses of the contract or based on transaction customs.[36] Put simply, Article 61 gives parties the option to reach a post-contract agreement to clarify any uncertain or missing terms in a contract. Transaction customs may be used as a secondary means for determining any uncertain or missing terms. Recall that Article 61 is a special provision applicable only to certain specified terms.

Due to the difficulties inherent in Article 61's application and the need for achieving uniform results, Article 62 contains more detailed provisions aimed at making determinations of uncertain or missing contract terms straightforward. Under Article 62, if the relevant terms of a contract are not clear, nor can be determined under Article 61, the following rules shall be applied:

1. If the quality requirements are unclear, State or industrial standards shall be applied; if there are no such standards, generally accepted standards or specific standards in conformity with the purpose of the contract shall be used.[37]
2. If the price or remuneration is unclear, the market price of the place of performance at the time of the contract's conclusion shall be applied; if a law requires that a government-fixed price or government-guided price be followed, the provisions of that law shall be applied.

---

36 *See* Contract Law, art. 61.

37 Unlike many other countries or international treaties where quality standards basically conform with samples or with the purposes of a particular contract, Article 62 of the Contract Law requires that State or industrial standards be met first. There is a similar provision in the 1986 Civil Code. Article 88 (1) of the Civil Code provides that if the quality requirements are unclear, State quality standards shall be applied; if there are no State quality standards, generally held standards shall apply. In its *Opinions on Several Question Concerning the Implementation of the 1986 Civil Code (Provincial)*, the SPC interpreted Article 88 (1) to mean that when the contract contains ambiguous requirements for the quality of a product, the parties have failed to reach an agreement, and there are no State quality standards, the standards set up by State ministries or commonly accepted professional standards shall be applied; in the absence of such ministerial or professional standards, the approved enterprise standards shall apply; if there are no approved enterprise standards, the trade standard of the same industry or the approved standards for the similar products shall apply.

3. If the place of performance is unclear, and the payment is in currency, the performance shall be effected where the party receiving the payment is located; if real estate is to be delivered, the performance shall be effected where the real estate is situated; for other subject matters of the contract, the performance shall be effected where the party fulfilling the obligations is located.
4. If the time limit for performance is unclear, the obligor may at any time fulfill the obligations, and the obligee may also at any time demand the performance, but the obligor shall be given a necessary preparation time period for the performance.
5. If the method of performance is unclear, the method that would best effectuate the contract's purpose shall be adopted.
6. If the burden of expenses for performance is unclear, the expenses shall be assumed by the obligor.[38]

Article 62 in most parts is simply a restatement of Article 88 of the 1986 Civil Code, which contains the provisions for determining uncertain terms concerning a contract's quality, time limit of performance, place of performance, and price. What is not covered in Article 62 of the Contract Law is the determination of the right to patent application and the right to the use of patent. Under Article 88 of the 1986 Civil Code, if a contract contains no agreement as to the right to patent application, the party who has completed invention-creation shall have such right; if the contract contains no agreement on the right to the use of patent, either party shall have the right of use.[39]

In the context of the Contract Law, Articles 61 and 62 seem to be more involved in contract performance because they are regarded as applicable only in the stage of contract performance.[40] In actual cases, however, Articles 61 and 62, as applied to contract interpretation, may very likely overlap Article 125. If overlap occurs, this necessarily raises the question of what provision should be applied first when a determination of uncertain or disputable terms is required.

Again, it is a jurisprudentially established rule that, if there is a conflict between a general provision and a specific provision, the special provision prevails unless the law provides otherwise. Because Articles 61 and 62 are designed to cope with specific terms of a contract, their application should accordingly

---

38 *See* Contract Law, art. 62.
39 *See* the 1986 Civil Code, art. 88.
40 Also note that Articles 61 and 62 differ from Article 126 with respect to determining contract terms. Articles 61 and 62 are aimed at dealing with determinations of uncertain terms while Article 125 applies when determining terms that are in dispute.

be attempted first. Keep in mind, however, that Articles 61 and 62 are limited in application to specific contract terms that are missing. The following case from the High People's Court of Beijing illustrates the interpretation mechanism employed in the courtroom under the provisions of the Contract Law.

Beijing Big Dragon Mechanical Engineering Co. Ltd.
v.
Beijing Kaibor Paddling Co. Inc.

High People's Court of Beijing[41]

On April 2, 2000, plaintiff and defendant signed an "Agreement on the 3rd Phrase of the Project of Excavation of Water Route." Under the Agreement, plaintiff was responsible for excavating, removing, and bulldozing soil, and for leveling riverbed as well as stacking rocks at the riverbank. The total workload was 572,000 cubic meters of soil to be measured by plaintiff and verified by defendant. The unit price of the project was RMB 4.80 per cubic meter. In addition, plaintiff was required to pay deposit of RMB 100,000 Yuan upfront as the fund to guarantee the quality and timely completion of the project. The contract was to be supervised by Beijing Jinze Municipal Mechanical Engineering Company.

After signing the Agreement, plaintiff made payment under the Agreement in the amount of RMB 100,000 to the project guarantee fund, and then started work on the project site on April 6, 2000. However, during the process of digging at the site, it was found that the water level underneath was rising, which required additional water-drain equipment for the proper drainage for the work on the project. As a result, both the difficulty to dig and the costs for the project increased. On May 20, 22, 23, and 25, plaintiff sent four letters to defendant reporting the completion of the project and asking for defendant's inspection. Defendant refused plaintiff's request for inspection on the ground that the project had not been complete and the progress of the project was affected by the technical problems plaintiff had confronted. Plaintiff then left the project site.

In July 2000, plaintiff brought a lawsuit against defendant at Beijing No. 1 Intermediate People's Court. Plaintiff alleged that it had a valid agreement with defendant on the project and had performed accordingly, but defendant refused to pay plaintiff for the complete project amounting to RMB 8,449,657 Yuan. Plaintiff asked the court to order defendant to make the payment and also to refund the RMB 100,000 Yuan deposit to plaintiff.

Defendant argued that the project had quality problems and was unfinished. In addition to asking the trial judge to dismiss plaintiff's claim, defendant filed a counterclaim against plaintiff. In its counterclaim, defendant requested the court to (a) render the Agreement void, (b) order plaintiff to pay RMB 1,990,000 Yuan for defendant's economic loss, (c) ask plaintiff to make public apology for the damage to defendant' business reputation caused by plaintiff's petition to the court for attachment, and (d) re-examine and re-appraise the quality of the project. Plaintiff argued that defendant's refusal of plaintiff's request for inspection in May was groundless, and there was no way to re-examine the project at the time of the lawsuit because the situation of the project site had changed.

---

41   The source of this case is from the First Civil Division of High People's Court of Beijing, A PRECISE ANALYSIS OF BEIJING CIVIL CASES 258 (Legal Press 2003).

During the hearing, the court asked Beijing Gaodi Investment Consulting Company Ltd. to make an appraisal of the value of the said project according to the then effective pricing parameter of Beijing City. The result of the appraisal demonstrated that the total value of the project was RMB 9,50,319 Yuan, of which the volume of machine-excavated earth was totaled at 617,277 cubic meters with the unit price of RMB 11.96 Yuan per cubic meter, and the volume of total debris removed by mechanical equipment was 12,000 cubic meters at the unit price of RMB 7.79 Yuan per cubic meter.

The arguments between plaintiff and defendants were centered on two major issues: the first issue was whether defendant was required to pay plaintiff for the project, and the second issue was how the price of the project should be determined if defendant was obligated to pay. The court held that the agreement between plaintiff and defendant was valid, but that during the course of construction, the river-level rose, which made it more difficult and more expensive for plaintiff to complete the project, and therefore it would be obviously unfair to require defendant to pay plaintiff on the basis of the agreed cubic meters of the soil (namely 572,000 cubic meters). Thus, according to the court, the appraisal by Beijing Gaodi Investment Consulting Company Ltd. on the price of the project was fair.

The court further held that defendant's argument about the incompletion of the project was not supported by any evidence, and therefore should be denied. The court also dismissed defendant's counterclaim because the counterclaim was based on the assertion that plaintiff did not complete the project. In its decision to dismiss, the court ordered defendant to pay plaintiff for the project in the amount of RMB 8,499,657 Yuan and to refund plaintiff's deposit of RMB 100,000 Yuan as well. Defendant appealed.

We hold that the standard of obvious unfairness as applied to a contract dispute has its limits. A contract that is obviously unfair normally refers to a contract that is concluded to the disadvantage of one party who clearly lacks experience or is in an emergent situation. In this case, the agreement reached between plaintiff and defendant was their true mutual intention and did not violate the law. Therefore, its validity must be upheld. For that reason, the unit price per cubic meter as agreed upon by the parties must be held effective, and the parties must be bound by what they had agreed. The trial court's decision requiring the project price to be adjusted on basis of the third party appraisal violated the parties' agreement and must therefore be reversed.

In reaching its decision on the project price, the trial court relied on Article 62 (2) of the Contract Law. Article 62 (2) provides that if the price or remuneration is unclear, the market price of the place of performance at the time of the contract's conclusion shall be applied; if a law requires that a government-fixed price or government-guided price be followed, the provisions of that law shall be applied. This case, however, does not fall within the coverage of Article 61 (2) because the parties have agreed on the price and the only thing not covered in the party's agreement as to price is the cost of the work that was unexpectly required under the water.

The trial court erred in applying Article 62 to an agreed-upon term with a specific subject matter. The trial court tried to use Article 62 to fill the gap, and thus confused contract interpretation with contract-gap-filling. The difference between contract interpretation and contract-gap-filling is that interpretation occurs when a term is provided but does not clearly express the meaning of the parties, whereas contract-gap-filling is needed when there is no agreed term. Here, the price term is clear with regard to all of the work not under the water, and what is needed is to figure out how much it would cost for the work under the water.

It is true that the rising of underneath water level resulted in an increase of the work difficulty and costs to plaintiff. For the increased costs, defendant shall compensate. The compensated amount can be determined under the appraisal of the third party. Thus, the order of the trial court as to the refund and the counterclaim is affirmed and the decision as to the payment required to be made by defendant is reversed and modified to the amount of RMB 3,364,021 Yuan.

4   Proof of the Terms of a Contract

Again, under the Contract Law, contract interpretation is needed whenever (a) a disputable term, (b) an uncertain or missing term, or (c) an inconsistent version of a contract that is made in different languages becomes an issue. In addition, special provisions in the Contract Law govern the interpretation of standard contracts. For purposes of contract interpretation, certain evidence is often sought, particularly when the parties make contradictory arguments as to the specific meaning of a term in a contract. To a certain extent, contract interpreation is a matter of proof.

One question regarding proof that arises is what evidence is permitted to help ascertain the meaning of a certain term or identify a term that is missing. At the center of this question is whether extrinsic evidence may be introduced to aid a contract's interpretation. Under Article 61 of the Contract Law, if certain terms of a contract are unclear, the parties may enter into a supplementary agreement to resolve any uncertainty as to such terms. But the supplementary agreement is something that the parties negotiate after the interpretation becomes an issue. Article 125 of the Contract Law is silent as to what the parties may bring up for the contract interpretation. Consequently, it is unclear whether other relevant evidence such as the records of negotiation, side agreements, or memos may be used to help interpret the contract.

In American contract law, there is a "parol evidence" rule that functions to bar the admission of any prior writing or oral agreement or contemporaneous oral agreement between the parties to vary or contradict the writing of the contract if the contract is intended to be complete and final.[42] No such concept ever existed in China. In Chinese courts, a controlling rule is "to seek truth from the fact." Applying this rule to contract interpretation, the courts hold admissible all evidence that may help prove the meanings of terms that was intended by the parties. In addition, the courts have held that some ancillary evidence or materials may be used to aid the interpretation of contract terms.

Ancillary evidence includes the history of the parties' contract negotiations.[43] In a book written by a group of judges of the Supreme People's Court to explain the Contract Law, it is suggested that, taking the contract as a whole, a contract's interpretation should not be limited to evaluation of the words of the contract. Rather, to determine the meaning of a disputed contract term, all materials related to the contract—such as previous drafts, negotiation records,

---

42   See Johnson v. Curran, 633 P.2d 994, 995 (Alaska 1981); see also UCC §2–202.
43   See Cui Yunning, supra note 21, at 35.

letters, telegraphs, and telex—shall be consulted, even though such material might contradict the current contract writing.[44] In conformity with this guidance, in practice, the Chinese courts are open to all relevant evidence when interpreting contracts. An important question the courts therefore face is how to ascertain the credibility of each piece of evidence that is introduced.[45]

5 Standard Terms

Standard terms are generally viewed as a special type of written contract, which may be part of a contract or the contract itself.[46] If all of a contract's terms are standard terms, the contract is called a standard contract. Standard terms may be contained in the contract document itself or in a separate document. Under Article 39 of the Contract Law, standard terms are defined as contract provisions that are prepared in advance for general and repeated use by one party and that are not negotiated with the other party in concluding the contract.[47] Article 39 is the first piece of contract legislation in modern Chinese history to recognize standard terms in contracts or standard contracts.

The statutory recognition of standard terms resulted from the recognition that, in many business transactions where the services or products provided are consistently the same or similar and the number of users is quite large, it would greatly increase business efficiency to allow for standard terms in contracts that could be continually used and that would help simplify the contract making process. Standard terms are normally used in contracts involving

---

44 See Li Guoguang, *supra* note 16, at 521–22.
45 In the Untied States, the parol evidence rule is intended to promote and enhance business stability. As Professor Calamari pointed out, the policy behind the parol evidence rule is "to give the writing a preferred status so as to render it immune to perjured testimony and the risk of "uncertain testimony of slippery memory." But the rule has received criticism for its complexity and rigidity.
46 Because of the fact that standard terms are not made through negotiation by the parties, but are rather made by one party unilaterally, there some disagreement about whether standard terms are contracts. Some argue that standard terms are the norms recognized by the law. Others label standard terms as civil rules or regulations adopted by legal persons. Some contend that standard terms should be deemed *de facto* contracts because they exist before the contract is concluded and are accepted by the contracting parties as facts.
47 This definition is consistent with UNIDROIT's Principles of International Commercial Contract (PICC). According to Article 2.19 of PICC, standard terms are provisions which are prepared in advance for general and repeated use by one party and which are actually used without negotiation with the other party.

insurance, transportation, and the use of public utilities. Keep in mind that the legal notion underlying standard terms is not that of "repeated-use" but rather, of "prepared-in-advance" by one party. Standard terms may be provided by business companies or by the government if the terms regard public utilities that are run by government agencies.

"Prepared-in-advance" is a typical feature of standard terms. Because these terms are created by one party, the fairness of both the terms and the dealings between the parties becomes an issue that requires special attention. In the sense in which standard terms normally are not the product of a negotiation between the parties, a contract that contains standard terms is often called a "contract of adhension." In most cases, an adhesive contract is a "take-it or leave-it" deal.

Due to concerns about their fairness, standard terms are generally subject to certain rules. First, standard terms, regardless of whether they themselves constitute a contract or are part of a contract, will not take effect unless and until the other party accepts. In addition, if standard terms are contained in a separate document, for the terms to be effective, a proper reference to the terms must be expressly made in the contract by the party intending to use them. Furthermore, no standard terms are allowed without the reasonable knowledge of the other party—meaning that standard terms may not come in the contract as a surprise to the other party.

The Contract Law seems to have incorporated these rules into its provisions regulating standard terms. According to Article 39 of the Contract Law, where standard terms are adopted in a contract, the party who supplies the standard terms shall define the rights and obligations between the parties according to the principle of fairness, shall make the other party alerted to the exclusion or restriction of its liabilities in a reasonable way, and shall explain these terms in response to the other party's request. Article 39 does not expressly mention "surprising terms." Nevertheless, it is widely understood as being implied from the notice requirement that the other party must not be surprised to see any standard terms that would adversely affect its interest.[48]

---

48 With regard to notice, the statutory standard under the Contract Law is "reasonable ways." According to Professor Wang Liming, reasonable ways should be judged from the following five aspects: (a) the outfit of the notice document—it should be good enough to attract the other party's attention; (b) the method of giving the notice; (c) degree of explicitness of the language used; (d) time of giving the notice—the notice must be given before the contract is concluded or in the process of concluding the contract; and (e) degree of the awareness of the other party—the notice must make the other party fully aware. *See* Wang Liming, *supra* note 1, at 394–95.

Additionally, Article 40 of the Contract Law specifies several situations in which standard terms are invalid. First, standard terms are null and void if there exists fraud; duress; illegal purpose; harm to the State, the collective, or individual or public interests; or violations of compulsory provisions of laws and administrative regulations. Second, standard terms are invalid if they contain exclusion provisions that are prohibited by law. Third, standard terms will be struck down if they are used for the purpose of exempting one party from liability while increasing the other party's liabilities and excluding the other party's major rights. Article 40, however, does not specify what constitute "major rights." One scholarly interpretation is that major rights are the rights a party normally would have in the type of contract at issue.

Despite the business efficiency advantage of standard terms, the use of such terms has a great impact on the interests of the other party, especially in consumer contracts. A major concern in this regard is standard terms' impact on the parties' freedom of contract. The question is whether a contract containing standard terms can truly be made freely and fairly, particularly when the party subject to the contract's standard terms is in a weaker position. Realizing that standard terms are often abused by the party having the greater power in the market, many countries have adopted laws or rules to help maintain the fair use of standard terms.

Article 39 of the Contract Law represents the legislative effort to regulate the use of standard terms in business transactions. The Law of Protection of Consumer Rights and Interests (Consumer Protection Law) provides a similar provision. Under Article 24 of the Consumer Protection Law, business operators are prohibited from imposing, through standard contracts, unfair or unreasonable restrictions on consumers, and from reducing or escaping their civil liability for their infringement of the legitimate rights and interests of consumers.[49]

Article 39 of the Contract Law, however, is being criticized as lacking actual legal effect. The criticism is that Article 39 only states what obligations the party making the standard terms has, but provides no liability for the failure to perform such obligations. A question this raises is what standard terms are unfair and unreasonable. This question is not properly addressed in the

---

49 The Consumer Protection Law of China was promulgated on October 30, 1993 and took effect on January 1, 1994. Under Article 24 of the Consumer Protection Law, no business operator shall, through such means as a standard contract, notice, announcement, entrance hall bulletin, impose unfair and unreasonable restrictions on consumers or reduce or escape their civil liabilities for harms caused to the legitimate rights and interests of consumers.

law or regulations. In 2003, the Chinese Association of Consumer Protection (CACP)—the national consumer protection watchdog—conducted a survey on unfair standard terms in Chinese business transactions. The survey focused on the four major business areas where standard terms are most heavily used—government-monopolized public utilities, insurance, real estate, and tourism. Based on the survey, the CACP concluded that a substantial number of the standard terms used were "despotic" and clearly violated Article 39 of the Contract Law.[50]

According to the CACP, standard terms are unfair and unreasonable if they are aimed at (a) exempting the party who makes the standard terms from being held liable for any consequences, (b) restricting or excluding the legitimate rights of the other party, (c) providing the party making the standard terms with additional rights in order to reduce its liability, (d) restricting the access of consumers to CACP for assistance, or (e) granting the party making the standard terms the ultimate right of interpretation of the contract terms.[51] However, given its very limited authority, the CACP's finding and opinion do not seem to have much impact on the unfair use of standard terms.

In its 2009 Contract Law Interpretations, the SPC singled out two circumstances under which standard terms may be cancelled or invalidated. The first circumstance is lack of proper notice or explanation. As noted, under Article 39 of the Contract Law, the party who provides the standard terms is required to inform the other party of the exclusion or restriction of the providing party's liabilities in reasonable ways and to explain the standard terms pursuant to the

---

50 These clauses were classified into ten major categories: (a) the clause giving telecommunication company power to set arbitrary expiration date for calling card with the purpose to "take" unused balance; (b) the clause providing that the monthly charge will still apply even if the cell phone service has been cancelled unless certain procedures have been followed; (c) the clause requiring that customers promise not to make a claim against the company if the transmitting signal for the use of the cell phone is not strong or interrupted; (d) the clause requiring customers to prepay the monthly fees for telephone services and to face the risk of suspending the use of telephone line if the telephone charges in any given month unusually exceed the prepaid amount; (e) the clause allowing the company to alter the contract terms unilaterally without notice; (f) the clause granting the company the ultimate right to interpret the contract; (g) the clause reducing the statutory period of business record keeping; (g) the clause requiring customers at their additional cost to only use provided box or materials for shipping; (h) the clause limiting customers' option for receiving the shipped goods in order to charge more; and (i) the clause prohibiting customers from making claims within reasonable period of time. *See* Xinhua News Agency report (July 28, 2003), available at http://people.com.cn/GB/jingji/1047/1988742.html.

51 *See id.*

request of the other party. According to the SPC, if the providing party fails to comply with Article 39 and this results in the other party's unawareness of liability exclusion or restriction terms, the people's court will cancel such terms if the other party moves for it to do so.[52]

Article 39 does not specify what constitutes reasonable notice or explanation. Under the SPC's interpretation, a term or clause within a standard term contract is reasonable if it both is made in such special marks as words, symbols, or fonts that are legible and sufficient to call themselves to the other party's attention, and is explained to the other party upon request.[53] The SPC emphasizes that the party providing the standard terms bears the burden of proving that it fulfilled its Article 39 obligation to inform and explain to the other party.[54]

An exemplary case of the application of Article 39 is *Liu Chaojie v. Xu Zhou Branch of Jiangsu Co. Ltd, China Mobile Group*, which was selected by the SPC as Guiding Case No. 64. The case concerned a dispute over a prepaid cellphone card service agreement. On November 24, 2009, the Plaintiff purchased a prepaid cellphone card from the Defendant. The service agreement provided by the Defendant allowed the Plaintiff to use the card for a cellphone up to the money amount in the card. The Plaintiff could continue to use the card by adding money to it.

Under the service agreement, the Defendant could suspend or restrict the Plaintiff's use of phone service if (a) the Defendant was unable to receive the Plaintiff's payment for the service due to the Plaintiff's bank account being attached or frozen, or because there were insufficient funds in the account; or (b) the prepaid fee was used up and no money was timely added.

On July 5, 2010, the Plaintiff added RMB 50 to the prepaid phone card. On November 11, 2010, the service was suspended, even though there was money left on the card. When consulting with the Defendant, the Plaintiff was told that the phone card could not be used because the valid period of the card had expired. According to the Defendant, the prepaid phone card had a fixed period of use, which began from one prepay to the next prepay. If no additional payment was made before the relevant expiration day, the card was suspended regardless of any residual amount of money paid to it.

The Plaintiff sued the Defendant for breach of contract. The district people's court ruled in favor of the Plaintiff. In its decision, the district people's court explained that under Article 39 of the Contract Law of China, when a contract

---

52 *See* the SPC, 2009 Contract Law Interpretation, art. 9.
53 *See id.*, art 6.
54 *See id.*

is made on the basis of a standard form, the form provider must define the parties' respective rights and obligations in accordance with the principle of fairness, and must inform the other party through reasonable means of any liability exclusion or restriction.

The district people's court held that the Defendant was liable because it violated the notice requirement of Article 39. The court based this conclusion on the fact that the Defendant suspended the Plaintiff's service on the basis of expiration of the prepaid phone card's fixed term of use, but failed to inform the Plaintiff at the time the Plaintiff signed the service agreement of the fixed period term. The Defendant's conduct, according to the district court, constituted a breach of contract.

By publishing this case as a guiding case, the SPC endorsed the lower court ruling as illustrating the rule that, if a business operation in its standard contract does not explicitly set forth limitations or conditions on a certain product or service, and the business cannot prove that it informed the consumer at the time of the contract of such limitations or conditions and obtained the consumer's consent to them, such limitations or conditions will have no effect as to the consumer.[55]

The second circumstance involves the violation of both the Article 39 notice requirement and Article 40 validity conditions. Under Article 40, standard terms are null and void if they fall within any of the situations set forth in Articles 52 and 53 of the Contract Law, which concern the voidance of contracts and exculpatory clauses, where a providing party attempts to exempt itself from liabilities while weighting the liabilities and excluding the rights of the other party. In accordance with the SPC, the people's court will hold standard terms invalid if they violate Article 39 of the Contract Law and also are found to be in one of the situations provided in Article 40.[56]

The SPC's interpretation appears to be at odds with Article 40 of the Contract Law, however. Article 40 does not reference Article 39, instead only referencing Articles 52 and 53. The SPC nevertheless seems to suggest that standard terms are subject to both Articles 39 and 40. In other words, if a proper notice or explanation was given under Article 39, a standard term will not necessarily be held invalid even if it should be under Article 40.

An additional issue regards the interpretation of standard terms, especially when the parties have different understandings of the terms. Standard terms have several distinctions from regular contract terms. One distinction

---

55   *See* the SPC, Guiding Case No. 64, http://www.court.gov.cn/shenpan-xiangqing-27571.html.
56   *See* the SPC. 2009 Contract Law Interpretation, art. 10.

commonly discussed is that the parties' intentions with respect to the meanings of standard terms may not be a proper parameter for determining the meaning of such terms because standard terms are often not products of the parties' negotiation. Another distinction is that standard terms normally involve a large number of users (i.e., consumers) and thus affect greater social and public interests. For this reason, the rules for interpreting standard terms necessarily incorporate policy concerns.

The Contract Law contains a special provision for interpreting standard terms. According to Article 41, if a dispute over the meaning of a standard term occurs, the standard term should be interpreted pursuant to its general understanding. If there are two or more kinds of possible interpretations, an interpretation unfavorable to the party supplying the standard term is preferred. When a standard term and a non-standard term are inconsistent, the non-standard term shall prevail.[57] Simply put, as articulated in Article 41, to interpret standard terms, the following three rules must be followed: the rule of "general understanding," the rule of "unfavorable to supplying party," and the rule of "non-standard term preferable." It is important to note that these three rules do not take any particular order, when applied to the specific cases.

For purposes of discussion, the application of Article 41 requires more elaboration. First, Article 41 may not be used to exclude the application of other contract interpretation provisions. This means that any of the principles relevant to contract interpretation in the Contract Law may also be applicable to standard terms' interpretation. Second, from a judicial point of view, application of the Article 41 rules is not unconditional. Whenever a difference between a standard term and a non-standard term exists, the non-standard term must be upheld. Third, the rule of "general understanding" is premised on the idea that interpretation of standard terms must be made both reasonably and objectively because standard terms are provided unilaterally.

An interesting question concerning standard terms is the effect of individually negotiated terms. This question becomes relevant when the parties have agreed to add certain terms into the standard contract and the added terms are inconsistent with the standard terms normally used to deal with the same or similar situation. The Contract Law provides no answer to this question, but there is a compelling argument that the individually negotiated terms should override the standard terms. The underlying rationale rests with the dictum *"lex specialis derogat lex generalis"* (special law derogates general law)—although when applied to the standard terms, this dictum is reversed.

---

57   *See* Contract Law, art. 41.

In the case below, additional (i.e., non-standard) terms that were agreed upon by the parties to a standard contract were upheld by a people's court. Interestingly, the High People's Court of He Nan Province treated the additional terms as a special agreement superseding the standard contract. According to the court, additional terms control if there is a discrepancy between them and the standard terms, so long as the special terms do not violate any provisions of law.

Kai Feng City Hong Tian Electronics Co., Inc.
v.
Mincheng Securities Co. Ltd

High People's Court of He Nan Province[58]

Plaintiff, Kai Feng City Hong Tian Electronics Company, Inc., brought this lawsuit on August 25, 2003 against defendant, Mincheng Securities Co. Ltd, concerning a dispute over a trustee agreement on assets management. Plaintiff demanded that defendant (a) pay plaintiff RMB 50.45 million Yuan for the entrusted fund and accrued interest, (b) pay stipulated damages in the amount of RMB 2.41 million Yuan for breach of contract, and (c) pay a fine at the rate of .004% per day for the belated payment of the fund from August 13, 2003 to the date of actual payment.

In its complaint, plaintiff claimed that on February 17, 2003, plaintiff entered into the "Agreement of Trustee on the Management of Assets" (Agreement) with defendant (the standard contract provided by defendant), and on the same day, plaintiff and defendant signed the "Additional Terms to the Agreement of Trustee on the Management of Assets" (Additional terms), and both the Agreement and the Additional Terms were concluded on the basis of the parties' mutual assent. Plaintiff alleged that on February 13, 2003 plaintiff remitted RMB 48.20 million Yuan as agreed into the special account of the defendant's branch located in Jin Shui road, and entrusted defendant to manage the fund. Plaintiff further alleged that after the agreed six-month period of trusteeship ended on August 18, 2003, defendant did not payback to plaintiff the principal of the entrusted fund and interest amounting to RMB 50.45 million Yuan in total.

Defendant did not submit a written answer to the Court. During the court hearings, defendant admitted facts stated in plaintiff's complaint but argued that the additional terms contained a minimum guarantee clause, which was void because it violated the prohibitive provision of the Securities Law. Defendant also argued that since defendant had prepaid part of the interest to plaintiff in amount of RMB 1.8 million, the actual amount of the fund remitted by plaintiff to defendant designated account was RMB 48.20 million Yuan, and therefore, the principal of the fund should be the amount defendant actually received.

In response, plaintiff argued that the RMB 1.8 million Yuan was prepaid interest on the basis of RMB 50 million Yuan and therefore the principal of the fund should remain unchanged. Plaintiff then contended that the Agreement and the Additional Terms are the standard terms provided by defendant, and adopted by the parties through consensus. Plaintiff further asserted that under the Agreement, defendant should provide plaintiff with an assets management report and an investment manager report, but defendant did not do so, nor did defendant make

---

58   See The Civil Judgment of High People's Court of He Nan Province, (2003) Yu Fa Min (2) Chu Zhi No. 24.

available to plaintiff any documents evidencing the financial status of the fund under trusteeship. Plaintiff also proved that according the Additional Terms, if there is a conflict between the Agreement and the Additional Terms, the Additional Terms control. ......

Defendant insisted that the Agreement was the standard contract in compliance with the Securities Law, but the Additional Terms were a result of the negotiations by the parties and should be invalid because of the illegal minimum guarantee clause. Defendant argued that it operated plaintiff's fund to make investments in the security market on behalf of plaintiff, and under the Securities Law, the parties should equally share profits and losses attributed to such investment operations. ......

The Court found that the actual remittance plaintiff made to defendant for the fund in trustee was RMB 48.20 million Yuan, and defendant did not actually pay Plaintiff RMB 1.80 million as interest.

It is held that under the provisions of "Securities Management Methods" of the China Securities Regulatory Commission as well as the scope of the business operation as stated on defendant's business license, defendant is legally qualified as a legal person to engage in assets management. The Agreement between plaintiff and defendant manifests the true intent of the parties and its contents are not in violation of any prohibitive provisions of law, and therefore shall be held valid. The Additional Terms shall be deemed a special agreement on the distribution of profits because it not only provides the rate of return for plaintiff at 4.5%, but also makes it clear that any amount exceeding 4.5% shall be paid 100% to defendant as a performance bonus. Since the Additional Terms truly reflect the parties' actual intention and because the case involves trusteeship for which there are no prohibitive provisions, defendant's argument against the Additional Terms lacks legal grounds and shall therefore be denied.

Under Article 8 of the Contract Law of the People's Republic of China, a contract that is established according to law shall be legally binding on the parties and the parties shall perform their obligations as agreed, and the contract so established shall be protected by law. Applying Article 8 to the present case, the Court holds that defendant's failure to provide plaintiff with the periodical report on the management and operation of the fund in trust under the Agreement during the trusteeship and the failure to report to plaintiff on the asset management and to pay plaintiff the principal of the fund and the interest after the trusteeship came to an end constitute a breach of contract.

In addition, pursuant to Article 75 of the Supreme People's Court's "Several Rules of Evidence Concerning Civil Litigation," if a party who holds evidence refuses to submit it without reasonable grounds and the other party asserts that the contents of such evidence are something disadvantageous to the holding party, the assertion may be assumed to be true. In this case, since defendant is able to but does not provide the asset management report, which renders no evidence that the fund in trust experienced any loss or did not reach the level of profit as agreed by the parties, plaintiff's demand shall therefore be granted. ......

With regard to the fund in trust, the agreed amount by the parties was RMB 50 million, of which a receipt of acknowledgement was issued by defendant to plaintiff. However, since the amount of the fund actually remitted to defendant was RMB 48.20 million, and the prepaid interest of RMB 1.8 million was nothing more than a promise defendant made to plaintiff and no transfer of such interest money took place, we conclude that the amount of the fund in trust is RMB 48.20 million.

Accordingly, it is ordered as follows:

1. Defendant shall, within 10 days after this judgment takes effect, pay plaintiff the principal of the fund in trust and accrued interest in the amount of RMB 50.369 million Yuan, and shall also pay the late performance fine for the period from August 4, 2003 to the date of this judgment at the rate of .004% of RMB50.369 million per day.

TERMS OF CONTRACTS 177

2. Plaintiff's other claims are denied.

Further, defendant shall bear the litigation fee of RMB 274,310 Yuan and the attachment fee of RMB 275,000 Yuan. If refusing to accept this judgment, either of the parties may, within 10 days after this judgment is served, appeal to the Supreme People's Court by submitting to this Court three copies of the appellate petition and paying appellate fee of RMB 274,310 Yuan.

6 Disclaimers

In contracts, a disclaimer is a term whereby the parties agree to exempt a party from liability in certain situations; it is also called an exemption or exculpatory clause. Disclaimers are often included in sales contracts as devices for minimizing sellers' liability by reducing the number of situations in which sellers can be found in breach of contract. Obviously, a disclaimer is a useful tool for a contractual party that wants to be cleared of certain liability. Once agreed upon by the parties, a disclaimer becomes part of a contract and has binding effect upon the parties unless its effect is invalidated by the operation of law.

Disclaimers are recognized in the Contract Law to the extent that they do not fall within prohibited categories. Under Article 53 of the Contract Law, an exemption clause shall be null and void if it exempts liability for (1) personal injury caused to the other party and (2) property damages caused to the other party as a result of deliberate intent or gross negligence.[59] In addition to these categories, it has been argued that an exemption is invalid if it exempts liability for breach of the contract due to failure to perform.[60] Note that Article 53 also applies to standard terms.

For a disclaimer to be valid, two other criteria must be satisfied. One criterion is that the disclaimer must be made expressly by the parties and may not be inferred or implied because, as noted, a valid disclaimer will bind the parties to the contract. The other criterion concerns the contents of the disclaimer. It is generally held in China that a disclaimer clause's contents must at least address the matter of disclaimer and the scope of disclaimer. The former refers to the situations to which the disclaimer will apply, and the latter indicates the type and degree of the disclaimer (i.e., partial exemption or complete exemption).

---

59 *See* Contract Law, art. 53.
60 The "substantial breach disclaimer" is a disclaimer is aimed at releasing the breaching party from liability in a case where there is a substantial breach of the contract.

CHAPTER 6

Contract Defenses—Validity Issues

A contract, once concluded by the parties, may not be enforced if defects exist that affect its validity. As discussed, the validity of contracts has received special attention in China and issues of validity are distinct from those of contract conclusion. For purposes of the Contract Law, the validity of a contract determines whether the contract will be effective and legally binding as to the contractual parties. In China, if a contract lacks an element that is essential to its effectiveness or validity, the contract will not be enforceable as a matter of law.[1] Practically, the validity of a contract is always a target to be focused on in order to challenge a contract or to resist a contract claim in a meaningful way.

The case below illustrates a battle over the validity of a contract after the contract is concluded. The case involves a contract for the transfer of shares. The issue is whether the transfer of certain shares requires the creditors' approval. On appeal, the High People's Court of Liao Ning Province affirmed in part and reversed in part the lower court's judgment. In its reversal, the Liao Ning High People's Court invalidated part of the share transfer contract on the basis that it violated the Company Law.

> Shen Yang International Technology and Industry Park Company, Ltd.
> v.
> Shen Yang Electronic Company, Inc.
>
> High People's Court of Liao Ning Province[2]

Appellant (plaintiff at trial court) appeals to this Court from the Civil Judgment "(2002) Shen Min (3) Chu Zhi No. 559" entered by the Intermediate People's Court of ShenYang City over a dispute over a contract of transfer of equity shares.

The facts as pleaded at the trial court are as follows. Appellant and respondent entered into a contract for the transfer of equity shares on September 24, 2000. Under the contract, appellant would transfer to respondent all 30% of the equity shares of Shen Yang New World Industry Company, Ltd. and the subscribed capital in the amount of RMB 4.2 million that appellant held. It was agreed that the payment of RMB 4.2 million Yuan should be made within ten days after the transfer of the equity shares was approved by the original approval authority and registered with the commerce and industry authority, and the legal process of the transfer was complete. The contract would take effect after the said approval and the registration.

---

1 See Jiang Bixin, *et al*, Understanding and Application of the Adjudication Rules of the Guiding Cases of the SPC (Contract, Vol. I), 100–101 (China Legal Publishing House, 2012).
2 See, Civil Judgment Document, (2003) Liao Min 2 He Zhong Zhi No. 314.

CONTRACT DEFENSES—VALIDITY ISSUES 179

After the contract was concluded, on October 30, 2000, the Development Bureau of Shen Yang Economic and Technology Development Zone issued a document of "An Official Reply to the Request for Transfer of Equity Shares of Shen Yang New World Industry Company, Ltd.," approving the transfer of 30% shares and the subscribed capital of RMB 4.2 million Yuan. The Reply required that a registration of change of the shareholder for the transfer be made with the relevant registration authority within thirty days after the transfer. On December 12, 2000, Shen Yang New World Industry Company Ltd. registered the change with the local commerce and industry authority. A year later, appellant launched this litigation asking the court to declare the transfer contract invalid on the grounds that the contract for the transfer of equity shares violated the Company Law and other provisions of law concerning the transfer of State-owned assets.

The trial court held that the contract for the transfer of shares was valid and should be observed because the intention of the parties as manifested in the contract was true and the contract was made voluntarily in full compliance with the law. The trial court dismissed appellant's argument that the contract was void because it violated the law, and because it not only infringed upon the lawful interests of the appellant but also caused a significant amount of State assets to run off.

The court reasoned that although the "Methods of Administration of State Owned Assets Appraisal" issued by the State Council on November 16, 1991 required an asset appraisal for the transfer of the assets possessed by the enterprise on behalf of the State, under Article 45 of the Detailed Rules for Implementation of the Methods of Administration of State Owned Assets Appraisal, promulgated by the State Owned Assets Administration Office of the State Council on July 18, 1992, such appraisal applies to the situation where the Chinese investor has 50% or more shares in an equity joint venture or contractual joint venture.

In this case, according to the trial court's finding, the equity shares to be transferred amounted to only 30% of the total shares of Shen Yang New World Industry Company, Ltd. and thus did not fall within the scope of required appraisal. And since the appellant had accepted the payment for part of the transferred shares, and the transfer had been approved by the relevant state authority and registered with the local commerce and industry authority, the contract for the transfer had become effective, and the parties were bound by the contract.

On that ground, the trial court, pursuant to Articles 44 and 52 of the Contract Law, dismissed appellant's complaint and entered a judgment (a) holding the contract for the transfer of the shares entered into by the parties valid and effective, and (b) denying other claims of appellant and respondent. In addition, appellant was ordered to pay the litigation fee in the amount of RMB 31,010 Yuan.

Appellant appealed. In its petition for appeal, appellant argued that the share transfer contract was void because it was not a manifestation of the parties' true intention and was without creditors' approval, and that the contents of the contract were unlawful because articles 6,7, and 8 of the contract were contrary to the provisions of the Company Law of China that require creditors' approval for the bearing of the existing debts of the respondent.

In its rebuttal, respondent asserted that the transfer was valid because it was agreed upon by the parties on a voluntary basis and approved by the relevant government authority. Respondent further argued that the debts did not exceed the amount of subscribed capital of the shareholders because the worth of the transferred shares was RMB 12 million Yuan and the debts to be born by shareholders were RMB 6 million Yuan, and due to the uncooperative conduct of appellant, some of the debts failed to obtain creditors' approval, but this should not affect the effect of the share transfer agreement.

The finding of this Court reveals that the share transfer contract was concluded on September 24, 2000 and according to article 6 of the contract, Party B (respondent) accepts the rights and obligations after the transfer. It is found that (a) as of the date of transfer, the total debts of Shen Yang New World Industry Company, Ltd. (New World Industry) were RMB 20 million Yuan, and as a consequence of the transfer, such debts would be born by new shareholders and beginning on the day of transfer, the respondent was to be responsible for RMB 6 million Yuan debts proportionate to respondent's prescribed capital.

In addition, article 7 of the contract states a promise of Party A (appellant) to guarantee the payment for the debts of the New World Industry, which provides that after completion of the registration of the transferred shares, if appellant fails to manage the transfer and then causes damages to the New World Industry, appellant shall be responsible for the payment of debts or the damages. Moreover, under article 8, which provides the methods and time limit of the guarantee, the New World Industry shall be a guarantor jointly and severally responsible for ensuring that appellant will keep its promise, and the time of the guarantee of New World Industry has a two-year limit from the date when creditors make claims to the New World Industry after the transfer is complete.

In light of the facts that the share transfer contract on September 24, 2004 was reached by consensus of the parties and was approved by the Development Bureau of Shen Yang Economic and Technology Development Zone, and the change of the shares was registered with the commerce and industry authority, we hold that, except for its articles 6 (1)(a), 7 and 8, the contract of the share transfer is valid and lawful, and accordingly, the appellant's argument about loss of State-owned assets and avoidance of the contract must be denied for lack of factual and legal grounds.

Under the Company Law of China, after making capital or property contribution to a company, the shareholders only have the ownership of the shares of the company but do not have the right to own the credit rights or control the debt liabilities that belong to the company. However, the shareholders as the contributor of capital have such owners' rights as benefiting from the assets of the company, making major decisions, and choosing managerial personnel for the company. On the other hand, the company has the property right of the legal person that is formed entirely by the shareholders' capital contributions, and it possesses civil rights and bears civil obligations according to the law. In a limited liability company, shareholders assume the company's liability to the extent of their respective capital contribution, and the company is liable for its debts to the extent of all of its assets.

Applying the above rules to this case, we conclude that in the share transfer contract, articles 6 (1), 7 and 8, concerning the agreement on the liabilities to be assumed by the New World Industry, violate the provisions of the Company Law for want of the creditors' approval, and therefore must be held void, and the appellant's request for the voidance of the contract is granted with regard to these articles. The trial court was right on the finding of facts but erred in part in the application of law, which must be corrected on appeal. In accordance with Articles 56 of the Contract Law, Articles 3 and 4 of the Company Law, and Article 153 (1)(b) of the Civil Procedure Law, it is so ordered:

1. Reverse and modify the judgment (1) in Shen Min (3) Chu Zhi No. 599 Civil Judgment of Shen Yang Intermediate People's Court: Articles 6 (1)(a), 7 and 8 of the share transfer contract entered into between appellant and respondent on September 29, 2000 is null and void, and the remaining provisions of the contract are valid and effective.
2. Affirm the judgment (2) in Shen Min (3) Chu Zhi No. 599 Civil Judgment of Shen Yang Intermediate People's Court.

In addition, the RMB 31,010 Yuan litigation costs at the trial court shall be paid by appellant in the amount of RMB 18,606 Yuan, and by respondent in the amount of RMB 12,404 Yuan. As to the appellate court costs of RMB 31,010 Yuan, appellant shall pay RMB 18,606 Yuan, and respondent RMB 12,404 Yuan. This judgment is final.

In the *Shen Yang International* case, the High People's Court of Liao Ning addressed the validity of the contract separately from the conclusion of the contract. In this case, the contract was duly concluded, but because certain contents of the contract were found to violate relevant provisions of the law, such contents were therefore held to be invalid and as a result unenforceable. In addition, an important legal implication of the case was that the invalidation of partial terms of a contract do not affect the validity of the contract's remaining terms if the invalidated terms can be isolated.

1   Issues at Stake

Given the significance of contract validity, Chapter 3 of the Contract Law is specially designed to govern all validity issues in light of effectiveness of contracts. Under the provisions in Chapter 3 of the Contract Law, a contract may be held valid, void, or voidable with regard to its legal effect, or its effect may be subject to a further determination. Generally, a contract, once concluded, will be effective and enforceable if (a) it is made by parties possessing the required legal capacity, (b) it is the product of the parties' real intentions,[3] and (c) it does not violate any law or public interest. In addition, the effectiveness of a contract may be impacted by the conditions agreed upon by the parties.

Issues affecting the validity of a contract involve several aspects. One aspect, as noted, is the requirement of approval and/or registration. Normally, in accordance with Article 44 of the Contract Law, a legally formed contract without defects takes effect upon its formation (conclusion). However, as discussed in Chapter 4 of this book, if an approval or registration for the contract is required, the contract will not become effective until the said approval or registration is obtained.

But, with regard to the approval or registration requirement, the SPC is quite lenient as to when the approval or registration shall be obtained. As noted, according the SPC, the parties may obtain the approval or registration if required for the contract up to the conclusion of the court hearing in the trial.[4] In addition, the SPC has narrowly interpreted the application of the registration requirement to the validity of contracts. In the opinion of the SPC, a failure to obtain the registration shall not affect the effectiveness of the contract, but only the transfer of the ownership of the contracted items or other related

---

3   As discussed, the question whether a real intention is the true or apparent intention of the parties requires an assessment of the parties' intentions.
4   See the SPC, the 1999 Contract Law Interpretation, art. 9.

property rights in cases where the law or administrative regulation requiring a registration for a contract does not explicitly provide that the contract shall take effect after the registration.[5]

The following case explains the situation where government approval is required for a certain contract and illustrates how the requirement rule is enforced.

He Nan Dayou Chemical Products Company Ltd.
v.
Shan Qian Fu Da Coal Mine

High People's Court of He Nan Province[6]

Plaintiff, He Nan Da You Chemical Products Company, Ltd (Da You), is a company with its business address at No. 30 Chengbei Street, Hui Xian City, He Nan Province. Defendant, Shan Qian Fu Da Coalmine (Fu Da), is located at Shan Qian Village, Zhang Zhuang Township, Hui Xian City.

The case was appealed from the civil judgment of Xin Xiang Intermediate People's Court concerning the dispute over the contract of joint business operation between Da You and Fu Da. The facts of the case, as the trial court found, are as follows:

On December 13, 1996, Da You, through Da You Coal Mine formed by Da You, obtained a mining license from local authority. Prior to that, Da You invested in the exploration of coal reserves in several areas of Shan Qian Village. From June 1998, Da You started negotiating with Fu Da for a joint operation of the coalmine. During the negotiations, Da You provided Fu Da with the coal reserves materials collected by Da You during the coalmine exploration, and Fu Da copied those materials.

Thereafter, Da You and Fu Da orally agreed as follows: (1) the parties would invest RMB 12.5 million Yuan to form a joint coalmine, of which Da You would invest RMB 2.5 million Yuan or 20% of the total investment, and Fu Da RMB 10 million or 80% of the total investment; (2) Da You's cost for the exploration would be priced at RMB 4 million Yuan and according to the investment ratio, Fu Da would refund Da You RMB 1.5 million; (3) the RMB 1.5 million Yuan refund would be made to Da You after Da You completed all information related to exploration and received a new mining license; (4) the joint coalmine would be operated according to the "Charter of Coalmine" adopted by the parties, and after the joint operation started, the name of the coalmine would be "Fu Da Coalmine"; and (5) during the first two years after the profit-making year, Da You would not participate in dividend distribution and would also not bear any risk, and after that, the parties would share the profits and bear risks in proportion to their respective investments.

Based on the oral agreement and according to the requirement of the Bureau of Mining Administration, Da You submitted to the authority an application for canceling the registration of Da You Coalmine. From July 17, 1999 to July 27, 1999, Fu Da made three payments to Da You in a total amount of RMB 390,000 Yuan and no additional payment was made thereafter. On December 30, 1999, the parties signed "Agreement of Joint Operation of Coalmine" (Joint

---

5   See *id*.
6   See, Judgment of High People's Court of He Nan Province, (2003) Yufa Min 2 Zhong Zhi No. 47.

Operation Agreement) that contained the terms and conditions of the oral agreement, and the parties affixed to the Agreement with their official seals. On March 8, 2000, Fu Da registered "Fu Da Coalmine" (the entity for the joint operation) with the Provincial Bureau of Commerce and Industry, but the nature of the entity as registered was a collectively owned entity in the name of Sha He Village without consulting with Da You Chemical. On February 25, 2001, per the request of Sha He Village, "Fu Da Coalmine" was renamed as "Shan Qian Fu Da Coalmine," of which Da You was not notified.

On December 17, 2001, Fu Da obtained the new mining license, which showed that Fu Da's scope of mining was expanded to include the mining areas of former Da You Coalmine, and Da You Coalmine was merged into Fu Da Coalmine. But after paying RMB 390,000 Yuan, Fu Da refused to pay to Da You the balance of RMB 1.11 million Yuan. Da You brought this lawsuit requesting the court to order Fu Da to continue performing the Joint Operation Agreement and to pay the overdue RMB 1.11 million Yuan.

The trial court held that the Joint Operation Agreement entered into between the parties did not violate any prohibitive provisions of the law and should be held valid. The approval was not required because there was no evidence that the nature of the contract was to transfer the right of mine exploration. In addition, it could be seen from the document of the Bureau of Mining Administration that the Bureau knew and allowed the merger of the two coalmines, and therefore, the approval of the Bureau could be assumed. Although the Joint Operation Agreement did not mention the merger of the two coalmines, merger should be regarded as the basis on which the Joint Operation Agreement was made. In addition, after signing of the Joint Operation Agreement, Fu Da actually expanded its mining operation to the coalmine that used to be owned by Da You and made three payments to Da You according the Agreement. These facts demonstrated that the parties had performed their contractual obligations, which proved that the contract had taken effect. Therefore, the trial court denied Fu Da's argument that the Joint Operation Agreement did not take effect because it was not approved by the Bureau of Mining Administration and the approval was required since the Agreement was to transfer the right of mine exploration.

Fu Da argued that the Joint Operation Agreement was invalid because Da You did not have the right to explore the mine reserves, and the coal reserves material obtained by Da You during its exploration was also invalid, which made it groundless for the parties to have the joint operation. By dismissing Fu Da's argument, the trial court held that the question whether Da You had the right of exploration should be reported to the relevant administrative authority for a solution, but should not affect the validity of the Agreement. Under the Contract Law of the People's Republic of China, the validity of a contract shall not be denied as long as the contents of the contract do not violate the prohibitive provisions of the State.

In its judgment for Da You, the trial court ruled that (a) the Joint Operation Agreement entered into by the parties was valid and the parties should continue performing; (b) within ten days after this judgment was effective, Fu Da should pay Da You RMB 1.11 million; and (3) the litigation fee of RMB 15,560 Yuan should be paid by Fu Da.

On appeal, Fu Da argued that the trial court erred in finding the Agreement valid and in determining the nature of the Joint Operation. The Joint Operation Agreement was in fact an agreement to transfer the right of exploration, the right of mining, as well as the sale of mine reserves. In accordance with the "Law of Mineral Resources" of China and relevant administrative regulations, only the geology and mineral resources departments of the State Council and provinces have the right to examine and approve the transfer of exploration and mining rights, and materials of exploration may only be used after approval by the mineral resource reserves commission of provincial level or higher. The merger of two coalmines must also be approved by the provincial mining administrative authority.

Fu Da further asserted that since Da You did not have the right of exploration, the exploration materials collected by Da You could not be used, and by using the illegal exploration materials to form a joint operation with Fu Da, Da You sought an exorbitant profit. Therefore, the Joint Operation Agreement was invalid because it concealed an illegitimate purpose. Even if the Joint Operation Agreement was valid, because Da You's illegal exploration activity was irreparable and it had lost capacity to perform, Fu Da had every reason to rescind the contract unilaterally. Fu Da also pointed out that the trial court's finding that the negotiations between the parties began in June 1998 was erroneous because the parties did not negotiate until summer 1999.

The appellate court finds that Fu Da and Da You negotiated the joint operation matter in summer 1999 and the Agreement of Joint Operation was concluded on December 20, 1999. The appellate court believes that the trial court's finding that negotiations began in June 1998 was a clerical error. The court also finds that at the time of the Agreement, both Da You Coalmine and Fu Da Coalmine had legal mining licenses, but not exploration licenses. According to Da You's explanation, at that time, the Hui Xia local geology and mineral resources administrative authority did not give an exploration license to any coalmines in the area of Hui Xia.

On the basis of its finding, the appellate court is of the opinion that, given the actual situation at the time of the contract, the issuance of a mining license by the Hui Xia local mining administrative authority to Da You should be deemed as an acknowledgement of Da You's exploration activity by a mining administrative authority, though Da You had no exploration license. On this ground, Da You's exploration materials shall be regarded to have been obtained legally. In addition, it is reasonable to conclude that both Da You's investment in the exploration and the result of the exploration constitute Da You's legitimate property right. Also, there was no violation of the law with regard to the agreement between Da You and Fu Da to price the property right at RMB 4 million Yuan, of which RMB 2.5 million was used as an investment to form the joint operation of mining with Fu Da.

It is therefore held that the Agreement of Joint Operation is valid and enforceable. The contents of the Agreement state that the form of the joint operation is a joint venture for establishing a new coalmine, as well as a transfer of exploration and mining rights. Although the merger of the two coalmines was not approved by provincial authority, it was approved by Hui Xian local mining administration authority. Also, although provincial approval is required, the lack of such approval can be remedied by obtaining such approval afterward, and this lack therefore does not affect the validity of the Agreement.

Fu Da's argument against the validity of the Joint Operation Agreement is denied and the judgment below is affirmed.

Other aspects pertaining to contract validity include the parties' capacity, fraud or duress, illegality, mistakes, as well as unfairness. Each of these aspects deserves particular attention because each is often used as a contract defense. In a contract dispute case, an important preliminary question is whether there is a contract or, if there is a contract, whether the contract is valid and enforceable. Any of the defenses, if successfully pleaded, defeat a contract claim because each defense constitutes a legal obstacle to either the formation or enforcement of a contract.

In the Contract Law, issues relating to contract validity are addressed in Articles 45 to 59. Note that since each validity issue has a particular impact on the validity as well as the effectiveness of contracts, it is governed by a different set of rules in the Contract Law. Note also that, in the minds of Chinese contract law scholars, a question of contract validity is essentially a question about how a concluded contract is to be evaluated and effectuated under the law enacted by the State legislature. Underlying this view is the notion that while the conclusion of a contract depends on the intention of the parties, the validity and effectiveness of a contract is subject to the will of the State.[7]

Under the Contract Law, a contract that has a validity issue may become void or voidable. In addition, the Contract Law recognizes a special category of contracts that are not necessarily void or voidable, but that require further determination as to their validity. Such a contract is said to have two distinctions: first, the effectiveness of the contract is uncertain, and second, the defect affecting the effectiveness is curable.[8]

2 Capacity of the Parties—Effect-to-be-Determined Contract

At the outset, for a contract to be enforceable, the parties to the contract must have the psychological and intellectual capacity to understand and appreciate the consequences of what they have bargained for. Strong social and public interests necessitate legal protection for those who lack such capacity or have limited capacity. Traditionally, as a general rule of contract law, a contract that is defective with respect to its parties' capacity is either void or voidable.[9] In China, however, the term of "effect-to-be-determined," instead of "voidable," is commonly used to characterize contracts whose parties have limited capacity.

The term "effect-to-be-determined" in China signifies that it is uncertain, before certain acts or facts are ascertained, whether an already-concluded contract is effective.[10] Thus, the doctrine of effect-to-be-determined is premised on the notion that the contract itself is good, but there is a problem with respect to the capacity of one or more party to the contract. In other words, the effect-to-be-determined does not affect the contract's conclusion or its contents, but rather involves the capacity of a party to the contract. Some,

---

7   See Wang Liming & Cui Jian Yuan, *A new Commentary on Contract Law—General Provisions* (revised edition), 233–240 (China University of Political Science and Law Press, 2000).
8   See Wang Liming, Contract Law of China, 97 (Wells, 2016).
9   See Joseph M. Perillo, Contract Law (7th ed), Hornbook Series, 259 (West, 2014).
10 See Wang Liming, *Study on Contract Law*, 540–541 (People's University Press, 2002). But others insist that an effect-to-be-determined contract shall specially refer to a contract where one party's capacity is limited and the contract's effectiveness therefore requires a relevant third party's affirmation. See Cui Yunling, *General View on Contract Law*, 139–140 (China University of People's Public Security Press) (2003).

however, argue that a contract's effect being to-be-determined directly affects the contract's conclusion because a party to the contract being of limited capacity precludes the contract from being concluded without certain actions as required by the law.[11]

The capacity to contract is a matter of civil capacity. As a creation of law, civil capacity contains two different forms: capacity to enjoy and capacity to exercise. The former refers to the ability to enjoy rights while the latter is about the ability to take action or the capacity for civil conduct. The concept of civil action capacity in China was first provided in the 1986 Civil Code, and was modified in 2017 when the 2017 GPCL was adopted. One of the major changes created by the 2017 GPCL is that the term "citizen" is replaced by the term "natural person." Another major change is that the age at which a natural person lacks capacity is decreased from ten to eight years old. Under the 2017 GPCL, a natural person has the capacity to enjoy upon birth, but whether a natural person has the capacity to exercise depends on the person's level of maturity as well as mental condition.[12]

Under Articles 17 to 20 of the 2017 GPCL, the civil capacity of a natural person is divided into three categories: full capacity, limited capacity, and no capacity. A natural person attaining the age of eighteen or older is an adult, and an adult has full capacity for civil conduct and may independently engage in civil activities.[13] A natural person who has reached the age of sixteen and whose main source of income is his or her own work shall be deemed as having full capacity for civil conduct.[14]

A minor aged eight or older is a person with limited capacity for civil conduct and must be represented by, or obtain the consent or ratification of, his agent *ad litem* for civil conduct, though he may perform civil acts purely beneficial to himself or appropriate to his age and intelligence.[15] A minor under the age of eight has no capacity for civil conduct and must be represented by his or her agent *ad litem* in all civil activities.

Pursuant to Article 23 of the 2017 GPCL, the guardian of a person without capacity or with limited capacity for civil conduct shall be the agent *ad litem* of such person. This provision is basically a replica of Article 14 of the 1986 Civil Code. It is required under Article 163 of the 2017 GPCL that an agent *ad litem* exercise agent power as conferred by the law.[16] In addition, pursuant to Article

---

11   See Xiao Xun, et al, *Explanations to the Contract Law of the People's Republic of China*, 185 (China Legal System Press, 1999).
12   See the 2017 GPCL, art. 13.
13   See *id.*, art. 17 and 18.
14   See *id.*, art. 18.
15   See *id.*, art. 19.
16   See *id.*, art. 163.

27 of the 2017 GPCL, the guardian of a minor may be parents, grandparents, elder brothers or sisters, or other individuals or organizations willing to act as a guardian.[17]

Note that as provided in the 2017 GPCL, the parents of a minor are the guardians of the minor, and only if both parents of the minor are dead or incapable of acting as a guardian, may the grandparents, elder brothers or sisters, or other individuals or organizations act—in that order—as a guardian.[18] Also, the guardianship of other individuals or organizations is subject to approval by such authorities as the urban residents' committee, villagers' committee, or civil affairs department of the place where the minor is domiciled.[19]

With regard to an adult with a mental illness, the 2017 GPCL follows the 1986 Civil Code and treats such a person in two different ways. First, if an adult is unable to cognize his or her own conduct, he or she shall have no capacity for civil conduct and shall in civil activities be represented by his or her agent *ad litem*.[20] This provision equally applies to minors aged eight and above who lack the ability to understand their conduct.[21] Second, an adult who is incompetent to fully cognize his or her own conduct shall have limited capacity for civil conduct and shall be represented by, or obtain the consent or ratification of, his or her agent *ad litem* for civil activities, but may independently undertake civil actions that purely benefit himself or herself or that are commensurate with his or her intelligence or mental health.[22]

Since minors and adults with mental illnesses are unable to reasonably guard their own interests, the law protects them from being taken advantage of by others. Thus, any civil activity that is engaged in by a person who has no capacity for civil conduct or whose capacity for civil conduct is limited and that is not consented to by the person's agent *ad litem* has no legal effect. Again, for purposes of civil conduct, the agent *ad litem* of a person without or with limited capacity is the person's guardian.

---

17   See the 2017 GPCL, art. 27.
18   See *id.*
19   See *id.*
20   For example, according to the SPC, the civil act of a person of intermittent insanity shall be deemed void if such civil act is proven to take place during the period of morbidity. And the civil act of a person during his state of unconsciousness shall also be deemed void. See the SPC, *Opinions on Implementation and Application of the General Principles of Civil Law of the People's Republic of China (Provisional) 1988*, art. 67 (hereinafter referred to as Opinions on 1986 Civil Code).
21   See the 2017 GPCL, art. 21.
22   See *id.*, art. 22.

Pursuant to Article 28 of the 2017 GPCL, the guardian of an adult with no or limited capacity for civil action may be the person's spouse, parents, child, other close relatives, or other individuals or organizations willing to act as the guardian. Similarly, if another individual or organization is to serve as the guardian for an adult, he, she, or it must have approval from the urban resident committee, villagers' committee, or civil affairs department of the place of the adult's domicile.[23]

In addition to the maturity and mental or health status of a person, capacity for civil conduct involves the power to represent (i.e., agent authority) and the power to dispose of the property of others. Thus, in light of the application of the Contract Law, contracts whose effect is subject to further determination include (a) a contract that is concluded by a person with limited civil capacity, (b) a contract that is entered into by an agent in the name of the principal without authorization, and (c) a contract concerning a property transfer that is made by a person without the right of disposition to the property. In any of these cases, the contract, although it is concluded, will have no effect unless and until further action as required has been taken.

2.1 Contract by a Person with Limited Capacity for Civil Conduct

Under Article 47 of the Contract Law, a contract concluded by a person with limited capacity for civil conduct shall be effective after being ratified by the person's agent *ad litem*.[24] This provision implicates that a contract made by a person with limited capacity for civil conduct is not necessarily void or voidable by the operation of law, but its effectiveness is subject to the ratification of the person's agent *ad litem*. Although the term "ratification" is not defined in the Contract Law, it is commonly understood in China to mean approval, acknowledgement, or affirmation. Some argue that ratification should also include the prior approval by the agent *ad litem*—even though Article 47 uses the term "after" in defining ratification—because the approval in advance may need to be confirmed or proved in order to render the contract effective.

Note that China and western countries like the United States sharply diverge in their conceptions of contract ratification. In American contract law, ratification is regarded as an effective surrender of the power of avoidance or disaffirmance, and the power of avoidance may generally be exercised only by the minor or mentally infirmed person, unless a guardian is duly appointed.[25] In

---

23 See *id.*, art 28.
24 See the Contract Law, art. 47.
25 See Calamari & Perillo, *the Law of Contracts* (4th ed), Hornbook Series, 296–305 (West Group, 1998).

China, however, ratification is deemed to be civil conduct empowering agents *ad litem* to protect the legitimate interests of those who have limited capacity for civil conduct, and the power of ratification rests with the agent *ad litem*. In one contract book, ratification is explicitly defined as "a manifestation of intent of the agent *ad litem* to acknowledge and accept the effect of the contract a person with limited civil capacity made with other people."[26]

However, under the Contract Law, there are two kinds of contracts for which ratification of the agent *ad litem* is not required when made by a person with limited capacity for civil conduct. Pursuant to Article 47 of the Contract Law, a pure profit-making contract or a contract concluded appropriate to the person's age, intelligence, or mental health conditions need not be ratified by an agent *ad litem* of such person. The term "pure profit-making" means to enjoy all the benefits without bearing any responsibility or liability, which include receipt of reward, donation, or payment. According to the SPC, no one may, in the name of a person without or with limited capacity for civil conduct, claim ineffectiveness of such person'a conduct to receive a reward, donation, or remuneration on the ground of the person's incapacity or limited capacity for civil conduct. [27]

The concept of "appropriate to age, intelligence, or mental health conditions" refers to conduct of which a minor or mentally ill person fully understands the nature in accordance with the person's given age, intelligence, and mental health condition. For a minor, civil conduct appropriate to his or her age is normally understood to include activities that do not involve special knowledge or sophisticated understanding or valuables, such as taking the bus or purchasing stationery for the study. For a person with a mental infirmity, conduct is deemed appropriate if it is performed in a manner permitted by the person's mental health and the person understands the nature and consequences of the conduct. A standard that is commonly used in the people's courts is to look at a person's ability to make judgments and to engage in self-protection when evaluating the person's mental health condition.

The Contract Law does expressly address what effect a contract that is a made by a person with no capacity for civil conduct has. But as provided in Article 20 of the 2017 GPCL, a minor under the age of eight is a person without capacity for civil conduct, and presentation, consent, or ratification by the agent *ad litem* is required for such a minor in all civil activities of any nature. The legal implication of Article 20 of the 2017 GPCL is that civil conduct of

---

26 See Su Haopeng, *Conclusion and Effectiveness of Contracts*, 251 (China Legal System Press, 1999).
27 See the SPC, Opinions on 1988 Civil Code, *supra* note 20, art. 6.

a minor under the age of eight has no legal effect unless certain exceptions apply. Thus, it can be reasonably inferred that a contract made by a person without capacity for civil conduct shall be void if not consented to or ratified by the agent *ad litem*.

For purposes of comparison, in American contract law, a contract in which a minor is a party is valid and enforceable unless the minor disaffirms it. In China, by contrast, such a contract has no legal effect unless and until an affirmative action is taken by the minor's agent *ad litem*. In other words, in the United States, the right to disaffirm a contract that would otherwise be enforceable is vested with the minor, while in China, the power to affirm a contract that would otherwise be void lies with the minor's agent *ad litem*.

2.2   Contract by an Agent without Due Authorization

A contract can be concluded by an agent acting on behalf of the principal, and such a contract will bind the principal if it is effective. But in order for an agent to bind the principal to a contract, the agent must have a due authorization from the principal. Such authorization may be made in advance or it may be acquired afterwards through the principal's ratification. Without such authorization, the agent will be an unauthorized agent and thus will have no power of agency. As a general pattern, an agent will be found to lack power of agency when (a) there is no authorization, (b) the scope of the authorization is exceeded, or (c) the authorization is terminated or expires.

Under Article 48 of the Contract Law, if a contract is concluded on behalf of a principal by a person who is not authorized, who exceeds the scope of the authorization, or whose authorization has been terminated, the contract will have no binding effect upon the principal without the principal's ratification, and the person who lacks the due authorization shall be held liable.[28] Thus, before the principal ratifies such a contract, the contract's effectiveness is still pending, and the contract accordingly falls within the effect-to-be-determined category.

A principal's ratification of an act of an agent can be made either by words or through conduct. Ratification by words constitutes express ratification while ratification through conduct amounts to implied ratification. According to the SPC's 2009 Contract Law Interpretation, where an agent enters into a contract on behalf of a principal without authorization, and the principal starts performing the obligations arising out of the contract, the principal's performance shall be regarded as the principal's ratification of the contract.[29]

---

28   See the Contract Law, art. 48.
29   See the SPC, the 2009 Contract Law Interpretation, art. 12.

Conversely, under Article 49 of the Contract Law, if the other party has reason to believe that the agent has due authorization from the principal, the act of agency shall be effective.[30] Article 49 governs an agent's apparent authority, which constitutes an exception to Article 48. Thus, in the context of the Contract Law, an agent's authority to make a contract on behalf of a principal can be either actual or apparent. Where an agent acts with apparent authority, the agent's activity in the name of the principal that would otherwise be invalid may become valid.

Apparent authority is authority that an agent is deemed to have in the mind of the other party regardless of the agent's actual status, except that the other party knows and should have known that the agent is not authorized. The standard for determining whether apparent authority exists is whether a reasonable third party would understand that an agent had authority to act. When apparent authority is established, the principal is bound by the agent's action, even if the agent had no actual authority, whether express or implied.

In *Fujian Wanxiang Real Estate Development Inc. Ltd. v. Weng Yanjin* (2016), defendant *Weng* was a shareholder and the chairman of the board of deirector of *Wanxiang*. During August 2009 and Feburary 2010, *Weng* successively borrowed RMB 2.45 million from *You Binqiong* and made a loan and agreement. Being unable to pay back the loan, *Weng* at the request of *You* signed a loan quanrantee contract in the name of *Wanxiang* and executed the contract with a forged company seal of *Wangxiang*. *Weng* was late charged with criminal offense of seal frogery and was sentensed to six months imprisonment. *Wangxiang* then asked court to invalidate the guarantee agreement and denied any liability arising therefrom.[31]

The courts in both first and second instances rejected Wangxiang's request. Wanxiang asked the SPC to intervene through the process of judicial supervision. In its affirming the lower courts' decision, the SPC held that given *Weng's* special duties and shareholder status in *Wanxiang*, it was sufficent to make *You* reasonablly rely on *Weng* without a substantive examination of the authenticity of the official seal. The SPC concluded that *Weng's* conduct constituted an apparant agent for Wangxiang, and therefore Wanxiang should be held liable for the guarantee liability under Article 49 of the Contract Law.[32]

In judicial practice, apparent authority under the Contract Law is considered to contain four basic elements. The four elements are: (a) the agent has

---

30 See *id.*, art. 49.
31 See SPC Civl Judgment, Zuigao Minsen No. 733 (2016), available at https://www.qichacha.com/wenshuDetail_com_9fad686fb0e4df39fb3d52698ec0741b.html.
32 See *id.*

no authorization from the principal, (b) the other party reasonably believes that the agent is duly authorized by the principal; (c) the other party is a *bona fide* person, and (d) the civil acts of both the agent and the other party are valid and legally effective. [33] In addition, there are three circumstances under which apparent authority will be found by the people's courts.

First, apparent authority will be found where the principal, despite lacking actual authorization, engages in conduct that creates an impression on the other party that there has been such authorization. This may occur, for example, when the principal does not authorize an agent to sign a contract but allows the agent to use the principal's official seal or use a blank contract form bearing the principal's seal. Apparent authority may also stand when the principal knows about the agent's activity on behalf of the principal without authorization, but takes no action to repudiate it.[34]

Second, apparent authority exists if there is a change in authorization with respect to the scope of the authority granted to the agent but the principal fails to make that change known to the other party. In such a situation, in the other party's belief, the agent still has the same authority as he or she used to have. Accordingly, in this circumstance the principal may still be held liable for the agent's conduct on the principal's behalf with regard to the other party's interests that are involved. A logical reason is that the principal's guilt of laches in failing to make the other party aware of the change of the agent's authority will not overcome the other party's reasonable belief that the agent still has the authority it started with.

Third, the people's courts will find that apparent authority occurs where an authorization granted to an agent has been terminated but the principal takes no action to publicly effectuate the termination to make it a known fact that the authorization does not exist anymore. To illustrate, when an agent's authorization is terminated, the principal must make a timely public notice in this regard and in the meantime must endeavor to invalidate the document certificating the authorization through such means as recall or cancellation. Failure to do so makes the principal still liable for the agent's conduct affecting the other party if the other party reasonably believes that the agent remains authorized by the principal (e.g., a belief based on the certificate of agency issued or signed by the principal). The following case further illustrates how apparent authority is determined.

---

33   See Jiang Bixin *et al, supra* note 1, at 197–98.
34   This is the situation where the principal's consent will be assumed. Article 66 of the 1986 Civil Code provides that if a principal is aware that a civil act is being executed in his name but fails to repudiate it, his consent shall be deemed to have been given.

Guang Zhou Swan Sports Goods Trading Company Inc.
v.
Beijing Photoelectricity Hardware Building Materials Store

Beijing No. 2 Intermediate People's Court [35]

In October 2000, Wu Sufeng, the owner of the two-floor building known as No. 29 Zhang Jia Cun, Feng Tai District, Beijing, signed a lease agreement with defendant, under which defendant would rent the building at RMB 60,000 Yuan per year for a term of six years. After that, Wu Sufeng orally agreed that defendant might sublet the building. In December 2000, Li Qian, in the name of plaintiff, entered into a lease contract with defendant. Under the contract, defendant agreed to rent to plaintiff a 210-square-meter space in the said building. The term of the lease was three years from December 25, 2000 to December 25, 2003 at an annual rent of RMB 120,000 Yuan, paid in two installments.

According to the contract, during the term of the lease, if for whatever reason plaintiff caused defendant to suffer damages, plaintiff would be responsible without condition. In addition, plaintiff would pay all of defendant's electricity and water bills that were actually incurred during the lease term. Moreover, any non-performance or incomplete performance of the contract would be deemed a breach of contract and the breaching party would be responsible for actual damages caused to the other plus 10% of the annual rent in that given year.

After conclusion of the contract, on December 15, 2000, Li Qian, on behalf of plaintiff, paid defendant RMB 5,000 Yuan as a deposit. On December 25, plaintiff wired RMB 55,000 Yuan via the commerce bank of Guang Zhou to defendant as the payment for the rent. In that month, defendant delivered the building to Li Jian for him to use. Part of the rented building was used as a store to sell sportswear. On February 4, 2001, at about 10:35 pm, Li Qian called police reporting that the windows of the store were smashed. On March 20, 2001, Li Qian wrote to Li Guo Jun, defendant's legal representative, requesting to terminate the lease because the door and windows of the building were repeatedly broken by someone and there was no solution although several efforts were attempted. In the letter, Li Qian also asked for a refund of the balance of the paid rent (from March 25, 2001 to June 25, 2001). Thereafter, Li Qian made no further attempt to negotiate with defendant on whether the lease ought to be terminated.

In April 2001, Li Qian moved out of the building. At the end of May 2001, defendant took back the building and at that time both the door and windows of the building remained damaged. Defendant then had all damaged doors and windows fixed at its own cost. In June 2001, plaintiff brought the lawsuit against defendant at Fengtai District People's Court, alleging that plaintiff had orally agreed with defendant to rent defendant's two-floor building, and plaintiff had wired to defendant the half-year rent in the amount of RMB 55,000 Yuan, but as of the lawsuit, defendant never made the building available for plaintiff to use. Plaintiff then sought to recover from defendant the rent payment of RMB 55,000 Yuan.

Defendant argued that defendant signed the lease contract with Li Qian, who represented plaintiff, and delivered the building to Li Qian after receiving the RMB 5,000 Yuan deposit from Li Qian and the RMB 55,000 Yuan rent payment from plaintiff, and therefore, there was no breach of contract on defendant's side. Defendant then filed a counterclaim against plaintiff, asserting that plaintiff terminated the contract during the term of the contract without defendant's consent, and that the termination constituted a breach of contract. In addition, defendant

---

35 See the No.1 Civil Trial Division, Beijing High People's Court, A Precise Analysis of Beijing Civil Cases, 170 (Law Press 2003).

argued that during plaintiff's use of the building, the door and windows of the building were all damaged, which cost defendant RMB 9,795.48 Yuan to repair, and therefore, defendant was entitled to damages of RMB 36,000 Yuan plus RMB 9,795.48 of repair expenses.

To rebut defendant's counterclaim, plaintiff asserted that plaintiff did not actually use the building, and Li Qian was not an employee of plaintiff, nor did Li Qian have any agreement with plaintiff concerning the lease of the building. The RMB 55,000 Yuan rent was wired per the request of plaintiff's local representative who had an oral agreement with defendant for leasing the said building for six months at RMB 110,000 Yuan per annum.

In the trial court, it was found that the lease agreement at issue was entered by and between Li Qian in the name of plaintiff and defendant, and thereafter Li Qian paid the deposit to defendant on the plaintiff behalf. During the hearing, the trial court further found that, after the conclusion of the contract and the payment of the deposit, plaintiff paid defendant part of the rent according to the lease contract, and Li Qian started using the building in the plaintiff's name. Based on the above finding, the trial court held that the conduct of both Li Qian and plaintiff in dealing with defendant was sufficient enough to make defendant believe that Li Qian was authorized to represent defendant, and therefore, plaintiff should be responsible for the legal consequences of Li Qian's conduct in the plaintiff's name.

The trial court also held that the lease agreement between Li Qian and defendant was legally concluded and valid with a binding effect on the parties, and that during the performance of the contract, Li Qian asked for an early termination of the contract, but since Li Qian did obtain consent from defendant in this regard, the contract should not be deemed as having been rescinded per Li Qian's request for the termination. With regard to defendant, the trial court concluded that, pursuant to the lease agreement, defendant was obligated to keep the building in good condition and was responsible for repairing the broken door and windows in a timely manner, and defendant's failure to do so amounted to a breach of contract for which defendant should be held liable.

In its judgment, the trial court, pursuant to Articles 49, 107, 114 and 102 of the Contract Law of China, ordered plaintiff to pay defendant damages of RMB 3,000 for breach of the contract, and dismissed plaintiff's claims as well as other claims made by defendant. Plaintiff appealed to the No.2 Beijing Intermediate People's Court, alleging that the trial court erred in finding of the facts.

On appeal, the appellate court agrees with the trial court in the finding of Li Qian's authority to represent plaintiff. The appellate court is of opinion that the facts of the case clearly indicated Li Qian's apparent authority to act on behalf of plaintiff, even though he might not actually be authorized. The apparent authority can be evidenced from the following conduct by plaintiff: (a) plaintiff wired RMB 55,000 Yuan to defendant as rent payment and the amount, plus the deposit of RMB 5,000 Yuan Li Qian made to defendant, matched the half rent of RMB 60,000 Yuan; (b) the building in question was used as plaintiff's local store as well as a distribution center for plaintiff's goods, and when Li Qian called local police reporting the damage of the windows of the building, he explicitly specified that the building was plaintiff's store; and (c) Li Qian wrote to the defendant's legal representative seeking to terminate the contract and the letter was sent in the plaintiff's name.

The above conduct by plaintiff constituted a legitimate ground on which defendant would believe that Li Qian was duly authorized by plaintiff. Therefore, the appeal is denied and the judgment of trial court is affirmed.

With respect to a legal person (i.e., a corporation or enterprise), its legal representative or person-in-charge is generally regarded as an agent fully authorized by and for the legal person unless a limited authorization is imposed by the legal person's charter. A limited authorization restricts the agent's power to act on behalf of the legal person.[36] In addition, as commonly asserted, the authority of the legal representative or person in charge for a legal person may not exceed the business scope of the legal person.[37]

If, however, the legal representative has made the representation beyond his or her authority, an issue that must be dealt with is whether the representation has any legal effect with regard to the legal person represented. In the past, the people's courts normally regarded such representation as invalid unless it was ratified by the legal person. The Contract Law, however, alterred this judicial practice. Article 50 of the Contract Law provides that, where a legal representative or person-in-charge of a legal person or other organization exceeds his or her power to conclude a contract, the act of such representation will be effective unless the other party knew or ought to know that the representation was beyond the authorized power.[38]

Article 50 is self-evident: apparent authority is presumed with respect to the legal person. Therefore, in connection with contracts, conduct by a legal representative that oversteps the legal representative's authorized power is now generally deemed valid under the Contract Law. In its 1999 Contract Law Interpretation, the SPC further affirms the validity of a contract that is made by a legal person's agent in a manner that exceeds the agent's authority.

Under Article 10 of the 1999 Contract Law Interpretation, where a contract is concluded by a legal representative who has overstepped his or her authorized business power, the people's courts may not void the contract on the ground that the representative exceeded his or her authority, unless the contract violates any restriction or licensing requirements imposed by the State on the relevant business transaction or operation, and/or law or administrative regulations prohibit the relevant business transaction or operation.[39]

2.3   Right to Request Ratification and to Rescind a Contract

Since ratification, once needed, will ultimately determine the validity and effect of a contract entered into by a person with a limited capacity for civil activities, or an unauthorized or not duly authorized agent, it is important that ratification is made in a timely manner in order to reduce the risk of

---

36   The legal representative is defined in Article 38 of the 1986 Civil Code as the person who acts on behalf of the legal person in exercising its functions and powers in accordance with the law and articles of the association of the legal person.
37   Under Article 43 of the 1986 Civil Code, an enterprise as legal person shall bear civil liability for the operational activities of its legal representatives and other personnel.
38   See the Contract Law, art. 50.
39   See the SPC, the 1999 Contract Law Interpreation, art. 10.

uncertainty that the other party may face. In addition to the concern about the other party's interest, the social need for stabilizing business transactions and maintaining a sound order of economic activities would also require efficient ascertainments of contracts with pending issues regarding effectiveness.

To that end, the Contract Law provides the other party with two options regarding a contract for which ratification is sought. One option is to ask for ratification or to "urge to ratify." Under Articles 47 and 48 of the Contract Law, if there is the need for ratification of a contract, the other party may urge the agent *ad litem* or the principal to ratify the contract within one month.[40] If the said agent *ad litem* or principal makes no expression of the ratification within the one-month period, it shall be deemed as a refusal of the ratification, and consequently the contract shall be regarded as void if made by a person without or with a limited capacity for civil conduct, or the agent shall be held liable if the contract is made without the principal's authorization.

The other option is to rescind the contract. As provided in Articles 47 and 48 of the Contract Law, if ratification is required for a contract, before ratification is made, the other party, if bona fide, has the right to rescind the contract. If the other party chooses to rescind the contract, the rescission shall be made by way of notice. Thus, for purposes of the Contract Law, the exercise of the right to rescind a contract for lack of ratification must satisfy two requirements: the rescission must be made before ratification is made and a notice of rescission must be given.

As a practical matter for the agent *ad litem* or principal, the one-month time period for ratification serves a two-fold purpose. First, it is the statutory limitation for making the ratification, and second, the right to ratify is waived if not exercised within one month and it may not be revived after one month has lapsed. For the purpose of ratification, the one-month period starts from the day that the request for ratification is made. The Contract Law, however, does not provide a time limit for requesting ratification, and thus it is up to the other party to decide whether a request for ratification is to be made. The term of bona fide is understood to mean that the other party did not know or have no reason to know that the party at issue had no or limited capacity for civil conduct or, alternatively, that the agent in question had no authority at the time of the contract.

Under the SPC's 2009 Contract Law Interpretation, ratification takes effect when the relevant party's manifested expression of ratification reaches the

---

40 As discussed, the term agent *ad litem* in China refers to a person who serves as the guardian for one who has limited or no civil capacity. See the Contract Law, Articles 47 and 48.

other party. After ratification occurs, the contract is considered to be effective at the time of its conclusion.[41] Moreover, according to the SPC, when a principal assumes liabilities arising from a contract signed by an agent who has exceeded his or her authorization, the principal may seek compensation from the agent for the losses resulting from the agent's activities.[42] In other words, the principal under such circumstances may seek indemnification from the agent.

2.4 *Contract by a Person with No-Right-to-Dispose*

No-right-to-dispose refers to the situation where a person who disposes of the other person's property through a contract has no right to do so. The Contract Law treats the no-right-to-dispose concept as a capacity issue because it involves the status of the person in question (i.e., the holder of the right). Under Article 51 of the Contract Law, if a person that has no right to dispose of another person's assets disposes of such assets through a contract, the contract will only be valid if the holder of the right to the assets ratifies the contract or the person that initially lacked the right of disposal acquires the right after the conclusion of the contract.[43]

In light of Article 51, the right stated in the rule of "no-right-to-dispose" is the property right or the right to a thing. Pursuant to Article 2 of the 2007 Property Law, the property right is a person's exclusive right to directly dominate a certain thing according to law.[44] The essential component of the property right is the right of ownership, although the property right also includes rights to the usufruct as well as to any security interests in the property. Under Article 39 of the Property Law, the right to property ownership consists of the rights to possess, use, benefit from, and dispose of the property.[45] In this context, Article 51 of the Contract Law is regarded as having incorporated the property law concept of "right to a thing" into the contract law.

Article 51 seems quite abstract on its face. Basically, it involves the effect of a contract for the transfer of property that is made by a party who is not entitled to enter into the contract. Consider, for example, if A borrowed a watch from B, and the next day A sold the watch to C without B's consent. Clearly, A was not the owner of the watch and had no right to dispose of (i.e., sell) the watch unless he was instructed to do so by B. B's lack of consent to the contract

---

41 See the SPC, the 2009 Contract Law Interpretation, art. 11.
42 See *id.*, art. 13.
43 See the Contract Law, art. 51.
44 See the Property Law of China, adopted on March 16, 2007, art. 2.
45 See *id.*, art. 39.

between A and C calls the effectiveness of the contract into question, as A's conduct infringes upon B's right to ownership of the watch. As to ownership, B should have every right to reclaim the watch if B had no reason to know about A's unlawful conduct.

Disposal under Article 51 refers to legal disposal, which means the determination of the fate of the property (e.g., whether the property will be sold or given away as a gift, or whether a mortgage will be taken against the property). As noted, full ownership encompasses such rights as the rights to possession, use, receipt of benefit, and disposal of the property. Under the civil law ownership doctrine, except for the right of disposal, all ownership rights may be separated from the ownership. Because of this, the right to dispose is regarded as the core of full ownership, without which full ownership does not exist.

To illustrate, assume that A owns a house. Based on the ownership, A has the right to possess, to use, to benefit from, and to dispose of the house. At his choice, A may lease the house to B. If A leases the house to B, A will transfer his right to possess and use the house to B, and B in turn will pay A for an agreed amount of rent. Despite this, A's ownership of the house will remain intact because A will retain the ultimate control of the property. If, alternatively, A transfers his right to dispose of the house to B, A will lose his ownership of the house since the transfer of the right to dispose will destroy A's status as the owner of the house.

Pursuant to Article 51 of the Contract Law, a contract made by a person who has no right to dispose of the assets referred to in the contract is valid only if (a) the contract is ratified by the holder of the right to dispose of the assets, or (b) the person that initially lacked the right to dispose of the assets subsequently acquires that right. The holder of the right to dispose of a certain asset includes the owner of the asset and the person who has the right to dispose of the asset (e.g., a fully-authorized agent or a bank in the case of foreclosure). Acquisition of the right to dispose may occur through inheritance, purchase, or donation. Thus, before ratification or acquisition is obtained, a contract that is made by a person that has no right to dispose is a contract the effect of which is yet to be determined.

In 2012, the SPC explicitly addressed validity issues with respect to sales contracts in light of Article 51. The SPC instructed that the people's courts will not uphold any claim that a contract is void because the seller did not have full ownership or the right to dispose of the subject matter at the time of the contract.[46] However, in the SPC's opinion, when a seller fails to obtain full

---

46 See the SPC, Interpretation on the Issues Concerning the Application of Law in the Adjudication of Disputes over Sales Contract (2012), art. 3.

ownership or the right to dispose of the subject matter of the contract, such that ownership of the subject matter cannot be transferred to the buyer on the basis of the contract, the buyer may ask the seller to bear liability for its breach of the contract or request a rescission of the contract in addition to compensation for damages.[47]

The concept of no-right-to-dispose and its impact on contracting is not embodied in the contract law of common law countries such as the United States. In the United States, to the extent that contracts are affected, the concept that bears some similarity to no-right-to-disposal is the warranty of a clean title for the good to be sold under the UCC. Pursuant to §2–312 of the UCC, in a contract for sale, the seller warranties that the title conveyed is good and its transfer rightful. Any defect in the warranty may constitute a breach of contract. Nevertheless, as compared with the UCC warranty provision, the major distinction of the no-right-to-dispose is that it does not necessarily make a contract invalid; rather, it only requires further assessment of what the effect of the contract is.

Not surprisingly, Article 51 of the Contract Law is very controversial because it tends to recognize the effect of a contract made by a party who has no right to dispose of the assets involved at the time of the contract. The problem is that Article 51 does not specify what effect such a contract has if the holder of the right to dispose of the assets involved refuses to ratify the contract or the party that made the contract while lacking the right to dispose of the assets fails to subsequently acquire that right. Of course, it might be assumed that without ratification or acquisition of the right to dispose, the contract is void. A more difficult question is whether the contract itself or, rather, the conduct of disposal, are invalid if neither ratification nor acquisition is secured. As a practical matter, if the contract itself is void, the contract has no effect from the very beginning; if the conduct of disposal is alternatively what is void, the effect of the contract is not impacted.

Given the difficulty in this regard, the Contract Law makes no attempt to specify the effect of a contract that is not ratified wherein one party to the contract lacks the right to dispose and fails to subsequently acquire that right. Nevertheless, there have been debates on how (and on what legal grounds) to protect the interest of a party who either receives property in good faith or is a bona fide purchaser in a no-right-to-dispose case.[48] Interestingly,

---

47 See *id.*
48 In drafting the Contract Law, the drafters attempted to solve the "no right to dispose" matter in a more specific way. For example, the January 1995 draft provided that a contract containing the disposal of the property right of the other person shall be valid from the very beginning if the disposal is ratified by the holder of the right or the right to dispose is acquired afterwards. However, such a contract shall be invalid if the right holder does

notwithstanding the debates and the absent provisions in the Contract Law, the people's courts in their judicial practice have a strong tendency to uphold the validity of a contract made by a person having no right to dispose if the interest of a third party who acted in good faith is involved.

The people's courts' position favoring parties who act in good faith as well as bona fide parties is legally derived from the SPC's opinions on the implementation of the 1986 Civil Code, and the UNIDROIT's Principles of International Commercial Contract (PICC). For example, Article 3.3(2) of the PICC clearly states that the mere fact that at the time of conclusion of the contract a party was not entitled to dispose of assets to which the contract relates does not affect the validity of the contract. Also, according to the SPC, during the existence of ownership in the form of joint tenancy, the act of some co-owners to dispose of the property subject to the joint tenancy without the consent of the other co-owners shall in general be deemed invalid. If, however, a third party acquires the property by making compensation in good faith, the legitimate interest of the third party shall be protected and the damages caused to other co-owners of the property shall be paid by the co-owner that disposed of the property without the others' consent.[49]

Thus, in handling contract cases involving no-right-to-dispose, the people's courts normally use two criteria to determine the validity of the contract. The first criteria looks to whether the third party is a bona fide party, or whether the party knows or ought to know that the person he or she is dealing with lacks the right to dispose of the assets concerned in the contract. The second criterion focuses on whether the transfer of the assets in question is made for value. If the third party in good faith acquires the assets through a purchase, the ownership of the property is transferred regardless of the original owner's ratification. If, however, the third party receives the assets without paying

---

not ratify or the right to dispose could not be obtained, but the invalidity shall not be used against a bona fide third party. In the 1996 draft, the provision was changed to an even more detailed one, which provided that a contract concluded to dispose of the assets of the other person by the person having no right to make such a disposal shall be void without the ratification of the right holder or acquisition of the right after conclusion of the contract. A contract to dispose of property under a joint tenancy by one owner without consent of other owners shall be void. However, a third party with good faith obtains through registration or payment the property disposed of by the person having no right to dispose or by a owner of the property under joint tenancy without other owners' agreement shall be protected by law. Those attempts, however, all failed due to the inability to obtain a majority in favor.

49 See the SPC, Opinions on 1986 Civil Code, *supra* note 20, art. 89.

value, the original owner has the right to reclaim the assets no matter whether or not the third party acted in good faith.[50]

It should be emphasized that good faith acquisition of property has gained a great deal of recognition in the people's courts. As a result, in order to protect the third party's interest, a contract concluded by a party having no right to dispose may still be held valid if, after the contract's conclusion, the right holder has not ratisfied the contract and the party has not obtained the right to dispose. It seems that the people's courts have incorporated into their judicial practice the doctrine that no-right-to-dispose affects only the validity of the conduct of disposal, not the validity of the contract itself.

This judicial practice is also recognized in the Property Law. Article 106 of the Property Law provides that if a person transfers to a transferee a piece of property that he has no right to dispose of, the transferee shall acquire ownership of said property under one of the following circumstances: (1) the transferee acts in good faith when the property is transferred to him; (2) the transfer is made at a reasonable price; or (3) the property has duly been registered as required by law, or has been delivered to the transferee if no registration is required.[51]

It is important to note that under the Property Law, in order for a bona fide purchaser's legitimate interest in acquiring real property (i.e., immovable property) to be protected, proper registration or delivery after the transfer must be made. With regard to other property (i.e., movables), the Property Law provides that after a bona fide transferee acquires a movable, the rights previously attached to that property extinguish, unless the transferee is or ought to be aware of the attached rights at the time of transfer of the property.[52] Additionally, the Property Law states that if the property transferred by a person who has no right of disposition cannot be reclaimed under the law, the original owner has the right to request the person to compensate for the losses.[53]

3 Void Contracts

A contract will not be enforced if it is void. Importantly, voidness retroactively applies to a contract from the date the contract was made. This rule is

---

[50] See Li Guoguang, *Explanation and Application of the Contract Law*, 216–218 (Xinghua Press) (1999).
[51] See the Property Law of China, art. 106.
[52] See *id.*, art. 108.
[53] See id., art. 106.

established pursuant to the maxim that a contract that is void now is void from its beginning. Generally speaking, a void contract is a contact that is concluded but that violates the law or regulations or that does not meet the requirements for the contract to be valid. Therefore, if a contract is void, it has no legal effect and is not binding. Under Article 56 of the Contract Law, a contract that is null and void has no legally binding force from its inception.

The question, then, is what makes a contract void. In China, the voidness of a contract must have a statutory basis. In other words, the reason or ground pursuant to which a contract is held to be void must be derived from a statute. The Contract Law sets forth a list of general situations in which a contract is void. According to Article 52 of the Contract Law, a contract is null and void in any of the following situations:

1. A contract is concluded under fraud or duress employed by one party to damage the interests of the State;
2. Malicious collusion is conducted to damage the interests of the State, a collective or a third party;
3. An illegal purpose is concealed under the guise of legitimate means;
4. Social and public interests are harmed; or
5. Compulsory provisions of the laws and administrative regulations are violated.[54]

Note, however, that the range of void contracts as provided in the Contract Law is narrower than that in the 1986 Civil Code.[55] The reason is that the 1986 Civil Code does not distinguish between void contracts and effect-to-be-determined contracts. For example, under the 1986 Civil Code, a contract that is concluded by a person with limited capacity for civil conduct is void; under the Contract Law, by contrast, such a contract is classified as one the effect of which is yet to be determined, which does not necessarily make the contract void.

54　See the Contract Law, art. 52.
55　Article 57 of the 1986 Civil Code provides that the following civil acts shall be null and void:
　　a. A civil act performed by a person without capacity for civil conduct;
　　b. A civil act that may not be independently performed under the law by a person with limited capacity for civil conduct;
　　c. A civil act performed by a person against his or her true intention as a result of fraud, duress, or exploitation of his or her unfavorable position by the other party;
　　d. A civil act performed through malicious collusion to harm the State, a collective, or a third party;
　　e. A civil act that violates laws or social and public interests;
　　f. An economic contract that violates the State mandatory plans; or
　　g. A civil act performed under the guise of legitimacy to conceal illegitimate purposes.

The 1986 Civil Code was criticized as providing the people's courts with overly broad discretion to void contracts. Critics suggested that the 1986 Civil Code's conferal upon courts of such wide latitude to void contracts increased the number of void contracts to such an extent that it has undermined accomplishment of the very objective of the 1986 Civil Code—to maintain the stability of economic transactions. The Contract Law was intended to mitigate this criticism by distinguishing between effect-to-be-determined contracts and void contracts.[56] The 2017 GPCL clearly restricts the void civil acts to those performed by the person with no capacity for civil conduct, excluding the person with limited capacity.[57]

Again, in holding a contract to be void, the people's courts are bound by statutes. No contract may be deemed void except as pursuant to a provision of law. Thus, unless the law provides otherwise, all contracts are assumed to be valid.[58] The voidness rule serves a two-fold purpose: preventing the abuse of power to invalidate contracts so that the parties' reasonable expectation will be protected, and helping to maintain the business transaction in good order.

3.1 *Fraud or Duress*

Under the Contract Law, a contract is null and void if it is concluded as a result of fraud or duress to the extent that the State interest is harmed. Keep in mind that in China, fraud or duress only become legal grounds for voiding a contract when the State interest is at issue. Therefore, the trigger for contract voidness in a case involving fraud or duress is harm to the State interest. This Contract Law framework differs signficantly from that of the 1986 Civil Code, pursuant to which a contract was void if fraud or duress was found, regardless of whether or not there was a harm to the State interest.

During the drafting of the Contract Law, many suggested that fraud or duress should render a contract voidable, but not void. Proponents of this suggestion argued that China should follow the common practice in many other countries of holding a contract voidable only in the event that fraud or duress was committed in the process of the contract's formation. This suggestion, however, was not accepted by the ruling force in the national legislative body, because the drafting authority believed that the State interest had to be specially protected and that the State had to have the power to interfere whenever

---

56 See Wang Liming, *supra* note 10 at p 639.
57 See the 2017 GPCL, art. 144.
58 See Cui Yunling, *supra* note 10, at p112.

State interests were affected by the parties making a contract—not to mention the importance of State ownership in the nation's economy.[59]

The hard issue is what constitutes a State interest. One scholarly interpretation is that the State interest mainly includes the State economic, political, as well as security interest, and that it excludes the interest of State-owned enterprises.[60] Another scholarly interpretation agrees that the State interest should not mean the interests of State-owned enterprises. This interpretation argues, however, that the State interest should be protected by public law such as criminal and administrative law, and that the State interest should be regarded as being harmed only in the event that a party or parties violate criminal or administrative law.[61]

Both interpretations preclude governmental interference with private contracting by placing the interest of State-owned enterprises outside the ambit of State interests. It is further argued that, to qualify as a State interest under Article 52 of the Contract Law, an interest must be specific, not general (i.e., it must be an interest in a particular area, such as the economy, politics, or national security).[62] In other words, any claim asserting State interests as the basis for voiding a contract must be stated with particularity.

Nevertheless, in most cases it is difficult to see how fraud or duress is related to any State political or security interest such that a contract arising out of such fraud or duress will be void. It is also too abstract a task to attempt to ascertain what State interests are actually harmed when fraud or duress occurs. Perhaps the legislative intent of the Contract Law reflects the whole purpose of Article 52. The stated intent of the Contract Law is that, in consideration of the co-existence of State-owned, privately-owned, and foreign-owned enterprises, the statute not only reserves a legal means for the State to interfere at its own initiative in order to maintain the State interest, but also fits all kinds of situations.[63]

One last issue is whether the interests of State-owned enterprises are part of State interests for the purpose of the Contract Law. This issue has generated a great deal of debate. In a recent case where a State-owned company was sued by another company for breach of contract but the State-owned company asked the court to find the contract void on the ground that it damaged State

---

59 See Sun Lihai, *Selection of Legislative Materials of the Contract Law of the People's Republic of China*, 48–49 Law Publishing House (1999).
60 See Wang Liming, *supra* note 10 at p 643.
61 See Cui Yunling, *supra* note 10 at pp 112–113.
62 See Jiang Bixin, *supra* note 1 at 175.
63 See Sun Lihai, *supra* note 59 at pp 48–49.

interests, the SPC explicitly holds that the interests of a State-owned enterprise do not fall within State interests as set forth in Article 52 of the Contract Law.[64]

The case was orignially filed in an intermediate people's court, and then appealed to a high people's court. It finally came to the SPC for re-trial through the judicial supervision process. The main argument of the State-owned company was that the performance of the contract at issue would cause damage to the interests of the company, and since the company was owned by the State, the contract should be voided under Article 52 of the Contract Law in order to protect State interests. The SPC rejected this argument.

According to the SPC, the Contract Law regulates the transaction relationship between parties of equal status. Although State-owned enterprises are the major market players in the national economy, the Contract Law pursuant to the principle of equality does not provide any special protection to State-owned enterprises distinct from the protections it affords to other market players.[65]

The SPC further holds that in the context of Article 52 of the Contract Law, State interests are the State's overall political, economic, and national defense interests. The SPC opines that the interests of a State-owned enterprise, however, represent the enterprise's own interests as an independent party in the market in light of the enterprise's contracts, and such interests must not be confused with State interests.[66]

It is, however, important to note that the 2017 GPCL does not distinguish between fraud and duress that harm state interests and those that involve no state interests. Instead, under Articles 148 and 150 of the 2017 GPCL, in case of fraud or duress that causes a party to undertake a civil action against his/her true intention, the party shall have the right to request a people's court or an arbitration body to revoke such civil action. According to the SPC, the provisions of the 2017 GPCL may supersede Article 52 (1) of the Contract Law and made the contract voidable rather than void even though the State interests are involved.[67]

---

64 *Middle School Students Study News Inc. v. China Newspapers & Periodicals Publishing (Zheng Zhou) Co. Ltd.*, the SPC, (2017) Zhui Gao Fa Min Shen No. 4336.
65 See *id.*
66 See *id.*
67 See the SPC, Notice of the Minutes of National Meeting on Civil and Commercial Trial Work of People's Courts, issued on Nov. 14, 2019. According to the SPC, the "Minutes" is not a judicial interpretation, and should not be cited as a basis for the judgment but may only be used to form the judgment "reasoning". The notice is available at https://www.chinacourt.org/article/detail/2019/11/id/4638096.shtml.

3.1.1 Fraud

Unfortunately, neither the 1986 Civil Code nor the Contract Law contains a definition of fraud. The 2017 GPCL makes fraud a defense to the validity of a civil action but does not define the term. Nevertheless, in the view of the SPC, fraudulent conduct occurs when a party deliberately provides the other party with false information, or conceals the truth in order to induce the other party to make a mistaken expression of will.[68] As interpreted by the SPC, the term "fraud" seems to include misrepresentations—or at least, the SPC does not distinguish between misrepresentation and fraud. What can be inferred from the SPC's opinion is that in a civil action in China, misrepresentation is not distinct from fraud. Consequently, in many contract cases in China, fraud may actually mean misrepresentation.

Under the SPC's interpretation, contract fraud contains four elements: (a) intent to deceive, (b) conduct of deceit, (c) reliance, and (d) mistaken manifestation of the will of the deceived.[69] In contrast with the American concept of misrepresentation, which focuses on concealment and failure to disclose, the concept of fraud as interpreted by the SPC has a stronger emphasis on willfully deceptive conduct and the mistakes induced. Moreover, in American contract law, an injury may be required to make an misrepresentation case actionable, and injury will be presumed if a misrepresentation is material.[70] In China, by contrast, injury seems irrelevant to the question of whether contract fraud occurred.

3.1.1.1 Intent to Deceive

According to the SPC, intent to deceive is an essential component of fraud. In evaluating whether there is intent to deceive, courts assess the state of mind of the party committing the fraud. Intent to deceive exists where the deceiving party knows that the information upon which the other party relies is false, and either endorses that false information or fails to correct it. As noted, fraud is a synonym for misrepresentation in many contract cases in China. Accordingly, the intent to deceive requirement means that an innocent misrepresentation, if made unintentionally, is not actionable in a contract case.

Courts consider two primary factors when determining whether intent to deceive exists: knowledge of falsity and purpose to induce. To be more specific,

---

68 See SPC, Opinions on 1986 Civil Code, *supra* note 20, art. 68.
69 Some argue that fraud consists of three elements: (a) misrepresentation of material facts, (b) reliance, and (c) intent. See Economic Law Research Division of the Office of the Standing Committee of the National People's Congress, *Explanation and Application Guidance of the Contract Law of the People's Republic of China*, 65 (China Democracy and Legal System Press, 1999).
70 See Scott & Kraus, *Contract Law and Theory* (3rd ed), 424 (LexisNexis 2002); See also Calamari & Perillo, *supra* note 25 at p 329.

intent to deceive will be found if a person knows or understands that the information he or she is to give to the other party is false or that the truth of the information is being concealed, and the use of false information or concealment of the truth is aimed at trapping the other party into a transaction or deal that the other party otherwise would not possibly make. On this ground, scholars in China believe that when committing a fraud, the deceiving party is maliciously motivated. They also point out that whether the fraud committed is to benefit the deceiving party or a third party will have no impact on the finding of such malicious motive of the deceiving party.[71]

A question of whether there is an intent to deceive arises when a party is not certain whether the fact is true or false, but nevertheless states it as a truth in order to induce the other party. For example, a seller wants to sell a painting at a high price, and he affirmatively tells a buyer that the painting is a genuine Tang Dynasty painting in order to induce the buyer to buy, but in fact the seller has no idea about whether the painting is a Tang Dynasty painting or actually a Ming Dynasty one, nor does he know whether the painting is a genuine one or a counterfeit. To deal with this issue, some suggest a doctrine of assumption of intent, under which the intent to deceive will be assumed if a party knowingly makes a statement to the other party about the fact that its truth is unknown to the party.[72]

3.1.1.2   Conduct of Deceit

The conduct of deceit is an action by the deceiving party to carry on the intent to deceive, or an action that turns such intent into an external motion. Mere intent to deceive does not have any practical significance in the finding of fraud unless and until certain action motivated by the intent has been taken, including, for example, intentional misrepresentation and deliberate concealment of material facts. Intentional misrepresentation is an active action in which the deceiving party knowingly tells the other party false or deceptive information, while deliberate concealment is a passive action where the deceiving party purposefully does not disclose to the other party the fact that is material and the deceiving party is under obligation to disclose.

There are two situations where Chinese scholars are debating whether the conduct of deceit may present. One situation is where a party at the time of contract knows with some certainty that he lacks capacity to perform but still enters into the contract. In practice, many courts have treated the act of the party as conduct of deceit because a material fact—capacity to perform the contract—is willfully concealed, and such concealment leads to the conclusion of the contract.

---

71   See Wang Liming, *supra* note 10, at p 641.
72   See *id.*

Such practice, however, was criticized as rigid and arbitrary because non-disclosure of insufficient performance capacity at the time of contract may not necessarily be fraudulent. If a party lacking performance capacity makes a contract with another party in order to cheat that party of deposit money or upfront payment, and the party never intended to perform, such conduct is clearly fraudulent. If, however, a party who is incapable of performing at the time a contract is made believes that he will have the requisite capacity at the time of performance and makes every effort to get ready for performance, the party should not be deemed as having committed deceit.[73]

The other situation involves silence of a party. The issue is whether a fraud was committed if a party did not tell or disclose essential facts or information. Generally, silence, standing alone, is not a sufficient ground for the finding of fraud. If, however, a party is under an obligation to tell or disclose, that party's silence may constitute fraudulent conduct. According to Chinese contract scholars, the obligation to tell or disclose may arise under the provision of law, trade customs, or agreement. For example, if a party is required by law to provide the other party or the public with certain facts or specifications of products or goods, that party's silence about such facts or specifications will be regarded as a violation of the law, which amounts to a fraud.[74]

To find the conduct of deceit, no distinction seems to be made in China between misrepresentation of fact and misstatement of opinion.[75] The issue often raised is whether a party who misrepresents a fact or erroneously states an opinion has the intent to deceive or defraud. As a practical matter, however, if the intent is found in connection with a fraud, it seemingly does not matter whether the fact or opinion is involved. Thus, as long as the other party is induced to do something which it otherwise would not do, in accordance with the deceiving party's expectations, either misrepresentation of fact or misstatement of opinion may be regarded as a fraud.

3.1.1.3   *Reliance*

Although intent to deceive and conduct of deceit are critical elements of fraud, to recover for fraud it must be proven that the deceived party was trapped to rely on the induction of the deceiving party. In this context, reliance means that the deceived party mistakenly believes the deceiving party with regard to

---

73 See Wang Liming & Cui Jianyuan, *supra* note 7, at p 270.
74 See Su Haopeng, *supra* note 26 at pp. 275–276.
75 In the United States, although the difference between fact and opinion is regarded as a logical absurdity, it is generally held that misrepresentation of fact rends a contract voidable, while erroneous statement of fact does not. See Calamari & Perillo, *supra* note 25 at p330.

the information deceptively given. For example, A wants to sell to B a counterfeit Rolex watch, and in order make the deal, A forged all documents evidencing the genuineness of the watch. If B believes that the watch is a real Rolex as a result of A's misrepresentation, B will be regarded to have relied on the information deceptively provided by A, which is the cause of B's misunderstanding.

In the context of the Contract Law, reliance concerns the state of mind of the deceived party where a fraud occurs. For the purpose of recovery, however, there must be a connection between deceptive conduct and reliance. There are two factors that are decisive in the determination of reliance. The first factor is relatedness. To justify the reliance, the misrepresentation or false information at issue must necessarily be related to the contents of the transactions. Without such relation, the reliance would not exist. The second factor is the cause of misunderstanding. To establish reliance, the misunderstanding of the deceived party must be the direct outcome of the induction of the deceiving party, not a result of the deceived party's own fault.[76]

3.1.1.4   *Mistaken Manifestation of the Consent of the Deceived*
Many Chinese contract scholars believe that the mistaken manifestation of the will of the deceived party is an essential element for an actionable fraud. At first glance, it seems to be a repetition of reliance. However, the emphasis here is not on the reliance itself or the state of mind of the deceived party, but the actual result of the reliance or the action of the deceived party. The idea is that the misunderstanding of the deceived party, without more, does not make the fraud actionable because if the deceived party does not take any action resulting from the misunderstanding, the fraud ends without producing any consequences that the law will readdress. The action required is that the deceived party mistakenly manifests his will to enter into a contract with the deceiving party and the contract is concluded accordingly.

Thus, the mistaken manifestation of will implicates the action of the deceived party who is induced to enter into a contract or undertake transactions with the deceiving party, and such action is taken in reliance upon the fraudulent conduct of the deceived. More precisely, the determination of the mistaken manifestation of the will of the deceived is to establish causation. The reason is obvious. In order to hold the deceiving party liable for fraud, it must be proved that the deceived party was in fact deceived by the misrepresentation or fraudulent conduct of the deceiving party and in reliance upon such misrepresentation or fraudulent contract, the deceived party entered into the contract.

---

76   See Wang Liming, *supra* note 10 at p 642.

A related issue is whether the fault of the deceived party in communicating with the deceiving party will affect the determination of fraud. To illustrate, assume that a draft contract provided by Party A contains a fraudulent statement. Party B signs the contract without reading it. Later, Party B challenges the validity of the contract on the ground of fraud. The question then is whether Party B's failure to read compromises his fraud claim. Under the majority opinion, although Party B has a duty to read, his failure to fulfill such duty should not affect the finding of fraud because the key is whether the mistaken manifestation of Party B's will is induced.[77] However, Party B's fault is relevant to the determination of the scope of Party A's liability or the extent to which Party A is to be blamed.[78]

With respect to the elements of fraud, the reliance and the mistaken manifestation of the will of the deceived may overlap in certain aspects. But at least one difference between the two is quite clear: the reliance deals with the question of whether the deceived party is willing, and has the reason, to rely on a fraudulent conduct or misrepresentation of the deceiving party, while the mistaken manifestation of the will of the deceived involves the question as to whether the deceived party has in fact relied on such fraudulent conduct or misrepresentation.

Once again, under the Contract Law, a contract is void on the ground of fraud only if the fraud has caused harm to the State interests. Thus, if no State interests are involved, a fraud found will not void a contract as a matter of law. One situation in which the issue of fraud is raised is where the contract is backdated by the parties. Under the SPC's decision in *Guabgzhou International Overseas Chinese Investment Co. Ltd. v. Jiangsu Changjiang Film Industries, Ltd.*, to have a contract backdated does not amount to a fraud if the backdating was made with the knowledge of both parties and the contract entered into by the parties does not damage any interest of the State, collective, or a third party, and does not adversely affect the interests of the performing party.[79]

3.1.2 Duress

It is a general understanding in China that duress occurs where the "free will" of a party is overcome by a wrongful act or threat. Since there is no provision in the Contract Law that defines the term duress, the people's courts have been following the SPC's interpretation to determine the existence of duress in the

---

77 See Jiang Bixin, *supra* note 1, at 143–144.
78 See *id.*
79 See *Guabgzhou International Overseas Chinese Investment Co. Ltd. v. Jiangsu Changjiang Film Industries, Ltd*, the SPC, (2001) Min Shan Zhong Zi No. 3., Vol. 5, the SPC Gazette (2004).

contract-making process. According to the SPC, if there is a threat to the life and health, honor, reputation, or property of a person or the person's relatives or friends, or to damage the honor, reputation, or property of a legal person in order to force the person to make a manifestation that is against the person's true will, duress will be found.[80]

Based on the SPC's interpretation, duress in the context of contracts is described as a threat to inflict personal or property damages, causing the fear in the mind of the other party, whereby the other party is coerced to enter into a contract. Note that in China, to find duress, the person to whom a threat is made includes both the contractual party himself and the relatives or friends of the party. The test under the SPC's interpretation is whether a party is left with no alternative but to enter into the contract against his will, or simply put, whether the will of the party is overcome by the threat inflicted. Since the SPC's focus is on the will of a contractual party, the test is basically a subjective one. As a result, the question of whether a reasonable person would be in fear under the same or similar circumstance is of no significance, if not relevance.

It has been argued that the threat in the context of duress as provided in the Contract Law comprises two situations. One situation is a threat that is to cause damage. In this situation, the damage so threatened may happen or may not happen because the threat as such is a "to do" threat. Thus, to determine whether there is a threat under this circumstance, it is important to see if the party involved really believes that the harms or damages are going to happen. If in the mind of the party, no damage will be caused, no threat will be found because the party to whom the "to do" threat is made is not in fear.

The other situation is the threat that is actually faced or encountered. Such a threat includes violent conduct, withholding property, or defaming. In China, it is called a "doing" threat, which is a threat that has caused or is causing fear in the party involved.[81] It is commonly held that a "doing" threat is an actual threat, but a "to do" threat is not necessarily a threat because it depends on the state of mind of the party to whom the threat is made. The reason is that in the "to do" threat situation, the threat may not actually happen.

Duress in China consists of four elements. The first element is intent to coerce. Such intent is found where the coercing party knows that his conduct will create fear in the mind of the other party and intentionally does so in a hope that the other party will have no choice but to do what is asked. To determine if such intent exists, the outcome expected by the coercing party through the means of coercion is decisive. But from the viewpoint of many Chinese contract

---

80   See SPC, Opinions on 1986 Civil Code, *supra* note 20, art. 69.
81   See Wang Liming & Cui Jianyuan, supra note 7 at pp 271–272.

scholars, the outcome does not include the actual benefits or interests the coercing party will obtain because seeking benefits or interests only reflect the motivation, not the intent, of the coercing party. Thus, the benefit the coercing party actually receives is irrelevant to the determination of intent to coerce.

The second element concerns the act of coercion. According to the SPC, to constitute duress, there must be a threat to cause harm or damage to a person or a person's property. A threat, as discussed, is action that the coercing party takes or will take to overcome the free will of the other party so that the other party enters into a contract or undertakes certain transaction involuntarily. However, there is a debate over the degree of the threat that is required to establish duress. As a result, two tests have been introduced: the fear test and the material test.

Under the fear test, the requisite threat for duress will be found if the coerced party is in fear of an outcome of the act of coercion taken by the coercing party. The material test not only looks at the fear in the mind of coerced party but also measures the degree of the harm or damage. According to the material test, it would be insufficient to find threat without the presence of material harm or damage to be caused. Proponents of the material test argue that the fear resulting from the threat will exist only when the act of coercion is material or grave enough.

The third element involves the wrongfulness of the coercion. In order to make a case of threat, it must be proved that the coercion has no legal basis or serves an illegitimate purpose. A dictum in China is that a threat to exercise legal rights that are granted by the law should not be deemed to be duress unless such rights are clearly abused. For example, a threat to bring a lawsuit to ensure that the legitimate rights of the party will be effectively protected in the transactions is not considered actionable. If, however, a threat to bring a lawsuit is used to achieve a purpose beyond the rights legally granted, the threat may become duress. Because of the concerns about possible abuse of rights in the case of threats, some Chinese contract law scholars strongly advocate that the threat to exercise legal rights should be regarded as duress if its purpose is found to be illegal.[82]

The fourth element is causation, which requires that fear be a real and natural result of a threat. To amount to duress, a threat must actually cause in the mind of the coerced party fear that the harm or damage threatened is so imminent and serious such that he or she has no other alternative but to make the contract according to the terms and conditions offered by the coercing party.[83]

---

82 See Wang Liming, *supra* note 10 at pp 646–647.
83 This element reflects China's acceptance of Article 3.9 of UNIDROIT's "Principles of International Commercial Contracts," which provides: "A party may avoid the contract when the contract's conclusion was caused by the other party's unjustified threat which, under

Two factors are determinative for a finding of such causation: presence of fear and direct result of fear. The questions that must be answered are whether the threat has led to fear and whether a contract or transaction has been entered into because of fear. Any broken chain in this regard will necessarily destroy a finding of duress.

To help courts better handle cases involving fraud or duress in practice, a group of judges at the SPC made interesting comments on how to differentiate fraud from duress. According to those judges, the differences between fraud and duress can be discerned from several perspectives. First, in the case of fraud, the contract at least on its face is made voluntarily between the deceiving party and deceived party, but in the case of duress, the coerced party is induced by fear to make the contract against his will. Second, the contents that are sought by the deceiving party may become part of the contract in a fraud case, while the fear of the coerced party will not be manifested in the contract when duress is committed. Third, fraud may be made by either action or omission, but duress may only be made through active conduct. Fourth, fraud in a contract refers to the conduct of a contracting party. Duress, by contrast, may be imposed upon a contracting party by a third person.[84]

As with respect to fraud, for a contract to be void on the ground of duress, harm to State interests must occur and be proved. Otherwise, the contract made under duress will not be void but rather, will be voidable.

3.2 Malicious Collusion to Damage the Interests of the State, a Collective, or a Third Party

In China, a contract will also be void if it is concluded under malicious collusion to cause harm to the interests of the State, a collective, or a third party.[85] Collusion refers to the deliberate collaboration of a party with the other. Under the Contract Law, if collusion leads to a contract between the parties that damages the interests of the State, a collective, or a third party for the illegitimate

---

the circumstances, is so imminent and serious as to leave the first party no reasonable alternative. In particular, a threat is unjustified if the act or omission with which a party has been threatened is wrongful in itself, or if it is wrongful to use the contract as a means to obtain the conclusion of the contract."

84 See Li Guoguang, *supra* note 50, at pp 226–227.
85 It is interesting to note that the Contract Law differentiates the State and collectives from third partys—a distinction that has been criticized as treating equal civil actors unequally. The argument against drawing such a distinction is that, as opposed to contract parties, both the State and collectivse are third parties.

benefit or gain of the parties in collusion, such collusion will be found to be malicious or in bad faith. [86]

Therefore, under the Contract Law, malicious collusion is a civil conspiracy through the means of a contract to achieve illegitimate goals. For example, malicious collusion exists if a bidder conspires with a bidding inviter to exclude all other competitors in order to ensure that the bidder will get the contract. Another example of malicious collusion is where a representative of a State-owned enterprise collaborates with the other party in a contract to sell the products of the enterprise at an unreasonably low price in exchange for certain benefits the other party has brought or may bring to the representative.

The essential elements of malicious collusion are "collaboration" and "bad faith." Collaboration has a two-layered meaning. At the first layer, the parties involved have an agreement aimed at carrying out an intended act with each other. The agreement may be in the form of either words or conduct. The second layer is that the parties collaboratively take action together to achieve the goal underlying the agreement. Whether the goal has actually been achieved does not affect the finding of collaboration. Bad faith implicates the knowledge and deliberateness of the parties who collaborate. If the parties know that their collaborative conduct is causing or will cause harm or damage to the State, a collective, or a third party's interest, and the parties deliberately cause this result, the parties are acting in bad faith.

Thus, under the Contract Law, where a defense to the formation of a contact on the ground of malicious collusion is sought, both collaboration and bad faith must be proved. In practice, however, it seems very difficult to obtain evidence that parties collaborated in bad faith because collaboration between parties is not always discernable. On the other hand, a contract made through malicious collusion will be void only if the contract is intended to damage the interests of the State, a collective, or a third party. The party claiming that malicious collusion exists has the burden of proving either intended or actual damages to such interests.

---

86   As noted, in China, public ownership is divided into two categories: State ownership and collective ownership. Article 6 of the Chinese Constitution (as amended in 2004) provides that the basis of the socialist economic system of the People's Republic of China is socialist public ownership of the means of production, namely ownership by the whole people and collective ownership by the working people." Under Articles 73 and 74 of the 1986 Civil Code, State property shall be owned by the whole people and property of collective organizations of the working people shall be owned collectively by the working people. Most collectives are rural collectives—i.e., farmers production associations.

In *Cargill International SA v. Fu Jian Jin Shi Vegetable Oil Production Co. Ltd., et al*, the plaintiff obtained an arbitral award issued by the Federation of Oils, Seeds and Fats Associations against the defendant for breach of contract on October 10, 2005. Since the defendant failed to make payment under the award, the plaintiff filed a request for enforcement of the award with the intermediate people's court of Xiamen, Fujian Province. On June 26, 2007, the court ruled that the arbitral award should be recognized and enforced.

In the meantime, from May 2006 to November 2009, the defendant entered into a number of contracts with its affiliate companies to sell and transfer its assets, including its building, equipment, and its land use right. As a result, the defendant was left no assets, which made it impossible to satisfy the court order for the enforcement of the arbitral award. The plaintiff then brought a suit in the High People's Court of Fu Jian to invalidate the transactions the defendant made with its affiliates. The High People's Court ruled against the defendant on the ground that the transactions were the result of the malicious collusion by the defendant and its affiliates to damage the plaintiff's interests.

On appeal, the SPC affirmed. The case then was selected by the SPC as a guiding case in 2014 (Guiding Case No. 33). According to the SPC, where a debtor transfered its principal property to the affiliate companies obviously at an unreasonably low price and the affiliate companies, with knowledge of the debtor's indebtedness, did not actually pay for the property, the debtor and its affiliate companies will be found to have colluded in bad faith to adversely affect the interests of its creditor. Therefore, the contracts for the property transfer were invalid under Article 52 of the Contract Law.[87]

3.3 Use of a Contract for Illegal Purpose

A contract, though legally concluded, will be null and void if it is intended to serve an illegal purpose. The difference between malicious collusion to damage the interests of the State, a collective, or a third party and the use of a contract for an illegal purpose is that the former deals with the means of making the contract and its consequences, while the latter involves the legitimacy of the purpose for which the contract is made.

When a contract is entered into for a concealed illegal purpose, the form of the contract and the contract itself are valid and legally permissible, but the goal that the contract is set to achieve is illegal or prohibited by the law. To illustrate, assume the parties make a contract to voluntarily transfer of a piece of

---

[87] See *Cargill International SA v. Fu Jian Jin Shi Vegetable Oil Production Co. Ltd., et al*, the SPC, Guiding Case No. 33. An English translation is available at https://cgc.law.stanford.edu/wp-content/uploads/sites/2/2015/09/GC33-English.pdf.

property between them. The contract, if not prohibited by the law with regard to the transferred property, is valid and effective. If the transfer of property is aimed at evading taxes or the payment of debts, however, the contract will be deemed as having concealed an illegal purpose (i.e., tax evasion or cheating) and therefore is void.

Pursuant to the Contract Law, the critical factor for determining whether an illegal purpose is concealed under a contract is the intent of the parties because from the outside, there is nothing wrong with the contract. Thus, if the parties intend to evade law or legal obligations through an otherwise legitimate contract, the contract will be considered to have a concealed illegal purpose. Such intent can also be inferred from the actual consequences of the contract—for example, the frustration of the debt payment as a result of the contractual transfer of the property by the debtor.

However, in a case where one contractual party has the intent to conceal and the other party has no knowledge about such intent, a question will be whether the innocent party should be compensated if the contract is held void. For instance, a thief entered into a contract with a student to sell a used bicycle to the student for RMB 200 Yuan. The purpose of the thief was to transfer the stolen good—the used bicycle—to the student for money, but the student knew nothing about the source of the bicycle. Clearly, the contract itself was fine but the illegal purpose—transfer of the stolen good—was concealed. Should the student be able to get his RMB 200 Yuan back if the contract is declared void when the stolen bicycle is discovered? What if the thief spent the RMB 200 Yuan already? There seems to have no ready answer in China to this question yet.

Another matter involves damages. The use of a contract to serve illegal purposes may or may not cause actual damages to other party. Under the Contract Law, to determine whether an illegal purpose is concealed under the color of a contract, the presence of actual damages is not required. Therefore, in Chinese courts, whether there have been any damages is not a concern for the finding of illegal purpose under the guise of a contract. However, when determination of the liabilities to be imposed becomes an issue, actual damages become a relevant factor to consider.

Another issue is whether a criminal offense will affect the validity of a contract when such offense coincides with the making of the contract. One example is where bribery is involved in the making of a contract. To illustrate, assume that an officer of a corporation makes a contract on behalf of the corporation with another party. During the contract negotiation, the officer receives certain payments or something of value from the other party as a kickback. The officer is later caught and charged with receipt of bribery, which is a criminal offense.

The question then is whether the contract remains valid. Under the SPC's opinion, a criminal offence committed in the process of making a contract will in general not affect the validity of the contract unless malicious collusion is found.[88] Accordingly, the contract in this circumstance will not be considered invalid because it does not necessarily serve an illegal purpose. In addition, the use of a contract for an illegal purpose requires the joint intent of the parties to evade the law, which is not the case in the situation where the criminal offense is involved when the contract is being made.[89]

3.4 *Harm to the Social Public Interest*

As discussed in Chapter 4, the protection of the social public interest is a stated contract principle in China that directly affects the validity of contracts. This is a typical area of contracting where the freedom of contract is subject to governmental surveillance in order to maintain public interests and social morals. Thus, under the Contract Law, a contract, though it is freely concluded by the parties, may not be enforced if it offends the social public interests that the government intends to protect.

According to Article 7 of the Contract Law, when a contract is concluded or performed, no social public interest may be damaged. In addition, it is mandated in Articles 55 of the 1986 Civil Code that civil conduct must not violate social public interests. Further, Article 58 of the 1986 Civil Code provides that civil conduct is null and void if it violates the social public interest. In the 2017 GPCL, social public interests are defined as public order and good morals. Under Article 8 of the 2017 GPCL, the parties must not conduct civil activities contrary to the public order and good morals.

In China, social public interest and public order are often interchangeably used in contract cases. But since both of the terms are very broad, it is often very difficult to tell what constitutes a social public interest or public order. As discussed in Chapter 3, in order to help better measure the social public interests, some Chinese scholars have listed certain types of conduct that are considered to be in violation of social public interests. In addition, it is generally agreed among Chinese scholars that the social public interests should be viewed from two aspects.

---

88 See the SPC, the Rules on Several Issues Involving Suspects of Economic Crime In the Adjudication of Cases of Economic Disputes, art. 3.
89 See Du Wanhua, *et al*, Adjudication Guides for Contract Cases, 173–178 (Law Press, 2014).

First, social public interests possess the nature of both commonality and integration. Commonality means that social public interests must be commonly shared values, morals, or standard. Integration suggests that in order to become a social public interest, an interest must belong society as a whole.[90] Second, a distinction should be made between social public interests and State or private interests. Social public interests mainly refer to the interests of all members of society while State interests are the interests that the State as a governing body enjoys, and private interests are the interests of particular members of society.[91]

In many cases, social public interests are reflected in statutory provisions. In this context, social public interests are often intertwined with the issue of contract legality. Thus, if a statute clearly prohibits the parties from making a certain contract that is contrary to particular social public interests, the statute then actually states the issues of both social public interests and legality. The unfair competition law may serve as a good example in this regard. The very purpose of the unfair competition law is to create an environment in which business operators will deal with each other fairly. Hence, if a contract is intended to impose an unreasonable restriction on competition, the contract not only may violate unfair competition law itself but also is contrary to social public interests—the interests of fair competition embodied in the law to promote the welfare of the general public.

In addition, a contract may be deemed null and void for damaging social public interests even if it violates no provision of existing laws or regulations. This is particularly true when social virtues are involved—though there is no readily applicable law. On the other hand, due to the wide range of social public interests, not every offense to such interests will render the contract void. Under the Contract Law, a contract is only void for violating social public interests if the affront to such interests is so serious that the public order and important social virtues are damaged.

3.5 Violation of Compulsory Provisions of Law or Regulations

As a settled rule, a contract's violation of compulsory provisions of law renders the contract illegal. If a contract is found to have violated the law, the contract is void and thus has no effect from its inception. In China, a contract's violation of compulsory provisions is generally viewed as a matter of illegality, distinct from the use of a contract for illegal purposes. It is believed that the issue of

---

90   See *id.*, at 130–133.
91   See Wang Limng, *supra* note 10 at pp. 652–653.

illegality differs from that of the use of contract for illegal purposes. The major difference is that illegality directly involves the subject matter or the contents of the contract, while the illegal purpose of a contract concerns the goal of the contract that may itself be legally made. Some, however, argue that illegality should consist of both illegal subject matter and illegal goal of the contract.

A few contract scholars in China also opine that illegality under the Contract Law additionally includes violations of the formalities mandated by the law or regulations. In their view, for example, if a contract is required to be approved under the law, without such approval the contract will be void because violation of the approval requirement will make the contract illegal in its formality. But under the majority opinion, the illegality goes to the substance of the contract.

With regard to the determination of illegality, the Contract Law takes a narrower or more restrictive approach than the 1986 Civil Code. Under Article 58 of the 1986 Civil Code, a civil conduct will be invalid if it violates the law. The Contract Law, however, limits the law to its compulsory provisions. In other words, a contract will be null and void only if it violates those provisions of the law that are imperative. The 2017 GPCL contains a similar provision that makes non-violation of the compulsory provisions of laws and administrative regulations a prerequisite to the validity of civil conduct.[92]

In terms of their effect, the provisions of law can be divided into two categories: mandatory provisions and non-mandatory provisions. A provision of law is mandatory if it includes a word such as "should," "must," "shall," or "prohibited." If a provision includes a word such as "may," "could," or "allowed," the provision is non-mandatory. In contrast to non-mandatory provisions that leave options, a mandatory provision of law requires full compliance and allows no derogation. The legality of civil conduct becomes an issue only if the conduct violates a mandatory provision of law.

Thus, under the Contract Law, to make a contract void for illegality, it must be proved that the contract violates a mandatory provision of the law. In other words, if a provision of law is non-mandatory, it cannot be the ground on which the legality of a contract is determined. With regard to a mandatory provision of law, there are, as a practical matter, two issues that arise in its application.

The first issue is what the "law" should be for purposes of making a contract void. At the heart of this issue is whether the local law should be included. As noted, China has a unified legal system—with the exception of Hong Kong and Marco, because of the historical status of these two regions. Under the Chinese Constitution (as amended in 2004), the primary legislative power rests with

---

92   See the 2017 GPCL, art. 143.

the National People's Congress. The National People's Congress (and its Standing Committee) is responsible for adopting and amending national laws. The executive branch, namely the State Council and its ministries, is empowered to stipulate regulations and rules of administrative nature at the national level. In addition, the people's congresses at the provincial level (including municipalities directly under the central government) and their standing committees have the power to make local law and rules that do not contravene the Constitution, national laws, or administrative regulations.

Many in China take the position that the law should refer to statutes passed by the national legislature in addition to administrative regulations adopted by the national government, and that it should exclude local laws or regulations because the Contract Law makes no indication of any local law or regulation in this regard.[93] In its 1999 Contract Law Interpretation, the SPC explicitly states that after the Contract Law takes effect, the people's courts, when voiding a contract, shall follow the law promulgated by the NPC or its Standing Committee and the administrative regulations adopted by the State Council other than local decrees or administrative rules.[94]

Some, however, argue that despite the requirement for the application of national law and regulations, if a contract contradicts local decrees or rules, it should be deemed void on the ground of harm to social public interests.[95] This argument seeks to leave room for local decrees or rules to play a role in the determination of the validity of contracts.[96] Given the strong tendency of local governments to protect local interests, the possible influence of local law and regulations on the validity of contracts should not be underestimated. In fact, since local courts are all required to report to the local people's congress, and court budgets are provided by the local government, it is not uncommon to see that court decisions are more driven by local interests. Therefore, because of the concern for the local interests, a contract violating local law or regulations may be deemed void.

The second issue involves the nature of mandatory laws and regulations. It is argued that the violation of a mandatory law or regulation should not necessarily render a contract void because a mandatory rule can be either prohibitive or managerial. A prohibitive provision directly affects the effect of a

---

93 See Wang Liming & Cui Jianyuan, *supra* note 7 at pp 278–279; Jiang Ping et al, *A Detailed Explanation of the Contract Law of Law*, 43 (China University of Political Science and Law Press) (1999); Yang Lixin et at, *Implementation and Application of the Contract Law of China*, 87–88 (Jilin People's Publishing House, 1999).
94 See SPC, the 1999 Contract Interpretation, art. 4.
95 See Su Haopeng, *supra* note 26 at 285.
96 See Du Wanhua, *et al, supra* note 88 at 143.

contract while a managerial provision is aimed at regulating business acts and punishing violations. According to the SPC, if a law or regulation is about the market access qualification of a party other than particular types of contract activities, violation of that law or regulation may not lead to the voidness of a contract. The same concept also applies to the case where the law or regulation has a focus on the conduct of a contract's performance but not on the substance of the contract.[97]

Since prohibitive provisions determine the effect of a contract, such provisions are also called effect mandatory provisions. Under the SPC's 2009 Contract Interpretation, as far as the validity of a contract is concerned, a mandatory provision shall mean an effect mandatory provision. But in actual cases, it remains difficult to differentiate between prohibitive and managerial provisions because of the lack of uniform standards in this regard. In addition, in order to help maintain stability of business transactions, the SPC tends to hold a contract valid if during the trial the violation of mandatory law or regulation is corrected and no State, collective, or individual interests are harmed.[98]

4 Voidable Contracts

It must be kept in mind that under the Contract Law, a contract is void on the ground of fraud or duress only if such fraud or duress causes harm to State interests. If, however, no State interests are involved, fraud or duress will only render a contract voidable. Once again, the underlying premise is supremacy of State interests in the Chinese economy. The major difference between void contracts and voidable contracts is that when a contract is void, it will take no effect without any action of the parties, but if a contract is voidable, the party seeking to void the contract must make a request.

Pursuant to Article 54 of the Contract Law, if a contract is concluded by a party against the other party's true intention by the means of fraud, coercion, or exploitation of the other party's unfavorable position, the injured party shall have the right to request the people's court or an arbitration body to modify or rescind the contract. Article 54 also provides that a party shall have the right to modify or rescind a contract if the contract (a) is concluded as a result of a material misunderstanding or (b) is obviously unfair at the time it is formed.

---

97 See the SPC, The Guiding Opinions on Several Issues Concerning Adjudication of Civil and Commercial Contract Diputes under the Current Situation, Fa Fa (2009) No. 40.
98 See Du Wanhau, *et al, supra* note 88 at 134–135.

Thus, under Article 54 of the Contract Law, a contract is voidable in China in any of the following five situations: fraud, duress, exploitation of other party's precarious position, material misunderstanding, or obvious unfairness. It is important to note again that a contract is voidable for fraud or duress only if it causes no harm to the State interest. Thus, a fraud in China can make a contract either void or voidable, depending on whether a harm negatively impacts State interests.

It is worth noting that under the Contract Law, the fraud being a ground to avoid a contract is limited to the one that happens only between the parties to a contract. The 2017 GPCL however expands fraud to include the one that is committed by a third party. According to Article 149 of the GPCL, in case a fraud is committed by a third party so as to cause a party to take a civil action against his/her true intention, the party shall have the right to request a people's court or an arbitration body to revoke the civil action if the other party knows or should have known the fraud so committed.

According to the Contract Law, when a contract is voidable, the injured party has two alternatives: to modify or to rescind the contract. In either case, the injured party must make a request. Although a court or arbitration body may upon the request of an injured party rescind or modify a contract, the court will not rescind the contract if the injured requests modification. The rationale is that a contract is the product of the free will of the parties and their voluntary and meaningful choice in deciding their contractual rights and obligations ought to be respected as much as possible.

In order to prevent abuse of the right to rescind a contract on the ground of voidableness, the Contract Law specifies two circumstances pursuant to which the right to request that a contract be rescinded will be extinguished. One circumstance is the one-year limitation. Article 55 of the Contract Law requires that the party having the right to rescind the contract exercise the right within one year from the day he or she knows or ought to know the causes for rescission.[99] A failure to comply with the one-year limitation will extinguish the right to rescind. The other circumstance is the waiver of the right. Under Article 55 of the Contract Law, the right to rescind a contract will also be exterminated when the party who has the right to rescind explicitly expresses or acts to waive the right after he or she knows the causes to rescind.[100]

---

99 See the Contract Law, art. 55.
100 See *id.*

4.1 Exploitation of the Other Party's Precarious Position

In the context of the Contract Law, exploiting the other party's precarious position means taking advantage of the other who is in a difficult situation (e.g., in an urgent need or a desperate situation) in order to seek unjustified benefits or to make unfair deals. According to the SPC, it shall be deemed as taking advantage of the other's difficult situation if a party with a purpose to seek illicit benefits compels the other party who is in difficulty to make a manifestation against his or her true will so that the other party's interest is seriously impaired.[101]

The prevention of a party from exploiting the other who is in difficulty is based on the notion that taking advantage of the other's precarious position vitiates consent to the contract and seriously undermines the voluntary choice of the parties. In 1986, when the Civil Code was adopted, the legislators took the position that a contract made by taking advantage of the other party's difficulty was void, and this position was fully reflected in Article 58 of the 1986 Civil Code. It was subsequently argued, however, that it would be overly restrictive and arbitrary to make void a contract resulting from a party's taking advantage of the other's difficulty.

The underlying idea is that because a contract is mainly a matter between the parties, it would be more appropriate to allow the injured party to decide how to proceed with such a contract. For that reason, the Contract Law alters the 1986 Civil Code and makes a contract voidable if it is made by one party having taking advantage of the other party's difficult situation. The 2017 GPCL also provides that if a civil act is taken as a result of one party's taking advantage of the other party's difficult or distressful situation, the aggrieved party has the right to request a people's court or an arbitration body to revoke the act.[102]

The question is how to define difficulty or difficult situations in this context. Under the SPC's interpretation, difficulty may refer to an urgent need or a desperate situation. A general view in China is that the exploitation of the other's dificult or unfavorable position is something that would not possibly happen under a normal circumstance and therefore should be determined objectively. For this purpose, there is a four-factor test for judging whether a difficult situation existed at the time of a contract.

The first factor is the difficult situation facing the other party. Because of the existence of the difficult situation, a party had the opportunity to take advantage of the other and to push through a deal that the other party would otherwise not accept. The second factor involves the action of exploitation. There must be some conduct or certain words through which a party compels the

---

101 See the SPC, Opinions on 1986 Civil Code, *supra* note 20, art. 70.
102 See the 2017 GPCL, art. 151.

other party to make an involuntary choice against the latter's true intention. As a factual matter, the act of exploitation is a two-sided issue. On the one hand, the exploitation is in fact undertaken, and on the other hand, the exploitation ultimately results in the other party's surrender of his free will.

The third factor concerns deliberateness of exploitation. The party taking advantage of the other knew that the other party was in a difficult situation and deliberately made the other party to have no choice but to accept a deal against his will. Thus, exploitation may not be found if the other party had alternatives despite the difficulties he or she encountered. The fourth factor is the damage to the other party as measured by the terms and conditions the other party had to accept to his or her disadvantage. It is true that exploitation may benefit the exploiting party, but what is more important is whether the other party suffers damages as a result of the exploitation.

To determine the difficult situation, the people's courts often look at whether the aggrieved party was in urgent need or a desperate situation. From the viewpoint of Chinese contract law scholars, urgent need means an imminent want for something to live through a difficulty, which includes both economic need (e.g., money) and want for living (e.g., service). A desperate situation concerns not only economic constraints but also hardships in life, health, or reputation.

It is therefore clear that economic compulsion or pressure is recognized in China as a ground for making a contract voidable under the category of exploitation of the other's unfavorable position. Although there are similarities between exploitation and duress (e.g., lack of meaningful and voluntary choice), the difference is that duress involves illegal threats or wrongful coercion, while exploitation involves one party taking advantage of the other party by conduct that is neither illegal nor wrongful.

4.2 Material Misunderstanding

It is interesting to note that in China the term "misunderstanding," rather than "mistake," is used as a legal reason for which a contract becomes voidable. Many insist that "misunderstanding" is a concept distinct from "mistake" because misunderstanding deals with the contract itself while mistake has to do with the fact on which the contract is based. The main point is that the existence of the mistake does not impede the parties from reaching a consent as to the contract.[103] Opponents argue that a misunderstanding actually means a

---

103   According to some Chinese contract scholars, misunderstanding differs from mistake in several aspects: (a) the concept of mistake has broader coverage than that of misunderstanding; (b) mutual mistake makes a contract void, but misunderstanding only renders a contract voidable; (c) mistake may be a unilateral or mutual mistake for which there will

mistake that is made by the parties in making the contract and therefore, the two terms should be deemed synonymous.[104]

Despite the arguments, there seems to have no practical significance to specifically drawing a line between misunderstandings and mistakes. In fact, in many people's courts, misunderstandings are generally referred to as mistakes. In a recurring fact pattern, the people's courts prefer to define a misunderstanding as a mistake that the parties make in cognizance of factual elements of the contract.[105] Additionally, when the Contract Law was being drafted, a misunderstanding was interpreted as a situation where the parties make a mistake or have no knowledge about the incompatibility (or imparity) between their intentions and actual facts or outcomes.[106] A more direct interpretation is to characterize a misunderstanding as a term equivalent to the concept of mistake that is commonly used in western contract law theory.[107]

In China, three elements are regarded as important to a misunderstanding. The three elements are: (a) an error in expression of intentions, (b) negligence causing the error, and (c) causation between the contract and the erroneous expression of the intentions. Under Article 54 of the Contract Law, however, a contract is voidable for a misunderstanding only if the misunderstanding is material. The materiality requirement set forth in the Contract Law is derived from Article 59 of the Civil Code. In Article 59 it is provided that a party shall have the right to request a people's court or an arbitration body to alter or rescind a civil act if the act is conducted with a material misunderstanding of the contents of the act.[108] However, Article 54 of the Contract Law emphasizes that, to render a contract voidable, the material misunderstanding must be made during the conclusion of the contract.[109]

Neither the 1986 Civil Code nor the Contract Law contains any provision as to what misunderstandings qualify as material. To resolve this matter, the SPC has provided certain guidance for the people's courts to follow in their practice. In accordance with the SPC, a misunderstanding is material when a party misunderstands the nature of conduct, the other party, and the type, quality, specification, and quantity of the objects in question, and this results

---

be a different consequence while misunderstanding contains no such distinction. See Wang Liming, *supra* note 10 at pp. 683–684.
104 See *id.* Wang Liming.
105 See Li Guoguang, *supra* note 50 at pp 231–232.
106 See Sun Lihai, *supra* note 59 at p 152.
107 See *id.*
108 See the 1986 Civil Code, art. 59.
109 See the Contract Law, art. 54.

in a consequence that is contradictory to the party's true intention and that causes the party "relatively serious losses."

Obviously, the SPC tends to define materiality through its interpretation. But in the meantime, the SPC is quite cautious in picking proper words by which to refer to materiality in the context of misunderstandings. The term "relatively serious loss" is not only awkward but also abstract. The question necessarily raised by this phrasing is what losses are relatively serious. This phrasing furthermore requires that the determination of whether a loss is serious must be determined on a case-by-case basis, which gives the people's courts considerable discretionary power.

Nevertheless, the SPC's interpretation has established a content-based test for the finding of material misunderstanding. To be material, a misunderstanding must involve the contents and nature of the contract, the other party, or the type, specification, or quality of the objects of the contract. What seems interesting is a party's misunderstanding of the other party. This happens when a party negligently errs in comprehending the other party's qualifications or skills for performing a certain contract. The case concerning a party's misunderstanding of the other party often involves a service contract whereby the other party's "personal qualifications" are at issue.

The basic notion underlying the SPC's interpretation with regard to material misunderstandings is that a misunderstanding is material if it affects the primary rights or obligations of the parties or the very purpose of the contract. Pursuant to this notion, the people's courts may not find a misunderstanding material enough to make a contract voidable if a party to the contract only misunderstood the quantity, means of performance, location of performance, or time period of performance of the contract. Therefore, a contract is voidable for the reason of material misunderstanding if the rights or obligations the contract creates, or the purpose the contract seeks to accomplish, are adversely affected.[110]

An unsolved question is whether a material misunderstanding can be mutual. The dispute over this question is whether a contract can be voidable by reason of a material misunderstanding if the parties to the contract each erroneously expressed his or her intentions by mistake. As noted, Chinese contract scholars disagree as to whether there is a conceptual distinction between misunderstandings and mistakes. Some scholars argue that a misunderstanding, as a ground for making a contract voidable, does not encompass a mutual misunderstanding because it refers to the error in manifestation of the intention of a party, and a mutual misunderstanding, if any, would make a contract void,

---

110   See Li Guoguang, *supra* note 50 at p 233.

not voidable. In practice, the people's courts tend to hold that a misunderstanding, like a mistake, can be either unilateral or mutual.

Also questionable is whether a misunderstanding relating to a law existing at the time of a contract gives a party the right to void that contract. In many western countries, a mistake of law has the similar effect as a mistake of fact in terms of rendering a contract voidable. In the United States, for example, a well-accepted contract principle is that relief is available for mistake of law when a contract is concluded.[111] A similar principle is adopted in UNIDROIT's Principles of International Commercial Contracts, according to which mistake is an erroneous assumption relating to fact or to law existing when a contract is concluded.[112] In China, however, it may be inferred—at least from the SPC's interpretation—that a misunderstanding of law is not a ground for rendering a contract void, but the basis for making it voidable.

4.3   Obvious Unfairness

In China, a contract is also voidable if it is found to be obviously unfair at the time when contract was made. An obviously unfair contract is a contract in which there is a gross disparity between the rights and obligations of the parties in violation of the principle of fairness of the Contract Law. According to the SPC, a contract is obviously unfair if a party uses his or her superiority or dominant position, or takes advantage of the other party's inexperience, to make the unbalance of rights and obligations between the parties so obvious that the principles of fairness and equal bargain are clearly violated.[113]

Indeed, this concept of obvious unfairness is aimed at protecting a party in a weak position from being unfairly treated by the other. Following the SPC's interpretation, Chinese contract scholars almost unanimously view obvious unfairness as including three major components. First, there must be a clear imbalance between the rights and obligations of the parties. If a party bears obligations excessively in proportion to the rights he or she has or at a cost of

---

111   Such a principle is regarded in the United States as an import from criminal law. In criminal law, ignorance or mistake as a matter of law is a defense if the ignorance or mistake negatives the purpose, knowledge, belief, recklessness, or negligence required to establish a material element of the offense. Model Penal Code, §2.04(1).
112   See UNIDROIT's Principles of International Commercial Contracts, art. 3.4 (Definition of mistake). In the official comment, it is further indicated that this article equates a mistake relating to facts with a mistake relating to law. Identical legal treatment of the two types of mistake seems justified in view of the increasing complexity of modern legal systems.
113   See the SPC, Opinons on 1986 Civil Code, *supra* note 20. The term "equal bargain" is normally translated as "to make compensation for equal value." This means that, when making a contract, what a party bargained for should be fairly equal to what he or she paid for.

huge losses to him or her, and the other party overly benefits, the rights and obligations of the parties will be found to be obviously imbalanced. Second, there must be a situation wherein the injured party is in a desperate situation or lacks experience at the time of the contract, and the other party takes advantage of such desperate situation or inexperience to make the contract at the extent of the injured party's suffering. Third, the imparity between the rights and obligations of the parties must be present at the time the contract is concluded.

Apparently, the notion of obvious unfairness does not include any risk commonly associated with business operations. Therefore, any imbalance between the rights and obligations of the parties after the conclusion of the contract, if it is caused by a change in the market (e.g., rise or fall of price), will be deemed as normal business risk. In such a situation, though imbalance exists, no relief will be granted with regard to the effect or validity of the contract.[114]

The concept of obvious unfairness seems to be intertwined at least in part with the concept of exploitation of the other party's precarious position because both concepts involve one party taking advantage of the other. A closer look at the two concepts, however, may help distinguish them. Unlike obvious unfairness, exploitation of the other party's precarious position has a clear focus on the difficulty facing the other party. In the case of obvious unfairness, the other party may not necessarily be in a difficult situation, though he may desperately need something.

In addition, what matters in finding obvious unfairness is the existence of imbalance between the rights and obligations of the parties, while exploitation of another party's precarious position mainly concerns the bad faith of a party in taking advantage of the other's difficulty in order to reap benefits. Moreover, obvious unfairness is closely related to the superiority of a party or inexperience of the other party, but the exploitation of the other party's precarious position primarily deals with the other party's difficult situation regardless of superiority or experiences.

Because of its emphasis on imparity between rights and obligations, the concept of obvious unfairness, as many argued, may only apply to onerous contracts (obligation in exchange for benefit), particularly bilateral contracts. If a contract is unilateral (in Chinese concept) or gratuitous (*nudum pactum*), the parties have no need to compensate each other, and thus the issue of imparity of the rights and obligations between the parties becomes irrelevant.[115] The basic idea of obvious unfairness is that in order for a contract to be protected

---

114   See Wang Liming & Cui Jianyuan, *supra* note 7 at pp 285–289; See also Yang Lixin, *supra* note 92 at pp 93–94.
115   See Li Guoguang, *supra* note 50 at p 233. See also Jiang Ping et al, *supra* note 92, at 45.

by the law, it should be the result of fair dealing between the parties as a result of their free and voluntary choice.

Although the SPC has specified in its interpretation what constitutes obvious unfairness, many still feel that it is necessary to further define what unfairness is deemed "obvious." Under both the Contract Law and the SPC's interpretation, for an unfair contract to become voidable, the unfairness must be obvious. The question is how to determine whether the unfairness is obvious. One proposition is that unfairness is obvious if the gain of a party by unfair means exceeds the limit imposed by the law. For example, in an employment contract, if the salary agreed to pay an employee is far below the level in the same or similar sector or industry, such a contract with regard to the salary payment is obviously unfair.[116]

Some scholars in China equate obvious unfairness with the concept of unconscionability in the U.S. contract law. Under the UCC, if a contract is found to have been unconscionable at the time it was made, the court may refuse to enforce the contract.[117] The basic test for unconscionability, as articulated by the official comment of the UCC, is one-sidedness in the light of the general commercial background and the commercial need of the particular trade or case. If one-sidedness means disparity between the rights and obligations of the parties, the U.S. concept of unconscionability and the Chinese concept of obvious unfairness share this as a commonality. Both concepts are accordingly policy-driven mechanisms to protect against unfair or unconscionable exercise of a legal right.

But, the concept of obvious unfairness in Chinese contract law seems to have a broader meaning than that of unconscionability. In certain cases, a contract that is unfair is not necessarily unconscionable. For example, if a contract is made by a party who lacks experience, the contract may smell bad if the inexperience is unfairly exploited by the other party, but the contract may still

---

116 See Wang Liming, *supra* note 10 at 692. In his book, Professor Wang listed the gain exceeding the limit of the law as a factor to find obvious unfair contract.
117 UCC §2–302 reads as follows:
   (1) If the court as a matter of law finds the contract or any clause of the contract to have been unconscionable at the time it was made the court may refuse to enforce the contract, or it may enforce the remainder of the contract without the unconscionable clause, or it may so limit the application of any unconscionable clause as to avoid any unconscionable result.
   (2) When it is claimed or appears to the court that the contract or any clause thereof may be unconscionable the parties shall be afforded a reasonable opportunity to present evidence as to its commercial setting, purpose and effect to aid the court in making the determination.

be a conscionable one. Also, the doctrine of unconscionability is intended to prevent two evils: "oppression and unfair surprise."[118] Obvious unfairness, as mentioned several times, is more concerned about the balance of the parties' rights and obligations.[119]

Another point worthy of note concerns the doctrine of undue influence. The Contract Law contains no such doctrine nor has the doctrine yet been accepted in China. In the view of many Chinese contract law scholars, the problem of undue influence can be dealt with either under the Contract Law provisions on duress or obvious unfairness. However, many point out that since the concept of undue influence refers to the situation where a party, by using his special relationship with the other party or his special status, imposes pressure on the other party during the contract making process, it is more likely to constitute obvious unfairness than duress.[120]

5 Consequences of Void and Voidable Contracts

Once again, when a contract becomes void, the contract has no effect from the very beginning. If a contract is voidable, the effectiveness of the contract is not affected until the contract is voided and such voidance takes effect retroactively. The issue that follows the voidance in either a void or voidable contract is the restitution or compensation that can be made to one party or to each other of the parties. In dealing with the consequences of void and voidable contracts, the Contract Law adopts a number of principles that are compatible with internationally accepted rules, as reflected mainly in the provisions of UNIDROIT's Principles of International Commercial Contracts and the United Nations Convention on the International Sale of Goods.

---

118   See Calamari & Perillo, *supra* note 25 at 373.
119   As seen from the interpretation of the Supreme People's Court, the concept of obvious unfairness is adopted in the Contract Law with a reference to the approach of gross disparity in Article 3.10 of UNIDROIT's Principles of International Commercial Contracts. Article 3.10 provides that:
   (1)   A party may avoid the contract or an individual term of it if, at the time of the conclusion of the contract, the contract or term unjustifiably gave the other party an excessive advantage. Regard is to be had, among other factors, to
      (a)   the fact that the other party has taken unfair advantage of the first party's dependence, economic distress or urgent need, or of its improvidence, ignorance, inexperience or lack of bargaining skill....
120   See Han Shiyuan, The Law of Contract, 198–201 (Law Press, 2011).

5.1   Avoidance from the Very Beginning

It is provided in Article 56 of the Contract Law that a contract that is null and void or rescinded shall have no legal binding force from the contract's inception. A contract having no legal binding effect means that the contract is ineffective and will not be enforced. Therefore, after the contract is voided, the contractual relationship between the parties ceases to exist. Note that since the voidance occurs after the contract was concluded, it may be made before, during, or even after the performance. But whenever the contract is voided, the voidance takes effect from the time the contract was concluded.

A similar rule is provided in the 2017 GPCL. Under Article 155 of the 2017 GPCL, a void or revoked civil act has no legally binding force from the outset. Moreover, according to the SPC, in contract cases, the validity of a contract shall be examined by the people's court *ex offcio*. In *Fenghuang County State Land Resources Bureau v. Hunan Deheng Power Co. Ltd.,* the contract entered into by the parties concerning transfer of a construction land use right was found to be invalid on the ground of malicious collision causing harm to the State interests. The SPC held that the review and examination of the validity of a contract are within the adjudicative power of the people's courts, and shall be undertaken by the people's courts even though the parties did not make such claim.[121]

5.2   Partial Avoidance and the Remaining Part of the Contract

What happens in reality is that in many cases, a contract as a whole is not void or voidable but certain clauses or terms of the contract are. In other words, only part of the contract becomes void or voidable. As a general principle, partial voidance of a contract is permissible. For example, under Article 3.16 of UNIDROIT's Principles of International Commercial Contracts, where voidance affects only particular terms of a contract, the effect of such voidance is limited to those terms unless, under the circumstances, it is unreasonable to uphold the remaining contract.

The Contract Law follows this principle. It is provided in Article 56 that if part of a contract is null and void without affecting the validity of the other parts, the other parts shall still be valid.[122] In addition, under Article 156 of the 2017 GPCL, if the partial invalidity of a civil act does not affect the validity of

---

121   See *Fenghuang County State Land Resources Bureau v. Hunan Deheng Power Co. Ltd*, SPC, (2014) Min Yi Zhong Zhi No. 277, available at http://www.court.gov.cn/wenshu/xiangqing-8321.html.
122   See the Contract Law, art. 56.

the other part, the other part of the civil act shall remin valid. Thus, a contract in China could be found invalid in whole or in part.

There is an argument that the partial voidance of a contract under the Contract Law must meet two requirements. One requirement is divisibility of the contract. The point is that if a contract is indivisible, the voidance, though partial, will still affect the whole contract. In this regard, divisibility means that the individual terms of the contract may stand independently from each other. One typical example is the disclaimer clause. As we have discussed, in accordance with Article 53 of the Contract Law, a disclaimer is void and null if it is intended to exempt one party from liability for causing personal injury or property damage to the other party as a result of deliberate intent or gross negligence. If a contract contains a disclaimer clause in this nature, the people's court will read the clause out of the contract so that the contract will remain valid because the disclaimer clause is normally independent from other parts of the contract.

The second requirement involves possibility of partial performance. If an individual term is voided, the voidance shall have no direct impact on the validity of remaining part of the contract, and after the avoidance, it is still possible for the parties to perform the valid part of the contract. If, however, the void term, though divisible, is so closely related to other part of the contract that the partial voidance would make it meaningless to have the contract, or unreasonable to continue performing the contract, the contract as a whole would be affected. Similarly, if it is found that after voidance of the individual term, the rights and obligations of the parties are grossly imbalanced, the ramining part of the contract may not be enforced because of the fairness concerns.

5.3 *Independence of a Dispute Settlement Clause*
The Contract Law treats a dispute resolution clause in a contract as a special and separate clause. This means that the dispute settlement clause will remain intact regardless of the legal effect of other clauses in a contract. Under Article 57 of the Contract Law, if a contract is null and void, rescinded, or terminated, the validity of the dispute settlement clause independently existing in the contract shall not be affected.[123] Here, independence is deemed to mean three things: (a) when a contract is voided, the dispute settlement clause remains effective; (b) if a contract is rescinded, the rescission does not apply to the dispute settlement clause; and (c) if a contract is terminated, the effectiveness of the dispute settlement clause shall stay unchanged.[124]

---

123   See Contract Law, art. 57.
124   See Yang Lixin, *supra* note 92 at p104.

The independence of a dispute settlement clause has practical importance with regard to the validity of a contract. Assume that a contract dispute is brought to a court, and the court jurisdiction is established on the dispute settlement clause, e.g., choice of court clause. After the hearing, it is found that the contract is void and the voidance shall apply retroactively to the time when the contract was concluded. If the dispute settlement clause is not independent from the contract, the voidance of the contract will make the court's jurisdiction groundless. Assume again that the parties have their dispute solved under the dispute settlement clause during their performance of the contract, but the contract was declared void and null later on. Then the validity of the settlement of the dispute between the parties will be challenged if the dispute settlement clause is to be affected by the voidance.

Two points on this matter need to be further addressed. First, if there is a dispute settlement clause in a contract, the clause shall be deemed to have independently existed. Second, a dispute settlement clause may take the form of either a clause in a contract or a separate agreement. As a practical matter, a dispute settlement clause in a contract may include all possible mechanisms for dispute settlement, such as amicable negotiation, mediation, arbitration, or litigation.

5.4   *Restitution and Compensation*

There is no doubt that when a contract is voided, the existing contractual relationship between the parties is terminated. In the meantime, however, after the voidance of a contract, a new debtor and creditor relationship between the parties may be established by the operation of law. The reason, which is self-evident, is that before the voidance of a contract, some performance may have already been made or a certain amount of money may have already paid (e.g., a deposit). Then, when the contract is void, restitution or compensation may become necessary in order to prevent unjust enrichment. In the United States, such a new relationship is termed a "quasi-contract," under which restitution can be sought for money paid, service provided, or damages caused. In China, there is no "quasi-contract" concept, but the remedy for restitution or compensation is available.

Pursuant to the Contract Law, there are three remedies in terms of restitution or compensation in cases where a contract becomes void. The first one is return of property. Under Article 58 of the Contract Law, after voidance or rescission of a contract, the property acquired as a result of the contract shall be returned. The very purpose of the return of property is to restore the parties to the position they would be in if there had been no contract.[125]

---

[125]   There is a disagreement among Chinese scholars as to the nature of the return of property. Some argue that the return of property is based on the right of ownership because

In light of restitution, the property includes both in kind and money received. And the return of property can be either unilateral or bilateral depending on whether only one party has received property from the other or the parties have received property from each other. If the parties acquired in kind or cash from each other, the return of property will be bilateral and the money mutually paid will be set off.

The second remedy is monetary compensation. Article 58 of the Contract Law further provides that where the property cannot be returned or the return is unnecessary in the case of contract voidance, a monetary compensation shall be made. In this context, the monetary payment is actually an alternative to the return of property if there are certain obstacles to the return. The specific money amount for the compensation will depend on the value of the property.

The property that cannot be returned is generally interpreted to refer to the property for which a return is either legally or factually impossible—which includes property that is lost and irreplaceable, or property that is seriously damaged and irreparable, or property in the form of know-how or services. The return that is unnecessary is a bit complicated because the determination of the necessity of the return all depends on whether, from the viewpoint of the parties, it would make any sense to have the property returned. [126]

The third remedy is damages. Damages are warranted when a party is at fault, and causes the other party to suffer losses. According to Article 58 of the Contract Law, after the voidance of a contract, the party at fault shall compensate the other party for losses as a result thereof. If both parties are at fault, each party shall be respectively liable. What Article 58 actually tells is that to claim damage in contract avoidance, two things must be proved: actual losses and the existence of fault. Actual losses may take place during the conclusion of the contract or occur in the performance of the contract.

It is important to emphasize that Article 58 of the Contract Law establishes a fault standard for determining damages when a contract is void or voidable. First, for the purpose of Article 58, the fault must occur in the process of making a contract. Second, the fault that leads to the voidance of a contract can be either unilateral or bilateral. Third, if the fault is bilateral, damages can be

---

when a contract is avoided, the party who acquired the property will lose his ownership of the property and the ownership will be restored back to the original party. Under this theory, the return of property is the return of ownership. Others disagree by contending that the return of property is based on the doctrine of unjust enrichment because it is a remedy on the ground of contract, not property.

126 See Li Guoguang, *supra* note 50 at pp 245–246.

offset. Fourth, the damages should be calculated in proportion to the degree of the fault committed.

The restitution as a result of contract avoidance and the fault standard are also provided in the 2017 GPCL. Under Article 157 of the 2017 GPCL, when a civil act is void, revoked, or determined to be ineffective, the property obtained by the actor from such act shall be returned. If the return is impossible or unnecessary, compensation shall be made at a proper price. The party at fault shall compensate the other for loss arising therefrom; but if both parties are at fault, they shall respectively bear the corresponding liabilities, unless otherwise provided by the law.[127]

But note that the remedies as a result of voidance of a contract are not available in the case where a contract is void for malicious collusion to damage the interests of the State, a collective, or a third party. In such a situation, the property acquired shall be subject to the State confiscation. It is provided in Article 59 of the Contract Law that if the parties have maliciously conducted collusion to damage the interests of the State, a collective, or a third party, the property so obtained shall be turned over to the State or returned to the collective or the third party. Article 59 basically intends to impose sanctions on the basis of public policy concerns regarding certain misconduct during the process of making contracts.

In addition, pursuant to the SPC's opinion, when a people's court finds a contract void under Article 52 of the Contract Law, the court shall then determine the proper remedies in accordance with Article 58. Thus, the people's courts will make a decision on remedies in Article 52 cases even if the parties make no such claims. On the other hand, there is no need for the parties to make a new suit for remedies when the contract between them is void for any of the grounds stipulated in Article 52 of the Contract Law.[128]

6   Conditions Affecting the Validity of Contacts

When making a contract, the parties may agree to certain conditions on which the contract will be affected. Distinctively, the condition for a contract in China is a matter of the effectiveness—which means that upon the occurrence or non-occurrence of the agreed conditions, the contract may take effect or become null and void. In this sense, a condition may be deemed to be a limitation

---

127   See the 2017 GPCL, art. 157.
128   See *Fenghuang County State Land Resources Bureau v. Hunan Deheng Power Co. Ltd, supra* note 120.

on the validity of the contract. To compare, conditions in American contract law are related to the performance of a contract. Section 224 of the Restatement of Contracts (2nd) defines a condition as "an event, not certain to occur, which must occur, unless its non-occurrence is excused, before performance under a contract becomes due."[129] In China, however, conditions are associated with the effect of a contract.

In Chinese contract literature, a condition is generally defined as an uncertain future fact. A popular view is that a condition in a contract is an auxiliary clause that is based on the occurrence of a uncertain fact to determine the effectiveness of the contract. Thus, for a fact to become a condition, it is required that (a) at the time of contract the occurrence of the fact was uncertain (i.e., the past or existing fact is not a condition), (b) the occurrence of the fact is possible (i.e., a fact that will never occur or will definitely occur is not a condition), (c) it is unpredictable or uncertain as to when the fact will occur, (d) the fact is chosen by the parties, not the one provided by the law, and (e) the fact is legal.[130]

The Supreme People's Court is also of the opinion that a conditional civil act shall be deemed invalid if the condition is in violation of the law or is impossible to happen.[131] In addition, although parties have the freedom to decide what should be the condition(s) for the effect of a contract, they may not provide as a condition certains provision of law or administrative regulations, or the power of a government agency. For example, the parties may not set in their contract the government's right to approve as a condition for the contract to take effect.[132]

Under the Contract Law, conditions are divided into two categories: effecting (or entry-into-force) conditions and dissolving (or come-to-a-stop) conditions.[133] An effecting condition is one without which a contract will not take

---

129   See the Second Restatement of Contracts, §224.
130   See Jiang Ping, *supra* note 92 at p 36.
131   See Supreme People's Court, Opinions on the 1986 Civil Code, *supra* note 20, art. 75.
132   In *Qingdao Laushan District State Land Resources Management Bureau v. Qingdao Nantai Estate Co. Ltd.*, the parties entered into a contract for transfer of the Right to the Use of State Land, which provided that the contract would take effect upon the approval of the provincial government of Shandong. In their disputes over the effectiveness of the contract, the SPC held that, despite the parties' agreement that government approval would be a condition for the contract to be effective, such approval was not a condition as defined in Article 45 of the Contract Law, and thus would not affect the effectiveness of the contract. SPC (2004) Ming Yi Zhong Zhi No. 106.
133   In American contract law, conditiosn is classified as condition precedents, concurrent conditions, and conditions subsequent. As Professor Rosett pointed out, a condition precedent is an event that must exist or occur before a duty of immediate performance of

effect. A dissolving condition is just the opposite; it refers to a condition upon the occurrence of which a a contract will be dissolved. Under Article 45 of the Contract Law, parties may agree on conditions upon which the effectiveness of a contract is contingent. A contract with an effecting condition shall take effect when such condition is satisfied. A contract that has a dissolving condition shall become null and void when such condition takes place.

Article 45 of the Contract Law also prohibits the parties from manipulating conditions. Under Article 45, if a party, for its own benefit, prevents a condition from occurring without justification, the condition shall be deemed to have occurred. Conversely, if a party unjustly makes a condition to occur, the condition shall be regarded as having not occurred.[134] The provisions of Article 45 of the Contract Law are adopted as Articles 158 and 159 of the 2017 GPCL to apply to civil acts in general.[135] However, there is an exception under Article 158 of the 2017 GPCL, which provides that no conditions may be attached to a civil act if the nature of the civil act does not allow for conditions to be imposed upon it.[136] The exception mostly applies to a civil act that involves personal status, e.g., marriage or adoption. Moreover, for certain civil acts, if the attached condition would harm the legitimate interest of a party, such condition should not be attached. For example, if a condition is attached to the endorsement of a check, the check may not be accepted for payment.

With an effecting condition, the effectiveness of a contract is contingent upon the occurrence of the condition. If the condition occurs, the contract will become effective; if the condition does not occur, the contract will be ineffective. Because the effecting condition impacts the effect of a contract, it is also called a "suspending condition" or "postponement condition." The very basic idea, as the term itself suggests, is that if an effecting condition is attached to a contract, rights and obligations of the parties are ascertained at the time of the contract, but the effectiveness of the contract is suspended until the occurrence of the condition.

For example, A asks B to contribute RMB 10 Yuan to buy lottery tickets, and A tells B, and B agrees, that if any of the tickets wins the lottery, A and B will equally share the prize. In such a situation, there is a contract between A and

---

       promise arises. Where the occurrence of an event extinguishes an existent immediate duty to perform, the condition is said to be subsequent. A condition is concurrent if a party's duty to perform is conditional upon a simultaneous tender of performance by the other. See Rosett & Bussel, *Contract Law and Its Application* (6th ed.), 693–695 (Foundation Press, 1999).

134 See the Contract Law, art. 45.
135 See the 2017 GPCL, art. 158 & 159.
136 See *id.*

B to share the money won from the lottery, and the effecting condition is the "winning ticket." Hence, the contract will not take effect until the parties have the winning ticket. In this contract, the winning ticket is the trigger for the contract to become effective.

A dissolving condition applies to the contract that has taken effect. Thus, when the condition occurs the contract will cease to be effective. Because the dissolving condition determines continuity of the effectiveness of a contract, such a condition is also referred to as an "extinguishing condition"—which means that the effectiveness of the contract will be extinguished upon the occurrence of the condition.

Assume that A agreed to rent his apartment located in City S to B. In the lease agreement, B agreed that if C returns to City S, the lease will be terminated. In this situation, the C's return to City S is the condition upon which the lease agreement between A and B is to be dissolved. Therefore, whenever C returns to City S, the contractual relationship between A and B will be extinguished because the agreed condition is satisfied upon C's return.

But the Contract Law is silent as to whether the condition attached to a contract must be made expressly or, rather, can be implied. The language of Article 45 of the Contract Law appears to suggest that if there is a condition it should be expressly stated in the agreement because Article 45 of the Contract Law seems only to recognize conditions agreed to by the parties.

Besides conditions, the Contract Law also allows the parties to subject the effectiveness of the contract to a time period. In a contract to which a time limit is attached, the effectiveness of the contract will be affected by the expiration of the time period. Again, under Article 160 of the 2017 GPCL, a time limit may also be attached to a civil act. But Article 160 also provides an exception under which no time limit should be attached if it is against the nature of the civil act.[137]

Like conditions, time periods are also split into effecting time periods and dissolving time periods. Under Article 46 of the Contract Law, parties may agree on a time period to be attached to the effectiveness of a contract. A contract subject to an effecting time period shall be effective when the period expires, while a contract subject to a dissolving time limit will become ineffective when the period comes to an end.

Both time periods and conditions affect the effectiveness of contracts. But the concepts are different in that a condition is an uncertain fact at the time of contract, while a time period is a certain fact at the time of contract. The

---

137 See *id.*, art. 160.

certainty of the time period means that when concluding the contract, the parties knew that the time would come at the particular point.

Assume, for example, that A enters into a contract with B to deliver certain goods from A to B. In the contract the parties agree that the contract will end on the day of the opening ceremony of the 2020 Summber Olympic Game in Tokyo. The contract then has a time period because the "2020 Summer Olympic" is an event that has a fixed day to open and therefore is certain. If, however, it is agreed that the contract will end on A's birthday next year, "A's birthday next year" is not a time period but a condition because A may die any time before his next birthday, and thus the upcoming "birthday" is uncertain, though the actual date of A's birthday is known.

Note also that the time period attached to a contract is different from the time period for performance. As discussed, the time period attached to a contract concerns the effectiveness of the contract because the contract may become effective or ineffective upon the expiration of the time period as agreed by the parties. The time period provided for performance, however, deals with the party's tender of the duty to each other after the contract takes effect.

CHAPTER 7

Performance of Contracts

Contract performance concerns fulfillment of legal duties or obligations that become due as agreed upon by the parties under the contract. In China, contract performance is defined as conduct that executes contractual duties or obligations. When such performance is completed, the parties are discharged from any further obligations. Performance is considered to be the core of contract law because it involves the achievement of a contract's purpose and the realization of the expected interests of the parties to a contract. Under the Contract Law, a contract, once effective, must be properly and completely performed.

Three points must be further addressed. First, as previously noted, the law in China follows the civil law tradition, pursuant to which statutes play a dominant role. As part of this tradition, legal principles derived from statutes require particular attention. In China, almost every contract law textbook extensively covers these statutorily derived legal principles.

Second, contract performance under the Contract Law involves many rules that are typically civil law-based. Because of this, substantial discrepancies exist in the area of contract performance between the civil law and the common law. Moreover, given the importance of performance, the Contract Law contains a specific chapter that governs issues relating to contract performance.

Third, contract performance is in principle covered in the General Provisions of the Contract Law. However, in the Special Provisions of the Contract Law, there are detailed provisions that are applied to the performance of specific contracts. In their application, both the general and special provisions are mutually supplementary.

1 Performance Principles

There are two major principles under the Contract Law that govern the performance of contracts—complete and adequate performance, and good faith performance. The very purpose of these principles is to ensure that a contract will be performed as agreed by the parties and that performance will be undertaken in a proper way. In addition, there are a number of rules that are aimed at safeguarding contract performance.

1.1 Complete and Adequate Performance

Article 60 of the Contract Law prescribes that parties to a contract must perform their obligations completely and thoroughly according to the contract's terms.[1] Since performance effectuates the realization of what the parties have bargained for, and is what the contract is all about, the Contract Law provides as a principle that a contract must be fully and adquately performed. A violation of this principle will constitute a breach of contract for which liability will be imposed.

Complete and adequate performance requires that the parties accomplish what they promised or agreed upon in the contract to the extent that all legal duties are completely fulfilled and all legal rights are satisfied. In this regard, performance is complete and adequate when the parties have performed the contractual obligations they respectively assume exactly in accordance with the terms and conditions of the contract. Although there is no such concept as perfect tender or the mirror image rule in China, the principle of complete and adequate performance defines how a contract should be performed in order for the obligations that arise from the contract to be discharged.

Thus, under the complete and adequate performance principle, any non-compliance with the required terms and conditions of a contract will render performance incomplete and inadequate. In addition, scholars in China have suggested that complete and adequate performance also means proper performance, which refers to the way in which a contract is performed. Performance is proper if a contract is performed by the correct party at the agreed time and place with conforming goods or service.[2]

Because of the requirement for complete and adequate performance, the doctrine of substantial performance does not apply in China under the Contract Law. Therefore, damages for breach of contract will be imposed if performance is found to be defective. There are two articles in the Contract Law that directly deal with defective performance. One is Article 71—which relates to advance performance—and the other one is Article 72—which concerns partial performance. Both of these articles apply to contracts with fixed or agreed upon time periods for performance.

Advance performance is performance that is made ahead of the agreed time to perform. Advance performance may occur either at the request of the obligee or at the initiative of the obligor. Article 71 of the Contract Law applies

---

[1] See the Contract Law, art. 60.
[2] To a certain extent, complete and adequate performance shares common elements with the perfect tender rule, which is incorporated in §2–601 of the UCC and requires the full tender of perfectly conforming goods.

to advance performance initiated by the obligor. Under Article 71, the obligee may reject an advance performance of the contract by the obligor. As a general rule, unless agreed by the obligee, advance performance by the obligor will be considered to be a breach.

But, there is an exception. Article 71 does not permit the obligee to reject advance performance that causes no damages to the obligee's interests. This exception is intended to help facilitate transactions and maintain the business relationship between the parties. However, if advance performance causes additional costs to the obligee (e.g., warehouse fees), the obligor shall bear those costs.[3]

Partial performance is deemed defective performance because it violates the principle of complete and adequate performance. Article 72 of the Contract Law explicitly provides that the obligee may reject the partial performance of the contract by the obligor. Once again, however, there is an exception. Under Article 72, partial performance may not be rejected if it does not damage the obligee's interests.[4]

In most cases, partial performance of a contract is permissible when the contract itself is divisible and can be performed separately. Partial performance is also acceptable if the parties agree to have a contract performed in different parts. For example, if the parties have an agreement that the delivery may be made in batches, each batch then will be regarded as a partial performance. In this case, partial performance does not constitute a breach of the contract. However, the obligor shall be responsible for any additional costs that the obligee may incur during the course of the partial performance.

1.2   Good Faith Performance

Good faith performance is closely related to complete and adequate performance. As noted, good faith is a general principle in the Contract Law, and is based on moral values and standards. In the context of contract performance, good faith means to perform the contract according to the nature and purpose of the contract as well as transaction usages. Since complete and adequate performance is the primary requirement for performing contractual obligations, good faith performance is used as a secondary and supplementary means to ensure that the performance is made completely and adequately.

Though the concept of good faith performance appears to be rather abstract, it is considered in China to have an irreplaceable function in helping

---

3   See the Contract Law, art.71.
4   See *id.*, art. 72.

to determine the completion and adequacy of contract performance. The requirement of good faith performance has particular significance in the case where the parties' agreement concerning performance contains ambiguities or has loopholes. In this regard, good faith plays an important role to fill the gaps.

It is provided in Article 60 of the Contract Law that the parties shall abide by the principle of good faith and shall perform such duties as notice, assistance, and confidentiality on the basis of the nature and purpose of the contract or according to transaction practices.[5] To be more explicit, the good faith performance principle under Article 60 of the Contract Law mainly involves two basic duties associated with contract performance. The two duties are commonly called in China the "attached duty" and the "other related duty."[6]

The attached duty is the duty subordinating to the main duties of the contract, and it entirely depends on the existence of the contractual relationship between the parties. The underlying theory is that since making a contact is cooperative behavior through which the parties agree to work together,[7] it is essential that the parties collaborate with each other. Collaboration is often made as required under the good faith principle, though it may not be explicitly provided in the contract.

Thus, the attached duty is the duty necessitated by the contract and is derived mostly from commonly accepted business standards and the parties' reasonable expectations. On this ground, to perform the attached duty is not to increase the burden of either party, but rather is the natural duty imbedded in the performance of the contract. During the course of contract performance, the attached duty arises to the extent that the contract will be performed as expected by the parties.

Under Article 60 of the Contact Law, the attached duty includes the duties to give notice, to assist, and to maintain confidentiality. The duty of notice necessarily occurs when a contractual relationship is established between the parties. The good faith principle requires that the parties during the contract performance must faithfully inform each other of all major events or changes that may affect the performance of the contract. The whole purpose is to help facilitate the completion of the performance.

---

5   See *id.*, art. 60.
6   To compare, section 205 of the Restatement of Contracts provides: "Every contract imposes upon each party a duty of good faith and fair dealing in its performance and enforcement." Similarly, UCC section 1–203 provides: "Every contract or duty within this Act imposes an obligation of good faith in its performance and enforcement."
7   See Rosett & Bussel, *Contract Law and Its Application* (6th ed), 697 (Foundation Press, 1999).

For example, if a party is unable to perform or cannot perform the contract in accordance with the contract's required terms or conditions due to an unexpected event such as a natural disaster or other reasons, the party shall timely notify the other party so that both parties can take informed steps to deal with the situation.[8] Changes that may affect contract performance include changes in the business structure as well as contact information of the parties. Under Article 70 of the Contract Law, if the obligee does not notify the obligor of its separation or merger, or a change of its domicile, which makes it difficult for the obligor to perform its obligations, the obligor may suspend performance or submit the subject matter of the obligation (or object of the contract) to a relevant authority.[9]

The duty to assist is considered to be an inherent obligation of the parties to a contract. Again, since a contract is the product of the cooperation of the parties, the good faith principle requires the parties to be cooperative with each other. Cooperation under the good faith principle implicates that the parties are obligated to assist each other in performing the contract and to facilitate the completion of the contract's performance.

According to Chinese contract scholars, the duty to assist has several aspects. In one aspect, a party, when performing his or her own contract obligations, shall try to pave the way that is necessary for the other party to perform and shall also be prepared to accept the other party's performance. In another aspect, if a party is facing a certain difficulty in performing a contract because of an objective reason, the other party shall give reasonable consideration to the situation the former party encounters and try to help the former party overcome the difficulty in the performance, and if necessary, shall negotiate the options with the former party.

---

8 Some scholars in China suggest that the duty of notice under the good faith performance principle should include notice of (a) means to use; (b) defects; (c) report; (d) danger; (e) business condition, (f) delay; (g) assignment/delegation; (h) event affecting performance; and (i) inability to pay. Many disagree because they think that several of such duties are not duties attached to the contract, but are rather duties provided by the contract. See Cui Yunling, *General View on Contract Law*, 158 (China University of People's Public Security Press) (2003).

9 The submission of the object of contract to a relevant authority (also translated as to deposit the object of the contract with a relevant authority) is a form of statutory relief in China that is available to obligors. As will be discussed in a subsequent chapter of this Book, this relief is normally used when the obligor cannot make delivery of the contracted item either because the obligee's whereabouts are unknown or delivery was refused by the obligee without a legitimate reason.

Moreover, in a case of breach of contract by a party, the other party shall take all measures that are needed to mitigate the damages. The duty to assist requires that the non-breaching party make all reasonable effort to minimize losses. It is also believed that under the duty to assist, the parties, when dealing with contractual disputes between each other, shall treat each other responsibly and shall not evade their respective obligations.[10] In addition, if the parties have divergent views with respect to the terms of performance, they shall work together to resolve the difference in good faith.

The Contract Law does not specify what legal consequences there will be if a party fails to carry out the duty to assist. In practice, however, such failure may result in certain remedies against the non-assisting party depending on the nature of the case.[11] For example, under Article 101 of the Contract Law, if the obligee refuses to accept the subject matter of the contract without a justified reason, the obligor may submit the subject matter to the relevant authority for escrow so that the obligor's obligation is thereby discharged.[12] Another example is Article 259 of the Contract Law, which involves contracts for hired work.

According to Article 259, if assistance from the ordering party is needed for hired work, the ordering party is obligated to provide such assistance. Where the ordering party fails to fulfill his or her obligation of assistance, and this prevents the contracted work from being finished, the contractor may urge the ordering party to perform the obligation and prolong the term of performance. The contractor may also rescind the contract if the ordering party does not perform his or her obligation within the time limit.[13]

The duty to maintain confidentiality is another important element of performance. In fact, it is an extension of the duty that arises at the time of contract negotiation. When making a contract, the parties have the opportunity to learn each other's business secrets, and it is critical that the parties maintain

---

10   See Cui Yunling, *supra* note 8 at pp 158–159; See also Wang Liming & Cui Jianyuan, *A new Commentary on Contract Law—General Provisions* (reversed edition), 320 (China University of Political Science and Law Press, 2000).

11   One Chinese scholar summarizes such consequences as include including categories: (a) transfer of risk—failure to timely pick up the goods; (b) stop accruing interest—failure to accept payment as agreed; (c) extinguishment of guarantee—refusal to accept timely payment; (d) payment for damage or expenses—failure to timely use the materials provided by the other party; (e) extermination of obligation—failure to accept timely performance; and (f) modification or rescission of the contract—failure to assist, which results in the impossibility of performance by the other. See Dong Ling, *Performance, Modification, Assignment and Termination of Contracts*, 20–21 (China Legal System Publishing House, 1999).

12   See the Contract Law, art. 101.

13   See *id.*, art. 259.

the confidentiality of the business information they obtain during the process of contract formation as well as performance. Confidentiality is also required by the mutual trust on which the parties make the contract between one another. A breach of the duty to maintain confidentiality implicates bad faith, for which contractual liability, and in many cases tort liability, will be imposed.

The other related duty is a "catchall" imposition, and it deals with all other obligations that are necessary for the performance of a contract, though such obligations may not be clearly stated or expressed by the parties. As noted, good faith performance in China is regarded as complementary. Thus, the other related "catchall" duty refers to a duty that is not specified in the contract, or is vaguely stated. In either situation, the imposition of such a duty upon the parties is required for complete and adequate performance of the contract.

For example, after conclusion of a contract, each party has the duty to be prepared, or to get ready, for the performance. Although such a duty may not be expressly stated in the contract, it is quite natural that each party is under an obligation to make good preparation for the performance. For either of the parties, a failure to prepare may constitute bad faith, particularly when the failure is made intentionally.

An important point to note is that neither the Contract Law nor the 1986 Civil Code distinguishes between non-merchants and merchants. In a country like the United States, contract laws impose higher standards on merchants than non-merchants. In China, however, merchants and non-merchants are treated the same under the Contract Law. For instance, in the U.S., the key element of good faith in contract performance is honesty. As applied to merchants in sales, however, the UCC requires that merchants must observe, in addition to honesty, "reasonable commercial standards of fair dealing in the trade."[14] By contrast, in China, the Contract Law applies unified good faith standards to all contracting parties, regardless of their business status.

2   Determination of the Obligations to Be Performed

As discussed, the Contract Law contains provisions that are aimed at helping fill in the gap between what the parties have agreed in the contract and what the contract requires. The gap-filling provisions become relevant when certain terms of the contract are either not explicitly provided or are unclear. Such

---

14   See U.C.C. §§2–103(1)(b) and 2A-103 (3).

provisions, though relevant to the interpretation of the contract, are primarily involved in the performance of the contract.

However, it should be noted that the gap-filling provisions are applicable only to those terms that do not affect the conclusion of the contract but may cause difficulty in performing the contract. The purpose of these gap-filling provisions is to ensure that a contract, once lawfully established, is performed as agreed, provided that there is no statutory exemption excusing non-performance. In other words, the gap-filling provisions are intended to help determine what the obligations are under the contract.

The gap-filling provisions relating to contract performance are regarded as necessary in China because the Contract Law requires that contracts be performed completely and adequately. The reality is that in many cases, certain contractual obligations need to be further determined at the time of performance because, at the time the contract was concluded, the parties overlooked some items or could not predict what would happen when the performance became due. Since the existence of such uncertainty makes it difficult to perform the contract, it is necessary to clear up the uncertainty in order to facilitate smooth performance.

The gap-filling provisions in the Contract Law set forth two basic approaches for the determination of the obligations to be performed. One is the consensual approach and the other one is the statutory approach.[15] The consensual approach is to allow the parties by agreement to resolve the uncertainties in the contract. Under Article 61 of the Contract Law, the parties may by agreement supplement a contract's terms relating to quality, price or remuneration, or the place of performance if those terms were not clearly specified or provided at the time of the contract. Trade practices may also be used to help determine such terms.[16]

The statutory approach applies when parties cannot reach an agreement pursuant to Article 61. The Contract Law provides that, absent the parties' agreement, Article 62 shall be applied. Article 62 contains a laundry list for determining terms concerning the quality, price and remuneration, place of performance, time period of performance, method of performance, as well as

---

15 In addition to Articles 61 and 62, there are more than twenty articles in the Contract Law that are directly affected by the application of Article 61 and 62 in determining the obligations for purposes of performance. According to one scholar's survey, the articles related to Articles 61 and 62 include: Articles 111, 139, 154, 156, 159, 160, 161, 205, 206, 226, 232, 250, 263, 310, 312, 338, 341, 354, 366, 379, 418, and 426. See Dong Ling, *supra* note 11 at p 26.

16 See the Contract Law, art. 61.

the expenses incurred in the performance. Unlike Article 61, which is based on the parties' agreement, Article 62 must be applied when no agreement is reached between the parties. In this sense, the provisions in Article 62 are also called statutory gap-fillers.

It might be helpful to examine some of the statutory gap-fillers listed in Article 62. The first one is the quality provision. According to Article 62, when the quality of contracted items is at issue, State or industry quality standards shall be used first. Only if there is no State or industrial quality standard available, may the common standard or the specific standard pursuant to the purpose of the contract be employed.[17] The common standard is the one that the products or goods in question must generally meet. If, however, the common standard is not readily accessible, the courts may look at the medium quality level of the same or similar products or goods that possess the general merchantability to determine an applicable standard.[18]

The second statutory gap-filler that requires further explanation is the place of performance. Article 62 specifically addresses this gap-filler because the place of performance may affect the determination of the parties' rights and obligations. From a conflict of laws perspective, the place of performance may serve as a "connecting point" establishing a court's jurisdiction or identifying the applicable law with regard to the contract performance. Pursuant to Article 62, the place of performance is: (a) the place of the party who receives monetary payment if the performance involves the payment in currency, (b) the place where the property is located if the performance is about the delivery of real estate, or (c) the place of the performing party if the performance concerns all other items.[19]

The third statutory gap-filler that is important and unique in China is price. Two prices may relate to a particular contract performance: market price and State price. As previously noted, the State price in China is divided into the State stipulated price and the State guided price. If a contract is covered by the State price, such a price must be accepted. Again, the difference between the State stipulated price and the State guided price is that the latter affords parties certain room to determine the price as they wish around the range of the State guided price. If a contract is not required to apply the State price, the applicable price shall be determined by the market price of the place of performance at the time of the contract.

---

17 See *id.*, art. 62.
18 See Li Guoguang, *Explanation and Application of the Contract Law*, 274–275 (Xinghua Press) (1999).
19 See the Contract Law, art. 62.

In practice, however, there is always a question about the determination of market price. The question involves two issues under Article 62: namely, the market place and the place of performance at the time of contract. The general benchmark for determining the market price of an item is the cost of the item plus the average profit margin. But since it is often hard to figure out the cost of a particular item and the item's profit margin, some have suggested that the market price should be determined under the most similar product standard in consideration of the cost of the item and its profit margin at the place of performance.[20]

The issue of the place of performance at the time of the contract concerns the geographic area of the place. Presently, the place is provided as the administrative district of county or above. But many scholars believe that it would be unreasonable and unfair to use counties as the basic unit for determining the place of performance because prices may vary significantly among townships within a county.[21] Thus, such scholars argue, it would be more practical not to have a set unit standard so as to allow the people's courts to decide on a case by case basis.[22]

In addition to Article 62, the Contract Law has a special provision that applies to the case where there is a change of the State price. In accordance with Article 63, for a contract that is required to apply the State stipulated price or the State guided price, where the State price is adjusted within the delivery period of the contracted items, the price at the time of delivery shall apply. If the delivery is overdue and the price goes up at the time of delivery, the price shall remain unchanged. And if the price goes down, the new price shall apply. In the event of delay in delivery of the contracted items or late payment, if the price rises, the new price shall apply; but if the price drops, the original price stays.[23]

3   Right of Defense to Non-Performance

The right of defense to non-performance of contract is a civil law concept that is designed to protect the obligor from being harmed by the abuse of right of the obligee. It applies only in a bilateral contract where the parties are mutually the obligor and obligee to each other. By definition, the right of

---

20   See Du Wanhua, Adjudicative Guidance for Contract Cases, 276 (Law Press, 2014).
21   See *id.*
22   See *id.*
23   See *id.*, art. 63.

defense is the right to defend against the claim of the other party or to deny the right asserted by the other party. To the extent the obligor may refuse to honor the obligee's request, the right of defense is also called the right of opposition.

Keep in mind that the right of defense to non-performance is not a denial of contractual obligations or a discharge of contractual duties. Rather, the right provides the obligor with a legal ground on which the obligor may refuse the obligee's request for performance. The underlying notion is that in a bilateral contract, the rights and obligations between the parties are reciprocally connected and mutually dependent. One party's performance is a prerequisite to the other party's performance, and each party, when enjoying its rights under the contract, correspondingly bears contractual obligations. Thus, in order to realize their contractual rights, the parties must each perform their respective obligations. Without one party's performance, the other party's performance will not occur.

Therefore, the right of defense to non-performance is a self-protection right that is created by the law in order to help maintain the balance of interests of the parties in the course of contract performance. Based on such right, a suspension of contractual performance by one party, where that party wants to ensure that the other party will properly perform, is not a breach of contract. In this regard, many Chinese contract law scholars regard the right of defense to non-performance as a guarantee of contractual rights.[24]

The right of defense to non-performance did not appear in Chinese contract legislation until the adoption of the Contract Law. In the past, a concept of "mutual breach" was widely used in judicial practice because, at that time, it was overly emphasized that a contract involves mutual obligations between the parties and that, whoever did not perform the contract would be held liable regardless of the reason for the non-performance. The enactment of the Contract Law altered this practice and made it possible for parties to protect their contractual interests through exercise of their right of defense without litigation.

Under the Contract Law, the right of defense to non-performance consists of two types of defenses: fulfillment plea and unrest defense. Once again, the right of defense is a civil law concept without an equivalent in common law contract theory or practice. This is the right of defense that is applicable only to contract performance.

---

24   See Dong Ling, *supra* note 11 at p 62.

3.1 Fulfillment Plea

Fulfillment plea is the right granted to a party in a bilateral contract to refuse to perform or to reject the request of the other party for performance before the other party performs or properly performs the contract. Under the fulfillment plea, since the parties to a contract are mutually responsible to each other and each bears a duty to the other to perform contractual obligations, any non-performance or non-conforming performance of one party will constitute a ground for the other party to refuse to perform.

To illustrate, in a contract in which the parties agree to the time at which one party will make delivery and the other party will make payment, if at the provided time, the delivering party fails to deliver, the other party then has the right to refuse the other party's request for payment.[25] A practical importance of the "fulfillment plea" is that it helps a court or arbitration body to draw a line between breach and non-breach of the contract, especially when a "contributory breach" defense is asserted because the non-performance by the party exercising the "fulfillment plea" is not a breach of contract.

The Contract Law divides fulfillment pleas into two categories: "simultaneous fulfillment pleas" and "orderly fulfillment pleas." A simultaneous fulfillment plea occurs where the contractual obligations of the parties are mutually implicative. As provided in Article 66 of the Contract Law, if the parties have obligations toward each other and there is no order of priority in performance, the parties shall perform the obligations simultaneously.[26]

Under the simultaneous fulfillment plea, a contracting party has the right to reject the other party's performance request before the other party performs, and also to reject the other party's corresponding performance request if the other party's performance does not meet the terms or conditions of the contract.[27] The Contract Law does not specify the contracts to which the rule of simultaneous fulfillment pleas may apply. But as a practical matter, the

---

25 The concept of a fulfillment plea is similar to the doctrine of current condition in common law systems. In the United States, for example, a concurrent condition is defined to exist where the parties are to exchange performance at the same time. The difference between the two concepts is that a fulfillment plea gives a party the right to refuse to perform, for which no breach of contract will be held, while under the concurrent condition, unless tender is excused, a party must perform or tender performance before the party has a claim. See Calamari & Perillo, *The Law of Contracts* (4th ed), 399 (West Group 1998).
26 See the Contract Law, art. 66.
27 The Principles of International Commercial Contracts of UNIDROIT contains a similar provision. Article 7.1.3 (1) of the Principles provides: "Where the parties are to perform simultaneously, either party may withhold performance until the other party tender its performance."

application of simultaneous fulfillment pleas mostly involves contracts for sales and leases.[28]

Pursuant to Article 66, in order to make a simultaneous fulfillment plea, four elements are required. The first element is mutual obligation. In order to qualify for a simultaneous fulfillment plea, the parties must be mutually obligated to each other in performing the contract. Therefore, as noted, because of the mutual obligation requirement, the simultaneous fulfillment plea only applies to bilateral contracts. The second element is the performance without an order, meaning that there is no requirement as to who performs first. In a contract where the performance is to be rendered in no particular order or the order of the performance cannot be determined by law, trade practices, or business dealings, the performance is deemed to be simultaneous.

The third element is the performance that is due. To assert a simultaneous fulfillment plea, performance must become due. If the time for performance has not arrived, there is no obligation to perform. The fourth element is non-performance or non-conforming performance by a party. A simultaneous fulfillment plea takes place where a party does not perform what he or she is supposed to. Note that non-performance or non-conforming performance refers to performance that is possible, which does not include performance that is excused under the law (e.g., on the ground of *force majeure* or frustration of purpose of the contract).[29]

An orderly fulfillment plea is a defense that can be asserted against a party that is required to perform first under a contract but fails to do so. In accordance with Article 67, where the parties have mutual obligations and the performance of those obligations takes an order of priority, the party who should perform second has the right to reject the performance request of the party

---

28 For example, Article 221 of the Contract Law provides: "The lessee may request the lessor to maintain and repair the leased property within a reasonable period of time when the leased property needs maintenance and repair. Where the lessor fails to perform the obligation of maintaining and repairing the leased property, the lessee may maintain it by itself, and the expenses for the maintenance shall be borne by the lessor. If the maintenance affects the use of the leased property, the rent shall be reduced or the lease term shall be extended correspondingly." This provision is said to give the lessee the right to exercise the simultaneous fulfillment plea when the lessor fails to perform its duty to maintain the leased property. See Wang Liming, *Study on Contract Law (Vol. II)*, 83 (People's University Press, 2003).

29 Some argue that the possible performance of the party should be the fifth element needed to make a simultaneous fulfillment plea. They believe that if the performance of a party becomes impossible, there is no ground for the simultaneous fulfillment plea, and the damaging party may have to seek for other relief. See Cui Yunling, *supra* note 8 at pp171–172.

who should perform first if that latter party fails to make timely performance.[30] In addition, if the performance by the party who has the duty to perform first does not meet the contract requirements, the other party has the right to reject the corresponding performance request.

The orderly fulfillment plea is intended to protect the interest of the party whose performance is subsequent to the performance of the other, and to urge the party who is supposed to perform first to fulfill his or her obligations. The orderly fulfillment plea applies where the first performing party does not perform or the performance is defective. It should be noted that the orderly fulfillment plea, like the simultaneous fulfillment plea, gives a party the right to withhold his or her performance until the other party performs.[31]

Therefore, when the first performing party performs after the assertion of the orderly fulfillment plea, the asserting party must then perform. In the case where the orderly fulfillment plea is made, the first performing party may be held liable for any delay in its performance. No liability, however, will be imposed on the other party for not being able to timely perform due to the first performing party's delay.

There is an ongoing debate among Chinese contract scholars as to how to categorize and define the orderly fulfillment plea. Although scholars agree that the orderly performance plea involves consecutive performance, no consensus has been reached as to how the orderly performance plea should be termed. Some argue that the orderly performance plea should be defined as a defense right for prior performance because it is the right against the party who should perform first but fails to do so.[32] Pursuant to this argument, the focus is on the performance that should take place first under the contract.

Other scholars disagree. They suggest that the orderly fulfillment plea should be called the defense right for subsequent performance. The reason offered by such scholars is that the orderly fulfillment plea is in fact the right of defense that belongs to the subsequently performing party.[33] However it may

---

30 See the Contract Law, art. 67.
31 The term "fulfillment plea" is not used in the Principles of International Commercial Contracts of UNIDROIT; rather, "withholding performance" is used instead. With regard to orderly performance, Article 7.1.3.(2) provides: "Where the parties are to perform consecutively, the party that is to perform later may withhold its performance until the fist party has performed."
32 See Dong Ling, *supra* note 11 at pp 75–77; See also Li Guoguang, *supra* note 10 at pp 294–296.
33 See Wang Liming, *supra* note 28 at pp100–104.

be termed, the orderly fulfillment plea under the Contract Law is the Article 67 right of defense.[34]

3.2 Unrest Defense

The defense of unrest allows the party who should perform first to, under certain circumstances, suspend its performance until the other party's performance is ascertained. This defense provides the performing party with the right to hold off its performance if the party believes with certainty that the other party will not be able to perform at the time agreed upon for performance. As a result of the performing party's exercise of the unrest defense, that party's performance is suspended unless and until the other party's performance is guaranteed or is proven to be certain.[35]

The right of unrest defense is set forth in Article 68 of the Contract Law. Under Article 68, the party who shall perform first may suspend its performance if it has conclusive evidence to prove: (1) the other party's business conditions are seriously deteriorating, (2) the other party diverted its property or takes out its capital to evade debts, (3) the other party loses its business credibility, or (4) other circumstances show that the other party has lost or is likely to lose its capacity to perform.[36]

The very purpose of the unrest defense right is to protect the interest of the party who is under the obligation to render its performance first in the case where it is clear that the other party's subsqunt performance is uncertain. The unrest defense differs from the orderly fulfillment plea in that the former intends to maintain the interests of the party who is the first to perform while the latter is just opposite, being concerned about the protection of the interest of the subsequent performing party.

Like the fulfillment plea, the unrest defense is available only in bilateral contracts. In addition, the unrest defense must also be made on the basis of privity of contract. This privity requirement means that the unrest defense becomes applicable only between the parties to the contract. In the SPC's opinion, the

---

[34] Few scholars categorize the unrest defense as the right of prior performance defense. See Cui Yunling, *supra* note 8 at p 172.
[35] Some scholars compare the doctrine of the unrest defense to the concept of implied anticipatory repudiation as used in the United States and believe that these two are substantially the same. Implied anticipatory repudiation refers to the "prospective inability" stated in UCC §2–609. See Dong Ling, *supra* note 11 at p 79.
[36] See the Contract Law, art. 68.

breach of contract by a third party should not be a ground for application of the unrest defense.[37]

Two factors are essential to the assertion of the unrest defense. First, the party who asserts the unrest defense must be obligated to perform first under the contract, with the other party being obligated perform thereafter. It is the consecutive performances between the parties that necessitates a mechanism for protecting from being impaired the preceding performing party's expectation of receiving due performance from the other party.

Second, there must exist definite evidence that the other party's ability or capacity to perform has been impeded so seriously that the performance is unlikely to take place. To justify an exercise of the right of the unrest defense, the impediment must be caused by any of the statutory reasons set forth in Article 68. If, however, a party asserts the unrest defense to suspend its performance without conclusive evidence, the asserting party, under Article 68 of the Contract Law, shall be liable for breach of contact.

The question remains what constitutes circumstances affecting the subsequent performing party's ability to perform such that the first performing party is entitled to the unrest defense. For example, under Article 68 of the Contract Law, the first performing party may suspend its performance if the other party's business conditions are seriously deteriorating. But in order for the first performing party to be able to assert the unrest defense, an issue that must be dealt with is whether the fact of the other party's deteriorating business situation must occur before the conclusion of the contract or afterwards.

It is generally held that the unrest defense applies where the situation has changed after the contract is concluded. The reason is that if the first performing party has knowledge of the other party's deteriorating business situation at the time of the contract, the doctrine of assumption of risk may prevent the first performing party from asserting any defense. It is suggested that even if a party makes a contract with the other party without knowledge before the contract is concluded that the other party's business situation has deteriorated, the party may seek rescission of the contract, but is not entitled to assert the unrest defense. [38]

Another question is whether the unrest defense must be asserted before the performance of the contract is due, or whether it can alternatively be asserted after the first performing party has started its performance. The Contract Law is not clear on this point. Article 68 only provides that the preceding

---

37 *Yu Chaixin v. Fujian Huachen Real Estates Co. Ltd & Wei Chuanrui*, the SPC, (2010) Min Yi Zhong Zhi No. 13.
38 See Wang Liming, *supra* note 28 at p 107.

performing party may suspend its performance if it has conclusive evidence that the other party is unlikely to perform. The general notion is that the unrest defense is also available after conclusion of the contract and before performance of the contract since the unrest defense serves as a safeguard for the first performing party against the possible harm caused by the other party's failure to perform.[39]

Some in China analogize the unrest defense to the common law concept of anticipatory repudiation.[40] Although there are some similarities between the two concepts—e.g., prospective inability of a party to perform and suspension of performance—the major difference between the concepts is that anticipatory repudiation occurs before the time for performance of the contract arises,[41] while the unrest defense may be asserted either before or after a party has started performing the contract. Another difference is that anticipatory repudiation normally requires a part's unequivocal statement or manifestation of intent not to perform,[42] whereas the unrest defense relies on objective events that adversely affect the other party's ability to perform.

Exercise of the unrest defense is subject to certain limits as delineated in Article 69 of the Contract Law. These limits have two parts: (a) when suspending its performance, the first performing party must notify the other party of the suspension, and (b) if the other party provides an adequate guarantee, the first performing party must resume its performance.[43] Therefore, without notice, the first performing party may not suspend its performance. An unreasonable suspension of performance after an adequate guarantee is provided may make the first performing party liable for breach of the contract.

In addition, Article 69 allows the preceding performing party to rescind the contract when the other party's ability to perform the contract is substantially impeded. According to Article 69, if the other party, within a reasonable period of time after the performance is suspended, is unable to reinstate its ability of performance and fails to provide an adequate guarantee, the party suspending the performance may rescind the contract.[44] Thus, the right to rescind the

---

39 But, some argue that the unrest defense may also be asserted by the performing party after its performance began. In other words, the performing party will not be held liable for breach of contract if it suspends its ongoing performance when it believes with evidence that the other party will not be able to perform. See Dong Ling, *supra* note 11 at pp 87–88.
40 See Wang Liming, Contract Law of China, 138 (Wells 2016).
41 See Jeseph M. Perillo, Contracts (7th ed), Hornbook Series, 454 (2014).
42 See *id.*
43 See the Contract Law, art. 69.
44 See *id.*

contract resides with the preceding performing party as a remedy in the case where the other party's inability to perform continues.

According to the SPC, the unrest defense also applies where one party has made full delivery but there is convincing evidence that the other party will be unable to pay. In such a situation, the party that has made full delivery may ask the people's court to urge the other party to perform the duty of payment even if the payment is not due yet. Under the SPC's view, in this case, absent a guarantee of payment provided by the other party, the payment will be deemed as becoming due, or the due day will be accelerated, if it can be proved with affirmative evidence that (a) the other party has expressly stated an intention not to pay; (b) the other party's business license has been revoked, invalidated, or cancelled; (c) the other party's business has ceased to operate; (d) the other party has transferred its assets or funds to evade liabilities; (e) the other party has lost business credibility; or (f) there is any other situation in which the conduct of the other party indicates its inability or unwillingness to pay.[45]

In addition, under the Contract Law, to avoid the rescission of a contract, the party against whom the unrest defense is asserted must meet two requirements: it must (a) reinstate its ability to perform and (b) provide adequate guarantee within a reasonable period of time. "Adequate guarantee" is understood to mean guarantee that the party is capable of bearing liability for damages if it fails to perform the contract. However, the question is what time period is considered reasonable. Unless the Contract Law provides otherwise, it is entirely up to the court or arbitration body to make this determination.

4   Protective Measures for Performance

As previously discussed, a contract in China is considered to be a relationship of *obligatio* between the parties, pursuant to which the parties are both obligor and obligee to each other. Therefore, once a contract is concluded, such an *obligatio* relationship is created between the parties, and the realization of the contractual interests of the obligee is the full performance of the contractual duties of the obligor.

Generally, under the *obligatio* relationship, the obligor is obligated to perform the contract. Thus, in cases where the obligee's contractual interests are, or are likely to be, adversely affected, the assets of the obligor may be used

---

45   See the SPC, the Opinion of Guidance on Several Matters Concerning Adjudication of the Disputes over Civil and Commecial Contracts under the Present Situations, Fafa, (2009) No. 40.

to guarantee the realization of such interests. The "guarantee" so provided is commonly called the protective measure for performance because it is used to protect against changes in the obligor's assets that may necessarily affect the contractual interests of the obligee.

The Contract Law provides two protective measures: the right of subrogation and the right of cancellation. Both rights are granted to the obligee and are intended to ensure that the obligee's expected interests under the contract will be realized. The protective measures, as provided in the Contract Law, provide the obligee a statutory mechanism for preventing the obligor from inappropriately reducing its assets in order to impair the obligee's contractual interests. It is important to note, however, that though both the right of subrogation and the right of cancellation belong to the obligee, the exercise of such rights may only be made by a court order. In other words, the obligee needs to bring an action in a court in order to take either of the protective measures.

4.1   *Right of Subrogation*

Aimed at protecting the obligee's contractual interests, the right of subrogation allows the obligee in its own name to exercise the obligor's creditor right against a third party who is a debtor of the obligor. To illustrate, assume that A owes B, and C owes A. If A fails to perform its obligation to pay B, B has the right under certain circumstances to ask C to pay B as if C pays A. The theory is the external effect of the *obligatio*, which allows B's contractual right to be extended externally against C, the third party.

As a general contract principle, the obligee can only ask the obligor to perform under the contract between them because the contract may not obligate a third party without the third party's express consent. However, if the obligor's conduct with a third party may adversely affect the realization of the obligee's interests, the obligee would under the law be able to take certain action against both A, the obligor, and C, the third party, for purposes of removing the harm.[46]

The right of subrogation is set forth in Article 73 of the Contract Law. Under Article 73, if the obligor is indolent in exercising its due creditor right against its debtor(s), and this damages the obligee's interests, the obligee may ask the people's court for permission to subrogate the obligor's creditor right and exercise that right in the obligee's own name, despite the fact that the creditor right exclusively belongs to the obligor. Subrogation can be exercised within the scope of the obligee's creditor right and the obligor must bear all necessary

---

46   See Jiang Ping et al, *A Detailed Explanation of the Contract Law of Law*, 61 (China University of Political Science and Law Press, 1999).

expenses incurred by the obligee in exercising the subrogation right.[47] In application of Article 73, the Supreme People's Court has explicitly explained how an action for subrogation should be taken.

4.1.1 Conditions for Subrogation

Shortly after the Contract Law was adopted in 1999, the Supreme People's Court issued its "Explanation to Several Questions Concerning the Implementation and Application of the Contract Law of the People's Republic of China (I)." In its opinions, the Supreme Court set forth the conditions that an action for subrogation should meet. In essence, subrogation is a legal right of the obligee to protect itself from being damaged by the obligor's inactivity or indolence in exercising the obligor's own creditor right that has become due.

Since exercise of the subrogation right involves a third party, it is important that there is a valid ground for subrogating. According to the Supreme People's Court, to seek a subrogation action in a people's court, four conditions must be met. The four conditions are: (a) the obligee's creditor right against the obligor is legal; (b) the obligor is indolent in exercising its creditor right, which causes damage to the obligee; (c) the creditor right of the obligor in question is due; and (d) that obligor's creditor right is not a personal right of the obligor.[48]

The condition requiring that the obligee's creditor right be legal means that there must be a valid contract between the obligor and obligee, on which the obligee's creditor right is based. If no such contract exists or if the contract is void or rescinded, there is no ground for subrogation. Some, however, argue that in addition to being legal, the obligee's creditor right as against the obligor must be certain. Certainty exists where either the obligor admits the obligee's creditor right, or such right is ascertained by the court or an arbitration body.[49]

The notion of indolence concerns the creditor right of an obligor that is due and should have been exercised. Scholars have debated what constitutes indolence in this regard. One opinion is that indolence refers to the failure to claim the right due because of intentional delay in making the claim.[50] The other opinion describes indolence as the failure of the the obligor to claim its creditor right, when such right becomes available, through the means of litigation or arbitration.[51]

---

47 See the Contract Law, art. 73.
48 See the SPC, the 1999 Contract Law Interpretation, art. 11, (1999).
49 See Wang Liming, supra note 28 at pp 134–135.
50 See Li Guoguang, supra note 18 at pp 313–314.
51 The reason supporting this opinion is that to require the claim of the creditor right to be made by means of litigation or arbitration will objectively help determine whether the obligor has been indolent in timely making the claim because the initiation of the

The major difference between these two opinions relates to whether resort to litigation or arbitration should be an element of indolence. The Supreme People's Court's Explanation comports with the latter opinion. Pursuant to the Supreme People's Court's Explanation, subrogation should be made only if the obligor fails to assert the creditor right that it is eligible to claim through either litigation or arbitration.[52]

The personal nature of the obligor's creditor right implies that the right exclusively belongs to the obligor and may not be subrogated. According to the SPC, rights that are personal include rights for payment arising from alimony, child support, maintenance (i.e., support of parents and grandparents), as well as inheritance, and the rights of claims relating to salary, retirement funds, pension funds, survivor's pensions, relocation settlement fees, life insurance, and damages for personal injury.[53]

Article 73 of the Contract Law explicitly provides that the personal right of the obligor shall not be subrogated. It is also important to note that under the Contract Law, subrogation becomes necessary only when the available assets of the obligor are not sufficient to satisfy the obligee's creditor right. If the available assets are sufficient, the obligee may simply seek to enforce the contract and there is no need to look for the obligor's creditor's right against a third party.

One point that deserves further discussion is the determination of any damages that the obligee becomes entitled to when seeking subrogation. The question that necessarily arises in this regard is how damages should be calculated. One argument is that, in the context of subrogation, the damages should be the actual damages that are caused to the obligee by the indolence of the obligor in exercising the obligor's credit right against the third party. The actual damages doctrine is grounded on the notion that because the obligor did not exercise its creditor right—and because of this the obligor's assets that were supposed to increase did not increase, which made it impossible to fully realize the obligee's interests—the obligee has the right to subrogate.

Another argument asserts that, in the context of subrogation, damages should be commensurate with the "likely danger" affecting the realization of the obligee's creditor right, and such danger should be measured by the obligor's delay in performing its contractual obligations as well as its indolence in claiming the obligor's creditor right against a third party. Under this argument,

---

litigation or arbitration will serve as an objective standard for the determination. See Wang Liming, *supra* note 28 at pp 137–138.
52   See the SPC, the 1999 Contract Law Interpretation, art. 13.
53   See *id.*, art. 12.

one factor that should be considered when determining whether damages have been caused is whether the obligor's performance is being delayed.[54] Between the two arguments is a suggestion that the damages to which the obligee seeking subrogation should be entitled should include both the actual and possible damages caused by the obligor's failure to claim its creditor right. Because of its failure, the obligor may not have any assets or at least sufficient assets to satisfy the debts it owes to the obligee.[55]

The SPC takes a moderate approach that does not specify whether the damages must be actual or likely. In the words of the SPC, the damages to the interests of the obligee provided in Article 73 of the Contract Law shall be the obligee's due creditor right that is unsatisfied as a result of the obligor's indolence in exercising its due creditor right and failure to claim the monetary payment on the basis of such right against its debtor through the means of litigation or arbitration.[56] Interestingly, the SPC seemingly intends to limit the claim via litigation or arbitration to the claim for monetary payment.

4.1.2 Action to Seek Subrogation

As noted, under Article 73 of the Contract Law, the exercise of subrogation shall be made through an action in a people's court. In an action seeking subrogation, several procedural issues arise. The first issue is court jurisdiction. In Chinese civil procedure, a general jurisdiction rule is that the plaintiff follows the defendant. Thus, since the defendant in the subrogation action is the obligor's debtor (or secondary obligor), the court of the place where the obligor's debtor resides has jurisdiction.

The second issue involves a pending lawsuit against the obligor. Under the Contract Law, a suit for subrogation is an independent action. Therefore, if the obligee has brought a lawsuit against the obligor, but there is a pending lawsuit against the obligor, the subrogation action is stayed until the court in the pending lawsuit makes a decision in that matter. The reason for this stay is that the court decision in the pending action may render the subrogation action unnecessary.

The third issue concerns the obligor as the third party in the subrogation action. Since subrogation is an action against the obligor's debtor, the obligor needs to be included in a subrogation action as a third party, given the relevance of the obligor to the suit. According to the SPC, if the obligor is not listed

---

54 See Wang Liming, *supra* note 28. at pp 139–143.
55 See *id.*
56 See the SPC, the Opinion of Guidance, *supra* note 45 art. 13.

as a third party joined in the action for subrogation against the obligor's debtor, the court may add the obligor as the third party.

The fourth issue is about the request for an attachment on the assets of the obligor's debtor. In order to help ensure that the court judgment against the obligor's debtor will be satisfied, the obligee in a subrogation action may ask the court to attach the assets of the obligor's debtor. It is required, however, that when making such a request, the obligee must provide as proper guarantee a certain amount of its assets.[57]

4.1.3 Defenses of the Obligor's Debtor

In a suit for subrogation, the obligor's debtor, as the defendant, may have certain defenses against the obligee. One defense is to deny the obligee's allegation about the obligor's indolence in exercising its due creditor right. If the obligor's debtor believes that the obligor has done nothing inappropriate with respect to claiming its creditor's right, the obligor's debtor may assert this accordingly. Importantly, when making the denial, the obligor's debtor bears the burden of proof as a matter of law.[58]

Another defense that the obligor's debtor may assert against the obligee is its own defense against the obligor. Since in the subrogation action, the obligee is allowed to stand in the shoes of the obligors to make a claim against the obligor's debtor, any defense that the obligor's debtor may have against the obligor would necessarily be used against the obligee. Of course, the obligor itself may also challenge the obligee's creditor right in a subrogation action. If the challenge is found to be true, the subrogation action will then be dismissed.[59]

4.1.4 Legal Effect of Subrogation

If an action for subrogation is established and a court decision is made in favor of the obligee, the obligor's debtor shall make the performance to the obligee to the extent that the obligee's creditor right is fully satisfied. And after the performance, the creditor-debtor relationship between the obligee and obligor and between the obligor and the obligor's debtor will be extinguished. With regard to litigation fees incurred in the subrogation action, if the obligee wins the action, the fees, according to the SPC, shall be borne by the obligor's debtor.[60]

Pursuant to Article 73 of the Contract Law, subrogation shall be exercised within the scope of the obligee's creditor right. Thus, if the monetary amount

---

57 See *id.*, articles 14, 15, 16, and 17.
58 See *id.*, art. 13.
59 See *id.*, art. 18.
60 See *id.*, art. 19.

in the obligee's subrogation request exceeds the debt the obligor owed to the obligee or the debt the obligor' debtor owed to the obligor, the exceeded part will not be considered by the people's court in the subrogation action. If, however, the obligor wants to sue its debtor for the residual amount of the debts after the obligee's creditor right has been satisfied, the obligor will have to file a separate action in a competent people's court for this purpose. [61]

4.2   Right of Cancellation

The right of cancellation is another right granted to the obligee by the law to protect the obligee's contractual interests. The right as such is to be exercised where the obligor intentionally gives away or reduces its assets in order to evade its debt obligations and subsequently harms the obligee's creditor right. In this case, the obligee may ask the court to intervene and through the judicial proceeding to cancel the transactions between the obligor and the third party who receives the assets. By "taking back" the assets of the obligor, the cancellation is aimed at restoring the obligor's performance ability to satisfy the obligee's creditor right. Once again, like the right of subrogation, the cancellation right may only be exercised through an action in a people's court.

The theoretical base for the right of cancellation is the subject of ongoing discussions among Chinese scholars. One point of view regards the right of cancellation as the right of claim, which means that the obligee has the right to ask a third party beneficiary to return the gained interests. The right of claim for cancellation arises when the obligor transfers its assets to a third party at a unreasonably low price such that the interests of the obligee are harmed. Thus, in order to protect the obligee's interest, the obligee may ask the third party to return the assets that are improperly transferred.

Others take the position that the right of cancellation is derived from the need to maintain the balance of interests between obligor and obligee. The notion is that a contract is a freely negotiated deal that reflects the expectation and reliance interests of the parties. The fairness principle requires that the rights of a party under the contract shall proportionally match the obligations the party will assume. Therefore, if a party is to evade its contractual obligations by transferring away its assets, the other party's interests will be impaired. The right of cancellation is intended to keep the rights and obligations between the parties balanced.

Another opinion argues that the right of cancellation is a device created by the law to safeguard the legitimate creditor right of the contract. It is believed

---

61   See *id.*, articles 20 and 21.

that the primary goal of the cancellation right is to help realize the obligee's creditor right.[62] Since performance is the key to achieve what the contract is made for, it is critical that the creditor right arising from the contract is protected and maintained. The right of cancellation intends to ensure that performance is proper and in accord with the parties' expectations.

In accordance with Article 74 of the Contract Law, the right of cancellation may be exercised by the obligee under two circumstances. Note that in either of the two circumstances, the third party or transferee has knowledge of obligor's motivation. First, if the obligor in a contract renounces its due creditor right or transfers its property rights gratis so as to damage the interests of the obligee, the obligee may bring an action and request a people's court to cancel the obligor's act.

Second, if the obligor through a transaction transfers its assets at an obviously unreasonably low price, thus damaging the interests of the obligee, and the transferee has knowledge of this effect, the obligee may request the people's court to cancel the transaction. In addition, Article 74 provides that the right of cancellation shall be limited to the scope of the obligee's creditor right. Under the Contract Law, necessary expenses caused to the obligee in its exercising the right of cancellation shall fall on the shoulder of the obligor.[63]

But whether the transfer of assets by the obligor was made at an obviously unreasonably low price can be a diffifult issue. According to the SPC, the people's courts shall determine the price on the basis of (a) the ordinary business judgment of the place of the transaction, (b) the guiding price of the local pricing department or the transaction price of the local market, and (c) other relevant circumstances.[64] In general, if the transfer price at the time of transaction was less than 70% of the local guiding price or market price, the price shall be deemed to be obviously unreasonable low.[65]

In addition, although Article 74 deals with a transfer of assets at an obviously unreasonably low price, the SPC allows the people's courts to grant, under Article 74, the obligee's request for cancellation of a transaction in which the obligor purchased assets from a third party at an obviously unreasonably high price.[66] The SPC holds that if the price of transfer was more than 30% of the

---

62   See Dong Ling, *supra* note 11 at pp. 105–107; See also Wang Liming, *supra* note 28 at p. 158.
63   See the Contract Law, art. 74.
64   See the SPC, 2009 Contract Law Interpretation, art. 19.
65   See *id.*
66   See *id.*

local guiding price or market price, the price will be considered obviously unreasonbly high.[67]

As provided in the Contract Law, there are three factors that are required for the exercise of the right of cancellation. The first factor is the obligor's conduct of renouncing its creditor right or transferring its assets. For the purpose of cancellation, the assets transfer includes a transfer gratis and a transfer at an unreasonably low price. Moreover, there is no legitimate reason to justify such transfer.

The second factor is the obligor's bad faith associated with the renouncement or transfer of its assets. The implication of the bad faith is that at the time of renouncement or transfer of its assets, the obligor knows or ought to know that its conduct will affect its ability to perform the contractual obligations owed to the obligee and, consequently the obligee's creditor right will be impeded.[68] Note that in the case of transfer of assets, the bad faith factor also applies to the third party who knows the purpose and the outcome of the transfer made at an unreasonably low price.

The third factor is the damage that is caused to the interests of the obligee. Damage in this context refers to the unsatisfied creditor right of the obligee. If there is no damage to the obligee, its request for cancellation will not be justified. But, as long as the obligor's conduct causes any incomplete performance of the obligor's obligations, the damage to the interests of the obligee will be found. The amount of damage will depend on the degree of impairment to the performance.

In its interpretation, the SPC seemingly intends to expand the application of Article 74 of the Contract Law. Pursuant to the SPC, in the case where an obligor gives up its undue creditor right or relinquishes the security interests on its creditor right, or extends with bad faith the performance period of its due creditor right, causing damages to an obligee, if the obligee brings a suit for cancellation under Article 74 against the obligor, the people's court shall take action in favor of the obligee.[69]

The effect of cancellation is to avoid the transactions the obligor made with the third party that were intended to frustrate the realization of the obligee's creditor interest. According to the SPC, in an action for cancellation of the obligor's act of announcing its creditor right or transferring its assets, the people's

---

67 See *id.*
68 Some argue that under Article 74 of the Contract Law, bad faith is assumed from the obligor's conduct. If the obligor's conduct causes damage to the interests of the obligee, the obligor will be deemed to have acted in bad faith. See Dong Ling, *supra* note 11 at p 114.
69 See the SPC, 2009 Contract Law Interpretation, art. 18.

court shall make a determination on the claim made by the obligee. If the cancellation is granted, the obligor's act is null and void from the very beginning.[70]

The implication of the SPC's opinion is multi-faceted. First, cancellation must be made by a court order upon the request of the obligee. Second, a cancellation order has a retroactive effect. Such an order traces back to the time the obligor's act was conducted. And third, if the transaction in question is cancelled through a court order, the third party is required to return the assets that it obtained from the obligor because the third party is not a *bona fide* purchaser.

There has been a debate on the actual meaning of the retroactive effect of cancellation. Under Article 74 of the Contract Law, cancellation renders a transaction in question void from the very beginning of the transaction in question. But the question is whether the "very beginning" in this context is to restore both the obligor and the third party to the position they would be in if there were no transaction between them or to require the third party to return assets to the obligee up to the amount that the obligor owed to the obligee. A majority view is that the obligee may not be paid directly by the third party.[71] If the obligee has suffered loss, it may file a suit against the obligor after the cancellation.[72]

In addition, although the right of cancellation belongs to the obligee, the exercise of the right must be timely made; otherwise the right may be extinguished. Under Article 75 of the Contract Law, the right of cancellation shall be exercised within one year from the day when the obligee is aware or ought to be aware of the causes for the cancellation. If the right of cancellation has not been exercised within five years from the day when the act of the obligor takes place, the right of cancellation is extinguished, regardless of the obligee's knowledge of the causes for the cancellation.

The statute of limitations as applied to the exercise of the right of cancellation is aimed at protecting the interests of the obligor. It also serves to help maintain business efficiency and transaction stability. Again, keep in mind that the one-year time limit is based on the obligee's notice of the obligor's act, while the five-year time limit deals with the actual occurrence of the obligor's act; whichever comes first controls.

The case below involves both the right of subrogation and the right of cancellation. Normally, the action for subrogation and the action for cancellation are deemed as separate causes of actions and ought to be litigated separately

---

70 See the SPC the Opinion of Guidance, *supra* note 45, art. 25.
71 See Du Wanhau, *supra* note 20, at 239–240.
72 See *id.*, at 241.

because in China the right of cancellation is characterized as "action for confirmation" (*actio confessoria*) while the right of subrogation is "action for payment". In this case, however, the court had the two actions consolidated and adjudicated them together.

China Agriculture Bank, Zhang Ping City Branch

v.

Zhang Ping Shuang Yang Supply & Sales Cooperative and Zhang Ping City Agricultural Capital Company, Inc.

The High People's Court of Fu Jian Province Ming Jing Zhong Zhi (2002) No. 290[73]

This case was appealed by appellant (plaintiff in the trial) from the judgment of Funjian Nongyan City Intermediate People's Court, *Yan Jing Chu Zhi* (2001) No. 083.

The basic facts of the case are as follows: On September 30, 1999, December 18, 1999 and March 31, 2000, defendant Agricultural Capital Company, Inc. (Agricultural Capital) borrowed RMB 2.45 million, 1 million and 4 million respectively from plaintiff, and defendant then defaulted in repayment of the loans. Plaintiff took a legal action against defendant Agricultural Capital and a judgment was entered in favor of plaintiff on December 8, 2000 by Funjian Nongyan City Intermediate People's Court, *Yan Jing Chu Zhi* (2000) No. 71. In that judgment, it was determined that defendant Agricultural Capital owed to plaintiff in a total amount of RMB 7.45 million plus interests. After the judgment, defendant Agricultural Capital only paid to plaintiff the interests of RMB 53,767 and was unable to pay the principal due to its financial inability to satisfy the judgment.

Defendant Agricultural Capital and defendant Zhang Ping Shuang Yang Supply & Sales Cooperative (SS Cooperative) had a long-term business relationship, and defendant Agricultural Capital was a holder of a creditor right against defendant SS Cooperative. On December 16, 2000, SS Cooperative and Agricultural Capital sign "the Agreement of Debts Offset for Properties" under which SS Cooperative sold to Agricultural Capital its Sawmill and other two warehouses at the price of RMB 1,048,038. On December 5, 2001, plaintiff sued the two defendants for their conspiracy to evade debts owed by Agricultural Capital to plaintiff on the ground that the actual value of the said properties was far less than the price specified in the Agreement.

Plaintiff claimed that the sale of the properties by defendant SS Cooperative to defendant Agricultural Capital was a setup manipulated by the defendants in bad faith and the whole purpose was to frustrate plaintiff's creditors right against defendant Agricultural Capital. Plaintiff asserted that defendant SS Cooperative owed to defendant Agricultural Capital in the amount of RMB 1,048,083, and defendant Agricultural Capital did not duly exercise its creditor right, but rather it colluded with defendant SS Cooperative to offset the debts by selling three buildings owned by defendant SS Cooperative to defendant Agricultural Capital.

Plaintiff argued that its creditor right was harmed by the deal between the defendants because given the fact that the real value of the Sawmill was no more than RMB 219,000, one warehouse was only worth RMB 127,000, and the other one was already occupied by a different entity, and therefore the offset was actually a disguised form of defendant Agricultural Capital's renouncing its creditor

---

[73] This case was selected in the National Judicial College & People's University Law School, *An Overview of the Trial Cases of China* (Civil and Commercial Cases 2004), 19 (People's Court Publishing House and People's University Press, 2005).

right against defendant SS Cooperative. Plaintiff requested the court (a) to cancel the Agreement of Debts Offset for Properties reached by the defendants and (b) to order defendant SS Cooperative to promptly pay off the debts of RMB 1,048,083 owed to defendant Agricultural Capital.

Defendant Agricultural Capital argued that plaintiff's request had no legal ground because the Agreement of Debts Offset for Properties it entered with defendant SS Cooperative was legal and valid, which did not infringe any interests of a third party. Defendant Agricultural Capital asked the court to dismiss plaintiff's claim for the reasons that it was not indolent in exercising its creditor right, but on the contrary, it had actively engaged in urging SS Cooperative to repay the debts, and that the Agreement of Debts Offset for Properties would best serve as a strong evidence in that regard.

Defendant SS Cooperative insisted that the Agreement of Debts Offset for Properties was a manifestation of the real intention of the parties to clear up the debts it owed to Agricultural Capital and the Agreement should be held valid because the value of the properties was determined on the basis of appraisal, and the transfer of the properties affected no interests of a third party. Defendant SS Cooperative also argued that plaintiff's exercise of the right of cancellation was groundless since the creditor-debtor relationship it had with Agricultural Capital would no longer exist after the full payment it made to Agricultural Capital through the valid sale of the properties to satisfy the debts in question. Defendant SS Cooperative further rebutted that plaintiff's assertion of the debt amount of RMB 1,048,083 was not supported by any evidence, and therefore there was no legitimate reason to support plaintiff's subrogation right.

It was found during the trial that as of January 1, 2001, SS Cooperative owed Agricultural Capital in a total amount of RMB 801,296.90, which was evidenced by the detailed ledger account of SS Cooperative, dated June 30, 2001, stating that SS Cooperative owed to Agricultural Capital RMB 801,296.90. It was also found that defendant Agricultural Capital owed plaintiff the debts of 7.45 million in total plus interests, and Agricultural Capital was financially incapable to pay off the debts, but it held matured creditor right against SS Cooperative. A further finding during the trial was that the actual value of the Sawmill and one warehouse, as appraised by the court designated appraisal agent, was RMB 346,000 all together, and the other two warehouses were possessed by other units, for which defendant SS Cooperative was compensated RMB 30,000. In addition, after defendant Agricultural Capital and defendant SS Cooperative singed the Agreement of Debts Offset for Properties on December 16, 2000, they did not close the deal and no settlement was ever made. In fact, however, on December 18, 2000, defendant Agricultural Capital leased back one warehouse to defendant SS Cooperative at an annual rent of RMB 1,000.

The trial court then held that there was no sufficient evidence to prove plaintiff's assertion of RMB 1,048,083 debts owed by defendant SS Cooperative to defendant Agricultural Capital, and then the actual amount must be based on the defendant SS Cooperative's ledger account, which was RMB 801,296.90. The court reasoned that absent evidence to the contrary, the record on the ledger account should be assumed to be the one that truly reflected the transactions between the defendants.

The trial court further held that the swap of the debts with the properties between the defendants was in fact intended to reduce the assets of defendant Agricultural Capital because the total value of the sold properties as appraised was unreasonably below the sale price of RMB 1,048,083, and by doing so defendant Agricultural Capital actually abandoned its due creditor right against defendant SS Cooperative. In addition, the facts of no-settlement of transactions and low rent of one warehouse to SS Cooperative clearly implicated that the transactions were never really executed and defendants colluded with each other in bad faith in order to evade the debt obligations of defendant Agricultural Capital. On this ground, plaintiff's request to exercise the right of cancellation under the provision of Article 55 of the Contract Law should be granted.

The trial court also came to a conclusion that although the agreement of defendants to offset the debts for properties between them ought to be cancelled due to their bad faith collusion, defendant Agricultural Capital still held the creditor right against defendant SS Cooperative for the debt of RMB 801,296.90, and the fact of signing the agreement between the defendants demonstrated that the debts were already matured. Thus defendant's failure to actively exercise its matured creditor right through litigation or arbitration would constitute an indolence that damaged plaintiff's creditor right, which justified plaintiff's right of subrogation.

The trial court then entered into the following judgment in favor of plaintiff:

1. The Agreement of Debts Offset for Properties reached by the defendants on December 16, 2000 should be cancelled;
2. Defendant SS Cooperative shall within 10 days after the judgment takes effect pay plaintiff RMB 801,296.90 that defendant SS Cooperative owed to defendant Agricultural Capital plus interests accrued from January 1, 2001 to the date of payment at an official rate set forth by the People's Bank of China for late payment; and
3. The litigation fees of RMB 22010 should be born by plaintiff in the amount of RMB 4010 and by defendant SS Cooperative in the amount of RMB 18,000.

Defendant SS Cooperative timely appealed the trial court judgment to this court. Defendant SS Cooperative argued that (1) the trial court erred in finding the transfer of the properties as defendant Agricultural Capital's abandonment of its creditor right, (2) SS Cooperative's internal ledger account should not be used as the basis for entering the judgment; and (3) the court's determination of defendant Agricultural Capital's indolence in pursing its creditor rights was not supported by sufficient evidence.

We, however, agree with the trial court that it is permissible to use the internal ledger account to help court make decision on the actual amount of debts, and as of January 1, 2001, the matured creditor right defendant Agricultural Capital had against defendant SS Cooperative was RMB 801,296.90. We find that defendant Agricultural Capital did not make active efforts to urge defendant SS Cooperative to pay the already matured debts that should have been paid, but instead it conspired with defendant SS Cooperative to sign a so-called "the Agreement of Debts Offset for Properties". We therefore hold that defendant Agricultural Capital's indolence and its bad faith collusion with defendant SS Cooperative indeed constituted a covert act of renouncement of its due creditor right against defendant SS Cooperative, and such act has caused damages to plaintiff's credit right.

Therefore, in accordance with Article 153(1)(a) of the Civil Procedural Law, it is ordered that the appeal be denied and the judgment below be confirmed. In addition, the appellant shall bear the cost of RMB 16250 to cover the fees for the appeal.

The *China Agriculture Bank* is a case where the Chinese courts uphold the right of cancellation and right of subrogation by focusing on the intent and conduct of defendants to make a determination of the bad faith collusion to evade the matured debts. Note that in this case the courts seem to suggest that the matured creditor right be exercised through litigation or arbitration or otherwise the right may be deemed as having not been actively exercised.

5   Guarantee of Performance

Besides the rights of subrogation and cancellation, the parties may set forth certain guarantees by agreement to ensure the performance of the contract. In addition, a guarantee for the performance may be provided by the law with regard to particular contract (e.g., a lien). Because of its purpose to ensure that the contract is performed, the performance guarantee is also called the guarantee of contract. The primary legal source of the performance guarantee is the 1986 Civil Code. Under Article of the 1986 Civil Code, a performance guarantee made by the agreement of the parties or by operation of law may take the form of suretyship, security interest, money deposit, or lien. In addition, the establishment of a guarantee is subject to the Guaranty Law of China.[74]

5.1   *Suretyship*

Suretyship is a personal guarantee provided by a third party to the obligee to ensure that the contract obligations will be performed. Such a personal guarantee is based on the third party's credibility or assets. Under the suretyship, if the obligor defaults in performance, the third party as a guarantor is obligated to perform for the benefit of the obligee or it will be held jointly liable for breach of the contract. According to Article 89 (1) of the 1986 Civil Code, a guarantor may guarantee to the creditor that the debtor will perform his obligations. If the debtor fails to perform, the guarantor shall perform the debt or jointly and severally bear the liability as agreed. After performing the debt, the guarantor shall have the right to claim indemnity against the debtor.

For purposes of suretyship, the guarantor may be a legal person, another organization, or a person who is capable of assuming debts. As a matter of law, however, no government agency or pubic affairs institute may serve as the guarantor in commercial contracts.[75] In addition, the branches or functioning departments of a business company may not act as guarantor unless expressly authorized in writing by the company. According to the SPC, a suretyship made by the branch of a company shall generally be deemed invalid, but the branch shall bear the property liability incurred thereof. If, however, the branch is insolvent, liability shall be borne by the company.[76]

There are statutory requirements relating to both the formality and contents of a suretyship. Under Article 13 of the Guaranty Law, to create a suretyship, a written contract shall be made between the guarantor and obligee.[77] But, the SPC seems to be flexible about the writing requirement. It is the SPC's

---

74   The Guaranty Law was adopted on June 30, 1995 and became effective on October 1, 1995.
75   Pursuant to the Guaranty Law of China, a government agency, as approved by the State Council, may act as a guarantor in the case of securing loans, for re-lending, from a foreign government or an international economic organization.
76   See the SPC, Opinions on Implementation of the General Principles of Civil Law of the People's Republic of China (1988), art. 107.
77   See the Guarantee Law, art. 13.

position that an oral guarantee made between Chinese citizens, if witnessed by more than two uninterested people, will be deemed to constitute a guarantee contract, unless otherwise provided by law.[78]

It is also required in Article 15 of the Guarantee Law that the suretyship contract shall include the follows contents: (a) type and amount of the principal claim guaranteed, (b) the time limit for the debtor to perform the obligation, (c) methods of guarantee, (d) scope of suretyship, (e) term of suretyship, and (f) other matters the parties deem appropriate.[79] Under Article 15, a lack of any of these required contents may render the guarantee invalid, but the parties are allowed to supplement to fill in any missing content.[80]

5.2   Security Interest

In order to guarantee the performance of a contract, the parties may agree that the obligor or a third party will provide the obligee with certain property as security by which the obligee may be compensated in the case the obligor defaults. In China, there are two major categories of security interests: mortgages and pledges. A mortgage is defined as an interest in real property or the right to the use of land that is provided by the obligor or a third party to the obligee as a guarantee for the debts without transferring the right of possession over the property.

The unique aspect of a mortgage is the right to the use of land. Again, in China, no individual may own a piece of land, as lands are owned either by the State or by the collectives. Since the right to the use of land possesses security interests on the land and is marketable, the right can be used as a mortgage in China to guarantee the payment of debt. Thus, it is important to note that a transfer of the right to use a piece of land does not affect the ownership of the land itself.

Different from a mortgage, which involves real property or immovables, a pledge is a guarantee on the basis of movables. A pledge means that an obligor or a third party transfers the possession of his movables to the obligee as a security for debts. In contrast to a mortgage, a pledge requires a transfer of possession of the property involved. In addition, the movables used as a pledge include negotiable instruments (e.g., stocks).

As provided in Article 89 (2) of the 1986 Civil Code, an obligor or a third party may offer a specific property as security for the performance of obligations. If the obligor defaults, the obligee shall, in accordance with the provisions of

---

78   See the SPC, Opinions, *supra* note 75 art. 108.
79   See the Guarantee Law, art. 15.
80   See *id.*

law, be entitled to use the property in its possession as a security to offset the debts or to the preferential payment out of the proceeds from the sale of the property pledged.[81]

Because of the requirement for the transfer of the possession of the pledged property, a pledge will not take effect until the delivery of the property. In addition, if the pledge consists of negotiable instruments, the right to the exclusive use of trademarks, or the property right in patents or copyright, which are transferable under the law, a registration is required in order for the pledge to become effective.

5.3 Money Deposit

A money deposit, also called earnest money, is a security in the form of an agreed amount of money put up front to guarantee realization of the obligee's creditor right. Under Article 89 (3) of the 1986 Civil Code, within the limits of the law, the parties to a contract may agree that one party will deposit with other party a certain amount of money as a guarantee for the performance of a contract. The money deposit guarantee has two distinctive features: (1) it must be in whatever amount the parties agree upon and (2) it must be in the hand of the party to whom the guarantee is made.

Since a money deposit guarantees the performance of a contract, the money so deposited shall be refunded or credited against the contract price after the contract obligations are performed. On the other hand, the depositor may not reclaim the money if he fails to perform the obligations under the contract. If, however, the party who receives the deposit fails to perform, the money shall be refunded. Under Chinese law, if the recipient of a money deposit defaults in its performance of the contract, the amount of refund is doubled.

Article 90 of the Guaranty Law mandates that the money deposit guarantee be executed in writing.[82] In the writing as required, the parties must specify the time limit for the delivery of the money deposit. The written agreement for the money deposit shall be effective upon the actual delivery of the money deposited. Also, pursuant to Article 91 of the Guaranty Law, the parties are free to determine the amount for the money deposit guarantee, but the amount is capped at 20% of the total price of the contract.[83]

---

81 See the 1986 Civil Code, art. 89.
82 See Guarantee Law of China, art. 90.
83 See *id.*, art. 91.

5.4 Lien

The parties to a contract may also provide a lien by agreement to ensure the performance of contractual obligations. A lien is defined in Article 82 of the Guaranty law as a form of security interest granted over the obligor's movables in the possession of the obligee to secure the performance of the contract.[84] If the obligor fails to perform, the obligee as the lien holder may retain the property or have priority in payment out of money converted from the property or the proceeds from sale of the property or an auction.

Although the lien appears similar to the pledge in terms of the obligee's possession of the personal property (i.e., movables) of the obligor, a lien and a pledge differ in substantial a way. The major difference is that property under a lien is in the possession of the obligee on or before the obligee's creditor right is created, while the pledge involves the transfer of property from the obligor to the obligee on or after the creation of the creditor right. In addition, a lien may only be made on the property of the obligor, but the pledge can be placed on the property of both the obligor as well as a third party.

According to Article 89 (4) of the 1986 Civil Code, if a party has possession of the other party's property according to the contract and the other party violates the contract by failing to pay a required sum of money within the stipulated time period, the possessor has the right of lien against the property and thereby may retain the property to offset the debts or have the priority of being compensated out of the proceeds from the sale of the property.[85] Contracts in which the obligee normally has the right of lien in the case of the obligor's failure to perform are contracts for storage, transportation, or processing.

6 Changes of Circumstances during Performance

In the Contract Law, two types of changes of circumstances are relevant when a contract is being performed. The first is the change in the parties. The most common phenomenon is the change in the management, business structure, company name, or address. The change also includes merger or split-up of the company. The second is circumstantial changes during the performance of the contract, which are unpredictable at the time of the contract or cannot be overcome after the occurrence. Circumstantial changes involve the doctrine of *Rebus Sic Stantibus*.

---

84 See *id*, art. 82.
85 See the 1986 Civil Code, art. 89.

6.1 Changes Related to the Parties

It is quite common that a company experiences changes in its business operation. Such changes, however, should not be used as an excuse to evade the company's obligations under a contract. Thus, under Article 76 of the Contract Law, after a contract becomes effective, the parties may not refuse to perform the obligations of the contract because of the change of the title or name of the parties, or change of the legal representative or person-in-charge of the parties.[86]

The importance of Article 76 is to maintain the consistence and continuance in the performance of contractual obligations regardless of any change in personnel or company structures of the parties. The purpose is to prevent the party or parties from evading contract obligations by making changes in the company or business settings. As far as an obligor is concerned, it is required under Article 76 that the obligor remain obligated to perform the existing contract during or after the course of the change(s) in its business operations.

On the other hand, if a change takes place as to an obligee, the Contract Law requires the obligee to provide the obligor with a notice about all the changes that may affect the obligor's performance. Article 70 provides that if the obligee does not notify the obligor of its separation, merger, or a change of its domicile, so as to make it difficult for the obligor to perform its obligations, the obligor may suspend the performance of the contract or have the subject matter of the contract submitted in escrow with a relevant authority.[87]

When Article 70 of the Contract Law applies, the obligor will be excused from performance and thus free from liability for breach of contract. In addition, if the performance is suspended under Article 70, the obligee shall bear the risk that the subject matter of the contract may encounter. The obligee may also be held liable for damages resulting from its late acceptance of the performance due to the suspension.

6.2 *Rebus Sic Stantibus*

One of the most controversial issues in drafting the Contract Law is whether the doctrine of *"rebus sic stantibus"* should be incorporated into the statute. Under this doctrine, one party may be excused from performance when a change in circumstances beyond the contracting parties' expectations and control has frustrated the original basis of the contract such that continuing

---

86 See the Contract Law, art. 76.
87 See *id.*, art. 70.

performance of the contract is obviously unfair. As a result, it is necessary to have the contract be modified or rescinded in such a situation.

Although *"rebus sic stantibus"* was not provided in any previous contract legislation, the doctrine was actually accepted in judicial practice. In *Wu Han Gas Company v. Chongqin Testing Instruments Factory* (1989), Plaintiff entered into a contract in 1988 with Defendant for purchasing 70,000 sets of J 2.5 gas meters at 57.30 RMB per set. The contract provided that Defendant should deliver 30,000 sets of the meters in 1988 and 40,000 sets in 1989 to Plaintiff. All meters were made of aluminum. Several months after the contract was concluded, the price of aluminum was adjusted by the States from 4,400–4,600 RMB per ton to 16,000 RMB per ton. Consequently, the cost for producing the meters was increased to 79.22 RMB per set. When Defendant asked Plaintiff to modify the contract or rescind it in order to avoid heavy loss, Plaintiff refused. After Defendant stopped delivering the meters, Plaintiff sued for breach of contract.

At trial, Wuhan Intermediate People's Court entered a judgment against Defendant. The court held that the change of price did not constitute a valid ground for Defendant not to perform its contractual obligations, and Defendant was therefore fully liable for the breach. On appeal, the judgment was reversed by the High People's Court of Hubei Province. In remanding the case for further proceedings, the High Court opines that if during the performance of a contract there is a material change that the parties could not have foreseen at the time when the contract was made, and if continuing performance would be manifestly unfair, the doctrine of *"rebus sic stantibus"* should be applied to preserve fairness.[88]

This opinion was upheld by the SPC. In its letter of judicial instruction issued on March 6, 1992,[89] the SPC held that for purposes of the instant case, due to the chance in circumstances, which could not be foreseen or prevented by the parties at the time of contract and during the performance of the contract, it would be obviously unfair if Defendant was asked to continue performing its obligations under the original contract. In 1993, the SPC further pointed out that if due to reasons for which none of the parties may be blamed, an unpredictable change in the circumstances on which the contract is based is so fundamental that it would be obviously unfair to enforce the original contract,

---

88   See Kong Xiangjun, Comments and Theoretical Study on Difficult Cases of the Contract Law (revised ed), 396 (People's Court Press, 2000).

89   The judiciary letter from the SPC is normally used by the Court to answer legal questions raised by a High Court concerning the interpretation and application of a specific law or regulation in a particular case. See *id.*

the people's courts may, upon the request of the parties, modify or dissolve the contract under the doctrine of *"rebus sic stantibus."*[90]

The *"rebus sic stantibus"* doctrine was included in early drafts of the Contract Law. This inclusion, however, met strong resistance. Opponents argued that the doctrine would be abused if provided in the Contract Law because (1) there is no commonly accepted definition for *"rebus sic stantibus"*; and (2) it is very difficult, if not impossible, to draw a line between *"rebus sic stantibus"* and normal commercial risk. As a result, the doctrine was ultimately deleted from the final draft of the Contract Law.[91]

But, the lack of actual legislative endorsement in the Contract Law of the adoption of *"rebus sic stantibus"* does not seem to have reversed the course of application of this doctrine in judicial practices. In order to clear up the doubt as to the validity of the use of *"rebus sic stantibus,"* the SPC takes the position that the doctrine of *"rebus sic stantibus"* will still be recognized and employed in judicial practice absent a provision to that effect in the Contract Law.

In its 2009 Contract Law Interpretation, the SPC restated the application of *"rebus sic stantibus."* In accordance with the SPC, when objective circumstances materially change after a contract has been formed, which could not be foreseen by the parties at the time of contract and was caused by the non-commercial risks falling outside the ambit of *force majeure,* if continuing performance of the contract will be obviously unfair to one party or will not achieve the goal of the contract, the party may ask a people's court to modify or rescind the contract. If the party so requests, the people's court shall make a decision on whether the contract should be modified or rescinded under the principle of fairness in consideration of realities of the case.[92]

The SPC's 2009 interpretation is considered as the formal adoption of the *"rebus sic stantibus"* doctrine into Chinese contract law. To apply the doctrine, however, certain conditions must be met. First, there must be a change in circumstances. Circumstances in this context refer to facts or objective situations on which the contract was concluded by the parties, including political, economic, legal, or commercial environment.[93] It is also believed that a change in

---

90 See the SPC, "Minutes on 1993 National Symposium on Trials of Economic Cases," May 6, 1993 Fa Fa (1993) No. 8.
91 See Sun Lihai, *Selection of Legislative Materials of the Contract Law of the People's Republic of China,* 54–55 (Law Publishing House, 1999).
92 See the SPC, 2009 Contract Law Interpretation, art. 26.
93 See Jiang Bixin, et al, Understanding and Application of the Adjudication Rules of the SPC's Guiding Cases (Contracts), 262–264 (China Legal Publishing House, 2012).

circumstances means abnormal variance or distortion in those facts or situations.[94]

Second, the change must occur after the contract was made. *"Rebus sic stantibus"* is a legal remedy to prevent unfairness in the performance of a contract. If there was a change in circumstances during the negotiation of a contract, it is expected that parties should have been able to deal with the change. Also, because of the fairness concern, the remedy of *"rebus sic stantibus"* will be considered to be inapplicable if a party delayed his performance without justification and a change in circumstances took place during the period of delayed performance.[95]

Third, the change in circumstances must be unforeseeable by the parties at the time of the contract. Unforeseeability means that the parties did not contemplate the changed circumstance when they entered into the contract. If the change occurred when the contract was concluded, the doctrine of *"rebus sic stantibus"* will be trumped by the assumption of risk. In addition, if the change was caused by the fault of a party or the parties, the *"rebus sic stantibus"* doctrine will not apply and, instead, the party at fault shall be liable for the damages arising from the change.[96]

Fourth, the change in circumstances must be material. Materiality exists when a change is so fundamental that the presumption on which the contract stands no longer exists or has been significantly altered. The idea is that due to the material change, certain justification will need to be made in order to avoid unfairness that would otherwise occur. Materiality is also a factor to be considered in differentiating a change in circumstances from a commercial risk. A commecial risk is the possibility of loss normally associated with the business operation, and such possibility in many cases should be or ought to be foreseen.[97]

Note, however, that since *"rebus sic stantibus"* is not addressed by any statutory provision, the SPC is quite cautious when it comes to applying the doctrine. Pursuant to the SPC's directive, the people's courts must carefully handle requests for modification or rescission of a contract on the ground of change in circumstances. According to the SPC, if the doctrine has to be applied in a particular case, the application requires approval by a high people's court and, when necessary, the case should be reported to the SPC for review.[98]

---

94 See *id.*
95 See *id.*
96 See *id.*
97 See *id.*
98 See *id.*

CHAPTER 8

Modification of Contract and Assignment

Once a contract is formed, a need may develop during the performance to make a change to the contract. Such a change may be effectuated in two different ways: a change to the contents of the contract and a change to the parties to the contract (which normally refers to the obligee or obligor in connection with the performance of the contract). In accordance with the provisions of the Contract Law, a change made to the contents of a contract constitutes a modification while a change that involves the parties to a contract constitutes assignment, including delegation.

Under the notion that a contract is a product of free and voluntary negotiations of the parties to carry out their business goals, the parties capable to make the contract are capable to modify the contract. Because a modification changes or alters the contents of an existing contract, a modified contract may differ from the existing contract in its contents. But the overall purpose and effect of the existing contract will in general remain intact after modification.

Contract modification can be made either by an agreement between the parties or by a court order upon the request of a party. In most cases, the modification is a consensual one, namely a mutually agreed modification. It is an internationally well-accepted common practice that a contract may be modified by the mere agreement of the parties.[1] Non-consensual modification is a change made to a contract through litigation in particular cases, which often requires a statutory basis. An example is the modification on the ground of *rebus sic stantibus*.

The Contract Law contains detailed rules for both modification and assignment of a contract. Since modification and assignment are provided in the same chapter of the Contract Law, they are often discussed together in Chinese contract law textbooks. Thus, modification is also classified into modification in a narrow sense and modification in a broad sense. Modification in a narrow sense means changes in the contents of a contract, including amendments, supplement, as well as limitations made to the terms of the contract. Modification in a broad sense includes the change of the obligee and obligor of the contract, meaning assignment and delegation.[2]

---

1 See, for example, Article 29 of the United Nations on Contracts for International Sale of Goods (A contract may be modified or terminated by the mere agreement of the parties).
2 In China, there seems to be no such concept as novation. Although the change of parties is discussed in the contract law literature, the discussion is more associated with modification

1   Modification

Again, contract modification may result from the agreement of the parties or a court order. In the context of the Contract Law, modifications are primarily made through the parties' agreement. Article 77 of the Contract Law provides that a contract may be modified if the parties reach a consensus through consultation.[3] Article 77 has several implications. First of all, the parties are free to modify the contract between them. Secondly, the modification shall be made by the agreement of the parties. And thirdly, the agreement for modifying the contract shall be reached by consensus of the parties on a voluntary basis through consultation.

In American contract law, the parties have the right to modify the contract as they wish, but for a modification to be effective and enforceable, it in general must be supported by consideration. It is held in the U.S. that all of the requirements for making a contract equally apply to a modification of the contract because the modification of an existing contract is actually an effort to create another contract.[4] In China, however, given the civil law tradition, consideration is not required for the modification.

However, modifications under the Contract Law are also subject to certain restrictions. One restriction is legality. The rule is that a modification must not violate the legality requirement of the contract. To be more specific, a contract modification cannot render the contract itself illegal. In other words, the legality is a matter of limits imposed on the parties to ensure that the enforceability of the existing contract will not be adversely affected.

This restriction to a certain extent also reflects the concern about excessive pursuit of individual self-interest of the parties or, in a more general sense, the public policy against abuse of right by the contractual parties. On the other hand, the legality requirement for the modification functions as a safeguard that the contract is not to be undertaken in a way that damages State or social public interests. Therefore, if the legality of the exisiting contract is affected by a modification, the modification will be invalid and unenforceable.

The other restriction is equal dignity. As applied to modification, equal dignity means that the validity of a modification shall be governed by the same rules that determine the validity of a contract. A highly notable example is the

---

or assignment. In the U.S., novation means a substitution of a new party which discharges one of the original parties to a contract by agreement of all parties. See Restatement of Contracts (2nd), §280.

3   See the Contract Law, art. 77.
4   See Jeff Perriell, Understanding Contracts (2nd ed.), 411 (2009).

requirement of approval or registration. Under Article 77 of the Contract Law, if the law or administrative regulations require that the modification to a contract must obtain approval or registration, that requirement must be satisfied before the modification becomes valid.[5] The approval or registration requirement for the modification normally depends on the contract itself. If a contract must be approved, approval is required for modification of the contract.

Related to the equal dignity rule is the issue whether an agreement in writing is required when a contract is to be modified. The Contract Law contains no provision in this regard. But in general, if a contract is made in writing, an agreement for modification must also be made in writing. It is believed that under the equal dignity rule, the formality requirements for the formation of a contract should also be applied to the modification of the contract.

Since the Contract Law does not mandate that modifications be made in writing, an oral modification might be held valid by the people's court. But note that in certain cases an oral modification is accepted by the court only if both of the parties admit. The admission is a clear indicator that the parties have expressly agreed to the modification. Therefore, as a practical matter, when the parties reach an agreement to modify the contract, the agreement should be produced into a writing. The reason is obvious. A writing has an evidentiary effect to prove the modification.

In addition, there are two doctrines in China that pertain to the modification of contracts. The first doctrine is called "non-substantial change." Under this doctrine, a modification is intended to make changes that are not substantial to the contract. If the change is substantial, it will then not be a modification but a replacement of the contract. Replacement means that a new contract will take the place of the existing contract.

Under the non-substantial change doctrine, the changes that are considered substantial to the existing contract include (a) a complete change of the subject matter of the contract, (b) a significant alteration of the performance, and (c) a material variation of the contract price.[6] Accordingly, if any of these changes is made to an existing contract, the existing contract will be deemed to have been replaced, rather than modified. The Contract Law, however, contains no such distinction between substantial and non-substantial changes.[7]

---

5   See the Contract Law, art. 77.
6   See Wang Liming, *Study on Contract Law* (Vol. II), 194–195 (People's University Press, 2003). Some argue that modification also encompasses changes in the subject matter of the contract. See Wang Jiafu, *Obligatio in Civil Law*, 358 (Law Publishing House, 1991).
7   Some argue that modification actually replaces an existing contract with a new contract because modification changes both the parties to the contract as well as the contents of the contract. This argument, however, seems to confuse the modification with novation

The other doctrine is named "unequivocal change." This doctrine is premised on the notion that modification imposes a consensual variation to the contract between the parties. Hence, since modification involves changes that may result in a mutual adjustment of rights and obligations between the parties, it is essential that a modification made by the parties to the existing contract is unequivocal or clearly stated.

The "unequivocal change" doctrine is adopted in the Contract Law. Under Article 78 of the Contract Law, if the contents of the modified contract agreed by the parties are unclear or uncertain, it shall be assumed that the contract is not modified.[8] In many cases, unequivocal change under Article 78 is a matter of burden of proof. According to the SPC, in a contract dispute, the party claiming that the contractual relationship has changed bears the burden to prove with evidence the facts of the change as such.[9]

The primary legal effect of a valid modification is that the performance shall be made on the modified contract. Since the contents of the contact have changed as a result of modification, a failure to perform the modified obligations will constitute a breach of the contract for which the breaching party will be held liable. In addition, modification will only affect the subsequent performance, and thus has no retroactive effect on the obligations already performed. By the same token, the parties may not avoid the previous performance on the ground that the contract has been modified.

A debatable question arising from the modification of a contract is whether the modification will affect the right of the parties to seek damages. The question mainly involves the damages caused by one party to the other before the contract was modified. From the debates, there developed an independent claim approach and a waiver doctrine. The independent claim approach argues that the party's right to the recovery of damages is an independent claim and thus shall not be affected by the modification. Thus, the aggrieved party may seek damages regardless of the modification agreement.[10]

The belief of the independent claim approach is that the absence of a provision pertaining to the damages in the modification agreement should not deprive the aggrieved party of the right to get compensated. The premise of the independent claim approach is Article 115 of the 1986 Civil Code. Under Article

---

and to blur the distinction between modification and assignment. See Dong Ling, *Performance, Modification, Assignment and Termination of Contracts*, 120–121 (China Legal System Publishing House, 1999).

8   See the Contract Law, art. 78.
9   See the SPC, Several Provisions on the evidences of Civil Litigation (2001), art. 5.
10   See See *id.*

115, a party's right to claim compensation for damages shall not be affected by the modification or termination of a contract.[11]

The waiver doctrine takes an opposite position. It asserts that the damages prior to the modification shall be dealt with by the parties in their negotiation for the modification. Thus, if the parties did not mention the damages in their modification agreement, the aggrieved party may not ask for the damages after the modification is made because the party's right to seek to recover the damages is deemed to have been waived.[12]

Those who uphold the waiver doctrine also try to narrow down the meaning of Article 115 of the 1986 Civil Code. They point out that the modification in Article 115 refers only to the modification made by court order or arbitral decision, excluding the modification by the agreement of the parties.[13] Therefore, in a consensual modification to the contract, if the parties have an agreement on the damages that have occurred, that agreement should be followed. Absent such an agreement, however, neither of the parties should be liable for the damages caused prior to the modification.[14]

Interestingly, although the proponents of the waiver doctrine believe that the way in which the modification agreement is made will lead to the different effect of the modification with regard to the prior damages, they take the view that the modification shall not affect the liability for breach of contract that occurred before the contract is modified.[15] This seems to suggest that the modification, depending on the parties' agreement, may affect the damages but not the liability for the breach of contract.

2 Assignment

As noted, in China an assignment is deemed to be a modification in a broad sense, which involves a change of the obligee or obligor. A change in terms of assignment is understood in China to mean a transfer of contractual rights or obligations. Under the Contract Law, an assignment may take three different forms: transfer of contractual rights, transfer of contractual obligations, and transfer of both rights and obligations of a contract.

---

11   See the 1986 Civil Code, art.115.
12   See Wang Liming, *supra* note 6, at 206–208.
13   See Cui Jianyuan, *Contract Law (4th ed.)*, 199 (Law Press, 2007).
14   See Han Shiyuan, *The Law of Contract (3rd ed.)*, 456 (Law Press, 2011).
15   See Wang Liming, *supra* note 6, at pp 207–208.

As a prereguisite for the transfer, there must be an effective contract. The primary notion is that no contractual rights or obligations will be transferred without the existence of a contract. The reason is quite obvious. It is the contract that creates the parties's respective rights and obligations. On the same ground, even though there is a contract, a transfer of the rights and obligations under the contract may be adversely affected if the contract becomes invalid.

There was no legal provision of assignment in modern China until the 1986 Civil Code was adopted. Under Article 91 of the 1986 Civil Code, if a party to a contract transfers all or part of its contractual rights or obligations to a third party, it must obtain the other party's consent and may not reap profits.[16] Based on Article 91, assignment was referred to as a transfer by a party of all or part of its contractual rights or obligations to a third party. Clearly, while permitting a transfer of contractual rights or obligation to a third party, Article 91 of the 1986 Civil Code imposes two restrictions on assignments. First, the transfer of either contractual rights or obligations made by one party must obtain the consent of the other party, and second, the transfer must not be made for the purpose of seeking profits.

Ever since its adoption, Article 91 has met strong criticism. The Contract Law revises Article 91 of the 1986 Civil Code and makes the assignment more appealing to the need of transactions. The revision contains two important aspects: (a) deletion of the prohibition of "profit-seeking" imposed on the assignment, and (b) elimination of the consent requirement for the transfer of contractual rights. In addition, the Contract Law separates the transfer of contractual rights from the transfer of contractual obligations.

The revision results in discrepancies between the 1986 Civil Code and the Contract Law. This creates a question about the application of law: which law, the 1986 Civil Code or the Contract Law, should the court apply when the determination of the effect of an assignment becomes an issue? A general holding in China is that under both the doctrine of "late-in-time" and the theory of "special law over the general law," the Contract Law shall take priority if its terms appear to be at odds with any terms of the 1986 Civil Code.[17]

The following case illustates how issues relating to contract assignment are being handled in the people's court. This case may not answer all issues involved in the assignment, but it states in detail the reasons for the decision made by the court to uphold the assignment that was in dispute, which in the

---

16 See the 1986 Civil Code, art. 91.
17 Under the "late-in-time" doctrine, if there is an inconsistency between two legal provisions, the legal provision that was adopted later is deemed to supersede the earlier provision. Moreover, under the "special law" doctrine, if there is a conflict between a provision of general law and a provision of special law, the special law provision governs.

past could not be seen in the decisions of Chinese people's courts. Not until 1999, when the first "five-year reform plan" was issued by the SPC, were adjudicative reasonings required in civil judgments.

Shen Yang Xu Ke Group, Ltd.
vs.
Tie Ling No. 2 Group of Northeast Jin Cheng Construction Installation Co.
The High People's Court of Liao Ning Province[18]

On August 18, 1995, the defendant entered into a contract with Shen Yang Railway Branch of China Construction Bank (Bank), under which the Bank was to provide a loan to the defendant in the amount of RMB 4.9 million with an interest rate of 10.05% per month for a term of one year. The loan was guaranteed by Jin Cheng Co. Inc. (Guarantor), who promised to repay the loan if the defendant defaulted. After the contract of the loan was signed, the Bank transferred into defendant's bank account RMB 4.9 million on October 10, 1995. However, after the repayment was due, both the defendant and the guarantor defaulted. On June 24, 1999, the defendant and the guarantor both acknowledged receipt of the notice of default issued by the Bank, and affixed their respective company seals to the notice as a proof of the acknowledgement.

In November 1999, the Bank reached an agreement with Shen Yang Branch of Xin Da Assets Management Co. (Xin Da) to assign its creditor right under the contract with the defendant to Xin Da. On November 3, the Bank and the defendant singed a verification of debts, which confirmed that the defendant owed to the Bank RMB 4.9 million and interest at 10.05%/month. On July 25, 2001, the Bank and Xin Da issued a public notice in "Liao Ning Daily" indicating the assignment and urging both the defendant and the guarantor to make prompt payment for the debts to Xin Da. The defendant, however, still made no payment.

On August 8, 2002, the plaintiff acquired from Xin Da the creditor rights through a public auction at the price of RMB 1,801 million against 10 sums of bad debts, including the one owed by the defendant. On September 5, 2002, Xin Da notified the defendant of the auction and the assignment of the creditor rights to the plaintiff. After several unsuccessful attempts to request the defendant to pay the debts, the plaintiff brought this action against the defendant at Shen Yang City Intermediate People's Court.

In its defense, the defendant argued that the assignment of the creditor rights from Xin Da to the plaintiff was illegal and therefore the plaintiff had no standing to make the claim. The trial court entered a judgment in favor of plaintiff, holding that the transfer of the creditor rights through public auction was valid, and failure to pay the debts constituted a breach of contract, for which both the defendant and the guarantor were jointly and severally liable.

In reaching its decision, the trial court reasoned that the contract between the defendant and the Bank and the agreement to guarantee the loan were both valid and enforceable, and being in default on the loan, defendant and the guarantor breached the contract, which infringed the creditor right of the Bank. According to the trial court, the assignment agreement between the Bank and Xin Da was also valid under the Contract Law because (a) it was reached on a voluntary basis, (2) its formality and contents did not violate the law, and (3) the Bank as the assignor performed its duty of notice.

---

18   See Civil Judgment of the High People's Court of Liao Ning Province, (2003) Liao Min 2 He Zhong Zhi No. 174.

The trial court denied defendant's argument neglecting plaintiff's standing for the lawsuit on the ground that the transfer of the creditor right from Xin Da to the plaintiff through the public auction was a valid transfer because the transfer, approved by the relevant authority, conformed with then-prevailing government policy and did not violate the law, and the notice of the transfer was properly given. In its judgment, the trial court ordered the defendant to pay the plaintiff the principal of the loan in the amount of RMB 4.9 million and interest in the amount of RMB 3,911,372.62, and also to bear the litigation fees in the amount of RMB 115,080.

On appeal, the defendant challenged the trial court's ruling. The defendant argued that (a) the trial court erred in determining the facts, and groundlessly denied defendant's right of first refusal; (b) the trial court made a mistake in application of the Contract Law because the loan was made before the Contract Law took effect; and (c) the trial court violated procedural law during the trial since the trial court ignored defendant's request for a closer review of legality of the process of the transfer of the creditor rights in question.

The defendant also asserted that there was no legal basis to allow the Bank to impose penalty interest, and the trial court erroneously dismissed the fact that the plaintiff and Xin Da conspired to commit illegal conduct in the transfer of creditor rights. The defendant alleged that the transfer had caused harm to the State interest and infringed upon the defendant's interest for the plaintiff's personal gains.

Plaintiff argued that the transfer of the creditor right was valid and effective. The argument was based on the following reasons. First, Xin Da, as a financial and assets management company, is a property entity authorized by the government to deal with all bad debts, and therefore it has the right in whatever means it sees fit to dispose of the debts it managed, including a public auction. Plaintiff acquired the Bank's creditor rights against defendant through the auction. Since the transfer meets the requirements of the law, it is therefore valid.

Second, before the transfer of the creditor right, Xin Da made a public notice in provincial newspapers about the public auction, which contained a detailed description of the defendant and its business situation. During the auction, the defendant did not attend the bidding, and then was regarded to have given up its right to purchase. Thus, none of defendant's rights were infringed in the transactions.

Third, the defendant provided no evidence to prove that the plaintiff and the Bank had maliciously conspired to damage the interest of the State. Also, since the agreement for the transfer of the creditor right was reached on August 30, 2002, which was after the Contract Law became effective on October 1, 1999, it is required that the Contract Law apply.

This Court agrees with the trial court's finding that the assignment agreement between the Bank and Xin Da was valid, and the guarantor was jointly and severally liable to the plaintiff for the debts owed by the defendant. With regard to the legality of the transfer of the creditor right from Xin Da to the plaintiff, under the State Council's "Regulations For Finance and Assets Management Companies," the asset company is the special entity created for acquiring, managing, and disposing of the bad debts that the State-owned commercial banks encountered.

The asset company, when transferring the assets under its management, may take the form of invitation for bids or public auction. In the instant case, because Xin Da chose to transfer the credit rights against the defendant through a public auction, pursuant which the plaintiff obtained the rights, and such a transfer was authorized by the State Council Regulations, the transfer is valid. On this basis, the Court concludes that the defendant's argument against the validity of Xin Da's transfer of the creditor right through the public auction must be denied.

The defendant's assertion of the right of first refusal shall also be defeated for the lack of legal ground. The Court holds that the right of first refusal is a legal right, which must be clearly addressed in the law. The current law in the country, however, contains no provision that would give the defendant the right of the first refusal in the case like the transfer of creditor right in question. With regard to the question concerning malicious conspiracy that causes harm to the State interest, it must be viewed within the four corners of the "Auction Law." Auction, as defined in the "Auction Law", means to transfer the specific item or property right in the form of publicly bidding to one who makes the highest bid.

Asset management companies are created to deal with the debts of State-owned enterprises. Since what the asset management company acquired in the instant case were the bad debts from the State-owned banks, there exists the difference between the original value and present value of the creditor right involved in the bad debts. Therefore, transferring the creditor right through public auction will not cause the State asset to lose, and on the contrary, it is the way in which the State asset credit rights can be maintained at the most optimal level as possible. For this reason, the legitimate credit rights the plaintiff obtained from the public auction shall and must be protected.

Equally, the defendant's accusation that the plaintiff conducted malicious conspiracy with Xin Da to harm the State interest in order to achieve personal gains shall also be denied because there is no factual evidence to support the accusation. In addition, the trial court did not err in application of Contract Law to the agreement of transfer of the credit rights between the plaintiff and Xin Da. The application is appropriate because the transfer agreement was signed after the Contract Law took effect.

For all reasons stated above, in accordance with Article 153 (1)(a) of the Civil Procedure Law of the People's Republic of China, it is so ordered:

The trial court judgment is affirmed with the appeal cost of RMB 62,285 to be paid by defendant. This judgment is final.

2.1   *Assignment of Contractual Rights*

For discussion purposes, the term "assignment" is used to specifically mean the transfer of contractual rights and the term "delegation" is employed to denote the transfer of contractual obligations—although in the Contract Law, no such distinction is explicitly drawn. Conceptually, assignment in Chinese contract law literature is a consensual transfer of an obligee's contractual right, and the relationship so created between assignor and assignee is a contractual relationship.

Under Article 79 of the Contract Law, the obligee may assign, in whole or in part, its rights under the contract to a third party.[19] Based on Article 79, an assignment can be defined as a transfer of a valid contractual right, in whole or in part, by the obligee to a third party. Article 79 of the Contract Law implies that the assignment can be made gratuitously, though most contract assignments are made for value.

As a result of the assignment, the assignor's interest in the contract are transferred to the assignee, and the assignor's right in this regard is terminated. After the assignment, the assignee is entitled to all claims the assignor has against the obligor. As a general rule, however, the right that the assignee may

---

19   See the Contract Law, art. 79.

obtain from the assignment shall not exceed the scope of the right that the assignor should have under the contract.

When an obligee assigns all of its contractual rights to a third person, the status of the assignee becomes a debatable issue among Chinese contract law scholars. One opinion is that if all of the creditor rights in a contract are assigned (i.e., full assignment), the assignee should be regarded to have replaced the assignor and become a party to the contract. [20] Under this opinion, after the full assignment, a new contract relationship is created between the assignee and the obligor, and the old contract will cease to operate. Consequently, the obligor is obligated to make performance to the assignee. [21]

Many, however, disagree. They argue that, even if all contractual rights are assigned, the assignor may still be under the obligation to perform the contractual duties it is supposed to perform. This argument is premised on the notion that although a full transfer of contractual rights by assignment terminates the right in the assignor, it does not necessarily extinguish the assignor's contractual relationship with the obligor. Rather, it only conveys to the assignee the assignor's right to receive the performance from the obligor.[22]

Indeed, the status of the assignor is of practical significance when a dispute arises between the assignee (the third party) and the other party (obligor) of the contract over the contract performance. A question often raised involves whether the other party (obligor) may have a claim against the assignor. Put differently, the question is whether the assignor may remain liable when the assignee breaches the contract.

As noted, under Chinese contract law, the parties to a contract assume mutual obligations. Pursuant to the mutual obligation theory, a party in the contract is an obligee in one respect, and is an obligor in the other, depending on the nature of performance. The point is whether a full assignment necessarily breaks the mutuality of the contractual obligations between the parties to the contract.

To illustrate, a seller has a contract with a buyer, under which the seller will deliver the agreed amount of grains to the buyer on a specific day. With regard to the delivery of the grain, the seller is the obligor and the buyer is the obligee. If, however, the payment is in question, the seller becomes the obligee and the buyer correspondingly becomes the obligor. Obviously, when the seller assigns its right to the payment (i.e., its creditor right) to C, the assignment may not

---

20   See Wang Liming, *supra* note 6 at p. 217.
21   See *id.*
22   See Yang Lixin, *Implication and Application of the Contract Law*, 153 (Jilin People's Publishing House, 1999).

necessarily make the seller home free, particularly if the grain delivered to the buyer turned out to be defective.

A partial transfer of the obligee's contractual rights (i.e., partial assignment) presents a different scenario. In the partial transfer, the obligee does not assign all of its contractual rights to a third party. Since the obligee remains a creditor, the third party will become a co-obligee after the assignment. Then, the obligor will need to make the performance to both the obligee (assignor) and the third party (assignee).

There has been a concern that partial assignment actually increases the burden of performance on the obligor since the obligor has to deal with more than one obligee after a partial assignment. The Contract Law has accordingly been criticized for allowing partial assignment but providing no specific rules regarding partial assignment. A suggestion is that if a dispute arises, the increased burden on the obligor arising from the partial assignment should be a factor for the court to consider.

Moreover, it seems hard to discern the nature of a partial assignment with regard to the relationship between the assignor and assignee. Basically, due to a partial assignment, the assignor and assignee possess a co-ownership of the contractual right, and each party is entitled to certain interests in the right. But the extent to which the parties divide their interests in the contractual right is dependent upon how the co-ownership is to be formed.

Thus, the nature of partial assignment is actually a question about the type of co-ownership of the right to receive the benefit from the performance of the contract. In Chinese contract law literature, the co-ownership created by partial assignment of a contract is generally divided into two categories: ownership in common and joint ownership.[23]

Ownership in common is also referred to as ownership by shares. With ownership in common, the assignor and assignee enjoy contractual rights in proportion to the agreed shares of the interests in the contract. When the ownership of contractual rights is in common, the assignor and assignee may only claim in proportion to their own shares, and may not reach beyond that. Conversely, the obligor may perform the duties to the assignor and assignee separately and the performance made to the assignor may not be carried over to the assignee. Consequently, the acceptance of the performance exceeding the shares of the interest by either assignor or assignee will be deemed to be unjust enrichment and is therefore subject to restitution.

---

23 See *id.*, at pp 152–153.

Joint ownership has a different feature. Under joint ownership, contractual rights are indivisible. If partial assignment causes a joint ownership to form, the assignor and assignee will jointly and severally own the interest in the contractual right. An interest owned jointly and severally means that either assignor or assignee has the right to request full performance by the obligor under the contact. Because of the joint ownership, the obligor may perform all of the contractual obligations to either the assignor or assignee, and completion of the performance will satisfy both the assignor and assignee.

Generally, when making an assignment, the parties may in the assignment agreement specify the type of ownership. Since ownership in common involves a particular amount of shares that the assignor and assignee may have, an agreement on the division of shares between the assignor and assignee is normally required. Therefore, if no specification is made in the assignment agreement or the specification is unclear to the effect of ownership in common, joint ownership will be assumed.

In the Contract Law, there is also no provision concerning multiple assignments of same right. Because the Contract Law does not prohibit multiple assignments, many suggest that a contract right can be assigned more than once. But, a question as to multiple assignments is how to determine the priority among the assignees. In other words, the question is who should receive the performance first. There are two approaches.

One approach is the "order of assignment." Under this approach, priority among the assignees shall be determined by the order of assignment, which means that the first assignee shall have priority over all subsequent assignees to benefit from the performance.[24] The "order of assignment" approach also contains two "supplementary orders." First, if the assignment is for value, it prevails over a gratuitous assignment. Second, when an assignment includes both full and partial assignments, the full assignment has priority over the partial one.

The other approach is called the "order of notice." This approach is derived from the so-called "English Rule," which provides that the first assignee to give notice to the debtor prevails.[25] The theory underlying the "order of notice" approach is that the assignee will not obtain the rights assigned until the obligor is notified of the assignment.[26] Therefore, the "order of notice" approach

---

24 See Wang Liming & Cui Jianyuan, *A new Commentary on Contract Law—General Provisions* (reversed edition), 424 (China University of Political Science and Law Press, 2000).
25 For a general discussion of the "English Rule," see Rohwer & Schaber, *Contracts In A Nut Shell* (4th ed), 373 (West, 1997).
26 See Wang Liming, *supra* note 6 at p 238.

is essentially a scheme of race notice. In this scheme, whoever provides notice first has the best position to claim benefits regardless of the order of assignment.

A related issue is the assignment of future interests in contractual rights. Future interests refer to interests that may appear in the future depending on the occurrence of certain facts. They are the interests that will be realized when the agreed condition is satisfied or the time for the interests to accrue comes. An example is the guarantor's right of indemnity against the obligor. Future interests may also be the expected interests that the parties agree to gain in the future.

The Contract Law is silent about this issue. The concern is that future interests might be too speculative to be certain. However, it has been argued that, although future interests seem uncertain at the time of assignment, such interests may still be assignable because they totally depend on the contract. Therefore, if the contractual rights are certain, the future interests that will arise from the contractual right may not necessarily be speculative.[27]

2.1.1   Formality of Assignment

Since assignment is a manifestation of the intent of the obligee to transfer its contractual rights to a third party, there must be an agreement for an assignment. But the Contact Law does not impose a writing requirement on the assignment, nor is there any special formality the parties must follow to make an assignment. Therefore, contractual rights in China may literally be assigned in the way both the assignor and the assignee see fit. In most cases, assignment takes the form of writing.

An exception, however, is the statuary requirement for approval or registration. Pursuant to Article 87 of the Contract Law, if laws or administrative regulations provide that an approval or registration is required for the assignment of contractual rights, such requirement must be met.[28] Normally, under the equal dignity rule, if approval is required for a contract, an assignment of the rights of the contract also requires approval.

As discussed, the Contract Law repeals the requirement, which was included in the 1986 Civil Code, that the obligor must consent to the transfer of the obligee's contractual rights. But, in order for an assignment to take effect, the Contract Law mandates notice to the obligor. Under Article 80 of the Contract Law, an obligee, when assigning its contractual rights, must notify the obligor. Without such notice, the assignment will have no effect as to the obligor.[29] The

---

27   See Dong Ling, *supra* note 7 at pp 138–139.
28   See the Contract Law, art. 87.
29   See *id.*, art. 80.

notice may be made orally or in writing as long as the obligor is informed of the assignment.

Article 80 of the Contract Law makes it an obligation of the obligee to send a notice to the obligor concerning the assignment, but contains no requirement for the time of the notice. There are two issues related to the time of notice: the first issue is at what time the notice will take effect to the assignment, and the second issue is when the notice should be sent out to the obligor.

The effective time of the notice, though not provided in the Contract Law, is determined by the rule of arrival. Thus, a notice of assignment will not take effect until it reaches the obligor. More explicitly, the effectiveness of an assignment is dependent upon the receipt of the notice by the obligor. The issue of when the notice should be sent seems less important practically to the effect of assignment because there is no valid assignment until the notice is received by the obligor.

Article 80 of the Contract Law has caused confusion in its application, however. Article 80 provides that absent notice, "the assignment shall have no effect as to the obligor." The confusion arises from the language "no effect as to the obligor." The issue is whether the "no effect" means ineffectiveness of the assignment agreement, ineffectiveness of the rights assigned to the assignee, or ineffectiveness of the assignee's claim against the obligor. There are also debates on this issue among scholars and practitioners.

The SPC takes the position that an assignment without a notice to the obligor has no effect to the obligor but does not affect the validity of the assignment agreement. In *Taibao Investment Management Co. Ltd of Shunde District of Foshan City v. Guangdong Zhong Ding Group Co. Ltd.*, the parties disputed the validity of the assignment of creditor rights because of the lack of required notice. The SPC held that when assigning its creditor rights, the assignor shall inform the obligor of the assigment; without such a notice, the assignment shall not take effect as to the obligor. Thus, the obligor has the right against the claim of the assignee, but the validity of the assignment agreement reached by the assignor and assignee shall not be affected.[30]

In certain cases, notice of assignment is a matter of proof. Since the Contract Law prescribes no specific means of notice, a practical question is whether notice can be assumed by the obligor's knowledge or awareness of the assignment. To illustrate, assume that it is unclear if a notice of assignment was given to the obligor, but there was a promise made by the obligor to perform

---

30 *Taibao Investment Management Co. Ltd of Shunde District of Foshan City v. Guangdong Zhong Ding Group Co. Ltd.*, See the SPC, (2004) Min Er Zhong Zhi No. 212.

for the benefit of the assignee. The issue then is whether the obligor's promise has an evidentiary effect as to the obligor's knowledge of the assignment so that the notice requirement is met. Some scholars suggest that such an effect should be recognized.[31] However, there has been no legislative or judicial endorsement yet.

Also related to notice is the revocability of an assignment. Under the Contract Law, an assignment becomes irrevocable when the notice of the assignment is sent. Article 80 of the Contract Law provides that notice of the assignment of the rights may not be revoked unless the assignee agrees.[32] Thus, once the assignment notice is dispatched, the revocability of the assignment is in the hands of the assignee.

However, since notice of an assignment is irrevocable after it is sent, it seems meaningless to base the effectiveness of the assignment on the arrival of the notice. Given the irrevocability of the assignment notice under Article 80 of the Contract Law, the assignor cannot do anything that may affect the assignment after the notice is sent, even if the assignor has the time to take the notice back before the assignee receives it.

2.1.2 Non-Assignable Rights

Generally, an assignor may assign all of its rights arising from a contract. There are certain circumstances under which the rights of a contract are not assignable, however. Under Article 79 of the Contract Law, the contractual right may not be assigned if the rights are non-assignable (a) according to the nature of the contract, (b) based on the agreement between the parties, or (c) as provided by law.[33] Thus, other than those listed in Article 79 of the Contract Law, all rights in a contract are assignable in China.

The nature of a contract refers to the distinction or character of a contract. A contract is not assignable by nature if it is made between the parties with a distinctive personal feature or particular relations, and the performance will be materially altered or the value of the performance will be substantially reduced when any of the contractual rights are assigned to a third party. Generally, there are three kinds of contractual rights that are considered to fall within this category: (1) rights that are based on personal trust and credibility, such as employment or agency; (2) rights arising from personal service contracts, such as entertainment performance; and (3) subordinate rights, namely

---

31 See Du Wanhua, et al, Adjudicative Guide on Contract Cases, 331 (Law Press, 2014).
32 See *id.*
33 See the Contract Law, art. 79.

the rights dependent on the main rights of the contract, such as rights in a guaranty contract.

The rights of a contract may also not be assigned if the parties by agreement prohibit the assignment. An anti-assignment agreement may take the form of an anti-assignment clause embodied in a contract or a separate agreement after the contract is made. The effect of an anti-assignment agreement is that any intended assignment will be ineffective unless the obligor consents to the assignment. In some jurisdictions, like the United States, an anti-asssignment agreement is subject to a restrictive interpretation. Thus, if the agreement generally prohibits assignment, it will commonly be construed to mean a restriction only on the delegation of duties.

There is no such restrictive rule in China. Under the Contract Law, as long as the agreement prohibiting assignment does not violate mandatory provisions of the law or public policy, it will be held to be valid and enforceable. In addition, a contract provision stating that the contract shall not be assigned prohibits both the assignment of rights and the delegation of duties.[34] The prohibition of assignment must be clearly stated in the agreement, however.

When a party breaches an anti-assignment agreement, and assigns its rights in a contract to a third party, there is a question about the effectiveness of the assignment if the assignee is a bona fide third party. In general, the assignee will be found to be bona fide in the assignment if it had no knowledge about the prohibition of the assignment at the time the assignment was made and the assignment is not gratuitous. Views vary, though, as to what effect an assignment to a bona fide third party by the assignor in violation of an anti-assignment agreement will have.

One opinion is that an assignment that is made to a *bona fide* assignee is effective regardless of the prohibition of the assignment in the contract. The idea is that, unless otherwise provided by the law, the assignment agreement shall only bind the parties given the privity of contract. Thus, when an assignment is made in violation of an anti-assignment agreement, the obligor may sue the assignor for breach of contract but has no claim against the *bona fide* assignee.

The other opinion takes a different view. It argues that the provisions of Article 79 of the Contract Law are mandatory. For that reason, an assignment shall not be enforced if it violates the parties' agreement prohibiting the assignment no matter whether the assignee is a *bona fide* third party or not. Pursuant to

---

34 In the United States, the non-assignment clause is strictly interpreted. The contract provision prohibiting assignment of the contract is normally construed to prohibit delegation of duties but not assignment of rights.

this opinion, the status of the assignee is irrelevent to the effectiveness of an assignment if there is an anti-assignment agreement.

With regard to legality, no assignment may be made if prohibited by the law. In China, contractual rights that are non-assignable under the law mainly include three kinds of rights. The first kind are the rights that are dependent on personal status or relation, such as family relation. Typical rights that bear personal status and are therefore not assignable are rights of claim for alimony, child support, or maintenance.[35] The second type of non-assignable right under the law is the right created and protected by the public law for public policy concerns. Such a right includes rights to claim a pension fund (for the disabled as well survivors), retirement fund, and labor insurance payment. The third right that is statutorily not assignable is a civil law claim right. The most common civil law claim is a tort claim. The right of a claim for an award arising from personal injury or dignitary damages may not be assigned.

2.1.3 Effect of Assignment

Under the Contract Law, the effect of assignment has two aspects. The first aspect concerns the relation between the assignor and the assignee as a result of assignment, and the second aspect involves the change both between the assignor (obligee) and the obligor as well as between the assignee and the obligor. Generally, an assignment will make the assignee a new obligee (if it is a whole assignment) or a co-obligee (if it is a partial assignment) of the contract. After a valid assignment, as noted, the assignee will take the place in part or in whole of the assignor, and enjoy the contractual rights accordingly.

With respect to the relation between the assignor and assignee, an important matter is the right that is subordinate to the assigned contractual rights, including rights to a security interest and accrued interest, claims for stipulated damage, and claims for remedies arising from the contract. The subordinate right itself is not assignable independently, but will be transferred to the assignee when the contractual rights are assigned.

It is a common rule that the subordinate right shall be automatically, without a specific indication, transferred to the assignee along with the assignment of the contractual rights. Since the subordinate right is attached to main

---

[35] In China, alimony refers to mutual support between spouses, and maintenance concerns the support provided by adult children to their parents (old parents in particular). Under Chinese law, children have the obligation to support their parents. For example, Article 49 of 1982 Chinese Constitution (as amended in 2004) explicitly states that parents have the obligation to raise and educate their children who are minors and adult children are obligated to support and assist their parents.

contractual rights, without the transfer, the contractual rights (e.g., the right to receive the performance as provided in the contract) would be affected.

There is a provision in the Contract Law that governs the transfer of the subordinate right. Article 81 provides that if the obligee assigns its rights, the assignee shall acquire the subordinate rights in relation to the contractual rights, except that the subordinate rights exclusively belong to the obligee.[36] If the subordinate right is inalienable from the obligee, it is deemed personal and therefore is not assignable.

For example, on the basis of prior dealings and an ongoing business relationship, an obligor granted an obligee some benefits (e.g., special status or privilege in relation to the performance the obligor is to make to the obligee) as a token of appreciation for the obligee's business. The right to claim such benefits may not be assigned with the contract because it exclusively belongs to the obligee.

Moreover, there is a concern in China about the right to dissolve the contract. Some believe that the right of contract dissolution is too personal to be assigned. Because the right of dissolution determines the fate of the contract, such right may not be separated from the obligee.[37] But in many others' view, this concern is irrelevant in a full assignment because when the assignment of a contract is made in full, the assignee acquires all rights in the contract, both primary and subordinate. Under this situation, the right of dissolution of the contract is included in the assignment.

The effect of the assignment as between the assignor and assignee imposes an implied duty on the assignor to guarantee that the rights assigned are free from any claims. If there exist defects in the assigned rights, which cause damages to the assignee, the assignor shall be held liable unless the assignee knew the defects at the time of assignment. In addition, the assignor has the obligation to provide the assignee with all documents necessary to prove the assigned rights. Furthermore, as noted, it is the assignor's duty to notify the obligor of the assignment in order to effectuate the assignment.

The change between the assignor and obligor mainly involves the obligor's performance of the contract. After the assignment, the obligor is responsible for the performance to the assignee, and, if the assignment is made in full, the assignor ceases to have the right to demand performance. On the other hand, the obligor must perform the obligations it owes to the assignee under the contract. If the performance is made to the assignor after the assignment

---

36 See the Contract Law, art. 81.
37 See Wang Liming & Cui Jianyuan, *supra* note 24 at p 423.

(except for the partial assignment), the contract will not be deemed to have performed. Also, the assignor may be liable for unjust enrichment if it continues to accept the obligor's performance of the contract that has been assigned.

2.1.4 Right of Defense in Assignment

After the assignment, the right of defense that the obligor has against the assignor remains intact, but may be exercised against the assignee. According to Article 82 of the Contract Law, after the obligor receives the notice of assignment of contractual rights, the obligor may assert its defense it would have against the assignor against the assignee.[38] The purpose is to protect the obligor's rights from being impaired as a result of the assignment. If, however, the obligee assigns all of its contractual rights to the assignee, the obligor's defense based on the contract may only be asserted against the assignee.

In addition, the obligor may acquire an independent right of defense against the assignee after the assignment is made. One example is that the obligor may refuse to perform the contract if the assignee's laches in exercising its contractual rights caused the lapse of the statute of limitation. Another example relates to the right to dissolve the contract. If the dissolution of the contract is based on the agreed upon conditions, the obligor may dissolve the contract against the assignee when the conditions are met.

Under the Contract Law, the obligor may also offset with the assignee the creditor's right that the obligor has against the assignor. The Contract Law has a specific provision that provides the obligor with the right to offset. Pursuant to Article 83 of the Contract Law, when the obligor receives notice of the assignment of contractual rights, if it has creditor's rights against the assignor, and such rights are due prior to the assignment of the contractual rights or at the same time as the assignment is made, the obligor may offset its creditor's rights with the assignee.[39]

The exercise of the right to offset, however, must meet certain conditions. First, there must be a bilateral contract in which the obligee and obligor have mutual contractual rights. In other words, the parties must be both obligee and obligor to each other. Second, the mutual contractual rights must be offsetable, which means that the offset must be made by the same or similar kind of thing or by money payment, and must not be prohibited by the law. Third, the obligor's contractual rights that are employed to offset the contractual rights assigned to the assigneee must become due prior to, or at the time of,

---

38 See the Contract Law, art. 82.
39 See *id.*, art. 83.

the assignment. The reason is obvious. If the contractual rights used for offset are not due, the offset will require an advance performance, which may harm the interests of the assignee.

2.2 Delegation of Contractual Obligations

Unlike an assignment, which generally means the transfer of contractual rights, a delegation means to delegate contractual obligations to a third party or to appoint another party to render the performance on behalf of the obligor. In China, delegation is generally defined as a transfer of debt obligations under a contract from the obligor to a third party without affecting the substance of the original obligations. Thus, an assignment involves contractual rights while delegation deals with contractual obligations.

In Chinese contract law literature, delegation may take the form of assumption of the debts or a substitute of the obligor to perform. Assumption of debts means a transfer of debts by the agreement among the obligee, obligor, and third party, and the transfer may be made in whole or in part. Substitute of obligor refers to the situation where a third party offers to take the place of the obligor to perform contractual duties without an agreement for the transfer of debts. In the context of the Contract Law, delegation mainly refers to a transfer of debts by agreement.

Also, in China, a delegation may render the the delegating party free from contractual obligations. In other countries, like the United States, by contrast, after a valid assignment, the assignor ordinarily no longer has any interest in the right that has been assigned, but when an obligation is delegated, the delegating party may continue to remain liable.[40] In addition, it should be noted that there is no such concept as novation in the Chinese contract law. Novation is a concept used in American contract law which means that the existing contract between the obligee and obligor is replaced by a new contract between the obligee and a third party to the extent of the contractual obligations to be performed.[41]

2.2.1 Delegation as a Transfer of Debts in Whole or in Part

The Contract Law allows for the transfer of debts. Article 84 provides that if the obligor delegates, in whole or in part, its obligations to a third party, it must obtain the obligee's consent. As a general rule, the obligor may delegate its obligations if the following conditions are met: (a) valid contractual obligations

---

40 See Joseph Perillo, Contracts (Hornbook 7th ed.), 665 (2014).
41 See *id.*, at 758–59.

exist, (b) the obligor and the third party agree to the delegation, (c) the obligee makes no objection to the delegation, and (4) the obligations are delegable.[42]

In contrast to assignment, where no consent is needed from the obligor, delegation requires the obligee's consent. Under the Contract Law, the obligeee's consent is not only the most important element for the delegation, but also a prerequisite for the delegation to be effective.[43] Therefore, without a valid consent from the obligee, no delegation will be permitted.

Chinese law distinguishes between a delegation in whole and a delegation in part. Delegation in whole is deemed to be a complete transfer of contractual obligations from the obligor to a third party. After such a transfer is complete, the original obligor is "exempted" from its contractual obligations and is replaced by a third party, the new obligor. In this context, delegation in whole seems to have the same effect as novation. Note, however, that in the U.S., novation requires the presence of a substituted contract that has a new party.[44]

A partial delegation is defined as a co-assumption of debts. In China, once the obligor delegates some of its contractual obligations to a third party, the obligor and the third party become jointly responsible for the performance of the contract. However, scholars continue to debate what the relation between the obligor and the third party that arises from a partial delegation is— although it is commonly believed that the obligor remains obligated for the performance of the contract.

One argument is that partial delegation simply adds the third party as a new obligor, and the original obligor and the third party each bear their own separate obligations.[45] Therefore, in a partial delegation, no obligor is responsible for the obligation of the other obligor. Opponents of this argument contend that partial delegation does not dispense the contractual obligations of the original obligor, but rather makes both the original obligor and the third party jointly and severally liable for the contract. Then, after the partial delegation, the obligee may ask either the original obligor or the third party for full performance.[46]

---

42 See the Contract Law, art. 84.
43 Article 84 of the Contract Law is derived from Article 91 of the 1986 Civil Code, which permits a delegation of contractual obligations in whole or in part by agreement. However, Article 84 substantially alters Article 91 by deleting Article 91's prohibition that the delegation cannot be made for profit.
44 In American contract law, a novation (1) immediately discharges a duty, (2) creates a new duty, and (3) creates a new party (the obligor or obligee). See Joseph Perillo, *supra* note 40 at 758.
45 See Yang Lixin, *supra* note 22 at p 160.
46 See Dong Ling, *supra* note 7 at p 149.

With regard to the consent of the obligee in the delegation of contractual obligations, there are no formality requirements in the Contract Law. It is generally understood that the consent may be made in writing or orally, and may also be implied from the conduct of the obligee. In addition, as mandated by Article 87, if approval or registration is required for delegation, no delegation shall be made without such approval or registration.

The case below supplies a good example of the situation where the conduct of the obligee was viewed by the people's court as an implied consent to the delegation.

China Great Wall Assets Mgmt. Co. (Zheng Zhou)
v.
Luo Yang Chaoli Lubricate Oil Co., Inc.

The High People's Court of Henan Province[47]

Appellant (Plaintiff in the trial) is Zhenzhou Branch of China Great Wall Assets Management Co., Inc.; Appellee (Defendant in the trial) is Chaoli Lubricate Oil Company, Ltd. in Luo Yang City. On November 23, 2001, the appellant brought a lawsuit against the appellee at Luo Yang Intermediate People's Court, asking the Intermediate People's Court to order the appellee to (a) pay the principal of the loan in the amount of RMB 1 million and interest up to the date of repayment, and (b) bear all litigation costs that incurred in the lawsuit.

At the trial, the trial court found the following facts: on November 14, 1995 and January 5, 1996, Luoyang Lubricate Oil Factory (the appellee's former name, hereinafter referred to as Oil Factory) put all of its assets in mortgage in order to obtain two loans from Luoyang Jianxi Branch of China Agricultural Bank (Bank) in the amount of RMB 1 million (RMB 500,000 each). Under the loan agreements, the term of each loan was half a year, with a monthly interest rate of 10.08%, and if the borrower defaulted when its payment was due, an additional interest of 0.6% per day was to be charged to any unpaid amount. After the agreements were signed, the Bank transferred the agreed amount of money fund into the Oil Factory. But the Oil Factory failed to pay the principal and interest under the agreements.

On June 7, 2000, the Bank transferred its creditor right against the Oil Factory to the Appellant, and on the same day, a notice indicating the transfer was sent to the Oil Factory. In the notice, it read: "the debts owned: RMB 1 million in principal and RMB 85,614 in interest. Since all of the loans and interests are past due, please responsively make a full payment for the loans and interest to China Great Wall Assets Management Co., or make an effective payment plan upon receipt of this notice." The receipt of the notice was acknowledged by the Oil Factory with the signature of the Oil Factory's legal representative as well as the Oil Factory's official seal on the return stub of the notice (also called the debts confirmation notice).

On July 27, 1999, the Oil Factory held a general assembly meeting of all workers, and a resolution was passed to the following effects: (a) the factory was to be restructured as a limited liability company, and its name was to be changed to Chaoli Lubricate Oil Company, Ltd. (Chaoli); (b) after the restructure, all of the legal rights and liabilities, including creditor rights and debts, of the Oil Factory were to be transferred to Chaoli; (c) based on the assets assessment

---

47   See Civil Judgment of the High People's Court of Henan, (2003) Yu Fa Min 2 Zhi No. 146.

conducted by He Nan Provincial Assets Appraisal Firm, the debts/assets ratio of the Oil Factory was 110.27%. After the transfer, new capital was to be added and Chaoli would have a registered capital of RMB 1 million, of which Chaoli Commodities Company was to own RMB 800,000, and Luoyang Chaoyuan Industrial Company Ltd. was to own RMB 200,000; and (d) the new company's address would be 41 Construction Road, Jianxi District, Luoyang City.

On August 18, 1999, Chaoli Commodities Company and the Oil Factory signed the Agreement of Merger of Luoyang Lubricate Oil Factory into Chaoli Commodities Company. Under the Agreement, the parties agreed that: (a) the Oil Factory was voluntarily acquired by Chaoli Commodities Company, and Chaoli Commodities Company accepted all assets and workers of the Oil Factory and assumed all credits and debts of the Oil Factory; (b) after the acquisition, the Oil Factory would transfer to Chaoli Commodities Company all of its assets, including land, buildings, machines, and equipment; (c) after the appraisal, the Oil Factory was certified to have total assets of RMB 4.2971 million and total debts of RMB 4.7386 million, and the Oil Factory's total net assets were RMB minus 441,500, and its debts ratio 110.27%. Therefore, the acquisition was an acquisition of zero assets burdened with debts.

The parties further agreed that: (a) after the acquisition, the legal person status of the Oil Factory would no longer exist, and the employees' collective ownership status would remain unchanged, and Chaili Commodities Company would use the name of the Oil Factory free of charge and the name would be changed to "He Nan Chaoli Commodities Company Luoyang City Lubricate Oil Factory," but the business/operation structure of the factory would be changed to a limited liability company; (b) Chaoli Commodities Company would invest capital to form "Henan Luoyang Chaoli Lubricate Oil Company, Inc.," which would become an independent entity of a legal person within one year after the Agreement; and (c) the newly formed Chaoli would be managed in the way Chaoli Commodities Company would manage its subsidiaries.

It was also found in the trial that (a) the Certificate of Change of Registered Name issued to Luoyang Lubricate Oil Factory on November 18, 1999 stated "the name of the enterprise is changed from "Luoyang Lubricate Oil Factory" to "Chaoli Lubricate Oil Company, Inc." On the same day, Chaoli Lubricate Oil Company, Inc. filed with the commerce and industry authority the application for registration, and on November 29, 1999, Chaoli Lubricate Oil Company, Inc. was authorized to be formed; (b) on December 17, 1999, Chaili Lubricate Oil Company held its inauguration ceremony, and the Bank as creditor sent a representative to attend the ceremony.

During the trial, the appellee admitted the debts that were owed to the appellant but argued that the appellant's claim was barred by the statute of limitation because the appellant did not assert its claim within the time period allowed by the law. The appellant rebutted that it (including the Bank) had no knowledge about the acquisition and the Oil Factory did not notify the creditors of its being acquired by Chaoli Commodities Company. The appellant also argued that on June 7, 2000, when the Bank transferred its creditor right to the Great Wall Asset Management Company, the Oil Factory was given a notice of the transfer and Oil Factory also signed the notice, therefore the statute of limitation was not an issue because June 7, 2000 should be the starting date for commencing the four-year limitation.

The trial court held that the loan agreement between the Bank and Oil Factory was valid. The trial court also held that the transfer of the debts through acquisition from the Oil Factory to the appellee should be regarded as valid based on the fact that the Bank attended the ceremony of the opening of Chaoli Lubricate Oil Company, Inc., which evidenced the appellant's knowledge of the acquisition. The issue then was whether the statute of limitation would bar the appellant from making the claim. The trial court denied the appellant's argument about the June 7, 2000 notice.

According to the trial court, the appellee was formed on November 29, 1999 and inaugurated on December 17, 1999. When the Bank transferred its creditor right to the Great Wall Asset

Management Company and dispatched the debts confirmation notice to the debtor on June 7, 2000, that notice should have been sent to the appellee, not the Oil Factory, since after November 29, 1999, the Oil Company as a legal person ceased to exist. For this reason, the trial court dismissed the idea that the June 7, 2000 notice should not operate to halt the statute of limitation.

In its decision, the trial court concluded that the appellant in this case had lost its right to make any claim against the appellee because the time period between the agreed repayment date and the date of this litigation was beyond the limit imposed by the statute of limitation set forth in the 1986 Civil Code and the appellant failed to prove the existence of any situation in which the state of limitation has been suspended.[48] The trial court then ordered that (1) the appellant's claims be dismissed, and (2) the appellant pay the litigation fees of RMB 15,345 as well other related fees of RMB 3,087. Then the appeal followed.

On appeal, the appellant argued that the trial court erred in finding the non-existence of the Oil Factory after the registration of the appellee because the registration only indicated the change of the name of the entity, and did not extinguish the entity. The appellant further argued that if the acquisition caused the Oil Factory to be extinguished, the appellee was obligated to send a notice to the appellant, and even if the Bank's representative attended the appellee's opening ceremony, it did not mean that the appellee had fulfilled its notice obligation. The appellant also argued that since the debts confirmation notice was signed by both the Oil Factory and its legal representative and in the acquisition agreement the Oil Factory agreed to allow the appellee to use all assets of the Oil Factory without charge, the signature shall be deemed binding to the appellee, which also indicated that the appellant had made a claim whereby the statute of limitation would be tolled.

To rebut, the appellee asserted that when the Great Wall Asset Management Company assigned its creditor rights to the appellant, it did not notify the appellee of the assignment, and the assignment therefore was not effective as to the appellee. The appellee insisted that the appellee's registration as a limited liability company was not simply a change of the name of entity, as the registration indicated a birth of a new company, and thus, after the registration the Oil Factory did not exist any more. The appellee also argued that the Bank had full knowledge of the acquisition by attending the appellee's inauguration, and there was no requirement that an acquisition be made public by a public notice in media.

Having reviewed the facts in this case and considered the arguments from both parties, we hold that the appellee shall be deemed as a new company, not the original entity with a changed name because the appellee was established by absorbing all assets and liabilities of the Oil Factory and the capital newly invested. It is our opinion that the acquisition process indeed was defective because the creditor was not notified in writing. However, the Bank's attendance at the appellee's opening ceremony was a clear indication of the Bank's knowledge of the acquisition and the delegation of the debts, which would cure the defect in the fulfillment of the notice requirement.

---

48   Article 135 of the 1986 Civil Code provides that, except as otherwise provided by law, the statute of limitation for claims to the people's court for protection of civil rights is two years. According to Article 136, the statute of limitation is one year in the following cases: (a) claims for compensation for bodily injuries, (b) sales of substandard goods without proper notice, (c) delays in paying rent or refusal to pay rent, or (d) loss of, or damage to, property left in the care of another person. Under Article 137, the statute of limitation is calculated from the date when the entitled person knows or should know that his or her rights have been infringed upon. See the 1986 Civil Code.

What really matters in this case is the debts confirmation notice. The undisputable facts reveal that at the time when the Bank assigned its creditor rights against the appellee to the appellant, the Oil Factory was already acquired by the appellee. Therefore, after the assignment, the Bank should have sent notice to the appellee. Unfortunately, however, the Bank sent notice to the Oil Factory and its former legal representative and obtained those entities' signatures upon their receipt of such notice. Although the former legal representative of the Oil Factory worked for the appellee at the time of the signature, he was not an authorized officer of the appellee. Hence, it is reasonable to conclude that the Bank made a mistake and sent the debts confirmation notice to the wrong person, which would result in an ineffective assignment of the creditor rights to the Great Wall Assets Management Company as far as the appellee is concerned because the appellee was not notified of the assignment.

Since there is no effective assignment of the creditor right against the appellee, the appellant does not have valid standing to make its claims, and all such claims must therefore be denied. The trial court judgment is affirmed, and the litigation fees of RMB 20,010 on appeal are to be paid by the appellant.

In this case, both the trial and appellate courts held that the obligee's attendance at the obligor's opening ceremony implicated the obligee's knowledge of, and consent to, the delegation of debts. Therefore, as a practical matter, even though no written notice of the obligee's consent to the delegation was given to the obligee, the obligee's consent could be inferred or implied from the obligee's conduct.

2.2.2   Subordinate Duties

When an obligor delegates its contractual obligations to a third party, the duties attached to the contractual obligation shall be also transferred along with the delegation. The duties that are deemed subordinate to the the principal obligations of the contract include the duty to pay interest, the duty to pay stipulated damages or earnest money for breach of the contract, and the duty arising from the guaranty that the obligor provided to ensure the performance of the contract. Since subordinate duties normally have significant impacts on contract performance, it is natural to require that they should automatically be assumed by the third party (i.e., delegate) in a valid delegation of contractual obligations.

Because of the importance of subordinate duties in a delegation, the Contract Law requires a transfer of such duties in every delegation. Under Article 86 of the Contract Law, if the obligor delegates its obligations to a third party (who then becomes a new obligor), the new obligor shall assume the subordinate duties relating to the principal obligations of the contract, excluding the duties that are exclusively personal to the obligor.[49] Exclusively personal duties mostly involve personal service. For example, if the parties agree that

---

49   See the Contract Law, art. 86.

the obligor may paint a portrait for the obligee as a payment for the interest accrued from the contractual obligations, the duty to paint the portrait will be regarded as personally exclusive to the obligor, and may not be delegated without the obligee's specific consent.

If, however, contract performance is under a guaranty provided by a third-party guarantor, the duty of guaranty will not be included in the delegation unless the guarantor expressly agrees to the continuance of the guaranty after the delegation. Otherwise the guaranty ends with the delegation. According to Article 23 of the Guaranty Law of China, if during the term of guaranty, the obligee allows the obligor to delegate duties, the guarantor's written consent must be obtained in order for the said guarantee to remain effective. Thus, if the duties are delegated without the guarantor's consent, the guarantor will no longer be responsible for the guaranty.

2.2.3   Non-Delegable Duties

Interestingly, the Contract Law in its General Provisions imposes no restrictions on the delegability of contractual obligations. Accordingly, literally speaking, as long as the obligee agrees, all contractual obligations are delegable under the Contract Law unless the obligations may not be delegated either because of the nature of the debts or because of the provisions of relevant laws. Also, if the contract contains a provision that explicitly prohibits delegation of obligations, no delegation shall be made unless otherwise waived by the obligee.[50]

In the Special Provisions of the Contract Law, there are certain obligations that are prohibited from being delegated to other persons. For example, under Article 272 of the Contract Law, which concerns construction contracts, the general contractor for a construction project is prohibited from delegating its duty to any sub-contractor on the construction of mainframe of the project.[51]

Obligations that are normally deemed personal, such as obligations for child support or alimony, are also not delegable. Moreover, the obligor may not delegate to anyone his or her obligations arising from civil liabilities imposed

---

50 In the United States, a contract provision that prohibits delegation will most likely not be interpreted to prohibit the delegation of a duty that is totally impersonal, such as the duty to pay money. See Rohwer & Schaber, Contracts In A Nut Shell, *supra* note 11, at 381. In China, no distinction in this regard is made. However, in practice, if a pure money payment is involved, a delegation to make such payment to the obligee may be recognized where the delegation is prohibited by the contract. In this situation, however, the delegated third party is under no obligation make such a payment because of the questionable effect of the delegation.

51 See the Contract Law, art. 272.

by the operation of law. Such obligations include, for example, rehabilitation of another's reputation, elimination of ill effects, or apology to others.

2.2.4 Transfer of Obligor's Defenses against Obligee

When an obligator delegates its obligations to a third party, any defense that the obligor has against the obligee will be transferred to the third party. Consequently, the third party may exercise the defense to the extent that the obligor is entitled to make it. A rule provided in Article 85 of the Contract Law is that if the obligor delegates its obligations to a third party, the new obligor may have the defense that the original obligor would have against the obligee.[52]

Note, however, that in order to effectuate such transfer, the right of defense that belongs to the original obligor in relation to the delegated obligations must accrue before the delegation is made. In other words, the third party or the delegate may not assert any defense that the original obligor may not have against the obligee before the delegation but acquired thereafter.

The transfer of the obligor's defenses also depends on the validity of the delegation. If the delegation is invalid or has not taken effect, the obligor's defenses will not be transferred. For instance, if the delegation requires the obligee's consent, a transfer of the obligor's defenses will not take effect unless the obligee agrees to the delegation of the contractual obligations. The simple reason is that without the obligee's consent, no delegation will be effective. Consequently, without an effective deligation, there will be no basis for the transfer of the obligor's defenses.

3 Comprehensive Assignment

In China, a comprehensive assignment occurs when there is both an assignment of contractual rights as well as a delegation of contractual obligations with regard to a particular contract. Under the Contract Law, comprehensive assignments are governed by the provisions relating to assignment and delegation. According to Article 88 of the Contract Law, the party to a contract may assign its rights and obligations together under the contract to a third party with the consent of the other party.[53] Accordingly, then, a comprehensive assignment of the contract is permissible, but the consent of the other party is required.

---

52 See *id.*, art. 85.
53 See *id.*, art. 88.

A comprehensive assignment may be made by agreement. To assign a contract by agreement on a comprehensive basis, two agreements are needed. One is the agreement between the original parties, in which a party's request for a transfer of all of its rights and obligations under the contract to a third party is agreed to by the other party. The other one is the agreement entered by the assignor and assignee, under which the assignee agrees to take over the rights the assignor has under the contract, and in the meantime to assume all obligations that the assignor is required to perform.

Under the Contract Law, for a comprehensive assignment to be valid, four elements are required. First, there must be a valid contract. Again, the existence of a valid contract is a prerequisite to assignment. Second, there must be a mutual assent between the assignor and assignee to the assignment. Third, an express consent must be obtained from the other party to the contract. And fourth, there must be no violation of law with regard to the assignment. For example, the contractual rights must be assignable, and the obligations must be delegable.

On its face, a comprehensive assignment may look similar to a novation in American contract law. The two conceps are similar because they both involve a change of the party to the contract. The major difference between comprehensive assignment and novation is that with novation, an agreement between the remaining original party and the assignee is required, but no such requirement is needed for a comprehensive assignment.

Put differently, a novation may not occur without the mutual assent of all three parties involved because the result of novation is that one of the original parties to the contract is removed from the transaction and a new party is substituted in the original party's place.[54] Thus, in novation, there will be a new contract between an original party and the new party such that the original contract is replaced. Apparently, comprehensive assignment under the Contract Law does not result in a new contract.

In China, a comprehensive assignment may also be made pursuant to the requirements of law. Such an assignment normally takes place where there is a merger or acquisition that affect the parties to the contract. Article 90 of the Contract Law requires that if one party to a contract is merged after the contract, the legal person or organization established after the merger shall exercise the contractual rights and perform the contractual obligations.

Article 90 also makes it clear that if a party to the contract undergoes a separation after the contract is made, the legal persons or organizations so

---

54   See Rohwer & Schaber, *supra* note 25 at p 398.

established after the separation shall exercise the contractual rights and assume the contractual obligations jointly and severally.[55] Thus, in either a merger or a separation case, the resulting person or entity shall take responsibility for the remaining obligations.

Article 90 seems hard to read. What the provision actually means is that if there is a merger, acquisition, or business separation, the newly established or organized business entity shall be liable for the existing contract that was made by its predecessor. Particularly in the case of a business separation, joint liability will be imposed upon the business entities that are born as a result of the separation.

The very purpose of Article 90 is to maintain the stability of business transactions and the continuity of existing contractual rights and obligations. Certainly, the provision helps to ensure that an existing contract will be performed. The legislative notion underlying Article 90 is that nobody may evade his or her contractual obligations through a change of either business structure or the type of operation.

---

55 See the Contract Law, art. 90.

CHAPTER 9

Rescission and Termination of Contracts

A well-established rule under the Contract Law is that a legally formed contract must be performed. The strict performance requirement is also underscored, at least in theory, by the traditional virtue of promises honoring in the country. Thus, any non-performance or incomplete performance of a contract will result in liability for breach of contract. If a breach occurs, remedies will follow either under the terms of the contract, a provision of the law, or both.

Non-performance, however, may be excused under certain circumstances. Excusal of non-performance leads to an alteration of the contract or a discharge of all contractual obligations. With an alteration, the contract is modified and performance continues on the modified basis. Discharge means that the contract is rescinded or terminated. Both rescission and termination bring to an end the contractual relationship. In China, however, there have been debates over the difference between the rescission of a contract and the termination of a contract.

One argument is that rescission and termination are the same, and rescission in essence refers to as advance termination of the contract by agreement of the parties or by operation of law. In general, rescission is defined as a discharge of contractual obligations by the manifestation of intent of a party or parties or upon the occurrence of legally prescribed events. Therefore, if a contract is rescinded under the parties' agreement or pursuant to the provision of law, the contract is terminated. With respect to the discharge of contractual obligations, there is no difference between rescission and termination.[1]

A different opinion, however, regards rescission as one of element of contract termination. Under this opinion, rescission differs from termination in several aspects. First, rescission may be followed by restitution in order to avoid unjust enrichment, but termination ends with the discharge of the contract. Second, rescission may retroactively affect past rights and obligations under the contract, while termination only deals with the present and future effect of the contract—i.e., it simply extinguishes the contractual relationship. Third, rescission is often used as a means to punish the breaching party (e.g., the non-breaching party is given the right to rescind the contract). Termination, by contrast, is mainly used in situations where there is no breach of contract.[2]

---

[1] See Wang Liming, *Study on Contract Law (Vol. II)*, 273 (People's University Press, 2003).
[2] See *id.*

Whatever its potential difference with termination, rescission, to speak loosely, mainly deals with cases in which a duty to perform a contract may be discharged without triggering liability for a breach of the contract. In China, some scholars have suggested that the distinction between rescission and termination lies with the buzzword "retroactive." If the discharge of the contractual obligations has a retroactive effect on the contract (e.g., restitution), the discharge is normally a rescission. Otherwise, the discharge is a termination.

The Contract Law, on its face, seems to designate rescission as one of the circumstances under which a contract may be terminated. For example, under Article 91 of the Contract Law, there are seven situations that cause a contract to be terminated. One of the situations is rescission. Although the Contract Law does not expressly distinguish between rescission and termination, it does contain several provisions that apply specifically to rescission only. Also, in Chinese contract law literature, rescission is often discussed separately from termination in general.

1 Rescission

Rescission of a contract, also called dissolution of a contract in China, is a mechanism provided by the parties or by the law to nullify the binding force of the contract. The legal effect of rescission is to reinstate the original position of the parties prior to the contract. In China, when a contract is rescinded, the relationship between the parties under the contract is dissolved, and the duties to perform the contract are dischared. In this context, a rescission terminates the contract. After the recission, the parties will no longer be bound by the contract and thus none of the parties have the right to ask any of the other parties to perform the contract.

Under the Contract Law, a contract may be rescinded either by an agreement or pursuant to a provision of law. The statute requires that the rescission of a contract comply with the agreement or the provision of law. According to the SPC, if rescission by a party is made on a ground that does not meet the condition as agreed for the rescission or does not fall within any of the categories as provided in the Contract Law to trigger the rescission, the rescission, though it is requested by the party, has no effect and thus the performance of the contract will not be interrupted.[3]

---

3 *Sichuan Jufeng Real Estate Development Co. Ltd. v. Dazhou University of Broadcast and Television*, the SPC, (2013) Min Yi Zhong Zi, No. 18.

1.1 Rescission by Agreement

Under the principle of freedom of contract, the parties to a contract may decide to rescind the contract as they wish. The Contract Law recognizes the right of the parties to rescind a contract on a consensual basis. Pursuant to the provisions of the Contract Law, a consensual rescission of a contract can be made in two different ways: (a) by an agreement, and (b) upon agreed conditions to rescind.

Article 93 of the Contract Law provides that a contract may be rescinded if the parties agree through negotiations.[4] Article 93 further provides that the parties to a contract may agree upon the conditions to rescind the contract by one party.[5] Rescission upon agreed conditions refers to the situation where the contract is rescinded by a party if the conditions as provided by the parties are met. Under Article 93, the party entitled to rescind the contract under certain agreed conditions may exercise its right to rescind the contract whenever the conditions are satisfied.[6]

Most consensual rescission cases are based on agreement. A rescission agreement refers to consent voluntarily reached by the parties to bring their contract relationship to an end after the contract is concluded, but before the contract is performed or the performance is complete. An agreement on rescission has three distinctions. First, it is an agreement that is aimed at ending the existing contractual relationship. Second, the agreement is made after the conclusion of the contract and before the performance or completion of the contract's performance. Third, the agreement must be made voluntarily and reflect the true intention of the parties.

Like a contract, a rescission agreement is also subject to various contractual defenses. For example, if an agreement of rescission is found to be made against the will of a party or in violation of law, the agreement will be held null and void. When the rescission agreement is void, it will have no effect and the parties shall remain responsible for the performance of the existing contract.

The effect of a valid rescission agreement is the extinguishment of the contract by which the parties are currently bound. The parties, however, may in the rescission agreement set forth a date on which their contractual relationship ceases to exist. If there is such a day in the parties' agreement for the rescission to take effect, the contract will remain in effect and the performance will continue until the date as agreed comes.

---

4   See the Contract Law, art. 93.
5   See *id.*
6   See *id.*

There are two issues that often arise with respect to a rescission by agreement. One issue is restitution. When a contract is rescinded, the parties may have to dealt with the benefits one party has already conferred upon the other during the performance or even in the course of formation of the contract. Restitution means that the benefit so conferred must be retuned. Restitution is considered as a neccesary remedy in the rescission because without it, the benefited party would be unjustly enriched after the contract is rescinded. The purpose of restitution is to maintain fairness.

The second issue is the damage that one party has caused to the other. In certain cases, a contract is rescinded by the parties due to a breach of the contract. When breach happens, damages occur. The damages can be either the losses caused by the breach or the expenses incurred during the performance or preparation for the performance. The damages are in fact a matter of compensation to which the aggrieved party is entitled as a result of the other party's breach.

These two issues become relevant only when the parties did not or failed to include the matters of restitution or compensation in their rescission agreement. Under Article 97 of the Contract Law, in the case of rescission, if the contract has been performed, a party to the contract may, in light of the performance and the character of the contract, request restitution or take other remedial measures. Article 97 also provides the aggrieved party with the right to seek compensation for the damages.[7]

However, there are different views as to whether Article 97 may apply to rescission that is made by an agreement. One view argues that the rescission agreement represents the will of the parties to end the contractual relationship between them. Therefore, if the parties reach an agreement to rescind the contract without mentioning restitution or compensation, the parties are deemed to have forgone the right to make such a claim, or the right of the parties to ask for restitution or compensation is regarded to have been waived.

Another view opposes the waiver. It contends that an agreement to rescind a contract shall not affect a party's right to claim for restitution or compensation. The argument is that to claim restitution or compensation in a case of rescission is the right granted by the law under Article 97 of the Contract Law. Thus, unless the party entitled to make such claim specifically gives it up, the right shall not be deemed waived if not mentioned or discussed in the rescission agreement.[8]

---

7   See *id.*, art. 97.
8   See Wang Liming, *supra* note 1 at 279–280.

In the middle is a moderate approach. This approach attempts to narrow down the difference between the two opposite views by focusing on the actual will of the parties. According to the moderate approach, in a rescission agreement, the intent of the parties with regard to restitution or compensation should be expressly stated. If the issue of restitution or compensation was never raised in the negotiations on the rescission agreement, the right to make such a claim is deemed waived. If, however, the parties discussed this issue in their negotiations but failed to reach an agreement in this regard, the right to make the claim shall not be deemed as being waived or abandoned.[9]

Rescission upon agreed conditions involves events agreed upon by the parties in a contract. An occurrence of any of the events enables a party to rescind the contract. Based on Article 93 of the Contract Law, the notable feature of the agreed conditions is that the conditions are contractually provided to give a party the right to end the contract upon satisfaction of the conditions as agreed by the parties. Satisfaction means the occurrence or non-occurrence of certain event.

Note that agreed conditions should be events that may happen (i.e., occur or not occur) in the future. For example, in a contract for a month-long entertainment performance, the parties may provide that if the income from the box office is less than $30,000 for the first three nights, party A (organizer) may at its own option rescind the contract with party B (performer). Then the "box office income less than $30,000 for the first three nights" (which may happen) is the agreed condition for rescission of the contract.

As discussed in Chapter 6, there is a concept of dissolving condition in Chinese contract law theory. If a contract contains a dissolving condition, the occurrence of the condition will necessarily terminate the contract. The common character of dissolving conditions and agreed conditions is that both are provided in the contract and are the agreed events that may affect the effectiveness of the contract. The two kinds of conditions, however, differ from each other in that the dissolving condition deals with automatic dissolution of the contract upon the occurrence of the condition, while the agreed condition may affect the contract only if the party having the right to rescind chooses to exercise the right.

To illustrate, in the above performance example, if the contract provides instead that the contract will cease to be effective if the first three-night income is less than $30,000, the box office income "less than $30,000 in the first three nights" is the dissolving condition. In this situation, the contract will be

---

9 See *id.*

terminated automatically because under the term of the contract the rescission is not dependent upon a request by a party.

1.2 Rescission by the Provisions of Law

Absent agreement by the parties, a contract may also be rescinded if certain events as set forth in the law occur. Rescission by operation of law takes place where the law allows a party to choose to cancel a contract when certain conditions are met. To compare, the rescission of a contract by agreement is a bilateral dissolution requiring both parties' consent, while rescission by operation of law is a unilateral dissolution that does not need consent from the other party.

Also, unlike rescission by agreement, rescission by operation of law is a statutory right that enables a party to dissolve a contract under specific conditions. The right is intended to effectively protect the legitimate interests of a contractual party by permitting the party to decide whether or not to stay with the contract. Note, however, that an affirmative action by the interested party is required to exercise the right to rescind a contract. In other words, the party able to rescind the contract under a provision of law must act to that effect in order to have the contract rescinded.

The Contract Law provides five conditions under which a contract may be rescinded unilaterally. Each of the conditions stands as the legal ground for the rescission of a contract. According to Article 94 of the Contract Law, in any of the following circumstances, a party may rescind the contract:

(a) The purpose of the contract cannot be realized due to *force majeure*;
(b) One party to the contract, before the expiry of the performance period, explicitly expresses or indicates through its conduct that it will not perform the principal obligations;
(c) One party to the contract defaults in performing its principal obligations under the contract and, after being urged, fails to perform such obligations within a reasonable period of time;
(d) One party to the contract defaults in performing its contractual obligations or commits other acts in breach of contract so that the purpose of the contract cannot be realized; or
(e) Other situations as stipulated by law.[10]

In short, Article 94 sets forth three types of statutory rescissions of contracts: (a) rescission due to *force majeure*, ((b)(c)(d)) rescission on the basis of

---

10   See the Contract Law, art. 94.

breach of contract, and (e) rescission by other statutory means.[11] Again, statutory rescission does not result in an automatic dissolution of a contract but it provides the legal ground on which a contract may be rescinded by a party. In many cases, statutory rescission requires a determination by the court, especially when there is a dispute over the justification of the rescission.

Since the Contract Law allows both consensual and statutory rescissions, a question is whether the two types of rescissions are mutually exclusive. The general view is that contractual rescissions and statutory rescissions can co-exist under the Contract Law and that a contractual rescission may be used as a supplement to a statutory rescission.[12] Supplement in this context means that, outside the scope of statutory rescissions, parties may still agree to directly rescind a contract or provide certain circumstances under which the contract may be rescinded. Also, as some suggest, the parties may by agreement provide what event may be considered as *force majeure*—a statutory reason for rescission.[13]

A related question is whether a contractual rescission may alter or limit the right to dissolve a contract under the law. Some argue that since Article 94 is not mandatory, the parties' agreement may supersede the statutory provision with regard to the contract dissolution.[14] For example, the parties may provide in the contract that no party may rescind the contract even if a party is in breach, or that the contract shall be rescinded as long as a certain duty is breached, regardless of materiality of the breach.[15]

1.2.1 Force Majeure

Force majeure is defined in Article 117 of the Contract law as objective circumstances that are unforeseeable, unavoidable, and insurmountable.[16] Such objective circumstances include natural disasters (e.g., a fire, flood, earthquake, or the like), abnormal social or political changes (e.g., social turmoil, a strike), and government action (e.g., a curfew).[17] In addition, change of law is regarded as an objective circumstance for the purpose of dissolving a contract.[18] For

---

11 See Dong Ling, *Performance, Modification, Assignment and Termination of Contracts*, 190 (China Legal System Publishing House, 1999).
12 See Wang Liming, *supra* note 1 at 278.
13 See *id.*, at 283.
14 See *id.*
15 See *id.*
16 See the Contract Law, art. 117.
17 See Jiang Bixin, et al, *Understanding and Application of the Adjudicative Rules of the SPC Guiding Cases (Contracts)*, 292 (China Legal Publishing House, 2012).
18 See *id.*, at 268–69.

instance, if a contract were to become invalid under a newly adopted law, the new law would be the cause of the contract's dissolution since the adoption of the new law would make it impossible to continue performing the contract.

Un-foreseeability is often a hard issue when determining the presence of *force majeure*. On the one hand is the matter of standard. There are two standards for assessing whether a particular event is foreseeable: the reasonable standard (i.e., ordinary people standard) and the professional standard (i.e., the standard for people with specialties or particular skills). The majority view is that un-foreseeability is determined under the reasonable standard of whether an ordinary person in the same or similar situation would reasonably foresee the occurrence of a particular event.[19]

On the other hand, there is a question of whether un-foreseeability means "totally unforeseeable" or "unable to accurately foresee." Chinese courts seem to hold that there is no substantial difference between "total un-foreseeability" and "inability to accurately foresee" in terms of *force majeure*. But when determining the effect of *force majeure* and the allocation of liabilities, the courts will treat the two differently.

In certain cases, a claim on the ground of *force majeure* will be granted even with respect to an event that is foreseeable if the event is considered to be unavoidable. In *Zhong Ji Tongyong Imports / Exports Co. v Tianjin Harbor Second Stevedoring Co. Ltd.*, the Tian Ji High People's Court opined that a tropic storm, notwithstanding the fact that it can be forecasted, constitutes *force majeure* because it remains unavoidable under the present level of science and technology. This decision was also endorsed by the SPC.[20]

Note, however, that the extent to which a particular event or circumstance is "unavoidable" and "insurmountable" must be justified in order for the event or circumstance to quality as *force majeure*. Whether the event or circumstance is justified is evaluated pursuant to a best-effort standard. Thus, an event is unavoidable when the parties have devoted all possible reasonable care but still could not prevent the event from happening. Similarly, an event that is insurmountable refers to the situation where the parties have made all possible efforts but remain unable to overcome the event's occurrence. Only if the event is proved to be objectively unavoidable and insurmountable, may a *force majeure* claim be granted.

Consequently, the *force majeure* may affect the performance of a contract in different ways. Under Article 117 of the Contract Law, *force najeure* can cause

---

19 See *id.*, at 278.
20 See the SPC Gazette, 5 (2000), https://www.chinacourt.org/article/detail/2002/11/id/18086.shtml.

three possible results: impossibility of performing the whole contract, impossibility of performing a part of the contract, or delay in performance.[21] Due to a concern that *force majeure* might not be properly asserted, Article 94 of the Contract Law narrowly prescribed *force majeure* as a ground for rescinding a contract. Under Article 94, a contract may only be rescinded on the basis of *force majeure* when the *force majeure* is so severe that the purpose of the contract cannot be realized.[22] The purpose of a contract is normally interpreted to mean the expected interest or benefit of the parties to the contract.

Generally, if an occurrence of *force majeure* makes it impossible to perform only partial obligations under a contract, that contract may be modified to the extent that the obligation to perform the affected part of the contract would be discharged. But, if the purpose of the contract is frustrated as a result of *force majeure,* the whole contract may be dissolved even though only partial performance is affected. The same rule also applies to a delay in performance caused by *force majeure.* Under 94 of the Contract Law, the bottom line is whether the purpose of the contract can be realized.

What appears questionable under Article 94 of the Contract Law, however, is whether both parties to a contract have the right to rescind the contract in the case of *force majeure.* In Article 94, the word "parties" is used to specify the rescission right. An argument is that since *force majeure* gives the performing party (debtor) a lawful excuse not to perform its contractual obligations, only the party receiving the performance (creditor) has the right to rescind the contract. Thus, Article 94 should be read to mean that that when the purpose of a contract is destroyed by *force majeure,* either of the parties has the right to seek rescission of the contract. The reason is that the frustration of the contract's purpose being effectuated affects the realization of both parties' expected interests.

1.2.2 Breach of Contract

Under the Contract Law, if a party is in breach of contract, the other party may rescind the contract as a legal remedy. Such a remedy, however, only applies to certain breaches of contract as specified in the law. Article 94 of the Contract Law permits rescission in three kinds of contract breaches: anticipatory repudiation, unreasonable delay in performance, and frustration of purpose of contract. If a breach falls within any of these three categories, the non-breaching party is entitled to the rescission of the contract.

---

21   See the Contract Law, art. 117.
22   See *id.*, art. 94.

1.2.2.1 *Anticipatory Repudiation*

Anticipatory repudiation is a common law concept that gives a party a legal right not to go forward with performance of a contract when the other party disclaims any intention to perform before the performance of the contract is due.[23] In American contract law, anticipatory repudiation serves as a legal ground under which a party's duty to perform may be excused. In the U.S., in the case of anticipatory repudiation, the non-repudiating party may suspend its own performance, bring a lawsuit immediately, rescind the contract, or ignore the repudiation and urge performance. In order to constitute anticipatory repudiation, the statement of intent (expressed or implied from conduct) not to perform must be clear and unequivocal.

The Contract Law borrows the concept of anticipatory repudiation from the common law system, and makes it a legal basis for the rescission of a contract. Article 94 (b) of the Contract Law provides that if a party, before the expiry of the performance period, expresses, either explicitly or through conduct, that it will not perform its principal obligations under a contract, the other party may rescind the contract.

Under Article 94 (b), three elements are required in order to find anticipatory repudiation. The first element is manifestation of intent not to perform. Such manifestation may be made expressly or implicitly through conduct. Although the word "unequivocal" is not used in Article 94, manifestation must be explicit and to the effect that the contractual obligation will not be performed. The second element is expiry of the time period for performance. To constitute anticipatory repudiation, the intent not to perform must be manifested on or before the day the performance period expires. The third element is non-performance of principal obligations. The intent not to perform must involve principal obligations of the contract; if it does not, the non-performance does not amount to anticipatory repudiation.[24]

Thus, although Article 94 (b) is modeled after the common law concept, anticipatory repudiation, as used in China, seems to have two distinctions. One distinction is the time of repudiation (or the time when the non-anticipating party's right arises). In the United States, where a party repudiates a contract before the time for the contract's performance, the issue of anticipatory repudiation arises.[25] By contrast, Article 94 (b) of the Contract Law prescribes the time of repudiation as the time when the period of performance expires. Admittedly, the term "expiry of the time period for performance," as used in

---

23   See Rohwer & Schaber, *Contracts In A Nut Shell*, 316 (West, 1997).
24   See the Contract Law, art. 94.
25   See Calamari & Perillo, *The Law of Contracts* (4th Ed), 477 (West Group, 1998).

Article 94(b), may cause confusion because in many cases it is difficult to tell when the performance period expires.

Some scholars argue that the "expiry of the time period for performance" means either the day before the performance is due or, where the due day and expiration day are not on the same day, the day after the performance is due but before the time for performance expires. For example, assume that the contract provides for a performance between May 1 and May 10. Then May 1 is the day the performance is due and May 10 the day the performance expires. If, however, there is clearly no performance period in the contract, the time will be the day when performance becomes due.[26]

Others disagree. They emphasize that anticipatory repudiation is a prospective breach of contract, and such a breach may only happen when it is clear that the performing party will not perform its obligations after the time period for performance ends. The reason is that the performing party has every right not to perform before the expiration day of the performance, and therefore the non-performance before that day does not and should not constitute a breach.[27]

Another distinction with respect to the concept of anticipatory repudiation between the Chinese and common law systems is the requirement of principal obligations. The Contract Law divides contractual obligations into principal obligations and non-principal obligations, and limits anticipatory repudiation's applicability to expressions of intent not to perform one's principal obligations under a contract. But the Contract Law contains no definition as to what obligations are deemed principal. A common understanding in China is that obligations are principal if they are the main focus or target of the contract, substantial to the contract, or determinative to the nature of the contract, and without their performance, the contract will not be performed or the purpose of the contract will not be effectuated. As a matter of fact, what constitutes principal obligations varies depending on the contents of the particular contract.

Article 94(b) allows the non-repudiating party to rescind the contract in a case of anticipatory repudiation. Note that under Article 94(b), the non-repudiating party may rescind the contract. The word "may" clearly indicates that the exercise of such right is at the non-repudiating party's choice. Therefore, even if an anticipatory repudiation occurs, the non-repudiating

---

26 See Dong Ling, *supra* note 11 at p 195.
27 See Yang Lixin, *Implication and Application of the Contract Law*, 183 (Jilin People's Publishing House, 1999).

party may choose to disregard the repudiation, and urge the repudiating party to perform the contract. In addition, the non-repudiating party may also regard the repudiation as a breach and bring a lawsuit. This remedy is provided in Article 108 of the Contract Law, which will be discussed in the next chapter.

1.2.2.2   Unreasonable Delay in Performance

Delay in performance of a contract is understood in China encompasses two situations: delay in delivery (including making a payment) or delay by obligor, and delay in acceptance or delay by obligee. Article 94(c) of the Contract Law deals only with delay in delivery because it is basically concerned with performance of obligations, while delay in acceptance mainly involves improper cooperation of the obligee with regard to the obligor's performance. In this context, delay in delivery is also called delay in performance. Delay in performance occurs when the obligor fails to timely perform the contract as agreed.

More specifically, delay in performance refers to the situation where the obligor is able to perform (as opposed to it being impossible for the obligor to perform) and willing to perform (as opposed to anticipatory repudiation), but without just reason fails to perform when the performance is due. Note, however, that if there is no agreed upon day or period for the performance of contractual obligations, the obligee may ask the obligor to perform any time, but the obligee must give the obligor a reasonable period of time to prepare for the performance. In this case, a determination of the delay in performance shall be made in consideration of a reasonable preparation period.

Once again, in a case of delay in performance, whether the obligee may rescind the contract is dependent on whether the delay affects the performance of the principal obligations of the contract. Article 94 (c) demands a showing of delay in performing the principal obligations in order for the obligee to be entitled to rescission of the contract. Therefore, if the delay in performance does not involve the performance of the principal obligations, rescission as a remedy is not available.

In addition, when there is a delay in performance, the obligee is required to "urge" the obligor to perform. To "urge" means to send a notice of performance to the obligor. The notice can be made either in writing or oral. After the notice, the obligor is allowed a reasonable period of time to prepare for the performance. Reasonable period of time is the time necessarily needed for the preparation according to the nature and customary practice of the particular transactions. In general, according to the SPC, the reasonable period of time after the notice and before the exercise of the right to rescind shall be no more than three months.[28]

Thus, to make an Article 94 (c) claim for the rescission of a contract, the following elements are required: (1) delay in performance, (2) of principal obligations, (3) without just reason, and (4) failure to perform, (5) within a reasonable period of time, (6) after a notice to urge is given. Obviously, the requirement of impact on principal obligations serves a twofold purpose: to assure that the aggrieved party gets what he has bargained for, and to avoid undue hardship (on the non-performing party) arising from the possible rescission of the contract.

1.2.2.3 *Frustration of the Contract Purpose*

Article 94 (d) grants to a party the right to rescind the contract if the purpose of the contract is frustrated as a result of the other party's delay in performance or other conduct resulting in a breach of contract. Apparently, Article 94 (d) is centered on the consequences of non-performance of the contract. In its application, Article 94 (d) can be triggered by two different causes: delay in performance and other breaches of contract. In either case, the key is whether the purpose of the contract is frustrated or destroyed.

With regard to the delay in performance, Article 94 (d) seems to provide an exception to Article 94 (c) to the effect that delay in performance itself, without more, suffices to rescind a contract if the delay frustrates the purpose of the contract. Put differently, if the time of performance is critical or essential to the contract and any late performance would render the contract meaningless, the delay will give rise to the right of the aggrieved party to rescind the contract regardless of principal obligations or notice to urge performance.[29]

Other conduct resulting in breaches of contract as the cause to rescind a contract are problematic because they are not specified in the Contract Law. One interpretation is that any conduct in breach of contract would fall within the coverage of Article 94 (d) if the conduct results in the frustration of the purpose of the contract.[30] The other interpretation defines "other conduct"

---

28 See the SPC, Interpretation of Several Legal Issues on the Application of Law in Adjudication of the Cases Involving Disputes over the Contracts of Sales of Residential Housing, art. 15 (2003) (absent legal provisions or agreement by the parties, the reasonable period of time for exercise of the right of dissolution is limited to three months after the notice to urge).

29 A similar concept in this regard in U.S. contract law is the doctrine of "time is the essence of contract." But the difference is that in order to assert this doctrine to hold the other party who delays in performance liable, it must be specified in the contract (i.e., there must be a phrase in the contract stating that time is the essence).

30 See Dong Ling, *supra* note 11 at pp 203–204.

to mean conduct, other than delay in performance, that breaches a contract, which includes impossibility, refusal of performance, improper performance, partial performance, and the like.[31] But whatever the other conduct may be, the determinant for the rescission is whether the purpose of the contract has been frustrated or destroyed as a result of the breach.

Some argue that Article 94 (d) actually infers the situation where there is a fundamental breach—the term most commonly used in western countries. In the United States, a fundamental breach is defined as a material breach, which justifies a cancellation of the contract.[32] Opponents of the notion that Article 94 (d) contemplates only those situations that result in fundamental breachs, however, view Article 94 (d) as a less restrictive version of the doctrine of fundamental breach. They believe that total breach is not equivalent to frustration of the purpose of contract because frustration under the Contract Law means a failure to achieve the goal or realize the benefits of the contract, while total breach can be caused by many other reasons. In addition, in certain cases, the standard for determining whether the liabilities of the breaching party may be reduced if a fundamental breach occurs is whether an ordinary person would reasonably foresee the result under the same or similar circumstances.[33]

1.2.3 Other Reasons Provided by the Law

Article 94 (e) of the Contract Law is a catchall provision under which a contract may be rescinded in other circumstances as stipulated by the law. The provision, on the one hand, requires a cross-reference to the relevant provision contained in another part of the Contract Law or any other existing laws. On the other hand, the provision leaves certain room for a late legislation. For

---

31 See Jiang Ping et al, *A Detailed Explanation of the Contract Law of Law*, 80 (China University of Political Science and Law Press, 1999). See also Wang Liming, *supra* note 1 at pp 292–294.

32 Generally, a breach is regarded material if, as a result of the breach, the aggrieved party does not receive the substantial benefit of what was bargained for. Although under the Second Restatement, a material breach justifies the suspension of performance, not necessarily cancellation of the contract, the aggrieved party may treat the contract as at an end and has the right to damages for breach of the contract. But if necessary to make a comparison, the delay in performance as provided in Article 93 (c) seems more like a material breach.

33 This argument is premised on Article 25 of the United Nations Convention on International Sales of Goods. It provides: "a breach of contract committed by one of the parties is fundamental if it results in such detriment to the other party as substantially to deprive him of what he is entitled to expect under the contract, unless the party in breach did not foresee and a reasonable person of the same kind in the same circumstances would not have foreseen such a result."

example, under Article 69 of the Contract Law, a contract may be rescinded by a party if the other party, after the performance is suspended, fails to reinstate its capacity of performance and to provide proper assurance for the performance within a reasonable period of time.[34]

But, the question is whether "other law" for the purpose of Article 94 (e) includes lower-level regulations—e.g., regulations adopted by the State Council, rules issued by various ministries, ordinances passed by local legislative bodies, or even government policies, as well as unpublished government directives. Since China's ascension to the WTO, it has been an established rule that no government policies or unpublished government directives and orders are to be applied in the people's courts.

Lower-level regulations do not fall within the scope of the "law" in the context of the Contract Law because only the statutes promulgated by the National People's Congress are characterized as the "law." In practice, the law is often broadly defined to include regulations, rules, and local ordinances. But according to the SPC's interpretation, as noted, when determining the validity of a contract, the people's courts shall only follow the law passed by the NPC and its Standing Committee, and the administrative regulations adopted by the State council. Thus, the State Council regulations are a part of the law but local ordinances are not.

A hard issue is whether the change of government policy may fall within the "other reasons" for which a contract may be rescinded. In the following case, defendant attempted to assert the "change of the State policy" as a defense to its rescission of the performance of the contract. The court affirmed the possibility of using the change of government policy as a condition to rescind a contract, but denied defendant assertion on a different ground.

Kun Ming Teng Si Lin Trade Company, Ltd.
v.
China Unicom, Inc. Yun Nan Branch

Kun Ming City Intermediate People's Court, Yun Nan Province

Kun Min Si Chu Zhi No. 007[35]

On February 17, 2000, plaintiff Kun Ming Teng Si Lin Trade Company, Ltd. and defendant China Unicom, Inc. Yun Nan Branch entered into the "Sales Agreement on Outright Purchase of '130 Teng Si Lin SIM Card' Utilizing China Unicom GSM 130". Under the Agreement, plaintiff would

---

34   Other examples in the Contract Law dealing with sales contracts are Articles 148 (defective quality of contracted goods), 165 (defective item among many items), and 167 (failure to pay in installment payments).
35   See the National Judicial College & People's University Law School, *An Overview of the Trial Cases of China* (Civil and Commercial Cases of 2004), 32 (People's Court Publishing House and People's University Press, 2005)

purchase and sell 100,000 China Unicom GSM 130 SIM cards with assigned phone numbers. Also, plaintiff was required to deposit "Credit Guarantee Fund" with defendant, and the fund would be refunded in proportion to the fees collected by defendant with regard to the use of the cards, such as basic charge, line subscriber fee, network charge and long distance call charge. In the Agreement, the parties agreed that if the sales of the cards could not continue due to the policy adjustment by the government, defendant should refund plaintiff the money of all unsold SIM cards at the price charged when plaintiff acquired the cards.

On February 23, 2000, plaintiff transferred to defendant's bank account RMB 1.6 mil- lion Yuan, and obtained from defendant some 2500 SIM cards. Plaintiff then started selling the cards immediately thereafter. On April 26, 2000, however, defendant sent a letter to plaintiff asking plaintiff to stop selling the cards, and attached to the letter was defendant's official document entitled" Emergent Notice Concerning the Unicom's Implementation of the State Policy on Charges and Fees". The document was issued in response to the Ministry of Information Industry's "Notice on Strengthening the Management of Charges and Fees for Cellular Phone Services".

Upon receiving defendant's emergent notice, plaintiff stopped all sales of the cards, and the parties managed to count unsold cards and negotiated on the matter of refund. By December 2000, the unsold cards, as counted by the employees of the parties, were 1192, and the money that should be refunded was RMB 896,000. But, defendant asked to deduct from the refund the unpaid fees associated with the use of the sold cards, to which plaintiff disagreed. After several unsuccessful negotiations, plaintiff brought this lawsuit against defendant for (a) RMB 896,000 that should be refunded to plaintiff plus late payment penalty, (b) RMB 358,760 of the loss of plaintiff expected interests caused by defendant's unilateral termination of the contract, and (c) litigation fees.

Defendant argued that the money to be refunded should be RMB 747,744.42 rather than RMB 896,000 because under the Agreement plaintiff shall be responsible for the costs such as mobile network charges and unpaid long distance charges related to the use of the SIM cards and such costs shall be deducted. Defendant also argued that although defendant shall refund to plaintiff RMB 747,744.42, the payment was withheld according to the court order on April 25, 2000, pending the disputes over the refund money. Therefore, defendant should not be asked to pay to any late payment penalty. Defendant further argued that plaintiff's claim should be dismissed because the rescission of the contract by defendant was not a breach of the contract because defendant had to comply with the State policy on charges and fees for cellular phone services, and the parties had agreed that the both parties would bear the risks due to the change of the State policy that makes the parties unable to continue selling the SIM cards.

It was found during the court hearing that the purchase agreement was signed by the parties on February 17, 2000, and after the sales was halted the total value of the unsold cards amounted to RMB 896,000 that should be refunded by defendant to plaintiff under the agreement. It was also found that there was no credible evidence to prove the costs that defendant claimed for deduction, and that the withholding of the payment of the refunded money was granted by the order of Kun Ming Intermediate People's Court (2000 *Kun Fa Jing Chu Zhi* No. 22).

The court then holds that defendant's assertion for deduction was not supported by evidence and therefore should not be accepted. The court further holds that defendant should not be penalized for the late payment of the refund because the delay in payment was granted by the court order, and for that reason plaintiff's claim for late payment penalty must be denied. With regard to the change of the State Policy, it is the opinion of the Court that defendant's rescission of the agreement was not a result of the change of the State policy because the fee standard employed by defendant was not in compliance with the State standard of changes and fees for the cellular phone serves, and the notice of the Ministry of Information Industries was aimed at enhancing the administration of the charges and fees applied by the cellular phone services provider, and thus the rescission had nothing to do with the policy change.

Therefore, the court concludes that defendant's rescission of the agreement did not fall within the coverage of the condition of the government policy adjustment as agreed by the parties because there was no change of government policy. On this ground, defendant's rescission of the agreement constituted a breach of contract for which defendant must be held liable. In the meantime, because of defendant's breach of contract, plaintiff suffered the loss of the expected interest of RMB 358,760 arising from the unsold cards. Thus, plaintiff's claim for the expected interest shall be granted.

In view of the above analysis and in accordance with Article 64 (1) of the Civil Procedure Law and Articles 93 (1), 97 and 113 of the Contract Law, it is ordered that:

1. The "Sales Agreement on Outright Purchase of '130 Teng Si Lin SIM Card' Linked to China Unicom GSM 130" entered by the parties on February 17, 2000 be rescinded;
2. Defendant China Unicom, Inc. Yun Nan Branch refund to plaintiff RMB 896,000 Yuan within 10 days after this judgment takes effect;
3. Defendant China Unicom, Inc. Yun Nan Branch pay plaintiff RMB 358,760 Yuan as plaintiff's loss of expected interests; and
4. Plaintiff's other claims be dismissed.

In the *China Unicom*, the court denied defendant's assertion of the State policy adjustment as the defense for unilateral rescission of the contract because, according to the court, to cure the defect in compliance with the State policy on charges and fees did not constitute a change of the State policy for which the unilateral rescission of the contract would be justified. The court decision, however, does suggest that the change of the State policy that affects a contract will be regarded as an agreed condition on which the contract is to be rescinded. But what seems typical in this case is that the court deemed "the change of government policy" as a "dissolving condition" provided by the parties in their agreement.

1.3 *Rescission Notice*

Under the Contract Law, to rescind a contract either by agreement or on statutory grounds, the claiming party must take action to that effect. In other words, rescission may only be made upon request. Pursuant to Article 96 of the Contract Law, if a party advances to rescind the contract, the party shall send a notice to the other party, and the rescission will not become effective until the notice of rescission is received by the other party. In the meantime, Article 96 gives the claiming party a cause of action to ask the court or arbitration body to affirm the validity of the rescission made under the contract or the provision of the law if the other party disagrees therewith.[36]

It is not clear in the Contract Law whether the notice of rescission must be in writing. Under the equal dignity rule, however, it is generally believed that if the contract is made in writing, the rescission notice shall also be in writing. Once again, for certain contracts that need approval or registration, approval

---

36 See the Contract Law, art. 96.

or registration is equally required for the rescission of such contracts. In these cases, without the "red chops" from relevant government authority to show the approval, no rescission will become valid. If only filing is required, however, failure to file will not affect the validity of the rescission, though it may result in administrative fines.

As discussed, rescission can be authorized by an agreement or by the law. But the exercise of the right to rescind is subject to a certain time limit. The time limit can be either statutory or consensual. Under Article 95 of the Contract Law, where the law stipulates or the parties agreed upon the time limit to exercise the right to rescind a contract, failure to exercise within the time limit will cause the right to be extinguished.[37] If, however, there is no legal provision or agreement on the time limit, Article 95 requires that such a right be exercised within a reasonable period of time after being urged by the other party. Otherwise the right will also be extinguished.

In addition, according to the SPC, if the other party objects to rescission, the objection must be raised within the time limit. The time limit may be set forth in the contract between the parties. Absent such agreement, the time limit is three months after the receipt of the rescission notice.[38] As noted, under Article 96 of the Contract Law, when the other party, upon receipt of the rescission notice, challenges the rescission, the claiming party may ask a court or an arbitration body for an affirmance of the rescission.

In certain cases, a party did not send a notice to the other party but instead took the case directly to a people's court for a rescission on the basis of terms as agreed in the contract or the provision of the law. Literally speaking, a notice to rescind is a manifestation of an intent to dissolve the contract. A question then is whether such intent can be manifested by the act of bringing a lawsuit. In other words, the question is whether a lawsuit for rescission meets the notice requirement of Article 96 of the Contract Law.

The answer to this question differs among Chinese scholars. Some believe that under Article 96, the right to rescind can only be vested after the notice is given, and the lawsuit may only be sought when the rescission is challenged by the other party. Others, however, argue that since Article 96 is mainly concerned with the manifestation of intent to rescind, the manifestation can be made directly via a notice and can also be made indirectly through litigation as long as the true intent is manifested. In addition, the service of court summons on the other party in a litigation for contract rescission is in fact a notice to the party.[39]

---

37 See *id.*, art. 95.
38 See the SPC, 2009 Contract Law Interpretation, art. 24.
39 See Jiang Bixin, *et al, supra* note 17 at 389–390.

1.4 Legal Consequences of Rescission

The legal consequence of contract rescission is to end the contract relationship between the parties. Under the Contract Law, rescission not only terminates the contract but also retroactively affects part of the contract that has been performed. Thus, Article 97 of the Contract Law provides two different outcomes of rescission. First, after a rescission, if the contract has not yet been performed, the performance is terminated. Second, if the contract has been performed, restitution, other remedial measures or damages may be claimed depending on the amount of performance as well as the nature of the contract.[40] It is important to note that the remedies in case of rescission are not the breach of contract liablities but civil remedies.

Obviously, if a contract has not yet been performed, rescission is simply a matter of termination of the performance. When the contract has been partially performed, certain complexities arise with respect to rescission because the performance may result in the conveyance of benefits between the parties. To deal with this situation, Article 97 provides the parties with three different alternatives: restitution, other remedial measures, or damages. Restitution seems to be simple. It is aimed at restoring the parties to the position where they were supposed to be in if the contract had not been performed. Therefore, restitution basically involves return of originals plus interests accrued and necessary expenses associated with the performance already made.

Other remedial measures require further explanation. On the one hand, they are not specified in the Contract Law, and on the other hand, there are different views on what falls within other remedial measures. Some suggest that other remedial measures mainly include repair and replacement to be used in the cases where it is impossible or extremely difficult to restore the original.[41] Others argue that other remedial measures refer to means such as reduction of price or payment, or claims for unjust enrichment.[42] A few regard other remedial measures as the way to supplement restitution.[43] For example, if restitution is not sufficient, the aggrieved party may also ask for stipulated damages. In practice, because of the lack of unified interpretation, the courts may view the other remedial measures in the way they see fit.

---

40   Keep in mind that the retroactive effect of dissolution only affects the contract or the part of the contract that has been performance. Where the contract or part of the contract has not yet been performed, retroactivity is not an issue.
41   See Wang Liming, *supra* note 1 at 308.
42   See *id.*
43   See Jiang Ping, *supra* note 31 at 82–83.

In the case of rescission, the aggrieved party may also ask for damages. In contract theory, there is a long lasting debate in China on whether rescission and damage may co-exist. In other words, the question is whether a party may make a claim for damages while rescinding the contract. Article 97 of the Contract Law seems to suggest that rescission and damages are not necessarily mutually exclusive.[44] In fact, Article 97 is based on Article 115 of the 1986 Civil Code, which provides that with modification or rescission of a contract, the party's right to seek damages shall not be affected.

The doctrinal basis for allowing damages in rescission is fairness. First of all, if a contract is rescinded due to a party's breach of contract, it is fair to ask the breaching party to bear the liability corresponding to its breach because the other party may have experienced the loss of benefits or interests caused by the breach.[45] Secondly, rescission frees the parties from their contractual obligations, but it does not necessarily mean that the damages the aggrieved party may have suffered are properly compensated without a remedy for damages. Thirdly, restitution alone as a legal remedy might not be sufficient because restitution restores the parties to their original position before the contract, but it may not cover the losses and damages, particularly when the contracted subject matter was destroyed and could not be returned, which would render the restitution meaningless.

Practically, the difficult issue is not whether damages shall be made available where a contract is rescinded but what should be covered in the damages. More specifically, a question involved is whether the aggrieved party may be compensated for both the damages in association with the restitution after the rescission and the damages that may incur as a result of non-performance of the contract. Another question is whether damages may include indirect damages, such as the loss of interests.

With regard to what the aggrieved party may be compensated in case of rescission, there are two different doctrines in China. One doctrine is called "complete compensation." Under this doctrine, the aggrieved party is entitled to all damages it may have suffered, including both damages caused by non-performance and damages related to restitution.[46] The other doctrine takes

---

44 Some believe that rescission and damages may not co-exist. The rationale is that rescission will only result in restitution, and because restitution restores parties to their original status, this would mean that the contract did not exist from the very beginning. Therefore, without the existence of the contract, there would no bases on which the damages may stand.
45 In this sense, if the dissolution is caused by *force majeure* without the fault of any party, the remedy for damages will become irrelevant.
46 See Wang Liming, *supra* note 1 at p 305.

a narrower view that the damages only cover the losses resulting from non-performance.[47]

The damages related to restitution are illustrated by some scholars in China to include (a) necessary expenses spent for the conclusion of the contract, (b) costs for the preparation for the performance of the contract, (c) opportunity costs, (d) losses caused by the failure to return the originals, and (e) other additional costs incurred to the aggrieved party as a result of the dissolution.[48] Non-performance damages normally refer to expectation interest and reliance interest.

In Chinese courts, however, there is a strong resistance against compensation for expectation interest with respect to contract rescission. The basic notion is that the primary legal effect of rescission is restitution while expectation interest may take place only after the contract has been performed. Thus, when the parties choose to rescind the contract, such choice implies that the non-breaching party is unwilling to continue to perform the contract. For that reason, the non-breaching party shall not be compensated for the interest that it is supposed to obtain after the completion of the performance of the contract.[49]

In addition, when a party asks for damages while rescinding a contract under either the agreement or the provision of the law, the people's courts will normally require the presence of the following elements before a decision is made: (a) the other party has acted in breach of contract; (b) the requesting party has chosen to rescind the contract; (c) the requesting party has suffered losses or damages; (d) there is a cauation between the dagames and the conduct of the breach of the contract; and (e) the requesting party is not at fault.[50] Therefore, although Article 97 provides damages as a remedy in the rescission of a contract, certain requirements must be met if damages are sought in a people's court.

2 Termination

Like rescission, termination has the effect of ending a contract, but for different reasons. Generally, termination discharges both the rights and obligations

---

47 See Dong Ling, *supra* note 11 at pp 217–218.
48 See *id.* at p 218.
49 See Li Guoguang, *Explanation and Application of the Contract Law*, 381 (Xinghua Press) (1999).
50 See Jiang Bixin, *et al*, *supra* note 17, at 400–401.

of the contractual parties, whereby the performance of the contract is called to a complete stop. In the civil law tradition, the termination of a contract extinguishes the *obligitio* because it brings to an end the relationship of contractual rights and obligations. But, as noted, the termination may only affect the contract to the extent of un-performed obligations. From this perspective, the termination will only make the contract ineffective from the date of the termination, but will not touch the effectiveness of the contract at the beginning.

The Contract Law provides a laundry list of causes justifying a termination of a contract. In accordance with Article 91 of the Contract Law, a contract is to be terminated under any of the following situations: (a) the obligations have been performed according to the terms of the contract, (b) the contract has been rescinded, (c) the obligations have been offset against each other, (d) the obligor has delivered the subject matter of the contract for an escrow under law, (e) the obligations have been exempted by the obligee, (f) the contractual rights and obligations have been integrated with the same person, or (g) there are other circumstances for termination as set forth in the law or agreed upon by the parties.[51]

As already discussed, Article 91 of the Contract Law lists rescission as a cause to terminate a contract. But because of its distinctive nature, recission is treated differently from termination based on other causes. In general, if a contract is terminated as result of rescission, the termination may retroactively affect the contract before the termination. In other words, with rescission, the restitution or non-performance damages that otherwise would not be available with termination may be sought.

More specifically, under Article 91 of the Contract Law, a contract can be terminated by performance, rescission, offset, deposit, exemption, assumption of both debts and credits, agreement of the parties, or operation of law. The legal effect of termination is to discharge all contractual obligations and extinguish the contract. But in China, there are at least two additional major effects that termination has on the contractual parties. The first effect is the right to seek for damages. Termination will not abrogate the right of a party to seek damages resulting from the breach of contract caused by the other party. On the contrary, under the Contract Law, after the termination, the aggrieved party is entitled to compensation for damages if the other party is found to have breached the contract.

In addition, if the contract contains terms for account settlement and clearance, the terms shall survive the termination, and remain effective. This rule is

---

51 See the Contract Law, art. 91.

also called the "settlement & clearance independence" rule, which is adopted in the Contract Law. Under Article 98 of the Contract Law, the termination of the rights and obligations of a contract may not affect the settlement and clearance clauses in the contract.[52] The same rule also applies to a dispute resolution clause, as to both litigation and arbitration, agreed upon by the parties.

The second effect concerns after-termination obligations. When a contract is terminated, the contractual relationship between the parties is extinguished. But in light of business interests, the parties are still required to bear certain obligations to each other. According to Article 92 of the Contract Law, when contractual rights and obligations are terminated, the parties to a contract shall under the good faith principle or transaction practices, perform such obligations as giving notice, providing assistance, as well as maintaining confidentiality.[53] Thus, notice, assistance, and confidentiality are three major obligations that the Contract Law imposes on the parties to a contract after the contract is terminated.

It has been argued, however, that after the termination of a contract, the remaining obligations are no longer contractual obligations because the contract has been extinguished. The question therefore is what the legal basis for imposition of after-termination obligations on the parties is. Put differently, it is a question about the cause of action that a party may rely on to sue the other party who fails to perform the after-termination obligations.

Under Article 92 of the Contract Law, after-termination obligations are premised on the good faith principle and transaction usages. Thus, a failure to perform such obligations is treated under the Contract Law as a violation of the good faith principle or transaction usages, which triggers certain liabilities. Despite Article 92, a different approach is to deem after-termination obligations as tort liabilities and to impose such liabilities in order to protect the parties' business interests from being infringed after the contract is terminated.

2.1 *Performance*

A contract is discharged after it has been fully performed. In China, for purposes of discharging contractual obligations, the performance is required to be appropriate, correct, and complete. A commonly used term that implicates full performance is "clear-off" of contractual obligations, or simply "pay-off." Once all contractual obligations are fulfilled as agreed, the relationship between the parties under the contract comes to an end.

---

52 See *id.*, art. 98.
53 See *id.*, art. 92.

"Appropriateness" means that the contract is being performed according to the conditions and terms agreed upon by the parties. It also means that the performance complies with the good faith principle or provisions of law where certain terms of the contract are not clearly defined. For example, under the Contract Law, if there exists ambiguity as to the place of performance or the time of performance, the ambiguity needs to be clarified under the good faith principle or the provision of law absent agreement of the parties.

"Correctness" requires that there be no defects in the performance. Normally, a contract is to be performed by the obligor to the obligee. But in terms of debt "clear-off," contractual obligations may be satisfied by the obligor. In certain cases, the performance can be made by a third party as long as the terms and conditions of the contract are met. From the obligee's point of view, what matters is whether the obligee's creditor interests will be realized. Thus, no matter who is going to fulfill the obligation, the realization of the obligee's creditor interests may be achieved only upon the completion of the performance. An exception to the third party performance is that the performance exclusively by the obligor is required.[54]

Additionally, to assure that performance is correct, the obligations should be cleared off by the delivery of the same items or services as agreed. However, there has been a discussion about whether the "clear-off" of obligations may be made by substitute items—for example, to pay off money debts by specific goods or the goods of a kind. A suggestion is that a substitute item should have the effect of satisfying the obligations as long as the substitute has the same value and is agreed by the obligee.[55]

"Completeness" means the satisfaction of the debts or achievement of the contract's purpose, by which the contract is terminated. According to many Chinese contract scholars, there is a slight difference between performance and "clear-off," though both are intended to realize the creditor's rights.[56] Performance is geared toward satisfying the creditor's rights in order to accomplish the purpose of the contract. "Clear-off" is aimed at discharging the contract (termination) through the satisfaction of the creditor's rights.[57] Indeed, it seems unclear what practical significance the difference would serve, but the

---

54   As noted, a contract may only be performed by the parties if (1) the third party's performance is prohibited by the agreement of the parties or (2) the nature of the contract precludes the performance by a third party.
55   See Dong Ling, *supra* note 11 at pp 179–180.
56   Few scholars deem "clear-off" to be legal fact, rather than conduct, because they believe that "clear-off" is a result of performance (e.g., delivery).
57   See Jiang Ping, *supra* note 31 at p 74.

idea is that for a contract to be terminated via performance, the performance must be fully complete.

2.2   Offset

Offset applies where the parties are mutually obligated to each other, and contractual obligations may be discharged to the amount that can be offset. To illustrate, if A owes B $1,000 for the goods B delivered, while B owes A $1,200 for the services A provided, the two debts may be offset because A and B are both obligee and obligor to each other. After the offset, the $1,000 debts A and B each owes to the other will be discharged, but B still owes $200 to A. An advantage to offsetting contractual obligations is the efficacy in clearing off contractual obligations.[58]

In addition to contracts, the offset in China is also used in the bankruptcy process. Under Article 33 of the Enterprise Bankruptcy Law of China (1986), if the creditor is liable for the debts of the enterprise in bankruptcy, the credits will be offset against the debts before the bankrupt clearance. The purpose is to prevent the occurrence of a dilemma that the party not in bankruptcy may face: it remains liable for the debts it owes to the bankrupted party, but it may have to realize its credit right through the process of bankruptcy depending ultimately on the availability of the assets left over from the bankrupted party.

The Contract Law adopts the offset mechanism and makes it a ground for the termination of a contract. As provided in the Contract Law, there are two kinds of offsets: offset by law and offset by agreement. Offset by law, also referred to as statutory offset, is one that meets the requirements of law and may be exercised through the operation of law. Under Article 99 of the Contract Law, where the parties to a contract have debts that are mutually due, and the type and character of the debts are the same, any party may offset his or her debts against the debts of the other party, except that such debts may not be offset pursuant to the provisions of the law or the nature of the contract.[59]

Article 99 of the Contract Law sets forth certain tests for application of statutory offset. The first test is mutuality. In order to offset, the obligations must be mutually owed by the contractual parties to each other. The second test is maturity. Offset obligations must be mutually owed as well as mutually due. If one party's obligation is due and the other is not, the two obligations can not

---

58   In China, some scholars view the offset to have the function of guaranteeing performance of the contract. The reason is that since the parties are both obligee and obligor to each other, the creditor right of one party would be safeguarded by his obligations owed to the other party, and *vice versa*.

59   See the Contract Law, art. 99.

be offset. The third test is identity. Identity requires that the obligations to be offset must be in the same category and have the same character (i.e., quality). For example, if the parties owe money to each other, those monetary debts can be offset because they are regarded as in the same category and being the same quality.[60] The fourth test is permissibility. If the obligations are not permitted to be offset either by the "provisions of the law" or by the "nature of contract," no offset is allowed.[61]

If all the above tests are met, any party may initiate the offset of the contractual obligations. But the Contract Law requires that the initiating party manifest his intent to offset by giving a notice to the other party. Under Article 99 of the Contact Law, a party advancing to offset the debts shall notify the other party, and notice shall take effect upon arrival at the other party. In addition, Article 99 provides that the offset may not be accompanied by any conditions or time limits. Thus, the Article 99 offset is a unilateral conduct of the initiating party and becomes effective when the notice of the offset is received. The preclusion of conditions and time limits derives from the unilateral character of the statutory offset because pursuant to Article 99, the statutory offset can be initiated by any party and the effectiveness of the offset as such is not dependent on the other party's assent but the arrival of offset notice at the other party. In addition, the manifestation of the intent to offset need to be certain and becomes operative as long as the legal requirements are met.

The offset may also be made by the agreement of the parties. According to Article 100 of the Contract Law, where the parties to a contract have mutual debts and the type and character of the debts are different, the debts may be offset against each other if the parties reach a consensus through negotiation. Obviously, consensual offset under Article 100 is less restrictive than statutory offset in terms of requirements. In consensual offset, the debt obligations in question may differ in type and character. In addition, maturity is not an

---

60 This matter will become more complicated if two non-monetary "things" are involved. If the two "things" both are specific items, such as the antiques, they may not be offset because they are unique and each could not be replaced. If the two things are the items of a kind, there may be an offset if they are in the same quality.

61 Generally, the obligations that may not be offset by the provisions of the law include, among others, (a) the debts for which the payment may not be coercively enforced—e.g., the debtor's money or assets that are necessity for living or family support; (b) wrongdoer's obligations arising from intentional torts; (c) the obligations that ought to be performed to a third party; and (d) the obligations serving the third party's interest. See Dong Ling, *supra* note 11 at pp 227–228. Some scholars also suggest that uncertain or conditional creditor rights should not be offset until the rights become certain or the conditions are met.

element in consensual offset, and thus a debt obligation that is due may be offset against the one that is not due, or two undue debt obligations may also be offset against each other under the agreement of the parties.

In practice, consensual offset may take different forms. The parties may offset their mutual debt obligations through an agreement that is separated from their contract. The parties may also include a provision or clause in their contract that sets the terms or conditions under which the parties' mutual debts may be offset. Of course, the parties may through their contract prohibit consensual offset of mutual obligations. In consensual offset, the parties often set forth procedures and accounting measures for conducting the offset. In sales contracts, for example, it is quite common that the parties agree to periodically offset their mutual debts obligations (i.e., delivery of goods and payments), and after the offset, whoever still owes a fraction of debts to the other party need only satisfy fractional debts.

2.3   Deposit

In the context of the Contract Law, deposit is a legal device by which an obligor may submit or deliver the unperformed contractual obligations or the subject matter of the contract to designated government authorities for an "escrow" so that the obligor's corresponding contractual obligation will be discharged.[62] Deposit is deemed necessary because in certain cases, for reasons beyond its control, the obligor may encounter difficulties in fulfilling its debt obligations under the contract. One situation is that the obligee refuses to accept the performance without a reasonable ground or justification.

The primary purpose of depositing the debt obligation or the subject matter of the contract with government agencies is to protect the legitimate interest of the obligor. Without such a device, the obligor would always be liable for unperformed obligations even when performance becomes extremely difficult for a cause attributable to the obligee. Since completion of the deposit directly results in the termination of a contract, the use of the deposit is limited to the situation in which the obligor is left with no meaningful way to perform.

Thus, in order to help release the obligor from remaining liable for the performance in the case where there is no way for the obligor to perform, the Contract Law allows the obligor to deposit the subject matter of the contract in the situation where the obligations are difficult to perform. Note that "difficult"

---

62   It differs from the regular escrow because deposit as used in the Contract Law is a legal means to hold the subject matter of the contract—e.g., payment—in the hands of government egency while escrow is generally an contractual arrangment in which a sum is kept in the custody of a third party on behalf of transacting parties.

as used in the Contract Law refers to the circumstances where the obligor is capable and willing to perform, but for certain reasons the performance cannot be conducted without the obligor's fault. The underlying rationale for having in deposit the subject matter of the contract is to help keep the interests of the parties to a contract fairly balanced.

To make a deposit of contractual obligations, there must be a legal ground as mandated by the law. In China, the deposit rule was officially adopted first by the Supreme People's Court in 1988 when the SPC issued its "Opinions (Provisional) on Several Matters Concerning Application of the General Principles of the Civil Law." According to the SPC, if the obligee, without good reasons, refuses to accept the performance of the obligor, the obligor may submit the subject matter or the object of the performance to a relevant authority for deposit, and after the deposit the obligations of the obligor shall be deemed to have been performed.[63] The SPC made it clear that the deposit has the effect of terminating a contract and the obligee's refusal of the obligor's performance without just cause is a legal ground for the deposit.

The Contract Law adopts the deposit rule in a way that reflects both the SPC's opinion and judicial practices. Article 101 of the Contract Law provides a number of statutory grounds by which the obligor may request a deposit. But no matter what ground it may be, the underlying notion is that the difficulty of performance is caused by the obligee, for which the obligor shall not be held liable. Once again, after the deposit, the contract is terminated.

Under Article 101, in any of the following circumstances, if the debt obligations are difficult to perform, the obligor may deposit its debt obligation:

> (a) the obligee refuses to accept the performance without justified reasons; (b) the obligee is missing; (c) the obligee is deceased and the inheritor is not yet determined or the obligee lost his civil conduct capacity and the guardian is not yet ascertained; or (d) other situations as provided by law.[64]

The obligee's refusal to accept performance without a justified reason normally involves the situation where the obligee should, and is able to, accept the performance, but refuses to do so. But the prerequisite for a deposit is that the obligor make the performance exactly according to the terms and conditions of the contract. If the obligee has the right to refuse to accept the

---

63   See, Supreme People's Court, "*Opinions (Provisional) on Several Matters Concerning Application of the General Principles of the Civil Law*" 1988, art. 104.
64   See the Contract Law, art. 101.

performance—e.g., the performance is improper or incomplete—the deposit rule will not apply.

It should be pointed out that under the Contract Law, refusal to accept performance implies a delay in acceptance. As a matter of fact, in the daft contract law, "refusal to accept" was actually defined as "delay in acceptance." The term later was rephrased as "refusal to accept performance without justified reason" when the Contract Law was adopted.[65] Thus, as some scholars explained, refusal to accept performance without justified reason as used in the Contract Law will necessarily lead to a delay in acceptance of performance. Put differently, the inevitable outcome of refusal to accept is delay in acceptance.[66]

A question that has been raised concerning the refusal to accept performance is whether the obligor may request a deposit when the obligee is anticipated to repudiate the contract (namely to refuse to accept the obligor's performance). A commonly accepted position is that a deposit shall not apply to anticipatory repudiation. The major reason is that deposit becomes relevant only when the performance is due, and the main theme of deposit is to help the obligor overcome the difficulty in performance caused by the obligee.[67] Therefore, even if the obligee has expressly stated that it will not accept performance before performance becomes due, the obligor's right to make the deposit will not arise until the due day for the performance passes.

Circumstances where the obligee is missing includes lack of information about the identity and address of the obligee, lost contact with the obligee, or total disappearance of the obligee. There are three related issues that are deemed important to determine whether there is a missing obligee to justify the deposit requested by the obligor. The first issue concerns the agent (including trustee or estate administrator) of the obligee. If the obligee itself is completely out of touch, but its agent is still available, the performance can be made to the agent of the obligee. In this case the performance of the contract by the obligor will not be considered difficult and therefore no request for deposit shall be permitted.

The second issue is the cause of the missing of the obligee. The obligor shall not commit any fault contrubuting to the missing of the obligee. If the obligee is missing as a result of the conduct of the obligor or his employees, the obligor is not entitled to the deposit. For example, if the obligee dissapeared when

---

65   See Sun Lihai, *Selection of Legislative Materials of the Contract Law of China*, 57 (Law Publishing House, 1999).
66   See Dong Ling, *supra* note 11 at p 237.
67   See Wang Liming, *supra* note 1 at p 336.

encountering a threat imposed by the obligor or his employees, the obligor may not seek to discharge its obligations through the deposit.[68]

The third issue involves the legal declaration of the missing obligee. If the obligee is deemed missing, there are two different views on whether the request for deposit should be granted. One view is that the status of the missing person must be determined through a legal proceeding and declared by the court. Therefore, in the case where the obligee is claimed to have been missing, no deposit shall be allowed until the obligee is declared to be missing by the court. The other view seems less restrictive. It argues that since the deposit is based on the difficulty in performance, the obligor shall have the right to request for the deposit regardless of the court declaration of the missing obligee as long as it can be proved that there is no way to find the obligee.

A harder question is the time for the obligor to make the deposit. This is a question about how long the obligor has to wait before the deposit can be requested when the whereabouts of the obligee are unknown. The Contract Law contains no provision on the matter of timing for the deposit. But for a person to be declared missing by the court, there is a statutory requirement of two years under the 1986 Civil Code. Article 20 of the 1986 Civil Code provides that if a citizen's whereabouts have been unknown for two years, an interested person may apply to a people's court for a declaration of the citizen as missing.

There is a belief, however, that since the deposit is provided in the Contract Law as a means to terminate a contract when the whereabouts of the obligee are unknown is not necessarily subject to a judicial determination that the obligee is missing, the two-year requirement does not apply. Instead, as it has already been the case in the practice, the deposit can be requested if the obligee cannot be found within a "reasonable period of time" during or after the performance period. The reasonableness of the time period often depends on the nature of transactions or trade customs.

A request for deposit may also be justified if the successor or guardian of the obligee cannot be ascertained when the obligee dies or loses capacity for civil conduct. To allow a deposit in this situation is based on the notion that the death or loss of capacity for civil conduct does not lead to the extinguishment of debt obligations. It is quite common that upon the death of the obligee,

---

68 As discussed in Chapter 8, according to Article 70 of the Contract Law, if the obligee does not notify the obligor of its separation, merger, or change of domicile, which makes it difficult for the obligor to perform the obligations, the obligor may suspend the performance or submit the object of the contract to relative authority for deposit. It is clear under Article 70 that the reason that cause the whereabouts of the obligee to be unknown must be something for which the obligee shall be blamed.

the performance of the debt obligations shall be made to the obligee's heir or appointed successor, and in the case of the obligee's loss of civil conduct capacity, the performance shall be made to the guardian of that obligee. However, if the successor cannot be identified after the death of the obligee or the guardian cannot be determined after the obligee lost its civil conduct capacity, the obligor may request a deposit in order to have the debt obligations timely discharged.

Uncertainty of heirs (successors) of a deceased obligee may arise in a couple of situations. One situation is that after the death of the obligee, there appear several successors who claim to be entitled to the deceased obligee's creditor right, and then the obligor has the difficulty to figure out to whom the performance shall be made. The other situation is where both the obligee and its heirs (or successors) die, and there is no feasible way for the obligor to determine who is the correct person to receive the performance. Normally, these multiple deaths will be followed by a judicial presumption of the sequence of the deaths in order to identify the eligible and legitimate successor(s).[69]

In many cases, a difficulty arises in designating a guardian for an incapable obligee. On the one hand, the range of persons who are eligible to become the guardian is very broad. According to Article 17 of the 1986 Civil Code, those who may serve as a guardian for mentally ill persons without capacity for civil conduct include (a) spouses, (b) parents, (c) adult children, (d) other close relatives, or (e) other related relatives or qualified friends. In practice, there always exist disputes over who should be the guardian.[70] On the other hand, if there is no legal (statutory) guardian or there is a dispute over the guardianship,

---

69   In its "Opinions in the Matters Concerning Application of the Succession Law of China," the Supreme People's Court offered special guidance for determining successors in the case of multiple deaths. Article 2 of the Opinions provides: "when several people who have inherent relationship to each other die in the same incident, if the time of the death one after another could not be determined, the person who has no heirs should be assumed to have died first; if the deceased each has heirs and each is in the different generation of the family, the elder member of the family should be assumed to have died first; If the decedents are all in the same generation, they should be assumed to have died simultaneously, and no succession will take place among them, but their each heirs will inherit them respectively."

70   As has been observed from judicial practice, disputes over the appointment of guardians include the following: (1) disputes among the deceased's relatives at the different levels of family relation who argue against each other for the guardian; (2) disputes among the relatives in the different levels of family relations who each tries to shift the guardianship responsibility onto the other; and (3) disputes among the family members either where all want to become the guardian or where all refuse to become the guardian. See Li Guoguang, *supra* note 20 at pp 392–393.

a guardian should be appointed. The appointment of the guardian has to go through certain legal processes, which takes time. [71]

The other circumstances under which a deposit can be made refers to the situations authorized by the law. One example is the Guaranty Law where a number of provisions permit a deposit. For instance, under Article 49 of the Guaranty Law, the proceeds obtained by the mortgager through transfer of the mortgaged property shall first be used to liquidate the claim secured by the mortgage or it shall be deposited with a third party agreed upon by the mortgagee. Another example is the Rules of Notarization of Deposit adopted by the Ministry of Justice on June 2, 1995. One of the situations where a deposit may be notarized under the Rules is that the parties agree in their contract to make payment in the form of a deposit.[72]

Still, there are certain questions concerning deposits. A significant question is what can be deposited. The terminology used in the Contract Law is "the object of the obligations" (or the subject matter of the contract), which seems ambiguous. A scholarly interpretation is that the object of obligations in the context of deposit mainly includes monetary items and other things suitable for deposit. Under the Rules of Notarization of Deposit, the items that may be deposited are currency, negotiable instrument, valuable notes, bill of lading, certificate of rights, precious articles, collaterals (money) or substitutes, and other items appropriate for deposit.

The items that are not regarded as suitable for deposit mainly involve those that are perishable or fast depreciable, such as food products. In addition, the deposit will also be deemed unsuitable if the costs for the deposit are too high. Under Article 101 of the Contract Law, if the object is not fit for deposit or the deposit expenses are excessively high, the obligor may auction or sell the object and deposit the proceeds obtained therefrom.[73] According to the SPC, if

---

71 Under Article 17 of the Civil Code, in the case of a dispute over guardianship, the work unit of the incapable person or the neighborhood or village committee of the incapable person's residence shall appoint a guardian among the person's close relatives. If a disagreement over the appointment leads to a lawsuit, the people's court shall make a ruling.
72 This practice seems like the creation of escrow account for the purpose of payment.
73 A dispute over the object of deposit is whether real property could be deposited. One view is that real property may not be deposited because of the immovable nature of the real property. When the obligee refuses to accept the real property, the obligor may not request deposit but may abandon it. The opposite view argues that the purpose of deposit is to end the debts relation between obligee and obligor, and thus the deposit shall not be denied as to real property because the real property cannot be moved, but can be sealed for purposes of deposit.

the obligor submits for deposit the proceeds from the auction or sales of the object of the contract, the deposit shall be deemed effective.[74]

Another question is the authority with which the deposit shall be made. The Contract Law does not identify the authority, but under the Rules of Notarization of Deposit, the notary public office is designated as the authority to accept deposit. Article 2 of the Rules provides that deposit notarization is the activity to take care of or take custody of the object of the debts or guarantees (including substitutes) submitted by the obligor or guarantor for the benefit of the obligee, and to return them to the obligee when required conditions are met.[75]

Relying on the provisions of the Rules of Notarization of the Deposit, many in China believe that the only authority designated for taking the deposit is the notary public office. Some, however, argue that despite the Rules, deposit authority includes those appointed by the court, such as a bank, trust institution, or warehouse. The notion is that the court has the discretionary power to appoint an authority for purposes of deposit.

To make the deposit, the obligor needs to make the first request with all supporting documents. When approved by the deposit authority, the obligor shall submit what would be deposited. After the submission, the obligor will obtain a certificate of deposit. The certificate will have an evidential effect that releases the obligor from its debt obligations. Under the opinion of the SPC, when the deposit takes effect, the obligor shall be deemed to have performed the obliations to the extent of the deposited object.[76]

However, in order to make the deposit effective, the obligor must satisfy the requirement of notice. According to Article 102 of the Contract Law, after the object is deposited, the obligor shall, except for the missing obligee, promptly send a notice to the obligee or the obligee's heir or guardian. Without such a notice, the deposit will be treated to have no effect.[77] If the deposit is not effective, the obligor shall remain liable for the performance of the obligation under the contract.

The primary legal consequence of the deposit, as discussed, is to free the obligor from its obligations to the obligee. Therefore, after a valid deposit, the obligee will have no claim against the obligor with regard to the obligations in question. Then, any request from the obligee in order to satisfy its creditor rights may only be made to the deposit authority other than the obligor.

74　See the SPC, the 2009 Contract Law Interpretation, art. 25.
75　See the Rules of Notarization of Deposit, art. 2.
76　See the SPC, the 2009 Contract Law Interpretation, art. 25.
77　See the Contract Law, art. 103.

Also, after the deposit is made, the burden of risk concerning the deposited object is shifted from the obligor to the obligee. Article 103 of the Contract Law provides that the risk of damage to, and loss of, the object after deposit shall be borne by the obligee. On the other hand, however, Article 103 requires that during the period of deposit, all interests accrued from the object deposited shall belong to the obligee. In addition, under Article 103, the obligee is responsible for all expenses related to the deposit.[78]

Keep in mind that the deposit as provided in the Contract Law shall by no means deprive the obligee of its rights to or interests in the deposited object. It is clear in Article 104 of the Contract Law that the obligee may claim the deposited object at any time. But such a claim by the obligee is not unconditional. Article 104 explicitly states that if the obligee is under a debt due to the obligor, at the obligor's request, the deposit authority shall deny the obligee's claim unless and until the obligee has performed its debt obligations or has provided a guaranty to its performance.[79]

Equally important is the statute of limitations on the obligee's right to claim the deposited object. Although the obligee's right to claim the deposited object remains after the deposit, the right will be lost if not exercised after a certain period of time. As Article 104 mandates, the claim to the deposited object must be made within five years after the date of deposit. A deposited object that is not claimed after the five-year time period expires shall become the property of the States minus the deposit expenses.[80]

2.4 *Exemption*

The obligations of the obligor to a contract may be exempted by the obligee in whole or in part, and after the exemption, the obligations are discharged with regard to the amount that has been exempted. Article 105 of the Contract Law provides that if the obligee exempts the obligor from its debt obligations wholly or in part, the whole or part of the rights and obligations of the contract shall be terminated.[81] Essentially, exemption of contract obligations occurs when the obligee willfully gives up or abandons its right to the performance of the obligations, and as a result the obligations so exempted are extinguished.

There are certain conditions that must be met for an exemption. First of all, an exemption must be voluntarily manifested by the obligee eligible to depose of the right to the performance of the obligations. The eligibility means

---

78   See *id.*
79   See *id.*, art. 104.
80   See *id.*
81   See *id.*, art. 105.

that the obligee has full civil capacity and his or her creditor right is free from any claims. For example, if the obligee is a minor or mentally retarded, the exemption must be made with the consent of his or her agent *ad litem*. Note that in China, an exemption of contractual obligations is regarded as unilateral conduct of the obligee, and therefore, the obligor's consent to the exemption is irrelevant.

Secondly, the manifestation of exemption must be made to the obligor. Through exemption the obligee forgives the obligor's obligations. Thus, if exemption is manifested to a third party, it will have no effect to the obligor and the obligor shall remain liable for the fulfillment of the obligations. With regard to the formality of exemption, the Contract Law contains no requirement as to whether the exemption must be made in writing. An inference is that as long as the exemption is manifested, it does not matter if the manifestation is made in writing or orally.

What seems disputable, however, is whether a manifestation of exemption can be implied from the obligee's conduct. For instance, assume that the obligee makes a loan to the obligor, and at the time repayment is due, the obligee does not ask for repayment but instead returns the receipt of the loan to the obligor. It is reasonable to hold that the return of the loan receipt manifests the obligee's intention to cancel the debt. In that case, the remaining debts will be considered to have been exempted.

Thirdly, an exemption may not be made as a bargain with the obligor. To exempt the debt obligations, the obligee may not ask the obligor for something in return. If the existing obligations are to be taken away from the obligor in exchange for other obligations to be imposed on the obligor or in exchange for certain value, there will be no exemption. The exchange will rather be deemed to be a modification of the contract or a substitute performance.

However, some suggest that the reason for the exemption may be a result of a bargain.[82] To illustrate, if the obligee reaches an agreement with a third party, pursuant to which the third party will exempt the obligor from its obligations on the condition that the obligee will be compensated by the third party, the exemption will be upheld even though there is a bargain between the obligee and the third party. But note again that, in order to be effectuated, the exemption must be manifested to the obligor by the obligee. In plain language, the obligee must tell the obligor that the obligations are exempted even if a deal (i.e., bargain) for the exemption is being made between the obligee and a third party.

---

82   See Dong Ling, *supra* note 11 at p 249.

Fourthly, the exemption may not affect the interests of a third party. Often third party interests will be involved when the creditor's rights in question have been pledged as security. The rule is that if the creditor rights of the obligee are encumbered with a security interest, such rights may not be given up without the consent of the holder of the security interest. Thus, the obligee may not exempt the obligor if the exemption will have an adverse impact on the third party's interest. For the same reason, the obligations of the obligor may not be exempted if the obligee is in bankruptcy.

An interesting question is whether a manifestation of exemption, once made, may be revoked. This question has not received much discussion, but in practice the courts tend to hold the manifestation of exemption irrevocable.[83] What seems problematical in this regard is whether the reaction of the obligor might need to be considered with regard to the revocability of the manifestation of exemption. But it would appear to be reasonable to allow the obligee to retract the manifestation if (a) the obligor has not received the manifestation; or (b) after receiving the manifestation, the obligor has not relied on the manifestation by detrimentally changing the obligor's position.

2.5 Merger

In light of contract termination, a merger means that the contractual rights and obligations are assumed by the same person as a result of consolidation of the parties or combination of contractual rights and obligations. One situation where a merger occurs is where the obligee and obligor in a contract become the same party through business restructuring (e.g. M&A). In the process of a restructuring, contractual rights and obligations are typically consolidated and the former debtor and creditor are integrated.

Another situation in which a merger of rights and obligations takes place is succession, by which the deceased is the creditor or debtor of the successor, or the decedents are the creditor and debtor to each other and they both are succeeded by the same person. As a result of the succession, the creditor's rights and debt obligations are combined and the successor becomes both the creditor and the debtor. Given this combination, the previously existing obligations or debts are assumed by one person, which renders the continuing performance meaningless.

---

83   Many judges in the SPC prefer to hold that the obligee's manifestation of intent to give up creditor rights shall not be retracted. The reason underlying this position is that the exemption is a unilateral act of the obligee and will take effect after it is manifested to the obligor, and therefore, once the manifestation is made, it becomes irrevocable. See Li Guoguang, supra note 48 at p 412.

Also a situation involving a merger of contractual rights and obligations is assignment in a contract. When creditor rights are assigned by the obligee to the obligor or the debt obligations of the obligor are assumed by the obligee, the contractual rights and obligations are combined to fall on the shoulder of one person. After the assignment, there will be no need for the assignee to perform the corresponding obligations he or she has assumed because the assignee becomes both the creditor and the debtor to the same obligations.

Thus, when contractual rights and obligations are combined or consolidated to be in the hands of the same person, the contractual relationship comes to an end. Consequently, the contract is terminated. This so-called "the merger rule" is provided in Article 106 of the Contract Law. Under Article 106, if the creditor's rights and debtor's obligations of a contract are assumed the same person, the rights and obligations of the contract shall be terminated.[84]

However, as an exception, the application of the merger rule may not inflict harm on the interests of a third party.[85] Therefore, if a third party interest is at stake, a merger of contractual rights and obligations will not lead to a termination of the contract. For example, if the creditor right of the contract is pledged to a third party as the security for a debt, the pledged creditor right shall remain intact despite the integration. In addition, a merger may also not affect the contractual obligations if so provided by law.

There appear to be several views on the nature of the merger for the purpose of contract termination. One view is called "impossibility." According to the impossibility approach, a merger will not result in the extinguishment of a contract, but will only render the performance of the contract impossible because of the merger of the obligor and obligee.[86] Another view is based on the theory of "clearance." This view argues that when contractual rights and obligations are assumed by the same person, the debts will be cleared up against the creditor, and the contract is then settled.[87] The third view focuses on "achievement of purpose." It emphasizes that the purpose of a contract is to perform the obligations whereby the creditor rights will be satisfied, and a merger of contractual rights and obligations has the effect of both performance and satisfaction. Thus, after merger the contract is terminated, because the purpose of the contract has been achieved.[88]

---

84 See the Contract Law, art. 106.
85 See *id.*
86 See Jiang Ping, *supra* note 31 at 88.
87 See Han Shiyuan, the Law of Contract (3rd Ed), 578 (Law Press, 2011).
88 See Jiang Ping, *supra* note 31 at 88.

In this spectrum there is also a view that a merger of debt and credit kills the creditor right because nobody may have a creditor right against himself. This view may be best described as the doctrine of "mutuality of contractual rights and obligations." Under this doctrine, there must be at least two parties to a contract, and each must have rights or obligations as to the other. Therefore, after the rights and obligations are assumed by the same person as a result of merger, it legally makes no sense to keep the contract alive.[89] This doctrine has been very well received and is also the underlying rationale of Article 106 of the Contract Law.[90]

---

89   See Wang Liming, *supra* note 1 at 348–349.
90   See *id.*

CHAPTER 10

Breach of Contracts and Remedies

The parties to a contract that is legally enforceable are mutually obligated to perform their respective obligations arising from the contract. A failure to perform without justification will constitute a breach of the contract for which the breaching party will be held liable. In the case of a breach, damages will be assessed and legal remedies available to the aggrieved party will be applied against the damages. Although the remedies for breach of contract can be a broad topic, the basic forms of remedies include monetary compensation and non-monetary relief. In either form, there are also different types or categories, depending on the nature of the breach.

1   Liability for Breach: a Chinese Concept

In China, a heavily discussed concept concerning the remedies for breach of contract is "liability for breach," a concept that is deemed native to China.[1] Generally, liability for breach is defined as civil liability that is derived from a violation of a contractual obligation or a failure to render the performance that is due under a contract. Thus, once a breach occurs, liability arises. The basic notion is that liability will be sought or imposed as result of the breach.

With respect to the question of how to define liability for breach, scholars in China take different views. One view is that liability for breach is the legal consequence that a party must face if the party fails to perform his or her obligations under a contract. Another view deems liability for breach as the responsibility of the breaching party to compensate the aggrieved party for damages suffered. A third view characterizes liability for breach as a legal sanction against the breaching party and thus treats the liability as a punishment imposed on the breaching party. A fourth view considers liability for breach to be a legal guarantee for the performance of the contract. The reason is that if a party defaults in performance, the other party may ask the court to enforce its contractual rights.[2]

---

1   See Xing Ying, *Liabilities for Breach of Contract*, 4 (China Legal System Press, 1999).
2   See *id.*, at pp 5–7.

Despite the differences in the views regarding liability for breach, it is widely acknowledged in China that liability for breach of a contract is governed by two basic rules. These two rules are also deemed to have fundamental impacts on the remedies available under Chinese contract law and in judicial practice. The first rule is the liability rule. Under this rule, a person shall be held legally liable as a matter of law for a failure to fulfill what he or she is obligated to do or not to do under a contract. The best example to illustrate this rule is Article 106 of the 1986 Civil Code. This provision provides that citizens and legal persons who breach a contract or fail to fulfill other obligations shall bear civil liabilities.[3] Similarly, under Article 176 of the 2017 GPCL, the parties to civil legal relations shall perform their civil obligations and assume civil liabilities in accordance with the provisions of laws and the agreements of the parties.[4]

Both Article 106 of the 1986 Civil Code and Article 176 of the 2017 GPCL suggest that imposition of liability ensures the fulfillment of obligations. An implication is that liability and obligation are two different concepts. Chinese contract scholars have also made efforts to differentiate between liability and obligation. In general, an obligation is defined as an engagement that a party is required to make either pursuant to law or under a contract, while liability is defined as a consequence that requires a party that has failed to fulfill its obligations to either continue performing or take other remedial action.[5] Therefore, liability is not simply an obligation, but rather, is the legal ramification facing the breaching party in case of breach of contract or failure to perform.[6]

The second rule is the rule of liability imputation. Liability imputation is the process of determining whether and to what extent the breaching party shall be responsible for the breach of the contract. In actual cases, if a party is alleged to have breached a contract, two questions must be answered before any liability is to be imposed. The first question is whether the breach is caused by the party in question. This is a question of causation. The second question is whether the liability shall be imposed on the party who is found to be in breach. This is a question of liability.

Two elements of the rule of liability imputation concern causation and liability. The rule of liability imputation requires that civil liability be imposed on a breaching party for what the party should be legally blamed. Thus, imputation means that if a party is found to be in breach of a contract, the extent to which the party should be held liable will be determined with regard to the

---

3   See the 1986 Civil Code, art. 106.
4   See the 2017 GPCL, art. 176.
5   See Cui Jianyuan, *Studies on Contractual Liabilities*, 3 (Ji Lin People's Publishing House, 1992).
6   See Wang Liming, *Study on Contract Law (Vol. II)*, 381 (People's University Press, 2003).

scope and the nature of the breach. In China, the rule of liability imputation is deemed to be of great significance in the determination of the liability for breach of a contract. Different approaches have developed as to the application of the liability imputation rule.

2 Liability Imputation

In Chinese contract law theory, there are two basic approaches commonly employed to impute civil liabilities. The two approaches, which constitute two basic standards for determining liability, are fault liability and non-fault liability. The major difference between these two approaches is whether the element of fault is required for the finding of liability. At the core is the issue of burden of proof.

The "fault" approach is centered on fault. It holds that a party who fails to perform the contract is not responsible in damages unless the party is found at fault. Under the "fault" approach, the imposition of liability is not simply based on the fact that a contract was breached; rather, liability is contingent upon on a finding of fault of the breaching party. The liability of the party who breaches the contract is therefore to be determined in consideration of both the breaching conduct and the underlying fault of the party in breach.

The non-fault liability approach, by contrast, does not require the presence of the fault in order to impose liability. It allows a party to claim damages if the other party fails to fulfill his or her contractual obligations regardless of fault. Pursuant to the non-fault liability approach, if the performance of a contract is due, any non-performance constitutes a breach and the fault on the breaching party is irrelevant. Since the non-fault liability approach makes no inquiry when determining liability into whether there is fault, it is often called a strict liability approach, a doctrine commonly used in torts law.

The rule of liability imputation is widely discussed among Chinese scholars with respect to the issues involving breach of contract. The rule is considered to have great impact on liability for breach in many aspects. In one aspect, the liability imputation rule prescribes what is needed to ascertain the liability for breach. For example, if the fault standard is applied, the fault of the breaching party must present in order to hold the breaching party liable. Another aspect, as noted, is the burden of proof. Under the non-fault liability standard, the aggrieved party only needs to prove the facts of breach, without specifying whether the breaching party is actually at fault or not. The fault standard, however, puts on the shoulder of the aggrieved party the burden to prove the fault of the breaching party.

Moreover, the liability imputation rule may also affect the excuses for non-performance. If the fault of the breaching party is a required element for imposing liabilities, the breaching party may be excused if it can be proved that the non-performance did not result from the fault of the breaching party. In addition, the liability imputation rule affects the scope of damages. Under the fault standard, damages are limited to what was predicted or ought to have been predicted by the breaching party at the time of the contract. If both parties are at fault, damages are determined with consideration of the degree of the fault of each party.[7]

The Contract Law on its face is quite vague about what standard of liability for breach it actually adopts. Before the Contract Law was enacted, the fault standard was generally considered to be the primary standard to determine civil liabilities in China.[8] Although this general view is subject to debate, the legislative history of the 1986 Civil Code revealed the intent of the legislature in this regard. When the draft civil code was submitted to the National People's Congress (NPC) for vote, the Standing Committee of the NPC, in its explanation to the draft, explicitly stated that the primary standard for determining civil liability in China was the principle of fault, and therefore civil liabilities were imposed only on those who were found at fault.[9]

Although the general inference in China was, and still is, that the fault standard is the underlying theme of the 1986 Civil Code,[10] Article 111 of the 1986 Civil Code, some have argued, does not seem to make fault a key element for civil liability imputation. Under Article 111, if a party fails to fulfill its contractual obligations or the fulfillment does not conform to the agreed terms in the contract, the other party has the right to demand performance or to take remedial measures and also has the right to claim compensation for losses.[11]

---

7   For general discussion, see Wang Liming, *id.*, at p 412–413. Another view is that the liability imputation principle may determine the means of damages, and that liquidated damages are the primary means for compensating damages under the negligence standard. See Li Guoguang, *Explanation and Application of the Contract Law*, 418–419 (Xinghua Press, 1999).
8   Article 29 of the 1993 Economic Law provided that if, due to the fault of one party, an economic contract cannot be performed or cannot be fully performed, the party at fault shall be liable for breach of the contract.
9   See Gu Angran, *Talks on Contract Law of China*, 44–46 (Law Publishing House, 1999).
10 For example, Article 106 of the 1986 Civil Code provides: "Citizens and legal persons who through their fault encroach upon State or collective property, or the property or person of other people shall bear civil liability. If stipulated by law, the civil liability shall still be imposed in the absence of fault." See the 1986 Civil Code of China, art. 106.
11 See *id.*, art 111.

The Contract Law also contains a provision that appears to be quite controversial pertaining to the standard of the liability for breach. Article 107 provides that, when a contracting party fails to perform its obligations under a conract or performs in a way that does not conform with the contract's terms and conditions, the party shall bear such liabilities for breach of contract as being required to continue performing the contract, to take remedial measures, or to compensate for losses.[12] The language of Article 107 is not hard to understand, but the issue behind Article 107 is whether it has actually abandoned the fault approach and adopted the non-fault liability approach instead.

The opinion at one extreme of the spectrum is that Article 107 of the Contract Law implicitly adopts the non-fault liability rule for contracts. Therefore, adherents to this opinion argue, the import of Article 107 is that an obligor, regardless of fault, bears liability for breach of contract if the obligor fails to perform its contractual obligations or performs in a manner that does not conform to the terms or conditions of the contract.[13] Proponents of this view further argue that the imposition of non-fault liability can also be seen in Articles 65 and 121 of the Contract Law, which deal with cases involving third parties.[14]

Under Article 65, where the parties agree to have a third party perform the contractual obligations to the obligee, and the third party fails to perform or the performance does not meet the terms of the contract, the obligor shall be liable to the obligee for breach of the contract. Article 121 provides that a party whose breach of contract is caused by a third party shall be liable for the breach to the other party; the dispute between the breaching party and the third party shall be settled according to the law or their agreement. A belief is that in both Article 65 and Article 121, the fault of either the contracting party or the third party is not an element for the imposition of liability.[15]

At the other extreme is the argument that the Contract Law is still within the system of the 1986 Civil Code, and the tradition of basing civil liabilities on the principle of fault persists.[16] A concern underlying this argument seems to be that changing the civil liability standard from the fault to non-fault standard will not only cause confusion among the judges who became accustomed to the concept of fault, but also create inconsistencies with the 1986 Civil Code. Subscribers to this argument contend that as a matter of fact, the Contract Law

---

12 See the Contract Law, art. 107.
13 See Han Shiyuan, the Law of Contract (3rd ed), 591–592 (Law Press 2011).
14 See *id.*, at 596–598.
15 See *id.*, at 597–598.
16 See Wang Liming, *supra* note 6 at 426–428.

upholds the fault principle in a number of areas such as pre-contractual liability, reasonably foreseeable losses or risks, mitigation rules, burden of risks, and the like.[17]

Between the two extremes is the opinion that the Contract Law in fact combines the fault and the non-fault liability standards as part of a developing trend. According to this opinion, the Contract Law in principle has departed from the traditional notion of fault, and has adopted non-fault liability as the primary standard for determining the liability for a breach.[18] This change, advocates of the opinion claim, reflects the need to follow the mainstream with respect to the practices of international business transactions. In this regard, the Contract Law is said to have followed the non-fault liability standard as used in both the United Nations Convention on Contracts for International Sale of Goods and UNIDROIT Principles of International Commercial Contracts.[19]

The majority view is that although the Contract Law designates non-fault liability as the major liability form for breach of contract, it does not abandon the fault approach embedded in the 1986 Civil Code. To the contrary, the Contract Law contains many rules that are fault-based.[20] For example, under Article 189 of the Contract Law, if in a donation contract the donated property

---

17   See *id.*
18   See Wang Linming, Contract Law of China, 217 (Wells, 2016).
19   For example, according to Article 7.4.1 of the Principles of International Commercial Contracts, any non-performance gives the aggrieved party a right to damages either exclusively or in conjunction with any other remedies, except where the non-performance is excused under these Principles. A similar provision can be seen in Article 45 of the International Sale of Goods, which provides that (1) if the seller fails to perform any of his or her obligations under the contract, the buyer may (a) exercise the rights provided in Articles 46 to 52; or (b) claim damages as provided in Articles 74–77. By this language, the Convention is said to have rejected the fault principle. See John Honnold, *Uniform Law for International Sales* (3rd ed), 276–277 (Kluwer Law International, 1999).
20   During the drafting of the Contract Law, the prevailing idea was that the liabilities for breach should be determined under the standard of strict liability, but the fault approach should still be used in such areas as pre-contractual liability, void contracts, and voidable contracts. See Sun Lihai, *Selection of Legislative Materials of the Contract Law of China*, 58 (Law Publishing House, 1999). For example, in the January 1995 draft, Article 138 provided that one party to a contract shall bear the liabilities for breach of the contract if it fails to perform the contract or its performance does not meet the requirements stipulated by law or agreed upon by the parties, except that the party itself is able to prove that it is not in fault. The "not in fault" exception was soon rejected because of the popular opinions in general in favor of strict liability. See Civil Law Division of the Standing Committee of the National People's Congress, Introduction to the Contract Law of China and its Important Drafts, 108–109 (Law Publishing House, 2000).

is destroyed or lost due to the deliberate intention or gross negligence of the donor, the donor shall be liable for damages.[21]

3 Breach

Breach of contract is a failure to fulfill contractual obligations. Under the Contract Law, a breach of contract occurs when (a) one party to a contract, before the expiry of the performance period, explicitly expresses or indicates through conduct that the contract will not be performed,[22] or (b) one party to a contract fails to perform its obligations under a contract or the performance fails to satisfy the terms of the contract.[23] The former is referred to as anticipatory repudiation while the latter is referred to as actual breach.

3.1 *Anticipatory Repudiation*

Again, the concept of anticipatory repudiation that is contained in the Contract Law is not a Chinese concept by origin. It is a contract law term borrowed from the common law system. In American contract law, for example, anticipatory repudiation occurs when a party repudiates, either explicitly in words or implicitly through conduct, a contract before the time for performance of the contract arises.[24] Thus, in the U.S., anticipatory repudiation is a breach that takes place before peformance is due or prior to the performance day. Once the perfornamce is due, any non-performance constitutes an actual breach.

As noted, under Article 94 (2) of the Contract Law, one party's anticipatory repudiation entitles the aggrieved party to assert a claim to rescind the contract. Article 108 further provides that where a party by an explicit statement or conduct indicates an unwillingness to performance a contract, "the other party may demand that the repudiating party bear liability for the breach of the contract before the expiry of the performance period."[25] Unlike Article 94 (2), which allows for rescission, Article 108 makes anticipatory repudiation a cause of action for breach of contract.

Pursuant to Article 108, in order to hold the repudiating party liable for breach of contract on the ground of anticipatory repudiation, it must be shown

---

21 There are many provisions in the Contract Law that embrace the fault standard. These provisions include such articles as 191, 222, 227, 265, 303, 320, 374, 406, and 425.
22 See the Contract Law, art. 108.
23 See *id.*, art. 107.
24 See Joseph M. Perillo, Contract (7th Ed), Hornbook Series, 454 (2014).
25 See *id.*, art. 108.

that (1) the non-performance is explicitly expressed by the repudiating party or can be clearly inferred from the repudiating party's conduct, and (2) such expression or conduct is made before the end of the performance period. Thus, in the case of anticipatory repudiation, the aggrieved party may either seek rescission of the contract under Article 94 (2) or directly sue for damages under Article 118 on the cause of action of breach of contract.[26]

As discussed, the language of "before the expiry of performance period" in both Article 94 (2) and Article 108 is confusing, however. It is not clear whether expiry means "before the time for performance has arrived" or "before the performance is completed." One scholarly interpretation is that Article 108 refers to a breach prior to the performance period because before the arrival of the performance period, the obligor has no duty to perform the contract.[27] A different view is that the performance period should include the period prior to the performance day and the period during the performance, and the expiry of performance period as provided in Article 108 is any time before the completion of the performance.[28]

In *Pearl Time Investments Ltd.,(Pearl Time) v. Tian Jin Metal Tools Co.(Metl Tools)* (2002), the parties entered into a joint venture contract in 1994, under which Pearl Time was to make a cash investment in the amount of 150,920,000 RMB, representing 51% of the total shares of the joint venture. According to the contract, the cash investment was to be made in five installments. The Pearl Time made three installment payments but withheld the payments for the last two installments. After several unsuccessful attempts to urge Pearl Time to transfer the rest of the investment money, *Metal Tools* brought suit against Pearl Time for breach of contract in Tian Jin High People's Court. Pearl Time filed a counterclaim on the basis of, among other things, anticipatory repudiation, alleging that Metal Tools failed to convey its property to the joint venture as the investment in kind.

Tian Jin High People's court entered a judgment for Metal Tools. Pearl Time appealed to the SPC. In its decision to affirm, the SPC held that since Metal Tools already allowed the joint venture to actually use, as Metal Tools' in-kind

---

26 See Wang Liming, Contract Law of China, *supra* note 18 at 220–221.
27 See *id.*, at 221.
28 See Han Shiyuan, *supra* note 13 at 417–418. See also Jiang Ping, A Detailed Explanation of the Contract Law, 90 (China University of Politic Science and Law Press, 1999) (explaining that a renouncement of a contractual duty before the expiry of the perforance period arises where there is either non-performance before the performance due date arrives or non-performance after the performance due day but before the end of the performance period).

investment, the buildings and equipment, Metal Tools should be deemed to have performed its major obligation under the joint venture contract, although some of the property was not transferred over to the joint venture. According to the SPC, when a party has performed its major obligations under a contract, there is no anticipatory repudiation.[29]

In the *Pearl Time* case, the SPC seemed to suggest that to constitute an anticipatory repudiation, the non-performance must involve major obligations under the contract, and the expression of such non-performance must be made after the contract is formed and before the performance period ends. The SPC, however, did not specify how the performance period should be characterized. Since it is not clear whether the SPC's decision in the *Pearl Time* implies that the performance period refers to the time before the performance becomes due, confusion remains. But, under the Contract Law, a party may choose to either rescind the contract or seek damages for breach of contract before the expiry of the performance period if the other party is believed to have definitely renounced its contractual duty.

3.2 Actual Breach

Actual breach is a failure to perform a contract after the contract's performance is due. Under Article 107 of the Contract Law, failure to perform, as noted, is divided into two categories: non-performance of contractual obligation and non-conforming performance. Non-performance is referred to as a complete failure to perform the contact's obligations, while non-conforming performance represents a partial failure in rendering performance. In addition, it is commonly held among Chinese contract scholars that an actual breach includes delayed performance.

In China, the terms non-performance and breach of contract are often used interchangeably in many places. But some suggest that non-performance should not be deemed synonymous with breach of contract. The argument is that breach is a violation of contractual obligations as a whole, but non-performance may only be a violation of some of such obligations.[30] In other words, a breach of contract may occur when performance is made in violation of a contract principle—e.g. good faith—and such a breach may not necessarily constitute non-performance.[31]

In Chinese contract literature, there is a general view that a breach of contract can be either fundamental or non-fundamental. A fundamental

---

29 See the SPC, (2002) Min Si Zhong Zi No. 3.
30 See Wang Liming, *supra* note 6 at pp 445–446.
31 See *id.*

breach is a concept contained in the United Nations Convention on Contracts for International Sale of Goods (CISG). Under Article 25 of the CISG a breach of contract is fundamental if it results in such detriment to the other party as to substantially deprive him of what he is entitled to expect under the contract. In China, it is believed that a fundamental breach, as embodied in the Contract Law, means that the failure of a party to perform the contractual obligations is so material that the goal of the contract is thereby destroyed.[32]

The relevant provision in the Contract Law for fundamental breach is Article 148. Under Article 148, a buyer may refuse to accept the goods or rescind the contract if the goods fail to meet the quality requirements so that the purpose of the contract cannot be realized.[33] It is commonly held in China that the test to ascertain whether the breach is fundamental is whether the purpose of the contract has been destroyed or whether the aggrieved party has suffered substantial damages.[34] The prevalent view is that under the Contract Law, if the beach is fundamental, the aggrieved party may either rescind the contract or refuse to accept the performance.[35] Therefore, if the breach of contract is not fundamental or in other words, the purpose of the contract is still attainable despite the breach, the aggrieved party may not rescind the contract or refuse to accept the goods but may seek damages suffered therefrom.

Non-performance of a contract may be the result of either impossibility of performance and refusal to perform. Impossibility is understood in China to mean that there is no way or no practical way to perform. The notion is derived from the classic maxim of *"impossibilium nulla obligatio est,"* meaning that there is no obligation to do impossible things. Performance may become impossible either objectively (e.g., as a result of the power of Mother Nature), or subjectively (e.g., it is impossible from the perspective of a contractual party to perform, even though the contract may possibly be performed by others). In general, the duty of the performing party is excused only when the performance is objectively impossible. If the performance is not objectively impossible, liability for breach of contract will be sought if non-performance occurs.[36]

---

32   See *id.*, at 490.
33   See the Contract Law, art. 148.
34   See *id.*, at p 490. See also Xing Ying, *supra* note 1 at pp 86–95.
35   One f the most commonly cited provisions in the Contract Law to support this argument is Article 148 of the Contract Law. According to Article 148, if the quality of the goods fails to satisfy the quality required by the contract such that the purpose of the contract cannot be realized, the buyer may refuse to accept the goods or may dissolve the contract.
36   See Han Shiyuan, *supra* note 13 at 413.

Refusal to perform refers to the situation where, after performance becomes due, the obligor who is able to perform does not, or does not want to, perform without reasonable grounds. Reasonable grounds in this regard consist of all legitimate reasons provided by law to allow the obligor not to perform. For instance, a party to a contract may refuse to perform under the defense of simultaneous fulfillment plea if the other party is mutually obligated to perform but fails to do so. Another example is a conditional contract. An obligor may refuse to perform if the conditions set forth in a conditional contract do not arrise or are not satisfied.

There is a debate in China as to whether impossibility of performance that is caused by or due to the fault of the obligor should be considered to be a refusal to perform. One argument is that whatever the reason for it may be, impossibility is not refusal. Others, however, argue that there is no need to distinguish between a contract being impossible to perform because of some act by the obligor and the obligor's refusal to perform because in either situation, the obligor does not have a justified reason for not performing. Thus, as long as there is no good reason for failure to perform, the obligor should bear the liability for breach of the contract.[37]

Non-conforming performance occurs where the obligor has performed the contract but the performance is either incomplete or improper because it does not conform to the requirements of the contract. In other words, non-conforming performance is performance that violates the principle of completion and properness. Performance will be deemed incomplete if only partial obligations of the contract have been performed during the required time for performance. Properness requires that the contract be performed such that that the quality, quantity, time, location, as well as manner of the performance match the terms and conditions as agreed upon by the parties to the contract.

Again, note that there are no UCC-type rules in China governing sales. As with every other contract, a contract for the sale of goods in China is governed by the general provisions of the Contract Law, though the Contract Law also contains a special chapter on such contracts. Therefore, there is no such rule as the "perfect tender rule" or "merchants" rule with respect to contracts for the sale of goods. All rules in the Contract Law (e.g., liabilities for breach) that apply to contracts generally apply equally to contracts for sales.

Improper performance also includes both advanced performance and delayed performance. Advanced performance is performance that is made before the performance date. It is in general deemed acceptable if performance

---

37   See Wang liming, *supra* note 6 at 496.

is made prior to the agreed time unless the obligee objects. As noted, delayed performance mainly refers to a delay by the obligor (e.g., delay in delivery), although it may also refer to a delay by the obligee (e.g., delay in acceptance).

Some in China consider delayed performance to be non-conforming performance. But others argue that delay in performance is different from non-conforming performance. Delayed performance occurs in the situation where the obligor is capable and able to perform but fails to do so when the performance is due, while non-conforming performance is performance that contains defects.[38] As discussed, under the Contract Law, delayed performance exists as long as the obligor fails to perform on the due day for the performance and the obligee is not required to to urge the obligor to perform. Note again that delayed performance is not a refusal to perform because a delay does not necessarily mean that the obligor intends not to perform. In most cases, when its performance is delayed, the obligor remains capable and is willing to continue to perform.

Nevertheless, no matter what the liabilities for breach and the types of breaches might be, a breach of the contract will arise under Article 107 of the Contract Law if a party fails to perform the contract or the performance does not meet the requirements of the contract. Therefore, after the performance is due, either non-performance or non-conforming performance will constitute a breach. Once there is a breach of contract, liability will be sought and a corresponding remedy will follow.

4   Remedies

Remedies, as provided in Article 107 of the Contract Law, take three forms: continuing performance, remedial measures, and damages. It is important to note that the Contract Law is considered to have refined the contractual remedies in at least three aspects: (1) there is no preferential emphasis on any particular remedy and all remedies are optional to the aggrieved party;[39] (2) the extent

---

38   See the Research Department of the General Office of the NPC Standing Committee, A Practical Guidance of Contract Law, 109–110 (Huawen Press, 1999).

39   Previously, contract legislation in China placed significant emphasis on the equitable principle of specific performance. The contractual parties in general were obligated to perform their contractual obligations and were not permitted to breach and pay stipulated penalties or compensatory damages instead of performing. Because of the State's controlling role in the economy, specific performance was deemed to be a dogma of contract law. See Wang Limin, *China's Proposed Uniform Contract Code*, 31 St. Mary's L.J. 7 (1999) at pp. 15–16.

to which the aggrieved party may seek remedies is broader than any previous contract legislation; and (3) many of the remedies provided for breach of contract are compensatory rather than punitive in nature.[40]

Thus, with respect to either non-performance or non-conforming performance, the aggrieved party may choose from the three liability forms for remedies. In addition, according to Article 112, if as a result of non-performance or non-conforming performance, the aggrieved party suffers from other losses, the breaching party shall, after performing its obligations or taking remedial measures, compensate for the losses. Furthermore, as noted, since the breach of contract can be in the form of anticipatory repudiation, the non-repudiating party may choose to sue the repudiating party for breach of contract.

4.1 *Continuing Performance*

Continuing performance requires that in the case of a breach, the breaching party, upon the demand of the aggrieved party, must continue to perform its contractual obligations if performance is possible. Since continuing performance is intended to effectuate the contract's performance as agreed, there should be no substitute performance. In this sense, continuing performance is also deemed to be specific performance or actual performance because it compels the breaching party to complete the performance of contractual obligations.[41] The ultimate goal of continuing performance is to help achieve what the parties have bargained for in their contract. Importantly, it should be noted that continuing performance in China is not an equitable relief but a statutory remedy.

Many scholars in China also refer to continuing performance as forced or mandatory performance.[42] The reason is that although continuing performance is intended to make the breaching party honor the contract, the performance is in fact compelled by the law as a remedy to satisfy the aggrieved party. Unlike performance under the contract, which is conducted by the performing party on a voluntary basis, continuing performance is a legal obligation that is enforced through compulsion.[43] It is on this ground that the Contract Law makes continuing performance a type of liability for the breach of contract.

In the past, however, continuing performance was employed in China mainly to ensure that the State plan would be accomplished. For example, Article 11

---

40 See the Research Department of the General Office of the NPC Standing Committee, *supra* note 38 at 105–106.
41 See Wang Liming, Contract Law of China, *supra* note 18 at 231.
42 See Han Shiyuan, *supra* note 13 at 600.
43 See Xing Ying, *supra* note 1 at p 126.

of the Economic Contract Law of China required that, if business transactions under a contract involved the State compulsory plan or projects, the contract had to be concluded in accordance with the plan issued by the State. At that time, due to the concern about improper implementation of the State plan, the continuing performance was perhaps the most practical device to handle the breach of contract.

A significant change in the Contract Law is that continuing performance is no longer the means to help implement the State plan but a contractual remedy available to the aggrieved party. What is unclear in the Contract Law, however, is how continuing performance should be enforced upon the aggrieved party's request. One scholarly interpretation is that such forced performance can be made directly, indirectly, or via a substitute means.[44]

Directly forced performance is performance through an exercise of governmental power. Indirectly forced performance is to use certain measure (e.g., increasing the amount of the interests to be charged against the nonperformance or imposing fines) to press the obligor to perform. Substituted performance is performance by someone other than the obligor at the cost of the obligor.[45] One example is the lessor's failure to repair the leased property. Under Article 121 of the Contract Law, if the lessor fails to perform the obligation of maintaining and repairing the leased property, the lessee itself may do so but the lessor shall bear the expenses.[46] In general, directly forced performance applies only to the monetary obligations.

Also unclear is whether the aggrieved party may directly ask a competent court to compel the breaching party to continue performing regardless of the arbitration clause in the contract.[47] Since a valid arbitration clause under Chinese law has the effect of precluding court jurisdiction,[48] it is likely that if a contract contains an arbitration clause, the judicial remedy will not be available unless the arbitration clause is found invalid or the arbitral award is set aside by a court.[49]

---

44 See Han Shiyuan, *supra* note 13 at 600–605.
45 See *id.*
46 See the Contract Law, art. 121.
47 The general rule is that an arbitration clause precludes courts' jurisdiction.
48 Under Article 5 of the Arbitration Law of China (1994), if the parties have reached an arbitration agreement, and one party institutes an action in a people's court, the people's court shall not take the case unless the arbitration agreement is null and void.
49 According to Article 9 of the Arbitration Law, if after an arbitration award has been made as to the dispute a party brings an action in a people's court for the same dispute, the people's court shall not take the case. If, however, an arbitration award is set aside by the people's court, a party may initiate a lawsuit in a people's court.

Note that continuing performance as provided in the Contract Law is not necessarily specific performance. In the common law system, specific performance is an equitable remedy by which a court orders the other party to complete performance of the contract. As a general rule, however, the specific remedy is not available unless and until the legal remedies are not adequate. In comparison, continuing performance under the Contract Law is a legal remedy and it applies to a much broader range of performance.

Under Chinese law, a claim for continuing performance must meet certain conditions. First, there must be a breach of contract because the continuing performance is a remedy that is available only in the case of breach. Second, the performance as requested must be possible to continue. If performance becomes impossible either as a matter of fact or as a matter of law, there will be no basis suitable for the continuing performance. Third, continuing performance must not be made at the court's initiative but rather must be requested by the aggrieved party.[50]

For purposes of the Contract Law, continuing performance primarily applies to monetary obligations; it is available for non-monetary obligations, but is subject to certain limitations with respect to such obligations. A monetary obligation, by definition, is an obligation that seeks, or can be satisfied by, the payment of a particular amount of money. A non-monetary obligation, as the term itself indicates, is an obligation that does not involve money payment. In the Contract Law, there are different requirements for continuing performance with regard to monetary, as contrasted with non-monetary, obligations.

4.1.1 Monetary Obligation

Continuing performance of a monetary obligation is governed by Article 109 of the Contract Law. Under Article 109, if one party to a contract fails to pay money for purchase or remuneration, the other party may request the party to make the payment.[51] The language of Article 109 is self-evident: in the case of a breach of a contract involving monetary payment, it is up to the aggrieved party whether to demand the breaching party to continue performing the contract.

There are two issues that have been raised with regard to application of Article 109. One issue is whether monetary obligations may be discharged by exemption. In general, a monetary obligation may not be exempted because of the highly fungible nature of money. But the question is whether a monetary

---

50   See Han Shiyuan, *supra* note 13 at 603.
51   See the Contract Law, art. 109.

obligation may be exempted on the ground of *force majeure*. There is no readily available answer in Article 109. In practice, *force majeure* is not a defense against the non-performance of monetary obligations. The reason is that lack of money does not render the performance of a monetary obligation objectively impossible. In most cases, the difficulty in paying money can be overcome through other payment alternatives such as an installment or extension of the payment period.

The other issue is whether the aggrieved party is entitled to other remedies when requesting the continuing performance of a monetary obligation. In other words, the issue is whether continuing performance can be used together with other remedies. A general holding is that that under the Contract Law, continuing performance and other types of remedies are not mutually exclusive. Therefore, while seeking continuing performance, the aggrieved party may still claim other remedies.

To illustrate, assume that A and B have a contract. Under the contract, A will deliver to B 1,000 cases of brand beers and B will pay A RMB 150,000 (approximately US $18,000) upon receipt of the delivery. Assume also that according to the contract, whoever is in breach of the contract will be liable for stipulated damages of 10% of the contract price. After the beers are delivered B defaults in making the payment. Under Article 109, A may request B to continue performing the contract (namely to make payment to A), and in the meantime, A is also entitled to stipulated damages as well as the interest that accrued between the date the payment was due and the date of actual payment.

4.1.2 Non-Monetary Obligation

Continuing performance as applied to non-monetary obligations is more complex. On the one hand, continuing performance is available with respect to non-monetary obligations mostly when money damages are deemed inadequate. On the other hand, a significant amount of non-monetary obligations are replaceable on the market, which makes continuing performance meaningless. In addition, there are certain kinds of non-monetary obligations that are not suitable for continuing performance, most of which are in the service areas. Consequently, as far as non-monetary obligations are concerned, the availability of continuing performance is always restricted.

Given this complexity, the Contract Law has different rules that apply to the continuing performance of a non-monetary obligation. Under Article 110 of the Contract Law, if one party to a contract fails to perform a non-monetary debt or the performance of a non-monetary debt fails to satisfy the terms of the contract, the other party may request the breaching party to perform, subject to certain exceptions as set forth in the law. The exceptions essentially function to narrow down the scope of the application of the continuing performance.

Article 110 of the Contract Law further provides that in any of the following situations, the request for continuing performance of non-monetary obligations will not be granted: (a) the performance cannot be made as a matter of law or as a matter of fact; (b) the object of the obligation is unfit for compulsory performance or the expenses for the performance are excessively high; or (c) the creditor does not make the request for performance within a reasonable period of time.[52] Therefore, continuing performance with respect to non-monetary obligations will be precluded if it falls within any of the statutory exceptions.

Pursuant to the Contract Law, in order to obtain the remedy of continuing performance of a non-monetary obligation, three conditions must be met. First, there must be non-performance or non-conforming performance of a non-monetary obligation that is provided in a valid and enforceable contract. Second, there must be no circumstances under which continuing performance is not permitted. Third, the request for continuing performance must be made within a reasonable period of time. The basic rules that govern the continuing performance remedy for non-monetary obligations include impossibility, impracticability, and rule of timing.

4.1.2.1 *Impossibility Rule*

As note, under the Contract Law a party may be excused from performance when performance becomes impossible. Here, the rule of impossibility applies when continuing performance is rendered impossible either by law or in fact (i.e., by uncontrollable circumstances). In its application, impossibility can be further divided into legal impossibility and factual impossibility. Legal impossibility means that for certain non-monetary obligations the continuing performance is prohibited or not permitted by the law.

A common example that has often been used to illustrate legal impossibility is where the object or the subject matter of the contract becomes illegal due to the change of law or regulations. Another example is where the obligor becomes bankrupt. In a bankruptcy case, if continuing performance is permitted, it may jeopardize other creditors' rights and then contravene the purpose of bankruptcy law.

Another example is where a transaction that is made for value involves a good faith third party purchaser. Assume A contracts to sell an antique to B for

---

52   See the Contract Law, art. 110.

RMB 10,000 (US $1,250). Before the delivery day, A sells the antique for RMB 15,000 (US $1,820) to C, who has no knowledge of the contract between A and B. C is the purchaser in good faith. Since the law protects the interest of a good faith third party purchaser, it would be legally impossible for A to make continuing performance by retrieving the antique from C and selling it to B under the contract.

The Contract Law and the 1986 Civil Code contain no provision concerning good faith purchasers, but in practice there is a well-recognized rule that a good faith purchaser for value has the right to refuse to return the item purchased.[53] Not until 2006, when the Property Law was adopted, was a good faith third party provided for in the law.

Under Article 106 of the Property Law, unless otherwise provided by the law, a third party retains the right of property, real or personal, he or she purchased from a person untitled to dispose of the property if (a) at the time of the property transfer, the party was in good faith; (b) the transfer was made at a reasonable price; and (c) the transfer was registered if required or the property was conveyed if no registration was required.[54]

Factual impossibility refers to the situation where the contract cannot possibly be performed despite the efforts the obligor can or is able to make to perform. To be factually impossible, the impossibility, viewed objectively, must be permanent and the occurrence of the circumstances that render the performance impossible must be out of the obligor's control.

A good example to illustrate is a contract for the sale of specific goods. Given their unique nature, specific goods are normally not fungible or replaceable in the market. Therefore, continuing performance by the obligor is needed and also necessary in order to help protect the interests of the obligee and realize the goal of the contract. However, if specific goods are lost or destroyed (e.g., by fire), there is no way to have them replaced or restored. Thus, in this circumstance, it will be factually impossible for the obligor to continue performing.

---

53 See Xing Ying, *supra* note 1 at p 131. Also, in its 1998 Opinions on the Several Issues Concerning Implementation of the General Principles of the Civil Law of China, the SPC explicitly stated an intent to protect the interests of good faith third partise. Under Article 89 of the Opinions, if during the period of existence of the co-owner relationship, some co-owners disposed of the property under the co-ownership without due authorization, such action shall be deemed invalid. If, however, the property was purchased by a third party in good faith, the legitimate interest of the third party shall be maintained. See the SPC, *Opinions on the Several Issues Concerning Implementation of the General Principles of the Civil Law of China* (Peovisional, 1998).

54 See the Property Law of China, art. 106.

When the remedy of continuing performance is not available as a result of impossibility, damages will be awarded as an alternative. In its Rules for the Matters Concerning the Work on the Enforcement of Judgments of the People's Courts (1998), the SPC explicitly addressed the issue of continuing performance in lieu of damages if the performance becomes impossible.

According to the SPC, where the matter that is subject to enforcement pursuant to a judgment is a specific thing, the delivery of the original of the thing should be required. If the original has been concealed or is illegally transferred, the court has the power to order the obligor to hand it over. If it is certain that the original has deteriorated in quality, has been damaged, or is lost, the court shall order damages equal to the converted value of the original or sequester the obligor's other property up to the amount of the original's value.[55]

4.1.2.2   Impracticability Rule

Continuing performance may become impracticable because of either the unique nature of the contract or prohibitively high costs. Contracts that are deemed unsuitable for continuing performance are normally those that are concluded on the basis of a personal relationship or personal trust (or credibility). A partnership contract, for example, is strongly dependent on the personality of the partners, and therefore continuing performance in the case of its breach may not be proper.

In China, contracts such as contracts for work or contracts for entrustment are regarded as relying heavily on the person of the obligor, and are therefore considered to be unfit for continuing performance. Moreover, continuing performance is not suitable with respect to a contract involving personal service because of the law or policy against any restrictions on personal liberty by means of a contract. In this regard, the unfitness for continuing performance mainly involves the person of the obligor.

Impracticability also applies to the situation where the cost for continuing performance is commercially prohibitive. Commercial impractibility is basically a consideration of the commercial burden or economic efficiency for continuing performance. The idea is that a contract represents a balanced interest between the contractual parties, and the duty of one party to honor the contract is to ensure the other party gets what is expected from the bargain. Thus, in the case of breach, if the breaching party ends up with paying much more than what ought to be paid as compensation to the aggrieved party, the

---

55   See the SPC, *1998 Rules for the Matters Concerning the Work on the Enforcement of Judgments of the People's Courts*, art. 57.

balance of interests between the parties will be destroyed and as result performance will become unduly burdensome.

The very purpose of the employment of the concept of commercial impracticability is to help protect the breaching party from bearing liabilities that are unnecessary and excessive. Under the economic efficiency doctrine, it is impractical for the breaching party to fulfill its obligation to perform the contract if such performance is too expensive to be rational. The basic test is whether the cost of performance and the benefit conveyed will be unreasonably disproportionate if continuing performance is made. In China, there has been a suggestion that if the losses of the obligee can be adequately compensated through monetary remedies such as damages or pecuniary awards, it is excessively burdensome for the obligor to be coerced into continue performing.[56]

Some in China argue that the impracticability rule should also be applied to the case where the time period for continuing performance is excessively long. This argument actually expresses a concern as to the role of the court in the case of the continuing performance. The reason is that since the continuing performance is a legal remedy granted by the court according to law, the court's supervision will be needed to ensure that the continuing performance will be made as ordered by the court. Therefore, if the continuing performance takes a long time, it might become impractical due to the excessive judicial time and effort that will be involved in the prolonged performance period. On the other hand, the court often may face difficulty in effectively supervising the performance.[57]

4.1.2.3 Rule of Timing

The rule of timing, or time rule, is a limitation on requests for continuing performance. Continuing performance is a form of claim-driven relief, which means that it may not be granted unless it is first requested by the aggrieved party. Under the Contract Law, however, a request for continuing performance must be made within a reasonable period of time after the breach of the contract occurs. A failure to make timely request will constitute a lashes, under which the right to make the request will be deemed to be waived.

The rule of timing serves a two-fold function. First, it is intended to prevent the breaching party from bearing undue difficulties when the non-breaching party makes a request for continuing performance after a unreasonable delay. Second, the rule helps maintain a rational relationship between the parties to

---

56 This is the suggestion from the judges of the SPC. See Li Guoguang, *supra* note 7 at p 438.
57 See Wang Liming, *supra* note 6 at p 579.

business transactions such that they deal with each other fairly. But there is no simple test or uniform standard for the "the reasonable period of time." In general, reasonableness must be determined on a case-by-case basis.

Some suggest that if the parties to a contract provide in their agreement a time period for the aggrieved party to make a request for continuing performance, such a time period should be followed. However, if the parties instead provide that in the case of breach, the aggrieved party may only ask the breaching party to pay for damages or bear liabilities for compensation, but may not request continuing performance, that agreement will in general be deemed valid and as an effective prohibition of continuing performance.[58] The reason is that if the parties agree not to pursue continuing performance in the case of breach, the aggrieved party should be estopped because its right to continuing performance is waived through their agreement.

As a practical matter, absent the parties' agreement on the time period for making a continuing performance request in the case of breach, reasonableness can be determined on the basis of the nature and purpose of the contract. In addition, trade customs or industrial usages are often the factors on which courts rely to resolve issues of reasonableness. Moreover, reasonableness can also be judged under the principles of good faith and fairness.

There is an argument that the rule of timing under the Contract Law should include a "grace period" for the breach party to perform. "Grace period" means that when making a request for continuing performance, the aggrieved party shall give the breaching party a reasonable period to complete the performance, and only if the breaching party fails or refuses to perform after the reasonable period, may the aggrieved party ask the court or arbitration body to compel or urge through litigation or arbitration.[59] Obviously, the proponents of the "grace period" opine that the reasonable efforts of the breaching party when the request for the continuing performance is made must be take into account.

As an alternative under the Contract Law, the aggrieved party may rescind the contract and ask for damages in lieu of continuing performance. But a

---

58   See Li Guoguang, *supra* note 7 at p 439.
59   See Sun Lihai, *A Practical Explanation to the Contract Law of China*, 174 (Industry and Commerce Publishing House, 1999). Many, however, disagree because they believe that Article 110 only sets a time limitation for the aggrieved party to exercise the right to make a request for continuing performance, and does not require the aggrieved party to give the breaching party more time to prepare for the performance after the request for continuing performance is made. On the other hand, since the breaching party is already at fault for not performing the contract, it should not be entitled to more time to make the performance.

drawback is that when the contract is rescinded, the remedy of continuing performance no longer exists. The reason is that rescission and continuing performance are mutually exclusive. However, if there is a delay in performance, the aggrieved party may seek damages and in the meantime make a request for continuing performance.[60]

4.2   Remedial Measures

Remedial measures are the remedies that are intended to cure the defects in the performance and simultaneously prevent further losses or damages that may incur in the breach of contract. Under the Contract Law, measures that are remedial mainly include repair, replacement, reworking, return of goods, or reduction of price or remuneration. Given their focus on the defective performance, the remedial measures mostly apply to non-conforming performance or performance that does not meet the standard, specification, or terms as agreed upon.

In China, non-conformance is also called incomplete performance. As noted, pursuant to Article 107 of the Contract Law, when a party's performance fails to satisfy the terms of the contract, the party is required to take remedial measures. For purposes of remedial measures, non-conforming performance often involves non-monetary obligations in which the quality is an issue. The major provision governing remedial measures in the Contract Law is Article 111.

Under Article 111, the aggrieved party may seek remedial measures from the other party when there is no agreement between the parties as to the liability for non-conforming quality of performance or such agreement is unclear, nor can the liability be determined by supplement agreement, contract provisions, or transaction practices.[61] Note, however, that though Article 111 mainly deals with defective performance in quality, remedial measures may also be applicable to continuing performance when non-conforming performance is involved. As a matter of fact, some of the remedial measures such as repair, replacement, and reworking are themselves sort of continuing performance because they are aimed at having the contract performed as agreed upon by the parties.

Return of goods is in fact a rescission of the contract, and in many cases a unilateral rescission. For purposes of the Contract Law, return as a remedial measure mainly applies to the case where the defects in the quality of the goods are so serious that the purpose of the contract will not be achieved as

---

60 See Contract Law, art. 114.
61 See the Contract Law, art. 111.

intended. As noted, under Article 94 (d), a contract may be rescinded if one party to the contract defaults in performing its contractual obligations or breaches the contract by other conduct such that the purpose of the contract cannot be realized.

Reduction of price or remuneration is an alternative to the return of goods, and is particularly appropriate when the aggrieved party has received defective goods but the defects do not necessarily frustrate the purpose of the contract. When the aggrieved party chooses price reduction, the reduced amount will be the difference between the contract price and the price the defective goods are actually worth. In the case of price reduction, once the aggrieved party accepts the defective performance at a reduced price, the performance will be deemed complete.

Repair, rework, or replacement is a remedy that is used to cure the defects in the performance. In both the 1986 Civil Code and 2017 GPCL, such a remedy is among the forms or methods of civil liability in general. Normally, the employment of repair, rework or replacement is dependent on the kind of performance and nature of the substance involved. If the aggrieved party accepts the remedy as such for the defective performance, the contract price for the performance must be paid.

However, the use of remedial measures does not preclude the breaching party's liability for other damages caused to the aggrieved party as a result of the breach. Under Article 112 of the Contract Law, the breaching party, after its taking of remedial measures, must make compensation for the losses incurred by the other party in connection with the non-conforming performance. In other words, the remedial measures and compensation are mutually supplemental.

In addition, if there are any costs associated with the application of remedial measures, the breaching party shall generally be liable for such costs. It should, however, be noted that if there is an agreement between the parties or a transaction practice that governs the non-conforming performance, the remedial measures should not be applied. Also, in order to make the use of remedial measures meaningful, two factors are important: (a) defective performance is remediable, and (b) the breaching party has the ability to take the remedial measures.

4.3 *Damages*

Damages are basically the monetary remedy to compensate the losses that the aggrieved party suffers from the breach of contract.[62] In this connection,

---

62　In certain cases, the damages may take the form of "in kind." But if the "in kind" damages are awarded, they must be something different from the object of the contract, or

damages are also called money damages that can be sued as substitute for performance. Compared with other remedies provided in the Contract Law, damages have at least two unique distinctions. The first distinction is the nature of general application. Damages are applicable to any case where other remedies are not suitable, available, or inadequate.

The second distinction lies with the function of supplement. Damages may always be used to fill in the gap left by other remedies or to supplement the losses that cannot be recovered by other remedies. As noted, according to Article 112 of the Contract Law, if one party to a contract fails to perform the contract or its performance fails to satisfy the terms of the contract, and if the aggrieved party has suffered other losses after the continuing performance or other remedial measures, the breaching party remains liable for compensating for such losses.[63]

As far as an award of damages is concerned, the scope of damages and causation are the two major issues that have been heavily debated in China. The scope of damages involves two sub-issues. One sub-issue is whether the damages in the contractual context should be limited to property damage. Put differently, the issue is whether damages should also include personal damages (e.g., mental distress).

Many in China hold the view that damages under the Contract Law only refer to property damages or economic losses of the aggrieved party. They argue that personal damages are almost impossible to predict at the time of contract and also are difficult to be measured in monetary value. They believe that non-property damages, such as personal or emotional damages, that are caused as a result of a breach of contract may only be dealt with separately under different causes of action.[64]

A different view emphasizes the interest of the aggrieved party by arguing that it should allow the aggrieved party at his own choice to seek personal damages in a contract claim if such damages can be quantified to a certain amount of money.[65] The theoretical basis of this view is that a claim for personal damages resulting from the breach of a contract can be treated as a

---

otherwise, the "in kind" would not be the damages, but specific performance.
63 A similar provision can be seen in the 1986 Civil Code. Article 111 of the Civil Code provides that if a party fails to perform its contractual obligations or its performance violates the terms of the contract, the other party has the right to demand the performance or remedial measures, and shall also have the right to claim compensation for damages.
64 See Xing Ying, *supra* note 1 at pp 151–152.
65 See Wang Liming, *supra* note 6 at p 599.

combined contract and tort claim, and the aggrieved party may choose to sue under either the cause of action of contract or the cause of action of torts.[66]

The third view is that the parties should be allowed to make a choice as beween contract claim and torts claim. This view is embodied in the Contract Law. Under Article 122, if the breach of contract by one party infringes upon the other party's personal or property rights, the aggrieved party shall be entitled to choose either to make a breach of contract claim against the breaching party under the Contract Law or to seek tort liability against the breaching party in accordance with other laws.[67] A similar provision is Article 186 of the GPCL, under which the aggrieved party has the right to request the breaching party to assume liability for breach of contract or bear torts liability if the breach causes damages to the personal or property rights and interests of the agrrieved party.[68]

In its practice, the SPC follows the Contract Law but takes a more flexible approach when dealing with personal damages in a contract claim. According to the SPC, if the aggrieved party requests to change or modify the cause of action after a choice is made pursuant to Article 122 of the Contract Law but before the trial at court in the first instance begins, the request shall be granted.[69] In other words, before the trial, the aggrieved party may choose a cause of acton as between contract and torts for personal damages, and may also modify the choice already made.

The other sub-issue deals with whether the harms beyond the direct losses of the aggrieved party should also be included in the damages. In China, losses for purposes of litigation are commonly divided into two categories: direct losses and indirect losses. What constitutes an indirect loss is often a debatable

---

66 The combined claim of both contract and torts refers to the claim arising out of the incident or conduct that concurrently violates the law of contract and the law of tort, which results in the concurrence of contract obligation and tort liability.
67 The Contract Law provides no guideline for the parties to make a choice in cases where both contract claims and tort claims exist. A scholarly suggestion is the test of interest. Under this test, if the personal interest of the aggrieved party is infringed in the breach of contract, a tort action is preferred because the remedy for personal damages is not available in a contract action. If, however, the interest in performance of the contract is the priority of the aggrieved party, a contract action should be chosen. See Xing Ying, supra note 1 at pp 281–285. Others also suggest that if the parties agree in advance not to make any claim other than a contract claim in the case of concurrence of different causes of action, the agreement should be upheld. If, however, there is special provision of law intended to reduce the duty of care of a party, such provision shall also be followed. See Sun Lihai, supra note 20 at pp168–169.
68 See the 2017 GPCL, art. 186.
69 See Supreme People's Court, *Explanation to the Questions Concerning Implementation and Application of the Contract Law of the People's Republic of China (I)*, 1999, art. 30.

question. The difficult part of the question involves the interests of the aggrieved party under the contract. In addition, often at the center of the dispute is the issue of causation between the breach of contract and the losses.

In the common law system, contract interests can be categorized as expectancy interests, reliance interests, or restitution interests.[70] In China, there is no such categorization, but expectancy interests—termed expected benefits or interests—seem to have gained broad acceptance. Under Article 113 of the Contract Law, in the case of breach of contract, the damages shall include the interests expected to be received from the performance of the contract.[71] In its 2012 Contract Law Interpretation, the SPC explicitly states that when a party in a sales contract breaches the contract, causing damages to the other party, and the other party claims the interests it expected to receive, the court shall on the basis of the claim determine such interests in accordance with relevant provisions of law.[72]

Neither the Contract Law nor the SPC's Interpretation define expected interests. Article 113 of the Contract Law imposes a ceiling on the damages to be compensated and provides that the total damages shall not exceed the probable losses as a result of a breach that was or ought to have been foreseen by the breaching party at the time of the contract.[73] Since foreseeable damages include both direct and indirect damages, it remains unclear what indirect damages are. But what can be inferred from Article 113 is that indirect damages must also be foreseeable at the time of contract.

The issue of causation concerns the relationship between the fact of breach of contract and the resulting losses. To ascertain causation, the Contract Law follows the rule of foreseeability, which prescribes that damages should only be awarded if they are the probable consequences of the breach and such consequences are foreseeable by the parties at the time of the contract. From many Chinese contract scholars' viewpoint, the rule of foreseeability essentially functions as a gauge to help keep the damages within a certain boundary. Under the rule, causation exists when the damages that are caused by the breach are foreseeable, and the breaching party is only responsible for the damages that could be reasonably foreseen.

There is no specific test in the Contract Law for determining the matter of foreseeability, however. Normally, to make a claim for damages for breach of contract, the aggrieved party must prove (1) the fact of breach, (2) losses, and (3) the connection between the breach and the losses. It is then up to the

---

70   See Calamari & Perillo, *The Law of Contract* (4th ed), 545 (West Group, 1998).
71   See the Contract Law, art. 113.
72   See the SPC, 2012 Contract Law Interpretation, art. 29.
73   See the Contract Law. Art. 113.

court to make a determination of what damages are foreseeable. The standard generally employed is whether the damages are the reasonable and natural outcomes of the breach and whether such samages would be contemplated by an ordinary person in the same or similar situation at the time of contract. If the aggrieved party wants to ask more than this standard, however, it must be proved that there is additional damage that is foreseeable under the special circumstances known to the parties.

Note, however, that Chinese contract law scholars almost uniformly endorse a damage principle called "full compensation." Full compensation means that in the case of breach of contract, the breaching party is responsible for all damages that have been caused to the aggrieved party. The view underlying this principle is that only when compensation is fully made, will the aggrieved party be restored to the position that he or she would have been in if there had been no breach. Thus, by requiring that the breaching party compensate the aggrieved party for both the direct damages and expected interest, the Contract Law is said to have adopted the principle of "full compensation."

Under the Contract Law, there are four different kinds of damages that are available in a breach of contract case: compensatory damages, liquidated damages, punitive damages, and earnest money. As indicated at the beginning of this chapter, contract remedies are in general compensatory by their nature. Therefore, punitive damages are available, if at all, only in very special and limited cases, and the imposition of such damages must be authorized by laws or administrative regulations.

4.3.1 Compensatory Damages

The most significant damages provided for in the Contract Law are compensatory damages. Damages are deemed compensatory if their purpose is to place the aggrieved party in the same position that the aggrieved party would have been in if the contract had been performed as agreed upon by the parties. As noted, according to Article 113 of the Contract Law, the breaching party shall be liable for damages that are caused to the aggrieved party by the breaching party's failure to perform its contractual obligations or by its non-conforming performance. The amount of damages shall be equal to the losses caused by the beach of contract, including the interest that would have accrued if the contract was performed properly.[74]

Article 113 of the Contract Law is the basic law of damages of a compensatory nature. As discussed, under Article 113, in the case of breach of contract, the

---

74   See the Contract Law, art. 113.

aggrieved party may recover from the breaching party its actual losses as well as those benefits or interests it expected to receive pursuant to the contract. Article 113 furthermore imposes a ceiling that limits compensatory damages to the amount of probable losses caused by the breach of contract. Again, probable losses for the purpose of Article 113 of the Contract Law are the losses that had been foreseen or should have been foreseen when the contract was made. Thus, the determination of compensatory damages is subject to the rule of foreseeability.[75]

There are some cases in which each party to a contract breaches the contract—i.e., a so-called "mutual breach" occurs. The Contract Law contains a special provision that governs mutual breaches. Article 120 of the Contract Law provides that if both parties breach a contract, they shall bear the liabilities respectively. If the liabilities are of the same kind in nature (e.g., money payment), they might be set off to the same amount that is mutually owed.[76] Article 120 of the Contract Law is actually based on Article 113 of the 1986 Civil Code, which addressed the mutual breaches involved in contracts.

Compensatory damages are subject to the rule of mitigation. Under Article 114 of the 1986 Civil Code and Article 119 of the Contract Law, if an aggrieved party in the case of a breach of a contract fails to take proper measures to avoid additional damages that otherwise would not arise, the party should not claim compensation for such damages. This limitation on damages is compatible with Article 77 of the CISG, under which the damages that a party who fails to mitigate is entitled to is reduced by the amount that would have been avoided had the party taken proper measures.[77]

4.3.2 Liquidated Damages

The parties to a contract may negotiate in their contract a certain amount of damages that the breaching party must pay to the aggrieved party as compensation in the case of breach. Such damages are referred to as liquidated, or stipulated, damages. One major characteristic of liquidated damages is that such damages are provided in advance and take effect when the breach occurs.

---

75   Article 113's limitation on compensatory damages is consistent with Article 74 of the 1980 UN Convention on International Sale of Goods. Under Article 74, damages for breach of contract by one party consist of a sum equal to the loss, including loss of profit, suffered by the other party as a consequence of the breach. Such damages may not exceed the loss which the party in breach foresaw or ought to have foreseen at the time of the conclusion of the contract, in the light of the facts and matters of which he then knew or ought to have known, as a possible consequence of the breach of contract.
76   See the Contract Law, art. 120.
77   See the CISG, art. 77. (1980).

Another notable aspect of liquidated damages is that such damages are not determined on the basis of actual losses but, rather, on the estimation of the losses caused to the parties as set forth in the parties' agreement. Liquidated damages may be made in the form of a specific amount of money or as calculated pursuant to a particular formula agreed upon by the parties.

Under Article 114 of the Contract Law, the parties to a contract may agree that, in the event of a breach of the contract, the breaching party shall pay stipulated damages of either a certain amount or an amount calculated by a certain method agreed upon by the parties.[78] Although Article 114 does not define liquidated damages, it nevertheless recognizes two forms of liquidated damages. Although some believe that liquidated damages are actually a guaranty for the performance of the contract, in the context of the Contract Law, they are a type of liability for breach and the parties may choose to use them as the parties wish.

Like other contract remedies, the primary function of liquidated damages is to compensate the aggrieved party. A question often raised, however, is whether liquidated damages should both compensate the aggrieved party and penalize the breaching party. In American contract law, liquidated damages are enforceable only if the contract provision by which they are set does not function as a penalty clause. Thus, the validity of stipulated damages in the U.S. to a great extent depends on whether the sum of such damages is a reasonable pre-estimate of the probable or actual loss. A measure of damages that appears to be punitive will not be enforced.[79]

By contrast, liquidated damages in China are available even if they impose a penalty on the breaching party. A common understanding in China is that an important function of liquidated damages is to deter breaches of contract. The notion is that, by agreeing to the imposition of liquidated damages in the event of breach, a party agrees to accept economic punishment if it does not perform its obligations under the contract. Under the Contract Law, when liquidated damages are provided for in a contract, a court or arbitration body may not set them aside without a successful request by the interested party. In addition, the liquidated damages, though agreed upon by the parties, may not preclude recovery of other damages that are allowed under the Contract Law.

The Contract Law provides a justification for liquidated damages. According to Article 114, if the agreed amount of damages turns out to be lower than the loss actually caused, the aggrieved party may make a request to a court or

---

78 See *id.*, art. 114.
79 See Joseph M. Peillo, Contract (7th ed), 558 (2014).

arbitration body for an increase. On the other hand, the breaching party may ask a court or arbitration body to reduce the amount of liquidated damages if the amount agreed proves to be excessively higher than the actual losses. Note, however, that under Article 114, if liquidated damages are agreed to with respect to a delay in performance, the breaching party will still be obligated to continue performing its obligations after the liquidated damages are paid. [80]

Although in China liquidated damages that appear to be punitive are not necessarily void, the Contract Law sets a boundary on the extent to which liquidated damages may be punitive. The SPC opines that stipulated damages shall mainly be a compensatory remedy and the punitive nature of such damages shall be supplementary.[81] The rationale underlying Article 114 is that liquidated damages shall be made on a reasonable basis reflecting an honest effort by the parties to stipulate the damages that would be the likely result of a breach. Accordingly, the limit on stipulated damages is one of reasonableness.

While the liquidated damages provision in a contract may be attacked on the ground of unreasonableness, the attacking party must make such an attack by means of a request to a court or arbitration body. A court or arbitration body may not make any change to the liquidated damages without first a request from a party. If the amount of the liquidated damages is found to be unreasonable, the court or arbitration body will not simply avoid the provision but will adjust the amount. The reasonableness limit applies to an amount of liquidated damages that is either too low or excessively high.

According to the SPC, if a party via a counterclaim or defense requests a people's court to adjust liquidated damages pursuant to a provision of the Contract Law, the court's decision whether to grant the request must be made according to certain rules. When the party requests an increase in the amount of liquidated damages, the total amount after the increase must not exceed the actual losses. It is important to note, however, that after an adjustment is made to the amount of the liquidated damages in favor of the aggrieved party, the party may not ask the other party for lost compensation.[82]

On the other hand, if a party requests a people's court to reduce the amount of the liquidated damages, the court is required to make a decision in light of fairness and good faith principles on the basis of actual losses with consideration of (a) the performance situation, (b) the degree of fault of the party, and

---

80   In China, many agree that in general, liquidated damages may become a substitute for continuing performance. Only in the case where performance is delayed may the aggrieved party ask for continuing performance after receipt of the liquidated damages.
81   See Du Wanhua, *et al*, Ajudicative Guidance of Contract Cases, 463 (Law Press, 2018).
82   See the SPC, 2009 Contract Law Interpretation, art. 27, 28.

(c) the expected interests of the party.[83] The standard for reduction is whether the stipulated damages are excessively higher than the actual losses. Under the SPC's interpretation, if the amount of stipulated damages is 30% higher than the amount of actual losses, the stipulated damages will be considered excessively high.[84]

4.3.3 Punitive Damages

Punitive Damages are not compensatory and the amount of such damages is usually much higher than the actual losses that the aggrieved party has suffered. Since punitive damages are intended to punish willful and wanton conduct in order to deter the wrongdoer or any other person from the same or similar conduct in the future, they are in general not available in contract claims.[85] In China, the award of punitive damages is not eliminated in contract cases but the use of such damages is strictly limited.

Under the Contract Law, the imposition of punitive damages requires a statutory basis. This means that punitive damages may not be granted in contract claims unless otherwise provided by the law. As provided in Article 113, the imposition of punitive damages requires a cross-reference to a specific law. The primary purpose of punitive damages it to punish fraudulent activities committed in business operations.[86] The 2017 GPCL explicitly makes punitive damages a form of remedies for civil liability. According to Article 179 of the 2017 GPCL, where a law provides for punitive damages for civil liability, that law shall be applied.[87]

The direct cross-reference in Article 113 with regard to punitive damages is the Law of Protection of Consumers' Rights and Interest (Consumers Protection Law). Promulgated on October 31, 1993, the Consumer Protection Law took effect on January 1, 1994. Under Article 49 of the Consumers Protection Law, if a business operator is found to have committed fraudulent conduct in providing goods or services, the damages for losses so caused to consumers shall be multiplied on the demand of the consumers. The increased amount of damages shall be equal to double the amount of the price of the goods purchased or services received.[88]

---

83 See *id.*, art. 29.
84 See *id.*
85 See Peillo, *supra* note 24 at 513.
86 See the Contract Law, art. 113.
87 See the 2017 GPCL, art. 179.
88 See the Consumer Protection Law, art. 49.

4.3.4 Earnest Money

Under the Contract Law, the parties to a contract may agree to provide a sum of money as security to guarantee the performance of the contract.[89] The sum of money so provided is labeled in China as earnest money. The amount of earnest money is normally a certain percentage of the contract price, and is made after conclusion and before performance of the contract. In contracts, the earnest money is used mainly to compensate the aggrieved party in case of breach, and is paid by one party to the other as agreed. As implicated in the Contract Law, earnest money is a security for performance and, up to the contract's conclusion, is a liability for breach.

Prior to the adoption of the Contract Law, earnest money was defined in both the Civil Code and the 1995 Guaranty Law of China as a type of security to guarantee creditors' rights. Contrastingly, the Contract Law defines earnest money as a remedy for breach of the contract. Under Article 115 of the Contract Law, the parties to a contract may, in accordance with the provisions of the Guaranty Law, agree that one party will pay earnest money as a guaranty of performance to the other. That earnest money shall be refunded or offset against the contract price after the contract obligations are performed.[90]

Article 115 also stipulates a rule pursuant to which earnest money is used against each party's non-performance. Article 115 applies to two different situations. If the payer of the earnest money fails to perform agreed obligations, he or she will have no right to reclaim the money paid. However, if the payee of the earnest money fails to perform its obligations, he is required to double refund the money being paid.[91] In the payee situation, the required double refund is punitive.

Thus, for the payer of the earnest money, failure to perform will result in the forfeiture of the earnest money. As far as the payee is concerned, his or her

---

89 In practice, earnest money may take different forms—namely, earnest money for conclusion of the contract, earnest money for rescission of the contract, and earnest money for breach of the contract. For purposes of Article 115 of the Contract Law, earnest money refers to earnest money for breach of the contract.
90 See *id.*, art. 115.
91 A similar provision is Article 89 (3) of the 1986 Civil Code. Under Article 89 (3), subject to the limits set forth by the law, a party may pay the other party earnest money. After the contractual obligations are performed, the earnest money provided may either be used as partial payment of the contract price or be refunded. If the paying party defaults in his performance, he shall not be entitled to demand the refund of the earnest money. If the receiving party fails to perform, he shall double repay the earnest money.

breach of the contract will lead to a penalty of being required to pay twice as much the earnest money as received.

Note that earnest money as provided in the Contract Law may not be used to replace damages. In other words, forfeiture of earnest money and recovery of damages are different, co-existing potential remedies. Therefore, in the event of a breach, the aggrieved party may not only keep the earnest money, but also demand other remedies. The aggrieved party, in addition to the earnest money, may ask the breaching party to continue performing the contract or seek damages if there are any losses resulting from the breach.

However, in order to avoid double jeopardy to the breaching party, the Contract Law prohibits the aggrieved party from claiming both liquidated damages and earnest money. Under Article 116 of the Contract Law, if the parties to a contract have agreed on both liquidated damages and earnest money, the aggrieved party may only choose to take either liquidated damages or earnest money when the other party is in breach of the contract. Therefore, it is permissible that the parties provide in their contract both liquidated damages and earnest money, but the aggrieved party may only claim one of them in the case where the other party breaches the contract.

There is a writing requirement for an agreement on earnest money. According to Article 90 of the Guaranty Law, an earnest money agreement must be made in writing. With regard to the delivery of earnest money, the parties are required to specify in their agreement the time for the delivery, and the agreement must not take effect until the day when the earnest money is actually delivered. Because of earnest money's security function, an agreement on earnest money is normally regarded as a side contract, although such an agreement is often seen as a contract clause or article. The existence of such an agreement is totally dependent on the underlying contract.

An issue that often recurs is the amount of the earnest money. The parties, of course, have the right to decide through their negotiations how much the earnest money should be on the basis of the contract price. But in order to prevent abuse of the right, there is a cap imposed by the law. In accordance with the Guaranty Law, the maximum amount of the earnest money as agreed upon by the parties shall not exceed 20% of the contract price. In practice, if the agreed amount of earnest money is over the 20% cap, the agreement will not necessarily be void, but the agreed amount will be reduced to the 20%.[92]

---

92   See the Guarantee Law of China, 1995, available at http://www.fdi.gov.cn/1800000121_39_3061_0_7.html.

5 Mitigation Duty

The rule of mitigation, also called the rule of "avoidable consequences," precludes the recovery of damages that could have been avoided with reasonable efforts and without undue risk, burden, or humiliation.[93] The duty to mitigate is recognized in the Contract Law and lies with the aggrieved party. The idea is that in the case of breach the aggrieved party must not sit idly by and allow damages to accumulate. In China, the mitigation duty is viewed as a fault-based duty, pursuant to which an aggrieved party will be found at fault if the party fails to take reasonable action to avoid further damages that otherwise could have been avoided.

The mitigation duty is set forth in Article 119 of the Contract Law. Article 119 requires the non-breaching party to take proper measures to prevent the aggravation of losses. If the non-breaching party fails to take proper measures and the losses are consequently aggravated, the party does not have a valid claim for compensation with respect to the aggravated part of the losses.[94] The breaching party is responsible for the reasonable expenses incurred by the other party for making efforts to prevent the loss aggravation. But according to the SPC, such reasonable expenses do not include the salaries or other remuneration for the services of the party.[95]

Under the Contract Law, the mitigation duty also arises in the situation where the contract cannot be performed due to *force majeure*. Article 118 provides that a party who is unable to perform the contract on the ground of *force majeure* must give prompt notice to the other party in order to reduce the probable losses to that other party, and must provide evidence in this regard within a reasonable period of time.[96] Simply put, the duty to mitigate under Article 118 is a duty to provide prompt notice.

6 Exemption of Liability

Derived from the traditional doctrine of *pacta sunt servanda* (agreement must be kept), a foundational rule is that a party who fails to perform a contract shall be held liable for breach. Such liability may be excused under certain

---

[93] See Goetz & Scott, *The Mitigation Principle: Toward a General Theory of Contractual Obligation*, 69 Va. L. Rev. 967 (1983).
[94] See the Contract Law, art. 119.
[95] See Li Guoguang, *supra* note 7 at p 497.
[96] See the Contract Law, art. 118.

circumstances, which are either agreed upon by the parties or identified in the law, however. If a party is exculpated from liability for breach pursuant to the agreed circumstances, the exculpation is called contractual exemption. When the liability for breach is excused under a provision of law, the exculpation is referred to as legal exemption. If a breach of contract falls within a legal exemption, the liability of the breaching party is exempted as a product of the operation of law, without reference to the agreement of the parties or the terms of the contract.

The only legal exemption of contractual liability in the Contract Law is the exemption on the ground of *force majeure*. Under Article 117 of the Contract Law, in a case where a contract cannot be performed because of *force majeure*, the liability for breach shall be excused in part or wholly in light of the effects of the *force majeure*. Recall that in Article 94 of the Contract Law, *force majeure* is a legal ground on which a contract may be rescinded. Here, upon the occurrence of *force majeure*, a party's obligation to perform the contract will be excused and the liability for breach will consequently be exempted.

Article 117 creates two exceptions to the legal exemption—namely *force majeure*—under the Contract Law. The first exception is where "the law otherwise provides." For example, under Article 34 of the Post Law, *force majeure* may not exempt the liability of the post office for the loss of money remittances or insured postal articles. The second exception involves delayed performance. Article 117 of the Contract Law provides that if *force majeure* occur after one party has delayed in performance, the liability shall not be exempted. The underlying reason is that delay in performance is a breach for which the non-performing party is liable, and *force majeure* should not exempt the liability of the party who is already in breach.

Quite often, parties to a contract prefer to negotiate into their contract a *force majeure* clause in order to better protect their respective interests. Note that in China, absence of a *force majeure* clause does not deprive a party of the right to claim exemption upon the occurrence of *force majeure* because of the Article 117 legal exemption. But, if there is a *force majeure* clause in the contract, the clause will be regarded as a supplement to the legal exemption and may be used to help allocate risks and ascertain the scope or coverage of the *force majeure*.

Again, as discussed, *force majeure* is defined in Article 117 of the Contract Law as objective circumstances that are unforeseeable, unavoidable, and insurmountable. To be exempted from liability for breach of contract on the ground of *force majeure*, the breaching party bears the burden to prove that the circumstance leading to the failure to perform meets the threshold of Article 117. On the other hand, in assessing whether a certain event constitutes a *force majeure*, the courts often take into consideration developments in the areas of science and technology.

For example, in *Zhongji General Import and Export Co. Ltd. v. Tianjin No.2 Port Co. Ltd.* (2000),[97] the Tianjin High People's Court held that a tropic storm in the sea constituted an event of *force majeure* based on the current state of science and technology, even though the storm was forecasted by the National Marine Forecast Station. The SPC endorsed this holding by publishing the judgment on the SPC's Gazette in the same year.[98]

---

97   The whole case is available at http://www.lawinfochina.com/display.aspx?id=64&lib=case.
98   SPC Gazette, Issue 5 (2000).

CHAPTER 11

Third Party Interests

With respect to a contract, a third party is a person who is not a party to the contract but is related to or has interests in the contract. A broad definition of third party includes any person other than the parties that may impact the contract's performance. The basic assumption in contract literature is that a valid contract has effects on, or produces consequences for, only the parties to the contract and does not externally affect others.[1] In contract jargon, this is the theory of "privity."[2] But third party theory penetrates the internality of contract affairs and brings non-parties' interest into the center of discussion by looking at external effects created by the contract.

Interestingly, in China the issue of third party interests has never received the attention it deserves. First of all, the Contract Law contains no special chapter dealing with third party interests and the law of third party interests can only be seen from the scattered provisions of the Contract Law. Secondly, almost none of the published contract books makes third party interests a separate issue or discusses third party interests in a specific way. Thirdly, there is a lack of symmetry among the rules that govern the relationships between parties and non-parties. The reasons attributable to this phenomenon may be many, but the most important one appears to be rooted in the traditional belief that a contract only involves the parties.[3]

Also, unlike the contract law of other countries, such as that of the United States, where third party interests include third party beneficiaries and assignment, Chinese contract law, as noted, considers assignment to be a matter of contract modification. In addition, the concept of third party beneficiary is seldom used in China. Even if a third party is characterized as a beneficiary in certain cases, no distinction is ever made between intended beneficiary and incidental beneficiary, or between creditor beneficiary and donee beneficiary.

---

1 See Robert Scott & Jody Kraus, *Contract Law and Theory* (3rd ed), 1127 (LexisNexis, 2002).
2 Privity is commonly defined in the law dictionaries as a connection or mutual interest between parties. As applied to contracts, it refers to the legal doctrine that a contract confers rights and imposes liabilities only on its contracting parties.
3 A predominant doctrine in China that places non-parties outside the scop of contracts is relativism of contract. Under this doctrine, only the parties claim their respective rights and bear their respective obligations arising from the contract. In this sense, relativism may actually mean or bear a great resemblance to "privity," though the term "privity" is not commonly used in China.

Before the Contract Law was adopted, issues relating to third parties often arose in connection with government action. At that time, a prevalent notion was that a contract was an agreement dealing with civil affairs and transactions between the parties, and the only possible non-party who could affect the contract was government authority. Therefore, concerns about non-parties were all centered on the authority of the government, and the discussions about third parties in contracts mainly involved governmental intervening power.

A notable legal provision pertaining to government conduct involved in contracts is Article 116 of the 1986 Civil Code. Under Article 116, if a party fails to fulfill its contractual obligations due to a reason attributable to a government authority, the party shall first compensate the other party for damages or take other remedial measures as agreed upon in the contract, and then the government authority shall be responsible for settling the losses caused to the party.[4] The purpose of Article 116 is to ensure that the aggrieved party will properly be compensated in the case where the breach of contract was caused by an act of government authority.

The Contract Law contains several changes to previous legislation pertaining to third parties. First, it expands the definition of third parties to include those to or by whom a contract is performed. Second, the Contract Law replaces the term "government authority" with the term "third parties" to cover in a more general sense the situation where the non-performance is caused externally by a non-party, including government authority. Third, the Contract Law further specifies how a third party is involved in a contract. But again, the Contract Law does not use the term third party beneficiary nor does it differentiate between the different types of beneficiaries.

Under the Contract Law, there are three situations in which a third party will become an issue. The first situation is the contract whereby the parties agree to make performance to a third party. The second situation concerns the contract under which the performance is to be made by a third party. The third situation deals with the breach that is caused by a third party. In addition, the Contract Law has several provisions that are particularly aimed at protecting the interests of third parties. For instance, according to Article 106 of the Contract Law, the rights and obligations of a contract may not be terminated as a result of the assumption of the rights and obligations by the same person if the interests of a third party are involved.

It might be argued that third party issues cannot be fully addressed without discussing assignment and delegation because an assignment or delegation

---

4 See the 1986 Civil Code, art. 116.

involves a transfer of contractual right or obligations from a party to a non-party. But as noted, assignment and delegation in China normally come up in the context of the modification of contracts. A common belief in China is that assignment and delegation are more closely related to modification than to the third parties. Thus, in the Contract Law, the provisions on contract assignment and delegation are provided in conjunction with those on contract modification.

1   Third Party Receiving Performance

Under the Contract Law, the parties to a contract may agree to have the contract performed to a third party. In the context of the Contract Law, a third party who is designated to receive performance consists of two kinds of person: (1) a person upon whom the benefits of the contract will be conveyed through performance, and (2) a person who will not benefit from the performance but rather receives the performance on behalf of an obligee for the benefit of the obligee. In the former situation, the third party is called the beneficiary, but in the latter case, the third party is actually an agent of the obligee to receive the performance for the benefit of the obligee. Therefore, a third party in China does not necessarily mean a third party beneficiary.

According to Article 64 of the Contract Law, where the parties agree that the obligor will perform its obligations to a third party, and the obligor fails to perform the obligations to the third party or the performance does not meet the terms of the contract, the obligor shall be liable to the obligee for the breach of contract. There are three points that can be inferred from Article 64. First, upon an agreement between the parties, a contract can be performed to a third party. Second, a contract to be performed to a third party is enforceable, and failure to perform constitutes breach of the contract. Third, in the case of breach, the obligee has a claim against the obligor for remedies.

However, Article 64 invites confusion. Based on its language, it is unclear whether the third party referred to in Article 64 includes both the third party "beneficiary" and the third party "agent," or only one of the two. On the other hand, an uncertainty arising from Article 64 is whether a third party to whom the performance is supposed to be made also has the right to demand performance in the case of non-performance or non-conforming performance. Put differently, the question is whether the third party has the same claim as the obligee against the obligor.

Some in China take the view that Article 64 is about a third party "beneficiary" because it governs the situation where a contract is made for the benefit of a third party.[5] Others insist that third party in Article 64 refers only to the third party "agent" who receives the performance for the benefit of the obligee. They argue that since Article 64 does not confer any right of claim to the third party and the performance to a third party is based on the intent of the obligee, its purpose is to satisfy the contractual interest of the obligee.[6]

In the middle is an argument that Article 64 should be interpreted to include the third party "agent," but whether the contract is made for the benefit of a third party "beneficiary" rather than the obligee via a third party "agent" depends on whether a right to a claim for the performance has been created for the third party. To further this argument, a three-test guidance has been introduced to help distinguish between the third party "beneficiary" and third party "agent."

The first test is the third party's independent right to make a claim. If the parties agree that the third party shall be entitled to the performance of the contract, such that the third party has an independent claim against the obligor for non-performance or non-conforming peformance, the third party shall be deemed a "beneficiary." If, however, the third party only helps accept the performance from the obligor for the obligee, the third party is an "agent."

The second test is the intention of the parties with regard to the performance of the contract. When performance is intended to be made to a third party and the right of the third party to the performance arises after conclusion of the contract, the third party is a "beneficiary," unless the third party rejects the performance. But if the performance to a third party is intended only as a change of the "route" of the performance and the beneficiary is actually the obligee itself, the third party is then an "agent."

The third test is the obligation to perform. If the performance under the contract is to be made to a third party but the obligor is responsible only to the obligee, not the third party, for the performance, the obligee other than the third party is the beneficiary. The reason is that in this situation, the third party will not benefit from the performance. The theory is that as a beneficiary, the third party should be the person to whom the obligor is obligated for the performance of the contract.[7]

---

5   See Jiang Ping et al, *A detailed Explanation of the Contract Law of China*, 54 (China University of Political Science & Law Press, 1999). See also Cui Yunling, *A General View on Contract Law*, 164–165 (China University of People's Public Security Press, 2003).
6   See Li Guoguang, *Explanation and Application of the Contract Law*, 282–283 (Xinhua Press, 1999).
7   See Wang Liming, *Study on Contract Law*, 56–57 (People's University Press, 2003).

Many, however, believe that Article 64 should include both the third party beneficiary and third party agent. On the one hand, Article 64 requires that the performance to a third party be made on the basis of the parties' agreement. That agreement may embrace an intent of the parties (the obligee in particular) to convey the benefit of the performance on the third party (beneficiary) or may just obligate the obligor to make performance to the obligee through the third party (agent). On the other hand, the language of Article 64 which states that the obligor shall be liable to the obligee for breach of the contract does not necessarily mean that the obligor is not liable for making the performance to the third party. The major argument is that Article 64 would be meaningless if it was interpreted to exclude the third party's right to make a claim against the obligor in the event of breach.[8]

In addition, there is an argument that performance to a third party under Article 64 contains three default features. First, the performance is made not to the obligee but rather to the third party because the obligee has agreed that the third party will be the recipient of the performance. Second, the third party acquires directly from the agreement of the parties the right to make a request to the obligor for performance, although the obligee's right to the performance remains. Third, the performance to a third party is not premised on the consent of the third party. In other words, to make the third party the recipient of the performance, the obligee does not have to consult with the third party in advance.[9]

The SPC has also recognized the dual coverage of Article 64—namely, the coverage of the third party beneficiary and the third party agent. Under its 2009 Interpretation of the Contract Law, the SPC opines that the people's courts may under the circumstances of each case treat the third party provided in Article 64 of the Contract Law as the third party having no independent claim right, but may not make *ex officio* such a party the third party with an independent claim right.[10] Apparently, the SPC seems to suggest that the status of a third part as a beneficiary or agent depends on the intent of the parties to the contract.

---

[8] See Li Guoguang, *supra* note 6 at p. 283. According to a different view, one of the legal effects of performance to a third party under Article 64 is that the third party has the right to ask the obligor to perform and such right is granted by, and exercised on behalf of, the obligee. See Jiang Ping, *supra* note 5 at p 54.

[9] See Sun Lihai, *A Practical Explanation to the Contract Law of China*, 86–87 (Industry and Commerce Publishing House, 1999).

[10] See the SPC, the 2009 Contract Law Interpretation, art. 16.

When a third party under the agreement of the contractual parties is the beneficiary of the contract, it is commonly held in China that the third party may choose to accept or refuse the performance. If the third party accepts, its right to request the obligor to perform is vested. The third party's acceptance may be assumed if no objection is made. When the third party refuses to accept the performance, the obligor is still liable to the obligee for the performance because as a result of the refusal, the right to the performance will automatically be regained by the obligee.

There are two questions related to the agreed performance to a third party. The first question concerns the additional expenses that may incur in association with the performance to a third party. Generally, the performance to a third party shall not increase the financial burden on the obligor or increase the level of difficulty in performing as compared with performance directly made to the obligee. A well accepted rule is that any additional costs for the performance to a third party shall be borne by the obligee or by the third party if the third party agrees.[11]

The second question is whether the obligor may still make the performance to the obligee after the third party agrees to accept the performance. Again, the answer to this question varies, depending on the type of the third party who receives the performance. If a third party beneficiary is involved, the performance may not be made to the obligee because under the agreement of the contractual parties the performance should be made to the third party. In this situation, the performance made to the obligee does not extinguish the obligor's duty of performance to the third party. But if the obligor has already made performance to the obligee, the obligor may ask the obligee for redemption.[12] If, however, the third party is simply an agent of the obligee for the purpose of receiving the performance from the obligor, the obligor may still make the performance directly to the obligee.

Note that under Article 64, the independent claim right of a third party beneficiary seems to be limited to the right to ask for performance. Article 64 does not give the third party beneficiary the right to hold the obligor liable in the case where the obligor fails to make the performance as agreed to the third party or the performance does not accord with the terms of the contract. Instead, Article 64 makes the obligor liable only to the obligee for a breach involving performance to a third party.

---

11   See Jiang Ping, *supra* note 5 at 54.
12   See Li Guoguang, *supra* note 6 at pp 283–284.

2 Third Party Performing the Contract

A well-established and classic maxim in the law of contract is that a contract may only bind the parties, and therefore, the parties are prohibited from imposing obligations on a third party. There is an exception in the case where the third party agrees to assume the obligations of the contract between the parties, however. As long as the third party consents to performing the contract, the effect of the contract will be extended to it. Literally, the assumption of contractual obligations by a third party may take different forms: third party performance, delegation, or novation.

In contract theory, a delegation occurs when a contracting party who is under a duty to perform (obligor-delegator) appoints a third party to render the performance to the obligee. By delegating its contractual duty, the obligor-delegator is transferring its obligations to the delegated third party (delegatee) who will then assume the obligations and perform the contract. After the delegation, the delegatee is in the position of the obligor in terms of performance but the obligor-delegator normally still remains liable to the obligee.

A novation is essentially a replacement of an original party to the contract with a new party by the consent of all parties involved. Typically, a novation will take place when an existing contract is overriden by a new contract as a result of a change of party. In the U.S., for example, a novation substitutes a new party and discharges one of the original parties to the contract by agreement of all parties.[13] Therefore, in a novation, because of the change of a party, mostly the obligor, a new contractual relationship is to be established between an original contractual party and a third party (new party).

Third party performance or performance by a third party, by Chinese definition, is different from delegation or novation. In the context of the Contract Law, third party performance involves no transfer of debt or change of party but only a surrogate for the performance of the contract. For the pruposes of performance of a contract, a surrogate means that a third party agrees to render the performance of the contract to the obligee on behalf of the obligor. The surrogate normally occurs when there is an agreement and contractual relationship between the obligor and the third party.

To illustrate, assume that A and B enter into a contract under which A shall make a payment of RMB 20,000 to B, and in the meantime, A and C have an existing lease where C pay rents to A. When A and B agree that the payment of RMB 20,000 shall be made by C, then in terms of performance of the contract

---

13   See Restatement of Contracts (2nd), §280.

between A and B, C will be A's surrogate. The reason why C agrees to make the payment is that the payment will off-set the rents C will have to pay to A.

Such a surrogate may also be found when a third party volunteers to offer the performance. The voluntary performance can be made with or without the knowledge of the obligor. For example, a father learns that his son owes a certain amount of money to A, and the father then pays A for the money owed without telling his son. Clearly, the father as a surrogate making the payment constitutes voluntary performance with regard to the money his son owes to A, and the performance releases his son from being obligated to pay A.

But, there is a debate as to the nature of voluntary performance by a third party. One view is that third party voluntary performance creates a *de facto* donation. In the above case, for example, what the father did by paying his son's debt was actually a gift he made to his son. The other view regards the third party's voluntary performance as conduct of *netotiorum gestor*—a person who voluntarily designates himself as an agent to take charge of an affair or concern for the benefit of another person without the knowledge or consent of the latter.[14]

The Contract Law adopts the concept of third party performance, but limits such performance to that arising from the agreement of the parties. The recognition of third party performance in the Contract Law derives from the notion that to allow a third party to perform on behalf of the obligor would help facilitate multiple business transactions that are related among each other. In this context, third party performance, like a delegation, is also an assumption of the obligation.

But, third party performance as set forth in the Contract Law is not delegation because, as noted, delegation results in the transfer of debts while there is no debt transfer in the case of third party performance. Therefore, some scholars in China prefer to call the third party who is designated by the parties to perform the contract as an "entrusted obligor" in order to differentiate such third party from a delegatee in the case of delegation.[15]

Under Article 65 of the Contract Law, when the parties agree that a third party will perform the contract's obligations to the obligee but the third party fails to perform or the performance does not satisfy the terms of the contract, the obligor shall be liable to the obligee for the breach of contract. Article 65 states the nature of third party performance and the relationship between the

---

14   See Wang Liming, *supra* note 7 at p 63.
15   See Chu Yunling, *supra* note 5 at pp 166–167.

third party and the obligor. More specifically, Article 65 contains a number of factors that are essential to third party performance.

First, third party performance is based on the consent of the parties to the contract. Second, third party performance does not need an agreement between the third party and the obligee or the obligor, though in many cases a certain relationship between the third party and obligor has already existed. Third, the third party, when making the performance, does not acquire the status of a party to the contract. Fourth, the third party may refuse to perform, and the obligee has no claim against the third party. And fifth, the obligor remains liable to the obligee until its obligations are fully performed.

The legal effect of third party performance under the Contract Law is that the performance made by a third party as agreed by the parties is deemed the same as performance rendered by the obligor itself. The practical importance of this effect can be seen from two aspects. In one aspect, third party performance accepted by the obligee will serve as a discharge of the contract between the obligor and obligee as if the contract has been fully performed by the obligor. The other aspect is that when the parties agree to have the obligations performed by a third party, the obligee may not refuse to accept the third party performance without justified reason. If the third party encounters an unreasonable refusal by the obligee to accept the performance, the obligee may be held liable for breach of the contract resulting from the delay in acceptance of the performance.

3   Breach Caused by a Third Party

It is not uncommon that a contract is breached not because of the fault of either of the parties but due to the conduct of a third party. To illustrate, assume that A and B have a contract by which A will deliver to B a machine on a specified day, and C is the supplier of a major component of the machine. A fails to make timely delivery of the machine because C did not provide A with the part as scheduled. Thus, A's breach of the contract with B is caused by C's failure to make the part available at the required time. Another example, which is typical in China, is that a party breaches a contract as a result of the conduct of government authority. In many cases, the breach of contract occurs when a party is asked to change a production plan or to accommodate local needs or interests.

As noted, the 1986 Civil Code contains a special provision, namely Article 116, which is intended to deal with action of government authority that affects the contract. The Contract Law basically follows the 1986 Civil Code and separates contract liability from other liability by requiring the breaching party to compensate the aggrieved party without citing the government action as an excuse. The only difference between the Contract Law and the 1986 Civil Code is that the Contract Law places the government in the same category as the third party. According to Article 121 of the Contract Law, a party who breaches the contract due to a reason attributable to a third party shall be liable for breach of the contract to the other party. And, the dispute between the breaching party and the third party shall be resolved separately pursuant to the law or the agreement between them.[16]

The fundamental notion underlying Article 121 is the doctrine of relativism of contract. Under the doctrine of relativism, a third party's conduct does not constitute a breach of contract because a contract is only a matter between the contracting parties. But such relativism does not mean that the third party is free from any liability for its conduct that is the cause of the breach of the contract. On the contrary, the third party will be liable to the breaching party who is affected by the third party in the performance of the contract the breaching party has entered with the aggrieved party.

Thus, when breach of a contract is caused by a third party, the liability of the third party will be dealt with separately and outside the contract between the parties. In this regard, Article 121 of the Contract Law is quite specific. First, if a contract is breached due to conduct of a third party, the breaching party is liable for the breach and the aggrieved party may not make any claim against the third party. Second, the breaching party may seek redemption from the third party for the money paid to the aggrieved party. Also, under Article 121, if there is an agreement between the breaching party and the third party, the dispute over the redemption shall be settled according to the agreement. If no agreement exists, the dispute shall be resolved under the provisions of the law.[17]

There are different categories under which a third party may become a cause of a breach of contract. In one category, the third party is a secondary performer of the contract. Secondary means that the third party assists the obligor in performing the contract. For example, A and B have a contract that A will build a house for B. During the construction, A asks his friend C to help with the ground paving for the foundation of the house. C, however, mistakenly uses wrong materials for the paving, which causes a significant delay in completion of the house. In this case, pursuant to the Contract Law, B may

---

16 See the Contract Law, art. 121.
17 See *id.*

only sue A for damages under the contract, and A may not assert C's mistake as a defense to the delay.

Another category involves the situation where the third party is contracted by a contractual party to perform the whole or part of the contract the party made with another contracting party. The most common case in this regard is the one in which the third party is a subcontractor. When an obligor engages a subcontractor, the engagement does not affect the contract between the obligor and obligee. If the subcontractor casues the obligor to breach the contract, the obligor rather than the subcontractor is liable to the obligee for the breach.

The third category is the superior authority or parent company of a party to the contract. In China, prior to the nation's economic reform in the late 1970s, almost every economic unit and enterprise was owned or controlled by the State under the planned economy. A significant aspect of the economic reform was separating the State from business operations by privatizing certain State-owned enterprises (e.g., allowing private individuals to own shares of a State-owned enterprise) or granting more power to the State-owned enterprises and other business entities to run their businesses.

But still, there are many cases in which the business operation of a company or enterprise is heavily influenced, if not controlled, by governmental authorities that were formerly the decision makers of those enterprises or entities.[18] As is often seen in reality, if a business or enterprise implicates strong local interests, its operation, to a great extent, must meet the need of local governments and even the tastes of local officials. It is very hard, if not impossible, for such a business or enterprise to stay free from the interference of local authorities.

Before the adoption of the 1986 Civil Code, when a contract had to be changed or the performance of the contract was affected as a result of the exercise of government power, the only choice available to the aggrieved party was to ask the superior government agency for approval of writing-off the damages. Then it would be up to the government agency to decide whether and how the aggrieved party should be compensated. The aggrieved party may not seek to hold the other party liable for the breach of contract.

---

18   In all State-owned enterprises—although many such enterprises have been converted into corporation-type business entities (either companies with limited liability or companies limited by shares)—business operations are somewhat under the control of the government through the appointment of top business executives (CEO or Chairman). For instance, in August 2004, the State Council appointed new ECOs of four major Chinese airlines (all of which are companies by shares) to replace the old ones who were discharged for different reasons.

The 1986 Civil Code permits the aggrieved party to request damages from the other party without making any plea to the relevant authority. By treating the government authority as a third party, the Contract Law requires the breaching party to first compensate the aggrieved party who suffers damages from the breach caused by a third party. After such compensation, the breaching party may seek redemption from the third party either under the agreement between them or according to the provisions of law, especially when the breach is caused by the action of the superior authority of the breaching party.

4 Bona Fide Third Party

The law involving *bona fide* third parties is regarded as another underdeveloped area in the contract law in China, although the concept itself has long been accepted in dealing with civil matters that concern the acquisition of movables. In the property area, there has been an established rule that if a piece of movable property is purchased by a third party who has no knowledge of imperfect title of the property in the transactions, the owner or the lien holder may not make the claim against the third party for the return of the property. This rule also applies to real property under common ownership.

Under the 2007 Property Law, common ownership refers to ownership under which real or movable property is owned by two or more entities or individuals.[19] Common ownership can be either co-ownership or joint ownership.[20] Co-ownership is also called ownership by shares, which means that the co-owners enjoy the ownership of the property according to their respective shares.[21] Joint ownership is referred to as ownership under which the owners share ownership interests in the property.[22]

According to the SPC, the disposal of property owned under joint ownership by one of the owners during the existence of such ownership without the consent of the other owners shall generally be held invalid. But if a third party acquires the property for value in good faith, the legitimate interest of the third party shall be protected. The owner disposing of the said property shall compensate the damages subsequently incurred by the other owners.[23]

---

19 See the 2007 Property Law, art. 93.
20 Note that China has not adopted such concepts as joint tenancy or tenancy in entirety in regard to marital property.
21 See the 2007 Property Law, art. 94.
22 See *id.*, art. 95.
23 See the SPC, *the Opinions on Several Matters Concerning the General Principles of the Civil Law of China* (1988), art 89.

Another area involving *bona fide* third parties is agency. There are several articles in the 1986 Civil Code that are aimed at protecting the third party in good faith with regard to the conduct of the agent. Article 65 of the 1986 Civil Code, for example, provides that if the power of attorney is unclear as to the authority conferred, the principal shall bear the responsibility towards the third party and the agent shall be held jointly and severally liable. But under Article 66 of the 1986 Civil Code, if an agent collaborates with a third party to harm the interests of the principal, the agent and the third party shall be held jointly and severally liable.

There is no definition of *bona fide* third party in Chinese legislation. A general understoodig, however, is that a *bona fide* third party is someone who is not a party to a certain transaction but is related in good faith to one of the parties in the transaction. During the drafting process of the Contract Law, there was a suggestion that the Contract Law should contain provisions on bona fide third parties. Consequently, the initial draft of the Contract Law included a provision on a *bona fide* third party with respect to a contract assignment.

The draft provision read: "a contract may not be assigned if the parties have the agreement prohibiting the assignment, but the agreement may not be used against a *bona fide* third party." This provision, however, met resistance from the legislators, and as a result the phrase "*bona fide* third party" was deleted from the final draft. There seemed to have been at least two concerns: one concern was that the term "*bona fide*" was not well-defined and therefore, it was feared, would cause confusion in its application. The other concern was the uncertainty about the standard under which a *bona fide* third party was to be determined.

In the 2017 Property Law, there is a provision concerning a *bona fide* third party purchaser or transferee of property. As noted, under Article 106 of the 2007 Property Law, where a party that lacks title to dispose of a piece of property transfers the property to a transferee, the owner has the right to recover the property. The transferee may acquire ownership of the property so transferred, however, if (a) the transferee is in good faith at the time of transfer, (b) the transfer is made at a reasonable price, and (c) a registration is made as required by the law for the property transferred or the property is delivered if no registration is required.[24]

The Contract Law has been criticized for not having properly covered the issue of third parties. The Contract Law not only fails to offer protection to the *bona fide* third party, but also contains very limited provisions relating to

---

24 See the 2007 Property Law, art. 106.

third party interests. Many suggest that, given their importance both in theory and in practice, the interests of third parties should be adequately addressed and protected either by future legislation or through judicial interpretation of the SPC.[25]

---

[25] See Li Guoguang, *supra* note 6 at 500–502.

CHAPTER 12

International Contracts

International contracts are commonly defined in China as contracts that involve "foreign elements." For this reason, international contracts in China are often called foreign contracts. If a contract is considered foreign, it will be dealt with differently than a domestic contract. Among the major differences, a foreign contract may involve an application of a foreign law or a law of foreign jurisdiction while there is no such issue in a domestic contract.

1   Foreign Elements

In general, a contract that is considered to have a "foreign element" is one of the following: (1) a contract in which at least one of the parties to the contract is a foreigner, stateless person, foreign enterprise or organization, or a person whose habitual residence is in a foreign country; (2) a contract that is concluded, modified, or performed outside the territory of China; (3) a contract that contains the subject matter (or the object of the contract) located in a foreign country; or (4) a contract that could be deemed foreign under certain circumstances.[1]

It should be noted that in defining foreign element, the word "foreign" normally implicates foreign countries or the places crossing the nation's borders. But for purposes of jurisdiction and application of law, Hong Kong and

---

[1] In China, a contract creates a civil relation between the parties. According to the SPC, in any of the following situations, the people's court will consider a civil relation to be a foreign civil relation: (a) one or both of parties are foreign nationals, foreign legal persons or other organizations, or stateless persons; (b) the habitual residence of one or both of the parties is located outside the territory of China; (c) the subject matter of the civil relation is outside the territory of China; (d) the legal facts that create, modify, or extinquish the civil relation occurs outside the territory of China, and (e) other situations in which a civil relation can be considered as foreign. See the SPC *Interpretation on Several Issues Concerning Application of the Law on the Application of Law Concerning Foreign Civil Relations (I)* (Dec. 28, 2012) [hereinafter *Choice of Law Statute Interpretation*]. Moreover, a British scholar defines "foreign element" to mean "simply a contract with some system of law other than that of the 'forum.' … Such foreign elements in the facts of a case are quite commonplace: a contract was made with a foreign company or was to be performed in a foreign country, or a tort was committed there, or property was situated there, or one of the parties is not English." *See* John H.C. Morris, The Conflict of Laws (5th ed), 2 (Sweet & Maxwell, 2000).

Macau—the two Special Administrative Regions (SARS)—though part of China, are both considered foreign under the one country with two systems scheme. Thus, a contract that involves the two SARS will be deemed a foreign or international contract. Similarly, Taiwan is also treated as foreign given its special status.[2]

Also important to note is that the determination of "foreign element" for a natural person is not based on the person's domicile but rather the habitual residence of the person. In China, domicile is normally understood as the place of household residence. Habitual residence, according to the SPC's interpretation, is the place in which the person has lived for more than one year and has used as the center of his or her living at the time the related foreign civil relation is created, changed, or terminated, except for seeking medical treatment, job dispatching, or business purposes.[3]

Before the Contract Law was adopted in 1999, international or foreign contracts, as noted, were governed by a separate contract law named the "Foreign Economic Contract Law." At that time, making foreign contracts was viewed as a business activity requiring application of special rules. For example, under the Foreign Economic Contract Law, a Chinese citizen was not eligible to be a party to a foreign contract.[4] The promulgation of the Contract Law unified Chinese contract legislation so that all contracts, regardless of whether they are foreign or domestic, are under the umbrella of the Contract Law.

International contracts possess some distinctions compared to domestic contracts, however. As mentioned, one distinction of international contracts is that the involvement of foreign elements in such contracts makes the choice of law an important issue that must be considered. Unlike a domestic contract that is completely within the domain of Chinese laws, an international contract may result in an application of a foreign law. Such application may arise at the choice of the parties or through the applicable choice of law rules.

---

2 For historical reasons, China treats Hong Kong and Marco differently from the Mainland. The structural format under which Hong Kong and Marco are being managed after the handover is referred to as "one country with two systems." As part of its scheme to reunite the country, China has been trying to employ the same idea to Taiwan, though there are tremendous resistances from Taiwan.
3 See the SPC, the Choice of Law Statute Interpretation, art. 15.
4 The Foreign Economic Contract Law applied to "economic contracts, concluded between enterprises or other economic organizations of the People's Republic of China and foreign enterprises, other foreign economic organizations or individuals." Clearly, Chinese individuals were foreclosed from making a foreign contract. See Foreign Economic Contract Law (1985), art. 2. An English translation is available at http://www.qis.net/chinalaw/preclaw20.htm.

In addition, an international contract may go beyond the reach of the judicial power of the people's courts even though the contract is concluded or performed in China. This is particularly true when the parties to a contract agree to choose a foreign forum to adjudicate the disputes arising from the contract. Of course, under certain circumstances, the application of Chinese law becomes mandatory, which leaves no choice to the parties to select a foreign law as the governing law. Also, in some cases, the people's courts have exclusive jurisdiction and no foreign court jurisdiction is recognized.

Moreover, since it raises issues of jurisdiction and choice of law, an international contract is not only subject to the Contract Law, but also governed by the Civil Procedure Law (CPL) and the Law of the Application of Law Concerning Foreign Civil Relation (Choice of Law Statute). The CPL was adopted in 1991 and amended three times in 2007, 2012, and 2017. Part IV of the CPL provides special procedures that apply to international civil litigations. Enacted on October 28, 2010, the Choice of Law Statute is the most recent choice of law legislation in China. It codifies all choice of law rules in the country.

2 Choice of Law in International Contracts

Choice of law inevitably becomes an issue when the contractual parties or the transactions involved are subject to the authority of more than one sovereign state or nation. In international business transactions, disputes may arise at any stage. To resolve the disputes, the most confronted matter for the parties and their lawyers is the governing law. When drafting an international contract, the lawyers often have to think ahead and get prepared for such questions as what law the contract will be subject to or under which rules the rights and obligations of the parties to the contract will be determined. With a well-drafted choice of law clause in the contract, the certainty and predictability about the outcome of any dispute resolution concerning the transactions will be greatly enhanced.

The choice of law governing business transactions with China is no exception in terms of its significance. In fact, it causes even greater concern to foreign businesses. Unfamiliarity with Chinese laws and legal system aside, a very common view among the West is that China is a country with no rule of law. Therefore, in spite of the incredible business opportunities provided by the Chinese economy's rapid growth (the fastest in the world) in the past few decades, consternation among foreign investors and companies about the legal climate in China still remains.

Despite the concerns, however, foreign business transactions in China have never stopped. To the contrary, the cross-border transaction volume has increased dramatically from year to year. When preparing an international contract, the parties, through their lawyers, often draft a choice of law clause carefully with a hope that their interests will be best protected in the case of a dispute. With regard to the governing law, lawyers often endeavor to have the contract governed by either the law of their client's own country, law that is similar to their client's national law, or at least by the law of a neutral country.

In certain cases, however, the parties, to avoid jeopardizing the deal that they really want, may choose to leave the choice of law issue open due to the difficulty in reaching an agreement on the governing law. It is not uncommon that the parties first enter into the contract and then negotiate and resolve the matter of choice of law at a later time. It is also often seen that the parties incorporate into the contract as governing rules the provisions of a particular treaty, existing trade usages, customs, or other internationally accepted rules.

In China, the choice of law in contracts with foreign elements were determined under the provisions of the 1986 Civil Code and the Contract Law prior to the adoption of the Choice of Law Statute in 2010. Like the 1986 Civil Code and the Contract Law, the Choice of Law Statute contains two basic choice of law rules for contracts: choice of law by the parties under the principle of party autonomy and, absent the parties' choice, the closest connection standard. In addition, the Choice of Law Statute provides certain default rules under the characteristic performance doctrine.

2.1 Choice of Law by the Parties

With respect to the choice of law in international contracts, a well-established rule is to allow the parties to choose the governing law. This rule is originated from the concept of freedom of contract, and is framed under the principle of party autonomy. Classically, freedom of contract was viewed as granting to the parties the power to regulate their own contracts. As Professor Kessler pointed out, as to the parties, the law of contracts is of their own making.[5] Under the party autonomy doctrine, if the parties have expressly chosen the law to apply to their contract, the law so chosen shall be used to govern the contract.

But when the choice is not made expressly, the issue is dealt with differently from country to country. In Great Britain, for example, if no choice of law is expressly made by the parties, the governing law may be inferred from the terms

---

5 See Kessler, *Contract of Adhesion—Some Thoughts About Freedom of Contract*, 43 Colum. L. Rev., 629–30 (1943).

of the contract by the court through "applying sound ideas of business, convenience, and sense to the language of the contract itself, with a view toward discovering from it the true intention of the parties."[6] However, in many other countries, the parties' intent in terms of applicable law may not be inferred.

In China, party autonomy is also an accepted principle governing the choice of law in foreign contracts. As noted, this principle has been incorporated into both the 1986 Civil Code and the Contract Law to give the parties the right to choose the law that they see fit to govern the contract. For example, under Article 145 of the 1986 Civil Code and Article 126 of the Contract Law, the parties to a foreign contract may choose the law applicable to the settlement of their contractual disputes except if otherwise provided by the law.[7] Article 41 of the Choice of Law Statute drops the "proviso" and simply provides that the parties may by agreement choose the law applicable to their contract.[8]

The implication of the choice of law provisions is that the law intended by the parties as a result of a fair bargain between them will govern their contract. In an international civil or commercial contract, the parties' choice of applicable law may be made either in the contract as a contract clause or outside the contract as a separate agreement. The former is commonly called a choice of law clause while the latter is referred to as a choice of law agreement. The two have the same legal effect in their application.

However, there are several questions concerning the choice of law by the parties that need to be further addressed. The first question is whether the choice of law must be made expressly by the parties or may be inferred from the provisions of the contract by looking into the "presumed intent" of the parties. Not until the enactment of the Choice of Law Statute, was this question ever answered in the law. In practice, the SPC has long taken a restrictive approach by limiting the choice of law to the one expressly made by the parties.

In its Answers to the Questions Concerning Application of Foreign Economic Contracts Law in 1987, the SPC explicitly ruled out the notion of implied choice of law by requiring that the contract law agreed upon by the parties be both the product of negotiation and made expressly.[9] The SPC's view against implied choice of law has also been endorsed by the Chinese Society of Private International Law (CSPIL). In 2000, the CSPIL published a Model Law of

---

6 See Morris, *supra* note 1 at p 323.
7 See the 1986 Civil Code, art. 145, the Contract Law, art. 126.
8 See the Choice of Law Statute, art. 41.
9 See the SPC, *1987 Answers to the Questions Concerning Application of Foreign Economic Contracts Law*, art. 2, See also *Gazette of the Supreme People's Court of the People's Republic of China*, Vol. 12 (1987).

the Private International Law of the People's Republic of China (Model Law), aimed at providing scholarly opinions for the legislature to reference in drafting future legislation.

Article 100 of the Model Law, under the title of Party Autonomy, provides that a contract is to be governed by the law agreed upon and expressly chosen by the parties except as otherwise provided by the law, or by treaties concluded by China or to which China is a member.[10] Based on the SPC's opinion and the Model Law, it has become a commonly accepted rule in China that the choice of law by the parties may not be implied by inference from the intent of the parties.

The Choice of Law Statute for the first time sets forth a statutory requirement that the choice of governing law by the parties must be expressly made in order to be enforceable. In addition, the Choice of Law Statute expands the application of party autonomy to civil relations in general. It is provided in Article 3 as a general rule that the parties may expressly choose the law applicable to a foreign-related civil relation in accordance with the provisions of law.[11] This expansion reflects the recent development of allowing the parties to choose the applicable law for both contractual and non-contractual obligations.[12]

Note, however, that the express choice of law does not have to be made in writing—though writing is preferred. Also, pursuant to the opinion of the SPC, if the parties each cite the law of the same country as the governing law and no objection is raised, the people's court may hold that the parties have already made a choice of law applicable to their foreign-related civil relation, and the court will apply that law accordingly.[13]

The second question is when the parties may make a choice as to the governing law. Neither the Contract Law nor the Choice of Law Statute contain a specific provision in this regard. But the SPC has taken a quite flexible approach that permits the parties to decide any time before trial what the law governing their contract will be. In the SPC's opinion, when the parties, prior

---

10   See the Chinese Society of Private International Law, *Model Law of the Private International Law of the People's Republic of China*, art. 100, published in 2000 by Law Publishing House (hereinafter referred to as Model Law); See also Han Depei, "Private International Law," Beijing Higher Education Press and Beijing University Press, 2000 at pp. 198–199.
11   See the Choice of Law Statutes, art. 3.
12   See EU Regulation on the Law Applicable to Non-Contractual Obligations, Regulation (EC) 864/2007 (Rome II).
13   See the SPC, the Rules on Several Issues Concerning the Application of Law in Adjudication of Foreign-Related Civil and Commercial Disputes (2007) (2007 Rules), art. 4; See also the SPC, Choice of Law Statute Interpretation, *supra* note 1, art. 8.

to the conclusion of the court hearing at the first instance trial, agree to choose a governing law or to modify the choice already made, the people's courts shall permit such choice or modification.[14]

Thus, according to the SPC, the parties to a foreign contract may choose the governing law at the time of contract, after the occurrence of disputes, at the time of case filing, or prior to the end of the court hearing of the first instance trial. In addition, in the SPC's opinion, the disputes arising out of a contract for which the parties may choose the governing law include those concerning conclusion of the contract, time for the conclusion, interpretation of contract terms, performance of the contract, and modification, suspension, assignment, dissolution, as well as termination of the contract.[15] But neither the capacity of the parties to the contract nor the formality of the contract is the issue listed in the SPC's opinion that can be resolved by the parties' choice of law.[16]

The third question concerns whether the law of the country that is chosen by the parties must relate to the contract or controversy. The relation requirement is used in some countries as a means to impose a limitation on the choice of law by the parties. In the U.S., for example, a relation between the state whose law is chosen and the parties or the transactions involved is considered an essential element for the choice of law by the parties. Under both § 1–301 of the UCC and § 187 of the Restatement (Second) of the Conflict of Law, an agreement of the parties on the choice of law applicable to a contract is enforceable only if there is a certain relation.[17]

In China, relation is not an element for the enforceability of the contractual choice of law. Article 3 of the Choice of Law Statute contains no limitation on the parties' choice in terms of relation. According to the SPC, if a party requests a people's court to hold invalid a choice of applicable law by the parties on the ground that the law so chosen has no actual relation with the foreign civil relation in question, the request shall not be granted.[18] Therefore, the parties may

---

14 See *id*. The SPC, Choice of Law Statute Interpretation.
15 See the SPC, the 2007 Rules, supra note 13, art. 2.
16 As a general principle, civil capacity, including the capacity to a contract, is determined by the "personal law"—that is, the law of the country of which the party is a citizen or a resident. Also, because the Contract Law has special requirements relating to contract formality (writing, oral, or other forms), compliance with the formality requirements is critical to the validity of a contract that is concluded in China and such requirements may not be bypassed by the parties' choice of governing law.
17 See UCC, § 1–301, and Restatement (Second), §187.
18 See the SPC, the Choice of Law Statute Interpretation, art. 7.

by agreement choose as governing law the Chinese Law, or the law of another country or region that is in force.[19] But the SPC requires that the people's courts render a choice of law by the parties invalid if the choice is made in the case where the law does not explicitly permit such choice.[20]

The fourth question involves choice of international treaty or international customary law. There is no clear provision in either the Contract Law or the Choice of Law Statute. The Model Law provides that the parties may choose as the law governing their contract international customs or international civil and commercial treaties to which China is a member.[21] The SPC seems to follow the Model Law and allows fo application of international treaties or customs. According to the SPC, when an international treaty or international customary rule is to be applied, the application shall be made under the relevant provisions of the laws.[22]

In addition, the SPC takes a further step by providing that if the parties choose as their contract's governing law a treaty that is not yet effective in China, the people's court may determine the parties' respective rights and obligations pursuant to the provisions of the treaty, provided that such application does not violate the social public interests of China or the mandatory rules of Chinese laws and administrative regulations.[23] However, the choice of an international treaty does not include the provisions to which China has made reservation. Under Article 142 of the 1986 Civil Code, in the application of international treaties, the provisions to which China has made reservation must be excluded.[24]

The fifth question relates to the parties' choice of different laws to govern different parts of the contract. This is a question of whether the matters of a contract may be split between or among different legal systems. Splitting a contract means subjecting different aspects of the contract, and disputes arising therefrom, to different laws. For example, splitting occurs where the parties agree that the validity of their contract is to be governed by the law of country A, while the performance of their contract will be subject to the law of country B.

---

19   See the SPC, *supra* note 9, art. 2.
20   See *id.*, art. 6.
21   See Model Law, supra note 10, art.110.
22   See the SPC, the Choice of Law Statute Interpretation, art. 4 &5, *supra* note 1. An exception concerns the IP treaty that is already transformed or would need to be transformed into the domectic law in order for them to be applied.
23   See *id.*, art. 9.
24   See the 1986 Civil Code, art. 142.

In conflict of law theory, the doctrine that permits splitting is called *"dépeçage."* In China, the Choice of Law Statute is silent about whether a *"dépeçage"* would be accepted in the parties' choice of applicable laws in a contract.[25] But in the conflict of laws literature, there has been strong voice calling for the adoption of the *"dépeçage"* doctrine, and a notable example is the Model Law. Under Article 100 of the Model Law, the parties may decide to apply the law they choose to the whole contract or only to one or several parts of the contract. There is also an argument that since the Contract Law separates the matters of capacity and formality of a contract from the matters of contractual disputes and allows the parties to choose the law that governs contractual disputes, the Contract Law itself subjects different parts of contracts to different laws.[26]

The last question goes to the scope of the chosen law. The question is whether the chosen law of a particular country refers to the entire law or only the substantive law of that country. More specifically, the question is whether the law of a country includes the country's choice of law rules. To illustrate, if the law selected by the parties refers to the entire law of a country, the law will include that country's conflict of law rules. In such a situation, *renvoi* (transmission or remission) may occur and as a result, the law chosen by the parties may be replaced with the law of a country that the parties never designated.

With respect to conflict of laws, *renvoi* is commonly called an "escape device" that renders the choice of law by the parties meaningless because it leads to an application of law that is not intended by the parties. Thus, to avoid *renvoi*, the choice of law rules must be excluded from the law that parties have chosen. In fact, many countries reject *renvoi* because the use of *renvoi* may produce an endless circle in the determination of applicable law.

China does not accept *renvoi* with regard to choice of law. The Choice of Law Statute prohibits the use of *renvoi*. Under Article 9 of the Choice of Law Statute, the law of a foreign country applicable to foreign-related civil relations does not include the choice of law rules of the foreign country.[27] The SPC has also made clear that the law applicable to a foreign related civil or commercial contract is the substantive law of the relevant country or region, not including the country or region's conflict of law rules or procedural law.[28]

---

25 There is a concern about the confusion arising from the application of *"depecage."* The problem that *depecage* may cause arises where the two chosen laws cannot logically be reconciled in their application to a particular situation. See Morris, *supra* note 1 at p 329.
26 See Li Shuangyuan, the Direction of the Private International Law in the 21st Century, 527 (1999).
27 See the Choice of Law Statute, art. 9.
28 See the SPC, the 2007 Rules, supra note 13, art. 1.

Again, choice of law by the parties is premised on the notion of freedom of contract. But keep in mind that the contractual parties' freedom with respect to choice of law is not unlimited. To the contrary, the freedom of contractual parties to determine the law applicable to their contract is restrained to the extent that the exercise of the freedom of choice must not be repugnant to the public policy of the forum country, and must not violate the mandatory rules of the forum or the country whose law will be applied absent the parties' choice. In either case, the law so chosen by the parties will not be applied.

The public policy exception is a safeguard device to exclude application of a foreign law in order to protect the state or public interests of the forum country. On the ground of public policy, the forum will deny the application of an applicable foreign law if the application is deemed to be offensive to the fundamental principles or policy of its country. Mandatory rules are rules that cannot be derogated from by agreement. Like public policy, the mandatory rule exception is also a common mechanism employed to preclude application of law that would otherwise be applied.

The public policy exception differs from the mandatory rule exception in two major aspects. First, to constitute public policy, there must something that is considered fundamental to social values and morals, principles of justice, and the public welfare. A mandatory rule involves a preempted area where the contractual choice of a different law by the parties is not permissible. Second, the public policy exception functions as a safeguard to exclude the application of foreign law, while the mandatory rule exception serves as a protective measure to deprive the parties of their freedom to choose other law.

In addition, a choice of foreign law will be excluded if such choice is aimed at evading Chinese law that otherwise would have to be applied. In the SPC's opinion, if a party deliberately creates a connecting point to a certain foreign-related civil relation for the purpose of evading mandatory provisions of Chinese laws and/or administrative regulations, the people's courts shall give no effect to the application of foreign law.[29]

The case below serves as a good example with regard to the effect of evasion of mandatory provisions of law. As noted, a contract that is characterized as foreign in China includes one involving Hong Kong or Macao. Thus, under the one country with two systems scheme, there is also a choice of law issue for a contract concluded between the Mainland and Hong Kong or Macau. Although within one country, due to the fact that the legal and social systems of the Mainland differ from those of Hong Kong or Macao in many aspects, the

---

29 See the SPC, the Choice of Law Statute Interpretation, *supra* note 1 art. 11.

application of the law of Hong Kong or Macao may be denied in the Mainland because of public policy concerns.

Bank of China (Hong Kong), Ltd.
v.
The Bureau of Foreign Trade and Economic Cooperation of Qinghai Province

The High People's Court of Qinghai (2003) Qing Min San Zhong Zhi No. 3

Plaintiff (Appellant), Bank of China (Hong Kong), Ltd. has its major business office in the Bank of China Tower at No. 1 Garden Road, Hong Kong. Defendant (Respondent), the Bureau of Foreign Trade and Economic Cooperation of Qinghai Province, is located at No. 25 Xishulin Lane, Xining City, Qinghai Province.

In July 1988, plaintiff and Haihu Trade Inc. Ltd. (Haihu Trade), a company incorporated in Hong Kong, established a credit relation under which plaintiff granted Haihu Trade a credit line of HK $17.5 million. On July 6 in the same year, Defendant issued an irrevocable Letter of Guaranty for Haihu Trade to guarantee the repayment of the loan. Haihu Trade defaulted in the loan repayment. On February 23, 1998, defendant wrote to plaintiff confirming that the Letter of Guaranty remained effective and the confirming letter also indicated that the guaranteed loan amount should not exceed HK$19.5 million. On March 6, 1998, in its "Letter of Commitment to Loan Repayment" sent to plaintiff, Haihu Trade admitted that the total amount of the loan owed to plaintiff was HK $19,021,625.04 and Haihu Trade promised to repay the loan in eighteen installments.

Haihu Trade repaid a portion of the loan and then defaulted again. In November 2000, plaintiff filed this lawsuit against defendant in Xi Ning City Intermediate People's Court, alleging that as of November 11, 2000, defendant owed plaintiff a total amount of HK $18,022,000. Plaintiff requested defendant (a) as the guarantor, to pay plaintiff HK $18,022,000, including both the principal and interests of the loan, and (b) to bear all litigation fees.

Defendant argued that it was a government agent, and was not allowed to guarantee any debts under the law. Therefore, according to defendant, the loan guarantee was invalid because defendant was lacked legal capacity as the guarantor. Defendant then moved to dismiss plaintiff's claim. At the court hearing, both plaintiff and defendant agreed that their disputes should be governed by the law of Hong Kong.

The trial court found that in March 2000, plaintiff brought an action against Haihu Trade at the Trial Division of Hong Kong High Court and asked the High Court to order Haihu Development Inc. Ltd. and other two individuals, Haihu Trade's guarantors in Hong Kong, to pay off the loan. In April 2000, Hong Kong High Court entered a judgment in favor of plaintiff, and the total amount of the unpaid loan was affirmed by High Court to be HK $16,247,546.78 (HK $14,460,586.96 plus interests). The trial court further found that due to their insolvency, Haihu Development Inc. Ltd. was liquidated on October 25, 2000 by the order of the Hong Kong High Court and other two individuals were declared bankrupt, leaving the loan unpaid.

The trial court was of the opinion that the conduct of the defendant as the guarantor not only violated the provisions of law of the Mainland, but also was in violation of the ordinances of Hong Kong. The trial court then held that because of its illegality, the guaranty in question should be invalid, and therefore plaintiff's requesting defendant to be responsible for the unpaid loan should be denied due to lack of legal grounds. Based on its holding, the trial court dismissed plaintiff's claim.

On appeal, plaintiff argued that the trial court erred with regard to the determination of the fact and application of law. Plaintiff asserted that the loan guaranty by the government agency did not violate the law of Hong Kong, and the trial court decision that there was no legal ground to support plaintiff's claim and governmental guaranty violated the law of Hong Kong was a clear error. Plaintiff also asserted that although the legal systems between Hong Kong and the Mainland were different, they each had a civil compensation system applicable to the situation where the voidance of a contract was caused by the fault of a party. Plaintiff alleged that defendant misstated its legal capacity as the guarantor for the loan, which led plaintiff to establish the credit line for Haihu Trade in reliance on defendant's Letter of Guaranty, and thus no matter whether the defendant's act as guarantor was valid or not, defendant was 100% at fault for which defendant should be held liable.

Defendant rebutted by arguing that the contract of guaranty was invalid and the invalid contract should not give rise to the cause of action for plaintiff's lawsuit. Defendant further argued that under the Hong Kong statutes and case law, if a contract is prohibited by law, or illegal on its face, it should not be enforced. Defendant stressed that because the guaranty contract in question was null and void, and there was in addition no evidence to prove that plaintiff had valid creditor rights against defendant, the appeal must be dismissed.

This Court finds that the facts and evidence ascertained by the trial court contained no error. Further, we are convinced that the total loan amount as specified in the judgment of Hong Kong High Court against Haihu Development Inc. Ltd. and other two individuals in Hong Kong should be HK $16,247,456.78, of which HK $14,460,586 was the principal. With regard to the evidence produced by plaintiff concerning Hong Kong ordinances, its contents mostly deal with city development and public utilities, and the provisions about the government guaranty have a special meaning and particular application that are all irrelevant to this case. Also, defendant's assertion of Hong Kong statutes and case laws should be denied as well because there is not sufficient evidence that such statute and case laws are applicable to the case in question.

Pursuant to Article 194 of the Supreme People's Court 1988 Opinions on Several Questions concerning Implementation of the General Principles of Civil Law (provisional), the conduct of the parties to evade the compulsory or prohibitive provisions of law of China shall give no effect to the application of foreign law. Under the law of China, it is imperative that a Chinese institute providing guaranty overseas must first obtain approval by, and register with, the foreign exchange administration authority, and a government agent is prohibited from becoming a guarantor. In the instant case, since the guaranty contract was not approved by the foreign exchange administration authority and defendant acted as a guarantor in the name of a government agent, defendant's conduct in fact evaded the compulsory and prohibitive provisions of law. On this ground, we hold that the application of Hong Kong law must be ruled out given the defendant's conduct of evasion despite the fact that the parties agreed that the contract should be governed and interpreted under the law of Hong Kong.

As far as defendant's 1998 reaffirmation of the validity of the Letter of Guaranty is concerned, it must be determined under the Law of Guaranty of China and relevant judicial interpretations. According to the Guaranty Law, this contract must be held invalid. However, as the facts of the case indicate, defendant, in its Letter of Guaranty, stated that it had all authority for the guaranty, but in fact, it did not comply with the required procedures for approval and registration. On the other hand, both parties knew or ought to have known that a government agent was prohibited from being a guarantor, but both parties ignored this provision and entered into the guaranty contract any way, which resulted in the avoidance of the contract. In this situation, both parties were found at fault. Therefore, we must hold that defendant should be liable for 50% of the unpaid loan of Haihu Trade.

Thus, in accordance with Article 153 (2) of the Civil Procedure Law of China and Article 7 of the Supreme People's Court Explanations to the Questions related to the Application of the Law of Guaranty of the People's Republic of China, it is so ordered:

1. The Ning Jing Chu Zi No. 81 Civil Judgment of Xi Ning City Intermediate People's Court be vacated;
2. Defendant the Bureau of Foreign Trade and Economic Cooperation of Qinghai Province be liable for the payment of 50% of the unpaid loan of HK $14,460,586.96 plus interest to plaintiff Bank of China (Hong Kong), Ltd., and the payment be made within one month after this judgment takes effect; and
3. The trial and appeal litigation fees in the amount of RMB 211,054 be borne by plaintiff and defendant each RMB 105,527.

The judgment of the Qinghai High People's Court in *Bank of China (Hong Kong), Ltd.* with regard to the liabilities of the parties was based mainly on Article 5 (2) of the Law of Guaranty of China. Under Article 5 (2), if a guaranty contract is determined to be null and void, the debtor, the guarantor, or the creditor who is at fault, shall bear civil liability according to their respective fault. But the important part of this case for our purposes is the exclusion of the law chosen by the parties on the ground of violation of mandatory or prohibitive provisions of law of the forum, namely Mainland China. Another interesting part of the case is that the appellate court heavily relied on the Supreme People's Court opinions and interpretations in making its judgment, which usually was not the case.

In its 2012 Interpretation, the SPC further addressed the mandatory rules. Pursuant to the SPC, for purposes of choice of law, mandatory rules are provisions that involve (a) protection of employees' rights and interests, (b) food or public health safety, (c) environmental safety, (d) financial safety including foreign currency control, (e) anti-trust or anti-dumping, or (f) other provisions that should have been considered as having mandatory effect.[30]

In the context of the Contract Law, mandatory provisions also include the requirements for exclusive application of Chinese laws. Exclusive application mainly deals with contracts concerning foreign investment enterprises. It is explicitly provided in Article 126 of the Contract Law that the laws of China shall apply to the contracts for Chinese-foreign equity joint ventures, for Chinese-foreign cooperative joint ventures, or for Chinese-foreign cooperative exploration and development of natural resources to be performed within the territory of China (JVs).[31] In addition, under the Detailed Rules (as amended in 2001) for Implementation of the Law of China on Wholly Foreign-Owned Enterprises (WFOE), for contracts between a WFOE and another company, enterprise, other economic organization, or individual, the Contract Law of China shall also be exclusively applied.[32]

---

30 See *id.*, art. 10.
31 See the Contract Law, art. 126.
32 *See* Art. 181 of the Detailed Rules on Implementation of the Law of China on Wholly Foreign-owned Enterprises, amended on April 21, 2001. A similar provision is also

The basic notion underlying the exclusive application of Chinese laws to JV contracts is that foreign investment has great impacts on the national economy and application of Chinese laws is needed to reasonably control foreign investments and effectively protect the nation's interests. On the other hand, it is commonly held that because of their business operations in China, JVs all have the most substantial connection with China, which provides the reasonable ground for the exclusive application of Chinese laws to them.

It is also argued that a JV or even a WFOE, once established in China, becomes a Chinese legal person. Thus, a contract involving a Chinese legal person is necessarily subject to both the jurisdiction and laws of China. It should be noted, however, that because of the Chinese legal person status of a JV, a contract between a JV and a foreigner (i.e., foreign company or individual) will constitute a foreign contract in which a foreign law may be selected by the parties as the governing law.

Another point worth noting is that like a contract, the choice of law by the parties must be made with mutual consent and on a voluntary basis. Therefore, any defenses to the formation of a contract will be equally applicable to the choice of law clause or agreement. If such a choice is made by fraud, duress, or any other means that violates the fairness principle, it will be held null and void. But under the independence principle that separates the choice of law clause from the rest of the contract, a challenge to the validity of a choice of law clause in a contract must be made specifically in order to be effective.

2.2 *Application of Law Absent the Parties' Choice*

If there is no choice of law by the parties, the governing law is determined by the choice of law rules based on the degree of relationship or nexus between the contract or parties and the particular country. In the U.S., abent the parties' choice, the governing law for a contract is mostly to be determined under the doctrine of the most significant relationship provided in the Restatement (Second) of Conflict of Laws (1971).[33] In Europe, the standard is the "closest connection" that was originally provided in the 1980 Rome Convention,[34] and

---

contained in the newly amended Law of China-Foreign Equity Joint Ventures and its Implementation Rules.

33 See the Restatement (Second) of Conflict of Laws (1971), §188 (1) (the rights and duties of the parties with respect to an issue in a contract are determined by the local law of the state which, with respect to that issue, has the most significant relationship to the transaction and the parties under the principles stated in § 6).

34 See 1980 Convention on the Law Applicable to Contractual Obligations, art. 4 (1) (to the extent that the law applicable to a contract has not been chosen in accordance with Article 3, the contract shall be governed by the law of the country with which it is most closely connected).

now is restated in the EU Regulation on the Law Applicable to Contract Obligations (known as Rome I).[35] In addition to the closest connection standard, Rome I provides as the default the applicable law to a particular contract under the characteristic performance approach.[36]

In China, the governing law for a contract without a choice by the parties is to be determined under the "closest relationship" standard. According to Article 126 of the Contract Law, which originates from Article 145 of the 1986 Civil Code, if the parties to a foreign contract make no choice of law, the law of the country to which the contract is most closely related shall apply.[37] The Choice of Law Statute expands Article 126 of the Contract Law to include both general and specific provisions for the determination of applicable law without the parties' choice.

The general provision is a combination of habitual residence, characteristic performance, and the closest connection. Under Article 41 of the Choice of Law Statute, absent choice by the parties, the law of habitual residence of the party whose fulfillment of the obligations best reflects the characteristics of the contract or other law that has the closest connection with the contract shall apply.[38] The implication of Article 41 is that for a contract the closest connection will be assumed if the characteristic performance is ascertained.

The specific provisions apply to special contracts given the particularity of such contracts. There are two kinds of special contracts for which the applicable law is provided in the Choice of Law Statute: consumer contracts and labor contracts. According to Article 42 of the Choice of Law Statute, consumer contracts shall be governed by the law of the consumer's habitual residence. If, however, the consumer chooses as applicable law the law of the place where the goods or services are provided or the business operator has no relevant business activities in the place of the consumer's habitual residence, the law of the place where the goods or services are provided shall apply. [39]

The applicable law for a labor contract is provided in Article 43 of the Choice of Law Statute. As discussed in the previous chapter, labor contracts in China are not covered in the Contract Law but rather in the Law of Labor Contracts. For purposes of the determination of governing law for labor contracts, Article

---

35 See EU Regulation on the Law Applicable to Contractual Obligations, art. 4 (4) (where the applicable law cannot be determined pursuant to paragraphs 1 or 2, the contract shall be governed by the law of the country with which it is most closely connected).
36 See *id.*, art 4 (1)(2).
37 See the Contract Law, art. 126.
38 See the Choice of Law Statute, art. 41.
39 See *id.*, art. 42.

43 of the Choice of Law Statute provides that labor contracts shall be governed by the law of the place where the employee works. But, if it is difficult to ascertain the working place of the employee, the law of the principal place of business of the employer shall be applied.[40] In addition, under Article 43, with regard to labor dispatching, the law of the place of dispatching may be applied as governing law.[41]

The determination of governing law on the ground of "connection" or "relationship" is a complicated matter because it in most cases involves an analysis of all related factors in order to find the "closest" connection, and the analysis is normally conducted by the court on a case-by-case basis. In China, the term "closest connection" is not defined in the 1986 Civil Code or the Contract Law. The Choice of Law Statute adopts the doctrine of charateristic performance but still leaves the term "closest connection" undefined.

In judicial practice, the people's courts, when determining the closest connection, have focused on the nature of the contract and type of transactions, which is akin to the concept of the "characteristics of performance." In fact, after the 1986 Civil Code was adopted, the SPC issued a choice of law guidance in 1987 for people's courts to follow for their ascertaining the applicable law under the closest connection test. The guidance provides a laundry list for the law applicable to different contracts in accordance with each contract's characteristics. [42]

---

40   See *id.*, art. 43.
41   See *id.*
42   The guidance was provided in the SPC's 1987 "Answers to Several Questions on Application of Foreign Economic Contract Law" (1987 Answers). Although the Answers were repealed after the Contract Law was adopted in 1999, the Opinions stated in the Answers are still authoritative resources for the practice of people's courts. According to the Supreme People's Court, in regard to contracts other than for sales, the laws determined by the people's courts under the closest connection standard shall be as follows: (a) contract for bank loan or guarantee—law of the place where the bank is located; (b) insurance contract—law of the place of the insurer's business office; (c) contract for product processing and work—law of the place where the contractor's business office is situated; (d) contract for transfer of technology—law of the place of the transferee's business office; (e) contract for construction project—law of the place of the project; (f) contract for technical consultation or design—law of the place where the commissioning party's business office is located; (g) contract for service—law of the place of service performance; (h) contract for supply of set equipment—law of the place where the equipment is installed and operated; (i) contract of agent—law of the place of the agent's business office; (j) contract for lease, sale, or mortgage of real property—law of the place of property; (k) contract for the leasing of chattels—law of the place of the lessor; (i) contract for storage and warehousing—law of the place where the storekeeper's business office is located.

In 2007, the SPC in its rules concerning applicable law in civil or commerical contract cases further addressed the determination of the closest connection on the basis of the nature of contract (2007 Rules).[43] According to the SPC, when detemining the law applicable to a contractual dispute under the standard of the closest connection, the people's courts shall take into account factors such as the particular nature of the contract involved and the obligation to be performed by a party that would best reflect such nature in order to make as applicable law the law of the country or region that is most closely connected with the contract. [44]

In addition, the SPC revised the 1987 launtry list to include a total of seventeen different contracts for which a default applicable law is provided. For example, under the 2007 Rules, absent parties' choice of applicable law, a contract for sale of goods shall be governed by the law of the place where the seller is domiciled at the time of conclusion of the contract. If the contract is negotiated and concluded at the place of the buyer's domicile, or the contract clearly provides that the seller shall fulfill its obligation of delivering the goods at the place of the buyer's domicile, the law of the place of the buyer's domicile shall apply.[45]

---

43 See SPC, the Rules on Several Question Concerning Application of Law in Adjudicating the Cases of Civil or Commercial Conractual Disputes, adopted on June 11, 2007 (2007 Rules).
44 See id., art. 5.
45 See id. UnderArticle 5 of the 2007 Rules, absent the parties' choice, (a) a sales contract applies the law of the place where the seller is domiciled at the time of conclusion of the contract; if the contract is negotiated and concluded at the place of the buyer's domicile, or the contract clearly provides that the seller shall fulfill its obligation of delivering the goods at the place of the buyer's domicile, the law of the place of the buyer's domicile shall apply; (b) a contract of material processing of assembly of parts, and other processing works applies the law of the processing contractor's domicile; (c) a contract for the supply of a complete set of equipment applies the law of the place of the equipment installation; (d) a contract of sale, lease, or mortgage of a real property applies the law of the place where the property is located; (e) a contract for the lease of movable property applies the law of the domicile of the lessor; (f) a contract for a pledge on movable property applies the law of the pledgee's domicile; (g) a loan contract applies the law of the borrower's domicile; (h) an insurance contract applies the law of the insurer's domicile; (i) a finance lease contract applies the law of the tenant's domicile; (j) a contract for a construction project contract applies the law of the location of the construction project; (k) a warehousing or storage contract applies the law of the place of the warehousing or the custodian's domicile; (l) a guarantee contract applies the law of the guarantor's domicile; (m) a entrustment contract applies the law of the trustee's domicile; (n) a contract of issuance, sale, or transfer of bonds applies the law of the place of issuance, sale, or transfer of bonds; (o) an auction contract applies the law of the place of auction; (p) a brokerage contract applies the law of the place of the broker's domicile; and (q) an intermediary contract applies the law of the domicile of the intermediaries. See id.

Note, however, that after adoption of the Choice of Law Statute, the SPC repealed the 2007 rules due to the conflict between the 2007 Rules and the Choice of Law Statute. An obvious conflict is the use of habitual residence instead of domicile in the Choice of Law Statute. Nevertheless, the choice of law concept for particular contracts as provided in the 2007 Rules continues to serve as guidance for the people's court in their determination of applicable law under the characteristic performance standard prescribed in Article 41 of the Choice of Law Statute.

In general, characteristic performance determines a default law applicable to a particular contract. In actual cases, a people's court will within its discretion make this determination on the basis of the facts of each individual case. Pursuant to the Choice of Law Statute, despite characteristic performance, if a contract is more closely connected with another place, the law of that other place will be applied.[46] In addition, according to the SPC, when a party's business place is relevant to the determination of applicable law, and the party has more than one business place, the people's courts shall apply the law of the place that is found to be most closely related to the contract. If there is no such business office, the law of the party's domicile or residence shall be applied.[47]

Once again, in order to avoid "*renvoi*," the applicable law determined by a people's court shall mean the existing substantive law of the country (place) specified, not including the conflict of law rules of such country. Also, under Article 6 of the Choice of Law Statute, when a foreign law is to be applied but within that foreign country different laws are applied in different regions, the applicable law shall be the the law of the region with which the contract is most closely connected.[48]

2.3   *Application of International Law*

Application of international law in international contracts encounters two basic questions: the first question is whether the parties may choose as the governing law an international law, and the second question is whether a court may apply an international treaty if no choice is made by the parties. In both

---

46   See *id.* (if a contract above is clearly more closely related to another country or region, the law of the other country or region applies).

47   See SPC, the 1987 Answers, *supra* note 9.

48   See the Choice of Law Statute, art. 6. Article 6 modifies Article 192 of the SPC's 1988 *Opinions on the Matters of Implementation and Application of the General Principles of Civil Law of China*, where the SPC stated that in a country which has different regions with difference laws, the applicable law shall be the law pointed by the conflict of law rules prevailing in that country, or the law of the region that is the most closely related to the contract absent the applicable conflict of law rules.

cases, an underlying issue is whether a domestic court may directly apply an international law to the controversy brought before it. A related issue is which law shall prevail if there is a conflict or discrepancy between international law and domestic law.

The sources of international law, as specified in the Statute of the International Court of Justice, include international treaties, international customs, the general principles of law recognized by civilized nations, and judicial decisions and scholarly treatises.[49] International treaties and customs are generally considered to be two major authoritative sources of international law. With regard to the application of international treaties in the domestic courts, countries differ from each other in the matter of how the international treaties should be applied.

Generally, there are three approaches to the application of international treaties in domestic courts. The first approach is called "monism" or direct application. Monism holds that the international law and the domestice law are within the same system of law, and international law does not need to be transformed into the domestic law. Under the monism approach, an international treaty can be directly applied in the courts of the country that is the party to the treaty except for those treaty provisions to which the country has made reservation because upon ratification, the international treaty is incorporated into, and automatically takes effect in, domestic laws.[50]

The second approach is named "dualism" or indirect application. Unlike monism, dualism considers international law and domestic law to be two different systems. Under the dualism approach, an international treaty may not be applied in the domestic courts without a process of transformation of the treaty into the domestic law. In other words, in order for a domestic court to apply an international treaty, a legislative action is required, which means that there must be a statute passed by the legislature to implement the treaty.[51]

---

49   Article 38 of the Statute of the International Court of Justice provides: "the Court, whose function is to decide in accordance with international law such disputes as submitted to it, shall apply (a) international conventions, whether in general or particular, establishing rules expressly recognized by the contesting states; (b) international custom, as evidence of a general practice accepted by law; (c) the general principle of law recognized by civilized nations; (d) subject to the provisions of Article 59, judicial decisions and the teachings of the most highly qualified publicists of the various nations, as subsidiary means for the determination of law." Available at http://www.icj-cij.org.

50   See Denza, Eileen, "The Relationship between International and National Law," in *International Law*. 4th ed. Edited by Malcolm Evans, 412–440 (Oxford 2006).

51   There are two theories that are intended to define the relationship between domestic law and international law, and they are called dualism and monism. Under dualism, domestic law and international law are two different systems regulating different subject

The third approach is called an eclectic approach because it is basically a combination of the above two approaches. Take the United States, for an example. In terms of their application, the treaties in the United States are divided into self-executing treaties and non-self-executing treaties. A treaty is enforceable directly in the courts of the United States only if the treaty is self-executing. If a treaty is itself non-self-executing, congressional action to incorporate the treaty into a federal statute is required. Therefore, a non-self executing treaty becomes enforceable only if the treaty has been implemented by the federal statute.[52]

In China, there is no provision in the Constitution or the law that prescribes the relationship between a treaty and domestic law, nor is there any rule or principle concerning how a treaty should be applied in the people's courts. Although the Model Law provides that the parties may choose as governing law international treaties or customs, there has been no statutory provision to that effect. With regard to the application of an international treaty, the only relevant provision is Article 142 of the 1986 Civil Code. Both the 2017 GPCL and the 2010 Choice of Law Statute are silent on the issue of treaty application.

Under Article 142 of the 1986 Civil Code, if any international treaty concluded or acceded to by the People's Republic of China contains provisions differing from those in the civil laws of China, the provisions of the international treaty shall apply, except for those to which China has made reservations.

---

matters, and neither legal order has the power to create or alter rules of the other. When domestic law provides for application of international law within the jurisdiction, this is merely an exercise of the authority of domestic law—an adoption or transformation of the rules of the international law. And therefore, application of international law in domestic courts is indirect. Monism, however, emphasizes the supremacy of international law and reduces domestic law to the status of pensioner of international law. Pursuant to monism, international law will be enforced directly in the domestic courts. See Weston, Falk & Charlesworth, *International Law and World Order, A Problem-Oriented Coursebook* (3rd Ed), 229–233 (West, 1997).

52 Although there is a general acceptance in the United States of the concepts of self-executing and non-self-executing treaties, the criteria used by the courts to distinguish self-executing treaties from non-self-executing treaties vary. One standard is to look at whether the treaty creates a private right of action. Under this standard, a treaty will be called non-self-executing if it does not create a private right of action. Another standard is the test used by the Ninth Circuit Court of Appeals in *Islamic Republic of Iran v. Boeing Co.*, 771 F. 2d 1279, 1283 (9th Cir. 1985). According to this test, to determine whether a treaty is self-executing or not, the following factors need to be considered: (a) the purposes of the treaty and the objectives of its creators, (b) the existence of domestic procedures and institutions appropriate for direct implementation, (c) the availability and feasibility of alternative enforcement methods, and (d) the immediate and long-range social consequences of self- or non-self execution.

Article 142 further provides that international customs may be applied absent any applicable law or international treaty. The provisions of Article 142 have been adopted *verbatim* in several other laws, including, for example, Article 95 of the Law of Negotiable Instruments, Article 268 of the Maritimes Law and Article 184 of the Law of Civil Aviation.

Article 142 of the 1986 Civil Code is ambiguous. First, under Article 142, a treaty will prevail if there is a conflict between the treaty and a domestic law. But it is unclear whether this can be interpreted to mean that a treaty can be applied directly in the people's courts. Second, Article 142 seems to acknowledge the application of treaties in people's courts. It is, however, uncertain whether Article 142 actually authorizes the people's courts to apply a treaty, without action by the NPC, to cases where such application becomes necessary. Third, it remains questionable whether later legislation may supersede the provisions of a treaty. Put differently, the question is whether a treaty should still prevail if legislation enacted after the treaty appears to be inconsistent with the treaty.

In judicial practices, however, the SPC seems to favor the direct application of the international treaties and customs under certain circumstances, at least for civil and commercial matters.[53] On April 17, 2000, in order to guide the lower courts, the SPC issued "Notice on Several Questions that Deserve Attentions Concerning Trial and Handling of Foreign Civil and Commercial Cases." In that Notice, the SPC explicitly instructed the lower courts to honor the choice of law clause made by the parties except if otherwise provided by the law, and to give priority to the application of international treaties, and in the meantime to make reference to international customs.[54]

As a matter of fact, there have been instances where international treaties were directly applied by people's courts. Such applications have mostly involved such treaties as the CISG and the United Nations Convention on the Recognition and Enforcement of Foreign Arbitral Awards (New York Convention). The following case shows how international treaties are being cited as legal authority by people's courts in their trials of foreign cases. The case

---

53 Some disagree with the direct application and argue that application of a treaty involves the exercise of national sovereignty and therefore shall not take place automatically in domestic courts without legislative authorization. But many suggest having the direct application limited to treaties of general civil and commercial matters, and suggest that treaties involving more policy matters, such as the WTO, should be indirectly applied. What they are concerned about is the complexity of policy-based treaties as well as the lack of knowledge and competency of the judges in this regard. See Cao Jianming, *The WTO and China Judicial Practices*, 254–258 (Law Publishing House, 2001).

54 See the SPC, *the Notice on Several Questions that Deserve Attentions Concerning Adjudicating and Handling of Foreign Civil and Commercial Cases* (2000).

concerns the application of the CISG, and is selected by Shanghai High People's Court for publication as a typical case of particular importance.

Shanghai Dong Da Import and Export Co., Inc. v. Laubholz-Meyer Company

Shanghai Yangpu District People's Court
Yang Jing Chu Zi No. 1179 (2001)[55]

On March 15, 2001, plaintiff Shanghai Gong Da Import and Export Co., Inc. (a Chinese corporation, note added) was appointed as an agent to enter into an import agency contract with Shanghai Chenchuan Industrial Company, Ltd. (Chenchuan) to import 15 cubic meters (+/-10%) of special timbers (known as Hornbeam) for Chenchuan. On the same day thereafter, plaintiff signed a contract with defendant (a German company, note added), under which defendant would provide required timbers according to the quantity, quality, price, and payment methods as agreed upon by the parties.

On May 28, 2001, plaintiff received 13.999 cubic meters of the timbers from defendant under the B/L No. HD-MUBMCH10030, for which plaintiff paid to defendant via L/C US $5179.63, or RMB 42,991 Yuan, plus custom duties of RMB 10,434.24 Yuan. However, an initial inspection indicated that the timbers received did not conform to the terms of the contract. Plaintiff then asked the local Entry/Exit Bureau of Examination and Quarantine for further inspection. On the Inspection Certificate issued by the Bureau on June 14, 2001, it was stated that among the imported timbers, about 192 pieces were not Hornbeam, amounting to 2.628 cubic meters, and about 52% of the timbers had poor quality. The Inspection Certificate concluded that the specification and the quality of the timbers imported did no meet the requirements of the contract.

Plaintiff brought this action against defendant at this court. According to plaintiff, due to the defendant's breach of the contract, Chenchuan, plaintiff's principal, was unable to deliver the digital piano keyboard to a Japanese company, for which Chenchuan had to pay the liquidate damages of RMB 100,000 Yuan. Plaintiff claimed that because of the breach, plaintiff and its principal suffered both economic losses and reputation damages. Plaintiff then asked the court to order defendant to pay to plaintiff (a) the contract price of RMB 42,991 Yuan, (b) custom duties of RMB 10,434.24 Yuan, (c) Chenchuan's economic damages of RMB 100,000 Yuan and reputation damages of RMB 50,000 Yuan, and (d) the fees of RMB 2,653 Yuan paid by plaintiff to the Shanghai Representative Office of German Industry and Commerce Chamber (German Chamber Fees).

Defendant challenged the legality and relevance of the Inspection Certificate on the ground that the Certificate could not prove the inconformity of the goods to the quality standard set forth in the contract. Defendant argued that plaintiff failed to make inspection according to statutory process upon arrival of the goods, but rather plaintiff made the inspection when plaintiff thought there were quality problems after the timbers were unpacked for use. In addition, defendant argued, the inspected timbers had been sorted by plaintiff and were heavily damaged. For this reason, defendant asked the court to quash the Inspection Certificate because, according to defendant, the inspected goods were not necessarily the goods under the B/L No. HD-MUBMCH10030.

Defendant further argued that the United Nations Convention on Contracts for the International Sale of Goods (CISG) should first be applied to this case. Under the CISG, defendant

---

55   See "*The 2003 Selected Cases Tried by People's Courts in Shanghai*," 166–170 (Shanghai People's Court Press, 2004).

asserted, its performance basically met the terms of the contract, and even if defendant was found in breach, its liability for damages should be limited. Defendant then asked the court to dismiss plaintiff's claim for the reason that the damages claimed by plaintiff were without legal grounds.

The court finds that plaintiff did not make timely inspection of the timbers and had the timbers inspected after the timbers arrived at the work site without the presence of defendant's local representatives. In this regard, plaintiff was at fault to a certain extent. But the court believes that the evidential effect of the Inspection Certificate shall not be denied only because of plaintiff's fault. First, based on the evidence provided by plaintiff, the timbers purchased by plaintiff were to be used to produce the customized products, and therefore the required timbers may not be substituted with other type of timbers. The contract between the parties was clear about the specification of the timbers, but defendant changed the specification without plaintiff's knowledge. And it was after being unpackaged that the timbers were found wrong. Therefore there is no evidence that plaintiff committed any fraudulent conduct in inspecting the timbers.

Second, the evidence before the court concerning Chenchuan's payment to the Japanese company for liquidate damages further indicated that both plaintiff and Chenchuan did not have any Hornbeam timbers from other sources in stock. Thus, it is reasonable and logical to infer that there is no basis for plaintiff to switch the timbers for the purposes of inspection. On this basis, it should be held that the timbers provided for inspection were imported from defendant and therefore the evidential effect of the Inspection Certificate should be affirmed.

With regard to the application of law, according to Article 2 of the Supreme People's Court's "the Notice on Several Questions that Deserve Attentions Concerning Trial and Handling of Foreign Civil and Commercial Cases" on April 17, 2000, except for the provisions of Article 126(b) of the Contract Law under which Chinese law must be applied, the applicable law to a contract should be determined exactly under the provision of law or the choice of the parties. The priority shall be given to international treaties, excluding the provisions to which China has made reservations, and the application of international customs may also be considered. In this case, the parties did not make the choice of law in the contract. But since the counties of which the parties are citizens are both the members of the CISG, the contract falls within the scope of the application of the CISG, and then the CISG shall first be applied.

Under the provisions of the CISG, defendant shall be held liable because defendant fails to deliver the goods that match the specification and quality provided in the contract and such failure constitutes a "fundamental" breach. But with regard to the liquidate damages Chenchuan paid to the Japanese company and the reputation damages claimed by plaintiff, plaintiff provided no evidence that defendant was in advance informed of Chenchuan and the transactions with the Japanese company. Plaintiff's claims in this regard therefore shall be denied.

The court hereby holds that after the contract is legally concluded, the parties shall fully perform the contract. But due to defendant's breach, plaintiff did not achieve what it had bargained for, and defendant shall of course be liable for damages. Plaintiff's claims for the returning of the goods delivered for a refund as well as the payment for the import duties as well as other fees in relation to the returning of goods should be granted because they are the consequences of breach that could be foreseen by defendant.

On the grounds stated above, in accordance with Article 142 of the General Principles of Civil Law of China, Article 25, Article 49 (1)(a), (2)(b), Article 51 (2), Article 81 (2), and Article 86 (1) of the CISG, it is now ordered:

1. Defendant Laubholz-Meyer Company refund plaintiff Shanghai Dong Da Import Co., Inc. RMB 42,991 Yuan within 10 days after this judgment takes effect;
2. Defendant Laubholz-Meyer Company pay plaintiff Shanghai Dong Da Import Co., Inc. RMB 10,434.24 Yuan of the import related costs within 10 days after this judgment takes effect;

3. Defendant Laubholz-Meyer Company pay plaintiff Shanghai Dong Da Import Co., Inc. RMB 2,653 Yuan of German Chamber fees within 10 days after this judgment takes effect;
4. Plaintiff's other claims be denied;
5. Defendant, within 10 days after Plaintiff Shanghai Dong Da Import Co., Inc. receive the above ordered payments from defendant, shall come to the place designated by plaintiff to pick up the Hornbeam timbers 11.371 cubic meters, and other timbers 2.628 cubic meters at its own cost; if plaintiff is unable to provide the timbers to the amount as specified above, plaintiff shall pay to defendant the difference at US $370/cubic meter.

None of the parties appealed in this case. When the case was selected for publication, the head judge who wrote the opinion made the following very interesting comments. First, this case involves a dispute over the specification and quality of contracted goods. During the trial the court had a clear focus on evidence by determining at the first place the validity and effect of the Inspection Certificate, and then the court made a determination on the matter of "fundamental breach" by defendant.

Second, under Article 1(a) of the CISG, the Convention applies contracts for sales of goods between parties whose places of business are in different States (a) when the States are Contracting States. In this case, the countries of both parties are the signatory countries of the Convention, and there was no choice of law made by the parties in their contract. Therefore, in accordance with the Supreme People's Court's Notice on April 17, 2000, the court must apply the provisions of the CISG to the case.

Third, under the provisions of the CISG, in case of a fundamental breach of contract, the damages for which the breaching party is liable shall be those suffered by the aggrieved party as a result of the breach, including profits. But the damages shall not exceed the possible amount the party in breach could or ought to foresee based on his or her knowledge and the situation at the time of the contract. It was on this ground that the court granted some of plaintiff's claims, and denied others.[56]

Despite, however, the direct application of the CISG in Chinese courts, the status of treaties in Chinese law remains a debatable issue. As noted, in March 2019, in order to unify foreign investment legislation, China adopted the "Foreign Investment Law" (FIL) to replace the three co-existing laws pertaining to foreign investment.[57] Under Article 4 of the FIL, the State undertakes the pre-entry national treatment plus negative list management system for foreign investment. If, however, international treaties or agreements concluded

---

56 See *id.*, at p 170.
57 The three laws are "Sino-Foreign Equity Joint Venture Law" (1979), "Foreign Wholly-Owned Enterprise Law" (1986), and "Sino-Foreign Contractual Joint Venture Law" (1988).

or participated in by the People's Republic of China provide more preferential treatment to foreign investors, the relevant treaty provisions may be applied.[58]

Article 4 of the FIL was widely contested during the drafting period. What was debated was the relationship between the domestic law and international treaties with regard to foreign investment. In the early draft, Article 4 of the FIL simply followed Article 142 of the 1986 Civil Code and required an application of the treaty when a conflict occurs between the treaty and domestic law.[59]

Some, however, argued that a mandatory application of treaty may adversely affect the uniformity of the law regulating foreign investment. Their concern was that the imperative language in the law pertaining to treaty application would provide an opportunity for foreign investors to challenge Chinese domestic law on the basis of an international treaty.[60] As a result, the final version of Article 4 of the FIL departed from Article 142 of the 1986 Civil Code and changed the word "shall" to "may," making it optional to apply the treaty that differs from the domestic law. In addition, those who shared this concern suggested that for foreign investment, a legislative action should be required to transform the treaty into a domestic law in order for the treaty to be applied in Chinese courts.[61]

3 Choice of Forum in International Contracts

Choice of forum occurs when the parties in their contract choose in advance a court before which any disputes arising out of or related to the contract will be brought. Doctrinally, the jurisdiction that a court obtains from the choice of forum clause is referred to as consensual jurisdiction. Jurisdiction by consent is recognized as a general jurisdictional basis in many countries. In the United States, the choice of forum by the parties was generally not enforced until 1972, when the U.S. Supreme Court in *Bremen v. Zapata Off-Shore Co.* rejected the traditional view that a forum choice clause tends to "oust a court of jurisdiction."[62] By vacating the lower courts' judgment, the *Bremen* Court held

---

58 See Foreign Investment Law of China, promulgated on March 15, 2019, effective January 1, 2020.
59 See Foreign Investment Law of China (Draft), published for the public comments on December 26, 2018, available at http://www.sohu.com/a/284665477_120052138.
60 As part of the drafting process, the draft FIL was published by the NPC for public comments from December 26, 2018 to February 24, 2019. A report of the scholarly debates on Article 4 is available at https://m.yicai.com/news/100108900.html?from=singlemessage&isappinstalled=0.
61 See *id.*
62 *Bremen v. Zapata Off-Shore Co.*, 407 U.S. 1, 92 S. Ct. 1907 (1972).

that a forum clause must be enforced unless there is a clear showing that "the enforcement would be unreasonable and unjust."[63] The Restatement (Second) also states that the parties' agreement as to the place of the action will be given effect unless it is unfair or unreasonable.[64]

Allowing contractual parties to choose a court beforehand rests with the idea that a choice of forum via agreement promotes certainty in dispute settlement and advances convenience to the parties. The assumption is that a choice of forum clause implicates both an attempt of the parties to ensure that the action will be brought in a forum that is convenient to both of them, and a commitment of the parties to binding themselves as to the place of litigation, whereby the certainty for the dispute settlement will be established. An argument, however, is that a choice of forum clause does not give the parties the power to alter the rule of jurisdiction, but rather only provides a ground on which a court may restrain from exercising jurisdiction.[65] Nevertheless, whatever arguments there might be, the choice of forum is in fact an extension of the freedom of contract to court jurisdiction.

Like in many other countries, a choice of forum by the parties is allowed in China. A choice of forum is subject to certain statutory limits, however. The jurisdiction of Chinese people's courts in civil cases is prescribed in both the Chinese Constitution (1982, as amended in 2004) and the Civil Procedural Law of China (CPL). With respect to foreign civil litigation, the jurisdiction of the people's courts is governed by both the general and special provisions of the CPL. In addition, the Supreme People's Court plays important role in determining the lower courts' jurisdiction pertaining to particular types of cases.

Before the CPL was amended in 2012, contractual choice of form in foreign civil litigation was provided in Articles 244 of the CPL. According to Article 244, the parties in disputes concerning foreign contracts or foreign property rights may choose by a written agreement the jurisdiction of the court that has actual connection with the disputes.[66] Under Article 244, a choice of forum is permissible, but subject to three conditions: (1) the agreement of choice of court must be made in writing, (2) the court so chosen must have "actual connections" with the disputes, and (3) the disputes must involve foreign contracts or foreign property rights.

---

63   See *id.*
64   See Restatement (Second) of Conflict of Laws, Section 80 (1971, as amended 1988).
65   See Restatement (Second), comment (a).
66   See Civil Procedural Law of the People's Republic of China (herein after referred as the CPL), art. 224. An English translation is available at http://www.gip.net/chinalaw/lawtranl.htm.

However, when the CPL was amended in 2012, the provision of Article 244 concerning contractual choice of forum was deleted. Instead, a general provision of contractual choice of forum was added as Article 34. In accordance with Article 34, the parties in disputes involving contract or other property interests may agree in writing to choose for jurisdiction a people's court of such place having real connection with the disputes as the place of the defendant's domicile, the contact performance, contract conclusion, plaintiff's domicile, the location of the subject matter, provided that the choice does not violate the provisions concerning the tier or exclusive jurisdiction of people's courts.[67]

"Tier jurisdiction" refers to the jurisdiction of the people's courts at different levels and it tells at which level of the people's court a particular case shall be filed with in the first instance. There are four tiers of courts in the Chinese judiciary: the SPC, the provincial high people's court; intermediate people's courts (at the prefecture city level); and district people's courts (at the county level).[68] Note also that judicial proceedings in China are conducted under a "two instance trial" system and in any given regular proceeding case there is one trial and one appeal only.[69]

Although Article 34 of the CPL (as amended) has a focus on the jurisdiction of Chinese courts, it is considered to be applicable to both domestic and foreign cases pertaining to choice of court agreements. In addition, compared with former Article 244 of the CPL, Article 34 is more specific about what the real connection should be referred to. In order to avoid confusion, the SPC in its 2015 CPL Interpretation specifically addresses the issue of a choice of foreign court in civil litigations, allowing the parties to choose a foreign court under Article 34 of the CPL.

According to the SPC, the parties in disputes involving foreign contracts or other property interests may agree in writing to choose for jurisdiction a

---

67 See CPL (as amended 2017), art. 34.
68 At present, the total number of people's courts in China is 3,568, including the Supreme People's Court. Moreover, there are thirty-two provincial high people's courts, 403 intermediate people's courts, and 3,132 district people's courts. Among these courts, ten are maritime courts, sixty railway courts, and eighty-eight military courts.
69 In most cases, the first trial begins at the county level, and the appeal will be made to the intermediate people's court. However, there are certain cases where the intermediate people's court or provincial high people's court will take the first trial. If a case starts at an intermediate-level court, the appeal will be heard by a provincial high people's court, and if a higher court takes the case for the trial of first instance, the Supreme People's Court will have to take the case if an appeal follows. For general information about Chinese courts jurisdiction, see Mo Zhang, *International Civil Litigation in China: A Practical Analysis of the Chinese Judicial System*, 25 Boston College Int'l & Comp. L. R., 59 (Winter 2002).

foreign court of such place having a real connection with the disputes as the place of the defendant's domicile, contract performance, contract conclusion, plaintiff's domicile, or the location of the subject matter.[70] The parties, however, may not by an agreement choose a foreign court for cases subject to the exclusive jurisdiction of the Chinese courts under Articles 33 and 266 of the CPL.

The exclusive jurisdiction of Chinese people's courts consists of two parts. The first part concerns the specific locales that the disputes will involve, and the actions thereof shall be under the exclusive jurisdiction of particular Chinese people's courts. In accordance with Article 33 of the CPL, (a) if a lawsuit is brought over a dispute concerning real estate, the people's court of the place where the real estate is located shall have jurisdiction; (b) if a lawsuit involves a dispute over port operations, the jurisdiction shall rest with the people's court of the place where the port is situated; and (c) if a lawsuit arises out of a dispute over succession, it shall be within the jurisdiction of the people's court of the place where the decedent was domiciled upon his death, or where the major estate is located.[71] In those cases, the jurisdiction of the court so designated shall not be altered by the choice of forum clause by the parties to a contract.

The second part of the exclusive jurisdiction of Chinese people's courts is the exclusion of the jurisdiction of any foreign courts. The CPL expressly denies foreign courts' exercise of judicial power over civil actions involving disputes over contracts of foreign investment enterprises (FIEs). Article 266 of the CPL provides that the people's courts of China shall have jurisdiction over civil actions brought over disputes concerning the performance within China for contracts of Chinese-foreign equity joint ventures, Chinese-foreign contractual joint ventures, or Chinese-foreign cooperative exploration and development of natural resources.[72]

Theoretically, Article 246 itself does not have the effect of extraterritorially prohibiting a foreign court from taking a case that concerns an FIE contract either initiated by a foreign plaintiff against a Chinese defendant or referred to by the consent of the parties. But the practical problem is that a judgment made by a foreign court involving an FIE contract will not be recognized or enforced in China because under Chinese law, the foreign court lacks subject matter jurisdiction over such cases.

Therefore, for a judgment to be enforced in China, the exclusive jurisdiction of Chinese courts must not be violated. Pursuant to the SPC, however, exclusive jurisdiction does not apply to arbitration agreements.[73] In other words, an

---

70   See the SPC, the 2015 CPL Interpretation, art. 531.
71   *See* the CPL. art. 33.
72   *See id.* art. 246.
73   See the SPC, the 2015 CPL Interpretation, art. 531.

arbitration agreement is not subject to the exclusive jurisdiction restriction. Thus, parties may still agree to choose a foreign arbitration institute to arbitrate disputes over which Chinese courts have exclusive jurisdiction.

An important nature of the forum choice agreement is the consent of the parties. Such consent may be expressed by the parties, and may also be inferred from the contents of the contract (e.g., from inclusion of a choice of law clause, or from the conduct of the party or parties). In China, an inference of the choice of forum may not be made from the terms of the contract, but may be presumed from the conduct of the defendant. Thus, in a civil action, if a foreign defendant raises no objection to the jurisdiction of a people's court and answers the complaint or otherwise appears in response thereto, the defendant will be deemed to have accepted the people's court's jurisdictional competence.[74]

Under Article 127 of the CPL, if a party does not raise any objection to the jurisdiction and files an answer and defends against the claim, the party shall be deemed to have agreed to the jurisdiction of the court over the case. Jurisdiction on the basis of no objection, however, must not violate the provisions of the tiers or exclusive jurisdiction of the people's courts.[75] The idea is that a party's attending the litigation in a court constitutes a surrender or waiver of the defense to the personal jurisdiction of the court, which implies the consent of the party.[76]

An issue that is often raised is the effect of an assignment or delegation of a contract on the choice of court clause in the contract. As noted, assignment or delegation in China may take the form of a partial or whole transfer of contractual rights or obligations to a third party (i.e., transfer of contract). According to the SPC, when a contract is transferred, the choice of court clause in the contract shall remain effective as to the transferee unless the transferee is unaware of the choice of law clause at the time of the contract transfer or the transfer agreement provides otherwise with the consent of the party in question to the original contract.[77]

74　See the CPL (as amended 2007), art. 255.
75　See the CPL, art. 127.
76　According to Article 268 of the CPL, a defendant who is not domiciled with the territory of China has thirty days to file his or her answer upon receipt of the plaintiff's complaint. Thus, if a defendant wants to challenge a people's court jurisdiction, he or she must do so within this statutory thirty-day period. According the Supreme People's Court, a third party to litigation may also challenge the jurisdiction of a people's court if the third party has an independent claim. Once the jurisdiction is challenged, the court has fifteen days to review the challenge and make a decision in the form of a court order. A court order on a jurisdictional matter is appealable.
77　See the SPC, the 2015 CPL Interpretation, art. 33.

For foreign lawyers, it is important to bear in mind that in Chinese judicial proceedings there is no such process as "special and limited appearance" as in many foreign courts for the purpose of challenging personal jurisdiction of the court or quashing service. If the jurisdiction becomes an issue in a Chinese people's court, it should be raised along with the submission of the answer to the complaint. In accordance with Article 127 of the CPL, after the people's court accepts the case, if a party disagrees to the jurisdiction of the court, the party shall raise its objection during the period of time the answer is submitted, and the court then will decide whether the objection is tenable.[78]

4   Dispute Settlement Mechanism

When a dispute over an international contract arises between the parties to the contract, there are four options for settlement of the dispute. Under Article 128 of the Contract Law, the parties may settle their disputes concerning the contract through conciliation or mediation. If the parties are unwilling to settle the dispute by reconciliation or mediation, or the conciliation or mediation fails, the parties may apply to an arbitration institution—Chinese or foreign—for arbitration according to their arbitration agreement. If there is no arbitration agreement between the parties or the arbitration agreement is null and void, a lawsuit may be brought to a people's court.[79]

Of course, the most ideal means to settle such disputes is for the parties to negotiate and reconcile the differences between them. The advantages of negotiation for dispute resolution are many. Through negotiations, the parties will be able to settle the dispute amicably and keep unaffected their business relations. As is often the case, negotiation provides a platform for the parties to communicate directly with each other and find out what their respective problems are. As a practical matter, negotiation is also a cost-efficient means for resolving disputes in business transactions. But for the settlement of disputes by negotiation to succeed, compromises from each of the parties are required.

Unfortunately, however, because of different or conflicting business interests and concerns, it is in many cases difficult, if not impossible, for the contractual parties to yield to each other, or the parties are unwilling or unable to reach a compromise. In this situation, the parties have to employ other means to resolve their disputes. In China, as prescribed by the Contract Law, parties

---

78   See the CPL, art. 127.
79   See the Contract Law, art. 128.

may engage a third party to mediate their dispute or submit their dispute to an agreed body for arbitration. Parties may also choose to litigate their disputes in a court. In many countries, mechanisms of dispute settlement other than litigation are collectively called "alternative dispute resolutions," or ADR.

4.1   Reconciliation

For purposes of the Contract Law, reconciliation primarily refers to negotiation, which is, as noted, the most desirable means for settling any dispute that may arise out of a contract between parties. In general, reconciliation is conducted between the parties or through their lawyers without the participation of any third party. Through negotiation, the parties in a dispute reach a settlement agreement on the basis of mutual understanding and mutual benefits. Note that negotiation, though highly desirable, is not mandatory. In other words, the parties may, as they wish, directly choose means other than negotiation to solve their disputes.[80]

In some cases, reconciliation takes place with the aid of a third party in whom the parties have trust and confidence. In this situation, however, the role of the third party is limited. In general, in order to help the parties to reconcile their differences and resolve their disputes, the third party serves as the negotiation facilitator bringing the parties together to a negotiation table. During the course of reconciliation, the third party normally will not put forward any proposal for the settlement of disputes between the parties. Instead, the parties will conduct negotiations themselves.

4.2   Mediation

Mediation is used where the parties have been unable to reach a settlement themselves but are willing to have their disputes heard by a third party. The difference between reconciliation and mediation is the role of the third party. In mediation, the third party plays an active role in making a proposal for how the parties can resolve their dispute. Mediation is widely employed in China as an effective means to help "melt" the differences between the disputing parties with mutual compromise. There are four kinds of mediations currently used in China: civil mediation, administrative mediation, arbitral mediation, and judicial mediation.

Civil mediation is commonly referred to in China as "people's mediation," which is non-judicial mediation. It is conducted by local people's mediation

---

80   See Li Guoguang, Explanation and Application of the Contract Law, 568–569 (Xinhua Press, 1999).

committees, which are usually by neighborhood or township committees. The purpose of civil mediation is to help settle disputes at a grass-root level. Under the 2010 People's Mediation Law (Mediation Law), people's mediation is defined as mediation by the people's mediation committee to help the parties voluntarily reach an agreement on the basis of equal consultation and to resolve civil disputes through persuasion and guidance.[81]

Pursuant to the Mediation Law, a mediation agreement reached by parties through mediation by the people's mediation committee is legally binding. Therefore, once a mediation agreement is agreed upon, the parties must perform in accordance with the agreement.[82] Meanwhile, the people's mediation committee is required to supervise the performance of the mediation agreement and urge the parties to perform their agreed upon obligations.[83] However, if the parties dispute either the performance under, or contents of, the medication agreement, one of the parties may file a lawsuit in the people's court.[84]

After a mediation agreement is reached through mediation by the People's Mediation Committee, the parties may jointly apply to the people's court for judicial confirmation of the validity of the mediation agreement within thirty days from the effective date of the agreement. After the court's confirmation, the mediation agreement will have a judicial effect. If one party refuses or fails to perform, the other party may apply to the people's court for enforcement. If, however, the mediation agreement is found invalid by the people's court, the parties can modify the original mediation agreement, reach a new mediation agreement through the people's mediation, or directly file a lawsuit in the people's court.[85]

The method of civil mediation is greatly favored by the Chinese government. The crown jewel of civil mediation is to help solve civil disputes in a timely manner. The idea is that the efforts to quiet or eliminate civil disputes at the grass-root level help maintain much wanted social harmony and stability in China. Despite its advantages, however, civil mediation may not be attractive to a foreign party in an international contract. A major concern is with local bias. Another concern is the effectiveness of such mediation in terms of enforcement of the mediation agreement.

---

81 See the People's Mediation Law, promulgated by the NPC's Standing Commettee on August 28, 2010, art. 1.
82 See *id.*, art. 31.
83 See *id.*
84 See *id.*, art. 32.
85 See *id.*, art. 33.

Administrative mediation, in the context of helping resolve contractual disputes, is mediation conducted by an administrative authority. In the area of contracts, administrative mediation is mostly conducted by the authority of commerce and industry management for mediation. Under the Methods of Administrative Mediation of the Disputes Concerning Contracts, which was issued by the State Administration of Commerce and Industry on November 3, 1997,[86] administration mediation will be instituted at the request of the contractual parties in disputes on a voluntary basis and will be conducted non-publicly unless otherwise asked by the parties. A successful mediation will produce a settlement agreement between the parties.

Like civil mediation, administrative mediation has a limited effect, however. A settlement agreement reached by parties through administrative mediation, though considered to be binding on the parties, is not enforceable in courts. In other words, if a party breaches a settlement agreement that was agreed to by the parties in an administrative mediation, the other party does not have the right to ask a people's court to enforce it. In the case of breach, the aggrieved party has to seek arbitration under the arbitration clause or, absent an arbitration agreement, file a lawsuit in the people's court to resolve the dispute.[87]

Arbitral mediation is referred to as mediation conducted by the arbitration body during the process of arbitration. Although mediation is not required in arbitration, it is strongly preferable in China that the mediation be conducted before the arbitral award is made. According the Arbitration Law of China, the arbitration tribunal may conduct mediation prior to making an arbitral award. If the parties are willing to seek mediation, the arbitral tribunal shall conduct the mediation.[88]

A major difference between arbitral mediation and civil or administrative mediation is that that a settlement agreement reached as a result of arbitral mediation has the same legal effect as an arbitral award.[89] Such an agreement is not only binding to the parties but also enforceable at law. If a party fails to perform a settlement agreement reached through an arbitral mediation, the aggrieved party may ask the people's court to enforce the settlement agreement.

---

86   See the State Administration of Commerce and Industry, Methods of Administrative Mediation of the Disputes Concerning Contracts, articles 3 and 5.
87   See *id.*, art. 20.
88   See the Arbitration Law of the People's Republic of China, art. 51. An English translation is available at http://www.gip.net/chinalaw/lawtranl.htm.
89   See *id.*

Judicial mediation concerns mediation by the court. Since government policy in China strongly favors mediation, a people's court is required by the law to conduct mediation before the judgment is rendered. Under Article 93 of the CPL, when hearing civil cases, the people's courts must conduct a mediation between the parties based on the voluntariness principle and the clear facts.[90]

It is further provided in Article 122 that where mediation is appropriate in a civil lawsuit in the people's court, the parties shall first go through mediation unless the parties reject it.[91] On appeal or the second instance trial, the appellate court may also conduct mediation. The mediation at the proceeding of appeals, however, is not required under the CPL (as amended).[92]

In accordance with Article 95 of the CPL, when conducting a mediation, a people's court may ask for assistance from relevant units or individuals. Once invited, the units or individuals shall assist the people's court in the mediation.[93] When an agreement is reached by the parties as a result of the mediation, the people's court shall issue a mediation statement signed by the presiding judge and the court clerk and affixed with the seal of the people's court. When served to the parties, the mediation statement shall come into force upon the signature of the parties.[94]

But, if no agreement is reached during the mediation or if a party repudiates the agreement prior to the service of the mediation statement, the people's court is required to promptly enter a judgment.[95] It is required under the CPL that the mediation agreement must be reached voluntarily between the parties without coercion, and the contents of the mediation agreement must not violate the law.[96]

In its 2015 CPL Interpretation, the SPC sets forth several rules on judicial mediation. According to the SPC, a people's court may with the consent of the parties directly proceed to conduct mediation upon acceptance of the case if it finds after review that the legal relationship involved is clear and the facts of the case are ascertained.[97] Under the SPC's Interpretation, the mediation process in civil cases shall not be made public unless public disclosure is agreed upon by the parties.[98] In addition, the contents of a mediation agreement

---

90 See the CPL, art. 93.
91 See *id.*, art. 122.
92 See id., art. Art. 172.
93 See *id.*, art. 95.
94 See *id.*, art. 97.
95 See *id.*, art. 99.
96 See *id.*, art. 96.
97 See the SPC, 2015 CPL Interpretation, art. 142.
98 See *id.*, art. 146.

must not be made public except where disclosure is necessitated by the protection of national interests, social and public interests, and legitimate rights and interests of others.[99]

However, mediation may not be conducted in the following cases: (a) cases subject to special procedures, procedures for urging performance of obligations, or procedures for the public summons for exhortation; (b) cases confirming marriage or other personal relationships; or (c) other cases unsuitable by nature for mediation.[100] Moreover, the parties must not maliciously collude with each other or attempt to use mediation to infringe upon the legitimate rights and interests of others.[101]

4.3 *Arbitration*

If all efforts for mediation are futile, a dispute will be submitted to either an arbitration tribunal or a court for decision. As in many other countries, in China arbitration is a popular device by which to resolve disputes in international contracts. As a matter of fact, a significant number of international contracts in China contain a special clause calling for arbitration if the parties cannot reach an agreement through negotiation and/or mediation. Such arbitration such may either take place in China or outside China; if takes place outside China, it is called foreign-country arbitration.

Within China, foreign arbitration refers to arbitration that contains foreign elements and is conducted by a Chinese arbitration body. In most cases, foreign arbitrations in the country are conducted by the China International Economic and Trade Arbitration Commission (or CIETAC). The CIETAC is headquartered in Beijing and has branches in Shanghai and Shenzhen, respectively.[102]

---

99 See *id.*
100 See id., art. 143.
101 See id., art. 144. Also, in its Rules on Several Issues Concerning Mediation of Civil Affairs in the People's Courts issued in 2004, the SPC specifically states in Article 12 that under any of the following circumstances, a mediation agreement shall not be accepted by the people's courts: (a) harmfulness to the national and social public interests, (b) infringement of the third party interests, (c) violation of the true intention of a party, or (d) violation of compulsory provisions of law and administrative regulations. A full text of the Rules is available at https://www.renrendoc.com/p-17036064.html.
102 Under the Arbitration Law of China, the CIETAC is organized by the China Chamber of International Commerce (CCOIC), and the CCOIC is associated with the China Council for the Promotion of International Trade (CCPIT). The CCPIT, though purportedly a non-government institute/organization, is a semi-government agency, and the top officials of CCPIT are all governmental appointees.

In addition, a few other local arbitration institutions—including Beijing and Shanghai Arbitration Commissions—may conduct foreign arbitrations if selected to by the parties.

There are a number of issues that affect foreign arbitration. The most important issue is the arbitration agreement because the agreement serves as a jurisdictional basis for the arbitration body—or, put differently, determines the competence of the arbitration body. Under Chinese law, an arbitration agreement can take the form of an arbitration clause in a contact, a separate arbitration agreement reached by the parties before or after a dispute arises, or other forms. For an arbitration agreement to be valid and enforceable, it must meet both formality and substance requirements.

With regard to formality, an arbitration agreement must be expressly made in writing because it is considered to be a manifestation of the parties' consent to resolving a dispute among them through an arbitral entity. In its substance, an arbitration agreement must contain three essential elements: (a) the parties' intent to arbitrate, (b) the matters subject to arbitration, and (c) a designated arbitration body. Any defect in the arbitration agreement may adversely affect the validity of the arbitration. In addition, China does not recognize foreign arbitration on domestic disputes. Thus, to be eligible for foreign arbitration, the dispute must contain a foreign factor.

The second issue involves the effect of an arbitration agreement. Under Article 271 of the CPL, no party may institute an action in a people's court if there exists a valid arbitration agreement that provides for arbitration in a Chinese arbitration body or other arbitration institution.[103] Thus, the major effect of an arbitration agreement, if valid, is the exclusion of the jurisdiction of the people's courts. If a party wishes to pursue litigation in a courtroom in lieu of arbitration in contravention of the contract, the party must succesfully challenge the validity of the arbitration agreement. A people's court will not take the case unless and until the arbitration agreement is found to be null and void, and thus is set aside by the court.

The third issue concerns the enforcement of arbitral awards. Once again, a foreign arbitration can be conducted either in or ourside China. If an arbitral award is made by a Chinese arbitral body, under both the CPL and the Arbitration Law, no party may institute an action in a people's court for the same dispute.[104] If a party fails to satisfy the arbitral award, the other party may apply for enforcement to the intermediate people's court of the place where

---

103   See the CPL, art. 271.
104   See *id.*, art. 273; Arbitration Law of China, art. 9.

the award debtor is domiciled or the place in which the property of the award debtor is located.[105]

However, according to the CPL, a foreign related arbitral award made by a Chinese arbitration body will not be enforced if evidence shows that (a) there is no arbitration agreement reached between the parties, (b) the award debtor was not given notice of the need to appoint an arbitrator or to take part in the arbitration proceedings or the award debtor was unable to state his or her opinions due to reasons for which he or she is not responsible, (c) the composition of the arbitral tribunal or the arbitration procedure was not in conformity with the rules of arbitration, or (d) the matters decided in the award exceed the scope of the arbitration agreement or are beyond the arbitral authority of the arbitration body.[106] Additionally, the arbitral award will not be enforced if the people's court determines that the enforcement would be against social and public interests.[107]

Enforcement of arbitral awards entered into by a foreign arbitration body is governed by Article 283 of the CPL. According to Article 283, if a party seeks to have a foreign arbitral award recognized and enforced in China, the party must directly apply to the intermediate people's court of the place where the party subject to the enforcement resides or has property located. Upon receipt of the filing, the people's court is required to handle the enforcement matter under the treaties concluded or acceded to by China or, absent relevant treaties, based on the principle of reciprocity.[108] For purposes of the enforcement of foreign arbitral awards, the New York Convention can be directly applied in a Chinese court. If there is a discrepancy between a treaty provision and a provision in domestic law, the treaty prevails.

It should be noted that to qualify as a foreign arbitral award, the arbitration must contain foreign elements, and the award must be entered by a foreign arbitration institution. In addition, the arbitration agreement, in order to be valid, must be in writing and contain the required essential elements. The competence of the arbitration body may be decided by the arbitration commission or the people's court at the parties' choice. In addition, the arbitrability of particular disputes is subject to Chinese law and the enforcement must not violate Chinese public policy.

Note also that an important component of the enforcement process for foreign arbitral awards is the internal reporting system established by the SPC

---

105   See *id.*
106   See *id.*, art. 274.
107   See *id.*
108   See id., art. 283.

in 1995.[109] Under the internal reporting system, when making a decision to deny recognition and enforcement of a foreign arbitral award, the intermediate court must report to the high people's court that has jurisdiction over the intermediate people's court for review. If the high people's court is to grant the denial, a report must be made to the SPC for approval.[110]

According to the SPC, the internal reporting system also applies where a party files a lawsuit seeking to have an arbitration agreement set aside. The intermediate people's court is not allowed to take the case without obtaining approval from the high people's court as well as the SPC.[111] In 1998, the SPC extended the internal reporting system to requests for vacating arbitral awards made by the CIETAC, the domectic arbitration body, in response to the increasing prevalence of Chinese parties seeking to deny the effect of arbitral awards entered by the CIETAC.[112]

The SPC in 2017 adopted several new rules concerning judicial review of arbitration awards. In order to streamline the enforcement of foreign arbitral awards in the China under the New York Convention, and to place all arbitration awards, foreign and domestic alike, under a unified machanim of judicial review, the SPC requires that both denial of enforcement of arbitral awards and invalidation of arbitration agreements must be reported internally to the high people's court and the SPC for review and approval.[113] In both cases, the SPC has the final say.

4.4   *Litigation*

Litigation is the last resort to dispute settlement. To initiate a lawsuit in a court, the threshold issue is the jurisdiction of the court. As noted, for a contractual dispute, the parties may by agreement select a court and the selection may be made in the form of a contractual clause or a separate agreement. Absent parties' choice, however, jurisdiction must be determined under the provisions of law. With regard to civil dispute cases that contain foreign elements, the CPL provides a specific statutory basis for the jurisdiction of people's courts.

---

109   See the SPC, *the Notice Concerning Handling by the People's Court of the Matters Involving Foreign Arbitration,* August 28, 1995, Fafa (1995) No. 18.
110   See *id.*
111   See *id.*
112   See the SPC, *the Notice Concerning the Matters To Vacate by the People's Court the Foreign Arbitral Awards,* April 23, 1998, Fa (1998) No. 40.
113   See the SPC, Provisions on the Issues Concerning the Reporting of Judicial Review of Arbitration Cases, issued on December 26, 2017.

In civil litigation, the general jurisdictional basis of the people's court, under the rule of "plaintiff following defendant," is the place of the defendant's domicile or habitual residence if the defendant's domicile is different from his or her habitual residence.[114] However, pursuant to Article 265 of the CPL, to bring an action on a contractual dispute against a defendant who is not domiciled within the territory of China, if the contract involved was formed or performed in China, the subject matter of the suit is located in China, the defendant's attachable property is situated in China, or the defendant maintains a representative office in China, the people's court of the place of contract, the place of performance, the place of subject matter, the place of the attachable property, or the place of the representative office shall respectively have jurisdiction.[115]

There are two issues that are often raised with respect to international civil litigation. One issue is parallel litigation and the other issue involves *forum non conveniens*. Parallel litigation occurs when a Chinese court and a foreign court have concurrent jurisdiction over a particular case. According to the SPC, when a court of China and a foreign court all have jurisdiction over a case, if one party files a lawsuit in a foreign court, and the other party a suit for the same case in a people's court, the people's court may take the case.[116]

To deal with parallel litigation, the SPC requires that a request by a foreign court or foreign party for recognition and enforcement of a judgment entered by the foreign court on the case must be denied when a judgment is to be entered by a Chinese court, except if otherwise provided by a treaty concluded or acceded to by China. If, however, a judgment or ruling entered by the foreign court has been recognized by the people's court and a party files a lawsuit on the same dispute with a people's court, the people's court must dismiss the lawsuit.[117]

There is no provision in the CPL regarding *forum non conveniens*. The SPC recognizes the doctrine of *forum non conveniens*, however. In its 2015 CPL Interpretation, the SPC opines that under certain circumstances, a people's court in a civil case that contains foreign elements may decide to dismiss the case and advise the plaintiff to bring the lawsuit to a more convenient foreign court.[118] It is important to note that the doctrine of *forum non conveniens* in Chinese courts applies only to civil cases that have foreign elements (i.e., foreign civil cases).

---

114   See the CPL, art. 21.
115   See *id.*, art. 265.
116   See the SPL, 2015 CPL Interpretation, art. 533.
117   See *id.*
118   See *id.*, art. 532.

In the SPC's opinion, circumstances that justify dismissal on the basis of *forum non conveniens* include: (a) the defendant raises a request that the case should be adjudicated by a foreign court that is more convenient or raises an objection to the jurisdiction; (b) there is no agreement between the parties selecting a Chinese court as the competent court; (c) the case does not fall within the exclusive jurisdiction of Chinese courts; (d) the case does not effect the interests of the State, citizens, legal persons, or other organizations of China; (e) the key facts of the dispute in the case did not take place within the territory of China, and the case is not governed by the laws of China, making it significantly difficult for the people's court to ascertain the facts and apply the laws; and (f) a foreign court has jurisdiction and is more convenient to adjudicate the case.[119]

It historically was, and remains, true that many foreign companies and their lawyers do not feel comfortable litigating in a Chinese court. One reason is their reluctance to engage in litigation in a legal system with which they are not familiar. The other reason is concerns about the lack of independence of the Chinese judiciary. The reality is, however, that in certain cases the foreign party, either as a plaintiff or as a defendant, may have to litigate in a court in China. Although in contract cases, the parties are allow to choose forum, the choice, as noted, is subject to two restrictions: connection between the forum and the contract or dispute, and non-violation of the exclusive jurisdiction of Chinese courts.

Therefore, when foreign lawyers draft contracts relating to business their clients are conducting with China, the lawyers have to think about different options for dealing with possible disputes. It is important to have a well-addressed dispute settlement clause in the contract. Equally important is the consideration of possible compromise in order to reach the desired outcome or ultimate goal. Thus, in certain situations, engaging in arbitration or litigation in China is not necessarily bad choice in terms of effective and adequate protection of foreign parties' interest. According to an old Chinese saying, if you don't go into the tiger's lair, how can you catch the cubs?

5 Statute of Limitations

The right to make a civil claim arises from a statutory basis. For example, a failure to perform contractual obligations gives a rise to the right under the

---

119 See *id.*

Contract Law to make a claim for breach of contract. But an exercise of such right is subject to a statute of limitations—a law that sets the maximum period for filing the claim arising under the right for judicial relief. If the claim is not filed before the statutory deadline, the right to make such a claim is lost forever. The length of time the statute of limitations allows, however, varies depending on the nature of the claim.

The statute of limitations in civil cases is provided in both the 1986 Civil Code and the 2017 GPCL. Under the 2017 GPCL, there are three different statutes of limitations: the general statute of limitations, the special statute of limitations, and the ultimate statute of limitations. The general statute of limitations applies to all civil matters unless otherwise provided by the law. The special statute of limitations is the maximun length of the time that falls within the category of "otherwise provided by the law." The ultimate statute of limitation refers to the maximum time period for making a civil claim.

The general statute of limitations is provided in Article 188 of the 2017 GPCL. Under Article 188, the statute of limitations for an action brought to a people's court for protection of civil rights is three years, except as otherwise provided by the law.[120]

The statute of limitations runs from the day when the obligee knows or ought to know that his or her right has been infringed upon and who the obligor is.[121] Under special circumstances as provided by the law, however, the statute of limitations is calculated in a particular way. For example, if a debt is to be performed in installments pursuant to the parties' agreement, the statute of limitations starts to run from the day when the performance period for the last installment expires.[122]

The Contract Law also contains a statue of limitations that applies to two kinds of contracts: contracts for international sale of goods and contracts for

---

120 See the 2017 GPCL, art. 188. Under the 1986 Civil Code, the general statute of limitations was two years. However, in the 1986 Civil Code, there are several civil actions for which the statute of limitations is one year, including (a) claims for compensation for bodily injuries, (b) sales of substandard goods without proper notice to that effect, (c) delays in paying rent or refusal to pay rent, or (c) losses or damages to the property left in the care of another person. Although the GPCL does not necessarily operate to repeal the 1986 Civil Code, the 2017 SPC is of the opinion that the three-year statute of limitations as provided in the 2017 GPCL shall supersede the limitation provisions of the 1986 Civil Code. See the 2017 SPC, Interpretaions for Several Questions Concerning Application of the Statute of Limitations Provided in the General Provisions of Civil Law, issued on July 18, 2018, http://www.court.gov.cn/fabu-xiangqing-108251.html.
121 See *id.*
122 See *id.*, art. 189.

import and export of technology. Under Article 129 of the Contract Law, the time limit for instituting an action or arbitration concerning a dispute over a contract for the international sale of goods or contracts for technology import and export is four years. The four-year limitation is calculated from the date on which the party knows or ought to know that his or her rights are infringed upon. This provision is compatible with the United Nations Convention on the Limitation Period in the International Sale of Goods.[123]

In addition, the Contract Law provides a special two-year statute of limitation for contracts for the sale of substandard goods. According to Article 158 of the Contract Law, with regard to sales of goods, (a) if there is no agreement between the parties in the contract regarding the inspection period, the buyer shall provide notice to the seller within a reasonable period of time after it finds or ought to find that the quantity or quality of the goods do not conform with the terms of the contract; if the buyer fails to provide such notice within a reasonable time period or within two years from the date of the receipt of the goods, it shall be deemed that the quantity or quality of the object has conformed with the terms of the contract; (b) if there is a quality guaranty period, such guaranty period shall be applied in lieu of the two-year limit; (c) if the seller knows or ought to know the goods to be supplied do not conform with the terms of the contract, the buyer is not subject to the time limit of the notice.[124]

The ultimate statute of limitation refers to the maximum time period for making a civil claim. The maxmum length of the period as provided in both the 1986 Civil Code and the 2017 GPCL is twenty years from the date of infringement of the right.[125] The twenty-year statute of limitation applies to all civil claims regardless of whether the aggrieved party knows or ought to know the damages or infringement. However, under special circumstances, the people's court may at its discretion extend the period of the statute of limitations upon the request of the obligee or claimant. According to the SPC, such "special circumstances" are cases in which the obligee could not exercise his or her right during the statute of limitations due to an "objective reason."[126]

---

123 The Limitation Convention entered into force on August 1, 1988. The Convention determines "when claims of a buyer and a seller against each other arising from a contract for the international sale of goods or relating to its breach, termination, or invalidity can no longer be exercised by reason of the expiration of a period of time." Art. 1. Under the Convention, the "limitation period" is four years. Art. 8.
124 See the Contract Law, art. 158.
125 See the 1986 Civil Code, art. 137. See also the GPCL, art. 188.
126 See the SPC, the 1988 Opinions on Several Matters Concerning Application and Implementation of the General Principles of Civil Law of China (Provisional), art. 169.

The statute of limitations may be tolled or suspended. Under Article 194 of the 2017 GPCL, the statute of limitations shall be tolled if the right to make a claim cannot be exercised during the last six months of the time limitation due to any of the followings: (a) *force majeure*; (b) the person without capacity or with limited capacity for civil conduct has no an agent *ad litem*, or his or her agent *ad litem* dies, loses the capacity for civil conduct, or no longer has the power to represent; (c) the sucessor or estate adminstrator cannot be ascertained after the commencement of the succession; (d) the obligee is controlled by the obligor or any other person; or (e) other obstacles result in the obligee's inability to exercise the claim right.[127] But once tolled, the statute of limitations shall expire six months after the cause for the suspension is eliminated.[128]

In addition, the statute of limitations will be recalculated in certain situations in which the time limitation is interrupted. In accordance with Article 195 of the 2017 GPCL, under the following circumstances the statute of limitations shall start all over again from the time when the interruption or relevant process ends: (a) the obligee makes a request to the obligor for performance; (b) the obligor agrees to perform; (c) the obligee brings a lawsuit or applies for arbitration; or (d) other situations arise that have the same effect as institution of a lawsuit or arbitration.[129]

Note, however, that for purposes of recalculating the statute of limitations, a request for performance does not have to be made to the obligor himself. According to the SPC, a request made by the obligee to the guarantor, the agent, or administrator/receiver of the property of the obligor will satisfy the requirements for a re-start.[130] In addition, the statute of limitations may start anew when the obligor or claimant makes a petition to the local people's mediation committee or relevant authority for the protection of his or her civil rights.[131]

One issue concerning the statute of limitations is how "ought to know" is to be determined. As a practical matter for contracts, the SPC has developed a guideline that is aimed at helping make such a determination. According to the SPC, the issue of "ought to know" can be determined differently in the following ways: (a) if the contract claim is attached with a condition or time limit, the limitation runs from the time that condition is met or the time limit ends; (b) if the contract has a time for performance, the limitation begins from

---

127   See the 2017 GPCL, art. 194.
128   See *id.*
129   See *id.*, art. 195.
130   See the SPC, Opinions on Several Matters Concerning Application and Implementation of the General Principles of Civil Law, issued on 1988, art. 173.
131   See *id.*, art. 174.

the expiration of the time; (c) if there is no performance time period, the limitation runs from the time the obligee or claimant makes a claim; (d) if there is a claim for restitution after the contract is void or rescinded, the limitation is calculated from the time of the voidance or rescission of the contract; (e) if the subject matter of the contract is a promise "not-to-act" or an "omission" (i.e., a passive obligation), the limitation starts from the time the obligation not-to-act is violated; or (f) if there is a claim for specific performance, damages, or liquidated damages due to a breach of contract, the limitation runs from the time of the breach.[132]

It is also important to note that under Article 196 of the 2017 GPCL, the statute of limitations does not apply to certain cases—such as a claim for cessation of infringement, removal of obstacles, or elimination of danger; a claim for restitution of property; and a claim for child support, elder parents support, or spousal support.[133] Equally important is Article 197 of the 2017 GPCL, which prohibits the parties from providing by agreement the period of limitation, method of calculation, or the causes of suspension or interruption. Pursuant to Article 197, the matters related to the limitations on the exercise of the right to bring a claim must have a statutory basis as provided in the law.[134]

---

132   See Li Guoguang, *supra* note 80 at pp 596–598.
133   See the 2017 GPCL, art. 196.
134   See *id.*, art 197.

CHAPTER 13

Labor Contracts

Labor contracts in China are not within the realm of the Contract Law but, rather, are governed by a different set of laws. As noted, a contract under the Contract Law refers to an agreement between the parties that creates, modifies, or terminates civil or commercial relations of rights and obligations. A labor contract, in and of itself, is also an agreement but it specifically deals with a labor or employment relationship. Although certain general principles of Contract Law (e.g., good faith and fairness) may equally apply to labor contracts, there are several differences between labor contracts and civil or commercial contracts.

One difference is that a civil or commercial contract by its nature is basically a private matter or a product of civilian conduct, while a labor contract is considered to be more involved in social or public affairs and thus is in substance subject to more government intervention. As a private affair, a civil or commercial contract is generally premised on the principle of party autonomy and the parties are empowered to determine their bargains as they wish. The labor contract, however, is often a mixture of the parties' will and government power. In other words, the contents of a labor contract, though spelled out by the parties themselves, would have to include certain terms mandated by the government. Also, the enforcement of a labor contract is always under the scrutiny of the government through the process of supervision and review.

Another difference lies with the relationship between the terms of a contract and the provisions of law in their application. With regard to civil or commercial contracts, the contractual terms as agreed upon by the parties normally take priority and legal provisions apply only when there is no contractual term, or the contractual term is found to be invalid. The labor contract is just the opposite—legal provisions are always applied first and the contract terms will govern when there is an absence of applicable legal provisions. For example, Article 62 of the Contract Law deals with how the terms of quality, price, performance place, time period, and method are to be determined. But the provision applies only if there is no agreement between the parties or the agreement is unclear pertaining to these terms. This is not the case with a labor contract.

The third difference concerns compensation. As a general rule, the damages awarded for breach of contract are compensatory. The purpose of compensation is not to punish the breaching party, but rather to restore the non-breaching party to the position the non-breaching party would have been in if the contract were fully performed. In a labor contract, however, a breach of contract may result in a penalty, especially when the breach is caused by the employer. In addition, in a civil or commercial contract, the parties may provide liquidated damages in advance as a forecast of estimated loss in the case of breach. But in a labor contract, the damages may not be stipulated by the parties but, rather, must be provided by the law. Simply put, the damages in labor contracts must have a statutory basis.

1   Labor Contract Legislation and Legal Framework

Labor contracts as a legal system did not exist in China after 1949 until the country departed from the planned economy in the late 1970s. Under the planned economy, all labor was arranged, allocated, and managed according to the State plan. The early regulation that involved labor contracts was the Provisions of Labor Management in Sino-Foreign Joint Venture Enterprises adopted by the State Council in 1980.[1] At that time, a labor contract was required only for employment in foreign joint ventures. Three years later, in 1983, the Ministry of Labor and Personnel issued a notice promoting the use of labor contracts in State owned as well as county-level collectively owned enterprises.[2] The formal use of labor contracts in the country began in 1986 when the State Council adopted the Provisional Rules of Implementation of Law Contracts System in the State Owned Enterprises, which required that labor contracts be used uniformly in all employment in the country unless otherwise provided by the State.[3]

The first piece of congressional legislation on labor is the Labor Law promulgated by the NPC on July 5, 1994. Effective January 1, 1995, the Labor Law makes a labor contract a statutory requirement for employment in the country.[4] It not only provides a definition of labor contract but also contains special

---

1 See the State Council, Provisions of Labor Management in Sino-Foreign Joint Venture Enterprises, issued on July 26, 1980. Under Article 2 of the Provisions, employment, dismissal, and resignation of employees of joint ventures, production, and work tasks, wages and rewards and punishments, working hours and holidays, labor insurance and living welfare, labor protection, labor discipline, etc., shall be stipulated by entering into labor contracts.
2 See the Ministry of Labor and Personnel, the Notice Concerning Actively Use of Labor Contracts on Trial Basis, issued on August 22, 1983.
3 See the State Council, the Provisional Rules of Implementation of Law Contract System in the State Owned Enterprises, adopted on July 12, 1986.
4 See the Labor Law of China, http://www.npc.gov.cn/englishnpc/Law/2007-12/12/content_1383754.htm.

provisions concerning labor contracts entered into either individually or collectively. Three years later, in 2007, the Standing Committee of the NPC adopted the Labor Contract Law (LCL), which took effect on January 1, 2008.[5] The enactment of the Labor Contract Law marked the establishment of a statutory system of labor contracts in China. In the same year, on September 18, 2008, the State Council issued the Rules of Implementation of the LCL (LCL Implementation Rules).

The current legal framework that governs labor contracts in the country consists of three layers. On the top of the layer is the Constitution, which protects the working right of citizens.[6] The second layer under the Constitution includes such laws as the Labor Law and the LCL passed by the NPC and its Standing Committee. The third layer contains administrative rules and regulations adopted by the State Council with regard to labor and labor contracts. In addition, the SPC's Interpretations, though not the law themselves, constitute an important legal source on which the people's courts often rely in their handling of labor contract cases.

The LCL is of course the most important legislation that governs labor contracts. With a total of eight chapters and ninety-eight articles,[7] the LCL applies to the formation, performance, modification, rescission, and termination of labor contracts.[8] The purpose of the LCL, as stated in Article 1, is to improve and perfect the labor contract system, to make explicit the rights and obligations of both parties to a labor contract, to protect the lawful rights and interests of laborers, and to build and develop harmonious and stable labor relationships.[9]

But ever since its promulgation, the LCL has met criticism. The most critical view is that the obligations imposed on employers—mainly to mandated insurance and funds contributed by the employer and required compensation for the termination of labor contracts or employment relationships—are too burdensome. It has been observed that while the Labor Law intends to strike a balance between employers' interests and the minimum protections of employees, the LCL was clearly weighted more toward employees.[10] Indeed, from

---

5   See the Labor Contract Law of China (LCL), http://www.npc.gov.cn/englishnpc/Law/2009-02/20/content_1471106.htm。.
6   See Constitution of China (1982, as amended 2018), art. 42.
7   The eight chapters include General Principles, Conclusion of the Employment Contract, Performance and Amendment of the Employment Contract, Rescission and Termination of the Employment Contract, Special Provisions, Supervision and Examination, Legal Liabilities, and Supplementary Provisions.
8   See the LCL, *supra* note 5, art. 2.
9   See *id.*, art. 1.
10 Virginia Harper Ho, From Contracts to Compliance? An Early Look at Implementation under China's New Labor Legislation, 23 COLUM. J. ASIAN L. 35, 68–71 (2009).

the legislative viewpoint, the LCL is designed to provide employees with greater rights and to make it easier for employees to enforce their rights in order to help create and maintain a harmonious society in the country.

In fact, after the LCL took effect, many employers used labor dispatch in lieu of labor contracts to hire workers or laborers in order to avoid the legal obligations facing them under the LCL. Labor dispatch is a kind of employment arrangement where an employee enters into a contract with a labor dispatch service firm and then is dispatched to work for the company that otherwise would be the actual employer. The widespread employment of labor dispatch practices raised concerns over the abuse of labor dispatch in violation of employees' rights and interests that the LCL is intended to protect.

As a legislative response, the LCL was amended in 2012 to limit the use of labor dispatch and narrow the scope of such service.[11] The amendments reinforce the concept of "equal pay for equal work" on which the Labor Law is premised in order to achieve pay parity for dispatched workers. In addition, it is required under the amended LCL that a company using dispatched workers must pay such workers the benefits related to their position without discrimination.[12] Furthermore, in order to implement the amendments, the Ministry of Human Resources and Social Security in 2014 issued the Interim Provisions on Labor Dispatch that sets restrictions on the types of positions dispatched workers may assume as well as the number of dispatched workers a company can utilize, and emphasizes the supplementary nature of the use of dispatched workers.[13]

2 Concept of Labor Contract

Under both the Labor Law and the LCL, to establish an employment relationship, a labor contract is required.[14] As noted, a labor contract is considered in China to be a special type of contract that combines private characteristics with a public nature. Therefore, though a labor contract, like a civil or

---

11 For general comments on the LCL amendments, see Virginia Harper Ho & Huang Qiaoyan, *The Recursivity of Reform: China's Amended Labor Contract Law*, 37 FORDHAM INT'L L. J., 973 (2014).

12 See the LCL, *supra* note 5, art. 62.

13 The Interim Provisions on Labor Dispatch was issued on January 24, 2014, effective march 1, 2014. Under the Interim Provisions, labor dispatch may be used only for "temporary, ancillary or replaceable" positions.

14 See the LCL, *supra* note 5, art. 10.

commercial contract, is in the domain of freedom of contract in many aspects, it is a statutory-based engagement intended to form an employer-employee relationship that is heavily regulated by the law.

2.1 Definition

A labor contract in China is defined in Article 16 of the Labor Law as an agreement that establishes the employment relationship between an employee and an employing unit and prescribes the rights and obligations of respective parties.[15] There are at least three implications in this definition. First, the parties to a labor contract are specified, namely the employee and employing unit. Second, the agreement is made on a voluntary basis and the parties have equal status in making such agreement. Third, the purpose of entering into a labor contract is to establish an employment relationship.

The term "employing unit" is commonly used in China to refer to an employer. Under Article 2 of the LCL, an employing unit can be an enterprise, individual economic organization, or private non-enterprise entity, and it also includes a state organ, public institution, or social organization.[16] Note that the type of an enterprise varies under Chinese Law. By ownership, an enterprise can be a state, collectively or privately owned. Structurally, an enterprise can be a limited liability company or company by shares. From the investment sources, an enterprise can be a foreign investment enterprise (FIE) or non-foreign investment enterprise (non-FIE). An FIE can be an equity joint venture, cooperative joint venture, or a wholly foreign owned enterprise (WFOE).

An employee is a natural person who has reached the legal age with a corresponding capacity to work and is able to engage in certain labor to obtain income as the main source of life. The minimum working age is China is sixteen years old. Under the Labor Law, employing units are prohibited from hiring minors under the age of sixteen, except where otherwise prescribed by the State [17] Also, as required under the Minor Protection Law, any organization or individual that hires minors who have reached the age of sixteen but not the age of eighteen shall observe State regulations regarding the types of jobs, working hours, intensity of labor, and protective measures. [18] The minors so hired shall not be assigned to any over-strenuous jobs, jobs exposed to toxic

---

15   See *id.*, art. 16.
16   See *id.*, art. 2.
17   Under Article 15 of the Labor Law, the institutions of arts, sports, and special crafts may recruit minors under the age of sixteen through the required process of approval under the law.
18   See the Minors Protection Law of China (1991, as amended 2006), art. 38.

or hazardous substances, or other jobs that imperil their physical or mental health, or nor may they be assigned to dangerous operations.[19]

In addition, an employee can be a Chinese citizen or foreigner. But, for a foreigner to be eligible to work in the country, a work permit is required. In terms of employment, a foreigner includes a foreign citizen and a stateless person. A work permit is also required for a person seeking employment in the Mainland who resides in Hong Kong, Macao, or Taiwan. According to the SPC, a foreign citizen, stateless person, or resident of Hong Kong, Macao, or Taiwan may not become a party to a labor contract without obtaining a work permit.[20] Thus, if such a person without a work permit requests a people's court to affirm his or her employment relationship based on a labor contract entered into with an employing unit in the Mainland, the request will be denied.[21]

2.2 Categories

Labor contracts in China can be divided into different categories. Depending on the employment form, a labor contract can be a contract for full-time employment or a contract for part-time employment. In contrast to full-time employment, part-time employment is defined in the LCL as employment that is paid on an hourly basis with average working hours not exceeding four hours per day and twenty-four hours per week.[22] In terms of employment period, a labor contract can be a contract for fixed term employment or non-fixed term employment. Fixed term means that there is a time stipulated in the labor contract for the termination of the employment,[23] while non-fixed term refers to employment for which no ending day is set in the labor contract.[24]

Moreover, with regard to the number of the parties in the contract, a labor contract can be an individual contract or a collective one. A collective contract is a contract entered into between an employing unit and a trade union on behalf of employees.[25] According to the LCL, collective contracts are concluded to mainly deal with such matters as remuneration, working hours, breaks and vacations, work safety and hygiene, insurance, and employee benefits.[26] The more detailed provisions of collective contracts will be discussed later.

---

19 See *id.*
20 See the SPC, Interpretation on Several Questions Concerning Application of Law in Adjudicating labor Disputes (IV), issued on February 1, 2013, art. 14.
21 See *id.*
22 See the LCL, *supra* note 5, art. 68.
23 See *id.*, art. 13.
24 See *id.*, art. 14.
25 See *id.*, art. 51.
26 See *id.*

A collective contract may also be made as a specialized contract to cover specific issues such as work safety and hygiene, protection of the rights and interests of female employees, and the mechanism for the adjustment of salary.[27] For such special sectors as construction, mining, or restaurant or catering services, an industrial or regional collective labor contract may be made for the same purposes.[28] But the LCL limits the use of industrial or regional collective contracts to the region at or below the county level in the country.[29]

3 Formation

3.1 *Requirements*

Under the LCL, to form a labor contract, certain statutory requirements must be met. First, the formation must follow the governing principles. As provided in Article 3 of the LCL, when making a labor contract, the parties are bound by the principles of lawfulness, fairness, equality and voluntariness, consensus, and good faith.[30] Lawfulness deals with the legality of the labor contract, which requires strict observation of the provisions of the law with respect to formality, substance, and the eligibility of the parties of a labor contract. Fairness concerns the contents of the labor contract with a focus on the balance of the rights and obligations of the parties as intended under the law. Equality and voluntariness emphasize the equal footing of the parties regardless of their bargaining power or social status, and the freewill of the parties in the contract making process. Consensus refers to an agreement resulting from thorough negotiations between the parties. Good faith requires that the parties be honest and responsible to each other.

Second, the formation of a labor contract must also comply with formality mandates. According to Article 10 of the LCL, a contract to establish an employment relationship must be in writing.[31] An exception to the writing requirement is a contract for part-time employment that may be entered into by the parties orally.[32] Note, however, that although a writing is required for a labor contract, the actual establishment of an employment relationship does

---

27 See *id.*, art. 52.
28 See *id.*, art. 53.
29 See *id.*
30 See *id.*, art. 3.
31 See *id.*, art. 10.
32 See *id.*, art. 69.

not necessarily start with the conclusion of a labor contract but rather runs from the time when the employee begins to work.

Nevertheless, it is imperative that if an employment relationship is established without a written contract, a written contract must be entered into within one month from the date when the employee's work commences.[33] On the other hand, if a labor contract is concluded prior to the employee's first work-day, the employment relationship is not established until the date the employee starts to work[34] The reason is simple: the establishment of an employment relationship means as a matter of law that the employing unit is obligated to pay the employee and is liable if it does not.

A failure to enter into a written labor contract will create legal consequences. Although the failure may be caused by either the employing unit or the employee, both the Labor Law and the LCL have a clear focus on the interests of the employee and make compensation a liability of the employing unit. Under Article 98 of the Labor Law, if the employing unit intentionally delays the conclusion of a labor contract, the administrative department of labor shall order it to make corrections; and if any damage has been caused to the employee, the employing unit shall be liable for compensation.[35]

The LCL further provides that if an employing unit fails to conclude a written labor contract for a period of more than one month but less than one year after the employee is hired, the employment unit shall pay the employee twice as much monthly salary.[36] Also, according to the LCL Implementation Rules, in addition to the payment of double the amount of monthly salary, the employing unit is required to sign with the employee a supplementary labor contract in writing.[37]

However, if an employing unit fails to sign a written labor contract with an employee for more than one year after the hiring, the employing unit and the employee will be deemed to have entered into a non-fixed term labor contract.[38] In the meantime, under the onerous provisions of the LCL implementation Rules, the employing unit shall (a) pay double the employee's monthly salary and (2) enter into a supplementary written labor contract with the employee.[39]

---

33   See *id.*, art. 10.
34   See *id.*
35   See the Labor Law, art. 98.
36   See the LCL, *supra* note 5, art. 82.
37   See the State Council, the LCL Implementation Rules, art. 6.
38   See the LCL, *supra* note 5, art. 14.
39   See the LCL Implementation Rules, art. 7.

Third, a labor contract in order to be valid and enforceable must contain the required terms. Under the Labor Law and the LCL, the terms of labor contracts are divided into three categories: required terms, optional terms, and prohibited terms. Required terms are mandatory and must be included in the labor contract. Pursuant to Article 19 of the Labor Law and Article 17 of the LCL, a labor contract must include the following terms:

a. The name, domicile, legal representative, and person-in-charge of the employing unit
b. The name, domicile, resident ID card, or other valid ID certificate number
c. Time limit of the contract
d. Work description and location
e. Working hours, breaking time, and vacations
f. Remuneration
g. Social securities
h. Work protection, conditions, and prevention of occupational harms
i. Labor disciplines
j. Conditions for the termination of the labor contract
k. Liabilities for the violation of the labor contract
l. Other terms that should be included in the labor contract under the laws and regulations.[40]

Optional terms are those terms that are not considered essential to a labor contract but may be included if agreed to by the parties. According to Article 17 of the LCL, in addition to the required terms, the employing unit and the employee may agree to include in the labor contract such terms as probation period, job training, confidentiality, supplementary insurance, and welfare benefits.[41] Optional terms, though not required, are binding if made by mutual consent of the parties.

Prohibited terms involve terms or contents that are deemed harmful to the interests of employees. The underlying concern is the abuse of bargaining power of the employing unit. For example, under Article 9 of the LCL, when it conducts hiring, the employing unit shall not detain the employee's personal identification card or other certificate, and shall not require the employee to provide guaranty or collect money or property from the employee on any grounds for the purpose of employment.[42] Article 25 of the LCL prohibits an employing unit from imposing stipulated damages in the labor contract on

---

40 See the Labor Law, art. 19., and the LCL, *supra* note 4, art. 17.
41 See *id.*, the LCL.
42 See *id.*, art. 9.

an employee in any situations other than those provided by the law.[43] Also, in accordance with Article 13 of the LCL Implementation Rules, the parties to a labor contract shall not agree on the conditions for the termination of the contract beyond the statutory conditions provided in the law.[44]

3.2 *Probationary Period*

The LCL allows an employing unit to provide a probationary period for new hires. The probationary period is a time frame for the employing unit to assess or evaluate whether the new hire is a good fit for the position. It is required under Article 19 of the LCL that the probationary period, if provided, shall be part of the employment term of the labor contract.[45] If, however, a labor contract only provides a probationary period, the probation provision shall be null and void, and the term of the probation shall be deemed a term of the labor contract.[46]

The probationary period may range from one month to six months. There are three types of probationary periods as provided in the LCL, depending on the term period of the labor contract. First, when the term of a labor contract is more than three months but less than one year, the probationary period may not exceed one month. Second, if the term of a labor contract is more than one year but fewer than three years, the probationary period may not exceed two months. Third, where the term of a labor contract is more than three years or is a non-fixed one, the probationary period may not exceed six months.[47]

However, a probationary period is not allowed if the term of a labor contract is fewer than three months or expires upon the completion of specific work.[48] Also, the probationary period may only be provided once between the same employing unit and the same employee.[49] Moreover, during the probationary period, the employing unit is prohibited from dissolving the labor contract unless otherwise permitted by the law. When a labor contract is dissolved by the employing unit under the provision of the law within the probationary period, an explanation shall be given to the employee.[50]

---

43 See *id.*, art. 25.
44 See the LCL Implementation Rules, art. 13.
45 See the LCL, *supra* note 5, art. 19.
46 See *id.*
47 See *id.*
48 See *id.*
49 See *id.*, art. 21.
50 See *id.*

In order to protect the interests of the employee working in the probationary period, the LCL sets forth a minimum salary standard under which the employing unit is required to pay the employee. Article 20 of the LCL provides that the salary of an employee during the probationary period shall not be lower than the minimum wage for the same position in the same employing unit or lower than 80% of the wage as agreed in the labor contract.[51] But in either case, the salary in the probationary period shall not be lower than the minimum wage standard of the place where the employment is located.[52]

3.3 Collective Contract

As noted, a collective contract is a contract made by the trade union with the employing unit to deal with particular matters concerning the interests and benefits of the employees involved. Also, depending on the nature of the sector in which employees work, a collective contract can be made individually or on an industrial or regional basis. Prior to the adoption of the LCL, collective contract was first provided in the Labor Law. In 2004, the Ministry of Human Resources and Social Security (MOHRSS) issued the Regulation of Collective Contracts, which contained detailed rules governing collective contracts.[53]

The LCL contains special provisions on collective contracts, which are condensed versions of both the Labor Law and the Regulation of Collective Contracts. Under the LCL, the formation and validity of a collective contract are not only subject to the limitations on coverage, contents, and the use of the contract as previously noted,[54] but are also required to follow certain procedures and requirements.

First, the formation of a collective contract requires administrative review. Pursuant to Article 54 of the LCL, upon its conclusion, a collective contract shall be submitted to a labor administration agency. Unless rejected by the said labor administrative agency, a collective contract shall take effect after fifteen

---

51 See *id.*, art. 20.
52 See *id.*
53 The Regulation of Collectivce Contracts was issued on January 20, 2004 and took effect May 1, 2004.
54 Under the Regulation of Collective Contracts, the contents of a collective contract may include: (a) labor remuneration, (b) working hours, (c) breaks and vacation, (d) work safety and hygine, (e) supplement insurance and benefits, (f) speccial protection of female workers and minors, (g) professional skill training, (h) labor contract management, (i) awards and pubishment, (j) layoffs, (k) term limits, (k) procedures of modification and rescission of the labor contract, (l) dispute resolution, (m) liabilities for the breach of a labor contract, and (n) other matters deemed necessary by the parties.

days from the date of the agency's receipt of the submission. Once effective, the collective contract becomes binding to both the employing unit and the employees. An industrial or regional collective contract has a binding effect on all employing units and employees in the local industry or region.[55]

Second, a collective contract must meet the required remuneration standard and working condition. It is mandated under Article 55 of the LCL that wage payments and working conditions as set forth in a collective contract must not be lower than the minimum criteria as prescribed by the local government. Likewise, the salary level and working condition stated in a labor contract between an employing unit and an employee must not be lower than those specified in the collective contract. Note, however, that the Article 55 standard is the minimum standard. Thus, the actual payment in a particular labor contract may exceed that standard.

Third, a dispute over a collective contract must be resolved through stipulated procedures. In accordance with Article 56 of the LCL, if a dispute arises over the performance of a collective contract, the parties shall negotiate first to resolve the dispute. If the negotiation fails, the labor union may apply for arbitration or bring a suit in a people's court. Also, under Article 56 of the LCL, if an employing unit breaches a collective contract that results in an infringement of the labor rights and interests of the employees, the labor union may require the employing unit to bear legal liabilities.

It is important to note that the LCL revises the dispute settlement procedures in two aspects as compared with the provisions in the Labor Law and the Regulation of Collective Contracts. The first aspect is administrative mediation. Both the Labor Law and the Regulation of Collective Contract provide for administrative mediation in a labor dispute in which the parties fail to negotiate. Mediation may be requested by any of the parties or initiated by a local labor agency. The LCL requires no such mediation.

The second aspect is litigation. Under the Labor Law and the Regulation of Collective Contracts, litigation may only be sought after the arbitration is conducted. In other words, only if the parties disagree with respect to the arbitration award, may the dispute be brought to a court for litigation. The LCL, however, makes arbitration an option. Pursuant to the LCL, if a dispute cannot be resolved through negotiation, the trade union may choose to apply for arbitration or directly initiate litigation.

Note also that with respect to the formation and performance of a collective contract and dispute settlement, a trade union has broad authority under the

---

55 See *id.*, art. 54.

law to deal with an employing unit on the employees' behalf. But given the trade union's relationship with the employing unit and with the local government,[56] it is often a questionable whether the trade union could effectively, adequately, and truly represent the legitimate interests of the employees in all cases.

3.4 Labor Dispatch

As noted, a labor dispatch is an employment arrangement by which an individual is dispatched to work in an employing unit under the agreement entered into with a labor dispatch agency. Under a labor dispatch agreement, the individual is hired by the labor dispatch agency but the real employer is the employing unit. Labor dispatch has been a quite attractive alternative for employing units, particularly FIEs, for hiring local employees given its flexibility and lower cost. For example, if an employee is dispatched from a labor dispatch agency, the employing unit is not responsible for certain statutory payments for the employee's benefits and welfare.

However, in order to ensure the proper use of the labor dispatch, the LCL, as discussed, was amended in 2012 to strengthen the critera for labor dispatch. In addition, on January 24, 2014, the MOHRSS adopted the "Interim Regulations on Labor Dispatch" to limit employing units from taking advantage of labor dispatch. The amended LCL and the MOHRSS regulations set forth certain restrictions on the use of labor dispatch, including the credentials of a labor dispatch agency, types of positions for the dispatched employees, the number of dispatched employees an employing unit may have, and discharge of dispatched employees.

For a labor dispatch, two agreements are required: an agreement between the dispatched employee and dispatch agency and an agreement between the dispatch agency and the employing unit (or host company). Under the amended LCL, a dispatch agency must have registered capital of at least two million RMB and have a fixed office place and facility for the dispatch services. In addition, before operating, the dispatch agency must obtain a service license and be registered with government authority.

In China, since a labor contract is the primary form of employment, the labor dispatch is deemed a supplementary form. Thus, as provided in the LCL, labor dispatch applies only to three types of positions: temporary, auxiliary, and substitute positions. A temporary position is a position with a term of no more than six months. An auxiliary position refers to a position that provides

---

56 Under the Trade Union Law, a trade union is required to work under the leadership of the communist party. Moreover, for the purpose of helping maintain social stability, the head of a trade union in most cases is a political or semi-polotical appointee rather then an elective one.

auxiliary services to the main or core business of the employing unit. A substitute position means a position that becomes available when a permanent employee is absent due to such reasons as on-leave study or vacation.[57]

It is also required that the labor dispatch agency inform the dispatched employee of the contents of the dispatch agreement concluded between the labor dispatch agency and the employing unit. The labor dispatch agency is prohibited from taking away any part, or making any deduction, of the remuneration the employing unit has paid to the employee under the provisions of the labor dispatch agreement. In addition, neither the labor dispatch agency nor the employing unit may charge or collect any fees from the dispatched employee.[58] If a labor dispatch agency violates the statutory provisions, it will face punishment.[59]

4   Validity and Enforceability

A labor contract, once concluded, becomes effective unless the contract is found invalid under the provisions of the law. Under Article 16 of the LCL, a labor contract is concluded when the employing unit and the employee reach an agreement, and it will take effect after the parties affix their signatures or seals to the contract. But the effectiveness of a labor contract is subject to its validity.[60] As noted, the conclusion of a contract and its effectiveness are viewed differently in China. The conclusion of a contract is a matter of the parties' agreement while the effectiveness of a contract concerns the enforceability of the agreement. A labor contract may not take effect and thus is unenforceable when its validity becomes an issue.

---

57   See LCL, *supra* note 5, art. 66.
58   See *id.*, art. 60.
59   See *id.*, Under Article 92 of the LCL, if a labor dispatch agency engages in labor dispatch business without a license, the labor administrative department shall order the unlicensed dispatch agency to stop operation, confiscate its illegal income, and impose a fine of one up to five times the amount of illegal income, or no more than 50,000 RMB if there is no illegal income. Where a labor-dispatch agency violates the provisions of this Law, the administrative department of labor and other competent departments concerned shall order it to rectify. If the circumstances are serious, a fine shall be imposed with not less than 5,000 Yuan but not more than 10,000 Yuan for each person, and its business license shall be revoked by the administrative department for industry and commerce. If harm is caused to the dispatched workers, the labor-dispatching unit and the labor-receiving unit shall bear joint and several liability for compensation.
60   See *id.*, art. 16.

There are certain requirements for the determination of the validity of a labor contract. First, the determination must be made on a statutory basis. As provided in the Labor Law and the LCL, a labor contract shall be invalid in whole or in part if (a) it is made or modified against the other party's will by the means of deception or coercion, or by taking advantage of the other party's difficult situation or vulnerability; (b) the employing unit disclaims its legal liability or excludes the employee's rights; or (c) it violates mandatory provisions of the laws or administrative regulations.[61]

Second, the determination shall be made by a competent government authority. In accordance with Article 26 of the LCL, if there is any dispute over the validity of a labor contract, the dispute shall be submitted for resolution to the labor dispute arbitration body or the people's court.[62] The labor dispute arbitration body is the arbitration commission designated to handle labor disputes. Under the Law of Mediation and Arbitration of Labor Disputes (Labor Mediation and Arbitration Law),[63] a labor arbitration commission is formed locally at the county level, and each commission is in charge of labor dispute arbitration within its jurisdiction territory.[64]

According to Article 17 of the Labor Arbitration Law, a labor dispute arbitration can be conducted by the arbitration commission of the place of the performance of the labor contract or the place where the employing unit is located. If, however, the parties apply for arbitration respectively to the arbitration commission of the place of performance and the location of the employing unit, the arbitration commission of the place of performance shall have jurisdiction.[65] In China, labor arbitration is not mandatory, but it generally is free of charge. Therefore, a labor dispute will often go to arbitration when the parties fail to solve their dispute by negotiation or mediation.

A major difference between labor arbitration and commercial arbitration is that a labor arbitration award does not exclude litigation. Put differently, either of the parties who disagree to an arbitral award may bring a case to a people's court for litigation. Thus, labor contract invalidation is a two-step process. The first step is arbitration by the labor dispute arbitration commission upon the request of either of the parties. The second step is litigation in a people's court when a party is not satisfied with the award made by the arbitration

---

61 See *id.*, art. 26; See also the Labor Law, art. 18.
62 See *id.*, the LCL.
63 See the Law of Mediation and Arbitration of Labor Disputes, adopted by the Standing Committee of the NPC on December 29, 2007 and effective May 1, 2008.
64 See *id.*, art. 17, 21.
65 See *id.*, art. 21.

commission. In this context, the people's court has the final say to the dispute over the validity of the labor contract.

Third, the parties bear certain liabilities when the labor contract is null and invalid. There are two major liabilities that may arise from the invalidation. One liability is payment for work already performed. According to Article 28 of the LCL, when a labor contract is found invalid, the employing unit shall pay the employee for the work done, and the amount of the payment shall be compatible with the salary paid to the employee in the same or similar position of the employing unit.[66]

The other liability is compensation. Under Article 86 of the LCL, in the case where a labor contract is invalidated, if any damage is caused by the fault of a party to the other party, the party at fault, either the employing unit or the employee, shall be liable for compensating the other party. Also, the LCL allows the innocent party to decide whether to rescind the labor contract.[67] If the employing unit is at fault, the employee may rescind the labor contract and seek compensation.[68] If, however, the employee is at fault, the employing unit may terminate the labor contract without making any compensation.[69]

As an alternative, after a labor contract is invalidated, the parties may agree to enter into a new labor contract. In this situation, the employment relationship between the employing unit and the employee will not be interrupted, but a different labor contract is concluded to replace the old one that has been found invalid. In addition, under Article 27 of the LCL, if a labor contract is found partially invalid, the partial invalidity does not affect the validity of the other parts of the labor contract and the other parts shall remain valid and enforceable.[70]

5 Performance and Modificatiom

5.1 *Performance*

Performance is fulfillment of obligations that each party has under the contract. Article 29 of the LCL requires that where there is a valid labor contract, the employing unit and the employee fully peform their respective obligations as stipulated in the contract.[71] It is commonly held in China that Article 29

---

66 See the LCL *supra* note 5, art. 28.
67 See *id.*, art. 38, 39.
68 See *id.*, art. 89.
69 See *id.* art. 39.
70 See *id.*, art. 27.
71 See *id.*, art. 29.

states at least two principles that govern the peformance. The two principles are full peformance and actual performance.

Full peformance is also called comprehensive performance. Under the full performance principle, the parties to a labor contract must perform all of their obligations as agreed upon and the performance must meet all of the terms and conditions of the contract. It is believed that only if the contract is fully performed, will the parties' expectation and bargains be realized. Actual performance requires the performance to be made in accordance with the methods and the standard provided by the contract. The purpose of actual performance is to ensure that the contract is performed properly.

The major difference between the full performance principle and the actual performance principle is that the former is concerned with the substance of the performance, while the latter focuses on the process of the peformance. However, given the social and public interests involved in labor contracts, the LCL contains several specific provisions pertaining to the performance. Those provisions are intended to prevent the employing units from abusing their bargaining power, and to protect the legitimate interests of the employees

Among the specific provisions is the provision of the employees' salary payment. In order to curb the employing unit's default or deferral in paying salary to its employee, Article 30 of the LCL mandates that an employing unit shall timely pay to its employee the employee's full salary according to the labor contract or the regulations of the State.[72] Under Article 30 of the LCL, an employing unit is obligated to pay to its employee the full amount of the employee's salary either as agreed by the parties or as provided by the law (e.g., minimum wage payment under certain circumstances).[73]

It is further provided in Article 30 that if the employing unit is in arrears on paying or fails to pay its employee's salary, the employee may ask a people's court to compel the payment.[74] Upon the request of the employees, the people's court shall under the law issue an order of payment.[75] If there is a dispute over the salary payment, the parties may negotiate for a settlement. The parties

---

72   See *id.*, art. 30.
73   For example, according to Article 40 of the Labor Law, in any of the following circumstances, the employing unit shall under the following standards pay its employees remunerations that are higher than those for normal working hours:
   (1) No less than 150% of the normal wages if an extension of working hours is arranged;
   (2) No less than 200% of the normal wages if work is arranged on off days and no make-up off days can be arranged; or
   (3) No less than 300% of the normal wages if work is arranged on statutory holidays.
74   See the LCL, *supra* note 5, art. 30.
75   See *id.*

may also seek mediation by the mediation committee within the employing unit or submit the dispute to the arbitration commission for arbitration.

In addition, if an employing unit defaults in making a timely salary payment, the affected employees may report it to the local labor administrative agency. Upon the receipt of the report, the labor administrative agency is required to make an investigation. When the employing unit is found to have owed unpaid salary to employees, the labor administrative agency shall urge the payment within a specific deadline. If the payment is not made before the deadline, certain fines will be imposed upon the employing unit. The amount of fines will be equal to the payable salary plus the damages of 50% to 100% of such salary.[76]

Another specific provision is concerned about the labor quota standard. In China, labor quota refers to the amount of labor consumption or working hours needed for completion of certain work tasks or production of a particular number of the qualified products per working day. It is provided in the Labor Law that the standard working hours for an employee are eight hours a day or forty hours a week.[77] Under Article 31 of the LCL, an employing unit shall strictly execute the labor quota standard and is prohibited from forcing any of its employees, directly or in any disguised form, to work overtime.[78]

Overtime working is permitted under the law if (a) there is a production need, (b) the employee is consulted and consents, and (c) the length of overtime working is less than one hour or in special circumstances no more than three hours per day. Article 31 of the LCL requires that if an employing unit arranges an employee to work overtime, it must pay the employee the overtime wage according the provisions of the law. The overtime wage is 150% of the regular hourly salary. If the employee is arranged to work during the non-working day, the overtime wage is 200% of the regular hourly salary. The overtime payment will be tripled or 300% of the regular hourly wage if the employer is asked to work during national holidays.[79] As an alternative, the employing unit may arrange a substitute break day in lieu of overtime payment for an employee to work in a non-working day except for national holidays.

The third specific provision is the employee's right to refuse. It is the right granted to an employee to reject the request or instruction from a managerial

---

76 See the State Council, the Labor Security Supervision Regulation, issued on November 1, 2004 and the Ministry of Labor and Social Security, Rules of Implementation of the Labor Security Supervision Regulation, adopted on December 31, 2004.
77 See the Labor Law, art. 30.
78 See the LCL, *supra* note 5, art. 31.
79 See *id.*

person under certain circumstances. According to Article 32 of the LCL, an employee may refuse to perform dangerous operations ordered by a manager of the employing unit who violates safety regulations or forces the employee to take a risk. Such a refusal, as provided in Article 32, shall not be deemed a breach of the labor contract.[80]

In addition, Article 32 makes it a right of an employee to criticize, make a report to relevant authority, or file a claim against the employing unit if the work conditions pose a danger to the life or health of the employee.[81] Under the Labor Law, an employing unit is obligated as a matter of law to provide employees with occupational safety and health conditions conforming to the provisions of the State and necessary equipment or items of labor protection. It is also required that the employing unit must provide regular health examinations for the employees who engage in work exposing them to occupational hazards.

5.2 *Modification*

Modification involves a change of the contents of the labor contract. Pursuant to Article 35 of the LCL, the employing unit and the employee may agree to modify the contents of a labor contract.[82] The modification agreement, in order to be valid and enforceable, must meet two conditions. First, the modification must be made by mutual consent without coercion or duress. Second, the modification agreement must be made in writing. Article 35 of the LCL also requires that the parties shall each be given a signed copy of the modified labor contract.[83]

The writing requirement for the modification of a labor contract, however, may be overcome by actual performance. According to the SPC, when the modification of a labor contract is not in written form, but the actual performance of the modified contract has been more than one month, if a party requests a people's court to invalidate the modification on the ground that the modification is made without writing, the request will not be granted.[84] But a condition is that the contents of the contract as modified must not violate the

---

80 See *id.*, art. 32.
81 See *id.*
82 See *id.*, art. 35.
83 See *id.*
84 See the SPC, *Interpretation on Several Legal Matters of Applicaton of Law in Adudicating Labor Dispute Cases (IV)*, issued on December 31, 2012, art. 11. (hereinafter referred to as Interpretation on Labor Dispute Ajudication).

law, administrative regulations, state policies, the public order, or good social morals.[85]

During the performance of a labor contract, the employing unit may undergo certain structural changes. Such changes, however, shall not affect the performance. The structural change of the employing unit may take place either when there is a change of name or managerial personnel, or in the situation where there is a merger or split. Article 33 of the LCL explicitly provides that the change of name, legal representative, key person-in-charge, or investor shall have no impact on the fulfillment of the labor contract.[86]

Under Article 34 of the LCL, in the case of merger or split of the employing unit, the original labor contract shall remain valid, and shall continue to be performed by the new employing unit that succeeds the rights and obligations of the previous employing unit as a result of the merger or split. [87] The significance of Articles 33 and 34 of the LCL is that they provide a statutory assurance for the continuity of labor contract performance regardless of changes that happen to the employing unit during the performance period. Such a statutory assurance is intended to prevent the employing unit from evading its obligations through structural changes.

6   Rescission and Termination

A labor contract may be rescinded either by an agreement or by the operation of law. The former is called consensual rescission while the latter is statutory rescission. Under Article 36 of the LCL, the parties may rescind the labor contract upon their agreement. The rescission by agreement requires mutual consent of the parties pertaining to the conditions or circumstances under which the contract is to be rescinded. In general, when the agreed conditions are met, or the agreed circumstances occur, either of the parties may rescind the contract. Theoretically speaking, contractual rescission is actually about the right to rescind. The rescission will be effective only if the right to rescind is exercised by a party under the contract.

6.1   Rescission
Statutory rescission is rescission that is effectuated under the provisions of the law without regard to the parties' consent, and it intends to protect the

---

85   See *id.*
86   See the LCL, *supra* note 5, art. 33.
87   See *id.*, art. 34.

respective interests of the parties, the employee's interests in particular. Thus, when any of the statutory grounds present, the protected party may unilaterally rescind the contract. Because the rescission of a labor contract requires a statutory basis, the LCL provides a list of situations in which a labor contract may be rescinded. Under the provisions of the LCL, statutory rescission of a labor contract may be made either by the employing unit or by the employee.

As provided in the LCL, an employee may rescind a labor contract either by advance notice or on any of the statutory grounds. Rescission by advance notice allows an employee to quit without giving any reason. Under Article 37 of the LCL, an employee may dissolve the labor contract when the employing unit is notified in writing thirty days in advance. But during the probation period, an employee is required only to provide the employing unit with a three-day notice in advance in order to rescind the labor contract.[88] The very purpose of Article 37 is to safeguard the employees who are normally in a weak position in their dealing with the employing units.

Rescission by statutory grounds is essentially an option for an employee to cancel the labor contract without incurring any liability. Such rescission may take two different forms: rescission with short notice and rescission without a notice. In either situation, the labor contract will be legally dissolved. Pursuant to Article 38 of the LCL, an employee may rescind a labor contract with short notice under any of the following circumstances:

a. The employing unit fails to provide labor protection or labor conditions as agreed in the labor contract;
b. The employing unit fails to timely pay the full amount of remunerations;
c. The employing unit fails to contribute social security premiums for the employee under the law;
d. The rules or procedures adopted by the employing unit violate the provision of law or regulation, and impair the employee's rights and interests;
e. The labor contract is concluded or amended against the employee's true intention by means of fraud, coercion, or taking advantage of the employee's unfavorable position; or
f. Other circumstances provided by the laws and regulations exist that authorize the employee to rescind the labor contract. [89]

Rescission by an employee without notice occurs in certain situations specifically stipulated by the law. Article 38 of LCL provides that an employee may immediately rescind the labor contract without notifying the employing unit

---

88 See *id.*, art. 37.
89 See *id.*, art. 38.

in advance if the employing unit forces the employee to work by means of violence, threats, or illegal restrictions on personal freedom, or if the employer violates the safety rules to order or force the risky operations that endanger the personal safety of the employee.[90] Because of the illegality of the conduct of the employing unit in those situations, an employee may promptly rescind the labor contract by simply walking away from the employing unit.

On the other hand, the LCL also provides grounds on which an employing unit may rescind the labor contract. Rescission by the employing unit may be made with cause or without cause. Under Article 39 of the LCL, an employing unit may rescind the labor contract unilaterally if it is proven that the employee (a) fails to meet the employment criteria during the probationary period; (b) seriously violates the rules or procedures adopted by the employing unit; (c) commits serious dereliction of duty or practices graft, which causes material damage to the employing unit; (d) establishes an employment relationship simultaneously with another employer and thus materially affects the completion of the work assignment, or refuses to rectify the situation when demanded by the employing unit; (e) causes the employing unit to conclude or amend the labor contract by means of fraud, coercion, or taking advantage of the employing unit's unfavorable position; or (f) has been charged for criminal offense according to law.[91]

Rescission of a labor contract without cause can be made by an employing unit under certain circumstances. As provided in Article 40 of the LCL, the circumstances that justify an employing unit's rescission without cause include: (a) the employee is ill or suffers a non-work-related injury, and cannot take original work or other re-assigned work upon the expiration of the legally stipulated period for medical treatment; (b) the employee lacks competence for the work and remains incompetent after training or a work adjustment; or (c) the objective conditions on which the labor contract was based have changed significantly so that the labor contract cannot be performed as expected, and the parties cannot reach an agreement to change the contents of the contract.[92]

Note that rescission due to a significant change of conditions is in fact an application of the *rebus sic stantibus* doctrine to the labor contract. As discussed, the Contract Law contains no such doctrine with regard to the performance of contracts but in practice the SPC through its judicial interpretation allows the use of such doctrine in the people's courts. Article 40 of the LCL is a statutory

---

90   See *id.*
91   See *id.*, art. 39.
92   See *id.*, art. 40.

recognition of *rebus sic stantibus* with regard to the contractual obligations in China. Also, under Article 40 of the LCL, in case of rescission without cause, the employing unit is required to provide the employee with a thirty-day advance written notice, or to pay the employee an extra month salary before the labor contract is rescinded.[93]

In addition, an employing unit may rescind a labor contract via an economic layoff. In accordance with Article 41 of the LCL, an employing unit may reduce its labor force if (a) the employing unit undergoes restructuring pursuant to the Bankruptcy Law; (b) the employing unit is confronted with severe difficulties in its production or business operations; (c) a need for the layoff of certain employees remains even after a modification of the labor contract in response to the change of products, important technical innovation, or adjustment of business operation methods; or (d) the change of circumstances is so great that the contract could not be performed.[94]

However, an economic layoff is subject to some restrictions. One restriction is the pre-condition for the layoff. Under Article 41 of the LCL, the employing unit may exercise an economic layoff only if there is a need to cut the number of employees by twenty or more, or by fewer than twenty employees but more than ten percent of the total number of the employees. Additionally, the employing unit shall make an explanation to the labor union or all employees about the economic layoff thirty days in advance for their opinions and shall thereafter file a report with the labor administration authority on the economic layoff plan.[95]

Another restriction is the type of the employees to be laid off. It is mandated in Article 40 of the LCL that, during the economic layoff, the following employees must be given priority with respect to being kept in the labor force of the employing unit: (a) an employee who is under a fixed term labor contract with a long period; (b) an employee who is under a labor contract without a fixed term; and (c) an employee whose family has no other employed person and has an aged or minor person to support.[96]

Another restriction is re-hiring. In a case where a layoff is made due to a business restructuring, if the employing unit intends to hire a new employee within six months after the layoff, it must notify the employee who has been laid off. It is required under Article 41of LCL that the said employee shall have priority to be re-hired under the same or similar conditions compared with

---

93 See *id.*
94 See *id.*, art. 41.
95 See *id.*
96 See *id.*, art. 40.

other candidates.[97] This restriction, however, does not apply to layoffs in other situations as listed in the LCL.

It is important to note that with regard to certain employees, a rescission without cause or a layoff for economic reasons is prohibited. This prohibition rests with concerns about the interests of the employees who deserve special protection. According to Article 42 of the LCL, rescission without cause or economic layoff may not be made to the employee who (a) is engaging the operation exposing to occupational disease hazards without having an occupational health check or is suspected to have contracted an occupational disease and is still under diagnosis or medical observation; (b) has contracted an occupational disease or suffered injury during work so as to be confirmed to have lost or partly lost the capacity to work; (c) is in the statutory medical period for having an illness or sustaining non-work-related injury; (d) is in the period of pregnancy, maternity, or nursing; (e) has consecutively worked for no fewer than fifteen years and is fewer than five years before reaching the statutory retirement age; or (f) is in other situations prescribed by laws and regulations.[98]

As a general requirement, when unilaterally rescinding an employment contract pursuant to the provisions of the LCL, the employing unit shall notify the labor union of the reason for the rescission in advance. If it is found that the rescission would violate the law, regulations, or provisions of the labor contract, the labor union has the power to require the employer to rectify. Upon receiving the opinions from the labor union, the employing unit is required to consider such opinions and notify the labor union of its decision in writing.[99]

6.2 *Termination*

Termination of a labor contract derives from different legal grounds. Unlike the Contract Law under which rescission is one of the causes of termination, the LCL as well as the Labor Law treat rescission and termination separately. A general understanding in China is that rescission of a labor contract requires the occurrence of certain actions or conduct by the parties, while termination of a labor contract normally results from expiry of the contract term or loss of civil subject status of one of the parties due to the death or bankruptcy of the party.

Thus, under Article 44 of the LCL, a labor contract shall be terminated under any of the following situations: (a) the term of the labor contract has expired; (b) the employee becomes entitled to the basic benefits of his or her pension

---

97 See *id.*
98 See *id.*, art. 42.
99 See *id.*, art. 43.

as a matter of the law; (c) the employee is dead, or declared dead or missing by the People's Court; (d) the employing unit has been declared bankrupt pursuant to the law; (e) the business license of the employing unit has been revoked, or the employing unit has been ordered to close down its business or has decided to liquidate and dissolve ahead of schedule; or (f) other circumstances as provided by the laws and administrative regulations.[100]

The termination of a labor contract under Article 44 (b) of the LCL refers mainly to the situation where the employee is eligible to retire on the basis of age. Article 21 of the LCL Implementation Rules specifically provides that a labor contract terminates when the employee reaches the statutory retirement age. In China, the statutory retirement age varies depending on the gender, health, work condition, and status of the employee. In general, the statutory age for retirement is sixty for male employees or fifty for female employees. The prerequisite condition is that the employee must have been continuously working for ten years.[101]

If a female employee is an officer, her retirement age is extended to fifty-five. For those who are engaged in underground, high altitude, high temperature, especially heavy physical labor work, or other work that is harmful to health for a consecutive period of ten years, the statutory retirement age is fifty-five for men and forty-five for women. In addition, if a male employee of fifty years old or a female employee of forty-five years old has completely lost his or her capacity to work, upon approval by the labor verification commission on the basis of a hospital certificate, he or she will be considered to have legally retired.

However, under certain circumstances, termination upon the expiry of the term of a labor contract shall be postponed until such circumstances come to an end. The circumstances that would trigger postponement of the termination when the contract term expires refer to the situations listed in Article 42 of the LCL in which rescission is prohibited. However, the termination of a labor contract concerning an employee who has lost or partly lost his or her work capacity as a result of occupational illness or a work-related injury shall be subject to the provisions of State rules on work-related injury insurance.[102]

A major issue that arises from rescission as well as termination of a labor contract is compensation. In China, compensation is described as the legal consequence of a labor contract rescission or termination, which often becomes the center of disputes between the parties. Depending on the cause of

---

100 See *id.*, art. 44.
101 A statutory retiree will start to receive retirement benefits upon his or her retirement.
102 See the LCL, *supra* note 5, art 45.

rescission or termination, the obligation to compensate may fall on the shoulder of the employing unit or the employee under the provisions of the LCL. In either case, compensation is a statutory requirement and must be made in legally prescribed means and amounts.

The LCL provides a two-way compensation mechanism: employing unit to compensate employee or employee to compensate employing unit. Under Article 46 of the LCL, the employing unit must compensate the employee in any of the following situations: (a) the labor contract is rescinded by the employee unilaterally due to the employing unit's fault as provided in Article 38 of the LCL; (b) the employing unit proposes to rescind the labor contract and obtains the employee's consent through negotiation; (c) the employing unit rescinds the labor contract pursuant to rescission without cause allowed by the law; (d) the employing unit rescinds the labor contract during an economic lay-off; (e) the term of the labor contract has expired unless the employing unit offers to renew the labor contract under the same or better conditions for the employee but the employee declines the renewal; (f) the labor contract is terminated due to the employing unit's bankruptcy, license revocation, or dissolution of business; or (g) other circumstances as provided by laws and administrative regulations.[103]

The amount of the compensation must meet the statutory standard, which is the minimum amount the employing unit shall pay to the employee for the compensation. In general, the compensation is calculated on the basis of the number of years the employee has worked with the employing unit. The standard is one-month salary per year of employment. For the purpose of making compensation, an employment period of more than six months but less than one year will be counted as one year. If the employment is less than six months, the amount of compensation will be a half of the employee's monthly salary.[104]

However, if the employee's monthly salary is more than three times the average monthly wage set for the preceding year by the local government of the place where the employing unit is located,[105] the level of compensation will be capped at three times the local average monthly wage, and the period of compensation period is capped to a maximum of twelve years. Note that for calculation of compensation, the monthly salary of an employee is the average

---

103 See id., art. 46.
104 See id., art. 47.
105 The local government refers to the government of the municipality directly under the Central Government or the municipality that contains districts.

monthly salary of the employee during the twelve months prior to the rescission or termination of the labor contract.[106]

When the employing unit rescinds or terminates the employment contract in violation of the LCL, the employing unit is mandated to continue performing the labor contract if the employee so demands. However, in the case the employee chooses not to perform the labor contract or such labor contract cannot be continuously performed, the employing unit must compensate the employee in an amount twice as much as the above statutory compensation standard.[107]

Since the number of actual working years of an employee is an important perimeter to calculate compensation in the case of rescission or termination of a labor contract, a dispute over compensation often occurs when the employee has been transferred between employing units. As often is the case, during employment, an employee may switch from one employing unit to the other for various reasons. But when the labor contract is rescinded or terminated between the employee and the new employing unit, a question that is necessarily raised is whether the employee's working years with the original employing unit should be counted for the determination of the amount of compensation.

According to the SPC, if an employee's transfer made from an original employing unit to a new one was not due to personal reasons of the employee, and no economic compensation was ever made by the original employing unit, the employee's previous working years with the original employer should be included to determine the compensation amount when the labor contract between the employee and the new employing unit is rescinded or terminated. Thus, if the employee makes such a request to a people's court, the request shall be granted.[108]

On the other hand, the LCL also imposes certain liabilities on the employee to compensate the employing unit. But the liabilities are limited to the employee's breach, or wrongful rescission, of the labor contract. As discussed, when an employee breaches a labor contract, the employee shall be liable for

---

106 See the LCL, *supra* note 5, art. 47.
107 See *id.*, art. 48.
108 See the SPC, Interpretation on Labor Dispute Adjudication (IV), *supra* note 84, art. 5. Under the SPC's interpretation, job transfer for non-personal reasons of an employee include: (a) the working place and position of the employee remain the same but the employing unit changes to a new one; (b) the employing unit arranges a job transfer for the employee in the form of assignment or appointment; (c) the employee's transfer results from such reasons as merger or split of the employing unit; (d) the employing unit and its affiliates enter into a labor contract in turn with the employee; or (e) the transfer is made under other reasonable circumstances.

stipulated damages as agreed in the labor contract. The LCL also provides that if an employee rescinds a labor contract in violation of the LCL, which causes damages to the employing unit, the employee shall compensate the employing unit for damages.[109]

7 Legal Liabilities

Legal liabilities arising from a labor contract are the liabilities imposed for any violation of the statutory provisions of the labor law and regulations. In China, depending on the nature of the offense, there are three different liabilities pertaining to labor contracts: administrative, civil, and criminal liabilities. Administrative liabilities result from violation of administrative rules or regulations. The penalty resulting from administrative liability includes a warning, fine, or revocation of a business license. While many of the administrative penalties are enforced by the labor administrative authorities, the revocation of a business license is within the power of the industrial and commercial departments.

Civil liabilities in the context of the LCL are the liabilities that arise as the legal consequences of a violation of a labor contract law that causes damages to the aggrieved party. The violation could occur either in tort or in breach of the labor contract. Under the LCL, the imposition of civil liabilities mainly takes the form of cessation of infringement or money compensation. Since the damages could be caused by the employing unit to the employee or *vice versa*, liabilities could fall on the shoulder of either the employing unit or the employee.

Criminal liabilities are the liabilities imposed against the most serious offenses that constitute crimes. For example, under Article 88 of the LCL, the employing unit shall be subject to criminal consequences if it commits a crime in forcing the employee to work by means of violence, threat, or illegal restriction of personal freedom.[110] A criminal offense may also be found if the employing unit's poor working condition or heavily polluted environment has caused severe harm to the physical or mental health of the employees.[111]

Given the focus of the LCL on regulating employment, the legal liabilities provided in the LCL involve mostly the conduct of employing units. The situation in which an employing unit will be held liable include: (a) violation of the law and regulations, (b) failure to include in the labor contract the required

---

109   See the LCL, *supra* note 4, art. 90.
110   See *id.*, art. 88.
111   See *id.*

terms or clauses or failure to provide the employee with a copy of the labor contract, (c) failure to conclude a written labor contract with the employee, (d) stipulation of a probation period with the employee in violation of the law, (e) seizure of the employee's personal ID card or other certificates, (f) failure to pay to the employee wage and economic compensation in accordance with the law, (g) causing damages to the employee as a result of invalidation of the labor contract, (h) rescission or termination of the labor contract in violation of the law, (i) infringing upon the employee's interests, (j) rescission or termination of a labor contract without providing a written document to the employee, and (k) operating business without license.[112]

As noted, the LCL also imposes certain liabilities on employees. Under Article 90 of the LCL, an employee will become liable for compensating the employing unit if the employing unit suffers damages resulting from the employee's rescinding the labor contract in violation of the law or the employee's breaching the agreement of confidentiality or non-competition as provided in the labor contract.[113] In addition, if an employing unit hires an employee whose labor contract with the other employing unit has not been rescinded or terminated, which causes damages to the other employing unit, the employing unit hiring the employee shall bear joint and several liabilities for compensation.[114]

One of the liabilities imposed on the employee is liability for violation of a non-competition agreement. Article 23 of the LCL allows an employing unit to reach an agreement with an employee to provide in the labor contract a non-competition clause.[115] Pursuant to Article 23 of the LCL, if an employee breaches an agreement on non-competition, the employee shall pay to the employing unit damages as stipulated in the labor contract.[116] In addition, under Article 23 of the LCL, if the parties agree in the labor contract that when after the rescission or termination of the labor contract, the employee shall be given monthly compensation within the period of non-competition.[117]

To implement Article 23 of the LCL, the SPC adopts a number of rules for the people's courts to deal with Article 23 cases. First, when a labor contract that contains clauses of non-competition restrictions and economic compensation

---

112 See id, art. 80–89, and 93.
113 See *id.* art. 90.
114 See *id.* art. 91.
115 See *id.*, art. 23.
116 See *id.*
117 See *id.*

is rescinded or terminated, if the employing unit requires the employee to fulfill the non-competition obligation, or the employee has fulfilled the requirements of the non-competition obligation, the employee's request for the payment of economic compensation shall be granted, unless otherwise agreed upon by the parties.[118]

Second, when the parties have agreed in the labor contract to non-competition restrictions and economic compensation, if the labor contract is resinded or terminated but the employing unit due to its own reason fails to pay the employee economic compenation for three months, the employee may ask a people's court for an order to lift the non-competition restrictions. When so asked, the people's court shall take an action in favor of the employee.[119]

Third, if within the period of non-competition as provided in the labor contract, the employing unit requests to rescind the non-competition agreement, the people's court shall honor the request. However, when the non-competition agreement is rescinded, if the employee asks the employing unit to pay extra three-month economic compensation and seeks a court order to that effect, the people's court shall require that the employing unit pay the compensation asked for.[120]

Fourth, if, however, an employee breaches the non-competition agreement, the employee shall pay the damages stipulated by the parties in the labor contract. After the stipulated damages are paid by the employee, if the employing unit requests the employee to continue fulfilling his or her obligations under the non-competition agreement, the people's court shall endorse the employing unit's request.[121]

In addition to the liabilities imposed on employing units and employees, the LCL has a liability provision that applies to government agencies or officials. Under Article 95 of the LCL, if a labor administrative or another competent department or its staff member neglects legal duties and fails to perform legal duties, or exercises legal duties or powers in violation of law, thus causing damages to an employee or an employing unit, such department or staff member shall be liable for compensation, and the directly liable person in charge and the other directly responsible persons shall be punished by administrative sanctions. It is further provided in Article 95 that if a crime is committed, criminal liability shall be sought against those who are found responsible.[122]

---

118   See the SPC, *Interpretation on Labor Dispute Adjudication (IV)*, *supra* note 84, art.7.
119   See *id.*, art. 8.
120   See *id.*, art. 9.
121   See *id.*, art. 10.
122   See *id.*, art. 95.

8 Dispute Settlement

With regard to a labor contract, disputes often occur when the parties disagree with each other pertaining to such matters as formation, performance, modification, rescission, or termination of the labor contract. But, given the weak bargaining power of the employee in the employment or the job market in general, it is not uncommon to see that the employing unit abuses its position to take advantage of its employees and thereby harms the employees' legitimate interests. Therefore, many labor disputes take place in situations where the employees have allegedly been treated unfairly and unjustly by the employing unit.

One example is the case where the employing unit refuses to sign a written labor contract with the employee or even denies the employment relationship that in fact already exists with the employee in order to evade its obligations. Another example is that the employing unit unreasonably uses short-term contracts or abusively expands the probation period to minimize its statutory liabilities or duties. In the first few years after the LCL was promulgated, employing units heavily hired employees through labor dispatch rather than through direct hiring due to concerns about the economic burden. This practice was criticized as the means to escape the legal obligations employing units owed to employees, which, among others, prompted the amendments made to the LCL in 2012.

Under the Labor Law, when a labor dispute between an employing unit and an employee arises, the parties may seek a settlement through the mechanism of consultation, mediation, arbitration, or litigation.[123] It is important to note that as a general rule, the settlement of a labor dispute is required to follow the principles of legality, justness, and promptness.[124] In the process of dispute settlement, if the parties are unable to reach an agreement through consultation, mediation is preferred. But since mediation is not required, any of the parties may directly seek arbitration. Again, as noted, arbitration in the settlement of a labor dispute is not necessarily final. Thus, when a party to a dispute is not satisfied with the arbitration award, the party may bring a lawsuit to the people's court within the time period allowed.[125]

But, except with respect to collective labor contracts, there are no dispute settlement provisions in the LCL. Nevertheless, the LCL Implementation Rules specifically provide that a dispute between an employee and an employing

---

123 See the Labor Law *supra* note 4, art. 77.
124 See *id.*, art. 78.
125 See *id.*, art. 79.

unit over the formation, performance, modification, rescission, or termination of a labor contract shall be resolved in accordance with the provisions of the Labor Mediation and Arbitration Law.[126] Thus, under the provisions of the LCL Implementation Rules, mediation and arbitration are the two primary means for the settlement of labor contract disputes.

In accordance with the Labor Mediation and Arbitration Law, labor dispute mediation can be conducted by a labor dispute mediation committee of the employing unit, local people's mediation organization, or other organization established by a township or neighbor community to mediate labor disputes.[127] When the parties reach a mutual consent after mediation, a mediation agreement shall be made. If a party fails to perform under the mediation agreement within the agreed upon period, the other party may apply for arbitration.[128] If, however, the mediation agreement calls for the payment of wages past due, medical expenses for work-related injuries, or economic compensation, and the employing unit fails to pay within the provided period, the employee may apply to a people's court for an order of payment on the basis of the mediation agreement.[129]

The arbitration of labor contract disputes is handled by the local labor arbitration commission, which is normally at a county level.[130] The process of arbitration is open to the public unless the parties agree otherwise or the matter to be arbitrated involves State or commercial secrets, or personal privacy.[131] The time limit for an employee to apply for arbitration is one year from the date the employee knows or should know that his rights have been infringed.[132] Unlike commercial arbitration, labor dispute arbitration in China, as noted, is free of charge, and all expenses incurred to arbitration commissions are covered by the government.[133]

Note again that a labor dispute arbitration award does not necessarily preclude litigation in a people's court. Under Articles 5 and 50 of the Labor Mediation and Arbitration Law, if a party is dissatisfied with a labor arbitral award, the party may within fifteen days from receipt of the award bring the case to a people's court for litigation. Put differently, a labor arbitral award will become

---

126 See The Labor Mediation and Arbitration Law, art. 37.
127 See *id.*, art. 10.
128 See *id.*, art. 15.
129 See *id.*, art. 16.
130 See *id.*, art. 17.
131 See *id.*, art. 26.
132 See *id.*, art. 27.
133 See *id.*, art. 53.

final and binding only if no suit is filed within the time period allowed by the law for litigation.[134] However, for certain matters, a labor arbitral award is final and becomes effective once the award is made.

According to Article 47 of the Labor Mediation and Arbitration Law, there are two categories of labor disputes for which the arbitral award is final, and which prohibit further litigation once the award is made. One category involves disputes over the payment of labor remuneration, medical expenses for work-related injuries, economic compensation or damages, and the total amount claimed does not exceed the sum of the twelve-month local minimum salaries. The other category is about the disputes pertaining to the execution of State labor standards in such matters as working hours, breaks and vacation, or social securities.[135]

It should be noted that under the Labor Mediation and Arbitration Law, the employing unit and the employee are treated differently in terms of the effect of Article 47 arbitral awards. Although an arbitral award made on matters listed in Article 47 is final, an employee may still file a suit in a people's court within ten days after the award is made if the employee is not satisfied with the award.[136] An employing unit, however, may not litigate again in a people's court if it disagrees with the award. But the employing unit may ask a people's court to cancel or set aside the arbitral award within thirty days after the award is made.[137]

However, a request by an employing unit to cancel any Article 47 arbitral award must be made on a statutory ground. It is provided in Article 49 of the Labor Mediation and Arbitration Law that an employing unit may make a cancellation request to the intermediate people's court of the place where the arbitration commission is located if any of the following situation presents:

(a) There is a definite error in the application of law or regulation;
(b) The arbitration commission making the award lacks jurisdiction;
(c) There is a violation of statutory procedure during the arbitration;
(d) The evidence upon which the award is made is forged;
(e) The evidence concealed by the other party is so material that the fairness of the award will be impaired; or
(f) The arbitrator has committed the conduct of seeking or receiving bribery, fraud for personal gains, or violation of law when making the arbitral award.[138]

---

134   See *id.*, art. 50.
135   See *id.*, art. 47.
136   See *id.*, art. 48.
137   See *id.*, art. 49.
138   See *id.*

The SPC, however, seems to take a more pragmatic approach and deals with the employing unit's challenge to an arbitral award on the basis of the award type. According to the SPC, if an arbitral award clearly indicates that the award is final, an employing unit may only file a cancellation request with a people's court if the employing unit does not like the award. If the arbitral award is ambiguous about its finality and the employing unit brings a suit in a people's court, the court will handle it differently depending on whether the award should be considered final.[139]

If after its review, the court finds that the arbitral award is not final, the case shall be submitted to adjudication. If, however, the arbitral award is found to be final, the case shall be dismissed. When dismissing the case, the court shall inform the employing unit that a request for cancellation of the arbitral award may be filed by the employing unit within thirty days after receipt of the dismissal. Again, the court competent to adjudicate the cancellation request is the intermediate people's court of the place where the arbitration commission entering the arbitral award is situated.[140]

9 Government Supervision and Review

Labor contracts in China are subject to government supervision and review. There are two layers of government authorities for labor contract supervision and review: State and local. At the State level, the labor administrative agency of the State Council is responsible for the implementation of the LCL and administration of labor contract systems nationwide. At the local level, the labor administrative department of the local government of the county level or above is empowered to conduct supervision and review of labor contracts within its administrative region.[141] Under the LCL, during the process of supervision and review, the local labor administrative department shall consult with labor unions, employing unit representatives, and relevant industrial administrations.[142]

The scope of supervision and review is quite broad. Under Article 74 of the LCL, labor administrative agencies have the authority to look into any matter that involves (a) rules and regulations established by employing units that directly affect interests of employees, and their implementation; (b) conclusion

---

139   See *id.*, art. 2.
140   See *id.*
141   See the LCL, *supra* note 5, art. 73.
142   See *id.*

and rescission of labor contracts between employing units and employees; (c) compliance with relevant regulations on labor dispatch; (d) employing units' observance of State regulations on working hours, breaks, and vacation of employees; (e) payment of the labor remuneration as provided in labor contracts, and the employing units' conformity with the minimum wage standards; (f) participation in the various types of social insurance for the employees, and the premium payments of or fund contributions to, such insurances; and (g) other matters subject to supervision and review as provided by the laws or regulations.[143]

When conducting supervision and review, labor administrative agencies have the right to access any materials that are related to labor contracts, including collective contracts, and to conduct on-site inspection of workplaces. For the purpose of supervision and review, employing units and employees are required to truthfully provide relevant information and materials.[144] In addition, government agencies at the country level or above that administer construction, health, work safety, etc. have the right to supervise employing units' implementation of the labor contract system in related areas.[145]

Any organization or individual may inform the government of violations of labor laws or regulations. Upon receiving such information, a labor administrative agency is obligated to verify, and cope with, such violations in a timely manner.[146] Any employee whose legitimate rights and interests are infringed upon may request the relevant authority to deal with the infringement, apply for arbitration, or bring a lawsuit in a people's court.[147] Again, for litigation over labor disputes, jurisdiction is vested with the people's court of the place where the employing unit is located or the labor contract is performed.

The LCL also requires trade unions to protect the legitimate rights and interests of employees and to supervise the performance of labor contracts by employing units.[148] It is provided that when an employing unit violates labor laws or regulations, or breaches a labor contract, the trade union concerned has the right to give its opinions or request correction. If an employee applies for arbitration or brings a lawsuit, the trade union has the obligation to provide the employee with the needed support and assistance.[149]

---

143 See *id.* art. 74.
144 See *id.*, art.75.
145 See *id.*, art.76.
146 See *id.*, art.79.
147 See *id.*, art.77.
148 See *id.*, art.78.
149 See *id.*

Index

Acceptance   128, 132, 134, 136
   agreement   1, 33, 41–45
   arrival rule   129, 133, 135
   communication   116, 130
      formality   138, 139, 143, 147
      made to offeror   130
      meeting of minds   43
      multiple offerees   116, 117, 131
      mutual assent   43
      non-intended offeree   116
      oral acceptance   130, 139
      reasonable period of time   130, 133, 318, 319, 364, 378
   contract formation   138, 139
   equal dignity rule   279, 280
      implied from conduct   131
      silence   131, 132
         act-attached   131
         non-act   131
   late acceptance   132, 133
   late arrival of acceptance   133, 134
   material alteration   129
   withdrawal   132
Adhesion contracts   168, 169, 174 *See also* Standard terms
Advertisement   117, 118, 121, 122 *See also* Offer
Agent   188, 190, 195, 382, 383, 384, 388 *See also* Agent at *ad litem*
   apparent authority   191, 192
   capacity and authorization   186, 188
   effect-to-be-determined contract   185
   guardianship   186, 187
   legal representative   187
   no right to depose   197
   ratification   188, 190, 195, 197, 199
Agreement   1, 33, 41–45 *See also* Acceptance; Agreement theory
   contract   34, 42, 49–55, 59, 64, 90, 93, 134, 136, 138, 151, 155, 158, 159, 167, 188, 190, 195, 197, 201, 221, 230, 235, 286, 297, 315, 397, 419
   intent to contract   115, 116, 117
   labor contract   36, 440, 442
   third parties   383, 384
Ambiguity   109 *See also* Interpretation

Anticipatory repudiation   13, 312, 316, 351, 352 *See also* Bilateral contract
   breach   345, 351, 353
   expiry of the time period for performance   352
   rescission   308, 309, 312, 323, 325, 458, 460
   termination   327, 328, 458, 462
Arbitration   429, 430, 469, 470, 471 *See also* Dispute settlement
Assignment and delegation   278, 282, 286, 297, 304 *See also* Assignment of rights; Contract rights
   comprehensive assignment   304, 305
   defenses   296
      assignor against assignee   296
      obligor against assignor   296
   definitions   282, 286, 297
   delegation of duties   297
      assumption of duty   297, 298
      consent of obligee   298
      non-delegable duties   303, 304
      subordinate duties   302
      transfer of debts in whole or in part   397
      writing requirement   290
   formality requirement   290, 291
   modification   279
   non-assignable rights   292
   notice   290, 291
   novation   305
   order of assignment   289
   order of notice   289
   redemption   392
   third parties   381, 383, 387, 389, 392
   transfer of rights and obligations   305
   transfer of rights in whole or in part   286
Avoidable damages   372, 378 *See also* Damages

Beneficiaries   381, 383, 384 *See also* Third parties
Bilateral contracts   54 *See also* Anticipatory repudiation
   fulfillment plea   251, 252, 253
   mutuality of obligation   54, 251

Breach of contract 315, 318, 320, 345, 351, 353
    See also Anticipatory repudiation
    actual breach 353
        non-conforming
            performance 353, 355
        non-performance 353, 354
        refusal to perform 355
    liability for breach 345
        fault liability 109, 347, 348
        non-fault liability 347, 349
        liability imputation 347
Business compulsion 210, 223 *See also*
    Duress

Cancellation 263, 265, 266, 269 *See also*
    Discharge; Performance
Capacity of the parties 185
    legal person 194, 195
    mental illness 187
    minor 186, 187, 188, 189
    natural person 186
Certainty 122, 162 *See also* Damages;
    Offers; Terms
Change of circumstances 273, 274 *See also*
    Conditions
    impossibility of performance 361
    impracticability of performance 363
    Rebus sic stantibus 274–277
CISG 14, 139, 354, 372, 418   *See also*
    International Contracts
Civil code *See* General Principles of
    Civil Law
    general provisions of civil law 14–17
Compensatory damages 371 *See also*
    Damages
Conditions 235, 259 *See also* Effecting
    condition
    dissolving condition 236, 237
    express condition 238
    occurrence of certain event 236
    time period as condition 238
Confucianism 34, 35
    customary rules 34
    moral means and virtues 35
    punishment of punitive nature 34, 35
Contract law 8, 11
    economic contract law 8
    foreign economic contract law 8
    general principles of the civil law 1986 9, 10

theories of
    agreement 41
    civil act 40
    economic means 39
    exchange 42
Contracts 34, 42, 55, 64, 68, 73, 87, 90, 93,
    106, 115, 134, 136, 138, 150, 151, 155, 158,
    159, 167, 178, 185, 188, 190, 195, 197, 215,
    221, 230, 231, 235, 278, 286, 297, 307, 315,
    319, 345, 387, 395, 397, 419, 439, 440,
    442, 449 *See also* Agreement
    acceptance 128, 132, 134, 136
    chinese tradition 34, 345
    civil law influence 36
    civil legal act 43
    contract and socialist market
        economy 59, 81
    contract and state plan 61, 81
    contract classification 49
        consensual and real contracts 51
        formal and informal contracts 50
        named and unnamed contracts 49
        onerous and gratuitous contracts 52
        unilateral and bilateral contracts 54
    contract concept 34
    contract theories 39
        agreement theory 41
        civil act theory 40
        economic means theory 39
        exchange theory 42
    labor contract 439, 440, 442
    mutual assent 115
    Obligatio 33, 34, 36, 37
    offer 115, 117
    Qi Yue 1, 33, 34
Course of dealing 157 *See* Interpretation
Course of performance 162, 163, 167 *See*
    Interpretation

Damages 378 *See also* Remedies
    avoidable consequences 378
    compensatory damages 371
    continuing performance 357
    duty to mitigate 378
    earnest money 376
    expected interests 371, 372
    foreseeability 370
    interests 370
    liquidated damages 372, 373, 374

INDEX 477

punitive damages   375
recovery, expenses to mitigate loss   378
redemption   392
reliance interest   370
remedial measures   366
Data-telex   135, 143 *See* Formality
Delegation   297 *See* Assignment and Delegation
Discharge   305, 329 *See also* Rescission; Termination
   completion of performance   329
   comprehensive assignment   304
   deposit of subject matter of contract   333
   dissolution   308
   payment   248, 251, 359, 360, 471
Dispute settlement   424, 469 *See also* International Contracts
   arbitration   429, 469, 470
   litigation   432
      Forum non conveniens   433, 469.470
      statute of limitations   434
   mediation   425, 469
      administrative mediation   427, 469, 470
      arbitral mediation   425, 427
      civil mediation   425, 426
      judicial mediation   425, 427, 428
   negotiation / reconciliation   425
   statute of limitations   434
Dissolution   308 *See* Rescission
Duress   203, 210 *See* Validity

Enforceable contracts   88, 89 *See also Obligatio*
   contract obligation   90, 91, 92
   enforceability   87, 88, 89
   equality principle   93
   fairness principle   96, 97
   good faith   96, 242, 393
   good faith principle   96, 97, 98, 99, 102
   legal compliance   79, 103
   legality   102
   observance of contract   106
   public interests   102, 105
   public policy   102, 103, 404, 431
   voluntariness principle   93, 95, 96
Excuse of performance   249, 250 *See also Force Majeure*
   fulfillment plea   251

impossibility of performance   361
impracticability of performance   263
Rebus sic stantibus   274–277
unrest defense   254
Express conditions   238 *See also* Conditions

Foreign contacts   395, 396 *See also* International contracts
Foreseeability   370 *See also* Damages
Formality   79, 103, 138 *See also* Freedom of contract
   formation of contract   115
   government approval   128, 132, 134, 136, 147, 168, 280
   other forms   139
   registration and filing   85
   writing   139, 140, 146
      Data telex (telegram, telex, fax, EDI, and emails)   143
Formation   115 *See also* Acceptance
   conclusion of contract   136
   effectiveness of contract   136, 137
   formalities   138
   government approval   84, 137, 147, 148
   reasonable reliance   89
   state plan   64, 147
Fraud   202, 203, 206 *See also* Validity
Freedom of contract   68, 71 *See also* Legal Compliance
   administrative supervision   81
   bird in cage   78
   freedom-given   72
   freedom-inherent   72
   government approval   128, 132, 134, 136, 147, 168, 280
   making contract voluntarily   70, 75, 77, 93
   party autonomy   69, 74, 77, 398, 400
   rights of the parties to contract   73
Frustration of purpose   319 *See also* Rescission
Fulfillment plea   251, 254 *See also* Performance
   mutuality of obligations   54, 251, 287
   orderly fulfillment plea   251
   order of performance   251
   simultaneous fulfillment plea   251, 252, 253

Good faith   96, 242, 393
   generally, performance   240
   Government approval   128, 132, 134, 136, 147, 168, 280 *See also* Freedom of contract
      formality requirement   138, 146, 280
      state plan   64, 147
   Guiding case   17, 18, 19, xii
      judicial interpretation   17

Habitual residence   409, 412

Illegality   79, 102, 215, 216, 218 *See also* Legal Compliance
   illegal purpose   215
Impossibility of performance   354, 361
   economic impracticability   363
   factual impossibility   361
   legal impossibility   361
Inquiry or invitation for offer   117, 120, 121 *See* Offer
Intent to contract   115, 116 *See also* Contract
   manifestation of   115, 117
   objective theory of   116
   reasonable man test   116
   subjective theory   116
International contracts   395 *See also* Foreign Contracts
   application of international law   421
   choice of forum   419, 420
      consensual jurisdiction   419
      exclusive jurisdiction   421
      tier jurisdiction of chinese people's courts   421
   choice of law   397, 398
      choice by the parties   398
         Dépeçage   403
         limitations   77, 404
         party autonomy   69, 74, 77, 398, 400
         Renvoi   403
         time to make choice   400
      determination by court or arbitration body   408, 409
         characteristic performance   409
         the closest relationship standard   409
      mandatory application of chinese law   407, 408
   CISG   14, 139, 354, 372, 418

dispute settlement   424, 469
foreign elements   395
international customs   402, 413
international treaty   400, 402, 413, 414, 421
Interpretation   155, 158, 159
   course of dealing   157
   interpretation approaches   155
      broad approach   156
      restrictive approach   156
   objective expression   158, 159
   plain meaning rule   157, 160
   purpose of contract   153, 156, 157, 162
   rules of interpretation and preference   155, 158, 159, 162
   standards of interpretation   160
   subjective intention   158
   true meaning   160
Invitation for offer   117 *See* Offer

Labor contract   439, 440, 442
   collective contract   444, 445, 449
   employing unit   443, 446, 447, 448, 451, 452, 453, 454, 456, 457, 460, 464, 466, 468, 469, 472
   labor dispatch   442, 451
   probationary period   448, 460
Legal compliance   79, 103 *See also* Formality
   compulsory rules   103
   government approval   128, 132, 134, 136, 147, 168, 280
   laws and administrative regulations   29
Legality   102
   customs   104
   law and regulations   103
   social and pubic interests   102, 105
Liability   345, 347, 378, 466 *See also* Contract
   exemption of liability   378
   fault liability   109, 347, 348
   labor contract   439, 440, 442
   legal liability   90, 106, 241, 345, 466
   liability for breach   345, 351, 467
   liability imputation   347, 349
   obligations   246, 297, 359, 360, 378, 454
Liquidated damages   372 *See* Damages

Manifestation of intent   115, 128 *See also* Intent to contract
Meaning of terms   155 *See* Interpretation

INDEX 479

Minors 186, 187, 188, 189 *See also* Agent at Litem
Mistake 224, 225 *See also* Misunderstanding
Misunderstanding 224, 225, 226
   error in expression 225
   materiality 225
   mistake 224, 225
Mitigation of damages 378 *See* Damages
Modification 279 *See also* Assignment
   changes by agreement 279
   government approval 280
   writing requirement 290
Mutual assent 43 *See also* Acceptance; Agreement; Offer
Mutuality of obligations 54, 251, 287 *See* Fulfillment Plea

Novation 305 *See* Assignment
   delegation 279, 297
   discharge 305, 329
   third parties 292, 381, 383, 387, 389

Obligatio 33, 34, 36, 37 *See* Contract
   law of obligations 246, 297, 359, 360, 378, 454
   observance of contractual obligations 106
Offer 115, 117
   advertisements 118, 119
   bilateral contracts 54
   counter offer 128
   indefiniteness 117, 118
   intent, manifestation of 117
   invitation for offer 117, 121
   irrevocability 125, 126
   lapse of time 127
   legal effect of offers 123, 124
   rejection 127
   revocation of offer 125
   termination of offer 124
   void offers 126, 127
   who may accept - specified person 116, 130
   withdrawal of offer 122, 123
Order of performance 251, 252 *See* Fulfillment Plea

Partial assignment 286 *See* Assignment
Performance 240, 242, 246, 257, 269, 273, 454
   change of circumstances 273
   change related to parties 274
      Rebus Sic Stantibus 274–275
   defenses to non-performance 249
      fulfillment plea 251–254
      unrest defense 254–257
   determination of obligations 246
   guarantee of performance 269
      lien 273
      money deposit 272
      security interest 271
      suretyship 270
   non-conforming performance 353, 355
   non-performance 353, 354
   principles of performance 240
      complete and adequate performance 241
         partial performance 242
      good faith performance 242, 243
      subordinating duty 243
         duty to assist 243
         duty to maintain confidentiality 243
   protective measures 257
      cancellation 263, 264
      subrogation 258, 259, 261, 262
      required order 258
Plain meaning rule 157, 160 *See* interpretation
Pre-contractual liability 107, 109, 126
   business secret 113
   contract liability 108
   tort liability 108
Price 21, 22, 153, 154, 163 *See* contract terms
   state guided price 23, 153, 163
   state mandatory price 153, 163
Priorities 289 *See* Assignment and Delegation
Profits 283 *See also* Assignment
   damages 367, 378
Punitive damages 371, 375 *See also* Damages

Quantity 151 *See* Terms

Rejection of offer 127 *See* Offer
Remedies 356 *See also* Damages
   compensatory nature 357, 371
   continuing performance 357, 358
      monetary obligation 359
      non-monetary obligation 360

Remedies (*cont.*)
  impossibility rule   361
  impracticability rule   363
  remedial measures
    reduction of price or
      remuneration   366, 367
    repair   366, 367
    replacement   366
    return of goods   366
    reworking   366, 367
  restitution   233, 234
  rule of timing   364
Rescission   308, 309, 312, 323, 325 *See also* Discharge
  by agreement   309
  causes for rescission   312, 320
    anticipatory repudiation   13, 312, 316, 351, 352
    breach of contract   315, 318, 320, 345, 351, 353
    frustration of contract purpose   319
    unreasonable delay in performance   318
    Force Majeure   85, 312, 313, 378, 379
  legal consequence of rescission   325
  by provision of law   312
  rescission notice   323
  retroactive effect   325
Restitution   233, 234
  avoidance   230, 231, 235
  rescission   308, 309, 312, 323, 325
  unjust enrichment   16, 233
Revocation of offer   125 *See* Offer

Socialist market economy   59, 60 62, 63
  economic reform   6, 11, 59, 60
  opening door policy   6, 60
  planned economy   2, 6, 13, 14, 42, 59
  state, collective and private interests   213
  state plan   8, 32, 81, 153
Standard terms   174 *See* Adhesion contract; *Terms*
Statute of limitations   434
  general limitation   346
  special limitation   346
  suspension   437
  tolling   437
  ultimate limitation   346

Termination   327
  deposit   333
  exemption   340
  merger   342
  offset   331
  performance   329
Terms   155, 157, 159, 162, 163, 167
  ambiguity   109
  disclaimers   177
  proof   167
  standard terms   168, 174
    adhesion contract   168, 169, 174
    despotic clause   171
  supplement agreement   162
    missing terms   162, 163
    uncertain terms   162, 163
  terms generally included   151, 152
    dispute settlement   424, 469
    liability for breach   345
    method for dispute settlement   76, 151
    method of contract   151
    name and domicile   151, 152, 153
    quality   151, 163
    quantity   151
    subject matter   151, 153
    time limit   151
Third parties   381, 383, 387, 389, 392 *See also* Assignment and Delegation
  assumption of contractual obligations   282, 387
  Bona fide third party   392, 393
  breach by third party   389
  government authority   382, 391
  relativism   390
  third party receiving performance   383
    agent   382, 383, 384, 388
    beneficiary   383, 384, 394
Threat   210, 211 *See* Duress

Unrest defense   254 *See* Performance

Validity   178, 181, 184 *See also* Agent
  effect-to-be-determined
    capacity to contract   185, 186, 188
      authorization   190, 191
      limited capacity   185, 186, 188
      no capacity   186

no-right-to-dispose 187
ratification 195, 196
conditions affecting the validity of contracts 235
legal compliance 79, 103
misunderstanding 224, 225, 226
legal consequences of void and voidable contracts 230
avoidance from the very beginning of contract 230
independence of dispute settlement clause 232
partial avoidance 231
restitution and compensation 233, 234
voidable contract 221
exploitation of other party's precarious position 223
material misunderstanding 224
obvious unfairness 227

void contract 201, 203, 205, 210, 213, 215, 217, 218
duress 203, 210, 221, 222
threat 210, 211
wrongful act 210
fraud 203, 221, 222
conduct of deceit 207
intent to deceive 206
mistaken manifestation of will of the deceived 209
reliance 208
illegal purpose 215
malicious collusion 213
harm to state, collective or third party interest 213
social and public interest 102, 105
violation of compulsory provisions of law 218

Writing 139, 140, 146 *See also* Formality